JOSÉ ORTEGA y GASSET
Circumstance and Vocation

José Ortega y Gasset

JOSÉ ORTEGA y GASSET

Circumstance and Vocation

By JULIÁN MARÍAS Aguilera

TRANSLATED BY FRANCES M. LÓPEZ-MORILLAS

196
Or8m

UNIVERSITY OF OKLAHOMA PRESS : Norman

BOOKS AVAILABLE IN ENGLISH
BY JULIÁN MARÍAS:

Reason and Life: The Introduction to Philosophy (translated by Kenneth S. Reid and Edward Sarmiento) (New Haven, 1956)

Miguel de Unamuno (translated by Frances M. López-Morillas) (Cambridge, Mass., 1966)

History of Philosophy (translated by Stanley Appelbaum and Clarence C. Strowbridge) (New York, 1967)

Philosophy as Dramatic Theory (translated by George Parsons) (University Park and London, 1970)

José Ortega y Gasset: Circumstance and Vocation (translated by Frances M. López-Morillas) (Norman, 1970)

INTERNATIONAL STANDARD BOOK NUMBER: 0-8061-0879-7

LIBRARY OF CONGRESS CATALOG CARD NUMBER: 71-88141

For LOLITA
who is on every page

ACKNOWLEDGMENTS

I am grateful to the Rockefeller Foundation, and particularly to Messrs. Charles B. Fahs, Edward F. D'Arms, and John P. Harrison, as well as to Dr. Jaime Benítez, President, University of Puerto Rico, for their help in the years of research which made possible this book.

I am also thankful to Don Carlos Prieto, whose generosity sponsored the accurate and sensitive translation of this book by Frances M. López-Morillas; and to the University of Oklahoma Press, which was so enthusiastic in accepting this study, for making this fine edition available to English readers.

JULIÁN MARÍAS

Madrid
February, 1970

ABOUT THE FOOTNOTES

References to Ortega's works give, whenever necessary, the exact title of the piece of writing quoted, in quotation marks when it is an article or essay, in italics when it is a book or autonomous part of a book, followed by the date of composition in parentheses, with a question mark where the date is uncertain. For all the writings included in the *Obras Completas*, an indication of volume and page follows; thus, VI, 343. I quote from the first edition, in six volumes, Revista de Occidente, Madrid, 1946–47. Where sufficient only this short reference is given.

CONTENTS

Contents

JOSÉ ORTEGA y GASSET
Circumstance and Vocation

"*There are no great probabilities that a work like mine—which, though its value is slight, is very complex, very full of secrets, allusions, and elisions, very much interwoven with a whole vital trajectory—will find a generous spirit who will really work hard at understanding it. More abstract works, detached because of their aim and style from the personal life within which they arose, can be assimilated more easily, for they require less interpretive effort. But each one of the pages collected here summed up my entire existence at the hour when it was written, and, put together, they represent the melodic line of my personal destiny.*"

ORTEGA: Prologue to his *Works*, 1932

PROLOGUE

Among the truths which Ortega taught about human life, the following two are numbered: that everything man does, he does *in view of the circumstances*, and that to each of the actions of our lives, its justification intrinsically belongs. This book could not be an exception. And, in fact, a careful consideration of the circumstances in which it is being written contains the core of its justification.

Ortega occupies a unique place, by virtue of his quality and character, in the history of Spain and, in general, the history of the Hispanic peoples; in him the Spanish-speaking peoples have had for the first time the full and authentic experience of philosophy. By this I mean that before Ortega, philosophy had had among us a penultimate and deficient character, from the point of view of philosophy as well as the point of view of its condition in Spain. Either there have been immature philosophical attempts (gropings, rather), intuitions which have not attained the level of strict theory, or simple utilization of alien philosophical structures—not thought out from inside Spanish circumstances —set in motion by the need to interpret reality from this irreplaceable perspective. In Ortega—and not before him or after him—something decisive happened to the Spanish mind as such, something which makes it different from what it had been before, and which conditions its future: the incorporation of philosophy. And this, of course, becomes a new determination of Hispanic reality, to the extent that philosophy has begun to function within it, in a double sense: as an element with which it will have to reckon in the future, and as a possibility which will be at its disposal from now on. Before Ortega, an analysis of the essential content of the form of Spanish historical life did not reveal philosophy, except in the relatively abstract dimension where philosophy formed part of Europe and the West, realities in which Spain is implanted. Ortega's work signifies the inclusion of philosophy in the very texture of things Hispanic. But when we speak of human things, we must keep in mind that insecurity belongs to them as a constitutive element; everything human can be won or lost, can go wrong, can degenerate or become falsified; when I speak of that inclusion, I am thinking of its possibility: its full and authentic realization depends on the measure in which that philosophy is possessed, assimilated, rethought, effectively incorporated into the structure of our collective life. But what is certain is that philosophy, whether we will or no, *has happened to us*, and we cannot go backward; what must be decided in the near future is whether it is to belong to us in an intense, purified, and fruitful form or in a residual and deficient form.

It might be thought that, even though this were correct, interest in Ortega's works would be confined to Spanish-speaking countries. I do not believe that this is the case, for an extremely simple reason: if it is true that philosophy has happened to the Spanish mind, it is no less true that the *Spanish version* of philosophy has happened to Western philosophy through the work of Ortega. I mean that twentieth-century European thought has become part of a new, *irreducible* perspective, which works back on all the other perspectives and changes them. What Descartes, and possibly Giordano Bruno, and Bacon, and Leibniz and Kant—both of them, for Leibniz did not write in German—have meant for modern philosophy, Ortega has meant in our time, for he has contributed *a new way of looking at things*, without which Western philosophical thought would be mutilated, incomplete, anachronistic, and, in short, *less than itself*. Since, moreover, Ortega's philosophy includes decisive aspects which are not found, not even in other forms or versions, in the rest of the philosophical systems of our time, their incorporation into the common property of Western philosophy becomes as necessary as it is urgent: given the rhythm of historical transformation in our century, certain anomalies began to be observed some years ago in European and American thought which endanger a large part of their best possibilities, and which a sufficient presence of Orteguian philosophy would have prevented from the start.

This means that its *effective possession* is an inescapable condition for making a Spanish philosophy possible and for a Western philosophy to achieve its proper level. In other words, we need Ortega in order to be fully ourselves, in order to have available all the possibilities of our future.

Does this suffice to justify the writing of this book? Is not Ortega's work there, before our eyes, so close to us that his death occurred only a few years ago? It is a fact—for the moment, a fact—that Ortega's philosophy, (and his intellectual work in general), is adequately possessed today by only a very small number of persons, and obviously it is not well enough known to the public at large. This suggests the existence of some kind of anomaly, either in Ortega's work or in the public's capacity for receptivity in our time, or perhaps in both. I shall anticipate by saying that this last hypothesis seems to me to be the true one; but for the moment I shall confine myself to pointing out that the first part is undoubtedly correct: Ortega's published work—and even his whole written work—is not what it should have been, what its author considered necessary. The reasons for this constitute one theme of this study, and not the least important one. In any case, we must keep in mind that Ortega's philosophy was never *expounded* by its author in the way he aspired, and desired, to do it for many years of his life. That, despite this, it was possible to grasp that philosophy, that some people had the strict obligation to have understood it, rethought it, and mastered it, is another matter. The necessity remains of confronting it in an even more active and creative way than that which the assimilation and comprehension of all philosophy demands; or, if you prefer, of supplying by our own intellectual action the deficiencies which the realization of Ortega's public work displays when it is compared with what his aim was, with what would have assured—at least on his part—the optimum conditions for its historical effectiveness.

This is, of course, the mission which falls to each generation in regard to its predecessors, the mission which makes possible the fruitfulness of historical continuity and prevents "Adamism." This demand of the circumstances is the one which justifies the writing of a book on Ortega, in which an attempt will be made, with all possible scrupulosity and rigor, to see him *from inside himself*; this implies going beyond his writings, beyond his doctrines (including all "data"), and presents no few difficulties and very serious risks. How to go about it? What must a book be like if it is to try to *give Ortega the fullness of himself and confer on him his own possibilities?* How to justify it, from the present moment—life is always of the present moment—from the position, that is, of the person who writes it and those who are to read it? And, lastly, what is the justification for the fact that it is I and not someone else who is setting himself to write it?

The first time that Ortega turned his attention to the whole body of his work, in 1932, he regarded it as the precipitate of his own life: "That is, seen from today, what remained of our frenzies: footprints! footprints!—slight chance impressions on soft earth. Is it not terrible that nothing is left of our magic journey but this—the mute stupidity of a footprint—and the rest has evaporated, has been blotted out of the universe?"[1] The only way to understand footprints is to see them as footprints—that is, to see them being made; to turn from the inert imprint in the sand to the footstep that left it there, a footstep weighted down (perhaps bowed down) by an existence, a footstep that was going somewhere, that arrived or did not arrive. Theory becomes intelligible only when it becomes rooted in the life for which it was at once possible and necessary. In Ortega's case this happens with double force and intensity, for in him theory was, thematically and deliberately, *dramatic*. Therefore this book, which is not and does not aspire to be in any way a biography, has one essential biographical component; or, if you prefer, it carries with it, as one of its philosophically essential elements, an attempt to penetrate or divine the drama—circumstance, project, plot, adventure, fate—in which Ortega's life consisted.

Only from this drama does the doctrine which arose from him acquire its meaning; but, conversely, only in that doctrine, taken in its extreme theoretical exactness, does the meaning of that life become clear. If we dispense with the strictest intellectual meaning of that work, all the rest is reduced to anecdote, in the last instance trivial. In a thinker who possessed a maximum of profundity and authenticity, as Ortega did, the deepest and innermost part of his life is expressed and "realized" in his work; though, naturally, it is only accessible if his work is taken in its complex reality. We must take seriously the need, formulated by Ortega, to see the work as "interwoven with a whole vital trajectory"; but no less seriously the second part of that sentence in which he states that "each one of the pages collected here summed up my entire existence at the hour it was written, and, put together, they represent the melodic line of my personal destiny."[2] Anything else

[1] Prologue to an edition of his *Obras* (1932), VI, 343.
[2] *Ibid.*, 349.

would be like thinking that we knew who Beethoven was, however many things we might be told about him, if we were unaware of his symphonies. When it is said that, whatever the biographical events history may discover, Shakespeare is the author of Shakespeare's plays, Cervantes the man who wrote *Don Quixote*, and Homer the Homeric poems, this does not mean—it ought not to mean—the selfish triviality that it is the works themselves which interest us; rather that, at that level of creation, they are the most refined and personal expression of their authors, the thing in which those authors, when they existed, most properly *consisted*; and that, therefore, that is what we properly understand by the names of Beethoven, Shakespeare, Cervantes, and Homer, on condition that we see these works as human productions in which was made manifest and realized that ungraspable and ultimate project to which each of them alluded when he said, making a vague gesture toward his heart, "I."

That project, program, or aspiration, that arrow aimed at a target, that voice (or vocation) which calls us, that destiny which is "ours" and which we fundamentally are, is not separable from, nor does it have concrete reality apart from, a precise circumstance which we may call "our world." This has always been true, but Ortega is the first man who has understood it philosophically and has made it the very root of his doctrine. This is why that condition of human life has been still more true in him; I mean that in him this inexorable condition was *accepted*; and instead of fabricating another, as almost all Western thought has done, he made it the starting-point of his philosophy, at once resistance and point of support, servitude and spur. Everything human is circumstantial, but in Ortega it was so deliberately. To say the same thing in other words, we may add that Ortega's philosophy consisted, and very formally—we will see later to what point this is literally true—in *freely deciding to be faithful to his destiny*. And this expression I have just written is perhaps the best possible definition of *authenticity*.

It is not possible, then, to enter into Ortega's work if we are not clear about his circumstance. This is perhaps the reason why foreign studies on Ortega have not had the depth and fruitfulness which might have been otherwise expected, the reason why, for example, the vast and fervent enthusiasm which Germany has dedicated to his writings has so far not been translated into a philosophically adequate understanding: it was extremely improbable that any non-Spaniard could be acquainted with and comprehend the Spanish circumstance into which Ortega was born, in which he grew up, had to live, and finally died, the circumstance which obliged him—in order to be who he was, that is, who he wished to be and *had to be*—to think and write and teach, and in so precise a way, that philosophy which now exists distilled into books. But, on the other hand, "every circumstance is enclosed in another, broader one." "A serious oversight, a miserable stupidity, to deal with only a few circumstances, when in truth everything is around us!"[3] Ortega had said as early as 1911. Knowledge of Spanish circumstances would be totally insufficient. Without knowing where Spain was, where the man was who began his attempt to think, which he had to do in Madrid, it is impossible to understand. The need to know what to hold to led Ortega to thought, and concretely to philosophical thought; but to which one? Not to his own, for it did not exist; not to bringing one into existence, unless the thought around him was of no use to him. When he did not find philosophical thought in his immediate Spanish circumstance, Ortega had to resort, in the second instance, to Europe: the first stage and the method itself of his public activity and his intellectual action consisted in this recourse, as we shall see. And if Ortega set his own thought in motion, if he made his own personal philosophy, it was like a forced landing after a second shipwreck on the inadequacy of European philosophy. "Consciousness of shipwreck," he once wrote, "when it becomes the truth of life, is already salvation. That is why I believe only in the thoughts of shipwrecked men. We will have to summon the classics before a court made up of shipwrecked men, so that they can answer certain peremptory questions which have a bearing on authentic life."[4] If Ortega can count in any sense as a classic writer, it is precisely because he has thought like a shipwrecked man; and he counts only in the measure in which he is seen in this light, arriving on the shore of his own doctrine, in an essential *anabasis* of the philosophy that he found reigning in Europe.

If we consider Ortega's written work, we will see that there are several points of inflection in it. In the first place, whereas in its early

---

[3] "Vejamen del orador" (1911), in *Personas, obras, cosas.* I, 557. See my annotation in *Meditaciones del Quijote*, Comentario de Julián Marías, Revista de Occidente (Madrid, 1957), 242–48.

[4] "Pidiendo un Goethe desde dentro" (1932). IV, 397–98.

stages the realization seems to coincide approximately with the projects, in the last stages a series of apparent chance occurrences constantly disturbs the plan and its configuration. In the second place, the continuity of aim, the sure fluency of the writer, is not always equally visible. Finally, on various occasions there are explicit references to the need for going to new forms of expression—and of intellectual creation—and it is never entirely clear whether this is what one is reading or whether what is before one's eyes is only a new postponement. At the end of his prologue to the first collected—though not complete—edition of his *Works*, he expressly stated this in a Platonic figure of speech: "A new task begins, then. Little boat, to sea once more! What Plato calls 'the second voyage' begins."[5] This *déuteros ploûs* began about 1932 and lasted until 1955, the year of his death. Only until then? The fact is—one more unlucky chance—that a large part of Ortega's work was unpublished on the day of his death: almost-finished books, fragments and odds-and-ends, essays, loose notes, lectures, and courses. Seen from the vantage point of today, the writings published between 1933 and 1955 take on an unexpectedly fragmentary character: they are the announcements, the promises, the anticipations of that "second voyage" which was only begun, its uncertain route camouflaged by all kinds of reefs and shoals.

It would be unjust and confusing, of course, to load onto the figure of Ortega, onto what he was in life, the mass of decisive writings which only now are coming to light, writings which were not available when we could see him and coexist with him; but it would also be arbitrary to weigh him down, from the start, with the indiscriminate accumulation of his earlier writings. This is why I have decided to study Ortega on a series of levels, in the effective stages of his intellectual biography, and to structure them into independent, but closely connected, volumes. At the end it will be necessary to come to terms not only with what really existed, but with "the Ortega who might have been"; with the man he will be if we are capable of asking him those peremptory questions which refer to authentic life; that is, if we are sufficiently authentic to go with him to the place he would have reached, and to go on alone, farther on, toward ourselves.

I asked before what could justify the fact that it should be I who

[5] VI, 536.

would undertake to write this book. It will be well to recall briefly the history of my intellectual relationship with Ortega. Although I had begun to read him about two years earlier, I first met him in 1932, precisely at that moment of important inflection of which I have spoken. Year after year, until I received my degree in philosophy in 1936, I was an assiduous student of his in his Chair of Metaphysics at the University of Madrid, and during those years a friendship gradually grew up between us. The Civil War and Ortega's absence from Spain separated us for eight years, precisely those years in which I began my personal activity and published my first five books. In all that long period of time, Ortega wrote me only two letters: the first, on the subject of the war, to remind me—and recommend to me—"the great Spanish serenity which so surprised the other Europeans in the sixteenth century," that "attitude of serenity which those of other nations called 'Spanish gravity' "; the second, five years later, to approve of what I had done in that period of solitude and to encourage me: "You are the only one who has found the right tactic for times like these: work, work, work . . . ."

In those eight years—during which I neither saw him nor received any guidance from him, in which I was alone with his books, his lecture notes, and memories of him, in which I had to mobilize my own personal thought—I progressively discovered the truth and fecundity of *his* thought. As I approached things, I felt that I was getting closer and closer to him. Far from any influence—exposed, rather, to every sort of adverse temptation—I was pushed by the very strength of things closer and closer to the very center from which Ortega's philosophy had sprung. Its connections gradually emerged as it was put to the test; the efficacy of his replies was discovered as I encountered them, not in a passive and inert way, but prodded by personal problems. Every day I felt myself to be more deeply installed, on a different level, in a philosophy which I had rethought, relived, extended toward the directions my own vocation was carrying me. This did not escape Ortega's notice, for years later he wrote me, "In reality, you made yourself a disciple of mine *after* I stopped being a professor, in these years of my absence and your reconcentration and maturation."

In 1944 and 1945, I saw him again in Lisbon; I spent a few weeks of almost constant association, of long conversations, settling of accounts, philosophical discussions, minute analyses of my recent books, of my way of understanding his books, of the possibilities of a philosophy which Ortega began at that time to call "ours." In 1945, after he returned to live in Madrid, at least for long periods of time, our friendship became more and more close and frequent, our deep-rooted sense of agreement even more profound, our discussions more impassioned and interminable. In reply to my commentaries on the manuscript of his *Leibniz*, he wrote me in 1947, "I have not had time—this is literally true—even to read the material that you have read. You are, then, *absolutely* its first reader. I have gone on producing without looking back, only with the sensation *a tergo* of what had been in each case previously enunciated in what I had already written." A year later we began our collaboration in the Institute of Humanities, in which he generously included me, taking advantage of both our mutual identification and our total independence, our common "having nothing to lose." And in the years which followed, up to the time of his death, long conversations—two every day—and walks through the green or golden Retiro Park, interminable letters during absences, constant adjustments in philosophy or in friendship, and always plans, plans, plans.

For me, the chief reason I am writing this book is that Ortega counted on it, and perhaps this gave him a certain sense of tranquillity about the hazards of life and history. I think that probably his generosity made him too confident, and this fear both restrains and incites me. If I did not write it, I would feel that I had defrauded him, had denied him what he deserved; were I to write it small-mindedly, I would be forgetting what he always taught: that in man nothing is sure, that there is nothing on which we can count without qualification, that intelligence and accuracy are problematical ventures; that whatever man does is utopian, and that it is enough to have tried to do it, so long as one puts his heart and soul into it.

And one word more: this book is, at least, necessary for me. I would have wished, to be sure, to write it when Ortega was still alive, when it would have been pleasant and encouraging to have gone on with the writing of it, counting on his reading it; and especially that it would not have been closed and finished, that I would have had to go back over it and add new things, maybe the best things. God has not willed it so. But this effort to rethink Ortega's philosophy, to realize its potentialities, to give an account of it vitally and historically from my own perspective—a filial one and therefore irreducible—is to make Orteguian philosophy, and at the same time it is the only way for me to be freely faithful to my personal destiny. Said in fewer words, the condition of being authentically myself.

INTRODUCTION

I.

SPAIN ON THE THRESHOLD OF THE TWENTIETH CENTURY

I. THE CRISIS OF THE *Ancien Régime;*
ENLIGHTENMENT AND POPULARISM

If we wish to understand a historical situation, we must look at it historically—that is, we must see where it comes from—and this always forces us to look back in time. An attempt to understand what Spain was, about the year 1900, demands that we cast a backward glance at the road by which she had arrived at that date. Where shall we begin? The indispensable point of departure is the date when a crisis occurred within the form of collective life in which Spain had been *installed* previously; this installation, however—and it is the first thing we must establish, for it constitutes an essential trait of our recent history—had not taken place during the whole course of the nineteenth century; we must go back to the "ancien régime," to the last decades of the eighteenth century, if we wish to find a form of collective life which was fully reigning and stable, which fits the term I have used, that of "installation." Obviously, having to go back so far imposes a stipulation required for the internal economy of this book, by its structure, and, especially, by its length: extreme abbreviation. Therefore I shall have to confine myself to statements which are excessively laconic and seemingly dogmatic, leaving to the reader the responsibility for fleshing them out, justifying them, or even correcting them by the use of materials he may be able to find in works where this subject is treated more directly.[1]

---

[1] A great deal of bibliography in Jean Sarrailh's excellent book *L'Espagne éclairée de la seconde moitié du XVIIIᵉ siècle* (Paris, 1954). (There is a Spanish translation, Fondo de Cultura Económica, Mexico.) Also, see Richard Herr's recent and admirable study *The Eighteenth-Century Revolution in Spain* (Princeton, 1958). [See also Julián Marías, *La España posible en tiempo de Carlos III* (Madrid, 1963), reprinted in *Obras*, VII.]

Whenever possible, I shall use Ortega's points of view as a basis—that is, whenever I can share them and when they refer to the question in a not too oblique way—not only because of their value and habitual perspicacity, but because, in the last instance, what we are trying to do is to understand *his* situation; and a decisive element in that situation is how he understood his own Spanish and European past.

Spanish society rested on a foundation of agreement, at least up to the end of Charles III's reign (1788); this does not mean, of course, that there were not tensions and struggles; all historical life feeds on these, and it is precisely in them that the basis of agreement which makes them possible, and upon which they rest, reveals itself. But the basic reigning ideas are generally accepted, and dissent from them relates to concrete matters which do not call into question the existence of society itself, of government, or of the principles which regulate life in common.[2] The tension introduced into this society by internal movement was the tension existing between popularism—in its extreme form, plebeianism—and the spirit of the Enlightenment. Strictly speaking, the state of struggle affected only the ruling *minorities*: the nation as a whole continued to be installed in its traditional forms of life—precisely those to which it felt particularly attached, and which had flavor and full *meaning* for it—which constituted the compartment wherein it believed happiness to be possible. This does not mean that the Spanish people were satisfied with their *situation* in the second half of the eighteenth century; this situation was unequal, but in many regions, and on a number of levels in all regions, it was fairly precarious, although since the latter part of Philip V's reign it had improved extraordinarily and was incomparably superior to all the previous situations that had existed since the sixteenth century; what I mean is that the people *adhered to their condition*,[3] and could think of changing their situation only in terms of and from the point of view of that condition. This feeling was what, in a certain sense, spread into the upper classes and made them take part in this adhesion, in ways which even reached the pitch of enthusiasm. A considerable fraction of the aristocracy and even the Court imitated and copied popular customs; it was not a question of merely "playing at being members of another class," as the courtiers of Versailles did when they dressed as shepherds

[2] See J. Marías, *La estructura social* (1955), chapter 3.
[3] See *ibid.*, chapter 4, pp. 47–49.

and milked goats, but that the ladies and gentlemen, the duchesses of Madrid, played—there is no doubt of that—*getting into the game*; that is, they really took part in those forms of life, in those styles of dress, of song, of dance, of entertainment, of going to bullfights and the theater, of speech. This is the root of that popularism and even plebeianism which constituted the great "downward thrust" of Spanish life, in contrast to the universal upward impulse—snobbery of the most arid sort—which characterized other European societies. (Of course, this "downward thrust" was *also* an impulse toward the deepest feelings, the roots, toward all that is most elemental and basic; and it would not be fair to forget that this has been one of Spain's greatest strengths, the one which undoubtedly has kept her, in spite of the many causes which have led her in that direction, from being completely annihilated as a nation, the strength which has always allowed her to have *some* hope, the strength which has made possible from time to time a resurrection to a new life, by activating certain ultimate springs of action and certain energies of pure historical vitality.)

The tension arose because another fraction of these select minorities (another fraction insofar as it formed a group, which does not exclude, as we shall see, the fact that in part the same persons were involved), had been incorporated for a number of decades into the spirit dominant in Europe—France in particular, but also, naturally, England, secondarily Holland, Prussia, and Italy—and felt itself called upon to overcome this plebeianism and establish new and higher standards: they were the "enlightened" folk, the rationalists, those steeped in the ideas of the Encyclopedia, the educators, those who wished to emerge from the decadence and routine into which Spain had sunk since the middle of the seventeenth century. This attitude began with Feijóo (1676–1764), whose *Teatro crítico universal* began to be published in 1726; this fact suffices to prove that he could not have derived the attitude from the Encyclopedia, but from the spirit which was dominant throughout the century. From the intellectual point of view, the justification for these groups was evident: Spanish decline, especially in the University and the science then reigning, was absolute, and the difference in level between Spain and the rest of Europe seemed almost impossible to overcome. The need to create effective guiding minorities, technicians in all disciplines, a population which would be educated and free from superstition was very pressing. There was also an urgent need to raise the morale of a people abandoned to pure improvisation—at best—and to passive routine in the classes which felt responsible for, and in fact exercised, a large part of the country's orientation. One might think, given these postulates, that the nation as a whole, or at least the most wide-awake segments of it, would naturally second enthusiastically this movement of enlightenment, led, moreover, by the most gifted people in Spain, some of them persons, like Jovellanos, of extraordinary dignity and nobility. And yet this is not what happened; far from it. Why?

It is clear that "popularism" had a much more immediate attraction than "enlightenment." In spite of its excellent qualities, the latter movement was relatively lacking in color. None of the men who represented it—though, I repeat, they were admirable in many senses—was possessed of great breadth of imagination, an originally creative personality, or the gift of inspiring others. All of them, from Feijóo to Leandro Fernández de Moratín, were receptive, passive, dependent on outside factors (especially French and English ones), rather timid, and rarely bold. The only man of *genius*—to take this word with complete seriousness—that Spain produced after the end of the seventeenth century was Goya; not an intellectual, but a painter; an elemental man, whose position in this tension between popularism and the enlightened faction, studied by Ortega with matchless penetration,[4] is revealing. The enlightened party "had the right on their side"; they were plausible, well-intentioned, even effective—the Friends of the Country, the Gentlemen of Azcoitia, Olavide and his colonization of the Sierra Morena region, the technicians and researchers, Jovellanos with his Institute of Gijón—but they did not have sufficient energy to convert all this into a national *undertaking*. Compared to the popular world—bullfights, the theater, popular music, popular farces, popular costumes in *fiestas* and in dress, dances, ways of speaking—their ideas lacked savor and stimulating force.

The proof is found in the fact that the enlightened folk themselves gave way to the enchantment which they officially resisted. Ortega has observed[5] how the enlightened faction became impregnated with "plebeian" style and vocabulary, "which shows the invading and penetrating

---

[4] *Papeles sobre Velázquez y Goya* (1950). Revista de Occidente (Madrid, 1950), 279ff. See also *Goya* (Madrid, 1958).

[5] *Ibid.*, 294.

strength possessed by plebeianism." "Jovellanos," he adds, "who detested bullfights, talks like a reporter for a bullfight magazine." Moratín, who represented the last generation prior to Romanticism in literature, and who in certain important aspects was already a Romantic, when he refers with ironic scorn to the forms of plebeian life, cannot, however, hide the fact that, for all his "European" refinement and "enlightenment," he feels their strength, their thrust, and "his eyes stray after them." In 1793, while traveling through Germany and Switzerland, he admires the high living standard and refinements, and compares them with the sordidness of the Spain praised by her "apologists" in reaction to the "enlightened" party: "I dined in Happenheim, a small village located at the foot of some mountains, absolutely delicious for its pleasantness and coolness; but in this insignificant hamlet of four houses, far from any opulent court, what an inn! What a soup with egg dissolved in it, German style! What a good roast of lamb! When there is something like this in Las Rozas, Canillejas, or Alcorcón, I am convinced that no one will waste time on writing defenses."[6] And a few days later, after listing the dishes of an excellent supper: "Apologists, can you find this in Villaverde at eleven o'clock at night?"[7] In 1797, Moratín wrote the following paragraph, which in five lines sums up the subject I have been discussing and seems to summarize entire chapters of Cadalso: "We reached La Luisiana, one of the new towns [in the repopulation of Sierra Morena]: the inn full of donkeys and mules and mule-bells: shouts, smoke, muleteers, a traveling friar, and a marquis from Ecija dressed as a coachman, who stood me a brandy, and he and the innkeeper addressed each other as *tú* with the greatest affection."[8] But in 1825, writing from Bordeaux to his faithful friend, Juan Antonio Melón, his nostalgia for all of that is plainly visible: "I live and grow old . . . . Meanwhile, I haven't a pain anywhere, and I enjoy that negative good health I told you of, eight years ago, when I was in Montpellier. I can only hope that you are in the same condition. Take care not to stuff yourself with the tripe, hardboiled eggs, blood pudding, fried sardines, chili peppers, pickled peppers, cheese, and cheap wine that you have such a taste for in those ghastly inns, swarming with flies and beggars and dead dogs. That's the life! and

[6] Leandro Fernández de Moratín, *Obras póstumas* (Madrid, 1867), I, 287.
[7] *Ibid.*, 298.
[8] *Ibid.*, II, 14.

then you can laugh at Apicius and Epicurus and Aristippus and all the gluttons praised in fame and history."[9]

We must present the situation clearly: there was tension and struggle between enlightenment and popularism; about 1790, Ortega says, "All of Spanish life was pure partisanship"[10]; he was referring to the partisans of the bullfighters Costillares or Pedro Romero, or the actresses María Ladvenant, *La Tirana*, *La Caramba*, or Rita Luna. But this partisanship flourished *within a common life* based on the agreement I spoke of before, with mutual admiration between the hostile factions and between the two great tendencies into which Spanish life was divided: if the enlightened folk "felt their eyes stray" to the popular strain which they abhorred in principle, the popular and even the plebeian faction admired and respected the figures who united exemplary conduct with intellectual prestige. The symbol of all this could well be Colonel Cadalso (1741–82), who died at Gibraltar, a Europeanist and a man of the Enlightenment, an imitator of Montesquieu, with an anguished concern for Spain, a reformist, who while he was writing his *Cartas marruecas* and agonizing over the evils of his country, was frequenting the Príncipe theater, where he was to fall in love with the actress María Ignacia Ibáñez.[11] If there had been no more than this, the spirit of the Enlightenment would have encountered resistance, would have become impregnated with popularism, and would have gained in authenticity and flavor; the transformation of Spain would perhaps have been slow—there would have been no lack of backsliding—but no more. The process which began at the end of Philip V's reign and became dominant under Ferdinand VI and Charles III would have continued its course, without any serious break in the general agreement, without any dissociation in Spanish life. To explain these factors, and with them the crisis which began at the end of the eighteenth century and perhaps has not yet ended, we must recall other factors.

2. "MODERN" SPAIN AND
"THE TWO SPAINS"

If we look at the total picture of the variations in the Spanish situation

[9] *Ibid.*, III, 55–56.
[10] *Papeles sobre Velázquez y Goya*, 303.
[11] See Dolores Franco, *La preocupación de España en su literatura* (Madrid, 1944), 61 ff. [New and expanded edition: *España como preocupación* (Madrid, 1960).]

throughout the eighteenth century, we will see that the points of view of the "enlightened" men continued to gain ground and achieve prestige and currency. Not only among the enthusiasts of the popular faction did a taste arise for certain intellectual refinements and the approximation of Spain to the level of Western Europe; but even among the elements who were most resolutely opposed to each other and, fundamentally, to the new tendencies, hostility was being mitigated and the distances between the two positions being diminished. Jovellanos felt that not much could be done with the dominant ecclesiastical authorities, but that, once the younger people were in positions of command, things would be easier, and a more refined, intelligent, and open religious feeling would be possible. A large part of the Church looked favorably on the progress—moderate as it was—of the spirit of enlightenment; the extremely pious courts of Ferdinand VI and Charles III also shared this attitude, first with Feijóo and later with Padre Isla, at least during the time immediately following the publication of *Fray Gerundio de Campazas* (1758). A few years later, however, things began to get a little more unfriendly; the Inquisition condemned *Fray Gerundio* in 1760; in 1767 the Jesuits were expelled, treated with unexpected harshness by a government which exiled them without warning and by the Papal authorities who refused to receive them into their states, threatened to bombard the Spanish ships filled with exiled Jesuits and made them sail for months along the coasts of Italy and Corsica without being able to disembark.[12] Very diverse motives entered into this expulsion: together with "encyclopedism"—which is the excuse usually given nowadays—there was "regalism," represented by Floridablanca, as well as the tremendous hostility of the other religious orders, made quite obvious in the case of Padre Isla. That is, both of the "parties" I spoke of before, the "enlightened" faction and the "plebeians," contributed energetically to the expulsion and later the dissolution of the Company of Jesus, which in its turn had engaged in activity hostile to both, in aspects which were very different and independent of each other. But in spite of all this, once the situation quieted down, common life was

[12] See Padre José Francisco de Isla, *Obras escogidas* (Biblioteca de Autores Españoles, Madrid, 1850), especially the "Cartas familiares." See also the Prologue, by Pedro Felipe Monlau. Interesting details in Antonio Ferrer del Río's *Historia del reinado de Carlos III en España* (Madrid, 1856), Volume II, book 2, chapters 4–5. See also Sarrailh, *op. cit.*, chapters 7–8.

reestablished, and the basic agreement of the century was not broken until very late in Charles III's reign.

We must point out, however, that the great majority of the Spanish "enlightened" party were sincere, often fervent, Catholics (like Jovellanos), and that even the anticlericals attacked the ecclesiastics *in the name of religion*—that is, insofar as they felt them to be unworthy of religion and its obligations—not attacking religion itself.[13] The anticlericals were enemies of the Inquisition, which seemed to them to dishonor religion and Spain; they wished to do away with many forms which were dominant in the practice of religion, in the theater, in education, because these seemed to be profanations of Catholicism and improper to the century, but they fully accepted Christian faith and ethics and the authority of the Church. They were also—at least the truly representative men among them were—extremely moderate in politics, conservative, and enemies of all subversion and violence. Naturally, some probable atheists in private could be found among them, some few libertines, and some rebellious spirits; but we must ask ourselves who they were and whether they counted in Spanish life, if it was against them that the "anti-enlightenment" offensive was mounted.

Jovellanos admirably expressed in a letter[14] the dominant opinion in intellectual circles at the end of the eighteenth century: "You express yourself very openly about the Inquisition: on this point I am very much of your opinion, and believe that many share it, that there are many who are in agreement with us. But how far this opinion is from being general! And as long as it is not, this abuse cannot be attacked directly; all would be lost: the same thing would happen as in previous attempts; its roots would be strengthened more and more, and its

---

[13] See Sarrailh, *op. cit.*, 617ff. See also the Prologue written by Moratín, about 1808, for an edition of Padre Isla's *Fray Gerundio de Campazas* which was never published (*Obras póstumas*, III, 200–10), and my article "Isla y Moratín" (*La Nación*, Buenos Aires, 1958). [In *Los Españoles* (Madrid, 1962). *Obras*, VII.]

[14] Letter to "an unidentified person," in *Obras*, B.A.E., II, 366–67. This letter can be accurately identified and dated; it was written to the English consul Jardine, and its date is June 3, 1794. In his *Diarios* (Oviedo, 1953), I, 436, we read in the entry corresponding to that day, "Letter to Jardines [*sic*] to be sent in tomorrow's post: 'that nothing good can be hoped for from the revolutions in the Government, and that everything can be hoped for from the improvement of ideas; that consequently they should arise out of general opinion; two consequences: *first*, against Mably, who defends the justice of civil war; second, against Jardines himself, who looks on the spirit of revolution as a sign of merit. Etc.'"

system would become more cruel and insidious. What is the solution? I find only one. To begin by wresting from them the power to ban books; to give this right only to the Council of State in general matters, and to the bishops in matters of dogma; to destroy one authority with the other. You cannot imagine how much would be gained by this. It is true that the councillors are as superstitious as the inquisitors, but the light would be brought to them sooner; their judges are dependent on the censors, the censors are found in our academies, and the academies contain what little enlightenment there is among us. There are better ideas even among the bishops. Ecclesiastical studies have improved greatly. In a few years Salamanca will be much better than it is now, and, though this is not much, it is a great deal better now than twenty years ago. *You will say that these solutions are slow. That is true: but there are no others; and if there should be one, I would not be for it. I have said it already; I will never consent to sacrifice the present generation in order to improve future ones.* You approve the spirit of rebellion; I do not; I openly disapprove it, and am very far from believing that it bears the stamp of merit . . . . I believe that a nation which becomes enlightened can make great reforms without bloodshed, and I believe that enlightenment can occur without the necessity of rebellion . . . . If the human spirit is progressive (though this single truth deserves a separate discussion), it is a constant that it cannot pass from the first to the last idea. Progress presupposes a graduated chain, and its course will be determined by the order of its links. The rest will not be called progress, but something else . . . . It is, therefore, necessary to carry out progress by degrees."

How, then, were the rupture, the discord, the dissociation produced which led to our being able to speak in some sense—and not before this time—of "the two Spains"? This is in my opinion a textbook case of the historical phenomenon which I have called elsewhere "induced radicalization," using the adjective in the sense it has in electricity. The "enlightened" Spaniards had a certain community of basic ideas and principles with *part* of the dominant ideas in Europe, especially in France; they were—with some exceptions which counted for very little—moderation itself; but toward the end of Charles III's reign a violent type of extremism arose *in France*, leading to the Revolution; and by means of "induced radicalization" the Spanish Enlightenment acquired a charge of electricity *which was not its own*, which it never wanted to have, perhaps less at that time than any other. But this is not important: to the men of the Enlightenment was attributed everything that happened or might happen in France; and under this pretext, Jovellanos was attacked as bitterly as if he were a Robespierre or a Collot d'Herbois. Any measures seemed justified against those who wanted to suppress the Inquisition, even though they might be men of deep religious feeling, who took the sacraments frequently; against those who aspired to make available foreign books on mathematics, physics, navigation, or philosophy, even though it was to raise the nation's standard of living; against those who wished to raise Spain's ethical and educational level, even though they were incapable of the slightest violence. Suspicion ruled everything. The prestige accumulated in fifty or sixty years of exemplary ethical practices, serious thought, and intellectual solvency was wrested from these men in view of the fact that excesses were occurring in France which they repudiated more than anyone else.

These excesses served to make the reactionary forces feel *justified*. They reasoned more or less in this way: the French have guillotined their king and queen; therefore modern science is an error and we must stick to fifth-hand Scholastic manuals. The Committee of Public Safety is criminal; therefore the Inquisition is admirable. The Jacobins attack religion; therefore theocracy is the only admissible system. Marat and Robespierre are execrable, therefore Galileo, Newton, Descartes, Locke, and Leibniz must be eliminated by every possible means. The Convention established the Terror; therefore we must insist on unrestricted absolutism. Voltaire has contributed to the development of the revolutionary spirit; therefore the torments and tortures he attacked are admirable and should be applied without scruple.

This is no caricature. A simple perusal of the *Gaceta de Madrid* from 1815 to 1820 or after 1823 gives us hundreds of examples of such inferences, both in theory and in the most effective practice.[15]

15 See, for example, the "Exposiciones dirigidas al Rey Nuestro Señor," which fill all the numbers of the *Gaceta* after the Royalist victory of 1823, presented by cities, towns, corporations, religious communities, even groups of Royalist women, asking for severe punishment for members of the constitutional party (including women), immediate re-establishment of the Inquisition, persecution of the "philosophers," etc. Also reports showing that these desires were being carried out, in accordance with the laws drawn up at that time, and that they went so far as searches of private libraries with the obligation of turning over banned books to the bishops of the respective dioceses, under civil penalties.

The evolution of Floridablanca (the man who was probably most influential in the disbanding of the Company of Jesus), recognized by all historians, is very significant of this "induced" radicalization to which I refer. "Too, the last years of the reign of Charles [III] were marked by a notable change in his spirit and conduct, and still more in those of his minister, Floridablanca, in regard to favoring, up to a point, their century's new ideas. This change arose from what was happening in neighboring France, where the political horizon was heavy with clouds and threatened a storm . . . ." "The King of Spain, already very old, was frightened to see the unrest in a state ruled by a monarch of his own family, and head of the family at that, and in a nation with which Spain had so much contact, and to which Spain's most intelligent and cultured sector owed so much, from the loftiest ideas to the most frivolous practices. If this was passing through Charles III's mind, what was going on in France aroused even more worry and displeasure in Floridablanca; and since he was a shrewd and despotic man, and along with this a man of so narrow a piety that it came close to superstition, he decided to pause in his career as a reformer, and, in opposition to the new French ideas, to uphold vigorously the cause of civil and religious tyranny."[16] Alcalá Galiano wrote in this vein in 1835. And when he refers to Floridablanca's policies under the new king, Charles IV (1788), he adds: "Extreme vigilance, therefore, was exercised in Spain over the actions of all private persons; writers who in past days had been protected were now restrained, and in the lowering suspicion which reigned every effort was made to avoid dealings with foreigners, and particularly with the French."[17]

But with all this, we must note that a relative cohesion was maintained in Spanish society even later than this, lasting until the early years of the nineteenth century. The war waged against Jovellanos and his undertaking in the Institute of Gijón was silent and stubborn, but it was still possible to resist.[18] In another area, as late as 1797, Jovellanos

---

[16] *Historia de España* (Madrid, 1845), V, 309–10.

[17] *Ibid.*, VI, 6; see also 11.

[18] "What can this be? Is it possible that some secret persecution of the Institute is going to begin? Of this new Institute consecrated to enlightenment and the public good? And are we to be so unfortunate that no one can assure such institutions against this kind of attack? And what attacks! Inspired by perfidy, issued in secrecy, sustained by hypocrisy and infidelity to all the sentiments of virtue and humanity. But I give them warning! I shall uphold my cause; it is sacred; there is nothing in my Institution, nor

had hopes that the Inquisition would be suppressed, and placed all his intellectual and *religious* confidence in it: "They say that Tavira will be Inquisitor General, and there are even some who say that the *Inquisition will be abolished.* Oh, how much letters would gain from this! How much customs! The fewer hypocrites, the better it would be. Faith would be better deposited in the hands of the Bishops, from whom it was torn; and this mark of infamy, suffered by only three Catholic peoples, would be uprooted forever."[19] Let us also recall the very small amount of violence in a government so absolute and so much attacked as that of Godoy, a real dictator but not a bloodthirsty one, whose most serious outrage was the imprisonment of Jovellanos, which was as long as it was unjust (1801–1808), but which cannot be compared with other kinds of cruelty that were to become extremely frequent a few years later.

The climate of violence did not erupt until the French invasion of 1808, first as a reply to it, but soon in the form of popular mutinies or uprisings. The occupation of the country by Napoleonic troops, the flight of the sovereigns and the government, the external destruction and internal defection of the whole State, left Spanish life at the mercy of the storm. Almost nothing fully acceptable was left. A small number of the "enlightened" men felt the temptation to carry out the desired transformation by accepting the change of dynasty, since the reigning one had shown such lack of dignity, without realizing that the French invasion was not a mere change of dynasty. The greater part of the nation, naturally including the "enlightened" sector, with Jovellanos in the forefront, organized national resistance and tried to reconstruct the State. "Far from renewing the Spain of former times," writes Alcalá Galiano, "all efforts were aimed at the creation of a new Spain."[20] But national accord was purely negative and did not imply *concord*; there was accord in rejecting Napoleon and defending independence, but the ambiguity which underlay this apparently unifying task soon became evident. Alcalá Galiano continues, "In free Spain two warring factions appeared, still *in accord* about waging war on the usurper and

---

in the Library, nor in my counsels, nor in my designs, which is not aimed at the sole object of discovering useful truths. I shall repel attacks, no matter what they may be, and *if necessary, I shall die in the breach.*" (*Diarios,* 5–IX–1795, II, 158–59.)

19 *Ibid.,* 338.

20 *Historia de España,* VI, 329.

his followers, but *in discord* among themselves, with every appearance and even the certainty of carrying the disagreement in opinion, offspring of opposing interests, to the extremes of bitter hatred and merciless struggle."[21] The innovators were at first inclined toward moderation and compromise; but when they were answered with a *total* and extreme rejection which would not accept the slightest transformation—or rather, conformation to what had lost all form—they reacted in their turn with irresponsibility and extremism. And after that time what was to predominate in Spanish public life was the negative, the controversial, the constant emphasis on difference and disunion. In other words, *life as partisanship* began, not as a game, but in the deepest strata of collective life.

3. PERIODS IN CONTEMPORARY SPANISH HISTORY

"Modern" Spain begins with the generation born about the year 1766, whose oldest representative was Moratín. It was, I believe, the generation in which Romanticism began.[22] It began, of course, in the individuals belonging to the avant-garde minority, and therefore manifestations of it began to show when this generation came into power, about 1810—just at the time of the Cortes of Cádiz. The Constitution of 1812 was to be the first generally recognized public reality of the "new" Spain, which was, in fact, Romantic Spain. According to my calculations the last Romantic generation, properly speaking, was that of the men born around 1811; for reasons a little too lengthy to be explained,[23] I believe that *authentic* Romanticism ended in 1849; but the Romantic "world" continued to hold sway as long as that generation stayed in power—in

---

[21] *Ibid.*, 359.

[22] See J. Marías, "Un escorzo del Romanticismo," in *Ensayos de convivencia* (Buenos Aires, 1955), 206ff. (*Obras*, III.)

[23] In 1849, Zorrilla presented his last play, *Traidor, inconfeso y mártir*, and retired, still a young man (he was born in 1817), from the theater, where he had had enormous success. Zorrilla was incapable of writing theater that was not Romantic, and public taste, which in the theater is shown in a collective and immediate form, was already turning in another direction. It is no coincidence that this drama was played by Julián Romea, who was to become a great actor of realistic comedy. And Zorrilla had his last great success by treating Romanticism *ironically*, in the only way possible for him: using a subject—the pastry cook of Madrigal or King Don Sebastian—whose substance was itself ironic.

all aspects of life; that is, until the crisis which immediately followed the revolution of 1868.

The second "period" in contemporary Spain is represented by the three following generations—let us take as probable dates the years 1826, 1841, and 1856—the generations of Valera, Galdós, and Menéndez Pelayo, to choose three highly characteristic names. It was the Spain of the Restoration. I have written "period" in quotation marks, for I doubt very much that this span of time was properly speaking a period; elsewhere I have demonstrated that the "minimal," or elemental, period—what we might call the chronological "intelligible area"—has to take in at least four generations; if historical variations affect a shorter space of time, they are not periods in the sense that a form of life is achieved in which society as a whole takes part, the social body in its entirety.[24] These periods give meaning to a much-used expression in history, which usually is a very trivial one: periods or stages "of transition." All time partakes of transition, for history consists in passing, or *transire*; but there are certain chronological spaces which are those *of transition between periods*; that is, they fill the interstices between the *full* historical forms which take place in close-knit societies, and which therefore presuppose a minimum of some sixty years.

The third period in contemporary Spain, this one worthy indeed of the name without qualification, is the present one, whose undoubted beginning is the so-called Generation of 1898; that is, the men born around 1871, the oldest of whom was Unamuno. This is the first generation of the twentieth century, the one in which certain original ways of reacting to problems, which were to be characteristic of our time, achieved their first effectiveness. But above all else, this generation, decisive in many senses, was destined to have a most delicate historical mission, which has made possible all the best that Spain has produced since, and which explains to some degree what otherwise would be totally inexplicable: the figure of Ortega in Spain and at the date when he appeared. This mission, the most important of his missions if I am not mistaken, was that of canceling out one anomaly in Spanish life, an anomaly with which that life had been burdened ever since the beginning of the "new regime," and which had introduced a tremendous factor of abnormality into the entire history of the nineteenth century,

[24] See my book *La estructura social*, II, 9.

to the point of sterilizing possibilities that could have been very fertile ones.

4. THE ROMANTIC PERIOD AND THE DIFFERENCE
IN LEVEL BETWEEN SPAIN AND EUROPE

At the end of the eighteenth century those Spaniards who were educated and aware of Europe knew very well that Spain was in a bad *situation*; backward, plagued with difficulties, passive in regard to what was being done in more prosperous countries, with a tendency to imitation rather than to original creation, and a low standard of living; but *nothing more*. It will be said that this was no small thing; but it is not so very important if compared with what those same Spaniards felt in the third decade of the nineteenth century, during Ferdinand VII's reign: they were convinced that Spain's *condition* could not be compared to that of other European countries, and, above all, that it could not be improved. Whereas formerly they had treated these countries *on a plane of equality*, even though they recognized their advantages and superiority, thirty years later they no longer even dreamed of catching up, and recognized with dismay that to cross the Pyrenees was to pass into another and different historical reality.

Nothing would be easier, or more suggestive, or more painful than to find documentary proof, in hundreds of texts, of what I have just written; but as this would take us too far afield, I shall cite only two or three brief passages; and to prevent all possible misunderstanding, I shall confine myself *to one person*: Moratín. In 1792 and 1793 he lived in England. His *Apuntaciones sueltas de Inglaterra* ["Scattered Notes on England"] show the degree of detachment with which he regarded and judged everything, and the lack of small-mindedness, hostility, or humiliation with which he confronted the habits and customs of the English, their good qualities and defects, the beauties or uglinesses of their country. When he refers to the frequency of drunkenness,[25] or makes fun of the twenty-one "implements, machines and instruments necessary in England to serve tea for two guests in any decent house,"[26] or admires the tolerance he finds,[27] or explains that

[25] *Obras póstumas*, I, 163.
[26] *Ibid.*, 171.
[27] *Ibid.*, 177.

"the mortal sin of the English, which envelops the whole nation and makes individuals so tiresome, is pride; but a pride so stubborn and incorrigible that it cannot be tolerated,"[28] or when he complains of the discourtesy and distrust of the English and misses "frankness, unselfishness, generosity,"[29] or praises the true charity which exists in England,[30] or takes pleasure in the inns,[31] he is behaving at all times like a European in Europe, one who belongs to the same family—a "poor relation" perhaps, one who has come down in the world, but of the same race after all.

Nor is his attitude toward France different; in spite of his notorious Francophile attitude, which was to carry him to a certain—and more than debatable—degree of "afrancesamiento," or overt sympathy toward the French invaders, he writes in 1787 to Cea Bermúdez, "The same genius that makes them the inventors of so many fashions, of so many mannequins, of so many graceful whims that turn our women's heads and make all Europe pay tribute to the rue Vivienne and the Palais Royal, this same genius, ill-applied to austere architecture, degrades it and corrupts it with novelties and monstrous extravagances . . . . This liberty is spreading so fast in Paris that whatever is most modern is worst . . . . They do not wish to imitate; they want to invent, always; and this desire, which is favorable to the advance of some arts, prejudices and ruins the others."[32]

But when a few years have passed, the attitude is very different. "There is no more time to read and write,"[33] he says dispiritedly in 1816. Two years later, from Montpellier: "I know nothing of Spain; I know only that it is a peninsula joined to the continent of Europe by a long chain of mountains called the Pyrenees; the rest of it, bathed by the Mediterranean and the Atlantic, and separated from Africa by only three leagues."[34] In 1819, from Paris, in a letter to Dionisio Solís: "Maybe it is the influence of the climate, maybe the effect of circumstances, maybe the Devil, who meddles in everything; but the truth is that our sweet country does not permit any of her sons to be outstanding with impunity, and rewards with bitterness the efforts of talent and hard work, at the same time that she gives prizes and honors to igno-

28 *Ibid.*, 180.
29 *Ibid.*, 204.
30 *Ibid.*, 204–206.
31 *Ibid.*, 218.

32 *Ibid.*, II, 109.
33 *Ibid.*, 253.
34 *Ibid.*, 300–301.

rance, error and crimes . . . . Up till now I have not felt the slightest impulse of repentance for having said farewell to my dear country and having changed it for a different soil, *Où d'être homme d'honneur on ait la liberté*."[35] And in 1823, after contemplating the blunders and extremism of the constitutionalists, and their imminent defeat by the Holy Alliance: "Doesn't it seem to you that after so many years of privations, of alarms, of hardships, of unrest, of persecutions, of robbery and abuses, that sensible and peaceful men who have had the misfortune to be born in that blessed land have come to a pretty pass! And don't think that it will end so soon; you will soon see what kind of outcome is in store for us from those men who threaten the whole world from Cádiz, and add to their frantic exaltation the exaltation of despair. I simply cannot imagine any other outcome than calamity, discord, and a long train of miseries."[36]

Even without counting the disturbances arising from the war against the French Republic, and against England in favor of Napoleon, ending in the disaster of Trafalgar (1805), from the beginning of the French invasion (1808) to the death of Ferdinand VII (1833), there was scarcely a moment in Spanish life resembling normality. Nor did normality begin after that date, for from 1833 to 1840 Spain was torn in two by the first Carlist war; and when that was over, a period began which was not exactly one of stability and peace. But during the reign of Isabella II, although unrest existed, at least there were also movement and possibilities; whereas the previous period had consisted by definition of throttling these. For a quarter of a century, by the shortest possible calculation, *nothing could be done* in Spain; and in fact nothing was done: neither culture, nor education of the country, nor industry, nor wealth, nor a bourgeoisie, nor a modern state. To Spain's undoubted backwardness at the end of the eighteenth century was added the forcible paralyzation of those twenty-five years, affecting a social body that was full of vitality. The result was a difference in level between Spain and Europe, of such magnitude that it seemed absolutely impossible to overcome.

In the years of Jena and Berlin, from Fichte to Hegel, the universities were not in operation in Spain. While the historical school flourished, while Auguste Comte began his work, while the English, French,

[35] *Ibid.*, III, 353.
[36] *Ibid.*, II, 460–61.

and German Romantics were writing, and Stendhal published *Le rouge et le noir*, Spanish presses could turn out only translations of mediocre novels, read and re-read by the myopic eyes of the censors, who banned one of Valbuena's poems which mentioned *breasts*, or a reference to *loosened clothing* in a translation of Horace, or Garcilaso's mention of *the shell of Venus*.[37] While parliamentary monarchies were being estab-

[37] *Ibid.*, III, 101 ff. José Gómez Hermosilla writes to his friend Moratín from Madrid, on July 12, 1827, about the vicissitudes of his *Arte de hablar en prosa y en verso*, then in the hands of the censors: "My dear Moratín: When I was about to answer the letter in which you spoke of my book, the order was given, which you have probably heard about already, to suspend its sale . . . . Having established the fact that it was *immoral and conducive to lasciviousness*, and should be banned, they began to seek means of achieving this . . . . It was, therefore, necessary to set in motion lofty and powerful persons, such as the nuncio and the Queen's confessor, and even the Council of the Realm itself; and all these, in a formal report which was handed up to the King, accused the work of being *conducive to unnatural crime*. However, five months had gone by, and nothing had been accomplished; but at last the confessor personally presented to the King a very short description in which he stated that, since various passages in the work were obscene, and in particular the line in the idyll reading
And perchance joining your lips to mine,
it was indecorous to have the Queen's name on the title page. This interpretation was passed on to Calomarde; he, frightened by even the name of the Queen, ordered that the sale of the work be suspended, and that it should be examined by no less a personage than the archbishop of Toledo, along with the patriarch and the bishop of León; but that in addition, before passing it on to these three, he wished to hear the verdict of the very reverend nuncio of His Holiness. He gave it promptly; and as it was his opinion that the work, *in its totality, was recommendable for erudition, delicacy and solidity*, he said that it was necessary to *strike from it* the poem *To Absence*, and also a verse of Valbuena's in which there was a mention of *breasts*. And it is worth noting that the nuncio himself had been the chief author of the conspiracy against the work, or rather against its author, and for five months had been urging the Queen's confessor to denounce it. The three prelates have delayed eight months in issuing their censure, but at last they gave it; and after also praising the work, and paying just homage to *the author's upright intentions*, they propose that the idyll be suppressed as *intolerable*; the *loosened clothing*, in one of the translations from Horace; the *breasts*, from Valbuena; the *shell of Venus*, from Garcilaso, repeated by Francisco de la Torre; my comments following Vergil's verses *Malo me Galatea Petit*; the words *resplendent light*, when speaking of the continued metaphor, and *irresistible necessity*, found in the treatment of the trope . . . ." I have quoted at length here because it seems to me that this passage reveals a situation in its entirety: it is not a question of chance, of an arbitrary action or an individual whim; what we see here is all of official Spain—the Court, the government, the Council of State, the Church in its uppermost hierarchies—examining for many months such small details of a treatise on rhetoric and poetry, becoming scandalized, and using the resources of temporal power against the figures of speech of the classical poets. And Moratín, writing from Bordeaux, after commenting wittily on the whole affair, concludes, "First of all, a piece of advice from a friend: show such censures and defense to only a few, and then prudently, so they will not think that you

lished all over Western Europe, and with them stability for many decades and a state based on law, in Spain the Inquisition was in control again and there was not the slightest personal security. During the years when the first European industrialization took place, from the textile industry to the first railways, the remnants of the Spanish industries—textiles, ceramics, furniture, clocks—which still flourished in the eighteenth century, were destroyed, and all the works of the Friends of the Country, of the ministers of Ferdinand VII and Charles III, of Olavide, Jovellanos, and even of Godoy, were annihilated. And, as a result of all this, Spain "skipped" the establishment of a bourgeoisie, which was to be the axis of life in Europe for the next eighty years; and because of this, the seemingly European forms adopted by Spanish society after 1833 fell upon a social body which was not capable of receiving them, and were a massive affectation—or, as in the felicitous Spanish expression, "hacer que se hace," ["to go through the motions"].

This explains how, in spite of the fact that Spanish life was Romantic at the same time as the rest of Europe, Romantic literature appeared in Spain with a lag of at least a generation: this was the great *décalage* which burdened Spanish culture, with respect to European culture, throughout the nineteenth century; and, what is perhaps even more serious, with respect to the deepest substratum of life in our country.[38] In an almost miraculous way, and one which must be studied, even though very briefly, this *décalage* was cancelled by the Generation of 1898, thus eliminating the essential anachronism which affected the Spanish mind throughout the nineteenth century. In some places, in a few individuals—not in general or anything approaching it—the Spanish mind (not society as such, of course) "caught up." This coincided with the early years of the twentieth century, and opened up possibilities which had not existed in the previous century, not even during the times when it seemed that the history of Spain "was progressing" and that the country was entering upon paths of normality.

5. SPAIN AS DISORIENTATION

The difference of level between Spain and Europe, the lack of an orig-

want to take revenge by that means, and give possible publicity to the affair. Suffer in silence; with the King and the Inquisition, mum's the word."

[38] See my essay, already cited, "Un escorzo del Romanticismo."

inal intellectual output in Spain, the total absence of anything which we could call "criticism," the inexistence, even, of mere *publicity*[39] most of the time, was translated into a result which has not been sufficiently emphasized: *irresponsibility*. Almost everything that was spoken and written in Spain in the first three quarters of the nineteenth century was purely capricious and arbitrary. If this impression is not the first one we receive, it is because, fortunately, time makes a selection as it passes, and what comes to the surface is that which had the deepest and most authentic roots. When we look at things without arranging them in any order of excellence, as Menéndez Pelayo deliberately did in his *Heterodoxos*, and place some next to others with no more justification than that they *existed*, the impression we receive is enormously depressing and even, at times, causes repugnance. Of course it would be a serious historical error to go no farther than this, for then we should have to give up trying to understand the period; but it would also be impermissible not to pass through this impression, naturally, in order to go beyond it and seek the objective hierarchy which things possessed. And—there is hardly any need to state it—we would have to complement the role of the *Heterodoxos* with other books which cast a glaring and sharply focused light on the zones of Spanish life which Menéndez Pelayo chose to leave conveniently in the shadow.[40]

The basic beliefs which supported the common life of society were broken down to an extreme degree; in part through attrition and attenuation, in part also because they had been constantly "formulated" —almost always very clumsily—and "brandished" as fighting weapons; but more than anything else, because they had become enveloped in dubious associations, which had soon dragged down their prestige. Thus there was a deep sense of *discord* in nineteenth-century Spain. On the

---

[39] I have studied the requisites of *publicity* in *La estructura social*, IV, 36, "Opinión privada y opinión pública."

[40] See, for example, Juan Rico y Amat, *Historia política y parlamentaria de España* (3 vols., Madrid, 1860); by the same author, *El libro de los Diputados y Senadores* (4 vols., Madrid, 1862); Antonio Pirala, *Historia de la guerra civil*; Fernando Garrido, *La España contemporánea* (Barcelona, 1865); A. Fernández de los Ríos, *Estudio histórico de las luchas políticas en la España del siglo XIX* (2nd ed., Madrid, 1879); *Historia de la vida y reinado de Fernando VII de España* (3 vols., many documents, Madrid, 1842); Alcalá Galiano's *Historia de España*, already cited, and of course the same author's *Memorias* and *Recuerdos de un anciano*, and other memoirs of the period. The available bibliography is very ample, but the works I have mentioned suffice for my purpose: to evoke a *complementary impression*.

other hand, there was no system of ideas worthy of the name to serve as orientation. At most there was a juggling of "pseudo-ideas," which had only the appearance of ideas. The lack of intellectual discipline, of information, and of strict standards is visible in almost everything that was written or spoken. For sixty years the instability of life—and especially of public life—made it impossible to set certain points of reference, certain norms of evaluation, some few firm and clear convictions which would permit men to know what to hold to, would serve as points from which to begin the crystallization of an intellectual order. The lack of continuity in teaching and the extremely low caliber of the universities[41] made impossible the establishment of schools of thought, or even the normal transmission of scientific disciplines. With all their limitations, with grave defects arising precisely out of this situation, the great merit of the Krausists was that they established the first entity in nineteenth-century Spain which could be called a *school*, and that with it they *initiated*—no more, but it was not a minor achievement—habits of scientific discipline and intellectual responsibility. When we read the writings of these men a century later, we see that most of them are of little interest, but they are usually *respectable*; they have to do with current problems and the state of science in their time; they do not

[41] See Menéndez Pelayo, *Historia de los heterodoxos españoles*, book 8, chapter 1: "Nobody thought of studying; the chairs were unoccupied; two or three Universities had ample revenues, considering the poverty of the times and the country, but the professors in the others were vegetating in indigence. The title of chair-holder was usually purely honorific, and served only as a title or merit for the highest positions in law or administration. No one felt obliged either to teach or to learn simply for the love of knowledge. Teaching was pure farce, a tacit agreement between pupils and masters, founded on mutual ignorance, indifference, and almost criminal abandon. The experimental sciences were forgotten, physics was learned without ever seeing a machine or a piece of apparatus, or rather it was not learned at all, for the students refused to make useless efforts, and presented themselves in the University only on matriculation day and on the day of the examination. If there was anything left of the old system, it was lack of discipline, disorder, rigged voting and competitive examinations. And do not believe that the Universities were *dens of the old obscurantism*; in reality, they were dens of nothing but barbarousness and neglect." And he concludes: "To sum up: in 1845, nothing that was left in the Spanish universities deserved to survive." (*Obras de Menéndez Pelayo* [Edición Nacional, Madrid, 1948], 275.) It must be noted that similar terms were used to describe the Spanish universities until well into the twentieth century: remember Costa's testimony, as well as that of Macías Picavea, Damián Isern, Unamuno, Baroja, Azorín, and even Ortega. The renaissance experienced by the universities from the early years of this century up to the Civil War is as exceptional as it is admirable, seen against the backdrop of a century-old tradition of incredible decline.

produce the hallucinatory impression of so many other books of the period, which seem to be the offspring of improvisation and caprice, of unreason and delusion, of the humor—often the ill humor—of the moment; in short, of irresponsibility.

Needless to say, it would be possible to find in that period some names untainted by irresponsibility, works full of intelligence and good sense; but not even this, although it is true, essentially modifies the situation. For that exceptional responsibility of mind and attitude *had no currency*, and thus it failed to have *public* and collective effects. Not only because all continuity was lacking, but because men scarcely distinguished between what was in fact justified and what did not even pretend to be so, to the point that the best men of the period, those who in their personal works were models of discretion (Valera, for example) automatically felt this discretion diminished when they acted publicly, and were by no means as responsible as they undoubtedly would have been under other circumstances. A vague and widespread skepticism was the expedient to which they appealed in order to attenuate the effects of this irresponsibility, which they stated with pain and disenchantment, but which they did not feel themselves energetic enough to weaken and vanquish. To take a concrete example, think of the reaction of Valera himself to Donoso Cortés' work[42] in 1856, and compare it with his attitude during the years of the Restoration: in the earlier period he still felt sure of himself, at least of his knowledge of affairs and of his good sense, and believed that he knew what to hold to and that he had the ability to persuade others of it; twenty years later he was content to smile ironically, to water the wine so that it would do less damage, and to mistrust everything.

But it would be an error to suppose that there were not vigorous beliefs in the Spain of that time. On the contrary, the first half of the nineteenth century is one of the periods in Spanish history in which certain reigning ideas were lived most energetically, and these give it an intensity unusual in other times. What happened was that these ideas did not affect the whole social body, but only some parts of it, and their very vigor became a factor for dissociation and discord. One

---

[42] "Ensayo sobre el catolicismo, el liberalismo y el socialismo, considerados en sus principios fundamentales, por D. Juan Donoso Cortés, Marqués de Valdegamas," in *Estudios críticos sobre literatura, política y costumbres de nuestros días* (Madrid, 1864), 1–46. (See my article "Una tradición olvidada," in *La Nación* [Buenos Aires, 1959].) [*Los Españoles. Obras, VII.*]

of these beliefs was *liberty*; the other was what might be called "life as *tradition*"—but we must immediately demolish some ambiguities which might confuse everything. The general breakdown of the forms and usages of the "Old Regime," the "life at the mercy of the elements" which was the condition of the century,[43] obliged the Romantics, if they were to be authentic, to be liberals, in a sense which came before politics and was deeper than politics: something resembling a commitment to personal inspiration, a forced abandonment to fate on the part of each of them. This was the vocation which kept their lives tense, which filled those lives and gave them shape, which sustained and fired them. Many men and some women lived and died—with great fearlessness and generosity—for this vocation; they were, in Ortega's phrase, "noble flames of endeavor." Since this was an aspiration, it became converted into a program: liberalism. It must be said that since it dealt with something deeper than politics, this liberal attitude or temper included many authentic reactionaries, who were, if the expression serves, liberally reactionary. And this puts us on the track of certain anomalies of the opposite belief, and helps to clarify it. It is obvious that there was a great difference in attitude between the absolutists of Ferdinand VII's reign and the Carlists who, from the day after the king's death, waged civil war against the liberals, supporters of María Cristina or Isabella. While the former produce unmixed repugnance today, the latter group —who seem to be just like them and in principle are so—do not arouse it, and frequently have an obvious appeal. It is another matter that we feel repugnance for their atrocities and cruelties, just as we do for those frequently committed at the same period by their adversaries as well. There is a linguistic fact, revealing as all such facts are, which can help us to understand: the absolutists of Ferdinand VII's time were often called (the phrase was apparently coined by Eugenio de Ochoa) "*serviles*"; this expression later fell into disuse and, so far as I know,

---

[43] See Alfred de Musset, *La Confession d'un enfant du siècle*, especially the first two chapters, where he describes this situation in particularly felicitous expressions: "Toute la maladie du siècle présent vient de deux causes; le peuple qui a passé par 93 et par 1814 porte au coeur deux blessures. Tout ce qui était n'est plus; tout ce qui sera n'est pas encore. Ne cherchez pas ailleurs le secret de nos maux." "Voilà un homme dont la maison tombe en ruine; il l'a démolie pour en bâtir une autre . . . . Et pendant ce temps-là cet homme, n'ayant plus sa vieille maison et pas encore sa maison nouvelle, ne sait comment se défendre de la pluie, ni comment préparer son repas du soir, ni où travailler, ni où reposer, ni où vivre, ni où mourir; et ses enfants sont nouveau-nés."

was not applied to the Carlists (though it would not matter if it were used occasionally, for it would have been as an exception and would have lacked true currency). Why? I believe, and have said so elsewhere, that the term "servile" responded to the suspicion that underneath this political attitude was hidden a desertion of personality. "When there is nothing with sufficient dignity to justify service," I have written,[44] "the decision to serve is merely servile." The servility during Ferdinand's reign was that of courtiers, of flatterers, and was exercised—except for the three years of constitutional rule, 1820–23—from above; moreover, it was an *urban* phenomenon. On the other hand, Carlism's favorite expression was "to take to the country"; and in fact it was chiefly a rural and village-level movement, and in addition a movement of struggle, opposition, and resistance. The city was liberal; the countryside was *popular*, and was still immersed in what I have called "life as tradition"; Carlism was made up of a clinging to this, of resistance to innovation, to everything that came from outside, to what was mistrusted. Nothing illustrates it better than the picture so marvelously sketched by Unamuno in *Paz en la guerra* ["Peace in War"]: the liberal Bilbao of the second civil war, surrounded by the Carlist countryside, asleep in its "eternal tradition," in what Unamuno himself called —though the expression is equivocal—"intrahistory." Servilism was unauthentic; Carlism was not. Unauthenticity—the second time—came over it when it was interpreted as *traditionalism*. For an *-ism*—that is, an ideology—is literally the opposite of life as tradition; I mean that it is the least traditional thing in the world, for it is precisely what appears when tradition no longer exists, when it is not possible. This *-ism* was also an urban phenomenon, created by politicians and "theoreticians," and was almost entirely imitative, no less French-inspired than the liberal ideologies, but with the difference that while these ideologies, when they had created it, were faithful to their program, the traditionalism of the ideologists reversed the profound significance of the force they were trying to interpret, and drained away its authentic content of tradition.

These two basic beliefs, since they were highly charged with energy and not shared by the whole of society, but simply by fragments of it, split society; and since there was no intellectual discipline capable of

---

[44] "Un escorzo del Romanticismo," in *Ensayos de convivencia*, 227. (*Obras*, III, 300.)

calling both to account and overcoming their division, preserving them as internal forces for a broader common life, both became progressively more negative, fed on reciprocal hostility and on taking a stand against the other position, and became more and more reduced to mere partisanship; this was what Spanish public life consisted of up to 1875—what would continue to beat under its surface, ready to surge forth at the first opportune moment, breaking the thin film of agreement being spread over the country through the efforts of a few groups. The program of collective life became more and more confused, and kept disappearing; less and less did men know what they wanted, and they kept wanting less and less; and what they wanted was not so much being as antibeing. A society is defined, more than anything else, by the things which are not possible in it, because the social body does not tolerate them; by the middle of the nineteenth century, anything was possible in Spain, which is the same as saying that nothing was viable: I call this *disorientation*.

6. THE RESTORATION AND ITS AMBIGUITY

The Restoration of 1875 and the Constitution of 1876 spelled a notable normalization of public life. Cánovas said—and probably believed—that what he was doing was "to continue the history of Spain." If what he meant was that this history, as a coherent trajectory, had been interrupted, he was obviously right; if he believed that the Restoration meant that this trajectory had been found, his error was more than probable. A few years later all discerning spirits, in the grip of disenchantment, felt that this was the case; the war with the United States in 1898 and the loss of the overseas territories made plain how illusory those appearances were. "This nation which we thought cast in bronze," wrote Joaquín Costa in 1898,[45] "has turned out to be a hollow reed. Where we thought we saw an army, a navy, a press, schools, thinkers, justice, parliament, credit, parties, statesmen, ruling classes, there was nothing but a painted backdrop, a Potemkin-style trick, which the roar of a few cannons has caused to slide almost noiselessly to the ground." And he stated even more clearly the following year: "Even before the war Spain was a country which, seen from the outside, was unstructured,

[45] *Reconstitución y europeización de España* (Madrid, 1900), 3.

without real and living institutions, without schools or universities, without an administration, without a parliament, without deputations or city councils or courts of law or registry or insurance or territorial credit, without a navy or an army or diplomacy, though it had the *appearance* of all this, as Sr. Silvela, with his farseeing intelligence, recognized years ago."[46] And he added in 1900, clearly referring to Cánovas: "Just as Cánovas del Castillo came upon the scene to continue not exactly Spain's history, but her decline, so his successors have come upon the scene to continue not decline, but catastrophe."[47]

Illusion, appearance, fakery, phantasmagoria—as Ortega was to say in 1914—this is the interpretation given to the task of the Restoration, which was a gigantic attempt at the "philosophy of as if." The ambiguity was based on that very word, "restoration." It would be unjust, from today's perspective, to forget everything Spanish public life gained after 1875, and for nearly a half-century after that date; the painful reconstruction of a legitimate monarchy and a state based on law, the normalization of the exercise of citizens' rights, in a way which was undoubtedly precarious—there was political bossism, administrative corruption, etc.—but unimaginable either before or after; the balance between authority and freedom, and therefore the considerable margin of activity enjoyed by both; the tremendous improvement in a sense of common life among Spaniards; a considerable rise in the standard of living, accompanied by a rapid increase in the population. But the lack of solidity of all this, the vulnerability of a society which appeared normal from the outside, the existence, revealed by later history, of a layer of discord even more serious than its predecessors—all this showed that, in fact, the Restoration was a superficial and deceptive phenomenon. When the Bourbon dynasty was restored, it was believed that a *restoration* in Spanish life was possible, and that this had been done with the Restoration. Strictly speaking, a reestablishment would have been necessary, a serious facing of the problems instead of considering them solved and covering them with a coat of varnish, a reconstitution of society, which had been disunited ever since the beginning of the nineteenth century at least, and of a state which since the days of the Old Regime had always existed in a form which was both precarious and out of its proper orbit, both oppressive and inefficient. The belief that it was enough to "rejoin," to connect up with a fictitious past, was

[46] *Ibid.*, 153.   [47] *Ibid.*, 275.

the fundamental error of those prosperous years; it was not entirely illusory, not merely an appearance, but it was feeble, superficial, constructed upon a system of falsehoods in the most literal sense of the term: upon the concealment of reality and its problems. What in easier circumstances might have sufficed, and by this I mean the simple exercise of a national normality—for that is what the best men of the Restoration were really attempting—which would have restored elasticity and health to the social body, was absolutely insufficient in a country affected to its very roots by long decades of disagreement, and by a profound difference of level between the country and its immediate world: Europe. To forget, or to refuse to see, this fact was the fundamental error of the Restoration, which left it wide open to the possibility of failure; not only the next failure (1898), but failure in the successive crises which, born of its spirit, were to threaten Spanish life in the following century.

For a long time, Spain had alternated between stagnation and spasm. Beginning with the War of Independence, and with scarcely a break, Spanish history had been a series of spasmodic movements, without continuity or coherence. Fear of this experience, the disillusionment of so much pointless agitation, weariness with partisanship—all this impelled the men of the Restoration toward immobility; peace at any price was in fact their program. That is, stagnation, which had been the constant companion of Spanish society for interminable periods during the seventeenth and eighteenth centuries.

In 1895—three years before the disaster—Unamuno had written a clairvoyant essay, "Sobre el marasmo actual de España" ["On the Present Stagnation in Spain"], the last of the essays in his book *En torno al casticismo* ["On Traditionalism"]. "A profound crisis has transfixed Spanish society," Unamuno said. "In its bosom lie inner readjustments, a brisk shaking-up of elements, a tumult of disorganizations and recombinations, and, beyond all this, a state of maddening stagnation."[48] "The dearth of internal freedom stands out all the more clearly when compared to the great external freedom we seem to enjoy because no one denies it to us. An enormous monotony is spreading and expanding throughout our whole present-day Spanish society, and the result is inertia, the dull uniformity of a leaden slab of massive vulgarity."[49] And then he added these penetrating words: "Every cultivated Span-

[48] *Ensayos*, I, 190.   [49] *Ibid.*, 192.

iard can scarcely be distinguished from any other cultured European, but there is an enormous difference between any Spanish social body and any other foreign one."[50] And he continued, indicating the point which was beginning to seem decisive, linking just those two subjects—European enlightenment and the pure popular strain—with which we saw that disunity had begun in the eighteenth century, "Is everything dying? No, the future of Spanish society waits within our historical society, in intrahistory, in the unknown people of the nation; and it will not arise as a force until it is awakened by the winds or tempests of the European atmosphere . . . . Spain is yet to be discovered, and only europeanized Spaniards will discover her."[51]

This is, formulated with all concision, the posing of the problem for those who wish, underneath appearances, to confront the true reality of Spain, masked by the hallucinatory calm of the Restoration.

7. "RECONSTITUTION AND EUROPEANIZATION OF SPAIN"

Under this title, and with the subtitle "Program for a National Party," the "Directorate" of the National League of Producers published a book in 1900. This volume was composed of a number of essays and speeches by Joaquín Costa, together with some documents relating to these, all from the years 1898 to 1900. The title of this book is the most felicitous formulation of the program of *regeneration*, the urgent necessity for which was vigorously upheld by a minority during the last decade of the nineteenth century. This book is not the place to study it in detail, though it well deserves study; here we will simply indicate its position as an integrating element in the Spanish situation at the turn of the century. The central figure in this group is undoubtedly Costa (1846–1911), whose influence on the young Ortega, as we shall see, was so great; but we should also take into account Ricardo Macías Picavea (1874–99), author of *El problema nacional: hechos, causas, remedios* ["The National Problem: Facts, Causes, Remedies"] (1899) and Damián Isern (1852–1914), who in that same year, 1899, published a bulky volume on *El desastre nacional y sus causas* ["The National Disaster and Its Causes"]; not to mention the

[50] *Ibid.*, 197.   [51] *Ibid.*, 211.

writers, especially those of the generation born around 1841, who shared the same spirit; and also, to a certain degree, Galdós.

As Laín Entralgo[52] has so shrewdly observed, these men were very much in the spirit of the seventeenth century *arbitristas*, both for good and for ill, in spite of certain scientific pretensions and, in some cases, an undeniable intellectual discipline. But underneath all this, they must be considered in two aspects. The first, common to all, is what we may call their "theoretical radicalism." This can be immediately explained as a reaction against the climate of the Restoration, against the easy optimism, the frivolity, a certain "felicity" felt during those years, in spite of the many sordid features of life, a reaction well reflected in the *género chico*, or popular theater. The "regenerationists" indulged in implacable, overwhelming criticism of everything in existence; in fact, they tried too hard, for if things had been as they painted them, Spain would not have existed and no one could have lived there. This does not mean that the regenerationists distorted or falsified reality; they were truthful men, and Costa was a person of incredible sincerity, uprightness, and good faith; they were given to data and statistics, and were always ready—like the good Positivists they still were—to bring "facts" to bear, and these facts were in large measure both accurate and distressing; but what happened was that they scarcely had eyes for any but lamentable things, which were many, and so they forgot that even in the most prosperous situations—for example, in the France, England, or Germany of 1900, which they considered the summit of perfection—innumerable stupid, faulty, unjust, and atrocious things existed. For these men, to invert the terms of Cánovas' formula, the great need was to go back to the beginning. Everything had sunk into the profoundest corruption and decline, and there was no other hope than an appeal to the great resources and profoundest depths of the Spanish soul. Hence no restoration would do; what was needed was a truly radical *regeneration*; that is, one arising from the very roots of society.

"Creeping paralysis and Hapsburguism," wrote Macías Picavea, "hold sway today, just as in the imminent crises of the reigns of Charles II and Charles IV, and with identical symptoms of barbarism, 'colorful' low-life, demoralization, theocracy, a surfeit of friars, and Caesarism.... Today we are disoriented, lost, astray, as never before. Healthy, vital, traditional Spain has vanished into time and is lost in the depths.

[52] Pedro Laín Entralgo, *Menéndez Pelayo* (Madrid, 1944), 99ff.

The deep, hidden, under-the-skin history Unamuno speaks of, which evolves and flows underneath our lives, grows increasingly more difficult to illuminate, as we dig ever deeper into the subsoil of the Spanish soul."[53] And when he sets out to present the "pathological chart" of Spain, he enumerates the following diseases: Hapsburguism ("the primary and initial disease," his great *bête noire*), Caesarism, ministerial despotism, political bossism, centralism, theocratism, universal Catholicism, intolerance, militarism, paralysis of evolution, idiocy, psittacism ("from *psitaccus*, parrot or parakeet"), atrophy of the organs of national life, the ignoring and supplanting of tradition, loss of personality, lack of orientation ("We have lost the polestar of our history, and do not know where we are going either from within or without. . . . every Spaniard is a man lost in the desert"), lack of culture, ideologism, vagrancy, poverty, barbarous ethical standards, decadentist irreligiosity, a regressive loss of civic sense. And the conclusion is "this implacable dilemma: either heroic treatment, or a hopeless prognosis."[54] The section devoted to "remedies" is unfortunately too vague—or too detailed. It is tinged with arbitrism and does not have great penetration or originality, although there is no lack in Macías Picavea of ideas—perhaps merely "bright ideas"—which surprise us by their acuity and which we shall have to recall later on.

The word most often repeated by Damián Isern in his book is "degeneration." With a great deal of statistical data, quotations from German, English, and French psychologists, sociologists, and politicians, he sketches an extremely somber picture to explain *The National Disaster*. The scope of his book is more limited than Macías Picavea's; but his assumptions are almost the same. The chief difference is that Isern is less rhetorical, less impassioned, and especially less hopeful. "I offer to the public," he says, "an album of photographs taken from social, economic, juridical, political, and military facts, and I am bound to add that in them I have paid more attention to careful observation than to preconceived ideas, to the strict need for exactitude than to the demands of art, to fidelity of expression than to the embroideries of elegant expression."[55] His work, he adds, has been written "not to dishearten our country, for, as Menéndez Pelayo has so correctly said, 'to

[53] Ricardo Macías Picavea, *El problema nacional* (Madrid, 1899), 366.
[54] *Ibid.*, 370–76.
[55] Damián Isern, *El desastre nacional y sus causas* (Madrid, 1899), 5.

help to dishearten one's mother is truly an impious deed'; but to point a finger at the causes of the disaster we have undergone, so as to make possible the cure for the present evils as well as for other more serious and transcendental evils of future times, which are inevitable if we follow the path which we unfortunately took not many years ago."[56]

Costa's position is more complex and more ambitious. He was gifted with extraordinary rhetorical power, was able to coin striking slogans (though frequently they were of low literary quality, sometimes very felicitous but in doubtful taste); and the word which time and again came to his lips was "thunder." Costa thundered against everything, and especially against the politicians and civil servants, against the "criminal frock-coats and lawyers' robes" who ought to be packed into the prisons. Sometimes his slogans did not express what he meant (for example, "a double lock on the tomb of the Cid"), and he was obliged to clarify them; others described a situation: "oligarchy and bossism"; others were programmatic: "school and pantry," "protect the tree," "hydraulic policy," "the surgeon with an iron hand." Occasionally his "arbitrism" appears, even in an extreme form: in 1904 he sent a postal card to a raffle organized by the Republican Brotherhood Society in Barcelona, in which he condemned its entire program. It is worth reproducing here:

"A natural patriciate, social authorities, but not bossism; self-government, government of the people by the people, but not parliamentarianism; army and Civil Guard, but not militarism; many and large amounts of capital, but not capitalism; freedom of trade, but not vampirism; religion and clergy, but not clericalism . . . .

"Double lock on the tombs of Torquemada and Calomarde, so that they cannot return with their 'purifications' to sully Spain and rot her away.

"Few things are so urgently needed here as to improve the spiritual direction of small and medium-sized localities by improving the staff of teachers and priests and making them two addends, instead of what they are today, one minuend and one subtrahend. —Joaquín Costa."[57]

The most novel factor in Costa's work lies in the second part or element of the program: *europeanization*. The realization that Spain was not wholly European had been obtruding painfully. Macías Picavea

---

[56] *Ibid.*, 3–4.
[57] Joaquín Costa, *Política quirúrgica* (Madrid, 1914), 59.

speaks of "our Galdós, the foremost novelist, by a wide margin, in Europe in this century . . . if Spain belonged to Europe."[58] Costa, no matter how much he might insist (like the other partisans of "regeneration") on the economic and administrative factors, did not lose sight of the fact that these were not the only, or most important, ones. "Morocco," he writes, "broke down as a nation centuries ago, although it has no public debt and its budgets never show a deficit; and we do not want to be a copy of Morocco or a duplicate of China. We want to breathe the air of Europe; Spain must quickly change her African atmosphere into a European atmosphere, so that we will not feel a nostalgia for foreign things—what a horrible reversal! Spaniards, yes, but Europeans."[59] His program is "to contain the backward movement and absolute and relative africanization, which is dragging us farther and farther from the orbit in which European civilization moves and develops; to carry out a total casting of the Spanish state into the European pattern which history has given us ready-made, and to whose forward thrust we have succumbed . . . to found without delay a new Spain in the Peninsula; that is, a rich Spain and one that has enough to eat, a cultured Spain and one that thinks, a free Spain and one that governs, a strong Spain and one that conquers; a Spain, in short, contemporaneous with humanity, a Spain that does not feel foreign outside her own borders, as if she had gone to another planet or another century."[60]

Costa's whole work, his tenacious effort, is a gloss on these words. The problem is transferred from Spain alone to Europe; that is, Spain in Europe. But the question is this: From what vantage point is this europeanization called for, so sorrowfully and nobly? From Europe, or perhaps only from Spain?

8. THE CRISIS OF 1898

"In 1898 the last remnants of the old Empire slipped out of Spanish hands, and Spain's fragile ships, laden with individual heroism, sank in far-off seas. For Spain there was no longer a shadow of the former power; now there were no more islands in the Caribbean Sea for self-

[58] Macías Picavea, *El problema nacional*, 363.

[59] *Reconstitución y europeización de España*, 159–60.

[60] Joaquín Costa, *Los siete criterios de gobierno* (Madrid, 1914), 57–58. See also *Crisis política de España (Doble llave al sepulcro del Cid)* (Madrid, 1914).

confident Spaniards, with their promises of golden pesos, lulled by playful breezes that linked the rhythms of the hammock and the fan . . . . There was no more white Cuba where the gentleness of the native wife and the fawning of the Negro servant made men dream of overlordship . . . . Nor were there the far-off Philippines, where a man could be carried in a litter and feel himself superior to yellow-skinned men . . . . And the country scorned for its lack of tradition, insolent with youth, had buried our ships and our sailors along with the last dreams of empire.

"This liquidation of past glory, this final defeat, sank the majority of the Spanish people into inertia, into their petty private interests, into their indifference . . . . People went mad over the next bullfight and sighed with relief because they did not have to *give* their sons *to their country*; the middle class criticized the government, insulted the Yankee, worried about whether it had influence with each new ministry, and did not believe in its country; the governments in power constantly sang the praises of past national glories and were based on insincerity. National life continued on its course without emotion, without pulse, without tension . . . . Everything was worn-out and lacking in vitality; obsolete forms persisted, but they were hollow and maintained the fiction of effectiveness; nothing had the strength to put forth new shoots.

"Such was the picture offered to the almost adolescent sensibilities of a new generation which approached life with open eyes and sensitive hearts. These young men came to be called the *Generation of 1898*, a generation conditioned by that unhappy date in Spanish history."[61]

This is the way Dolores Franco has described, in her anthology *La preocupación de España en su literatura* ["The Preoccupation of Spain in Spanish Literature"], the situation within which the Generation of 1898 began its historical life. And I say the Generation of 1898, and not simply the situation of Spain in 1898, because to say Spain alone is an abstraction: inherent in the situation, as one of its constituent ingredients, is the aspiration of the man for whom the situation exists,[62] and therefore at any given moment there are at least as many historical

---

[61] Dolores Franco, *La preocupación de España en su literatura*, 255–56. [*España como preocupación* (1960), 287–88.]

[62] See my *Introducción a la Filosofía*, I, 9; and from the point of view of collective life, *La estructura social*, I, 6.

situations as there are active generations coexisting at that moment. As we have seen, the disaster of 1898 affected the men of previous generations: most fully, the generation of men who were representative of the Restoration, those who were "in power" (Cánovas, Sagasta, Valera, Echegaray, and Castelar had recently died) and those who were struggling to take their places (Costa, Macías Picavea, Giner de los Ríos, Azcárate, Galdós); in a less immediate sense—perhaps because of their generation's collective vocation as "scholars," in Laín's opinion,[63] and in any case because of their lesser *historical* responsiblity—Clarín, Hinojosa, Ramón y Cajal, Ribera, Menéndez Pelayo, Cossío, Emilia Pardo Bazán, Palacio Valdés, Ortega Munilla, Maragall. For all these men, the "national disaster" was something that took place in their lives, within those lives, that became part of their trajectories, in the case of some almost spent, in the case of the others well launched at least. For some it was the confirmation of what they had foreseen, for others a rude awakening. But for the very young, for the men of the generation which was to receive the name of that year, it meant the *horizon* of their lives, the conditioning factor of their vital plans. In a certain sense, they were going to have to imagine and project those lives "from that point," and thus their lives were made of that substance, were intertwined with the national concern from their very beginning, were sentimentally affected by the "painful emotion" in which that generation of literary genius expressed itself.

This means that, for those who were beginning to act in history at that time, the fiction on which the Restoration had been based was no longer possible. The assumptions upon which Spanish life had rested for the last twenty-five years, and those on which it was going to continue to be based, even in the form of dissent, for the men of previous generations, *were no longer in force* for the new generation. Remember Costa: he *thundered* against each and every one of the elements of the Restoration, but he was conditioned by them, he lived by opposing them, he needed them to be who he was—their adversary. Observe also the early impression of "old age" that the men of the generation of 1856 were so soon to give; as an extreme case, Menéndez Pelayo, who was born in that year, and who, even in his early years, seemed "ancient" long before his death in 1912. The men of 1898, however, did not really take the Restoration seriously, and if they engaged in polemics with it,

---

[63] Laín Entralgo, *Menéndez Pelayo*, 97ff.

this was to continue the tradition of their elders and to go on at once to *something else*. The fact is that, precisely because the currency of those assumptions had ended, a new period, in a strict sense, began *in Spain* with the Generation of 1898: the present period. (In Europe the present period began a generation earlier, precisely with the generation of 1856, that of the *innovators* in every field, one of the most extraordinary generations in modern history, and the one out of which what we may call *our time* arose.)[64] Hence the function *hors pair* of the Generation of 1898, of which I shall have to speak later, and the surprising sense of contemporaneity which it maintains today, sixty years after the "disaster" which conferred its name upon it. It is a historical phenomenon which can be explained only because the essential principles on which it based its form of life are still in existence—in other words, because we are still in the same period which those men initiated.

It would be well, however, to describe the situation in a little more detail, for confusion here is easy and has been frequent. How often there has been insistence on the relatively small importance of the events of 1898 on the writers of that generation, when it has been demonstrated that many of them were already writing—and in their own style— several years before, and others not until some years afterward, when the year 1871 is proposed as the central birth date, and 1901, in consequence, as the date of the beginning of its historical action (and this is precisely my opinion); but even though all this is true and important, the importance and significance of the date 1898 has not been destroyed or diminished, for that date is different; it is not generational. I mean that the "event" of the war with the United States and the loss of the rest of the Empire does not define a generation, which attains its proper level because of general historical reasons,[65] with a certain independence of concrete happenings. What the year 1898 signifies is the revelation of the emptiness of the basic assumptions of previous generations, the discovery of the falsehood on which Spanish life had been based, under a thin film of favorable appearances. In other words, 1898 is no more than the *developer* (in the photographical sense) that showed what the

[64] See my article "La generación de 1856," in *El oficio del pensamiento* (Madrid, 1958).

[65] The theoretical justification of this will be found in my books *El método histórico de las generaciones* (Madrid, 1949) and *La estructura social*, II, "Dinámica de las generaciones." [*Obras*, VI.]

true situation in Spain was; after that, Spain could live *authentically* only by recognizing this fact, and therefore by beginning a new era.

9. SHIPWRECK AS A POINT OF DEPARTURE

Were I to summarize in a single expression the representative attitude of the men of 1898, I would choose this one: *acceptance of reality.* Therefore, the first thing these men did was to *take possession* of Spain. First, physically, and thus they were to be the inventors of a landscape, creators of a "literary Castile" more real than the physical one, and after that creators of a whole Spain; they were to travel from one end of Spain to the other, to emphasize and collect to the last detail her poverty as well as the most profound of her charms; they were to read and reread her classics and bring them to life; they were to discover, to investigate and rethink her history; they were destined, above all, to dream of her—that is, to take possession of her profoundest and most essential reality: namely, what she possessed of a plan or project.

When I say *acceptance of reality*, I do not mean "conformity," still less "conformism," but quite the opposite: acceptance of reality *exactly as it is*; and they found that that reality, paradoxically, was *unacceptable.* By this I mean that they were to take it precisely as something which they could not leave as it was, but from which they must go forward. The shipwreck in which Spanish reality *consisted* was to be their point of departure. We could quote hundreds of texts from Unamuno, Azorín, Baroja, and Antonio Machado to prove it;[66] but I merely wish to recall some rather late words of Azorín's, in 1913, in which he draws up a balance sheet of the attitude of the whole group: "It is not *chiefly* a literary orientation, in my opinion, which brings us together here. Aesthetics is only a part of the great social problem. For those of us who live in Spain, who feel her sorrows, who participate—with so much faith—in her hopes, there is a supreme, anguished, tragic interest which is above aesthetics. We will desire the renewal of literary art; we will anxiously await a revision of all the traditional artistic values; but these hopes and longings are contained within and scattered through other ideals which are more impelling and more lofty. It would be vain for

---

[66] See Dolores Franco, *La preocupación de España*, part 5, pp. 255–417. [*España como preocupación*, 285–506.]

us to pursue the less important if we did not first make every effort to achieve the more important."[67]

Only this can explain a fact which is fully obvious today: that beginning with the Generation of 1898 a sudden concentration of genius appeared in Spain, what we have been calling—overhastily, or mistrustfully?—"a golden *half*-century." From Quevedo and Calderón in the seventeenth century to the beginning of the twentieth century, there was only one man of genius in Spain, if we take the word genius in its strictest sense; and this man was not an intellectual, but a *visual* and *manual* person, a painter and artisan: Goya. This is an excessive dearth of genius for a period of 250 years, especially in a country where the previous 50 years had seemed to lavish genius to an almost disturbing degree. How is it understandable that about 1900 things changed so suddenly, and a *superior* Spanish quality arose so abruptly, so portentously? I do not believe that it can be explained as a mere matter of "gifts"; a people's gifts are approximately the same throughout their history, at least for very long periods. We will have to look for reasons on the more properly human—that is, the biographical—side, and on the collective, historical side. It is *life* as such which had a point of modulation about 1900, and which *did something new* with the same psycho-physical elements, the same gifts.

The men of 1898 produced literature, art, history, science, *because they could do no other*, because they had started off with a shipwreck and needed to know what to hold to. No external reason—economic advantage, social prestige, political opportunities, automatism of institutions—led them to the intellectual life; it welled up from inside them, from the profoundest depths of their authenticity, because they needed it *to be themselves within that Spanish reality which they had accepted*. In these men intellectual life became fresh and new, as it has done very few times in history; they produced it as the pre-Socratics might have, with equal intensity, purity, and efficacy. It may be said that what they produced was, more than anything else, *literature*, that they were a "generation of literary men"; this is true, but I see in this fact, far from being coincidental, the deepest and most revealing facet of their historical destiny, a point to which I shall have to return later.

Even those who were within the tradition of a scientific, philological, or historical discipline, those who were apparently concerned only with

[67] *Fiesta de Aranjuez en honor de Azorín* (Madrid, 1913), 44–45.

its technical demands—Menéndez Pidal, Gómez Moreno, Asín Palacios—who for a long time have been felt to be detached from the group
of "writers" in the strict sense, turn out to have been united to them
by a profound link, to have been imbued with the same concern, moved
to the very fiber of their being by the same impulse which inspired the
work of the novelists and poets. The careful research which led to
the identification of the origins of the Spanish language, the survival of
the *Romancero*, the Arabic elements in Spanish and European culture,
the art and archaeology of our country are only the tactical path, according to the vocation of its authors, leading to the same point where, by
other paths, Azorín's literary evocation, Antonio Machado's lyricism,
and Unamuno's *excitatio Hispaniae* lead. When we consider the end
result of Menéndez Pidal's highly scientific work, for example, we find
that its deepest motivation was the need to clarify the meaning of Spain's
history, to *begin again*, but not from zero—indeed, precisely after
having taken into account this unacceptable reality which had formerly
been accepted as fate is accepted.

This is why all these men, faced with the general skepticism of the
Restoration, faced with its attitude of "going through the motions"
and ultimately taking nothing seriously, could not be satisfied with
less than the truth. For each of them the truth inherent in their
specialty: philological truth, historical truth, the aesthetic truth of the
authentic man of letters. These shipwrecked men who recognized themselves as such, felt that only the truth could keep them afloat.

10. THE PROBLEM OF INTELLECTUAL METHOD

But here the most serious question arises. Spain had lost all her own
intellectual tradition a long time before. Not only had she lacked all
strictly scientific or original philosophical thought ever since the seventeenth century, but since the end of the eighteenth, she had not even
been up-to-date in a receptive sense. She was very far from possessing,
in any adequate way, what was being done in Europe. The few who
really knew the intellectual output of the leading countries at that
time—Valera, for example—held a view of it which was purely one
of "enjoyment" (or if not, a scholar's view); I mean, it was passive,
and had no connection with personal, real, and authentic problems.
Given these assumptions, there could be no possible real *incorporation*

of foreign culture, or any way of overcoming the nineteenth-century *décalage*. The enormous reading range of Valera and Menéndez Pelayo, the great keenness of the former and the tenacity of the latter, the intellectual probity of Giner de los Ríos, the passion of Costa, could not achieve this incorporation in spite of all their effort and all their worth.

This is the point at which we must introduce upon the scene the literary character of the Generation of 1898. I have already said that I considered this to be no coincidence, but the most revealing factor in its historical destiny. The literary quality of the authors in this group is *intrinsic*, not a result of the mere coincidence of being great writers, as in the case of Valera himself. For the *vital* approach to the themes these writers had taken as their own was made in a literary way. I mean, out of a literary *temper*: literature is not a joke, but an essential human possibility—and necessity. The radical innovation of the men of 1898 in literature—I mean the innovation common to all of them, the one which contrasts them with the most representative men of the Restoration, even with the greatest of this generation, Galdós, and explains their coldness toward him—is what I have called the "sense of style";[68] and this is achieved when a certain idea exists of what it is to write, and therefore what it is to be a writer, which the nineteenth century had not possessed. "There can be a sense of style," I have said, "only when the author is present in every written line. I mean when *he* has written it, and not other alien and impersonal powers. These powers can be so diverse that their common root, which is always the same, cannot be discovered. Galdós' carelessness, in which the author is almost always replaced by 'what is said,' is as apparent as the formula-based preciosity of noncreative Baroque writers. No one doubts that splendid edifices can be built with bricks—and that is what Galdós' work consists of—but it is not easy to forget that the edifice has something of the bourgeois house about it." Authors who have a sense of style—no matter how abysmal the distance between them, no matter what their period or language—"those authors have been there, on the page, moment after moment, thinking, inventing, singing, recounting, and never letting 'people' speak for them. And this is why, when we read that isolated page, it seems as though we have felt for a moment the warmth of their hand between our own two hands."

[68] "Calidad de página," in *Ensayos de convivencia*, 155–57. (*Obras*, III, 241–43.)

This is the situation of the writers of 1898, from Ganivet to Baroja and Valle-Inclán. The personal literary temper is what confers communicative authenticity on their subjects, and what, in turn, emerges from that radical authenticity which was their very essence. What I should like to emphasize is that only with such literature was the "reappropriation" of intellectual life in Spain possible. And therefore everything which has been authentic among us—even science and the strictest theory—since that time, has been accomplished by being incarnated in exceptionally effective literary forms. And if I am not mistaken, this has been one of the great Spanish accomplishments of our century, one of our most fruitful contributions to contemporary culture, still to be achieved by other countries where the situation is different. In the nineteenth century, a tradition of scientific discipline excused them from literary achievement—not without failures which quickly became apparent; in Spain, doctrine acquired its *personal* (and in consequence, authentic) character only within this immediate and creative literary situation, and ever since then has been a useful means of measuring the degree of intensity and plenitude of that character. If we look backward, and think of the precarious nature, in a literary sense, of works as admirable as Balmes' or Sanz del Río's, what I have just said acquires an unexpected corroboration; and analogous observations could be made about our more recent intellectual output.

But this, though absolutely necessary, was not sufficient. Mere scientific discipline is not enough either, at least as it is achieved in the humanities. The information given to us by science is fragmentary and is reduced to specific objects. Under the best of circumstances, this gives us a number of partial certainties, whose relative value and mutual connection is likely to be problematical. Mere observation gives us only isolated elements, insufficient for us to know *what to hold to*. And in fact, this was precisely what motivated the whole heroic intellectual action of 1898. The lack of *theory*, strictly speaking, placed under interdict the success of that splendid undertaking.

The situation was all the more serious because the only men of that generation who had a theoretical vocation, Ganivet and Unamuno,[69]

---

[69] It must be noted that some of the most earnest and scrupulous *research men*—such as, for example, Miguel Asín Palacios and Ramón Menéndez Pidal—inspired by the very force of the things they knew so thoroughly, would later make discoveries and attain points of view which had strict theoretical value. On the case of Menéndez Pidal,

never succeeded in fulfilling it adequately. The former, of course, because of his premature death at thirty-three, in that same year of 1898; the second because, for reasons I have studied in depth elsewhere,[70] he made his intellectual attitude consist in *avoiding theory*. The irrationalism dominant in European thought at the turn of the century made unlikely the birth of a strict theory—that is, a rigorous philosophy—in a country in which for exactly three hundred years— Suárez' *Disputationes metaphysicae* dates from 1597—not one single original philosophical work fully worthy of the name had appeared.

These are, in my judgment, the terms of the problem. When the authenticity of intellectual life and the literary temper which made it communicable and fruitful had been recovered, when the difference in level between Spain and Europe which Spain had dragged like a fetter throughout the nineteenth century had been cancelled—at least in the minds and attitude of a very small minority—when a really determined effort had been made to accept, possess, and interpret Spanish reality, then *disorientation* reappeared, in a more subtle form: precisely that of the European form of *despair of reason*. Was not the European solution perhaps an ultimate and even thornier problem?

a truly exemplary one, see my articles "La poesía juglaresca en su realidad histórica" and "La idea de estado latente en el método de Menéndez Pidal" (in *Insula* [Madrid, April–May, 1958].) [*Los Españoles. Obras*, VII.]

[70] *Miguel de Unamuno* (Madrid, 1943) [English translation, Harvard University Press, Cambridge, Mass., 1966], and *La escuela de Madrid* (Buenos Aires, 1959). (*Obras*, V.)

II.
EUROPEAN THOUGHT
ABOUT 1900

II. PHILOSOPHY AND LEVEL: THE CRISIS OF PHILOSOPHY IN THE WAKE OF GERMAN IDEALISM

"More than anything else in life, philosophy is level," Ortega has written somewhat abruptly.[71] We must take this expression seriously, for I think that it contains an important truth. Philosophy itself, when it came into existence, meant that a certain level had been achieved, very different from the levels on which prephilosophic thought had moved. Its radical innovation consisted in this. Pre-Socratic "thought," at least up to Parmenides, was quite simple and elementary, certainly much more so than other previous forms, incomparably richer and more complex, both inside and outside of Greece, as well as in Egypt, Mesopotamia, and Iran. What Thales represents—and, in another category, Hecataeus of Miletus—is the taking up of questions *at another level* (and within that level, for the moment, with obvious poverty of thought). This "other level" uncovers a new stratum of reality, which in principle is resistant to exploration, an exploration begun, naturally, with very crude mental techniques. This explains the fact of the very noticeable "primitivism" of a thought which, however, seems to us to be superior in another sense: its superiority corresponds to its *level*, even though within that level the results are crude and elementary.[72]

Within philosophy (that is, throughout its history) something similar occurs—and this is why philosophy can properly have a history, not a mere succession of exertions and discoveries. Every philosophy operates at a precise level, which has been "achieved" and which constitutes its ultimate substance. Since every form of thought is partial, because it

[71] *Prólogo para alemanes* (1934) (Taurus, Madrid, 1958), 34.
[72] See my *Biografía de la Filosofía* (*Obras*, II), especially I, 1–2.

is conditioned by a perspective which pays heed to certain areas of reality and ignores others, it often happens that a series of elevations of level are followed by an abrupt "descent." Within the totality of a given form of life, this is usually justified: we are dealing here with a peculiar "turning back" to take in areas of reality which had been abandoned when an idea "took off," as all philosophic thought does, especially in its more abstract forms. This is precisely the historical meaning of the philosophy which immediately follows Parmenides, somewhat later of Sophistry, and lastly—and this the most important and characteristic example—of Stoicism and the other Hellenistic philosophies after Plato and Aristotle.[73] That is, lowerings of level are likely to be produced when the previous level has become *impossible to sustain*—almost always owing to an excess of abstraction, which leads to a loss of contact with the problems, or through neglect of an essential part of those problems, which then reclaim their rights. The fact that the theoretical consequences of such descents are sometimes extremely serious does not mean that they are not historically justified. Their full and positive significance is that of elevating to the achieved level the portions or dimensions of the real which had been superseded. When further progress in one direction is no longer possible, an "assumption" has been exhausted, and it becomes necessary to take a step backward in order to "incorporate" the rest. Clearly, on some occasions when this is done, especially if causes extraneous to philosophy interfere or if the process lasts too long, the very meaning of the *theory* is lost, and that is when a real loss of level takes place: these are the authentic *crises* of philosophy, in which philosophy's existence is threatened, with no assurance of being able to survive (in all human creations, and even more so in the case of so subtle and delicate a reality as philosophy, there is a constitutional risk of this: man and everything which is truly his, I mean all that is human, are always exposed to two radical possibilities: to be lost or to be saved).

The problem of philosophical *level* comes even more sharply into focus when philosophy is forced out of an ambit in which it has germinated and goes into different ones—or, which is the same thing, when access to philosophy occurs in peoples who have not created it originally. The first example in history is Rome, which had not *arrived* at the

[73] See *ibid.*, I–III.

level on which Greece had faced problems; this condemned Rome's philosophy to relative unauthenticity precisely with regard to its level— that is, previous to all its doctrinal contents. *Mutatis mutandis*, the Arabs' access to philosophy (Greek philosophy, of course) in the Middle Ages is a similar occurrence; and in yet a third different form, something similar occurs in Jewish and Christian Scholasticism. (In two directions, let us not forget: if it is true that from the point of view of strict theory there is a lowering of level in the Scholastics when they are compared with the Greeks, and hence the inevitable uneasiness produced by medieval Aristotelianism in everyone who knows Aristotle well, it is no less certain that Christianity represents a still greater radicality, though in a different line, and therefore poses questions at a more profound level—notion of creation, idea of person, etc.; the serious side of the matter is that the Scholastics, quite aware that they had not achieved the level of the Greeks, and especially of Aristotle, and longing to place themselves on the same level with the Greeks, did so as much upwards as downwards—that is, as much by forcing themselves to achieve an adequate form of theory as by sacrificing their own demands for radicality, adapting themselves to a "Greek," though relatively superficial, way of facing very profound and fruitful Christian themes. The history of Western thought has still not been able to overcome this unfortunate "act of leveling.") Lastly, and in fact during our time, this is the problem which to me seems decisive when we consider the possibilities and risks of philosophy (initially European) in America: on what level is it to be taken? In what measure does the fact that philosophy is located from the outset on the level where it is placed when it is "received" suppose unauthenticity?

To me, this point of view seems necessary for the proper understanding of nineteenth-century European philosophy. Its history could be interpreted as a series of efforts to recover the level lost after the decline of German idealism (if a date is required, let us say 1831, the year of Hegel's death). But we would first have to give an accounting of this loss. Hegelianism represented the culmination, the perfection, of one line of thought. It could go no further along that line. At the same time, perfection signified the concluded, the finished nature of it. Of course there was no lack of attempts to advance in other directions; the three most important, if I am not mistaken, were the following: the thought of Marx, that of Schelling in his old age, especially in his

Philosophie der Mythologie,[74] and that of Kierkegaard. But all three were still too much "inside" the ambit of idealism, in its "element," as Hegel himself would have said. On the other hand, Marx advanced only in one particular direction, leaving to one side the traditional body of philosophy; Schelling's work, though of an innovating kind in many senses, suffered too much from the characteristics which made Hegelianism "indefensible"; lastly, Kierkegaard is too "anti-Hegel" (and consequently excessively "parasitical"), focused on religion, and in addition extremely "provincial," in the sense Ortega has demonstrated.[75]

Only Positivism made possible the effective continuation of philosophy, although precisely "at another level." Auguste Comte was no longer "inside" the Hegelian ambit; rather he carried Hegel "inside" himself. His thought, composed of renunciations, abandoned the plane of *absolutes Wissen* and fell back on the area of "science." But, in changing his assumption, he did not fail to accept, transposed, the whole *globus intellectualis*, which survived within his intellectual edifice as a reflection upon the positive sciences.

The serious part of the matter was that philosophy was presented as a negation of itself, disguised as science, and tried to define itself by the attributes of science. That is, it was no longer a question of a change of level *within philosophy*, but of *an abandonment* of the *philosophical level* as such. This did not happen in Comte himself—and the orientation of his chief work, the *Système de politique positive*, is good proof of this—but the Positivists took this abandonment seriously (we need only recall Littré's reaction to Comte's book);[76] they made it the method of philosophy, and in so doing destroyed their own theoretical possibilities. The effort toward recovery of the authentic level of philosophy was disturbed from within by its very assumptions. The manner in which problems were posed conditioned, as always happens, their solutions, and the greatest difficulty faced by all attempts to return to philosophy in the full sense of the term was simply to claim the *rights of problematicalness*. The greatest enslavement which took place in philosophy was the limiting of its question, the amputation of

[74] Lessons of 1842–48, published in 1856–57. Re-edition, Wissenschaftliche Buchgesellschaft (2 vols., Darmstadt, 1957).

[75] *La idea de principio en Leibniz y la evolución de la teoría deductiva* (Buenos Aires, 1958), § 31, "El lado dramático de la filosofía."

[76] *A. Comte et la philosophie positive* (Paris, 1863).

what it had been, which was precisely the condition of its existence: its *radicality*. No matter what demands are piled upon philosophy, this does no more than to make it more intense and refined—that is the function which Socrates, Plato, Aristotle, Suárez, Descartes, Hume, and Kant have successively performed; but if an attempt is made to make it *penultimate*, that is, to deprive it of the right to question, under the pretext that such questions have no answer, then a total inversion of its meaning occurs.

In other words, when philosophy began to be content with very little, a simple lowering of level took place: Stoicism compared to Aristotle, the Enlightenment compared to Descartes and Leibniz. When men begin to be content, not only with "not much answer" but with "not much question," when they limit philosophy's problematism and condition this to the possibility of reply—to the possibility of success, in short—this means the nullification of philosophy in its particularity, the loss of that *radical* form of theory which deserves to call itself philosophical.

This was the meaning of the Positivist crisis. I believe that it is in this context that the strange historical phenomenon of *irrationalism* can best be understood—I shall have to return to this point at length later on—and for which insufficient explanations are usually given. It cannot be properly understood unless it is made to originate in this limitation of questioning; it is a desperate escape from the *narrowing of problematicalness*. Reason expands in the face of difficulties and demands; the more that is asked of reason, the more it affirms itself as it is forced, as it tries to give that measure. But if the area of what the question can be is limited, if the horizons of reason as a problem, as an organ of problematicalness and interrogation, are limited—no matter what the solutions may be—then the inescapable excess of question, the radical problematism, must reject reason thus understood in order to find an ambit where it can be accommodated. The deepest source of irrationalism is not, therefore, a conviction of the impotence of reason, but rather the limitation of its aspirations, its consignment to a domesticated and attenuated problematicalness, one which of course is capable of being overcome, to objects which have previously been established as "rational" and controllable; whereas the proper function of reason is to inquire into reality, *no matter what it may be like*, without deciding in advance that it must also be rational or even accessible—

that is, without taking for granted that an answer to its unrenounceable questions is attainable.

12. NEOISMS

When there is an attempt to recover, not simply a certain philosophical level, but *the* level of philosophy, the chief difficulty is that there is no term of reference. I shall try to make myself clear. The sentence I have just written, apparently plausible and unobjectionable, conceals an imprecision, and it is just there that we find the root of the real difficulty in the second half of the nineteenth century: for "the level of philosophy" must always be "a certain level"—that is, the level of a concrete philosophy. Since such a philosophy did not exist, the indeterminateness of that level was the first obstacle, a very difficult one to overcome, encountered by the men who could no longer be Positivists.

When some thinkers began to feel an ultimate dissatisfaction with what was being done around them, and realized the need to achieve a new idea of the philosophy they felt to be within themselves, they did not know what yardstick to use in order to measure their own demands. Hence the inner uncertainty that characterizes the truly *inspired* thinkers of the years from 1850 to 1900, in all ranks, from Lotze and Dilthey to Brentano, Nietzsche, and Guyau. Properly speaking, they did not have anything to relate to, they were not "installed"; they have an unmistakable air of "Robinson Crusoeism" (not "Adamism," for none of them felt like a "first man," but "exiled," like castaways on the desert isle of Positivism, their only equipment the remnants of a philosophical tradition).

The solution that came to hand was what Ortega has called "going back to school; that is, to the classics."[77] The European thinkers of 1850 to 1870 relearned philosophy from the example of the classics; they rethought their techniques, they recovered that level—a concrete level

[77] As early as 1924 he had written, "The neo-Hegelian philosophy of Croce, the neo-Fichtean philosophy of Rickert, and the neo-Kantian philosophy of my teachers at Marburg belong to this philosophical fauna. The *neo-* prefixed to many of them shows how archaic they are. They are the suits of old systems re-tailored for other bodies. They made sense during their time, because the previous generation had completely lost the technique of philosophy and it had to be learned again. But at the same time, they reveal an incapacity to construct the new synthesis of life in any original way." (III, 253.) The sentence quoted in the text is from *Prólogo para alemanes*, 38.

in each case. Ortega recalls that even Trendelenburg had seized upon Aristotle. It was the period of all the "neoisms"; neo-Kantianism, neo-Fichteanism, neo-Hegelianism, and also—let us not forget, for this is its place—neo-Thomism. (It must be noted that the nineteenth-century thinker who had the sharpest and most accurate perception of the problem was Gratry: he too "went back to school," but not to the school of a *magister* chosen somewhat arbitrarily, though not without reasons: he went back to the school of *history of philosophy*; that is, he attempted to reintegrate himself into a total and continuing tradition, from Plato to Leibniz at least; if Gratry, whose philosophical talent was great, had possessed greater mental discipline and had not become too fond of certain bright ideas, if he had been in a somewhat different historical medium—if he had been German, perhaps, instead of French—he could have anticipated by a couple of generations the reestablishment of an adequate and not anachronistic philosophy, and we would have been spared a number of knotty problems which still harass us today.)[78]

Neo-Thomism, neo-Kantianism, and neo-Hegelianism are strictly coetaneous (their first important appearance took place between 1860 and 1870, and their development was strongest in the thirty or forty years after that). In all three cases there was an attempt to "go back" to a classic philosopher who was considered "safe," and at the same time one who had been forgotten or misunderstood by the recent past. It should be noted that, contrary to what is commonly believed today, the primary intention of neo-Scholasticism—neo-Thomism in particular —was not primarily to oppose modern philosophy, but to restore the doctrine of the Scholastics, especially that of Saint Thomas, within ecclesiastical thought, in the seminaries, etc. It was not that the Scholastics tried to fight against outside tendencies, but that their task was to make Scholasticism return to a form of thought which medieval tradition had abandoned a long time before. A passage from Gratry written in 1853, which I have quoted on other occasions, is particularly clear: "But Saint Thomas Aquinas needs to be understood! There are heights, depths, accuracies in him which contemporary intelligence is far from being able to suspect, and which will perhaps be understood within a few generations, if philosophy rises up, if wisdom reappears among us.... Philosophy has been discovered by Plato and Aristotle, by Saint

---

[78] See my book *La filosofía del P. Gratry* (*Obras*, IV), especially chapters 1–2. See also *Biografía de la Filosofía*, IV, 28–31.

Augustine, by Saint Thomas Aquinas, by the seventeenth century, but it has been lost in the intervals. Today, among ourselves, it is completely lost. We read the old monuments without understanding them; we do not know their language, we do not penetrate their meaning . . . . Such is the state of contemporary philosophy with regard to the noble philosophy of the past and the wisdom of the great centuries; it possesses all their monuments, but it does not have their comprehension, and still less their faith."[79]

The attitude of Otto Liebmann in 1865 is no different (*Kant und die Epigonen*) when he repeatedly proclaims the need to "return to Kant"; the difference is that the neo-Thomists and neo-Kantians demanded a return to Saint Thomas or Kant, and Gratry the return to Saint Thomas—and not only to him but to all the "first-rank" classical writers, to all who seem to him to be fully philosophers—that is, each one in his historical place.

I believe that it is essential to emphasize these affinities among the different neoisms, but now their differences must be indicated. Neo-Kantianism split up into various schools (especially those of Marburg and Baden); it originated in Germany—though it was not confined to that country—and operated in the centers of greatest philosophical intensity and intellectual prestige. But because of this very quality, its rapid rise was followed by a quick decline, as soon as—and in large part through its own influence—a recovery of the effective philosophical level had been achieved, and other doctrines which were more persuasive or more penetrating, in any case more in accord with the current situation, burst upon the scene. On the other hand, neo-Scholasticism was for a long time restricted to ecclesiastical thinkers and had little radiating effect outside the Church; for many years its presence was not noticed outside the centers of ecclesiastical education or those very directly influenced by the religious orders; but, on the other hand, its connection with the ecclesiastical organization, its relationships with theology, its growing "institutional" character, the ample resources of every type which sustained it—all this caused it to preserve a vitality and a development which the other neoisms could not have. If what is wanted—and it is what we want here—is to understand the situation of European philosophy during the second half of the nineteenth century,

[79] *El conocimiento de Dios*, trans. by Julián Marías, p. 188. See also the passage cited in the previous note.

we must keep in mind what the situation of all the "neoisms" was *then*, a situation much more similar than their later and very different fates would lead us to suppose.

Immersion in a great classic thinker always produces a sort of intellectual bedazzlement. To "install oneself" inside a powerful and creative mentality, and to try to philosophize from within it, raises considerable problems. To begin with, the first task to be undertaken is that of *understanding* the classic in question. To a certain degree, the classic becomes the equivalent of what, in a "direct" philosophy, is reality. When I say "direct" I do not mean a philosophy without tradition, for there is no such thing; the past which is immediate and *in continuity* or the remote past, historically linked—that is, in continuity also—with the present, does not deprive thought of a "direct" character: all of that past is "inside" the man who thinks, and he produces it out of himself, a self integrated with all of that tradition. On the other hand, when this continuity is lacking, when one "goes" to the remote classic writer—whether more or less remote—one is "inside" him and sees reality only from *his* perspective, not from one's own, which naturally should include him in his historical and not exclusive place. That this has been a decisive factor in nineteenth-century European thought is something which cannot be forgotten, because it conditions the form in which the most representative philosophies of that time originated, as well as those which appeared soon afterward as a reaction to that attitude.

13. SCIENCE AND PHILOSOPHY

In the second half of the nineteenth century there was the culmination of a tendency which had dominated all *modern* philosophy, as opposed to ancient: its claim to be a *science*, in principle a science "like any other," after the eighteenth century, a science such as physics, which seemed the exemplar, whose "sure path" Kant misses in metaphysics. After that time, philosophy was to feel that it was in a progressively more precarious situation, in the measure that it sensed that this scientific character was slipping away from it. In a certain sense, German idealism inverted the question, claiming for philosophy a primarily scientific character—Fichte's *Wissenschaftslehre* and Hegel's *Wissenschaft der*

Logik, where this *Wissenschaft* is not "science" in the sense of the "positive" sciences—but after the decline of idealism the primacy of the sciences was indisputable, and philosophy tried again and again to achieve this condition, which constantly eluded it. This situation lasted at least until 1911, when Husserl published his famous programmatic article *Philosophie als strenge Wissenschaft,*[80] although for some years a certain amount of uneasiness had been felt about the subject.[81]

Not even logic seemed to be independent of the positive sciences, except that *Wissenschaft und Logik gehören zusammen* and some few principles or theses of logic remained unchanged by the progress of scientific knowledge.[82] The invasion of all philosophy by *psychologism,* against which Husserl was to fight so hard, meant chiefly—though not exclusively—the attempt to associate it with a positive science, to sanction scientifically the establishment of problematical philosophical knowledge.

But the model continued to be physics. For the school of Marburg, Oesterreich was later to say,[83] in principle, basically, only the exact science of nature—physics—is science. And to the extent that philosophy is not and cannot be that, it seems destined for relatively vague functions of "synthesis," perhaps as a creative (*schöpferische Synthese,* as Paulsen was to say) reflection on science, the theory of theories, in short: theory of knowledge (scientific knowledge, of course).

That is, philosophy seemed oriented toward the "mode of thinking" of the sciences. When this was denied to some degree—as in the different irrationalist doctrines—it was done more as "an act of despair" or a "challenge," as an act of bravado, than as the statement of philos-

[80] In *Logos,* Band I. Heft 3. (Tübingen, 1911).

[81] See, for example, what Friedrich Paulsen says in his study *Die Zukunftsausgabe der Philosophie* (in *Systematische Philosophie,* 417, in the series *Die Kultur der Gegenwart,* herausgegeben von Paul Hinneberg [Berlin und Leipzig, 1907]): "Mit allem bisher Ausgeführten ist gegeben, dass die Philosophie nicht in demselben Sinne Wissenschaft sein oder jemals werden kann wie eine Einzelwissenschaft; sie hat einen anderen, einen universalen Charakter sowohl in Hinsicht auf ihr Ziels als auf ihren Gegenstand. Ihr Gegenstand ist die Wirklichkeit überhaupt, ihr Ziel eine ideelle Nachschöpfung des Universums, soweit sie denn mit menschlichen Anschauungen und Gedanken möglich ist."

[82] See Alois Riehl, *Logik und Erkenntnistheorie, ibid.,* 77.

[83] T. K. Oesterreich, *Die philosophischen Strömungen der Gegenwart* (in *Systematische Philosophie,* 3. [Auflage, 1921], p. 359): "Die Marburger Schule versteht unter Wissenschaft von vornherein im Grunde nur die exakte Wissenschaft, die Physik."

ophy's different character. Think of Kierkegaard's title: *Afsluttende Uvidenskabelig Efterskrift til de Philosophiske Smuler* ("Concluding Unscientific Postscript to the Philosophical Tidbits"), which bears as a subtitle, less often quoted but no less significant: "Mimical-Pathetical-Dialectical Composition, Existential Contribution." For many decades philosophy made *amende honorable* for its Hegelian pretensions and adjusted itself to the discipline of the sciences, without stopping to think whether it could be such a thing, whether such an aspiration made any sense. Let us recall the discussions, which lasted into our century for a couple of decades, and a stray whiff of which still reaches us from time to time, concerning whether or not philosophy is *Weltanschauung*, whether it differs from it or not: the very fact that the problem is posed can be understood only from a scientific concept of philosophy as reality, or at least as ideal. The same basic conviction underlies certain chapters of the philosophy of thirty or forty years ago; for example, the doctrine of "regional ontologies," and even the form acquired by the theory of values, which has been responsible, if I am not mistaken, for its relative sterility. A new departure would be possible in this discipline, starting from totally new assumptions which would return to it a fruitfulness that it lost very early. Heidegger's ill-humored attitude toward "values,"[84] no matter what opinion might be held of their own possibilities as a "departure," justly responds to this sense of unease in present-day philosophy.

For the important point, the one I am interested in pointing out in this context, is that *present-day* philosophy is formally opposed, and for very profound reasons, to the scientific mimetism of the philosophy of the nineteenth century, and therefore arises out of a violent wrenching of that deeply rooted attitude. But not in order to fall back on the idea of a "prescientific" philosophy (we must not forget that, as Ortega has reminded us, "its ancient 'mode of thinking' was what gave rise to the sciences; that is, that the earliest philosophy was too 'scientific' "),[85] but rather to recapture its own irreducible state. Without this, we would not be able to understand fully the turn which philosophy took in the twentieth century, the effective *level* at which it placed itself, and, consequently, the meaning of the ideas of Ortega, in whom this trans-

[84] For example, see his *Brief über den "Humanismus" in Platons Lehre von der Wahrheit* (Bern, 1947), 99–100.

[85] *La idea de principio en Leibniz*, § 4, p. 45.

formation operated in the fullest manner, more profoundly than in any other philosopher, to the point that, as we shall see later, the reproach he was to make to the philosophy of the nineteenth century still extends, no doubt in a residual form, to almost all of the European thought of our own century.

14. THE REIGNING PHILOSOPHY ABOUT 1900

Reigning philosophy does not mean the same thing as philosophy in existence: when we look back at any period in the past from the vantage point of today, we tend to take everything we find there at the same valuation; but its reality at the moment when it was current admitted very profound differences. If this is forgotten, a historical situation loses its outline, and still more if we project upon it the system of our present preferences and valuations, which usually do not coincide with things as they really were. For example, we know that Husserl's phenomenology dates from 1900; and in view of this, and of the fact that it seems of very great importance to us, we tend to think that the philosophy of the first two decades of the twentieth century was chiefly phenomenology. The facts are somewhat different. "A reigning idea," I have written elsewhere, "is that which is in force, that which has life, vigor, or strength; all that which I find in my social surroundings and that which I have to take into account. The vigor of reigning ideas depends on this quality. If a reality exists in my social world about which individuals do not have to take a position, from which they can detach themselves, which, in a word, they do not have to take into account, then it is not a reigning reality."[86] Very well, then: if we think about the books published in the first twenty years of the twentieth century on contemporary philosophy as a whole, we find something of a surprise compared to our usual picture of it. In J. Baumann's book *Deutsche und ausserdeutsche Philosophie der letzten Jahrzehnte* (Gotha, 1930), we do not find the names of Cohen, Natorp, and Husserl; H. Höffding, *Moderne Philosophie*, in the German translation (Leipzig, 1905), leaves out neo-Kantianism and phenomenology; they are also omitted in O. Külpe's *Die Philosophie der Gegenwart in Deutschland* (6th ed., Leipzig, 1914); and lastly, the still later book

[86] *La estructura social*, chapter 3, p. 16.

by Harald K. Schelderup, *Hauptlinien der Entwicklung der Philosophie von Mitte des 19. Jahrhunderts bis zur Gegenwart* (Oslo, 1920), totally omits phenomenology. That is, the work of Husserl and his school *was not yet reigning* in 1920, not even in Germany or in books written in the German language, and it was possible to write summaries of *contemporary* philosophy without saying a word about it.[87]

The most responsible and up-to-date German treatment of the intellectual situation in the first decades of the century was the series entitled *Die Kultur der Gegenwart*, edited by Paul Hinneberg. The volume called *Systematische Philosophie* admirably reflected the philosophical situation *in the world*, as seen from Germany. The first edition was published in 1907; its collaborators were W. Dilthey, Alois Riehl, Wilhelm Wundt, Wilhelm Ostwald, Hermann Ebbinghaus, Rudolf Eucken, Friedrich Paulsen, Wilhelm Münch, and Theodor Lipps. A third edition was published after World War I, in 1921, brought up to date and containing new monographs by various collaborators. The changes are significant: Ostwald's *Naturphilosophie* disappears, an unmistakable sign of the loss of currency of Monist Positivism; *Ethik*, *Pädagogik*, and *Asthetik*, by Paulsen, Münch, and Lipps, are turned over to Bruno Bauch, Theodor Litt, and Moritz Geiger. These are quite significant changes, especially in the case of the last named; finally, Paulsen's chapter on *Die Zukunftsausgaben der Philosophie* is replaced by a longer and more important one by T. K. Oesterreich, *Die philosophischen Strömungen der Gegenwart*, which we shall have to examine with some care.

In the first edition *there is no mention whatever* of thinkers like Brentano, Bergson, Simmel, Husserl, and William James, and only once is there a simple mention of Dilthey as a historian (aside, of course, from his own contribution on *Das Wesen der Philosophie*); and remember that this is 1907. If we compare 1907 with 1921, we must first of all make a distinction: if we disregard Oesterreich's study, whose *subject* is precisely the *present-day philosophical currents*—that is, if we consider only the descriptions of the different philosophical disciplines, in which each of the authors refers to what is to be found in his field—we find only *one* mention of Bergson; all the other philosophers I have mentioned appear only in Oesterreich's treatment— that is, as a *novelty* which those who are describing the *present-day*

[87] See T. K. Oesterreich, *loc. cit.*, 395.

situation (we must keep the adjective in mind) of logic, metaphysics, ethics, or the theory of knowledge do not need to speak. That is, none of these philosophers *was as yet "reigning" in Germany in 1921.*

What was the reigning philosophy, then, at the beginning of the present century? When we try to pin it down, we have a moment of hesitation; it would be well not to pass over this, but to take it precisely as our point of departure. Was there no reigning philosophy? Our hesitation arises from the fact that it was *not very fully philosophy.* Not a few traces remained of Fechner, Lotze, and even Schopenhauer and Herbart; Wundt, Eduard von Hartmann, Fouillée, Vaihinger, and Sigwart, who dominated logic, together with Mill, Spencer, Haeckel and Ostwald, Mach and Avenarius, Volkelt, Lipps, Taine, Renan, and Durkheim, were all in full flower; an incipient state of currency was being attained by William James, Windelband, Renouvier, and—in a peculiar form, so peculiar that it would need considerable explanation— by Cohen, and in a still stranger way, by Nietzsche, whose currency was enormous, but was not a strictly philosophical—or at least an extra-academic—currency, in a period when philosophy was produced mostly in the universities.

And Dilthey? Brentano? Bergson? Do not the great philosophers of the time appear? They have no *currency* whatever. The esteem—a very different matter—enjoyed by Dilthey was as a psychologist and especially as a historian of ideas, but there was no suggestion of his having a philosophy. In May, 1883, Dilthey sent his good friend Count Yorck von Wartenburg his *Einleitung in die Geisteswissenschaften,* dedicated to the Count, as we know; in October he wrote him, "I have not seen any reviews of my book as yet."[88] And in June, 1884, more than a year after the appearance of this work of genius, he wrote to him again: "Have you read Julian Schmidt in *Nationalzeitung* on my book? There was also a comment in the widely circulated *Nation.* Julian Schmidt's review was respectful, but he has no comprehension, unfortunately, and much to my surprise, no capacity for understanding a rather difficult complex of ideas. Conclusion: I shall have to make the second volume much more simple and accessible."[89] In the autumn

[88] "Von meinem Buch noch keine Recension gesehen" (*Briefwechsel zwischen Wilhelm Dilthey und dem Grafen Paul Yorck v. Wartenburg 1877–1897* [Halle/Saale, 1923], 35.)

[89] "Haben sie in der Nationalzeitung Julian Schmidt über mein Buch gelesen? Auch

of 1885, the first volume had netted Dilthey 100 *thaler*.[90] As late as 1920, Vörlander gave him twenty lines in his *History of Philosophy*, and in those twenty lines there was room to list his disciples; Bréhier does not even discuss him; the list of omissions, or little better than omissions, could be prolonged *ad infinitum*, up to about 1930.

Brentano, whose influence on a group of disciples who turned out to be of exceptional quality was so profound, was even less known, and sometimes five lines suffice to list him in a history of philosophy. Bergson began to be known only about 1912, when his work was treated as "une philosophie nouvelle" (the phrase is Le Roy's), in spite of the fact that he had been publishing since 1889. And Ortega has told us that he could never persuade Cohen to read him, in spite of the fact that both were Jews. However, during the World War, and especially about the year 1920, Bergson was the best known and most influential of living philosophers, more than any of the Germans at that time.[91] Brentano would have to wait until fame and a peculiar posthumous "currency" were reflected upon him by Husserl's phenomenology, and we have already noted that phenomenology in its turn achieved a state of currency rather late; Brentano's currency came in the form of an already superseded "antecedent," as the source of a school which extended from the theory of objectivity to the theory of values, from Meinong, von Ehrenfels, and Husserl to Scheler and his peers and disciples.

By the end of the nineteenth century and even in the early years of the twentieth, the lack of a reigning philosophy was expressed by the customary formula of "anarchy of philosophic systems"; as the present century went on, a surprising unity began to be apparent, a coherence among the different orientations which, however, did not take the form of great all-embracing systems, which nobody had attempted after Wundt and Eduard von Hartmann. Another fundamental change was that, whereas until shortly before the War of 1914 the different countries relied on their own resources and were acquainted with those

---

in der freisinnigen 'Nation' war eine Besprechung. Respectvoll, doch nirgend Verständnis, leider auch bei Julian Schmidt zu meiner grossen Überraschung keine Fähigkeit mehr, einen schwierigeren Gedankenzusammenhang aufzufassen. Schlussergebnis: ich muss den zweiten Band viel einfacher und fassbarer schreiben" (*ibid.*, 41–42).

90 *Ibid.*, 53.

91 See Oesterreich, *loc. cit.*, p. 353.

of other countries only in very limited measure (in Germany "philosophy" was almost synonymous with "German philosophy"), after that date the presence of a community extending beyond national borders began to make itself felt. Bergson's reputation was a decisive factor, but so was the influence of James's pragmatism, and, secondarily, the presence of other Americans such as Emerson, Royce, Dewey, F. C. S. Schiller (as a professor in the United States), and Peirce, little known as yet. Germany had lived off the consciousness of a philosophical superiority which had been absolute in the first half of the nineteenth century, during the dominance of German idealism, and this attitude persisted even when the true state of affairs had become quite different. A proof of how great this currency was is offered by the enormous unbalance of Volume V of Überweg's *Grundriss der Geschichte der Philosophie*, dealing with "Foreign Philosophy in the Modern Period" (after 1800), whose last edition contained little more than four hundred pages, compared with more than seven hundred (of incomparably superior quality) in Volume IV, covering German philosophy during the same period.

Were we obliged to seek an expression describing the common currency of philosophy in the early years of our century, we should have to use the term *critical philosophy*. In widely different forms, all the important schools—which had a currency *sui generis*, not full and "established," but polemical and avant-garde, yet which had to be *taken into account*—took up the Kantian theme. First of all, naturally, in the neo-Kantians, those of Marburg—Cohen, Natorp, later Cassirer—as well as those of Baden—Windelband, Rickert, Jonas Cohn, Münsterberg. But it was not only these men; there was also *critical realism*, so influential for several years, with Külpe, Messer, Frischeisen-Köhler, Stumpf, Oesterreich, and to a certain degree Meinong himself. And not far distant from them, the neocritical realists, Riehl or Volkelt. And the *empirical criticism* of Mach and Avenarius, not far removed from Ziehen. And outside Germany, the so-called neocriticism took in tendencies of the greatest prestige, from Renouvier to those who tended toward a "physicalism," such as Poincaré, Duhem, or Enriques. Nor should we forget—even though it is not what interests us *today*—the *critical* approach to the theme of sciences of mind in Dilthey or Rickert: when the former, in his dedication of the *Introduction to the Sciences of Mind* to Count Yorck, says that some time previously this book could still have presumed to call itself *Critique of Historical Reason*, we feel a temptation to underline *Historical Reason*, investing the phrase with the meaning which Ortega has given to this expression; but what Dilthey and his readers had in mind, what to them seemed presumptuous, was the word *Critique*, with its close resemblance to the *Critique of Pure Reason*; that is, the ambitious attempt to do "the same as Kant" for the other half of the *globus intellectualis*.

15. THE NEW THEMES: EXISTENCE, LIFE, HISTORY

The chief innovation that took place in philosophy was that its attention came to rest on the reality of *human life*. It seems paradoxical that until well into the nineteenth century there should have been no ingress into philosophy, as a theme with full rights, for the theme which soon was to seem its primary, and sometimes almost exclusive, one. In my *Introducción a la Filosofía* [English edition: *Reason and Life*] and elsewhere I have tried to explain the reasons which make comprehensible this strange "backwardness" lasting fifteen hundred years.[92] But there is yet more: the discovery of human life as reality, and consequently as a philosophical problem, has been obscured by the fact that the word "life" has been avoided since the beginning. Kierkegaard, as we know, was the one who introduced the term "existence," altering its traditional meaning, to denote the reality of human life. By employing this term he wished to point out its quality of being "a synthesis of the infinite and the finite, the eternal and the temporal"; but the clearly arbitrary use of this expression, which had always borne a very different meaning, masked for a long time in the greater part of European philosophy the life which had been discovered, for it simultaneously *"covered"* that life. Walter Lowrie has already observed that it would have been much easier and more intelligible to use the word "life" instead of existence, and added, " 'Existence' is a far more abstract term than 'life,' and I suppose that the word 'life' was eschewed because of its romantic, sentimental, and even biological associations."[93]

---

[92] *Introducción a la Filosofía*, VI, 50. *Biografía de la Filosofía*, VI, 36. (*Obras*, II.)

[93] "We must habituate ourselves to S. K.'s use of the word 'existence.' He means by it the conditions of a truly humane life. He means specifically the good life in its practical aspects, and his gravest complaint against the Hegelian system is that it 'abbreviates

The question was not simply one of terminology: a name is already an interpretation; it is the *foreshortening* in which a reality is presented. Since life was entirely unexplored and furthermore is essentially multilateral (*mehrseitig*), the foreshortening was decisive, and Kierkegaard's decision—perhaps more literary than anything else—launched the philosophy of the following century onto a very necessary but perhaps not very reliable path.

It is true that "life" is also spoken of in the philosophy of the nineteenth century and the early years of the twentieth; I have tried to show in another book[94] the prehistory of this idea from the end of the eighteenth century. But even in the cases in which it does not appear "disguised"—under the guise of consciousness, "will," etc.—it yet appears theoretically interpreted from certain points of view which hinder access to its naked reality, precisely what Ortega was to discover as "radical reality," *underneath all the theories*. This happens when the assumption that "life" means, to begin with, "biological life" creeps into one's concept—as in the case of Bergson—and, from biological life, comprehension of human life is attempted; or when the "values" of certain forms of life are considered, perhaps the primary value of "vitality"— as happens in Nietzsche, without his noticing that vitality only has meaning and even reality *within life*, and must be understood from life and not the reverse; or, lastly, when one studies "historical life"—and this is the case of Dilthey, even though there is more than this in his thought—understanding by this something other than human life, pure and simple: that is, trying to understand life from history instead of discovering historicity as a characteristic of life itself.

Similarly, attention to the peculiarity of the knowledge of human realities as distinct from natural ones led, from many different perspectives, to the discovery of history as a reality irreducible to nature. The so-called moral sciences, Dilthey's *Geisteswissenschaften*, the contrast between *Natur-* and *Kulturwissenschaft* in Rickert, the new points of view in psychology—the idea of intentionality in Brentano as well as

existence' to such a degree that it leaves out ethics. It would often be far easier and more intelligible were I to use the word 'life' instead of 'existence'—and say, for example, that the truth must issue in a life conformable to it. But I adhere scrupulously to our author's terminology. 'Existence' is a far more abstract term than 'life,' and I suppose that the word 'life' was eschewed because of its romantic, sentimental, and even biological associations." Walter Lowrie, *Kierkegaard* (Oxford, 1938), 302.

[94] *Biografía de la Filosofía*, VI.

the notion of stream of consciousness in William James, or Dilthey's "descriptive and analytic" psychology, inseparable from the paired concepts of *Erlebnis* and *Verständnis*, and even Freud's psychoanalysis, which above all meant the methodical introduction of biography into psychological studies—all these were different paths by which these realities (nothing less than human life and history), almost unknown before and lacking in theoretical citizenship rights, entered the horizon of European science for the first time and with surprising fascination. With what consequences for that very theory which would have to confront those realities?

16. THE CRISIS OF SPECULATIVE REASON AND IRRATIONALISM

Rationalism had had difficulty in assimilating history ever since the seventeenth century. Remember the attitude of Descartes and, in even more acute form, that of Malebranche. Throughout the eighteenth century, and in spite of the fact that, strictly speaking, this period was the one in which historical science became truly established,[95] the opposition between the rational and the historical was kept alive. But in case of conflict, history was always sacrificed. Without difficulty, almost gaily, up to the end of the eighteenth century; with tremendous efforts to achieve a conciliation from that time up to the decline of German idealism; but it was always history that gave in at the last moment, and was either disqualified or subjected, not without violence, to logical reason.[96] From Voltaire to Hegel, even up to Comte, the predominance of reason was decisive.

Something different happened in the second half of the nineteenth century. History and human life had thrust themselves onto the intellectual horizon; full "experience" of these realities had, we might say, been achieved, and appeared to be unrenounceable. If there had to be a choice between them and reason, this did not solve the problem either; certainly a "rationalist" attitude was to persist, similar to that of the previous 150 or 200 years; but a new and very different

[95] See, for example, E. Cassirer, *Filosofía de la Ilustración*, chapter 5, "La conquista del mundo histórico" (Mexico, 1943).

[96] See *Introducción a la Filosofía*, V, 46, "La razón y la historia."

attitude arose, willing rather to sacrifice reason and adopt an irrationalist posture. Why?

The previously reigning assumption was that if history does not turn out to be fully accessible to reason, it is because of a defect in history; that is, a deficiency of its reality. What does not enter into the rational scheme of things—the men of the seventeenth and eighteenth centuries came to believe—is worthless; it is no more than a residue to be disdained. Malebranche was only interested in what Adam also could have known; though in a less extreme form, the other thinkers of the time, even Voltaire, the father of historiography in the modern sense of the word, were not too far from holding the same belief. Voltaire sets apart, among the many elements of history, "ce qui mérite d'être connu" as a philosopher; that is, he was ready to leave out everything which could not be adjusted to a rigid rational pattern.

Now the opinion was going to be, rather, that what history and life possess which is rationally knowable is what they possess of a "product," of a mechanism, what is least alive or least historical—in a word, what is *least real*. Far from renouncing what is peculiarly historical or vital, to retain only the nucleus which coincides with reason, these new thinkers—Kierkegaard, Nietzsche, Bergson, Spengler, and even Unamuno, already in the twentieth century—were to affirm the *integrality* of these realities and abandon reason as an inept method for knowing them.

But we must ask ourselves rather seriously why this was so. I have already said that it was not a question of a mere "difficulty" of certain subjects; if this were the case, it would only set a higher purpose in reason's path, toward which she would have to strive. It would not be understood that—in a period in which science had tackled the most difficult and exalted tasks, in which the most thorny and complex subjects had been attacked—science could have taken a backward step in the face of a demand for higher intellection. Rather, it was a question of the contrary phenomenon: reason, molded by the positive sciences, especially by physics, an exemplary science in Newton, to which Kant primarily refers, was above all *explicative* reason; its function consisted in beginning with what was "given"—data—and "explaining" those data; that is, elucidating them, reducing them to their elements, causes, or principles. This task may be more or less complicated or difficult to accomplish; in some cases it is extraordinarily so. But let us suppose that it is achieved: what is its result?

The explanation goes from a patent "datum" to an element—or cause, or principle, depending on the case—which is latent, from which it is possible to return to the reality which has been explained in order to manipulate it in different, purely cognitive, ways—to identify it, differentiate it, classify it, understand it genetically, etc.—or in technical ways; to manipulate it, produce it, use it for different purposes. It is taken for granted that the elements achieved by means of the explanation, those to which the thing has been *reduced*, are, in some sense at least, more important than the thing. But in any case this cognitive process has its limitations: in the first place, any explanation or reduction is adjusted to a "scheme" from which, and as a function of which, it is executed; that is, it affects one dimension of the reality which is explained, which is only a reality in this "line," leaving out all other possible lines; in the second place, this same schematic quality means that *individual* reality is never attained—remember the interminable discussions on the possibility and meaning of historical laws, for example; finally, the explicative reduction tears reality out of its context and makes it abstract, in greater or lesser degree; therefore it is stripped of concretion and circumstantiality.

This means that the explanation *leaves out the thing itself*; yet more, it consists in this leaving-out, in order to go to its elements or causes, from which it can be manipulated. This is, in fact, what science sets out to do. Science is not so much interested in *knowing*, in the firm sense of the word, as in *manipulating* things mentally—and secondarily also in a real, that is, a technical, manner. But as soon as the reality being considered has interest *of itself*, all "reduction" turns out to be insufficient, for the thing presents itself precisely as *irreducible*.

This is what happens with life and history: if I "explain" them, I reduce them to *something else*; and it is they themselves which interest me. In other words, the scientific explanation gives me in return for reality something which it considers to be more valuable, but which is not that reality; and when this exchange is unacceptable, the explanation has no function. If reason is identified, as was done in the nineteenth century, with *explicative reduction*, then the inevitable result is that reason supplants those realities, annuls them, putting in their place an abstract and inert diagram which cannot be adequate. This was the starting point of *irrationalism*, which was not, as it is often considered, a *renunciation of understanding,* but rather the opposite—a refusal to accept the idea that understanding was simply explaining.

Oesterreich accurately observed that what had led some philosophers to a departure from conceptual thought was the "vacuity of content of the philosophy of the last decades and the spiritual hunger for vital content" ("die Inhaltsleere der Philosophie der letzten Jahrzehnte und der geistige Hunger nach Lebensgehalt").[97] It is admitted that there are other forms or sources of knowledge besides thought, ones that are more efficacious, or at least ones which put us in closer contact with reality itself. The inevitable temptation was, of course, the association of those forms with perception, and so there was a return to the old notion of *intuition*, in different forms.

Elsewhere[98] I have indicated the formulas arrived at by Bergson, Spengler, and Unamuno to express their irrationalist attitude. Bergson also influenced William James—the influence was mutual, in fact; Dilthey was considered an irrationalist until some time after his death, and in two senses: not only in the one we have mentioned, of considering explicative reason insufficient for the understanding of life and history, but also in the sense that for him reality itself is irrational: "Er hält die Wirklichkeit selbst für irrationaler Natur," writes Oesterreich.[99] A vast segment of twentieth-century philosophy consists in trying to go beyond the situation created by this irrationalism. Its partial but very obvious justification could not be overlooked; the difficulties in which philosophy was entangled were no less obvious. Furthermore, in the descent into irrationalism and the urgent need for going beyond it, the relationship we mentioned before, that of science and philosophy, was also being debated. The identification between reason and the particular form of reason used by the sciences was what caused philosophy to arrive at an irrationalist posture. Was it possible to reject the "scientific" condition without decreasing rationality? Were there other "sciences" apart from those so called by antonomasia, with methods of their own which would be more suitable for grasping the reality of life and history? Could these be called, in some sense, reason?

[97] Oesterreich, *loc. cit.*, 378.
[98] *Introducción a la Filosofía*, VI, 46. *Ensayos de teoría*, "La razón en la filosofía actual." (*Obras*, IV.) Commentary on *Meditaciones del Quijote* (Madrid, 1957), 343–45.
[99] Oesterreich, *loc. cit.*, 378.

Attempts were made in several directions to escape these difficulties. They were contradictory on essential points, and were sometimes formally opposed. However, underneath the differences it is easy to discern a still deeper common aim; this was not, of course, that of solutions, but that of the problem itself and the level at which it was posed. And this was precisely the starting point of what was to be the philosophy of our century.

17. INNOVATIONS: *a*) *Lebensphilosophie*

About the year 1900 there was a good deal of talk in Germany about *Lebensphilosophie* in a broad sense, which took in all the thinkers, of any period, who had emphasized the study of man rather than giving predominance to the Cosmos or Nature. Thus, even some of the pre-Socratics were included—for example, Empedocles; still more clearly, the Skeptics, Epicureans, and Stoics, namely Cicero, Lucretius, Seneca, Epictetus, and Marcus Aurelius.[100] But, in a closer sense—precisely the sense which made philosophers look back to such remote antecedents— the point of departure was chiefly Schopenhauer. In a remote corner of his writings[101] he distinguishes between two forms of *Lebensansicht*, of consideration or view of life: according to the *transcendent* view, life is so brief, so small, and so fleeting, that nothing in it makes our actions or our struggles worthwhile; according to the other, the *immanent* view, life appears to the intellect so long, so important, so all-in-all, so serious in content, and so difficult that we cast ourselves wholeheartedly into taking part in its richness, assuring ourselves of its rewards and imposing our plans. Ovid's expression *non est tanti*, adds Schopenhauer, serves to describe the first, or better still Plato's: οὐδέ τι τῶν ἀνθρωπίνων ἄξιόν ἐστι μεγάλης σπουδῆς (*nihil, in rebus humanis, magno studio dignum est*); for the immanent view, what Gracián means by "taking the act of living very seriously." Man is great or small, Schopenhauer concludes, according to the predominance of one or the other view of life.

Life appears to be united to a certain "mode of seeing it," and consequently of esteeming it or valuing it. Thus, while Schopenhauer places absolute value on nonliving, Nietzsche—so close to him in his way of

---

[100] See W. Dilthey, *Das Wesen der Philosophie* (*Gesammelte Schriften*, V, 351).

[101] Schopenhauer, *Parerga und Paralipomena*, II Theil, Kap. XXVI, 337. (Grossherzog Wilhelm Ernst Ausgabe, V, 654.)

posing the question—inverts the solution and places living in the position of absolute value. Corresponding to Schopenhauer's negation of life as a definitive value is the elevation and intensification of life as a definitive value in Nietzsche.[102] At the beginning of his *Aphorismen zur Lebensweisheit*, Schopenhauer says that he takes this concept *gänzlich im immanenten Sinne*, completely in an immanent sense; this cannot be properly understood if we do not keep the previously discussed passage in mind. In order to take this view, that of *eudemonology*, which affirms the value of life, Schopenhauer must draw away from the higher, metaphysical-ethical point of view to which his authentic philosophy leads him ("von dom höheren, metaphysisch-ethischen Standpunkte, zu welchem meine eigentliche Philosophie hinleitet").[103]

What I wanted to show was this: that *Lebensphilosophie* originated out of a consciousness of *valuation*, and still more out of a change of valuation; the terms *Umwertung*, in an extreme form, naturally a Nietzschean one, and *Umsturz aller Werte*, are characteristic. It was a question of affirming polemically the rights of life as opposed to other things and other valuations: reason or abstract thought, cosmic nature, the spirit, all that is solid and geometrical, etc. After Schopenhauer and Nietzsche came Dilthey, Simmel, Bergson, James, Troeltsch, Klages, Keyserling, Spengler, even Unamuno in a certain sense. The *reactive* character of *Lebensphilosophie* has been energetically, and rightly, emphasized by Heinemann,[104] though some of the qualities which he attributes to it could be found, in a different context, in other philosophical tendencies of the most varied inspiration.

But if these philosophers are asked what they understand by *life*, what they are talking about when they proclaim it, things turn out to be less simple. One has the inescapable impression that they are not all talking about the same thing, and that it is not always easy to know what they *are* talking about. *Lebensphilosophie* never entirely succeeded in deserving the name of philosophy, even though some of its representatives were famous philosophers, and naturally we can find among them views about life itself which are of the highest value. The constant mixture of biological and vital factors in the meaning of human

[102] See Georg Simmel, *Schopenhauer und Nietzsche*, 7. Vortrag: "Wie Schopenhauer nur einen einzigen absoluten Wert kennt: Nicht-Leben—so kennt Nietzsche gleichfalls nur einen: Leben."

[103] Schopenhauer, ed. cit. IV, 373.

[104] Fritz Heinemann, *Neue Wege der Philosophie* (Leipzig, 1929), 157ff.

life, the accentuation of "vitality" and the arbitrary identification of vitality with some very partial forms of it ("vital values," life as "practical life"), opposition to the "mind" (let us recall Klages' book: *Der Geist als Widersacher der Seele*)—all this clouded considerably the phenomenon they were trying to study; but, in particular, none of them had an adequate *method* for the apprehension of that reality they claimed to have discovered, and which, in fact, could only be found intellectually by following the path in which that method consisted. *Lebensphilosophie* started off from various interpretations of life—that is, from theories already held about it—and it was never able to reach that aspect of life which is irreducible reality.

b) PRAGMATISM

This does not mean that the concern for method was foreign to the philosophers possessing these orientations; indeed, to a certain degree their thought was directed toward the discovery of new methods which would be capable of apprehending the realities in which they were interested. This occurred in an extreme form with pragmatism, as much in its first, less popular and less well-known version (Peirce's), as in its second and much more famous version (James's).

We know that pragmatism dates from 1878—from an article by Charles Sanders Peirce, "How to Make Our Ideas Clear," published in the *Popular Science Monthly* in January of that year—although this term was not used in the article; it appears in James's writings, and in Peirce's, after 1898. In 1906 Peirce referred to the nucleus common to all the pragmatist positions and their principal tendencies. "Suffice it to say once more that pragmatism is, in itself, no doctrine of metaphysics, no attempt to determine any truth of things. It is merely a method of ascertaining the meanings of hard words and of abstract concepts." And a little farther on he explains that he uses the word "hard" in its strict mineralogical sense, whatever would resist the edge of a knife. F. C. S. Schiller's conception of *humanism* probably falls between Peirce's own conception of pragmatism and James's personal one.[105]

[105] See *The Philosophy of Peirce*, edited by Justus Buchler (London, 1950): "Pragmatism in Retrospect; a Last Formulation," 271 ff.

As for James, he is no less insistent on the methodical nature of pragmatism. Theories become instruments, he says, not replies to enigmas on which we can rest. And this method is anti-intellectual, antirationalist. It does not predetermine the content of the doctrines which are to be reached, but only the path to be followed to get to them. Properly speaking, it has no dogmas or doctrines; as a method, it is compatible with many, and very different, dogmas and doctrines. It is the "attitude of drawing away from first things, principles, 'categories,' supposed needs; and of looking toward last things, results, consequences, facts."[106]

A whole current of American (and English) thought, with no few repercussions in Europe—especially in France and Italy—arises out of this attitude. It was given different names: pragmaticism in Peirce himself (to distinguish his position from others which used the same name), instrumentalism in Dewey, humanism in Schiller; pragmatism's connections with some tendencies of personalism are evident. The insufficiency of almost all these positions was very soon recognized, but we must also point out the injustice and superficiality with which they were treated by many, especially in Germany. What happened most often was that some particular point of view was chosen, some isolated thesis (an extremely weak one whose context the chooser had no intention of reconstructing), to demonstrate the inanity of pragmatism; and *all* tendencies were rejected—Lovejoy has traced and isolated thirteen different forms of pragmatism—on no other basis than this isolated point in one of them. For example, the pragmatist notion of truth, whose formulations were almost always infelicitous, served to disqualify a movement which had considerable possibilities, though these were menaced by very profound and almost unsalvageable deficiencies.[107] And very rarely was there an attempt to see what the profound intuition was which inspired that same idea of truth.

In any case, pragmatism, like *Lebensphilosophie*, had to seek the unfolding of its possibilities by going beyond itself to other deeper and more radical forms of theory.

[106] W. James, *Pragmatism* (1907): "What Pragmatism Means." See my *Historia de la Filosofía* (10th ed.) (*Obras*, I, 387–92).

[107] See, in *Diccionario de Filosofía*, by José Ferrater Mora (4th ed., Buenos Aires, 1958), the articles on pragmatism, Peirce, James, Schiller, Dewey, etc.

c) BERGSON

Although Bergson may be considered, in a broad sense, to be one of the representatives of *Lebensphilosophie*, his work, like Dilthey's, has dimensions that are totally original and cannot be reduced to any general "current," and this fact converts them into decisive innovations within philosophic thought at the turn of the century. His connections with pragmatism are substantial. The introduction written by Bergson shortly after James's death for the French translation of *Le Pragmatisme* (1911) shows very clearly his attitude of affinity and friendly feeling for the work of the American thinker.[108]

At the end of his career as a thinker, Bergson made certain explanations about the genesis of his philosophy. The excessive distance between theories and reality seemed to him to lie in lack of precision. Systems serve either for reality as it is or for another reality which might be very different: for they are abstract and vague to an extreme degree. "Ce qui a le plus manqué à la philosophie, c'est la précision. Les systèmes philosophiques ne sont pas taillés à la mesure de la réalité où nous vivons. Ils sont trop larges pour elle. Examinez tel d'entre eux, convenablement choisi; vous verrez qu'il s'appliquerait aussi bien à un monde où il n'y aurait pas de plantes ni d'animaux, rien que des hommes; où les hommes se passeraient de boire et de manger; où ils ne dormiraient, ne rêveraient ni ne divagueraient; où ils naîtraient décrepits pour finir nourrissons; où l'énergie remonterait la pente de la dégradation; où tout irait à rebours et se tiendrait à l'envers. C'est qu'un vrai système est un ensemble de conceptions si abstraites, et par conséquent si vastes, qu'on y ferait tenir tout le possible, et même l'impossible, à côté du réel."[109] Very well then: the doctrine which seemed an exception to the young Bergson was Spencer's and in the beginning he adhered to it. "La philosophie de Spencer visait à prendre l'empreinte des choses et à se modeler sur le détail des faits."[110] The *First Principles* certainly seemed very weak to Bergson, but he thought that he could dig deeper and go beyond them, and this led him, he says, to the idea of time. The traditional parallelism in philosophy between

---

[108] Reproduced in *La Pensée et le mouvant* (Paris, 1934), 267ff., under the title "Sur le pragmatisme de William James. Vérité et réalité."

[109] *La Pensée et le mouvant*, 7.

[110] *Ibid.*, 8.

time and *space* very soon came to seem like a disturbing error. Bergson was obliged to separate them from the outset—and in a certain sense to contrast them—to "despatialize" time and thus attain an internal vision, deeper and more intimate, of *movement*; and not only movement as something which affects an object susceptible of motion but of reality itself which *moves*; that is, of the moving, *le mouvant*.

In 1889 he had published his thesis, *Essai sur les données immédiates de la conscience*; in 1896, *Matière et Mémoire*—one of the books most difficult to understand in all contemporary philosophy—and in 1900, a short book, of secondary importance though significant: *Le Rire*. In 1903 he published in the *Revue de Métaphysique et de Morale*, a long essay entitled "Introduction à la métaphysique," where the central ideas of his philosophy, at least those of its early maturity, appear very clearly, precisely those ideas which indicate the greatest innovation in early twentieth-century thought, those which already anticipate the ideas of the more important *L'Évolution créatrice* (1907).

Bergson distinguishes two profoundly different ways of knowing a thing: to circle around it and to enter into it; the first depends on the *point of view* and the *symbols* through which it is expressed; the second takes *no* point of view, nor does it depend on any symbol; Bergson calls the first way *relative* knowledge; the second, when it is possible, achieves *absolute* knowledge. Bergson uses the example of the character in a novel and one's knowledge of him: "Description, histoire et analyse," he says, "me laissent ici dans le relatif. Seule, la coïncidence avec la personne même me donnerait l'absolu."[111] "Il suit de là," he adds, "qu'un absolu ne saurait être donné que dans une *intuition*, tandis que tout le reste relève de *l'analyse*. Nous appelons ici intuition la *sympathie* par laquelle on se transporte à l'intérieur d'un objet pour coïncider avec ce qu'il a d'unique et par conséquent d'inexprimable. Au contraire, l'analyse est l'opération qui ramène l'objet à des éléments déjà connus, c'est-à-dire communs à cet objet et à d'autres. Analyser consiste donc à exprimer une chose en fonction de ce qui n'est pas elle."[112] And, as a result: "La métaphysique est donc la science qui prétend se passer de symboles."[113]

We must keep clearly in mind these characteristics of knowing as

[111] *Ibid.*, 204.
[112] *Ibid.*, 205.
[113] *Ibid.*, 206.

Bergson understands it, in order to comprehend later in what form Ortega's thought differs essentially from his. All that has traditionally been called conceptual or rational knowledge (science, in brief) is interpreted by Bergson as analysis, and this consists precisely in the *reduction* of reality to elements which are not reality; when we find ourselves in the presence of that which interests us for its own sake—and which for that reason is irreducible—analysis, and hence symbols or concepts, have nothing to do, and nothing is left but intuition. What Bergson was later to call *true empiricism* (we shall soon see the reappearance of this idea of empiricism in various forms), is a kind of *spiritual auscultation*, and that empiricism is the true metaphysics.[114] One can pass from intuition to analysis, but not from analysis to intuition,[115] and, "with concepts or points of view, nothing will ever be done."[116]

The reality which we apprehend from within, by intuition and not by analysis, is "our own person in its flow through time."[117] Inner life cannot be represented by *images*; still less by *concepts*; "that is, by abstract, or general, or simple ideas." The image, at least, keeps us within the concrete. Concepts are "symbols which take the place of the object that they symbolize," for "the concept generalizes at the same time that it abstracts." Certainly, concepts are indispensable to metaphysics, but the reason Bergson gives for this—let us keep it well in mind—is that "all the other sciences ordinarily work on concepts, and metaphysics cannot get along without the other sciences." "But metaphysics is not properly itself except when it goes beyond the concept, or at least when it frees itself from rigid and ready-made concepts in order to create concepts that are quite different from those which we customarily manipulate; I mean flexible, mobile, almost fluid representations, always ready to mold themselves upon the fleeting forms of intuition."[118] "Ou il n'y a pas de philosophie possible . . . ," Bergson concludes, "ou philosopher consiste à se placer dans l'objet même par un effort d'intuition."[119]

The method of intuition, which has as its immediate object the mobility of *duration*, should not reduce philosophy to "watching itself live," "comme un pâtre assoupi regarde l'eau couler," says Bergson,

114 *Ibid.*, 222.
115 *Ibid.*, 229.
116 *Ibid.*, 224.

117 *Ibid.*, 206.
118 *Ibid.*, 210–14.
119 *Ibid.*, 226.

recalling a line from Musset. The analysis of duration leads to the recognition of an exterior reality which is, however, immediately given to our spirit; this is *mobility* (although Bergson expressly warns that this in no way eliminates *substance* and that his doctrine cannot be compared to Heraclitus's); ready-made things do not exist, but rather things that are being made, and all reality is *tendency*. Our intelligence, when it follows its natural inclination, proceeds by means of solid perceptions and stable conceptions and thus it allows the real to slip away from it, for there is no way of reconstructing the mobility of the real with the fixity of concepts; therefore "to philosophize is to reverse the habitual direction of the effort of thought." Symbolic knowledge through preexisting concepts—which goes from the fixed to the moving (or, better perhaps, to the *self-moving*, which would be the closest translation of *le mouvant*)—is relative; on the other hand, the intuition which installs itself in the moving and adopts the very life of things achieves an absolute.[120]

This is the presentation of the problem in the Bergson of early maturity, in the man who was to influence European philosophy in the early part of the century. We shall add a few more statements from *L'Évolution créatrice* (1907), the masterwork in which he expresses his philosophy and which consolidated his prestige, where he neatly formulates his position in regard to concept and reason: "*Notre intelligence, telle qu'elle sort des mains de la nature, a pour objet principal le solide inorganisé.*" "*L'intelligence ne se répresente clairement que le discontinu.* Bornons-nous à dire que le stable et l'immuable sont ce à quoi notre intelligence s'attache en vertu de sa disposition naturelle. *Notre intelligence ne se représente clairement que l'immobilité.*" "*Nous ne sommes à notre aise que dans le discontinu, dans l'immobile, dans le mort. L'intelligence est caractérisée par une incompréhension naturelle de la vie.*"[121] Such is Bergson's innovation in regard to method.

d) THE DISCOVERY OF OBJECTIVITY (BRENTANO AND HIS SCHOOL)

At first sight, Brentano (1838–1917) represented the opposite of all that was beginning to be done around him: while the most penetrating

[120] *Ibid.*, 233–44.
[121] *L'Évolution créatrice*, 166–79.

thinkers of the period were trying to seek a new method for human and historical reality, while Dilthey was working out his notions of *Verständnis, Auslegung,* and *Hermeneutik* in order to establish "sciences of mind" quite different from those of nature, while the pragmatists were trying to find new means of access to reality and Bergson was arriving at the doctrine of intuition and disqualifying—no less—both intelligence and the concept, serviceable for things and natural knowledge, Brentano was proclaiming the thesis that *vera philosophiae methodus nubla alia nisi scientiae naturalis est.*[122] In fact, Brentano placed himself in opposition to the idealist tradition and attempted to base himself on Descartes and Leibniz, and beyond them on Saint Thomas and, especially, on Aristotle.

What Brentano extracted from his tradition and affirmed as a method was *empiricism,* in the sense of opposing all the forms of constructive thinking and the speculation of the idealists, in order to hold to the observation of phenomena and a rigorous analysis of them. This led Brentano to fix his attention chiefly on psychology, and within psychology on the rediscovery of intentionality; in the hands of his disciples—Stumpf, Meinong, von Ehrenfels, Marty, Kastil, Kraus, Höfler, Twardowski, and especially Husserl—this method became the reconquest of objectivity, as opposed to idealism, and of essences as opposed to the Positivist form of empiricism, with its tendency to reduce everything to facts.

The result was that this "sobriety," paradoxically, enriched the world prodigiously. The firm proposition to hold to the reality of things, and not to substitute mental constructions for it, led to the discovery of a whole multitude, not only of objects, but of modes of objectivity, of ways of being. Fidelity to the real was a sort of magic wand which made new realities spring up everywhere: the world of ideal objects, which made possible a new logic; values; meanings as such; essences, in a very different function from that which this notion had had in Aristotelian thought and Scholasticism; and through this, in a perhaps unexpected way, the discovery of the "intentional" condition of man, a new setting-forth of the problem of the external world and even of the doctrines concerning "existence" or human life. But in order to achieve this, naturally, the tendency which proceeded from Brentano

[122] See *Die Zukunft der Philosophie* (Spanish trans., *El porvenir de la filosofía* [Madrid, 1936], 37).

had to link up with other orientations, especially with the one proceeding from Dilthey.

We must note, however, that Brentano followed Positivism very closely in certain especially important aspects, such as his withdrawal from metaphysics—an attitude which coincided with Dilthey's; that, from the point of view of the demands of phenomenology, his "empirical" method would emerge as shaky and insufficient; that, on the other hand, the phenomenological philosophy in which Husserl's doctrine debouched was, beyond its method, a falling back into idealism; and that, lastly, the consequences which Husserl's disciples extracted from phenomenology were to be repudiated by Husserl as unfaithful to the assumptions and the inspiration of phenomenology. We will do well to keep this in mind, so as not to link together in a precipitate and exaggerated manner doctrines which were not free from contradiction and opposition, and so as not to take as the philosophy of 1900 or its "immediate consequences" what has only been established, with great effort and many struggles, during a period of more than half a century.

The philosophy of the past few decades is the result of an original thought which was *conditioned* but not determined by the philosophical innovations I have just enumerated. And the divergencies within that thought which we can call fully *present-day* have acted upon the reception of that common tradition and have resulted in the fact that, in spite of that tradition and of moving on the same "level," the different philosophies of our time are quite distinct and, in a certain measure, irreducible to each other.

18. THE PROBLEMS POSED AND THE PHILOSOPHICAL PERSPECTIVE UP TO 1914

The inadequacy of the neo-Kantian theory of knowledge gradually became realized as the twentieth century advanced. Its alliance with natural science became ever harder to sustain. Two new demands militated against it: on the one hand, Diltheyan thought; on the other, phenomenology. But again, we must not be hasty or take these two words to mean what comes to our minds today when we hear them.

Neo-Kantianism had continued in the conviction that an *a priori* foundation had to be given to knowing, and had maintained that physics was the model of science. Dilthey's chief theme was that of basing the "sciences of mind" philosophically, of filling out theoretically the work of the historical school. His *Introduction to the Sciences of Mind* begins with these words: "The book whose first part I am publishing here unites a historical with a systematic method in order to resolve, with the greatest degree of certainty accessible to me, the question of the philosophical bases of the sciences of mind."[123] After discussing the discoveries and results of the historical school, he adds, "But the historical school has not, up till now, broken through the internal limits which obstructed its theoretical perfection as well as its influence on life. Its study and evaluation of historical phenomena lacked any connection with the analysis of the facts of consciousness; and therefore it lacked philosophical foundation."[124] "Exclusively in internal experience, in the facts of consciousness, did I find a firm base on which to anchor my thought, and I hope that no reader will pass up the demonstration of this point. All science is of experience; but all experience has its original connection and validity, determined by that connection, in the conditions of our consciousness, within which it arises, in the totality of our nature. We call this point of view—which sees logically the impossibility of retreating behind these conditions, of seeing, if it can be expressed that way, without eyes or directing the eye of knowledge behind the eye itself—the *gnoseological* point of view; modern science cannot recognize any other . . . . Real blood does not flow through the veins of the cognitive subject constructed by Locke, Hume, and Kant, but only the thin fluid of reason as mere mental activity. But occupying myself (historically as well as psychologically) with the whole man led me to place him, in the multiplicity of his faculties—this being who loves, feels, and has ideas—also as a base of knowledge and its concept (such as external world, time, substance, cause), although knowledge appears to weave its concepts only out of the material of perception, representation, and thought. The method of the essay which follows is, therefore, this: I contrast every element of abstract, scientific, present-day thought with the entirety of human nature as experience, the study of language, and history show it, and I seek their connection. And this is what happens: the most important elements of our image and our knowledge of reality, such as the vital unity of the person, the external

[123] *Introducción a las ciencias del espíritu*, trans. by Julián Marías, p. 3.
[124] *Ibid.*, 4.

world, individuals outside ourselves, their life in time, and their inter-action—all these can be explained from that whole human nature, whose real, vital process in loving, feeling, and representing simply has different aspects. Not the supposition of a rigid *a priori* in our faculty for knowing, but only the evolutive history which arises from the totality of our being can give answer to the questions which we all must ask of philosophy."[125]

But it must be stated that the program which these paragraphs seem to formulate did not develop into a philosophy, and especially into a philosophy that was destined to be communicated and known. "Until now," says Oesterreich, commenting on the passage I have just quoted, in 1921, ten years after Dilthey's death, "these ideas have not achieved a greater influence, outside the closed circle of the Diltheyan school."[126] He considers Dilthey to be a representative of *irrationalism*, and in a particularly forceful sense; for Dilthey "considers the very reality of nature irrational" ("Er hält die Wirklichkeit selbst für irrationaler Natur"). And he adds that the fight against metaphysics has reached its peak in Dilthey. He represents an *irrationalist skepticism* ("Ihren Höhepunkt hat der Kampf gegen die Metaphysik in Dilthey erreicht. Er vertritt einen *irrationalistischen Skeptizimus*").[127] And he further concludes that instead of giving an idea of the world, philosophy becomes a theory of the ideas of the world. His last word is skepticism ("Anstatt selbst Weltanschauung zu geben, wird die Philosophie zur Lehre von den Weltanschauungen. Ihr letzes Wort ist der Skeptizismus").[128] It is important to keep in mind this way of looking at Dilthey's philosophy in 1921, and by a man of the same generation as Ortega's (Oesterreich was born in 1880 and died in 1949).

At more recent dates, however, the influence of phenomenology was much greater. Oesterreich could say in this same study that phenomenology had dissolved neo-Kantianism.[129] It represented an intellectual instrument of incalculable precision, capable, first, of transcending psychologism and bringing logic into its own; in the second place, capable of reconquering essences and giving back to philosophy one of its most important functions, which had been placed under interdict for

[125] *Ibid.*, 5–6.
[126] Oesterreich, *loc. cit.*, 378.
[127] *Ibid.*, 380.
[128] *Ibid.*
[129] *Ibid.*, 376.

more than half a century. But very serious problems, difficult ones to solve, continued to arise.

The first piece of writing in which Husserl sets forth the *theory* of phenomenology was published in 1911 (the year of Dilthey's death), in a review called *Logos*: the essay "Philosophie als strenge Wissenschaft." Husserl discerns two *dangers* which threaten philosophy: *naturalism* and *historicism*. The first is a result of the discovery of nature, in the sense of "a unity of the spatio-temporal being according to exact natural laws." Up to this point, Husserl can go along with Dilthey; but he immediately adds that, analogously, as a phenomenon consecutive to the "discovery of history" and the establishment of new sciences of mind, historicism has arisen.[130] The allusion to Dilthey could not be clearer. And if this were not enough, he then refers to him by name, and with the greatest insistence. And his objections are the most serious that can be made, from the point of view of the assumptions of phenomenology.

Historicism, says Husserl, takes up its position in the sphere of facts (*Tatsachensphäre*), of empirical spiritual life (*des empirischen Geisteslebens*), and this leads to a *relativism* which is very close to *naturalistic psychologism*, and hence to a *historicist skepticism*. If one is acquainted with Husserl's work, in particular Volume I of his *Logical Investigations*, one understands what these reproaches mean when he expresses them. He at once mentions Dilthey specifically, and especially his last work, recently published, on *Die Typen der Weltanschauung*.[131] In contrast to the essences of phenomenology, facts; over against pure consciousness, empirical spiritual life; over against the absolute validity of truths, their historical conditioning. There could be no greater reversal than the one Husserl is attempting to make. "It can easily be seen," he adds, "that historicism, consistently developed, turns into extreme skeptical subjectivism. The ideas of truth, theory, science, like all ideas, would then lose their absolute validity." "Historical bases can only give historical consequences. To base or refute ideas with facts

---

130 "Der Naturalismus ist eine Folgeerscheinung der Entdeckung der Natur, der Natur im Sinne einer Einheit des räumlich zeitlichen Seins nach exakten Naturgesetzen ... Ganz ähnlich ist später, als Folgeerscheinung der 'Entdeckung der Geschichte' und der Begründung immer neuer Geisteswissenschaften der Historizismus erwachsen." (*Philosophie als strenge Wissenschaft, Logos*, Band I, Heft 3, p. 294.)

131 *Ibid.*, 323–24. See my translation of Dilthey's book *Teoría de las concepciones del mundo* (Madrid, 1944).

is a contradiction in terms—*ex pumice aquam*, as Kant quoted."[132] Dilthey must have confused empirical comprehension (*empirisches Verstehen*) with the essential phenomenological attitude (*phänomenologische Wesenseinstellung*). Only *phänomenologische Wesenslehre* is capable of forming a basis for a philosophy of mind. And, *in opposition* to the *Weltanschauungsphilosophie*, he is going to affirm *Philosophie als strenge Wissenschaft*.[133]

This is the problem, very shrewdly formulated. The need for establishing sciences of mind, historical and human sciences, led Dilthey to his *historical* and essentially empirical method. From Husserl's point of view, which had just given philosophy its most precise and felicitous instrument, this leads to skeptical relativism and, in the end, the annulment of the authentic meaning of philosophy. But if this demand of Husserl's is accepted, *reality* as such is lost, the *system* becomes impossible, and we fall back on consciousness and therefore on a refined form of *idealism*. This is, in its deepest nucleus, the problematical horizon of European philosophy about 1914, when Dilthey had died and Husserl had come into possession of the theory of phenomenology.

---

[132] "Man sieht leicht, dass der Historizismus konsequent durchgeführt in den extremen skeptischen Subjektivismus übergeht. Die Ideen Wahrheit, Theorie, Wissenschaft würden dann, wie alle Ideen, ihre absolute Gültigkeit verlieren." (*Loc. cit.*, 324–25.) "Aber historische Gründe können nur historische Folgen aus sich ergeben. Aus Tatsachen Ideen sei es begründen oder widerlegen wollen, ist Widersinn—ex pumice aquam, wie Kant zitierte." (*Ibid.*, 326.)

[133] *Ibid.*, 328.

Part One

THE GERFALCON

I.
ORTEGA AND HIS
CIRCUMSTANCE

19. HIS FAMILY WORLD AND EDUCATION

In the two preceding chapters, which constitute the Introduction to this study on Ortega, I have not spoken of him, and have scarcely made any reference to him. In those two chapters I have studied the situation in Spain and the situation of European thought at the moment when Ortega began his active life and with it his work; and, given the dynamic nature of every situation, this has obliged me to go back to the point of origin of each of those situations: back to the crisis of the *"ancien régime"* at the end of the eighteenth century, back to the crisis of German idealism in the first half of the nineteenth, in the other case.

In this Introduction I have omitted Ortega insofar as possible; I have written these two chapters *as if* they had nothing to do with him, as if I were simply trying to explain and present the situation *of Spain and of philosophy*, respectively. It was necessary to do it that way, for the important point was to show reality *previous to Ortega*, the reality with which he must have had to deal beginning in the early years of the present century. Any introduction of the viewpoints, doctrines, or particular interests of Ortega would have vitiated and obscured the image we must possess if we are to understand him; for without this it would be entirely illusory to believe that we can understand Ortega's significance, or even the "technical" content of his philosophy. But, could it be said that this Introduction "has nothing to do" with Ortega? Could it be a separable piece of work, independent of him? By no means. A situation is *always* the situation of someone;[1] the selection which the two preceding chapters have made, out of the *totality* of historical reality, has been determined and influenced by the *who*, the someone whose portion of resulting reality was to form the situation—in the form of present surroundings or recent past. There-

[1] See my *Introducción a la Filosofía* (*Obras*, II), I, 9, 20, 21; III, 35; IX, 68; X, 70. Also, *La estructura social*, I, 6.

fore, Ortega was already present in the Introduction, but precisely in the form of not appearing in it; in other words, it was necessary not to put him into its contents, precisely so that the situation described could be truly *his*; that situation with which he had to deal, and of which, consequently, he formed no part. Ortega's "absence" was the condition of his effective presence, for the situation I have described was that which was necessarily *other than he*, that as a result of which he had to be *himself*.

I have attempted, therefore, to clarify those areas of historical reality, both Spanish and European, which are at once united and isolated from the rest by Ortega's biographical trajectory. But—be it clearly understood—it is not a question here of those things which Ortega *found* and those with which he had to *deal*, with things he perhaps spoke and wrote about. Most of the elements which have entered into this Introduction are previous to Ortega; he never mentioned many of them; he did not even know, perhaps, about a large number of them. This is not the decisive point: the point is that they *acted on him*. Especially, of course, in the apparently passive form of the *configuration* of his world, and, consequently, of his biographical trajectory. Some of the factors mentioned up to this point are *material* ones—in the Aristotelian sense of the "of what" or *ex hoû*—those with which he could make his life; others, still more subtle, are the determining conditions of his *possibilities*, those by whose light we can understand his reality; that is, what he in fact *did*.

A similar criterion must guide us now. As we arrive at Ortega himself, as we begin to speak of him, we must pay attention to what he in fact found around him. But this is not the sum of what there *is* or was in the world in which he began to live. We must keep in mind only that which conditioned his personal life *a tergo*, and the factors *with respect to which* he was obliged to successively imagine and choose and realize that life. We must limit ourselves, then, to his *circumstance* in the strict sense of the term.

José Ortega y Gasset[2] was born in Madrid on May 9, 1883. The

[2] This is the way Ortega always signed his writings. The use of the two surnames was traditional in his family, and therefore "Ortega" was used successively in alternation with others; thus, José's grandfather was Ortega Zapata, his father Ortega Munilla; José Ortega *y* Gasset undoubtedly inserted the *y* for reasons of euphony; his younger son calls himself José Ortega Spottorno, and his son José Ortega Klein. For a long time our author called himself Ortega y Gasset; it gradually became customary,

Restoration was in its middle phase: Alfonso XII was king and Posada Herrera, prime minister; in England, the liberal Gladstone was prime minister under Queen Victoria; in Germany, under William I, Bismarck's hand ruled the Empire; it was the time of President Grévy in France, and Leo XIII was head of the Church. It was the year of Wagner's death; Dilthey had published his *Einleitung in die Geisteswissenschaften*, and Nietzsche *Also sprach Zarathustra*. Menéndez Pelayo was beginning publication of his *Historia de las ideas estéticas en España* ["History of Aesthetic Ideas in Spain"], while Emilia Pardo Bazán and Juan Valera were discussing naturalistic novels in *La cuestión palpitante* ["The Burning Question"] and *Apuntes sobre el nuevo arte de escribir novelas* ["Notes on the New Art of Writing Novels"]; and, in addition to these two, Galdós, Alas, and Palacio Valdés were writing novels.

Ortega was the son[3] of José Ortega Munilla and Dolores Gasset. On both sides of his family he belonged to circles which were very representative of the culture and politics of the Restoration. Ortega Munilla (1856–1922) had been born in the same year as Menéndez Pelayo, and was very close in age to Pardo Bazán, Picón, Palacio Valdés, Padre Coloma, and Leopoldo Alas. He had been born in Cárdenas (Cuba), but had lived in Spain since childhood, and was one of the literary figures who enhanced and gave prestige to journalism in Spain. Ortega Munilla, a writer, novelist, and short-story writer of no mean skill, became a member of the Spanish Academy of Letters in 1902, but was, above all, a journalist. *El Imparcial*, a newspaper founded in 1867 by Eduardo Gasset y Artime (a liberal monarchist), the most important

in the circle of his close friends and acquaintances, to call him simply "Ortega"; up to 1940 and even a little later, the use of one or the other form usually indicated whether a person belonged to the circle of his personal friendship or to the "public." In latter years, since those of us who have written about him have stressed the use of the first surname only, its use has become a great deal more general.

[3] Ortega's parents had four children: Eduardo, José, Rafaela, and Manuel. Rafaela died, unmarried, in 1940; Eduardo and Manuel live at present [1960] in Caracas and Madrid, respectively. Eduardo participated actively in politics and was a Republican deputy to the Cortes; in the last few years he has written a number of articles about his brother José, in particular recounting memories of his childhood or youth; he has also published the book *Monodiálogos de Don Miguel de Unamuno* (Ediciones Ibérica, New York, 1958), his memories and commentaries concerning the Rector of Salamanca, whom he knew well, and in which he frequently mentions Ortega. Manuel, a mining engineer, has occasionally written also: *Figuración* (Ensayo Folletinesco) (Madrid, 1948).

newspaper of the Restoration, was his chief rostrum. A contributor to and later the editor of *Los Lunes del Imparcial*, the most prestigious literary publication of that period, he had very considerable influence on Spanish letters. His cordiality toward the young writers of the Generation of 1898, many of whom he brought to public attention, was a decisive element in the renewal of literature, a factor of some weight in the consolidation of the new tendencies. Ortega was within journalism from a very early age, living in a family where public life—both letters and politics—was an immediate concern. Thus he could say that he was born on a rotary printing press. His mother was the daughter of Eduardo Gasset, founder of *El Imparcial*, who was minister of foreign affairs for some time, and the sister of Rafael Gasset Chinchilla, who was editor of the paper later and had a distinguished political career; he was a deputy and minister many times, an advocate of hydraulic works in Spain, and also a writer. It is important to keep in mind the conditions of this family atmosphere, which explain in some measure the sensitivity to *public* affairs which characterized Ortega's whole life.

Ortega's childhood, spent in Madrid, soon acquired a considerable Andalusian influence. His family had a house in Cordova, and spent long periods there during the winter from the time Ortega was four or five year old. But in particular, in October, 1891, at the age of eight, he entered the school which the Jesuits had founded in Miraflores del Palo (Málaga), and stayed there until 1897. He spent his summers in Madrid and Málaga. "I too was an *emperor*," Ortega recalled in 1910,[4] "in the school maintained by Jesuits in Miraflores del Palo, near Málaga. Does the reader know it? . . . There is a place blandished by the Mediterranean, where the earth loses its elemental value, where the water of the sea stoops to the duties of a slave and turns its liquid vastness into a shimmering mirror that reflects the only thing that is real there: Light. When one leaves Málaga following the undulating line of the coast, one enters the empire of light. Reader, for six years I was an emperor within a drop of light, in an empire bluer and more splendorous than the land of the Mandarins." Ortega returned to the memory of his school days when he compared them with those described by Pérez de Ayala in his novel *A. M. D. G.* This is perhaps the only place in which he refers specifically to his early education, and we would do well to dwell with some care on his description.

[4] "Al margen del libro A.M.D.G." (1910). I, 524.

Ortega's memory, at twenty-seven, of the pedagogy practiced by the Jesuits of Palo is neither pleasant nor inspiring: "When I read Ayala's book, that lost childhood came skipping back to me with dangerous speed, and now I can no longer distinguish between what the pages of this novel tell me and what they remind me of. I find only one difference: Ayala sets the scenes of his boyhood in a northern landscape, which accords very well with the melancholy and grief of the life he describes, whereas the framework of a childhood subject to Jesuit teaching comes to me under the embroideries of a magnificent southern landscape. But I fling up my hand like a visor to shade my eyes against that excessive radiance that bathed my early childhood, and then I discover *the same sad and thirsty childhood* that formed the trembling heart of *Bertuco*, Ayala's little hero."[5]

Why? Ortega has three chief reproaches to make to that method of teaching. The first refers to the effect on a sensitive, wide-awake, precocious, imaginative child, capable of becoming—keeping his childhood intact, one of Ortega's themes to which I shall have to return later—one of those men "who are the salt of the earth," capable of loving common things, of being "philanthropic and active, respectful of error and confident of man's innate capacity for betterment";[6] the effect caused by the content and style of an education which is in large part negative or devoid of meaning: "Laughter," he says, "is the expression of a healthy and resilient soul, one which is unified and has its functions all complete. If this be true, a sensitive soul must have profound faith in three things if it is to be able to permit itself the luxury of laughter: faith that there is a science worthy of the name, that there is an ethic that is not an absurdity, that art exists. Well then: the Jesuits will lead him to sneer at all the classics of human thought: Democritus, Plato, Descartes, Galileo, Spinoza, Kant, Darwin, etc.; they will give him the habit of calling ethics a vast number of rules or exercises which are both stupid and superstitious; and they will never speak to him of art at all."[7]

The second reproach, which Ortega thinks even more serious, is the suppression of human brotherhood by means of "a savage, incalculable, anarchic word: *our people* .... *Our* people are not like other men: *our* people are themselves alone."[8] And the third reproach, which Ortega

[5] *Ibid.*, 524–25.
[6] *Ibid.*, 525–26.
[7] *Ibid.*, 526.
[8] *Ibid.*

brings forward as an explanation for the other two, as the key to the others, is "ignorance,"[9] "intellectual incapacity."[10]

His opinion is peremptory and adverse. But we must establish a couple of things in order to fill out this opinion and make its meaning clearer. Ortega speaks of the teaching in a Spanish Jesuit school, the one he has known directly; the question remains to what extent the characteristics of this type of education were exclusive to these schools and how far they extended to those of other religious orders, or, even beyond them, to large sectors of Spanish education. It is a problem of no little interest, but one which goes beyond the scope of this book. On the other hand, the effects which Ortega feared, if they ever appeared in him, were soon overcome; Ortega was not "like those who went down to Saint Patrick's purgatory";[11] he was able to laugh again, and with the healthiest and fullest laugh imaginable, with a deeply felt cordiality, with inexhaustible confidence in reality and in man. He always retained much of the eager child, open to any kind of stimulus, and this characteristic recurred again and again in his writings.

Very early, however, he lost the Catholic faith in which he had been reared. He makes his first public appearance without it, as a matter of fact; in none of his youthful writings—and the earliest of these date from 1902, when he was nineteen—does a positive religious attitude appear; on the contrary, we shall have to go further along in his life to find more positive and intense personal references to the Christian religion, and these became progressively deeper, more profoundly felt and intimate, in his years of maturity and in the last years of his life. The first times that we find some allusion to his religious situation in his youthful writings, they give the impression of an *evaporation* of an *already outworn* faith. At twenty-five he writes, speaking of Fogazzaro's *Il Santo* ["The Saint"], "I owe a debt of gratitude to this book; in reading it I have felt what I have not been able to enjoy for some time now: Catholic emotion. The religious unrest which thrusts through the world, trembling and burning, the soul of Pietro Maironi, all oppressed with mysticism, a sponge soaked in charity, has revived some ashes which perhaps had lain hidden in the chinks of my spiritual hearth. My mystical ashes have not burst into flame; probably they never will. But this formula for a future Catholicism, as it is preached in *The Saint*, gives those of us who are separated from any church something to

[9] *Ibid.*, 527   [10] *Ibid.*, 528.   [11] *Ibid.*, 526.

think about: if Catholicism were like this, could we not also be Catholics some day? Could we not rejoice in this gentle good news that Faith bestows on those whom it visits? This good news is full consolation for the great sense of melancholy and more stringent discipline for the will: how can it not be tempting?"[12]

This passage is revealing. Ortega is talking about something long past; and as he is twenty-five years old, he must be referring to his adolescence. Hidden ashes, that do not come to the point of catching fire; an unequivocal yearning for a faith he would like to have. No less unequivocal dissatisfaction for what Catholicism is "like"; that is, as he finds it around him—perhaps Ortega did not go deeply into the question of whether Catholicism was in fact "like that"; if he had done so, he might have found that it was different, in which case he might have been able to feel authentically a part of it. There appears not to have been any specific and precise rupture with the faith of his childhood; no "conflict," as the usual phrase was then. This is why I have spoken of "evaporation." The form of religion in which Ortega was educated seemed to him inconsistent, inadequate, from the beginning, before he had any personal philosophy, before he went to Germany, perhaps even before he started serious University studies. After the solid Catholic education of his childhood and early adolescence, Catholicism seemed to him to be *what he had received*. When he looked around him, when he felt the need to choose, to have to adhere *personally* to those contents, he felt that they conveyed nothing to him, that he did not feel them authentically, that for him they *were not religion*. And when he encountered the writings of the modernists, about 1908, his reaction was one of grateful surprise: so it was not only that? Could there be other forms of Catholicism? And he felt that what he had lost was perhaps not entirely lost. Those who interpret negatively the young Ortega's fellow feeling toward the modernists commit not only an injustice, but a crass error. That modernism was a danger for Catholicism, no one doubts; that in large measure it was a movement imbued with faith and religious spirit, that "antimodernism" was also, in the hands of many, a religious danger and had grave consequences, no one is unaware today: the sophistical inference that the *partial error* of the modernists implied the justification of *all antimodernism* was perpetrated at every step. In any case, the misgivings which could be

[12] "Sobre *El Santo*" (1908). I, 425–26.

felt about modernism *from within orthodoxy and the Church* could not be expected in one who, *from outside the Church*, saw it as an open door, a possibility of *return*.

Ortega's attitude could not be more indicative of this yearning: "I cannot conceive that any man who aspires to expand his spirit indefinitely can renounce without pain the world of religion; for me, at any rate, to feel excluded from participation in that world is profoundly depressing . . . . For it cannot be doubted that when anything is sublimated to its extreme, there comes a moment when science ends and the thing does not; this nucleus of trans-scientific things is their religiosity."[13] And he recalls—as he was to do so often later—the motto *fides quaerens intellectum,* and harshly rejects the doctrine of "double truth," and brings to his mind and takes as his own Goethe's statement that "men are not productive except so long as they are religious; when the stimulus of religion is lacking, they are reduced to imitating, to repeating, in science, in art, in poetry." And he concludes: "Let us go on thinking that we must raise our people to that noble religiosity of problems, to that inner discipline of respect, the only discipline capable of justifying the existence of a race on this earth. Think how terrible and menacing it is to see our anemic national consciousness oscillating for centuries between uncritical faith and equally uncritical skepticism. If the former moves me to compassion, the latter is apt to turn my stomach; both, however, make me feel ashamed."[14]

Ortega's religious education turned out to be exceedingly weak. The disappearance of his faith did not arise from a personal doctrine, which he was not to have until many years later—and which was destined to bring him, at least, incomparably closer to religion—or from an irreligious attitude, or from an aversion to rigor and discipline (for this last was precisely what he missed and found attractive in the Catholic faith). It was simply a result—on the human plane of the question, the only one into which it is proper to go—of his first contact with harsh reality, with the need a young man feels, whether he will or no, to personally "revalidate" his faith, to "accept" it from within himself: the human level to which the sacrament of confirmation corresponds. This situation was not infrequent; if we pass in review the religious positions of the men of Ortega's generation and even those of the two or three generations previous to it, his own position is placed in a

[13] *Ibid.,* 426. [14] *Ibid.,* 433.

proper perspective, and he can be seen as one of those who were closest and most friendly to Catholicism, even at the times when he felt most distant from it. The more favorable attitudes were usually mingled with nonreligious factors, the larger part of which were not to the taste of the significant men of that time; I say mingled, and not simply coexistent, because the utilization of religion to support other interests was, and has continued to be, constant. From within faith, precisely as it partakes of a supernatural gift, all distinctions are possible and proper —I do not say easy; from outside it, with purely human resources, they are so difficult that they exceed anything that could be demanded. In this same early piece of writing we find some words of his which are so harsh and full of bitterness that they produce a painful impression when read after his death: "The fanatics will perhaps commit the indelicacy of thinking that this friendly feeling toward the modernists is nothing but the natural exhilaration in the face of a serious illness which has attacked the Church. Not at all: the origin of our feeling is much more noble and genuine . . . . Probably the fanatics will persist in disbelieving that our intentions are so honorable; in general, I have observed that men of much faith consider themselves exempt, in actual practice, from the exercise of good faith."[15]

Since faith is very difficult to measure from without, Ortega was thinking, when he referred to "men of much faith," of those who declare themselves to be such, those who present themselves as such and feel qualified to define and measure others. And it must be said that these words, in Ortega's own case, turned out to be prophetic, for throughout all his life and even after it, he has been the target of very remarkable religious interpretations made from the vantage point of "the exercise of good faith." I mean that, if we look at things humanly, he found nothing but obstacles to a return, so greatly desired at the age of twenty-five, to a faith which was so insecurely inculcated and lived that it vanished with melancholy and sorrow shortly after Ortega left the classroom to go out into the world.[16]

[15] *Ibid.*, 427. Regarding what Ortega meant by this expression and to what degree it could have had confirmation, see my writings *Ortega y tres antípodas* (1950), and *El lugar del peligro* (Taurus, Madrid, 1958). Naturally, when he speaks of "men of much faith," Ortega refers to those who proclaim themselves as such and define and call into question the faith of others.

[16] In the book by Padre Joaquín Iriarte, S.J., *Ortega y Gasset. Su persona y su doctrina* (Madrid, 1942), 30, there is this note: "Ortega's stay in Deusto was marred

Into what sort of world did Ortega go? At what level did he become a part of it? In other words, what were the generations that defined the different levels of reigning ideas with which he was going to have to deal, and what was his own level? Let us begin with Spain as a whole.

Of Valera's generation (to give it a meaningful name), whose central date we can fix as the year 1826 (that is, including those born between 1819 and 1833 approximately, and leaving room for empirical data which may necessitate corrections), there were only a few *survivors*: Valera himself, whom Ortega once saw,[17] Echegaray, Pereda, Manuel del Palacio; except for Echegaray, all of them died during the first years of Ortega's literary activity; that is, they were not an actively participating generation, but simply the remains of one which was definitely past, almost as much so as Alarcón, Castelar, Cánovas, or Sagasta, who had all died a short time earlier.

The following generation is Galdós's, which we shall call the generation of 1841. Most of its members were still living when Ortega started his writing career, but not at the time he began his effective historical action. Giner de los Ríos, Gumersindo de Azcárate, Galdós, Beruete, Costa, and Francisco Silvela are the most representative names. Ortega witnessed what we might call their "going into the reserves" during the first phase of his personal activity. It was the generation that was "in power," but which had been replaced by the following generation by

by a deplorable incident, whose origin must be sought in the politico-religious questions which were so exacerbated at that time. If his filial love was the victim of some imprudent sentence on the part of one of the professors, he knows very well that he was given due apology in the study of the rector, Padre Aniceto Casado. His heart was wounded, however, and this was given expression in a piece of writing which represents all the members of the Jesuit school dividing people on the sectarian basis of 'ours' and 'not ours.' " This article and its meaning have been discussed in the text. As there is not a single text from Ortega's youth in which he appears as an orthodox Catholic (rather, at the age of twenty-five he refers to his faith as something "old," to which he would like to return), it seems probable that his faith evaporated before he left Deusto; perhaps it did not have enough defensive capacity to withstand the negative impact to which Padre Iriarte refers.

[17] "But I have never seen Campoamor, and Don Juan Valera only once, in a reception at the Academy, tricked out in a uniform embroidered in gold, his breast covered with ribbons, above which rose a pleasant but not very expressive face; a classic blind man's face turned indecisively toward the light shed by a window. Practically speaking, then, as if I had never seen him." ("Una polémica" [1910]. I, 156.)

the time he really began. He did not need to do battle with it; rather, it exercised on him a somewhat distant prestige.

The generation that was really "in power," the one with which Ortega had to reckon, was the genealogically preceding one—that of his father—which historically was two generations away from his: that of 1856, which we may call the generation of Menéndez Pelayo. In Europe it was an extraordinary generation;[18] in Spain, because of the *décalage* of a whole generation insofar as intellectual life was concerned, the role which this European generation played belongs in large part— though not entirely—to the following one. Besides the man whose name I have used as its eponym, the members of this generation were Eduardo Carracido, Leopoldo Alas, Cossío, Emilia Pardo Bazán, Palacio Valdés, de Hinojosa, Julián Ribera, Ramón y Cajal, Torres Quevedo, Ferrán, Picón, Rodríguez Marín, Salvador Rueda, Maragall, Alcover, Ortega Munilla, Gaudí, Regoyos, Albéniz, Rusiñol, Moreno Carbonero, Tomás Bretón, Vital Aza, López Silva, Maura, Romanones, Dato, Ferrer Guardia; and, though he died shortly after Ortega's birth, it was that of Alfonso XII. A generation of considerable intellectual density, with a notable group of research men, who represented an idea of science with which Ortega was to measure his personal and historical demands. And, on the other hand, the last generation in the nineteenth century, the one which defined the level of reigning ideas of the *fin de siècle*, the generation which was confronted, as a profound innovation, spurred by the crisis of the year that gave it its name, by "the Generation of 1898."

This generation, if we follow our chronology, was that of 1871. Its eponym is *plural*: the group of outstanding personalities who are commonly called the Generation of 1898 and who are merely the representation of the whole generation, out of the millions of men and women who were born within its "area of dates" (1864–78, probably) and who lived at this historical level. Unamuno, Baroja, Azorín, Valle-Inclán, Benavente, Antonio and Manuel Machado, Maeztu, and (outside this more representative "eponymous" nucleus) Ganivet (who died in 1898, and therefore did not share intellectual life with Ortega), Arniches, Blasco Ibañez, Rubén Darío, Gabriel y Galán, Gómez Moreno, Menéndez Pidal, Asín Palacios, the Quintero brothers, Enrique

---

[18] See my article "La generación de 1856" in *El oficio del pensamiento* (1958). [*Obras*, VI.]

Granados, Zuloaga, Manuel de Falla, La Cierva, Primo de Rivera, and Alcalá Zamora. Later we shall have to speak at length about this generation.

Ortega's is that of 1886, if we accept this calculation. His affinities with the preceding generation are very close; undoubtedly his was one of the "cumulative" generations of which he himself was later to speak. It was inevitable that this should be so: modern-day Spain begins with the Generation of 1898, an innovator in so many things, but especially in a new way of regarding national reality and intellectual themes; the following generation added its own efforts to those of its predecessor, and took part in the same undertaking, with tonalities of its own and a well-marked personality. To this generation belong the men who are coetaneous with Ortega in the strict sense: Gabriel Miró, Eduardo Marquina, Villaespesa, Pérez de Ayala, Azaña, Juan Ramón Jiménez, Picasso, Eugenio d'Ors, Marañón, Alfonso XIII, Solana, Angel Herrera, Ramón Gómez de la Serna, and "at bottom," in spite of so many appearances,[19] Pedro Salinas and Jorge Guillén. I do not wish to add many names here of such a recent generation, with which Ortega was linked all his life: for their large number, if I listed them here, would weaken their distinguishing characteristics. The rest of the important names of the generation will come in as they have a "role" in the various chapters of the book; that is, as they enter one by one into Ortega's biographical trajectory, along with their undertakings, their struggles, or the specific content of their work.

As a term of reference, I shall list the names of some philosophers belonging respectively to the generations I have mentioned:

1826: Marx, Engels, Lasalle, Renan, Spencer, Wundt, Lange, Sigwart, Teichmüller.

1841: Dilthey,[20] Brentano, Cohen, E. von Hartmann, Nietzsche, Windelband, Volkelt, Frege, Avenarius, Mach, Riehl, Peirce, James.

1856: Husserl, Bergson, Dewey, S. Alexander, Santayana, Whitehead, Blondel, Natorp, Rickert, Lipps, Vaihinger, v. Ehrenfels, Meinong,

---

[19] See my article "Constelaciones y generaciones" in *Ensayos de convivencia* (*Obras*, III). Because they did not begin writing early, and, consequently, because of their younger "social age," Salinas and Guillén, though historically they belonged to the same generation as Ortega, were largely "incorporated" into the following generation, forming part of its "constellation."

Durkheim, Lévy-Bruhl, Guyau, Meyerson, Mercier, Sombart, Simmel, Royce, Veblen, Freud, Eduard Meyer, Planck.

1871: Unamuno, F. C. S. Schiller, Troeltsch, Croce, Driesch, Brunschvieg, Klages, Russell, Scheler, Cassirer, Jung, Buber.

1886: Spengler, Keyserling, Litt, W. Jaeger, Kelsen, N. Hartmann, Maritain, Spranger, Lavelle, Ortega, Jaspers, C. I. Lewis, Gilson, Karl Barth, R. Guardini, C. D. Broad, W. Koehler, Morente, Jean Wahl, Collingwood, Wittgenstein, Heidegger, Gabriel Marcel, Toynbee, Heimsoeth.

21. THE SPANISH INTELLECTUAL SITUATION

It is not my intention here to draw a complete, or even an abbreviated, picture of Spanish culture at the beginning of this century; I have done so in an extremely succinct form in the Introduction to this book in order to sketch out the backdrop against which the figure of Ortega would be made intelligible. Here I shall refer only to the capital elements in Spain's intellectual situation *as ingredients in Ortega's circumstance*; that is, those which he found on his horizon as possibilities, models, obstacles—those in view of which, in one sense or another, he began his intellectual task.

a) KRAUSISM AND ITS DERIVATIONS

Few subjects have been treated with less accuracy and veracity than Spanish Krausism. For many years, partisanship has obscured the shape, the scope, and the content of an intellectual movement which has aroused strange passions. The history of the controversies over Krausism is one of the most lamentable, and revealing, chapters in the history of our intellectual life. And yet, on this subject as on many others—and this is a fact which it is very important to retain and to emphasize—some

---

[20] We should not look for *mathematical exactness* in human phenomena, but rather *historical strictness*; if we pay attention to the pure numerical mechanism, we should count Dilthey, who was born in 1833, within the generation of 1826 (in its last year); but note that he was born on November 19—that is, on the numerical boundary between the two generations—and chronologically he could as well be included in one as in the other. If we add that Dilthey began his career rather late, his inclusion in the generation of 1841 is more than justified.

time ago we arrived at a clarity and an agreement which consist in letting the facts speak for themselves. Today we know what to reckon with in Krausism, as we do in many other important points in Spanish history. As soon as certain rigorous standards have been applied to the investigation, as soon as a group of thinkers has arisen, ready to see things as they are and to state them firmly, the shape of our past has begun to be enormously clarified, and it is to be hoped that within a few decades the image which Spain presents to Spaniards will be one of such a different degree of clarity and veracity that it will represent a door open toward the future instead of a source of confusion and discouragement. For there is no doubt in my mind that not knowing, or not wanting to know, about our history has been one of the decisive factors in the shutting-off of our future, of the plugging-up of its possibilities.

It would be unfair to forget that in the nineteenth century Valera made very laudable efforts to understand Krausism and assess its value. Apart from many references, sometimes quite humorous ones, especially when he spoke of the Krausists' literary style and terminology, Valera dedicated three long essays to the subject, and the accuracy of his observation is in contrast to almost everything that was being written about them at the time. In the midst of the famous controversy about "living texts" in 1864, Valera wrote *Sobre la enseñanza de la filosofía en las Universidades* ["On the Teaching of Philosophy in the Universities"];[21] in that same year, in his letters to José Luis Albareda *Sobre la política de El Contemporáneo* ["On the Politics of *The Contemporary*"],[22] he again spoke of Krausism in detail; a decade later, in 1873, after Sanz del Río's death, he wrote a long philosophical study in the form of a dialogue, on *El racionalismo armónico* ["Harmonic Rationalism"].[23] It must also be remembered that in his famous debate with Campoamor, in 1890, *La metafísica y la poesía* ["Metaphysics and Poetry"], he turned back to these previous studies and summarized, in a page which is particularly interesting, his judgment of Krausism, at a time when the movement was almost entirely passé.[24] Valera's

---

[21] *Estudios críticos sobre política, literatura y costumbres de nuestros días*, II, 361 ff.

[22] *Ibid.*, 400 ff.

[23] *Obras completas*, XXXV, 102–215.

[24] *Obras completas*, XXXVI, 335–36. Valera says of Krause: "His doctrine is the one most similar to the Scholastic Aristotelianism so much in vogue today, and the one

moderation and understanding are in contrast to some of the foolishly exalted praises of Krausism within the school, as well as to the pages, filled with errors of detail and erroneous interpretations, of Menéndez Pelayo in his *Historia de los heterodoxos españoles* ["History of Heterodox Thinkers in Spain"],[25] which are still blindly quoted today as

which most spiritedly and subtly upholds the objectivity of knowledge. At the end of the Analytics, God does not demonstrate himself, but shows himself. His manifestation, His real vision, is like that conceived by the Christian mystics, and is an abyss away from the creation of the absolute I, of the Idea, of the identical Being and all the rest, of Fichte, Schelling, and Hegel. Krause is not a pantheist, but a panentheist. And his panentheism resembles what Padre Ripalda expresses simply in his *Doctrina cristiana*: *God is in every place, by essence, by presence, and by power.* Although Scholasticism had not yet revived in Spain, Sanz del Río brought Krausism from Germany, acclimated it among us, and created a school from which brilliant personalities emerged. Few are still faithful to the master's doctrine. I say this with sorrow.

"In the course of some jests incurred by the Spanish Krausists' severe technicism, which caused them to indulge in some extravagant behavior and peculiarities of language, I defended the Krausists many years ago from the unjust attacks of traditionalist Catholics. Today I am proud to remember the defense I made in the newspaper *El Contemporáneo*, when I see that the most learned and profound Thomists of today agree with me. Msgr. van Weddingen says that Krause's panentheism does not differ, except for some lamentable excesses of language, from the theistic thesis of omnipresence, and the intervention of the First Cause in cosmic agents. And then he adds, 'It is an instructive spectacle to see the wisest adversary of critical philosophy approach the teaching of the most positive of the philosophies of past ages, predestined to all the rejuvenations and perfecting techniques of modern science.'

"Msgr. van Weddingen understands, finally, that the future of philosophy lies in establishing as its base the generating principle of knowledge, as the firmest thinkers— from Aristotle and the solidest Scholastics to Krause—have indicated, for the purpose of attaining the complete distinction between the subjective and objective elements of knowledge, and between the fatalism of material agents and the autonomy of the spirit, and for the purpose of recognizing the reality of the First and Infinite Cause and its incessantly active presence in the beings of the universe and the soul of man."

Valera met Msgr. van Weddingen in 1886, when he was the Spanish minister in Brussels; he spoke about him at length to Menéndez Pelayo, and sent him van Weddingen's books. The letters written by the two men between November 13 and December 7, 1886, are extant; in almost all of them van Weddingen and his writings are discussed. Menéndez Pelayo thought well of him also, and wanted to get in touch with him. It is curious that neither of the two best books on the Spanish Krausists—Msgr. Pierre Jobit's *Les Éducateurs de l'Espagne contemporaine* (Paris-Bordeaux, 1936), and Juan López-Morillas' *El krausismo español* (Mexico, 1956)—makes any reference at all to van Weddingen, or, which is still more curious, to the text by Valera quoted in this note. (The letters of Valera and Menéndez Pelayo may be seen in their *Epistolario* [Madrid, 1946].)

[25] *Heterodoxos*, VI, 366ff. See also *Historia de las ideas estéticas en España*, IV, 267. (Edición nacional de las Obras de Menéndez Pelayo.)

if they were definitive, in spite of the fact that their insufficiency and lack of scientific value have been demonstrated again and again.[26]

By the time Ortega could have encountered Krausism, it no longer existed as a philosophical school. It had been many years since the disciples of Sanz del Río (who died in 1869) had turned to other philosophical orientations: neo-Kantianism, Hegelianism, or Positivism in particular. Spanish Krausism was affected by an essential anachronism. Its chief significance was that Sanz del Río, when he made his famous trip to Germany in 1843, established Spain's first serious and direct contact with German philosophy, about which its only information up to that time had been indirect and very superficial. But there were certain abnormal circumstances about the nature of this first contact: Sanz del Río, already oriented toward Krausism, went to Heidelberg to work with Krause's disciples Leonhardi and Roeder; a few months after his arrival, he had made up his mind to dedicate all his energies to that philosophy and its acclimatization in Spain; the blunder he made in choosing Krausism, among the different German systems of the period, is clear and has been emphasized a thousand times; but in addition, we must remember that not only at that date, but many years later, at least until 1873, the expression "novísima filosofía" still appeared among the Krausists, referring to the philosophy of Krause and his disciples; that this philosophy, the last remnant of German idealism, was not "novísima" is obvious; however, we should not forget what I demonstrated in chapter 2 of the Introduction to this book with regard to the *reigning quality* of doctrines and the tremendous delay they often undergo before they achieve this quality: that is, Krausism was not current even then, but it was not so archaic as it appears to us *today*.

Its role in Spanish intellectual history was, however, unique. Whatever esteem its doctrinal content may merit, the incorporation of the Spanish mind into the German philosophical style dates from Krausism; and it was an open door to the comprehension of intellectual forms which had been totally alien to us, and which in the nineteenth century were the most highly regarded in Europe. The possession and (relative) assimilation of a German philosophical system was an experience of

[26] See the two books mentioned in note 24. See also my essay "El pensador de Illescas" (1950), in *Ensayos de teoría* (Barcelona, 1954) (*Obras*, IV).

prime importance, one which made possible the developments that have come to pass in our century. Spanish philosophy today has scarcely anything to do with Krausism, and of course is very far removed from its philosophical content; in many senses, as we shall see later, modern Spanish philosophy has inverted its order of assimilation; the difference in style could not be greater; we simply cannot insist too much on this point; but we must make clear that, in spite of all this, without the work of the Krausists—or others who would have done something analogous —this philosophy would not have been possible; and it is a fact—no more, but no less either—that it was the Krausists who accomplished this broadening of the Spanish mind.

Ortega recognized this, in passing, in an article written in 1911, when he wrote, "With the exception of the Krausists, Spaniards swallowed the dogmas of that *foreign* philosophy without thinking them through, *like buying medicine in a pharmacy*, and more or less consciously allowed themselves to become permeated with its substance."[27] And in that same year, writing to Baroja from Marburg, he referred to the Krausists in a way which revealed both his esteem for them and how far away from them he was, especially in the way in which he thought of them as outmoded. After expressing serious reservations about German imperialism, Ortega added, "But the important thing, for you as well as for me, is the cultural rapprochement of Spain with Germany .... Something of the sort was attempted once. In the 1870's the Krausists, the only intellectual force Spain has enjoyed for the last century, tried to submit their countrymen's intellect and hearts to German discipline."[28] His personal references to the Spanish Krausists —Sanz del Río, Azcárate, Giner—are usually of the same kind: esteem and distance. In 1908, he mentions Azcárate very critically, for having shared "the Anarchist reasoning which lies at the base of all old-style individualistic liberalism: that man in his native state is good; that regimented society makes him bad; destroy it, and human goodness will arise from its ruins like an immortal mustard seed."[29] Two years later, in more detail this time, he writes, "And there is Don Gumersindo de Azcárate, who still believes in the organic, spontaneous, sincere

27 "Observaciones" (1911). I, 167.
28 "Una respuesta a una pregunta" (1911). I, 212.
29 "Pidiendo una biblioteca" (1908). I, 84.

impulses of our people! What an agreeable and respectable man! How true it is that his heart is worth a great deal more than his sociology."[30] And a few lines later: "But, when will Spencer's law begin to operate? Perhaps even Don Gumersindo de Azcárate does not know when, in spite of the fact that he is the last Spencerian left on earth."[31] But when Azcárate died in 1917, Ortega turned his attention, more seriously this time, to a whole group within Spanish society, and wrote some serious words in which both distance and esteem are forcefully emphasized.

Ortega speaks of "the men who were active in the period previous to the Restoration, and who seemed to us something like the survivors of an epoch which appeared to us more heroic, more energetic, with greater spiritual zeal, whom a flood of corruption, cynicism, and despair had overcome. 'They are all dying off,' we told ourselves. And then, 'But Azcárate is still left!' Spare, taller than the average, with silver beard and melancholy face, we watched him pass by, moved by the sight, as of a Don Quixote who had come to his senses. The shades of Castelar and Cánovas, Salmerón and Giner, went by with him. When he came and went, a vast whisper of ideal enthusiasms came and went with him, a warm gust of essential patriotism and transcendent humanity . . . . Perhaps nothing indicates better what the future of Spain is to be than to note the fact that we men whose shield as yet bore no device felt a greater affinity with the men of 1869 than with the generation of the Restoration. And it certainly was not their Republic that attracted us, but their ethical sense of life, their zeal to know and to meditate."[32]

In Ortega's writings the name of Giner de los Ríos always appears in a context of cordiality, and he recalled Don Julián Sanz del Río, as late as 1932, with unequivocal esteem for his efforts—though not without a touch of irony when speaking of his old plan to write a "salvation" such as those he planned about 1912, entitled *El pensador de Illescas* ["The Thinker of Illescas"], "in which he combined, making one figure of them, El Greco's Saint Ildefonso in the Charity Hospital of that town with Don Julián Sanz del Río, who lived there meditating and doing Swedish gymnastics on the soil of the province of Toledo . . . . On the other hand, when someone was asked, 'Has there been thought in Spain, in nineteenth-century Spain?' he answered, 'I don't know,

---

[30] "Planeta sitibundo" (1910). I, 149.
[31] *Ibid.*, 153.
[32] "Don Gumersindo de Azcárate ha muerto" (1917). III, 11–12.

I don't know; but they say that sixty or seventy years ago a gentleman named Don Julián Sanz del Río sometimes wrapped himself up in his cape and set himself to thinking.' "[33]

b) THE POSITIVE DISCIPLINES

The young Ortega's point of departure was a very great esteem for science, to which must be added his consciousness of its absence in Spain. In his early youth, at the age of twenty-three, he stated his point of view very clearly:

"We should all yearn for the day when, in the course of time, the Spanish spirit gives a good harvest of wisdom; and we should do more than yearn; we must weave our individual lives in such a way as to become wise in some area. We need science by the bucketful, in floods, so that our dried-up, hard, and rocky brains will soften like irrigated lands. But those who preach the gospel of science most often have not noticed that they want us to have German science or French science, but not Spanish science.

"When Menéndez Pelayo was young and brash, he broke those famous lances on behalf of Spanish science; before he wrote his book, it was already suspected that there had never been science in Spain; after it was published, it became perfectly clear that there never had been. Science, no; men of science, yes . . . .

"As we have made our history after the manner of an earthquake, so we have made and will make all the rest. 'We don't look ahead, we don't look ahead,' Navarro Ledesma kept telling us. Do we want to have a disciplined science? This presupposes continuity of effort, and in Spain science and scientists are monolithic, like her painters and poets: they are beings unto themselves, born without precursors by spontaneous generation, from the fine (though somewhat muddled) mothers of our race; and they die the death of their bodies and their work, and leave no disciples."[34]

This attitude becomes clearer if we take into consideration another text, also a very early one, from the year 1908, in which Ortega establishes a clear hierarchy among the intellectual disciplines. He points

[33] "Prólogo-conversación a *Goethe desde dentro* (1932). IV, 384–85.
[34] "La ciencia romántica" (1906). I, 41–42.

out that Menéndez Pelayo, in a note to the second edition of his *La ciencia española* ["Spanish Science"], observes that there has been a lack of mathematics in Spanish culture, but that on the other hand we have cultivated the biological sciences very extensively. And Ortega comments, "Why? Does it matter? Are they co-ordinated subjects, of equal significance in the intellectual sphere? I think that the simile of a sphere is very applicable to culture; a culture also has a center and a periphery. Mathematics, together with philosophy, is the center of European culture, which is what we are discussing . . . . If we have not had mathematics—'the pride of human reason,' as Kant called it—if, as a result, we have not had philosophy, we can say very plainly that we have not even made a beginning as far as modern culture is concerned."[35] In the same year he again expresses himself categorically: "If Europe in some manner transcends the Asiatic type, the African type, she owes it to science . . . . Europe = science: all else she shares with the rest of the planet."[36] "The Spanish problem is, certainly, a pedagogical one; but what is real and distinctive about our pedagogical problem is that we need first to educate some few men of science, to create at least a shadow of scientific concern, and that without this previous step the rest of the pedagogical activity will be useless, impossible, senseless. I think that something analogous to what I have been saying could be the necessary formula for europeanization."[37] We do not know what to hold to with regard to our own misfortunes because we have no science, historical science this time: "since we have no brain we have not been able to weave our own history. We are a people of legends, not history, that is, a *ci-devant* people, like the Indians or the Egyptians!"[38] And thus Spain is "the land of interjections."[39]

I have emphasized these early texts because what I am interested in, for the moment, is Ortega's initial situation in his Spanish circumstance. All the writings of the early years cry out for science, in the sense of strictness, discipline, veracity, continuity, hierarchy. We shall see later to what degree this attitude conditions others which are only indirectly

[35] "Pidiendo una biblioteca" (1908). I, 83.
[36] "Asamblea para el Progreso de las Ciencias" (1908). I, 102.
[37] *Ibid.*, 103.
[38] *Ibid.*, 105.
[39] *Ibid.*, 108.

connected with it. And when he criticizes what seem to be, in a certain sense, contemporary scientific achievements, we notice, if we keep in mind what I have just demonstrated, that what Ortega does is to measure those achievements against the level of the demands of the hour—what he was always to call, in a theme repeated throughout his whole life, "the level of the times"—and against *real* possibilities which seemed, in his situation, to be possibilities and which in fact turned out to be such.

His praises of Hinojosa and Cajal are mixed with the consciousness of their exceptional, and in a certain sense anomalous, quality. Ortega refers to the absolute lack of books in Madrid in all the public libraries, in that same year of 1908: Fichte's works are not there, nor were those of Kant up to *a few days before*; those of Harnack or Brugmann do not even exist: "Let those I have mentioned suffice," he adds, "to prove that there is not the shadow of science in Spain. There may have been a scientist or two . . . . The case of Cajal, and still more the case of Hinojosa, cannot mean a source of pride for our country: rather, they are a source of shame, for they are a coincidence."[40] That is, Ortega starts off, at the outset, from a question of *level*, the level of a form of *collective* life. In that life there simply is no science, and this is the point Spain must start from: from its lack, its urgent need, its realization as a national undertaking. We shall see to what degree these thoughts, expressed at the age of twenty-five, have been decisive in Ortega's trajectory—and in Spain's.

c) COSTA

I have spoken at some length of Joaquín Costa in the Introduction to this book (I, 7) with regard to concern for the "reconstitution and europeanization of Spain"; I have already stated that he had exercised no little influence on Ortega in his youth; now we shall have to return to Costa in order to see him in this new perspective: as an element of the world Ortega encountered, as an influence on him at the beginning of his career.

There are a couple of references to Costa in Ortega's youthful writings which should have made us realize that Costa is a necessary element

[40] *Ibid.*

for the understanding of Ortega's thought and style. In 1908, Ortega says, "For a good many years now people have been talking about 'europeanization' in Spain: no word is considered to be more respectable and fruitful than this one, nor is there, in my opinion, any other word which more accurately sums up the Spanish problem. If there were any room for doubt that this is the case, it would suffice if we were obligated to meditate over the fact that Don Joaquín Costa, that Celtiberian whose soul vibrates more times per second than any other, has placed it on his ensign."[41]

The second reference is still more interesting. In a lecture given in *El Sitio*, a club in Bilbao, in 1910, Ortega says in his programmatic conclusion: "The word *regeneration* did not come into the Spanish consciousness by itself: scarcely had regeneration begun to be mentioned when europeanization also began to be spoken of. Don Joaquín Costa, energetically linking these words together, carved forever the escutcheon of those Spanish hopes. His book *Reconstitution and Europeanization of Spain* has guided our hopes for twelve years, while we were learning from him political style, historical sensitivity, and the best Castilian prose. Even when we depart in some essential points from his way of seeing the national problem, we shall always turn our faces reverently toward that day on which his enormous intellect—solitary, broad, square—rose like a castle above the desolate moral and intellectual steppe that was Spain."[42]

The admiration for Costa revealed in these words is very great; but it also explicitly shows an influence which has not been much observed: in politics, in a sense of history, in the Spanish language—that is, in style. Costa's ethical example, his energy, his zeal for going to visceral problems, his conviction that Spain's ills went back a long way, his constant reference to Europe, his feeling that it was not enough to spread a certain level of culture in the country, but that it was necessary to create culture and to work in science—all this served as an orientation for Ortega for a number of years. But there is also an influence in literary style. Costa was a splendid rhetorician . . . sometimes. His lapses

---

[41] *Ibid.*, 99.

[42] "La pedagogía social como programa político" (1910). I, 512–13. See also the article "La herencia viva de Costa" (*El Imparcial*, 20–II–1911), written on the occasion of his death and referring to "the sentimental mush that has been spattered recently on that influential name"; in it, Ortega quotes the essential part of his previous commentary.

are frequent; his bad taste, at times disturbing; sometimes he is guilty of vulgarity or triviality. But the aptness of his expressions is also frequent, his figures of speech are bold and forceful, occasionally unbalanced because of a certain poverty or inexactness of meaning. It is hard not to see a forerunner of Ortega's style in some of Costa's expressions; Pedro de Luna is "that great stammerer of history."[43] "Looked at as a whole, the governing of Spain has been a vast and constant omission, a vast negligence!"[44] Sometimes it is a question of a turn or contexture of phrase, enlivened by an image or a literary transposition: "Since the death of Cisneros, the Spanish State has lived in perpetual Sabbath";[45] "with no more ideals in their souls than the ass or the ox who accompany them, poor Simons of Cyrene, in their Calvary."[46] Sometimes the expression and the programmatic idea are combined: "to pass the sponge over the provinces and their odious organisms of every kind; to call the historical regions to new life."[47] Sometimes Costa mingles felicitous literary turns of phrase with unclear and pedestrian expressions in the same paragraph: "To make works of charity a matter of public law. To govern sadly, like Ferdinand VI, watching over and consoling the sadness of the governed." But he continues: "To bring down the price of our country, so that the condition of the Spaniard will no longer be bad business . . . to pull out the cork for the people." And finally, inexactness, the deficient style which says what it does not mean: "A double lock on the tomb of the Cid so that he cannot ride again."[48]

This is what Ortega received at one period in his life, as a stimulus, and which he refined from a superior and more demanding sensibility. A similar operation took place in the area of ideas. Let us not forget that in the paragraph from Ortega we quoted above, when he praises Costa so highly, he says he differs from him on some *essential* points of his way of looking at the national problem; the adjective *essential* cannot be wiped out by the vague warmth of "some points." Ortega's reservations begin as far back as the first piece of writing we have quoted, in 1908. "In my opinion," he says then, "the Agricultural Assembly of Upper Aragon committed this error in its message of 1898. The demand

[43] Joaquín Costa, *Crisis política de España* (3rd ed., 1914), 39.
[44] *Ibid.*, 96–97.
[45] *Ibid.*, 120.
[46] *Ibid.*, 121.
[47] *Reconstitución y europeización de España* (1900), 33.
[48] *Ibid.*, 20.

for culture and the demand for civilization cannot be presented together, and much less can we ask for science on the same plane and after agriculture and internal colonization, credit, property rights, public faith, registry, industry and commerce, viability, social reforms, and education."[49]

But the most serious and fundamental objections, those which have to do with Costa's intellectual limitations, refer to his *historicism*, which gives a "contradictory duality" to his program. "A jurist and philologist, as a scientific man; native, as an instinctual man, of a Spanish region which preserves certain obstinate traits of the race in a more marked from than anywhere else, Costa became saturated in the historicist atmosphere, in the romantic dogmas; and, letting his heart and brain go in the direction toward which they naturally tended, he dedicated his austere and diligent life to the study of the Spanish *people*, of the irrational Hispanic masses. Adjusting himself to *foreign* principles, which he had accepted without pausing to question, he believed that every people had its historical mission, its unbreakable metaphysical character and its absolute justification . . . . The opinion that Costa formed of the Spanish problem, under such an influence, is easy to anticipate: strictly speaking we do not need to read his books in order to become acquainted with this opinion, for he himself did not acquire it by studying in Spain; but, on the contrary, he studied Spain under the prejudice—in the best sense of the word—foreign philosophy had instilled in him. He thought about Spain what Renan, Taine, Treitschke, etc., thought about their countries."[50] In Ortega's view, Costa saw the national decline as an internal problem for Spain, the result of the deviation of the *spontaneity* of the race by an inadequate thinking minority. Therefore Costa believes that Spain must return to ethnic spontaneity and by so doing must *reconstitute* the spontaneous unity of classical Spanish reactions. To Ortega this seems romantic, a return to the idea of *Volksgeist*, which exists only in the books of an outmoded philosophy. This is *reconstitution* as a return to the most intimate, the most spontaneous, the most native. "We shall see," Ortega concludes, "whether the word *europeanization* does not mean something like a way of seeing the problem, and as a solution of it quite the opposite."[51]

[49] "Asamblea para el Progreso de las Ciencias" (1908). I, 107.
[50] "Observaciones" (1911). I, 168.   [51] *Ibid.*, 169.

Elsewhere he speaks again of Costa, "whose program some of us should like to keep defending in all its material integrity, although modifying its arrangement and changing its accents."[52] And when the coincidence of their ideas appears greatest, as when Costa speaks of "the pseudo-country" and the "true country,"[53] and one naturally thinks of Ortega's "official Spain" and "real Spain," this is where the distance between them appears most clearly: Costa understands by "pseudo-country" the ruling classes, and by the true country all the others, who do not constitute an active subject, who do not have dealings with the politicians or listen to them; whereas Ortega writes in 1914, "This is why I do not think like Costa, who attributed Spain's decline to the sins of the governing classes, and therefore to purely political errors. No; for centuries the governing classes—except for short periods—have governed ill not by chance, but because the Spain they governed was as sick as they . . . . *An entire Spain—with its governors and its governed, with its abuses and its uses—is at the end of its dying.*"[54] This is *official Spain*—not simply the government—as opposed to a *vital Spain* "perhaps not very strong, but vital, sincere, honorable, which cannot enter fully into history because it is hampered by the other one."[55]

These are not the only traces of Costa that we find in Ortega. Later we shall have to point out others, when we seek the origin of some of Ortega's ideas or clarify the meaning of certain allusions or rectifications. But what I have noted will suffice to clarify the function exercised by Costa in regard to the young Ortega, prior to 1914: in various senses, he serves as an example, a stimulus, and even a program. At an early moment in his life, Ortega considers himself to be a follower of Costa. He takes over the bulk of an attitude which seems to him extremely noble and, taken as a whole, accurate. The preoccupation for country—one of the mainsprings of Ortega's work—is first realized within the molds created by Joaquín Costa; it can be said that no Spanish figure aroused greater adhesion in the youthful Ortega than the declining Costa, during the last years of his life. But Ortega soon begins to feel the insufficiency of his *doctrine*; from the viewpoint of Europe—simultaneously from the viewpoint of the idea of Europe and European

[52] "Libros de andar y ver" (1911). I, 181.
[53] *Los siete criterios de gobierno* (1914), 38–39.
[54] *Vieja y nueva política* (1914). I, 274–75.
[55] *Ibid.*, 272–73.

thought made fully his own—Ortega finds that Costa does not suffice; and, paradoxically, he discovers that he does not transcend Spain, that he turns out to be in some measure *domestic*, because he has been nourished on *outside* ideas, ideas which have been borrowed, not thought out *from inside Spain on the level of Europe*. This criticism, thus formulated, was later to become an essential part of Ortega's own method.

d) MENÉNDEZ PELAYO

The figure of greatest intellectual prominence in Spain during the last decades of the nineteenth century, Don Marcelino Menéndez Pelayo, was an element in the young Ortega's circumstance with which he found it necessary to reckon. Not as a teacher, however, for Menéndez Pelayo, appointed director of the National Library in 1898, left his university teaching just at the time when Ortega might have been his student. But Ortega has left proof of his awareness of Menéndez Pelayo as an author —almost always with reservations which clearly indicate a *disappointment*. This is the impression given by most of his references to Don Marcelino, which reveal what we might call an *unfulfilled expectation*. That is, Ortega measures Menéndez Pelayo against himself, his actual stature against his pretensions; and thus he finds him wanting, inferior to his own self, a man who had not fulfilled his lofty possibilities. The justification of this attitude need not be gone into directly here;[56] the important thing is to detail the manner in which Ortega thought of Menéndez Pelayo in his formative years and at the beginning of his personal activity.

"When I was a boy," writes Ortega in 1914, "I read Menéndez Pelayo's books transfixed with faith in them."[57] Then Ortega goes on to recall and reject the famous contrast between "Germanic mists" and "Latin clarity." What is important here is his confession that he read those books as a boy, *transfixed with faith*; that is, believing in them wholeheartedly, completely hopeful of their value. But as early as

---

[56] See what Ortega says in the *Meditaciones del Quijote*, and my commentary on the passage, where I cite some texts by Menéndez Pelayo, in my edition of that book: *Meditaciones del Quijote. Comentario por Julián Marías* (Ediciones de la Universidad de Puerto Rico, Madrid, 1957), 134–35, and the commentary, 372–74.

[57] *Meditaciones del Quijote* (1914). I, 341.

1910 he had said, "To say Europe is . . . to take with equal respect a most erudite book by the great Menéndez Pelayo and to write in the margin of the last page: *Non multa sed multum*."[58] Although he concluded an article written in the same year with these words: "And now, friend reader, read the third volume of the *Historia de la novela en España* ["History of the Novel in Spain"], which has just been published. There is a splendid study on the *Celestina* in it, where Menéndez Pelayo says . . . ."[59]

Ortega feels two chief objections with regard to the great historian of Spanish letters: first, that he allows himself to be carried away by a nationalism which beclouds the issues and distorts the shape of our intellectual history; this occurs with the problem of *Spanish Science*: when he speaks of the notes to its second edition, Ortega makes this clear in an explanatory parenthesis, "notes which show a little more restraint in the nationalism of its author";[60] second, that he shares certain defects of his time, the Restoration, which cause him to suffer from "lack of perspective," and to applaud mediocrity because he has had no experience of anything deeper; Ortega extends this criticism to Valera, and adds in a note: "These words do not imply any capricious scorn on my part for these two authors, for that would be incorrect. They merely indicate a serious defect in their work, which coexisted, however, with no few virtues."[61]

But what is most serious, what Ortega really finds lacking in Menéndez Pelayo, is an adequate sense of *theory*. Menéndez Pelayo's philosophical bases—the Scottish philosophy of common sense—seem to Ortega to be seriously weak. And the result is that Menéndez Pelayo's work, in spite of its enormous breadth and its very real merits, as a *mode of knowing* does not exceed the limits of *erudition*. Now, for Ortega erudition is one of the great dangers: it is a form of science which has had its hour, but which is not "at the level of the times"; its survival is a hindrance, an obstacle to the opening up of the Spanish horizon toward the future. One of the great tasks he proposes is to surpass erudition, to go beyond it, precisely to attain *theory*. Later we shall have to present this problem thematically. And Ortega felt from

---

[58] "Nueva revista" (1910). I, 142. Ortega is referring to the review *Europa*.
[59] "Shylock" (1910). I, 518.
[60] "Pidiendo una biblioteca" (1908). I, 83.
[61] *Meditaciones del Quijote* (1914). I, 339.

a very early period the risk involved not only in Menéndez Pelayo's limitation, which did not exclude the valuable part of his work, but the *use* which was to be made of it, shutting off with its very bulk any possibility of transcending and going beyond itself, to the high seas of effective theory.

22. THE GENERATION OF 1898 AND ORTEGA'S GENERATION

Closer to him, very close indeed, Ortega found the men of the Generation of 1898. His first impression with regard to them is unequivocally one of "belonging." We should, however, not pass too hastily over this point, and should try to analyze in what the impression consisted.

It is not a question of "coincidence" or "resemblances": the distance separating Ortega from the most representative men of 1898 is considerable; his human and personal figure, his formation, his intellectual aspiration, all these things were different from what can be considered as *common* to the men of 1898—and which did not exclude, of course, enormous differences among them. Nor is it a question of community of "level," for it is precisely the distance between two generations which always excludes this. Nor is it a question of concurrence in opinions: Ortega's differences from his elders, and theirs from him, were frequent and sometimes had to do with very serious matters. There was no agreement between them, but there was *concord*, above and beyond which differences, disagreements, and even controversies took shape. And this concord was based, if I am not mistaken, on the fact that both sides felt that they were participants in the same *undertaking*. This undertaking was what they all belonged to, each generation in its own way, each at its own level. Thus a sharp difference of opinion was possible between them, analogous to that often found within the same generation, but one which does not cancel out a basic and fundamental concord.

Those of previous generations—Valera or Galdós or Giner or Azcárate or Costa or Menéndez Pelayo—are *something else*; they may be admirable, they may be deficient, they may be a model or an obstacle; but they are *the past*, even though it be a surviving, still active past. They represent another stage: that is, another *period*. But not the men of 1898; they were the ones who began the period in which Ortega found himself, the period in which it fell to him to live. No matter how great the innovation which Ortega carried out in so many aspects, and even though it was the greatest innovation that had operated in Spain for a long time, we must begin by imposing a limitation on it; that innovation did not begin with the period, but was found already installed in an innovation begun by others who were somewhat older. Ortega was a coparticipant in certain reigning ideas, aims, and hopes which he found *already* there when he opened his eyes to the historical world.

This is what explains the frequent error which at times places Ortega in the Generation of 1898. Ortega, for the moment, merely *joined it*, enlisted under its banner, made his own the undertaking to which that generation was committed, in which that generation *consisted*. Ortega has distinguished between *cumulative periods* and *eliminatory and polemical periods*, which he has also called "combat generations." "In the first sort of period," he says, "the upcoming young men, having a feeling of solidarity with their elders, are held in subjection to them: in politics, in science, in the arts the old continue to rule. These are times for the elderly. In the second sort, as it is not a question of preserving and accumulating, but of casting aside and substituting, the elders are swept away by the youngsters. These are times for the young, ages of initiation and constructive belligerence."[62] The Generation of 1898 was clearly "eliminatory and polemical," an innovating generation, a generation of combat. Ortega's—that of 1886 as a central *birth* date—was at once, and in two different senses, eliminatory and cumulative: the former in regard to the past—the Restoration, the nineteenth century, and everything they represented; the latter, in regard to the immediately preceding generation, that of 1898. It adopts, therefore, an attitude of *continuity*, but one which consists in *continuing* discrepancy and with it innovation.

Ortega *adheres*—one of his favorite words—to what the men of 1898 represent: he feels united to Unamuno—despite everything, as we shall see later: even against Unamuno, and in Unamuno's name— from the time he took his first steps in the world of letters; the first article he produced, in 1904, is dedicated to Valle-Inclán and is full of enthusiasm for him, though not without reservations;[63] beginning

---

[62] *El tema de nuestro tiempo* (1923). III, 149.
[63] "La *Sonata de estío*, de Don Ramón del Valle-Inclán" (1904). I, 19ff.

in that same year he warmly praises Rubén Darío;[64] Azorín and Baroja are very soon to be his friends, and he will study them with more attention than any of their contemporaries;[65] we also find admiring references to Benavente;[66] he writes of the Machados, especially of Antonio, with deep admiration and warmth;[67] his friendship with Maeztu is very close and intense for a number of years, and is the most meaningful friendship of Ortega's early years; nor should we forget his attitude toward Zuloaga, the painter of the Generation of 1898.[68]

There is another reason which explains the fact that Ortega has sometimes been included in the Generation of 1898: his precocity, his early success—that is, his greater "social age,"[69] which caused him to have a public figure very early, almost at the same time as the younger members of the Generation of 1898; his authority, which caused him to deal with them—except perhaps in the case of Unamuno—on an equal plane from the beginning, and the fact that more or less all of them—even Unamuno—soon recognized a certain quality of leadership in him which we shall investigate later on.

Within his generation, Ortega was close to the center, in the first of its two age groups or semigenerations. Differences of a few years, which seem to disappear with time, are very important in a man's youth. We must take this into account if we are to understand Ortega's youthful relationships with Pérez de Ayala or Juan Ramón Jiménez on the one hand, and with Gómez de la Serna on the other. Ortega, specifically an intellectual, a man of theory and discipline, used up an enormous

---

[64] *Ibid.*, 27. Also in "Algunas notas" (1908), I, 113, and in "Los versos de Antonio Machado" (1912), I, 564, where he says, "There is no bridge from ordinary conversation to poetry. Everything has to die in order to be reborn later, changed into metaphor and reflection of feeling. Rubén Darío, the divine Indian, tamer of words, driver of the steeds of rhythm, came to show us this. His verses have been a school for forging poetry. He has filled ten years of our literary history."

[65] Apart from innumerable references, "Ideas sobre Pío Baroja" (1915) (in *El Espectador*, I), an essay to which he soon added another, earlier one, "Una primera vista sobre Baroja" (1910), II, 67–123. And "Azorín: primores de lo vulgar" (1917) (in *El Espectador*, II). II, 153–85.

[66] "Only Señor Benavente has managed to do something quite respectable, and at the same time has pleased the public." ("Asamblea para el Progreso de las Ciencias" [1908]. I, 106.)

[67] "Los versos de Antonio Machado" (1912). I, 563.

[68] Especially "La estética del Enano Gregorio el Botero" (1911). I, 529–38.

[69] See my study "Generaciones y constelaciones" in *Ensayos de convivencia* (*Obras*, III).

proportion of his youthful years in study, even in its strictest form, as a university student in Germany. This made him delay, in spite of his great precocity, his mature written production: his first book, *Meditaciones del Quijote* ["Meditations on Quixote"], was published in 1914, when he was thirty-one years of age; by that date Gabriel Miró had published a number of books, among them *Del vivir* ["On Living"], *La novela de mi amigo* ["Novel of My Friend"], and *Las cerezas del cementerio* ["The Cherries in the Cemetery"]; Pérez de Ayala was the author of a book of poems, *La paz del sendero* ["The Peace of the Footpath"], and six novels: *Tinieblas en las cumbres* ["Shadows on the Mountaintops"], *La pata de la raposa,* ["The Vixen's Paw"], *A. M. D. G., Luna de miel, luna de hiel* ["Moon of Honey, Moon of Gall"], *Los trabajos de Urbano y Simona* ["Trials of Urbano and Simona"], *Troteras y danzaderas,* the latter such an important book for the understanding of these two generations and their mutual relationships; Juan Ramón Jiménez had published innumerable books, among them *Jardines lejanos* ["Faraway Gardens"], *Pastorales* ["Pastorals"], *Poemas mágicos y dolientes* ["Sad and Magic Poems"], *Laberinto* ["Labyrinth"], *Melancolía* ["Melancholy"]; that is, his poetic personality was well defined and assured.

But, on the other hand, the theoretical level of Ortega's writings (articles and essays) and the breadth and solidarity of his culture, his position as a professor after 1908 in the College of Education, and after 1910 in the University of Madrid as holder of the chair of Metaphysics—all this gave him from the outset an authority which was quickly recognized. The "young meditator," to use Antonio Machado's expression, had the respect of his own age group as well as his elders from the age of twenty. Figures of great prestige, at the peak of their fame, attended Ortega's courses. Those who were sufficiently sure of themselves or those who were modest enough and disposed to recognize levels of excellence, promptly gave him their support and a peculiar sort of intellectual headship, at first that of his own generation; those who lacked these attributes found him insufferable from the beginning. More than half a century later, even after Ortega's death, this pattern continues to be valid.

The generation of 1886 is much less sharply delineated than its predecessor. Whereas the representative men of 1898 formed a group in which their affinities were clear—to the point that the more efforts made by some of the members of the generation to deny their existence, the more evident these affinities have become—in the following generation, the situation was not the same; there were several different "directions" in it, which disturb the homogeneity of the level common to all of them. The oldest members—Miró, Marquina, Villaespesa, all born in 1879, on the borderline between the two generations—are in the line which was called, rather vaguely, modernism, and in a purely literary attitude; this could also be said in some measure of Juan Ramón Jiménez, although he, through his personal connections and the orientation of his work, is linked much more closely with what we might call the nucleus of the generation; Pérez de Ayala, Ortega, Marañón. Around Juan Ramón Jiménez a close periphery was formed, wavering between incorporation and resistance—which has sometimes alternated in the same person throughout his life: Martínez Sierra, Teófilo Hernando, Américo Castro, Madariaga, Fernando Vela. Some very important figures are affected by "excentricity" with respect to the central nucleus: Eugenio d'Ors because he was a Catalan, and especially because of his vacillation between that circumstance and the general Spanish circumstance, between Barcelona and Madrid, with the eventual desire to escape from both; Azaña and Angel Herrera because of the predominance in them of the political over the intellectual factor, without, however, renouncing the latter; and lastly, Ramón Gómez de la Serna, owing to the constitutional eccentricity of his figure rather than a voluntary attitude, for fidelity to the Generation of 1898—especially to Azorín and Valle-Inclán—and to Ortega has been constant in him. As for the younger members, at some distance from the rest of the generation, Antonio Marichalar, Melchor Fernández Almagro, Claudio Sánchez Albornoz, Pedro Salinas, and Jorge Guillén, they pose a curious problem: because of this distance and their lack of precocity, they have had a "social age" which was less than their affective and historical one, and thus they have gravitated toward the border generation between them and the next, and often seem to belong to it, forming a "constellation" with it; this occurs especially with the last-named poets, who are usually considered as coetaneous with García Lorca, Alberti, Dámaso Alonso, Aleixandre, Gerardo Diego, etc.

Only now, at a certain distance from them, does the profile of this generation of 1886 begin to become clear, underneath its multiple differences; and the community of "level," and consequently of historical image, appears. And just as what I have called the *literary temper* was characteristic of the Generation of 1898, what we might call the *theoretical attitude* appears as a trait of its successor. All of them, from different points of departure, from lyrical poetry or philology or scholarship or politics, tend in the long run at least, toward theory: Juan Ramón Jiménez theorizes his poetry; Ramón Pérez de Ayala, a novelist, slides in the direction of the essay and criticism; a philologist such as Américo Castro and an empirical and scholarly historian such as Sánchez Albornoz arrive at interpretive syntheses of Spanish history whose aims are strictly theoretical; the poets in their turn are also critics, theoreticians of their own and others' lyric poetry, professors; and even their own poetry is characterized by a theoretical lucidity for which we seek in vain, except in a few exceptional cases, either before or after them; not to mention, naturally, those such as Ortega, Manuel García Morente, Eugenio d'Ors, etc., who made theory itself their particular discipline; nor should we forget the theoretical bent which characterizes the politics of the members of this generation—during the times when politics has existed—and of the intellectual pretensions which they did not abandon so long as this was possible for them.

Given these characteristics, Ortega's significance within his generation becomes clear. For it was precisely Ortega who raised Spanish intellectual life to a *theoretical* level, to a form of theory which had never been attained before. Every form of intellectual knowledge was referred, as if to a certain level, to Ortega; all Spanish thought—whatever its content—formally appeared as "Orteguian" or "pre-Orteguian" (and in this latter case, as insufficient). In this concrete sense, which is not a mere valuation, Ortega is, both because of the content itself of his work and the character of his generation, its *eponym*; this did not occur with equal strictness in the Generation of 1898, despite certain intellectual excellences of Unamuno's, because from the *literary* point of view, which was the decisive one for his generation, Unamuno represented only one dimension, certainly an essential one, but not higher or more representative or more fruitful than those corresponding to other writers.

And this is precisely the point at which Ortega is going to have to take an innovative, and to some degree controversial, position with regard to the Generation of 1898. Its attitude toward theory was soon to seem to him to be deficient *from the point of view of theory*; I mean that, so long as the men of this group did other things, they seemed admirable to him; when they behaved like men of thought, he had some reservations to make; when they attempted to impose their own way of understanding this function, he found them inadmissible.

23. MAEZTU

The fraternal friendship between Ortega and Ramiro de Maeztu is well known; between 1908 and 1911, there are frequent and friendly references to Maeztu in Ortega's writings; as late as 1914 he dedicated the *Meditations on Quixote* "To Ramiro de Maeztu, with a fraternal gesture"; and Maeztu was a frequent contributor to *España* in 1915, while Ortega was its editor. But differences of opinion soon began to appear, along with their friendship, and especially an *intellectual discontent*, a discontent with regard to intellectual conduct. And this is, of course, personal when intellectual life is not a pastime or a mere profession, or a platform, or a mask, but purely and simply a *life*.

In an article published in *Faro*, the youthful review of those years, in 1908, Ortega takes Maeztu to task, though still in a friendly way, regarding the comments made by the latter to a previous article, "¿Hombres o ideas?" ["Men or Ideas?"], and through Maeztu takes to task a whole interpretation of the intellectual life. This previous article had alluded in its turn to a comment Maeztu had made on another previous article of Ortega's; that is, it was a discussion which had spread from one magazine to another, from *Faro* to *Nuevo Mundo*, from London, where Maeztu was, to Madrid or Marburg. "When I read this article," writes Ortega with noticeable disillusionment, "I began to think of the times, not very far off, when we two walked along these crooked streets in Madrid united by a close friendship, like an elder and a younger brother,[70] weaving our pure and ardent daydreams of ideal action. And I simply cannot understand how that still unbroken feeling of fraternity can have declined so much that today you make me say and think such inept things. No, my dear Ramiro; intellectual-

---

[70] Maeztu, born in 1875, was eight years older than Ortega, who was twenty-five at the time he wrote these words.

[71] "¿Hombres o ideas?" (1908). I, 434–36.

ism (?), and the idealism which I defend, do not lead me to believe that
ideas can move by themselves.

"A habit of mind which I have not succeeded in overcoming impels
me to see all things systematically. I believe that among the three or
four things men possess which are immutably true is that Hegelian
statement that truth can exist only in the form of a system. Hence the
enormous difficulty which the truth finds in shining through an article
or a speech in Parliament . . . ."

And he continued: "Years ago—do you remember?—we used to
enjoy setting our imaginations aflame over a page of Nietzsche, and
since this chatterer of genius has the gift of all the Sophists to flatter
the reader and make him conceited, the suspicion may have occurred to
us after reading him that maybe there was something in the two of us
of those great men who make history, isolated and adamantine, beyond
good and evil. A remembrance of that time, so pleasant and so devoted,
often sweeps over me. But in the end we emerged from the torrid zone
of Nietszche, whom we of course badly misinterpreted then: today we
are two ordinary men for whom the ethical world exists."[71]

Immediately after this, in the new article, Ortega continued: "Nothing can give me such pleasure as disputing with Ramiro de Maeztu on
subjects that are apparently superhistoric. We must try, each in his own
way and according to his energies, to enrich the national consciousness
with the largest possible number of ideal motives, of viewpoints. Difference of opinion, therefore, seems to me very desirable, and I am
wounded by dogmatism in any form. I believe that I can only reserve
the right to state that a precise and sharp opinion is not always a dogma,
that systematism can be miles away from dogmatism, and that finally,
when certain fundamental questions are reached, the contradictor should
not evade technical discussion.

"The possibility of resisting technical strictness is for me the criterion
of veracity, a quality that weighs infinitely more with me than mere
sincerity. The sincere man says what, in fact, his nerves are feeling, and
thinks that is enough. The truthful man thinks of this perpetual auto-
biography as a sin we all commit at times, and tries to rise above the
tendency of his nerves to what he really is, the Platonic $\tau\grave{o}\ \check{o}\nu\tau\omega\varsigma\ \check{o}\nu$. . . .

"Maeztu may believe," he continues, "that it was no effort for me
to construct more or less pleasant-sounding and harmonious paragraphs

in praise of vagueness, of imprecision, of the twilight life of the soul which is, undoubtedly, the most entertaining and pleasurable for each individual. But the indisputable right to make good literature does not exist in our country today: we are too much obliged to convince and to be concrete. If a man does not feel capable of anything more than literature, let him make it as best he can, and if he succeeds we will crown him with flowers and heap him with honors. I cannot understand the horror of art for art's sake that afflicts some contemporary Spanish thinkers. Aesthetics is a dimension of culture, equivalent to ethics and science . . . .

"So long as there is no power of choice, the moral dilemma does not arise. If we can make good literature, but also feel capable of science, our inclination must be unequivocally inclined toward this last, without a pact of any kind with literature . . . . A man should either cultivate literature or cultivate precision or shut up."

Maeztu had objected to Ortega's systematism and felt a great many fears in regard to it, and he said: "But if there is something no longer immutable, what can be immutable in this world, which takes so many turns? If there is any idea which has put down deep roots in the modern world, it is that of the evolution of systems, of schools and dogmas." And to this opinion of Maeztu's—note that *it is Maeztu's*—Ortega answered: "Hegel's statement does not exclude that of development; rather, as you know, Hegel has constructed the system of evolution more profoundly than anyone else. To demand a system, as I do, has nothing to do with the Scholasticism of the Sorbonne . . . .[72] But it is necessary at every instant that the truth of the world be a system; or, what is the same thing, that the world be a *cosmos* or universe.

"System is unification of problems, and in the individual it is unity of consciousness, of opinions. This was what I meant. It is not licit to leave opinions floating in the spirit like drifting buoys, without any rational links between them." And he concluded: "System is the thinker's honor."[73]

The discussion continued: a new article by Maeztu in *Nuevo Mundo*

[72] This was precisely Maeztu's fear. He wrote, "I do not need to bring up again the danger of synthetic systematizations. As soon as these doctrinaire ideas were forced a bit, they would lead us to repeat the dictum of the Scholastics of the University of Paris, when they denied that any fact was worthy of belief compared with Aristotle's teachings." Times change, indeed.

[73] "Algunas notas" (1908). I, 111–15.

(September 3, 1908), a new article by Ortega in *Faro* (twentieth of the same month). Cordiality continued: "fraternal hearts," "this Maeztu, an affable and fervent man, our dear and torrential optimist"; "I particularly appreciate Maeztu's intentions, and his patriotic fire"; "he is very affectionate toward my modest incipient person; and, in general, he is a pleasant person—he radiates benevolence and tender feelings toward all the griefs of this race, which has neither good fortune nor hopes." But the intellectual discontent also persisted: Ortega rejects Maeztu's opinion that virtue, morality, is "an almost blind impulse, with little of the intellectual about it, a vague call of the spirit"; for Ortega, on the other hand, "the moral is, by definition, that which is not instinctive." He censures Maeztu for the "lack of respect with which he touches upon questions which can only be resolved by technical means that are hard to improvise." And he bitterly concludes: "Here everything is allowed except to be exact, to seek precision, to weigh one's words, to rectify comparisons."[74]

This youthful attitude of Ortega's is already his innovative reaction against one aspect of the Generation of 1898. But he is very careful—as we shall see elsewhere—to affirm that generation, to establish not only his admiration for it but his solidarity with it. This forces him to correct it, to rectify it; at the age of twenty-five, he does not yet fully grasp the fact that what he is doing is *going beyond it*, taking a new step, installing himself in a new attitude which is another level; in sum, he is innovating, achieving the coat of arms belonging to his own generation. His esteem for literature, the invitation to make literature if one does not wish to make precision, coexists in him with the consciousness that something else is necessary, that one cannot content oneself with literature if one is *capable of science*. Ortega calls for *doctrine* and *system*; to him, it seems inconsequential and false to call for intellectual life and to reject its requisites. Obviously, the literary demand *in science* does not yet seem entirely clear to him, but it will reappear in a new form within his own work. Then the relationship between literature and theory will arise again, but in a different form than in the Generation of 1898, because the function of each will have changed, thanks, of course, to the work of that generation, which had made possible what had not been possible before. All this was very sharply posed when Ortega confronted Unamuno.

[74] "Sobre una apología de la inexactitud" (1908). I, 117–23.

I believe that Unamuno was by far the most important intellectual element in Ortega's youthful circumstance. For many years, perhaps throughout their lives, Unamuno and Ortega mutually interested and upset each other, were more important to each other than they cared to admit—and, if the truth be told, they did admit it to a considerable degree. For a long time only a few references to each other were known in their printed works; but when old essays, unknown or forgotten, and some letters were edited in book form, a few more direct and intense mentions appeared; there has been a tendency to settle on these and to believe that they clarify the relationship. In my opinion, this is an obvious error, in two senses: because these known manifestations are still extremely *partial*, and if they are taken to be a sufficient expression of an intellectual and personal relationship, this relationship is distorted; in the second place, because there is a tendency to consider them from today's point of view, forgetting the assumptions, the forms of shared life, and the literary style of the authors and especially of the period. An adequate study of the relationship between Unamuno and Ortega is extremely interesting and will have to be made some day; but this is not the place for it, because to be truly illuminating it would require details incompatible with the internal economy of this book. Let us content ourselves, therefore, with clarifying here how Unamuno appeared within Ortega's youthful circumstance, how Ortega came to grips with the most prestigious intellectual figure who existed in Spain in the early years of this century. Later we shall find it necessary to bring Unamuno into the picture so that we can understand certain of Ortega's actions and doctrines.

It will be well to keep in mind that Unamuno, born in 1864, was nineteen years older than Ortega. Although he did not begin to write at an unusually early age, when he and Ortega came into contact, he was already an author of important work and great prestige; Ortega, however, was a boy; aside from some possible contact in Salamanca in 1898, when Ortega took examinations at the University, by 1903, when Ortega was twenty and Unamuno thirty-nine, they were carrying on a long and friendly communication by letter. In May, 1904, Unamuno, in an article entitled "Almas de jóvenes" ["Souls of the Young"],[75]

[75] In *Ensayos* (Edición de la Residencia de Estudiantes, Madrid, 1917), V, 9–36.

transcribes two long letters "from my young friend J. O. G., who has already taken up arms, to the applause of all good men." The first of the letters is dated January 6, 1904, and begins with an apology for the delay in answering an affectionate letter from Unamuno; when he comments on the second, Unamuno gives the full name of its author, "my young friend José Ortega Gasset"; the article and the letters discuss the Machado brothers, Maeztu, and Grandmontagne: these are the "young" whose souls interest Unamuno.

After that date, the friendship between him and Ortega continued to be very much alive: at the end of 1906, in Marburg, Ortega says that the only letters he receives from Spain, besides those of his fiancée and family, are Unamuno's. Ortega speaks of him often in his writings, from a very early age—both favorably and unfavorably, with enthusiasm and with bitter censure, with adhesion and reproach; as the two men grow older, references to Unamuno become less frequent; Ortega scarcely mentions Unamuno again until after his death, and even then his words are full of very perceptible silences. Why? As one gets older, there are more things to say; what at first scarcely seems to have "thickness," and thus is to a certain degree transparent, gradually becomes dense and opaque; it becomes more and more difficult to say what one wants to, for one would have to say too much; and also, a fear, almost a certainty, begins to take root in one's soul, of being misunderstood, that *something other* will be understood than what has been said. Hence that silence which comes over the responsible intellectual, at least in regard to some areas of his life, as he advances in years and experience. This is why an author's work cannot be understood unless we place side by side what he has said and what he has not said. In Ortega's case this is true to a very high degree, and on the concrete point of his relationship with Unamuno it is the first thing we must keep in mind.[76] Far from calling on the texts as "evidence," therefore, or considering them to be sufficient, one must understand them by combining them with those silences, and especially with a final silence of which I shall soon speak.

From the beginning, Ortega felt enthusiasm for Unamuno. Imagine what it must have been for him to find on his horizon that enormous spiritual promontory rising above the Castilian plain. We must measure the hopes Ortega placed on Unamuno in order to correctly judge his

[76] See what I say below about Ortega's attitude toward my studies on Unamuno.

disillusionment, in the measure that he was forced to feel it, his indignation against Unamuno insofar as he felt that this disillusionment was unnecessary, that it was the result of Unamuno's own choice, of Unamuno's lack of fulfillment of what Ortega felt to be his mission. Paradoxically, he was faced with someone older than he, with a teacher; for Ortega's attitude was very like that of the father or the teacher who, in regard to his son or pupil, feels that he has not come up to his promise, that he has been less than himself or that he has strayed from his proper path. Thus, from the first years of their dealings with each other, and in a tone which is surprising if we think of the difference in age and social figure, Ortega makes criticisms of Unamuno which are sometimes reproaches: "Well, today I'm scolding you," he ends a very affectionate letter at the age of twenty-three, to the tremendous master who had already published *En torno al casticismo* ["On Traditionalism"], *Paz en la guerra* ["Peace in War"], *Amor y pedagogía* ["Love and Pedagogy"], *Vida de Don Quijote y Sancho* ["The Life of Don Quixote and Sancho"] . . . .

Ortega found in Unamuno depth, passion, courage, probity, a broad and deep erudition, the capacity to do new things, an understanding of Spain, a sense of what Spain needed, political possibilities, and religiosity in a different sense from the habitual and lifeless concept of it in the Spain of 1900. He also found sympathy for Europe. There is no error here; we are likely to forget that Unamuno was in the advance guard of Europeanness and the europeanization of Spain, and one of those who have done the most to ensure that Spain would again take possession of that European condition which she not only "has" but has *wished* to have, century after century, in spite of the fact that she has not simply been given it. We forget that these words are Unamuno's: "The soul of Castile was great when she opened herself to the four winds and spread all over the world; then she shut herself up again, and we have not yet awakened. While the race was still fertile, it did not recognize itself as such in its differences; its ruin began on the day when, crying 'my I, they are tearing away my I,' it tried to shut itself away. Is everything dying? No, the future of Spanish society awaits within our historical society, in intrahistory, in the unknown people of the nation, and it will not arise in strength until the winds or tempest of the European atmosphere awake it . . . . Spain is still to be discovered, and she will only be discovered by europeanized Spaniards . . . . I should like to suggest to my reader as forcefully as possible the idea that the awakening to life of Spain's diffuse and regional masses has to go along with, and be linked with, opening wide the windows to the fields of Europe so that our country may be well aired out. We must become europeanized, and cobble together a people . . . . Faith, faith in our own spontaneity, faith that we will always be ourselves, and then bring on the flood from outside, the cold shower!"[77]

If I am not mistaken, Unamuno's abandonment of the pro-European position was owed to the fact that he had made too many partisans; Unamuno never resigned himself to not going against the current, even though that current had been started by him. As early as 1907 Ortega speaks, still cordially and good-humoredly, of "some disputations I am composing against the 'Africanist' deviation begun by our master and hermit D. Miguel de Unamuno."[78]

In the following year, probably the date at which Ortega's enthusiasm, even his devotion, to Unamuno reached its height, the year in which his letters brim with affection and adhesion, he has to make distinctions in order to avoid confusion in his readers. Ortega states, *à propos* of discussions or controversies with "fraternal hearts," "We risk having the careless public believe that we are in total disagreement, and especially that our intentions and plans diverge, when they are more united than ever. This very day—I should like to take this weight off my mind as soon as possible—I have published some paragraphs in *El Imparcial* about Unamuno's last speech. I thought I had composed in them a prudent defense of the political action which the rector of Salamanca has been exercising on our dead nation with such steadfastness and firmness. Nor could I do otherwise, when Unamuno's political ideas are exactly the same as those which I am trying to defend with the puny modern lance of my pen. Nevertheless, some persons have succeeded in seeing some kind of invective against the great publicist in those paragraphs which intended to honor and applaud. We Spaniards have a spirit that was made for total admiration, and, since we have no critical habits, any withholding of praise seems like general censure to us . . . . Unamuno, the politician, the champion of causes, seems to me to be one of the last bulwarks of Spanish hopes, and his words are

[77] "Sobre el marasmo actual de España" (1895), in *En torno al casticismo* (*Ensayos*, I, 211–14).
[78] "Sobre los estudios clásicos" (1907). I, 64.

usually our vanguard in this new war of independence against the stolidity and selfishness that surround us. It seems that a stingy divinity has given to him alone all of the light-bearing task—*Aufklärung*—which a Lessing, a Klopstock, a Hamann, a Jacobi, a Herder, or a Mendelssohn did for Germany in the eighteenth century. And though I do not agree with his method, I am the first to admire the strange attraction of his figure, the out-of-step silhouette of a mystic fanatic who casts himself into the sinister and sterile depths of our Peninsular vulgarity, battering Celtiberian heads with the oaken trunk of his personality. But if Unamuno says, as he did not long ago in *Faro*, that Madrid is the only European spot in Spain, and then a little later, in Bilbao, that Madrid is a patrimony of frivolity, I reserve the right to think that these flighty psychologies of cities are foolishness, imprudence, or injustice. Unamuno's spirit is too turbulent, and drags in its racing current, along with some gold dust, many useless and unhealthy things. We must be careful about how much we swallow."[79]

The critical date in the relationship between the two writers is 1909. Ortega's fears were being confirmed: Unamuno persisted in his "Africanism," in sincerity beyond discretion, in his sarcastic comments about what was "European" and the "Europeanists." It would be well to read his essay "Sobre la europeización (arbitrariedades)" ["On Europeanization (Whims)"][80] written in 1906, where, in spite of the title, Unamuno shows a good deal of caution, which he was to abandon progressively, half-boastful and half-exasperated, over the next two or three years. He contrasts the "modern European" with the "ancient African," whom he exemplifies, a bit superficially, in Saint Augustine and Tertullian (without inquiring of himself, of course, how it is possible to get from them to us, if there is some bridge linking them with us that is not Europe). "Europeanism" had begun to be a cliché, that is, common property; in those hands, it irritated Unamuno, though he would have been one of the first to enlist under its banner. "I come back to my senses after a number of years," Unamuno says, "after having made a pilgrimage through various fields of modern European culture, and I ask myself, alone with my conscience: am I a European? Am I a modern? And my conscience answers: no, you are not a Euro-

---

[79] "Sobre una apología da la inexactitud" (1908). I, 117–18. Ortega is referring to his article "Glosas a un discurso" (*El Imparcial*, II–IX–1908).

[80] *Ensayos*, VIII, 157ff.

pean, what is defined as a European; no, you are not a modern, what is defined as a modern."[81] Notice that when Unamuno is about to deny his condition as a European and a modern, he seems to hesitate, and not quite dare to say so; the two repetitions, *what is defined as a European, what is defined as a modern*, are stylistically unequivocal. And later in the article he adds, "But this business about the attempt to hispanize Europe; the only way in which we can europeanize ourselves in the measure that is needful—or rather, so that we can digest the part of the European spirit that can be made our spirit—that is something we must deal with separately."[82]

As Unamuno warmed to his task, as he piled up passion and arbitrariness, Ortega felt his reservations, his alarm, his disenchantment growing stronger; in 1909 he writes, "An extreme symptom of Philistinism can be found in the zeal for sincerity we all feel nowadays; it is a fad which has been imposed on us, to whose success that supreme hermit, Don Miguel de Unamuno, has contributed not a little; for among the echoing stones of Salamanca he is initiating a torrid youth into fanaticism."[83] And a few months later, in September of that same year, a very violent difference of opinion occurred between the two thinkers.

In a letter to Azorín, published in *ABC*, Unamuno had spoken of the "simpletons" who were under the spell of "those *Europeans*." He had declared, "If it were impossible for a country to have produced both a Descartes and a San Juan de la Cruz, I would have chosen the latter." He had spoken of "our present superiorities," and in connection with European philologists had cited the merit and prestige of Menéndez Pidal. According to what Ortega says, he had not intended to answer, but decided to do so influenced by the strong demands of others: "I intended not to speak of this lamentable letter; but I have received so many letters inciting me to protest!" And in particular he cites some impassioned pages from Américo Castro[84] which are very

[81] *Ibid.*, 161.

[82] *Ibid.*, 174.

[83] "Renan" (1909). I, 457.

[84] Américo Castro says, among other things, "Grossly mistaken are those who shuffle the facts to suit themselves, facts difficult to prove for most people, those who aspire—with boastful, hastily-put-together words of supposed love for their country— to cover with the mask of an illustrious name the heinous sin of intellectual felony. This, and nothing else, is what it means to place the name of Don Ramón Menéndez Pidal

hostile toward Unamuno, in fact much more so than Ortega's article. Ortega says, "I am fully, wholly, one of those simpletons; I have scarcely written a page, since I have been writing for the public, in which the word *Europe* has not appeared with symbolic aggressiveness. For me, all the sorrows of Spain begin and end with this word." The whole article is bitter, indignant, harsh, and filled with tremendous disillusionment. And after quoting Américo Castro's pages, he ends with this paragraph, whose meaning is clear only after what I have just described:

"The number of persons who wish, like us, that personal quarrels would give way in Spain to more honest and virtuous discussions on the real truth, is slowly increasing. In the shipwreck of our national life, a shipwreck in the muddy water of the passions, we calmly interpose a new cry: Let us save ourselves in things! Ethics, science, art, religion, politics have ceased to be personal questions for us; our field of honor is now the familiar battleground of logic, of intellectual responsibility. Thinking of all this, I have preferred the technical observations of my great friend Américo Castro over all my indignant prose. Thanks to them I can state that on this occasion Don Miguel de Unamuno, that fanatical Spaniard, has fallen short of the truth. And this is not the first time we have wondered whether the red and fiery color of the towers of Salamanca does not come from the blushes of the venerable stones as they listen to what Unamuno says when he takes his afternoon walk among them.

"And yet, a great sorrow comes over us when we see the errors of that great spiritual machine, a deep feeling of melancholy . . . .

" 'God, what a good vassal, had he a good lord!' "[85]

One would think, in terms of present-day customs, that this would have meant a total break between Unamuno and Ortega. But things are more complex, richer, and more flexible. Six months after the article I have quoted, in March, 1910, Ortega wrote, "This is the tradition that Europe offers us; therefore the path from sorrow to joy which we are traversing will be, under another name, europeanization. A great

---

between the praise of a Chilean who 'prefers' him to the Germans, and a thoughtless censure of those who, outside Spain, have concerned themselves long before Sr. Unamuno could have thought of doing so, with making a study of our language." And then he gives an extremely well-documented summary of the studies in Romance philology done in foreign countries, and concludes, "Well then, if Sr. Unamuno knows all this in his capacity as professor of philology, why does he write the letter to the *ABC*?"

[85] "Unamuno y Europa, fábula" (1909). I, 128–32.

native of Bilbao has said that africanization would be better; but I do not know how this great Bilbaíno, Don Miguel de Unamuno, can come to terms with himself; for though he presents himself to us as an africanizer, he is, whether he likes it or not, because of the strength of his spirit and his solid cultural fervor, one of the prime movers in our European aspirations."[86] That is, he reclaims and affirms Unamuno in spite of himself, and passes over his arbitrariness because of his reality.

For his part, Unamuno, in a 1911 article, "Sobre la tumba de Costa" ["At Costa's Tomb"], which is so full of allusions to these problems, speaks of the peculiar Spanish despair, and to clarify what he means ends by saying, "It is a desperate hope, the impatience of hope, perhaps hope without faith. It is what José Ortega Gasset calls the Quixotic madness."[87] And that same year he sent Ortega his *Rosario de Sonetos líricos* ["Rosary of Lyric Sonnets"] with a dedication which I have discussed elsewhere,[88] in which he tells him, "I know that you do not enjoy my poetry, and it is a weakness of mine to believe that either I am a poet or I am nothing. I do not boast of being a philosopher or a thinker or a scholar or a philologist; I am vain only of being a good professor and a man of feeling or a poet." Ortega answered briefly and somewhat dryly, but the next year we find this sentence in an article on Machado: "I find in Machado the beginnings of that very new type of poetry, whose greatest representative would be Unamuno—if he did not scorn the senses so much. Eyes, ears, touch, are the patrimony of the spirit; the poet very particularly must begin with a broad cultivation of the senses."[89]

Naturally, matters did not end here. Unamuno, accused by Ortega of intellectual irresponsibility and arbitrariness, seized an opportunity, with obvious delight, to "pull out the thorn" and return the thrust of a few years back. In an article written in 1913 on "La supuesta anormal-idad española" ["The Supposed Spanish Abnormality"],[90] he comments on another article by Ortega, published in *La Prensa* of Buenos Aires, in which Ortega had said that Spain was the most abnormal country in Europe. And he says, "Why? I asked myself; how can this categorical statement be made just like that, so arbitrarily and caprici-

[86] "La pedagogía social como programa político" (1910). I, 512.
[87] *Ensayos*, VII, 209.
[88] "Dos dedicatorias" (in *El oficio del pensamiento* (1958), 235–41.
[89] "Los versos de Antonio Machado" (1912). I, 564–65.
[90] Published in *De esto y aquello*, III, 525ff.

ously, so totally lacking in proof, so unphilosophically; that is, so Spanishly? What is the measure of normality? What is the norm? Does Señor Ortega y Gasset possess it? Does he see it with the naked eye? Does he see it through lenses bought outside Spain and without having tested his eyes or tested the lenses?" And throughout the article he continues to emphasize the haste, the lack of justification and proof, of Ortega's article; that is, his having written it very little in the European style, and too *Spanishly*.

In time, however, the deep esteem in which the two great writers held each other blossomed again. From the first moment, Ortega counted on Unamuno's collaboration in the new review, *Faro*, in 1908; also in *España* in 1915; and lastly, when he was about to found the *Revista de Occidente* in 1923. In all three cases he offered to pay him the maximum rate for his contributions (Unamuno did contribute to *Faro* and *España*, but not to the *Revista de Occidente*). When Unamuno had difficulties with the government in 1912, and especially when he was removed from the rectorship of Salamanca in 1914, he found most energetic and firm support in Ortega, and active collaboration in the struggles which were aroused at the time. On his side, Unamuno was to offer Ortega genuine praise on many occasions. Thus, in 1922, he comments in an article entitled "Teatro y cine" ["Theater and Cinema"],[91] on one of Ortega's, "Elogio del Murciélago" ["In Praise of the Bat"], calling it "clever and subtle like everything he writes," and then recalls that "Ortega y Gasset has written before, with his habitual skill and subtlety, on the cinema, or rather, in praise of the cinema"; and then he says *à propos* of reading and listening, "And Ortega y Gasset himself knows the difference very well, for he is a superb lecturer, a marvelous reader or reciter of his essays. Does he believe that, even for a man capable of perceiving the superior qualities of one of his, Ortega's, essays, it is the same thing for him to read it when he is alone, in his house and silently, or to hear Ortega, its author? Of course not."

And at the end of his life, in January, 1933, Unamuno again comments on Ortega, in an affectionate tone, more affectionate perhaps than that of his early maturity, which coincided with the philosopher's impassioned youth. The article is called "Eso no es revolución" ["That Is Not Revolution"], and refers to what Ortega had said on the occasion

[91] *Ibid.*, IV, 384 ff.

of the centenary of the University of Granada. Now Unamuno is entirely in agreement. He refers, without mentioning the title, to "an article by our José Ortega y Gasset concerning the celebration of the University of Granada's centenary. And in that article our teacher demonstrated irreproachably the position, the spiritual position, of those of us who happen to call ourselves intellectuals." He follows the text step by step, agreeing with it, extrapolating it; and then he says again, "What will happen tomorrow? I ask myself with our Ortega, our teacher. What will happen tomorrow? What will happen to intelligence tomorrow?"[92]

Years later, in 1940, after Unamuno's death, Ortega alluded in a rather elusive way to this commentary: "Only that old fox Unamuno—he said that every Basque carries a fox inside him, but that he had two—saw the incipient prophecy and wrote several articles about this essay of mine. Unamuno, from whom I had been estranged for twenty years, came closer to me in the last days of his life, and until not long before the Civil War and his death he used to heave into sight, early in the evening, at the *tertulia* of the *Revista de Occidente*, with his distinguished figure, very bent by then, like a bow ready to shoot its last arrow. Some day I shall tell of the cause of this renewal of our friendship, which honors us both."[93]

He never got around to telling it. But—as almost always—there are sufficient "data" in an author's writings, if we know how to interpret them, to guide us to some degree at least. The ultimate root of the dissatisfaction Ortega felt about Unamuno in the early days was the belief that he had not been true to his role, his mission, his duty. Beginning with his first known letters, written at the age of twenty, Ortega expresses his faith in doctrine, in theory, in responsible intellectual effort, in system, and the fear aroused in him by the absence of all this, even in the name of very stimulating attitudes. There is a revealing sentence in the first letter quoted by Unamuno: "I feel that underneath my consciousness unknown ideas are moving, and fulfilling their functions; now and then one comes up for air, like a fish, and I see him; *but as I do not see the rest of his family, he is of no use to me*."[94] That is, an occasional idea, unconnected, is useless; it is a

---

[92] *Ibid.*, IV, 434 ff.

[93] Prologue to *Ideas y creencias* (1904). V, 375–76.

[94] Unamuno, "Almas de jóvenes" (in *Ensayos*, V, 16). The italics are mine.

"happening," and truth exists only in the form of *system*. Ortega preaches to Unamuno that he should concern himself with objective cultural problems; he warns him against the "anti-scientific" attitude; he wants him to become professor of philosophy of religion in Madrid and have the intellectual discipline not to fall into fanatical mysticism; when Unamuno complained[95] that in 1906 not a single real book had

[95] "La cultura española en 1906" (in *De esto y aquello*, I, 221 ff). Unamuno finds scarcely any interesting new productions. Only Marquina's *Elegías*, and in Catalan the collection entitled *Enllá*, by the great poet Juan Maragall, of whom he thought very highly. Unamuno's opinion with regard to the recent past and the present is wholly pessimistic: "Our times are times of struggle; God willing, we will not go back to the sad years of the so-called Restoration, in which the peaks, the shining lights of Spanish thought, were hidden in the fog of banality; those years of Campoamor's and Valera's conservative Voltaireanism, Nuñez de Arce's theatrical self-doubt. And during those same years in Italy, Carducci was raising one of the greatest monuments to the spirit of sacred simplicity and love for a free and united country. The great poet of disdain—as he has been called—described the country he loved as *vile*; and thus, by insulting it, he raised it high. This poor modern-day Spain of ours cannot even be called *vile*. She does not rise so high as vileness; she is only shamelessly crude and stupid. She is eaten up, as if by lice, by her unscrupulous exploiters. And our poor country, walled up in traditions of brick and plaster, runs the risk of dying, rotted away by her own excreta. Long ago, one of our kings was called 'the bewitched'; today it seems that the whole nation is bewitched. And we speak of culture?"

In 1906, Juan Ramón Jiménez had published his *Olvidanzas*, and Baroja *Los últimos románticos*. Eugenio d'Ors had begun his *Glosario*. It was not an extraordinary year, certainly, though today it does not seem one to be entirely despised. But in the immediately preceding years, in the decade that had passed since 1897, the following books, among others, had been published in Spain: *Misericordia, Electra*, and *El Abuelo*, by Galdós; *Idearium español, La conquista del Reino de Maya, Los trabajos de Pío Cid*, and *Cartas finlandesas*, by Ganivet; Ramón y Cajal's *Reglas y consejos sobre investigación científica*; Benavente's *La comida de las fieras*; *La barraca*, by Blasco Ibáñez; Costa's *El colectivismo agrario* and *Reconstitución y europeización de España*; *Hacia otra España*, by Maeztu; the first volumes of *Orígenes de la novela en España*, by Menéndez Pelayo; Menéndez Pidal's *Manual de Gramática histórica española*; Baroja's *Vidas sombrías, Idilios vascos, El mayorazgo de Labraz*, and *La lucha por la vida*; Valle-Inclán's *Sonatas*; his *Flor de santidad*; *La voluntad, Antonio Azorín, Las confesiones de un pequeño filósofo, La ruta de Don Quijote*, and *Los pueblos*, by Azorín; Manuel Machado's *Alma*; Antonio Machado's *Soledades*; Juan Ramón Jiménez' *Jardines lejanos* and *Pastorales*; Miró's *Del vivir*; *Paz en la guerra, Amor y pedagogía*, and *Vida de Don Quijote y Sancho*, by Unamuno himself. And in the two years which followed 1906, nothing less than his *Poesías* and his *Recuerdos de niñez y de mocedad* awaited, as well as Antonio Machado's *Soledades, galerías y otros poemas*; Baroja's *Las tragedias grotescas*; Juan Ramón Jiménez' *Elegías puras*; Valle-Inclán's *Romance de lobos; El Greco*, by Cossío; and the beginning of the edition of the *Cantar de Mio Cid*, by Menéndez Pidal. Can this be called a bewitched, crude and stupid country? Does it not seem to us like the beginning of a golden age? Yet that is the way Unamuno saw it,

been published in Spain, Ortega retorted that he had lost the thread of the battle and was doing little jobs fit for a common soldier, instead of thinking of overall strategy; for he had done what his disciples ought to have done, and that was what disciples were for. This was an accurate prophecy, let it be said in passing, for Unamuno never really had disciples. Sometimes, when he believed that Unamuno was going to take up a stand for science, clarity, rigor, Ortega was moved to the point of tears; when he saw this hope vanish, he felt overwhelmed and suffocated by a bitter disillusionment, an indignation in the name of Spain and of Unamuno, the Unamuno who might have been, who ought to have been. He felt tempted never to forgive him for not having fulfilled Pindar's maxim: *become what you are.*

In the end, however, after Unamuno's death, when Ortega first commented on his death in grief-stricken, emotional, and heartfelt terms and then reflected on his total significance, he thought of the fate of every generation, of the limitations each has, of the chiaroscuro of personal vocation; then Ortega seemed to accept his friend and adversary, his broken hope, the teacher who someday would call him to himself.

When the news that Unamuno was dead reached Ortega by telephone in Paris on the evening of New Year's Day, 1937, he wrote that he was sure that Unamuno had died from "the disease of Spain." "He has inscribed his individual death in the innumerable death which is Spanish life today. He has done the right thing. His trajectory was finished. He has placed himself at the head of two hundred thousand of his countrymen and has emigrated with them beyond all horizons...." "Now Unamuno is with Death," he continued, "his perennial friend and enemy. All of his life, all his philosophy, has been, like Spinoza's, a *meditatio mortis.* Today this inspiration is triumphant everywhere, but it must be said that Unamuno was its precursor. Precisely in those years when Europeans were most distracted from that essential human vocation which is 'to have to die,' and most diverted by the things that are within life, this great Celtiberian—there is no doubt

and he grieved over it. This invites us to disqualify *both* views; Unamuno's, too close, which feels the negative impacts and passes over the creative work being done all around him; ours, which retains only that work, and attributes *historico-social existence* to what did not possess such an existence, to what had not risen above what we might call its *threshold,* which is the quality of being "in force."

of that—both in the good and in the bad made Death his beloved."
"Unamuno belonged to the generation of Bernard Shaw . . . ."[96] It was
the last generation of 'intellectuals' convinced that humanity exists with
no more lofty purpose than to serve as a public for their juggler's tricks,
their arias, their polemics . . . . They had not discovered the tactic and
the delight it is to the true intellectual to hide himself and not to exist."
"But all this, be it understood, in a superlative degree. There is always
a great deal of gigantism both in Unamuno's virtues and his defects. To
this idea of the writer as a man who offers himself as a spectacle to
others, must be added a fuse of enormous dynamism, even of ferocious
dynamism. For Unamuno was, as a man, possessed of limitless courage . . . . He was a great writer . . . . Unamuno knew a great deal, and
much more than he seemed to know, and what he knew, he knew very
well. But his pretensions to being a poet made him avoid all doctrine.
In this, too, his generation was different from those which followed it,
and especially from future generations, for whom the inescapable
mission of an intellectual is, above all else, to have a rigorous unequivocal doctrine, and one, if possible, which is formulated into strict and
easily intelligible theses. For we intellectuals are not on this planet to
play sleight-of-hand tricks with ideas and show people the muscles of
our talent, but to find ideas with which other men can live. We are not
jugglers: we are artisans, like the carpenter, like the mason." And he
ended: "Unamuno's voice sounded without a break through all the
ambits of Spain for a quarter of a century. Now that it has ceased for-

---

[96] See also the "Prólogo a *Cartas finlandesas y Hombres del Norte*, de Angel Ganivet" (1940). VI, 370 ff. Ortega takes Ganivet's birth date to be 1862, a date which has
circulated in many books, but which is not accurate: he was born in 1865, a year later
than Unamuno. Taking the year 1857 as the central birth date for a generation, Ortega
includes in it Ganivet, Unamuno, Shaw, and Barrès; those called the "writers of 1898"
would belong in the following generation, and therefore would be separated from Unamuno and Ganivet. I see things differently; for reasons which it would take too long to
explain, I place the central date in 1856; Unamuno—and with greater justification Ganivet, once his birth date has been corrected—are then the oldest members of the generation of 1871, called the "Generation of 1898," and not excluded from it. Nevertheless,
almost everything that Ortega says of that generation, in which he includes simultaneously Shaw and Barrès, Unamuno and Ganivet, seems justified to me; the reason is
that the role played *in Europe* by the generation of 1856 corresponds in Spain, because
of the *décalage* mentioned previously, to the following generation: they are the men
who *initiate the present period*. See my article "La generación de 1856" (in *El oficio
del pensamiento*).

ever, I fear that our country will be afflicted by a period of terrible silence."[97]

In 1943, I published my book *Miguel de Unamuno*; I shall not go into detail here about the extent to which it has contributed toward the formation of the image of Unamuno which reigns today; I must say that without Ortega's intellectual discipline, comprehension of Unamuno would not have been possible. When I saw Ortega in Lisbon in 1944, after eight years of separation and lack of communication, I found that he had read all of my writings with great care except that one, which he consistently refused to read. "For you Unamuno is a *subject*," he told me; "for me he has been a slice of my life; I can't stir up all those things now by reading your book about him." But he listened with great attention to the lecture in which, at just that time, I expressed my view of Unamuno in Lisbon. And years later, in Madrid in 1951, he came one day into the room where I was giving a course, and the theme happened to be Unamuno again. He refused to give details, scarcely even to speak, but I knew the profound meaning that it all had for him.

25. ORTEGA'S ADMIRATIONS

I have gone into considerable detail about the relationship between Unamuno and Ortega, not only because of its intrinsic importance—for it bore upon the lives of both of them for so many years and with such unusual intensity, and we shall have to speak of it concretely many times in the course of this book—but because it is representative. Few things were of no concern to Ortega. His life was a constantly impassioned one, and cannot be understood if this is forgotten. Enthusiasm, demand, disappointment, trust ruled and dominated his life. Very late in that life, speaking emotionally and enthusiastically of Polybius and Scipio Aemilianus and their friendship, Ortega wrote with an unmistakable tone of confidence and "taking final stock": "It is not a question of academic *'beatería'* [superstition]. Above and beyond the fact that I created the expression 'cultural superstition,' there is the fact that I have pursued culture unflaggingly in every nook and cranny. For almost forty years, while I have lived, I have stretched myself thin, day after day, to push my compatriots and everyone who speaks Spanish toward

[97] "En la muerte de Unamuno" (1937). V, 261–63.

a culture without superstition, in which everything would be alive and authentic, a culture that would esteem what was estimable and dispense with everything false. But people need to leave off being stupid and learn to shudder when the hour comes to tremble; and that is not only at the hour of death, but whenever some symptom of sovereign humanity comes into view. Anything else is provincialism and stolidity."[98] Hence his demand for clarity in *hierarchies*; without a proper system of values an alert, fruitful, and truthful coexistence is not possible. On occasions Ortega could behave disdainfully, but this was precisely because he had always been unstinting in offering applause, and had even praised applause and its theory: "When something perfect passes in front of a man and he does not feel the need to applaud, then he is a man from whom little can be expected; note that this phenomenon of applause is one of the strangest, deepest, and rarest qualities of the human species: that the qualities of an object which neither belongs nor will belong to one should, in themselves, result in that instinct to open one's arms wide, as if wishing to take in the whole world, to bring them together energetically, to loose that strange bird of applause, of ovation, the specific sign of man's which enlivens history. Applause opens the heart; that is why the first gesture of the man who applauds is to open his arms."[99]

This enthusiasm, this wish for applause, is precisely the explanation of Ortega's harshest sayings. When they occur in his work, they are almost always preceded by praise, possibly excessive praise, by a trust generously granted and perhaps defrauded. Ortega always lived under the sign of expectation and hope; he needed admiration, self-surrender, a heartfelt outgoingness toward people, things, ideas, beauty, countries, as he needed air to breathe. And when the backwash of disenchantment, of disappointment, reached him, he was also incapable of deceiving himself, of continuing without faith or hope in an insincere attitude of esteem. And he had the habit of measuring everything by his own aspirations, by those of each reality; thus he was always tolerant and encouraging with limited and modest but authentic realities, and implacably scornful of pretense and mere posture. And he felt really

98 "Prólogo a *Veinte años de caza mayor*, del Conde de Yebes" (1942).
99 Speech in the Cortes, July 30, 1931. *Rectificación de la República* (Madrid, 1931), 50-51.

pained by failures: in the presence of what, capable of being more, contented itself with being less; in the presence of a person who preferred the lower path; in the presence of the man who flagged and lost his morale. Nothing pained and dismayed him like aborted possibilities.

When something or someone mattered to him—and almost everything that went on around him and entered the area of his life mattered to him very deeply—one could see him watching carefully, full of tense expectation, wanting to see it fulfill its promise, his eyes shining in response to success and good progress, ready to "warm the cockles of his heart" if the thing were accomplished; and anxiously scrutinizing the disturbing gesture, the bad symptoms, fearing to see the unstable fabric of those hopes break down, always greatly discouraged when he had to say—or perhaps mutter under his breath—that phrase which he once made famous: "That's not it, that's not it!"

It is true that he soon got over his disappointments and discouragements. Ortega had tremendous vitality, an inexhaustible capacity for incitement and enthusiasm, for beginning all over again. Like Lope de Vega, whom he must have resembled in more ways than one, he was always willing to set off on a new undertaking, to open another, larger credit, to hurl himself into a new enthusiasm. But it would be a mistake to believe that he could console himself easily after the most profound of past failures: all of them left a scar, and the painful ache of some stayed with him to the day of his death.

If we do not keep this in mind, we run the risk of misunderstanding Ortega's whole work in one essential dimension; not only his written work, but all his actions, the story of his undertakings, the whole configuration of his life's trajectory. Therefore, when occasional opinions of his are "gleaned"—when one forgets that, strictly speaking, he had no "opinions," that his mission was to establish in Spain a mental reaction to things which was not simply to opine about them—opinions about a man, a country, about his Spain itself, about an art form, a doctrine, a type of religion, if we are not clear about what those attitudes mean within the vital (historical, dogmatic) system of his admirations, they are disfigured, even with the best faith in the world. Not to mention the times when good faith is just what is lacking, when the motivating force for this isolation of his judgments is a deliberate wish to disfigure.

In a lecture given at the Ateneo on October 15, 1909, Ortega referred "to those who have not had masters, those who have the courage to confess to themselves that they have learned scarcely anything in Spanish that has made them more sensitive, more intelligent, or more virtuous." And he added, "Spaniards who have now reached fifty years of age have not accomplished the europeanization of Spain. As a generation they have failed." In this text, probably the first in which Ortega concerned himself with the idea of generations, he was referring unequivocally to the generation I call that of 1856, the one which immediately preceded that of 1898. And he was not using the term "generation" vaguely, for later on in the same lecture he added, "The historical reality of a generation consists in its being the point of intersection between a previous generation which has prepared it and another, subsequent, one which arises and derives from it: each generation is the disciple of an older one and the master of a younger one."[100]

The balance is certainly negative. Ortega recognizes the fact that he has had no masters, and even that he has learned little in Spanish which has increased his quality. Observe that these words follow closely upon his disillusionment about Unamuno, whom he probably implicates in the failure of europeanization (Ortega, though he did not make it entirely hard-and-fast, usually included Unamuno in the generation he called the generation of 1857, the one I consider to be the generation of 1856, *but precisely excluding Unamuno from it*. As I see it, Unamuno initiates the generation of 1871; that is, the so-called Generation of 1898).[101]

After finishing his studies for the baccalaureate degree at the school in Palo, Ortega went to the Jesuit university in Deusto (province of Bilbao) and began to study the courses of law and philosophy and letters there in 1897–98, taking his examinations at the University of Salamanca. In Deusto his professors were, besides Padre Gonzalo Coloma,

[100] Text from an unpublished manuscript.

[101] See note 96. Observe that, on the one hand, Unamuno was at that time forty-five years old, and that, on the other, Ortega makes absolutely no mention of the other writers of the Generation of 1898. The generation to which he alludes is clearly the previous one, though perhaps he vaguely tends to include Unamuno in the reproach.

who taught him classical languages, and the professor of Greek, Julio Cejador, who was at that time also a Jesuit, Padre E. Ugarte de Ercilla and Padre F. Echeverría. In Deusto, Ortega encountered some friction with regard to his father, and this confirmed his low opinion of that type of teaching. In May, 1898, shortly after his fifteenth birthday, he took his examinations in Salamanca before a board which included Unamuno; this must have been their first encounter, probably an impersonal one at this time.[102]

The next year Ortega continued his studies in Madrid, at the Central University; as was traditional at that time, and for a long time afterward, a student of philosophy and letters took law studies simultaneously; but Ortega did not go on with this latter career, and got a degree only in the former, in 1902—the same year which saw the publication of his first article in *Vida nueva*—at the age of nineteen. His university experiences were profoundly disappointing. In an article he wrote for *El Imparcial* in 1909, commemorating the five hundredth anniversary of the University of Leipzig, Ortega gave supreme importance to the institution of the university—and the lack of it. "If the army is, in appearance, the instrument of war," he wrote, "then the instrument of peace is indisputably the university; of that peace, I repeat, which can coexist with the greatest convulsions and pass through them without falling apart, without a break. It can be said without risk of error that there is just as much peace in a state as there is university; and only where there is something of a university is there some element of peace.

"Many readers will believe, and rightly, that this makes no sense: what comes to their minds under the name of university, is a most mournful reality: a dingy and featureless building, a few solemn men who, repeating dead words, foist their ineptitude and inner gloom onto the younger generations; some schoolboys who play billiards, loudly demand the score, and, twice a year, are classified into 'passed' or 'failed.' The reader is quite right: if that is the university, instead of finding anything resembling peace there, we should have to consider it as something resembling utter Philistinism.

"But now Germany is celebrating the fifth centenary of an institution called '*Universitas, Universitas studii*,' and which has a dignity and a value very different from that dreadful shame of ours in the street called Ancha.

[102] See J. Iriarte, *Ortega y Gasset. Su persona y doctrina* (1942), 22ff.

"And meanwhile, in our ghostly University the shade of a professor fiercely calls the roll of the shades of a few students."[103]

A year later Ortega was to recall: "A few years ago I went out one day fleeing from the rampant Philistinism of my country, and like a medieval scholar I arrived on another day in Leipzig, famous for its bookstores and its university."[104] And in 1930, when he was about to study—this time with troubled hope—*The Mission of the University*, and referred to what had been gained, although insufficiently, since his student days, the word which came to his lips again and again to explain the old Spanish university, the one which was then being improved upon, was Philistinism, the opposite of *things as they should be*.

From his student years Ortega did preserve one insecure, unsatisfactory devotion: Julio Cejador (1864–1927), an Aragonese, exactly the same age as Unamuno, a Jesuit, Ortega's professor in Deusto. He later left the order, was a professor at the Instituto in Palencia, and finally, after writing a work of great erudition and learning, though highly prejudiced in nature, taught at the University of Madrid. Ortega speaks of Cejador several times in his youth, and always affectionately. In 1911 he said of him: "Don Julio Cejador is one of the men whom I most love and respect among my compatriots: he was my teacher of Greek in the sad year of 1898, and later continued to be my teacher in many and important subjects during the long years of our common acquaintance. I feel toward him that emotion of loving distance which befits a disciple in the presence of his master. I also admire greatly his colossal knowledge, and even though I lack the most elementary notions which would enable me to judge his linguistic discoveries, the brute mass of information stored in Señor Cejador is so great that it seems shameful to think that no government has carried him off to the University, where he has the right to a position gained by merits weighing a good many more carats than the dubious ones of competitive examination."[105] For some years Ortega had been taking care, with obvious solicitude, to bring his old teacher's works to public attention: in 1906, the *Diccionario del Quijote* ["Dictionary of the Quixote"];[106] in 1907, the *Nuevo método para aprender el latín* ["New Method for Learning

103 "Una fiesta de paz" (1909). I, 125–27.
104 "Una primera vista sobre Baroja" (1910). II, 116.
105 "Observaciones" (1911). I, 164.
106 "La ciencia romántica" (1906). I, 38ff.

Latin"], in an article in which Ortega took good care to emphasize Cejador's copious production, and to add: "After a great deal of effort, Señor Cejador attained a chair of Latin in the Institute of Palencia. And there he is, teaching preterites and supines to little Celtiberian angels."[107]

The young Ortega felt other devotions, too, in his Spanish circumstance. One of the liveliest was for Francisco Navarro Ledesma, a professor in an institute, an obscure, and above all obscured, writer, who had wasted himself on writings inferior to his quality—author, nevertheless, of a valuable and strangely attractive book: *El ingenioso hidalgo Miguel de Cervantes Saavedra* ["The Ingenious Hidalgo Miguel de Cervantes Saavedra"], a literary biography of Cervantes which was by no means far removed from Ortega's Cervantine enthusiasms. Navarro Ledesma, who had been born in 1869, died very young, in 1905. Ortega wrote a sorrowful article about him, in which he lamented Navarro Ledesma's bad luck, which had kept him from carrying out his proper work, and in which he let slip some important confidences. Apart from a few paragraphs on death, of which I shall speak later, he wrote with brilliant insight about the factors of accomplishment in human life— "Time, hope, and freedom are the three demiurgi who work out the plans of the poet"[108]—and sketched out a theory of what the historical reality of a human figure may be and what one person may be to another. "In the history of thought," he says, "names sometimes appear to whom their contemporaries showed great respect, but who left behind no work on which we can definitely reconstruct that venerable soul today. Let Socrates be an example. But what was Socrates? And you will see that we must answer: Socrates was Plato and Xenophon; Socrates belongs a little to all of us who have been getting born for twenty-five centuries with some Socratic chords within the doubtful harmony of our spirits. But, for us, Socrates is an idea taught us by Plato; whereas for this divine philosopher, Socrates was an adventure—better still, *the* adventure, that moment in individual life which polarizes, which crystallizes in a definite form the rest of that individual life.

"Navarro Ledesma was my adventure," continues Ortega; and before explaining this, he must prepare the reader to understand it, taking him into his confidence with all the seriousness, untainted by irony, of youth.

[107] "Sobre los estudios clásicos" (1907). I, 63 ff.
[108] "Canto a los muertos, a los deberes y a los ideales" (1906). I, 59.

"You, friend reader, will read this sentence with indifference, but perhaps you do not know what a bundle of thistles and bitterness, what a breeding-place of anxieties, what a heap of painful yearnings, of doubts, of desperate attempts, of impossible ambitions, makes up what we call the soul of a twenty-year-old Spaniard. If you do not know, I ask for noble respect about a thing which is a mystery to you, and promise that some day I shall try to make it plain to you." And he explains that Navarro Ledesma was an adventure for him because he was gifted with "the two highest modern virtues: the carrying out of obscure duties, and imperishable idealism."[109] Is this not a key to the understanding of Ortega's admirations, his adhesions, his disappointments?

Here and there in Ortega's youthful pages we find names marked by appreciation, respect, or enthusiasm: all the men of 1898—Valle-Inclán,[110] Azorín,[111] Baroja,[112] Machado,[113] Menéndez Pidal;[114] some-

---

[109] *Ibid.*, 59–60.

[110] See the article mentioned above on the *Sonata de estío*, I, 19–27; also "Algunas notas" (1908), I, 113, where Ortega rejects, however, "the young poets who, without being Valle-Inclán or Rubén Darío, imitate them badly instead of shuffling the archives and reconstructing the history of Spain, or commenting on Aeschylus or Saint Augustine." There is an interesting reference to Valle-Inclán, "a great artist of our land who, like a great artist, possesses a genius's intuition of the essence of art," in "La estética del enano Gregorio el Botero" (1911), I, 535. Lastly, see an allusion to Valle-Inclán's "esperpento" as a literary genre in "La estrangulación de *Don Juan*" (1935), V, 243.

[111] From 1906: "Remember the 'Epilogue' which ends the book *Los pueblos*, by Martínez Ruiz. Could there possibly be anything more simple, more willowy, more insubstantial, or with greater imaginative restraint? Could there be anything more classical, either? Nothing at all happens, and yet, between the lines, the sound of Death speaking with his companion Oblivion, reaches us from an ideal distance." ("Moralejas. II. Poesía nueva, poesía vieja, I," 52.) In 1911 he fears for Azorín: "The best thing that has been done in Spanish literature in the last ten years has been the essays of *salvation* of the vulgar small-town social clubs, of the useless old women, of the anonymous dwellers in the provinces, of the courtyards, of the inns, of the dusty roads —composed by an admirable writer, who has not published for four years, and who signed with the pseudonym *Azorín*." ("Arte de este mundo y del otro," I, 200.) In fact Azorín, after *La ruta de Don Quijote* (1905), had written only *El Político* and *España*. And in 1912, as soon as he published *Lecturas españolas*, Ortega wrote an article about him, "Nuevo libro de Azorín" (I, 239–44), in which he expressed his pleasure and enthusiasm: "One of the best books I have read in Spanish is this one which Azorín has published, calling it *Lecturas españolas* . . . ." And after great and perceptive praise: "In this book Azorín arises from his parliamentary ashes and flows through the whole book as if he severely repented of those activities. The poet has spent four years in idle pursuits . . . ." We must also recall, naturally, his offer of the "Fiesta de Aranjuez en

what behind them, Sanz del Río,[115] Azcárate,[116] Hinojosa,[117] Cajal,[118]

honor de Azorín," in 1913 (I, 262ff.), and the extraordinary study from which I quoted above, "Azorín: primores de lo vulgar," among many other texts.

[112] The article in question, "Una primera vista sobre Baroja," was written in 1910 but not published until 1915. The article "Una respuesta a una pregunta" (1911), I, 211 ff., dated in Marburg, is a reply to one by Baroja, "¿Con el latino o con el germano?" In the *Meditaciones del Quijote* he announces, as early as 1914, his "salvations" on Azorín and Baroja, and says of the latter, "In Pío Baroja we have to meditate on happiness and on 'action'; really, we have to talk about a little of everything . . . . For this man, rather than being a man, is a crossroads." (I, 235.) The "salvation" called "Ideas sobre Pío Baroja" is even today the most penetrating study which has been made on this writer, and is full of admiration and liking, though Ortega does not spare objections reconcilable with very high esteem. And throughout his life Ortega always expressed his friendship and admiration for Baroja, and an irrepressible liking for him. Baroja, to be sure, responded with a respect and esteem which were absolutely exceptional for him: see his *Memorias*.

[113] See the article mentioned above, "Los versos de Antonio Machado," in which Ortega comments on the publication of *Campos de Castilla* at the time it appeared.

[114] "The name of Menéndez Pidal is so noble, so exemplary, so severe, that it is worth a hundred arguments" ("Unamuno y Europa, fábula," I, 130). See also Ortega's note to "La epopeya castellana," I, 146. And, besides many mentions full of admiration and gratitude, the article on "Orígenes del español" (1927), which begins, "Honor where honor is due. I am extraordinarily pleased to initiate this series of bibliographical notes with some remarks on one of Menéndez Pidal's books. Great gestures of admiration, of enthusiasm for the giant work—lesser gestures of curiosity, of doubt; then, an expression of minor dissatisfaction." (*Espíritu de la letra*, III, 511 ff.) Ortega relates Menéndez Pidal's works to his points of view in *España invertebrada*. I will discuss this point elsewhere in this book.

[115] See IV, 384, section 21a.

[116] See the passages quoted in section 21a (notes 29–32).

[117] See I, 85, 108, 113.

[118] See the last two passages quoted in the previous note. What Ortega says about Ramón y Cajal in 1927 is very interesting: "I will be told that there are cases of enormous and respectful popularity, and I will specifically be informed of the constant homage of the most diverse social classes to a man like Ramón y Cajal. But I deplore the fact that this example sinks me still deeper into what may be my error. That exception, unique in a certain sense, which is made of Ramón y Cajal, bearing him to and fro like the corpse of San Isidro, in the form of a magical fetish to placate the ire of the demon Intelligence, who may have been offended, is something that is done only in countries where normal, close, and nonmagical contact with intellectuals is not desired. One is chosen to free people, by excessive and unintelligent homage to his person, from all obligation to the rest. The fact that it is precisely Ramón y Cajal who is chosen accentuates—better still, it uncovers almost obscenely—the ridiculous secret obscured by such apparent fervor. For almost no one has the slightest idea of what the admirable conquests of the great scientist are. On the other hand, histology is a science so remote from public consciousness, so neutral and colorless, that it seems deliberately chosen for apotheosis by a nation which considers intellectual work a superfluity, when it does not think of it as a sort of conjurer's trick. If Ramón y Cajal

Giner de los Ríos,[119] Alcántara,[120] Rubén Darío,[121] Pablo Iglesias;[122] not forgetting, of course, Costa, Unamuno, and Maeztu, of whom I have spoken at length.

In other cases the admiration is more troubled, and mixed with discontentment; I spoke before of the case of Menéndez Pelayo; with Valera, Ortega oscillates between friendly feeling and dissatisfaction;[123] something similar occurs with Maura;[124] discontentment clearly predominates in his image of Cánovas;[125] his view of Galdós[126] and Ganivet[127] becomes more positive and cordial with the passage of time.

---

were to write a single page that affected the Spanish soul a bit more closely, we would witness the ominous evaporation of his social power." ("El poder social," III, 494–95.)

[119] See section 21a.

[120] Ortega considered Don Francisco Alcántara as extraordinarily knowledgeable about Spain and art. See I, 200, 469; II, 547; V, 475.

[121] See note 64.

[122] See an article from *El Imparcial*, May 13, 1910, which Ortega never included in a book; quoted by Padre J. Iriarte, *op. cit.*, 60–61. See also a mention in *Vieja y nueva política*, I, 274, and a much earlier mention in the article, which never appeared in book form, "El recato socialista" (*El Imparcial*, 2–IX–1908).

[123] In 1904 there is a short and penetrating characterization: "Don Juan Valera belongs to the eighteenth century; he has the cold malignance of the Encyclopedists, and their noble way of expressing himself" (I, 19). In the same article he calls him "this smiling, blind God Pan, who survives in the sterile garden of our *belles-lettres* like the broken white statue of a pagan deity." (I, 26.) The most important text is "Una polémica," referring to Valera's debate with Campoamor on *La Metafísica y la Poesía* (I, 155–63); it is a critical and somewhat negative article, probably more so than was called for; but we should not forget that it ends with this sentence: "When we see Campoamor in motion, however, Valera will seem historically justified to us." I have already referred to certain reservations which he had in regard to Valera's criticism and that of Menéndez Pelayo.

[124] See, for example, *Vieja y nueva política* (I, 294–95). In *España invertebrada* (1921) there is a page about Maura which sums up many things and a number of political attitudes: Ortega says that Maura was "a stager of *coups d'état* in a frock coat" (III, 84). In Ortega's political articles, with which I shall deal in a following book on Ortega, there are frequent, concrete references to Maura's activities.

[125] It is summed up in the famous sentence: "The Restoration, gentlemen, was a panorama of ghosts, and Cánovas the great impressario of fantasy." (*Vieja y nueva política*, I, 281.) See also p. 292. But Ortega's harsh judgment of Cánovas was founded on esteem for his qualities: "Cánovas, gentlemen, was not an innocent babe; I sincerely respect his enormous talent, perhaps the greatest of his century in Spain with regard to ideological questions, if he had been able to dedicate his life to them . . . " (*ibid.*, 281–82). Add to this what Ortega says in I, 167 and 215.

[126] See "La muerte de Galdós" (1920). II, 30–31: "Galdós was the man of genius. Campoamor was the ingenious man . . . . The nation knows that the greatest and most

Taken all together, there is little hostility in Ortega's work, and in particular a minimal amount of personal hostility. His aversions were, rather, objective: aversion to the uncalled-for, the anachronistic, the unauthentic; thus, to the spirit of the Restoration, rather than to its individual men, with regard to whom he often feels indulgence if not benevolence. But Ortega always wrote and spoke with unusual sincerity, without annoyance, without *arrière-pensée* (without "redroideas," as he once wrote to Unamuno, using a word he had evidently borrowed from him), with consummate literary *effectiveness*. Since this contrasted with the more sinuous and insinuating habits of the period—and the periods which followed it—it has often been thought that Ortega's words carried a charge of hostility which they did not have at all; it has been thought that, when he said what he said, he must have been thinking terrible things; but it was not so, rather the opposite: he was thinking just what he said, and perhaps the shape of his sentence, always so expressive, increased what would have been, from another pen, reduced to a restriction, a slight irony, a shade of displeasure that no one notices.

27. THE PLANES OF CIRCUMSTANCE AND ORTEGA'S INITIAL ASPIRATION

We have seen to what extent Ortega was linked, from his earliest years, with the immediate Spanish circumstance; not only for personal reasons, but also for others which went beyond the individual factor: first, because of the presence of national concerns—especially politics, journalism, and literature—in his family home; above all, because he had opened his eyes to historical life in 1898, the critical date for the Spanish

gifted of its princes has died . . . . There will be a deeply felt and sincere grief which will unite all good Spaniards before the tomb of our unforgettable master."

[127] In 1908, Ortega had written, "Ganivet—of whom I have a very different opinion from that commonly held among the young, but which I keep quiet about, so as not to seem uselessly out of step—read a little book, a very bad one to be sure, by Th. Ribot, who was in vogue at the time; he became enthusiastic about it, and tossed off the thesis of Spanish *abulia*." ("Algunas notas," I, 113.) Two years later he still can say, "Thus, for news of the Spanish mission on earth I am more in debt to Maurice Barrès than to Ganivet, for Ganivet did not succeed in raising himself to a supranational point of view, and his opinions are marred by a provincial vision of the universe." ("Viaje de España" [1910]. I, 521.) See also a reference in II, 175. The opinion I have just quoted is substantially corrected in "Prólogo a *Cartas finlandesas*" (1940), VI, 370 ff., which I quote in section 27.

consciousness. His immediate elders, the men who in one form or another were to serve as his models, the men we call the "Generation of 1898," had made Spain their theme, their drama, their fate; they had found aspects in Spain that were intact; they had initiated a different view of her past; they were giving her both color and depth; they were literally *recreating* her, making of her an unknown reality, at once painful and impassioned.

But, additionally, they were liberating her. From what? From the "outside," as Ortega himself was later to say, using a singularly expressive and accurate word.[128] For Spain, just because she was outside her time, had in the end become alienated in a strange world which was, in fact, all of it, *outside*. She communicated with this world—or rather she was under the impression that she was communicating with it—through France. This was what changed radically at the end of the nineteenth century, through the efforts of a handful of men of the Generation of 1898, who accomplished what a few older men had thought necessary; Sanz del Río and Giner, Valera, the mature Menéndez Pelayo (not the young one, whom the older Menéndez Pelayo could never sufficiently rehabilitate, for he had unleashed a "partisanship" which overtook the older Menéndez Pelayo as well as the memory of him, and has sterilized both the young one and the old one).

In his maturity at least, Ortega was fully aware of the function the Generation of 1898 had fulfilled. It was his point of departure: still more, it was the generation which had traced the curve of his vital horizon. The space within which Ortega moved from the outset was no longer the confined space of the Restoration, from which one set out, at best, on a disturbing intellectual *excursion*, to alien worlds. It was the world. Here is what Ortega says in 1940:

"If we now go back to Ganivet and Unamuno in their Spanish orbit, we observe the gigantic broadening of the Iberian horizon which they represent. France had influenced Spain constantly ever since 1750, but this influence had worked from a position of superiority. Ganivet and Unamuno are the first whose dealings with French production are those of equal to equal. They are more thoroughly acquainted with it than the previous generations, but they are not invaded or colonized by it. This liberation from the bondage of French teaching was owed to the fact that both men were the first to penetrate beyond it and have direct

128 "Europa ha de salvarnos del extranjero." "Nueva revista" (1910), I, 145.

contact with the work of the nations of Northern and Central Europe. England, Denmark, Scandinavia, Finland, and Germany helped them to put in its place, an honored but restricted, limited, place, the French spirit which up till then had enjoyed an exclusive influence; and because exclusive, unlimited.

"As more time passes, the more lofty seems the feat performed by these two men and others of their Peninsular generation, for they made universal the horizon of Spanish culture. Since then the writer and professor in Spain have been present in the intellectual life of the whole world. This universalization of the horizon has later become much richer, more precise, formal, and solid, but its radius has not grown larger, because there was no more radius. And it is curious to note that this fabulous expansion of the horizon produced, in Ganivet as well as in Unamuno, a precipitate of fierce Spanishness."[129]

Ortega is thinking, beyond Spain, of the periphery of the European nations. These are not seen *through* France, but directly, side by side with her. Naturally, the situation which Unamuno and Ganivet created is not the same as that of thirty or fifty years later; but Ortega finds, as he frequently does, the *mot juste*: "The writer and professor in Spain *have been present* in the intellectual life of the whole world." To a certain degree, Valera had already done this, *especially up to about 1870*, but the weight of Spanish provincialism had pressed down upon him progressively, had limited his own view, and, above all, had caused the presence of that wider horizon not to be fully operative inside Spain—that is, when Valera stayed *at home* and really began to live and to think. The pressure exercised from Europe was still too weak, unable to give form to Spain's national interior. This was what was *beginning* to happen with the Generation of 1898; but these men, who really were in the outside world, who were present at what was happening in it, when they began to *create*, fell back on themselves and went back into the constricted Spanish ambit; or, if they tried to avoid this, they stayed *outside*, expatriated—whether or not they actually left Spain— vaguely "cosmopolitan," rootless within their own country, no matter how great their desire for traditional Spanish values, which was sometimes considerable.

It was precisely Ortega who was to initiate a new attitude. We shall spend many pages seeing in what this attitude consists. Making it

[129] "Prólogo a *Cartas finlandesas*, etc." VI, 374–75.

possible occupied a good part of his effort, his work, his theory. For he really had to change the situation in which a Spanish intellectual found himself, and this was only possible by inventing a new aspiration which had not existed before. This aspiration, as we shall see, included philosophy, the only instrument which in its turn was capable of carrying out the transformation, the card on which Ortega had staked his life from the beginning.

II.

THE CIRCUMSTANTIALITY OF
ORTEGA'S THOUGHT

28. KNOWING HOW TO "KNOW WHAT TO HOLD TO":
THE SPANISH INTERPRETATION OF THE WORLD

Ortega felt himself rooted in Spain from his beginnings. There is not a
single moment in all his work when this condition disappears, when he
confronts reality from "outside" his Spanish circumstance. He never
for an instant had the so frequent illusion that when he went outside
his country he placed himself in a different point of view and abandoned
his original one: the illusion of the "foreignophiles" of all countries and
all times, which in a less crude form is that of "cosmopolitanism," the
illusion of the man who feels like a "citizen of the world."[1] When
Ortega left Spain—first mentally, in thought and in books, and very
soon in truth, when he went to Germany to study—he continued to
be aware of himself *as Spanish*, not less but more than before: what
happened then was that Spain had been "put in its place," circum-
stantialized in its turn, integrated into the ambit where it really was;
expressed from another point of view, Ortega's circumstance had expanded, had broadened, but it had not become "utopianized"—quite
the contrary: it had gained in circumstantiality. It was no less Spanish
because it began outside the country; but Spain now functioned in its
own *context*, not abstractly. Ortega went through the world "wearing"
Spain, if the expression serves, like that immediate portion of circumstance which permits us to have other portions, through which all the
others can live. Just as happens with one's body, and in general with
one's psychophysical reality: because I am "embodied," so the form of
historico-social "embodiment" is one's own country, and through it
Ortega was to confront all the rest of the universe, which appeared,
circumstantially, as its "periphery."

[1] See my essay "Marco Aurelio o la exageración," in *San Anselmo y el insensato*
(*Obras*, IV).

{ 159 }

Knowing, in its primary and radical sense, is "knowing what to hold to" with respect to reality, and this means with respect to the situation in which one finds oneself; therefore this knowledge is possible only from the standpoint of one's own circumstance. This idea—later we shall see its genesis in Ortega's thought, and its implications—stayed with him throughout his life. In 1932 he solemnly wrote, when he recapitulated one stage of his life and work, "Since life is in its very substance circumstantial, it is obvious that, though we may believe the contrary, everything that we do is done *in view of the circumstances*. Even when we create the illusion that we are thinking of something, or wanting something, *sub specie aeternitatis*, we do so through circumstantial necessity. Yet more: the idea of eternity, of the unconditioned, ubiquitous being, arises in man because he needs it as a saving *contrast* to his unescapable circumstantiality. It grieves man to belong to one time and one place, and the moan he makes over this assignment to the spatio-temporal glebe echoes in his thought under the guise of eternity. Man would like to be eternal precisely because he is the opposite of eternal. What I was to be I had to be in Spain, in the Spanish circumstance."[2]

He had written many years before, "The individual cannot get his bearings in the universe except through his race, because he is submerged in it like the drop of water in the passing cloud."[3] By "race" Ortega understands a historical manner of interpreting reality, an original version of humankind. Only by accepting the circumstance can one have a *real* and not a utopian abstract knowledge; yet more: only in that circumstance, by rooting oneself in it, can one *be* who one is authentically. Any attempt to avoid the circumstance is a supplanting of one's own reality, and this leads to the falseness of all knowledge, which becomes illusory.

We must keep this in mind in order to understand Ortega's whole fight against the "village" attitude of mind and "provincialism," which first showed in his zeal for "europeanization." Quite different, and sometimes contradictory, attitudes have circulated in Spain—and, analogously, in other countries—under this name. I cannot go here into a study of the europeanizing tendencies in the Spain of the early twentieth century, though there are many indications of it in the preceding pages;

[2] "Prólogo a una edición de sus *Obras*" (1932). VI, 350.
[3] *Meditaciones del Quijote* (1914). I, 361.

what we must now establish is that when Ortega confronted "traditional" and "intra-Spanish" attitudes—such as those he even reproached Menéndez Pelayo for—he did so not in the name of *something other than Spain*, but quite the contrary: in the name of *Spain in her true reality*; that is, in the concrete world in which Spain exists and has meaning. The dual temptation, which he resisted from the outset, is this: to *shut oneself up* in the immediate circumstance, or to *escape from it*. Ortega saw from the beginning that both positions are at once illusory and unfaithful to the circumstance: the first because it mutilates the circumstance and affects it in its own circumstantial quality; the second because it loses the circumstance, and one no longer has a point of view. The man who wants *only to be a Spaniard* is not even a Spaniard, because *Spain is not alone*; the man who believes he can be *something other than a Spaniard* tears himself up by the roots and renounces the point of view that has been given him, the one from which he is able to know reality. In the one case as well as the other, it becomes impossible to "know what to hold to."

When Ortega contrasts "Europe" with "abroad," he means that Europe is not something foreign or alien, and that to "europeanize" oneself is not to leave Spain, but to expand, to dilate one's own reality.[4] But not, of course, to "shut oneself in" either, as Ganivet, for example, had advised. Ganivet had written, "A restoration of Spain's whole life can have no other starting point than the concentration of all our energies within our own territory. We must close with bolts, keys, and padlocks all the doors through which the Spanish spirit escaped from Spain to scatter itself to the four points of the compass, and from which she hopes today that salvation is to come; and on each of those doors we will not place a Dantesque sign saying *Lasciate ogni speranza*, but this other sign, more consoling, more human, very deeply human, paraphrasing Saint Augustine: *Noli foras ire: in interiore Hispaniae habitat veritas*."[5]

It was precisely Ortega's diagnosis, from early in his life until his death, that the most serious evils of our country in the modern period lay in what he called the "tibetanization of Spain"—her seclusion within

---

[4] "España como posibilidad" (1910). I, 138.

[5] Angel Ganivet, *Idearium español* (*Obras completas*, Suárez ed., I, 151). On the problem of Europeanization, see Dolores Franco, *La preocupación de España en su literatura*, 1944. [*España como preocupación*, revised edition, 1960.]

herself, her detachment from the reality around her—a theme which we shall have to take up in detail elsewhere. What Ortega wanted can be expressed very succinctly in a sentence written in his youth: "We want the Spanish interpretation of the world."[6] What precisely does this mean?

29. PREOCCUPATION FOR SPAIN AND THEORY

The Generation of 1898 had felt the preoccupation of Spain as no other generation had done. Strictly speaking, we may say that this is its *theme*, and also that it is the only generation—not merely some individual authors—defined as such by that preoccupation.[7] Ortega is the inheritor of this position; on this point, his attitude is "cumulative," of a continuing kind; in this respect—though only in this one—he can be included unequivocally among the men of 1898; much more, certainly, than any of the other men of his age, in whom such an attitude is much less intense or, even when it has greatest energy, comes late and in large part aroused by Ortega himself, sometimes as a response to his personal action.

We saw earlier[8] that the work of the Generation of 1898 was set in motion by an imperious, sharp need *to know what to hold to* with regard to Spain; but that this undertaking was compromised in that generation by the lack of *theory* in the strict sense, justified to a certain degree by historical factors, not only in the Spanish situation itself but also in the irrationalism dominant in European philosophy. Thus the preoccupation found its outlet in that generation in *contemplation*, in the effort to comprehend aesthetically and sentimentally the reality round about. Literature continued to be the Generation of 1898's great instrument; first, in order to achieve a spirit of authenticity and communicative power; in the last instance, in order to comprehend in a form that was not theoretical. It is no coincidence that the most philosophically gifted person among the men of that generation, Unamuno, should have made poetry, and still more the novel, his personal method of knowledge.[9]

---

[6] I, 138.

[7] See *La preocupación de España*, 255–417.

[8] Introduction, section 10.

[9] See my *Miguel de Unamuno* (1943) (*Obras*, V), especially chapters 3–5.

Ortega's innovation with respect to these men whom he had joined was not to turn his attention to theory, and stop there. This would have meant an orientation toward *European* theory—Spanish theory there was none—and an abandonment of the need to root oneself in circumstance. He was to construct a theory born out of that shared preoccupation, one deeply moved by that generation, brought to life by it. And that theory was to have as its primary object the Spanish circumstance, and its aim was truly to attain, in an adequate way, without renouncing intellection, knowledge of what to hold to with respect to himself, since—let us not forget—"the individual cannot get his bearings in the universe except through his race."

But precisely because of this, when he confronted the problem *theoretically*, he felt the need of achieving a more rigorous philosophy. He was soon to see that, just because of the circumstantial nature of reality, the consideration of Spain was absolutely insufficient for understanding Spain: "Every circumstance is contained within another, larger one . . . . A serious oversight, a miserable stupidity, to deal with only a few circumstances, when in truth everything is around us!"[10] This is the exact starting point of Ortega's philosophy. His personal way of feeling concern for Spain, the level of his demand with regard to it, obliged him to mobilize his efforts toward theory, to try to give an account of Spanish reality *in its effective connections*, therefore beyond itself. The prologue to the *Meditations on Quixote* ends with these words, the key to its interpretation and to the meaning of its author's intellectual labor:

"One last word. The reader will discover, if I am not mistaken, even in the remotest corners of these essays, the heartbeats of patriotic concern. The person who writes them and the people to whom they are addressed have their spiritual origin in the denial of an outworn Spain. But denial all by itself is an impiety. When the pious and honorable man denies something, he assumes the obligation to set up a new affirmation, or at least to try to do so.

"Thus it is with us. Having denied one Spain, we find ourselves in the honorable dilemma of finding another, and honor will not let us rest until we do. Therefore, if the most intimate and personal of our meditations are explored, we will be surprised in the act of making

10 "Vejamen del orador" (1911). I, 557.

attempts at a new Spain with the humblest gleams of our souls."[11] "All my work and all my life," he said eighteen years later (when he drew up the balance sheet of his "first voyage,") "have been service to Spain. This is an incontrovertible truth, even though it may turn out that I have accomplished nothing."[12]

Attempts at a new Spain, service to Spain. And what of theory? What of strict philosophy? May it not be, as has happened so many times in our history, that the Spaniard, because he feels obliged to make his position clear with respect to his country before he embarks on creating science, doctrine, or theory, consumes his time and energy in that and never succeeds in creating the rest? Ortega's method—a natatory method, as he says in one of his favorite figures of speech—was to consist in *supporting himself in a difficult element.* His radical philosophical innovation—the adequate study of which is in large part the theme of this book—is, neither more nor less, that of converting this biographical and historical need of his—of coming to terms with his compelling circumstance—into *a method of philosophy.* In a letter written to Unamuno from Marburg, on January 27, 1907, he expresses his disappointment with the intellectual state of Germany, with the dulling of its vision, with the deficient way in which the intellectual task was realized there, owing to lack of immediacy and personality; Germany's cultural decline seemed undeniable to him. And he adds these revealing words: "You are going to laugh when I tell you that in my innocence the following thought contributed a good deal toward my launching myself on this miserable path of philosophy and scientific philosophy: 'What the devil! Wouldn't it be interesting to see how this strange business of philosophy crystallizes inside a Spanish noggin?' Like an uncle of mine who is eighty-seven years old, and every day before he has his soup says, 'Let's see how far a well-cared-for man will stretch.' I say to myself too, 'Let's see how far a philosopher-Spaniard can stretch, or what a Celtiberian noddle can get out of philosophy.' The fact is that we come to it with fresh eyes, like barbarians, to take a look at this worn-out spectacle which is only new, only renewed, when looked at by new men."

"It is only new when looked at by new men." This is the whole point. Ortega is to raise to the level of theory what he finds, what he himself

---

[11] *Meditaciones del Quijote.* I, 328.
[12] "Prólogo a una edición de sus *Obras.*" VI, 353.

is: a man lost in his Spanish circumstance, a man who does not know what to hold to. And he is going to take the matter literally: his circumstance is Spain, but it does not end there: Spain is in Europe. And Europe is—as he was to say categorically—science.[13] This is why he could have written the following paragraphs to Unamuno, at the age of twenty, and only in this context do they acquire full significance:

"You may tell me that one doesn't need to know in order to think, but I have to confess that that classically Spanish mysticism, which appears among your ideas from time to time, doesn't convince me; to me it seems to resemble moss, which gradually covers up slightly solitary souls like yours, excessively inner-directed (don't be cross with me) and preoccupied with good and evil as a sort of intellectualistic vice. Only a man of formidable intuition can make a temple with only a few bits of knowledge, with a few stones; and if he has no knowledge, he will build something anachronistic and brutal (like Mohammed). And, if he does not have that tremendous intuition, he will build only absurdities. That is what the thirty-year-old gentry have done, and what we twenty-year-olds were *starting* to do. They brought in a breath of fresh air and antiliterary life, and broke into the field of ideas like an invasion of barbarians. Something is better than nothing, of course. But I, and I say it frankly, can't squeeze myself into the role of a barbarian, and no matter how much they praise the muscles in my arms and my good color, I think I am capable of being a frank, good, just, open-air man, at the same time as I am well-informed, enthusiastic, studious, slow, and a bookworm . . . .

"Maybe there is no truth in what I am saying, but who would dare to criticize me when, not having anything better to do, I spend nine or ten hours a day over my books, and believe that if I do this for a few years, I *can* think better than if I had not done so?"[14]

Ortega's "Europeanism" is to arise out of this attitude. He will have to be a European in order to be truly a Spaniard; he will have to be a technical philosopher, in the European style, in order to be able to understand what Spain is; and as a result of this he will find a new European philosophy which is precisely, unexpectedly, *Spanish*: his own. Knowing what to hold to with respect to Spain is going to oblige him to make, permit him to make, *the Spanish interpretation of the world*.

[13] I, 100.   [14] Unamuno, "Almas de jóvenes" (in *Ensayos*, V, 16–19).

30. EUROPE AS A CONDITION OF SPAIN; SPAIN AS A EUROPEAN POSSIBILITY

"In other countries," Ortega said in Bilbao in 1910, "it may perhaps be legitimate for individuals to permit themselves fleeting abstractions of national problems: the Frenchman, the Englishman, the German live in the midst of an established social atmosphere. Their countries may not be perfect societies, but they are societies endowed with all their essential functions, and served by organisms in running condition. The German philosopher can afford to ignore (though I am not saying that he ought to) Germany's destinies: his life as a citizen is fully organized without any need for his intervention . . . . What could possibly stand in the way of the German's launching his own skiff into the sea of eternal, divine things, and spending twenty years thinking exclusively about the infinite?

"With us, things are very different; the Spaniard who attempts to escape from national preoccupations will be made prisoner by them ten times a day, and in the end will understand that for a man born between the Bidassoa and Gibraltar, Spain is the primary, plenary, and peremptory problem."[15]

And at the end of this speech, after invoking Unamuno and Costa, he finds the felicitous phrase: "Regeneration is inseparable from europeanization; this is why, as soon as the reconstructive emotion, or anguish, shame, and yearning were felt, the europeanizing idea came into being. Regeneration is the desire; europeanization is the means of satisfying that desire. Truly, it has been seen very clearly from the beginning that *Spain was the problem and Europe the solution.*"[16]

But that solution—that is, that very formula—involves no few problems. For we must ask: what is Europe? That is, in what measure, from what foreshortening does it present itself to us as a solution? And then we must still add: solution for what? I mean, for what Spain? What is the idea of Spain, Spain as a postulate, that we must attempt to reach by way of Europe? Only if all this is made clear can we understand what Ortega meant when he called for europeanization.

Very early, Ortega pointed out the lack of a "definition of Europe"[17]

---

[15] "La pedagogía social como programa político." I, 497–98.

[16] *Ibid.*, 513. Italics mine.

[17] *Ibid.*, 99.

in the usual programs calling for it. And he emphasized a fact which has often been passed over: the constant penetration of the foreign into Spain ever since the seventeenth century. For this is the paradox: since the middle of the seventeenth century, Spain had, in a certain sense, shut herself up within herself; it was the period of what Valera called "the Great Wall of China," with which Spain surrounded herself at the time of the last Hapsburgs, the "tibetanization of Spain," as Ortega liked to say, during the reign of Philip IV. Spain, whose presence extended all over the world, drew back into herself, isolated herself, broke her links with the European reality in which she was rooted. But it happened that just at that time she began to be drained of her national substance, began to become "foreignized," to imitate, to copy, not to be herself. "Is there perchance no room for hesitation," Ortega asked himself, "about what Europe is? Is it not this age-long hesitation, this not knowing from one century to another exactly what Europe is, which has kept Spain in perennial decline and annulled so many honorable, though shortsighted, hopes? Did not Spain begin in the seventeenth century to speak ill of Spain, to look about in search of the foreign, to proclaim the imitation of Italy, of France, of England? Has not all, or nearly all, foreign legislation passed bit by bit, throughout the last century, through the pages of the official Spanish *Gaceta?*"[18]

Ortega rejects the belief that Europe is the railway and the good police force, good hotels, a state with expert civil servants, trade, industry. There were no railways in the eighteenth century, and Europe was just as much Europe then as at any other period. Europe is not civilization, but *that from which all this comes.* And he arrives at the uncompromising formula: "Europe = science: all the rest is common to the rest of the planet."[19] Thus, when he speaks of europeanization, and recognizes that it is a *pedagogical* problem, he takes good care to emphasize that "the genuine, the characteristic factor in our pedagogical problem is that we first need to educate some few men of science, to arouse even the merest shadow of scientific concern, and that without this previous effort the rest of the pedagogical action will be useless, impossible, meaningless. I think that something analogous to what I have been saying could be the necessary formula for europeanization."[20]

[18] *Ibid.*
[19] *Ibid.*, 102.
[20] *Ibid.*, 103.

When he asks himself about optimism and pessimism, Ortega makes the following distinction: "European optimism and a certain provincial pessimism limited to the affairs of our country are compatible within a single heart." For if Europe is "ciencia" ["science"], Spain is "inconsciencia" ["unconsciousness"].[21] For "in Spain there is nothing but its people,"[22] says Ortega, anticipating at the age of twenty-five one of the fundamental ideas of *España invertebrada* ["Invertebrate Spain"]. We do not know where our misfortunes come from because *we have not been able to weave our own history*; we are a people of legends, and without history. The conviction that it was essential to make history, concretely that one of Spain's most urgent tasks was to make her own history, runs through Ortega's writings and all of his intellectual activity. And to a considerable degree he oriented his efforts toward the formation of a body of historians, and, in particular, created the method which he considered essential for it: *historical reason*.

His definition of Europe gradually takes shape. "Collaboration is the way of life which characterizes the Europeans."[23] And, still more rigorously: "An age-old tradition and exercise of the human factor has gradually laid down deep spiritual secretions: philosophy, physics, philology. The enormous accumulation looms likes an Asian mountain: from its summit there is a view of unlimited spaces. *That ideal height is Europe: a point of view*."[24]

What Ortega understands by europeanization now begins to be clear: "*Europe* is not only a negation: it is the start of a methodical attack on our national Philistinism. Just as Descartes employed methodical doubt in order to establish certainty, the writers of this review use the symbol of Europe as a methodical attack, as a renewing ferment which will bring to life the only possible Spain.

"Europeanization is the way to make this Spain, to purify it from all exoticism, all imitation. *Europe must save us from the 'outside.'* "[25]

This is another of those expressive and apparently paradoxical formulas, whose meaning is now transparently clear: Europe, when it becomes ours, when we reach that level, that point of view in which it consists, broadens *our* horizon, our field of vision, and thus it saves us from the

---

21 *Ibid.*, 104.
22 *Ibid.*, 105.
23 "Nueva revista" (1910). I, 143.
24 "España como posibilidad" (1910). I, 138. Italics mine.
25 "Nueva revista," I, 144–45.

"outside," from the strange and alien. It has not been realized—and this is the lamentable drama of Spanish history since its obliteration in the seventeenth century—that when a people is surrounded by stockades, there is nothing to do but peer out through the cracks. One whole aspect of our national life for three hundred years has consisted in this, in this stealthy looking out behind the backs of the guardians of a presumed "purity." And even today we must keep on defending our right and duty to make our national life something other than this.

"Today we are frenchified, anglicized, germanized," Ortega continues. "Lifeless chunks of other civilizations are being brought into our national body by a fatal current of insensibility. The fact that we import more than we export is only the commercial result of the much wider and graver fact of our having been 'foreignized.' *We are a cistern, and we ought to be a spring.* We are brought the products of culture; but the culture which is cultivation, which is labor, which is a highly personal and conscious activity, which is not a *thing*—microscope, railway, or law—remains outside us. We shall be Spaniards when we distill, through the vibration of our nerves, *human and Celtiberian substances of universal significance*—mechanics, economics, democracy, and transcendent emotions."[26]

Europe as science, as creative capacity for culture, as accumulation of efforts which rise like a mountain, a level; Europe as an *attainable* point of view—that is Spain's condition. Spain can only be what she authentically is, what she has to be, by europeanizing herself, by placing herself on that level *which is hers*, by ceasing to be, not below the level of other nations, *but below the level of herself.* "What do we care about foreign things," concludes Ortega, "the number of ethnic and historical forms that culture may take in other places? Precisely when we postulate the europeanization of Spain, we want nothing other than the obtention of a new form of culture different from French culture, different from German . . . . What we want is the Spanish interpretation of the world."[27]

But at the same time the other side of the question becomes clear to him. What is the meaning of another *European* form of culture, pre-

[26] *Ibid.*, 145. Italics, except for the word *thing*, mine.

[27] "España como posibilidad" (1910). I, 138. See also what he writes in "El *pathos* del sur": "When I speak of Europeanization, however, I do not wish in any way whatsoever to accept the German form of culture: what for? There are forty million Germans in Germany already. But that form of culture is capable of being superseded,

cisely the *Spanish* culture, different from French, English, or German culture . . . ? Does this not mean, perhaps, seen from the other side, an enrichment of Europe, a broadening of Europe, a European possibility? A quotation from Meier-Graefe, the German art critic, in his *Journey through Spain*, proves Ortega's point: "We were very much at ease in Spain," Meier-Graefe had written. "Europe is gradually becoming so small that one feels grateful for the sense of open spaces where body and spirit can move with freedom." And Ortega explains, "The only thing I am interested in here is to comment upon this general interpretation of Spain as a possibility for the immigration of European sensitivities. How? Do the Europeans need Spanish emotions? Would our Europeanism therefore be an error?"[28] And then, after replying to what he had brought up before, and affirming the possibility and necessity of this Spanish interpretation of the world, he concludes with these words, which sum up all of his thought about europeanization:

"We ask no more than this: that the European point of view fix its attention on Spain. The sordid Iberian reality will be stretched to the infinite; our realities, of no value now, will take on a weighty significance in human symbols. And the European words we have left unsaid for three hundred years will arise all at once and crystallize into a song. Europe, tired in France, exhausted in Germany, weak in England, will take on new youth under the strong sun of our land.

"Spain is a European possibility.

"Only when looked at from Europe is Spain possible."[29]

This is the briefest expression of what Ortega intended to attempt when, on his return from Germany, he was about to enter the Spanish University.

31. THINKING AS CIRCUMSTANTIALIZATION

Ortega's theory of *circumstantial thinking* is one of the keystones of his philosophy, which we shall have to study in its proper place. In this

---

or, at least, of having human breadth enriched by placing another culture beside it, as energetic, as fruitful, as progressive as itself. My ambition—I cannot content myself with less—is a Spanish culture, with a Spanish spirit. And this does not exist; for my part, I doubt whether it has ever existed. What Unamuno has called *the spirit of Spain*, in an English publication, is simply . . . *pathos* of the South, reflex movements, instincts, barbarism, Basque or Catalan physiology." I, 492.

[28] I, 137.   [29] I, 138.

chapter what interests us is merely to observe the birth of this concept: how it originated within this radical installation of Ortega's in circumstantiality, which is a basic *assumption* of his personal philosophy. There is a quite early statement of his which is highly significant: "And this is philosophy: rather than a system of crystallized doctrines, it is a discipline of inner liberation which teaches us to triumphantly liberate individual and living thought from all dogmatic bonds."[30] To think—and the young Ortega was to feel this from the outset—is precisely to establish oneself within the circumstance, to submerge oneself in it, to use it as an instrument for salvaging our own reality and thus escaping all the elements of limitation and oppression contained in that same circumstance. One can liberate oneself from one's own circumstance only by accepting it, by making it function as such, by converting it, from the prison that it was, into a means of liberation.

In Ortega's first known piece of writing, in the ingenuous, inexperienced article entitled "Glosas," which he published in the review *Vida Nueva* on December 1, 1902, at the age of nineteen, when he had just received his degree in philosophy and letters; in that article in which—with something more than a mere coincidence—the themes which he was later to define in his work abound, he said, "So, gentlemen, justice is an error of perspective; it means looking at things from afar, from the other side of life. But, is it possible to go outside of life?"[31]

The *adequate* reply to this question was to be Ortega's philosophy in its most original and creative aspect, the element which led him *from the beginning* to place himself beyond the subtlest error of contemporary European philosophy, the error which to a certain degree had rendered sterile the genius expressed in phenomenology and made it fall back into idealism.

Ortega had insisted a great deal—and we have seen this in detail—on the lack of theory which had afflicted Spanish life; and he had done so with the realization that he was exaggerating. In 1911, in an article aimed at Baroja, he wrote, "Though it is not good, in fact rather a Don Juanesque thing to do, to risk everything on one card, I continue to repeat, with meritorious insistence, that the decline of Spain consists purely and simply in a lack of science, in the absence of theory . . . . Your generation, and mine, and the coming generation all share this tempera-

[30] "Prólogo a *Pedagogía general,* etc., de Herbart" (1916). VI, 266.
[31] "Glosas" (1902). I, 14.

ment; and it is to be hoped that if we accept that interpretation of the history of Spain, reform will begin." But he took good care to add, "In fact, there is no practice without theory, or a country without men of ideas, unless we understand by a man of ideas someone who tells tall tales, in which case he is a trickster. Theory is nothing but the theory of practice, just as practice is nothing but the *praxis* of theory."[32]

At about the same date, commenting on a "criticism of the orator," precisely in the name of philosophy, Ortega defends oratory *because of its circumstantial content.* "The criticism of the orator formulated by Señor Cuartero has, I believe, seized the banner of philosophy, and indeed I think that he has gone a little further than is justified in his fierce enmity toward oratory. In my opinion, Señor Cuartera treats Demosthenes and Mirabeau with a severity which is not only excessive but historically erroneous. Because *the orator is always the man who takes accurate stock of the circumstances* . . . I am not in sympathy with the madman and the mystic: *the man who grasps the circumstances* arouses all my enthusiasm, provided that he does not forget a single one."[33]

In a more theoretical form, he had written at the early date of 1910: "There are as many realities as there are points of view. The point of view creates the panorama."[34] And *in a political speech*—I think it is essential to emphasize this (that is, the circumstantial determination of this thesis)—in "Vieja y nueva política" ["Old and New Politics"], he was to speak these words, in which he anticipated his philosophical method: "The abstract is no more than an instrument, an organ, to see the concrete clearly; its goal is in the concrete, but it is necessary. So long as the abstract idea and the concept of the unreal are synonymous for Spaniards, all attempts at rebirth will fail. For culture is nothing but that premeditated, cunning turn taken by thought—which is generalizing in nature—in order to throw the chain securely over the neck of the concrete."[35]

To do this, to do it with full reality and effectiveness, to be able to take integral possession of his Spanish circumstance and *with it* to make

[32] "Una respuesta a una pregunta" (1911). I, 214–15.
[33] "Vejamen del orador" (1911). I, 556–57. Italics mine.
[34] "Adán en el Paraíso" (1910). I, 471.
[35] I, 285.

philosophy in the strict sense—so much so, that it would allow him to *give an account* of that circumstance itself—Ortega had to go to Germany, like a medieval scholar. What did he do there? What did this journey mean—for him, for Spain, perhaps ultimately for Germany?

III.

ORTEGA AND GERMANY

When we think of Spain's intellectual relations with the rest of Europe during the nineteenth century, it is easy to fall into two errors of opposite kinds: the first, to suppose that Spain knew only France, and that she knew very little of the other countries, and those always through France; the second, after establishing a whole series of proofs of familiarity with English, German, and Italian culture, to conclude that the presence of Europe in Spain was effective. We must point out, on the one hand, the degree of penetration of these influences, their extent, their intensity, their configuration within national life and its different groups; on the other, we must keep in mind the variation in these influences throughout various stages during the nineteenth century.

France, of course, constitutes the *foreground* of the picture throughout the century. The upper classes in Spain had known the French language since the eighteenth century, and the reading of French books had always been frequent. Translations were also very numerous, partly because it was easy to find translators from French, partly because readers had formed a taste for French literature and French forms of thought, both of which had been familiar to them for some time past; added to this was the fact that the bulk of French production was known, that some Spaniards traveled to Paris, that the worldwide prestige of everything French was very high.

However, English Romanticism entered Spain very early. Walter Scott and Byron were enormously popular. A few German or Italian names managed to get into the circle of reading. But the differences between these and anything French were very great. Above all, so long as French culture was present as such, other national cultures were known only through isolated names: instead of the coast and the interior, there were only promontories which swam into view and left the rest in shadow. Moreover, whereas in the case of France a considerable *minority* knew the language, read the books directly, explored the culture, etc., only a few *individuals* knew English, and very few knew German; in other words, French culture had *arrived*; one could in some sense "be located" in it even though only as a visitor; the other cultures were known only as unconnected moments, almost always by hearsay; there could not be even minimal "installation"; the allusions made by English or German authors to their respective traditions, to the world behind their writings, awoke no echoes in Spanish readers.

About 1830, an interest in German culture began to awaken in certain small circles. From then until the middle of the century its prestige—almost always by way of French sources—was to become very great. Germany was a peaceful and tranquil country, much given to the demands of culture: philosophy, literature, and music. This was the picture which began to penetrate into Spanish minds, though, of course, sketchily and in little detail. López-Morillas has pointed out how often the epithets "cultured Germany," "learned Germany," and "erudite Germany" were used, as well as the gratitude felt toward the attention some German scholars had begun to pay to Spanish matters, especially to our classical literature, and which contrasted with the disdain felt by the French for anything outside their own culture.[1] This interest—whose bulk must not be exaggerated, however—became crystallized in the fact that in 1843 the minister Gómez de la Serna gave funds to Sanz del Río to study philosophy in Germany. What was to happen at that time was not a penetration of German culture into Spain but something quite different: the penetration of a Spanish group into German culture.

This group, a very small one certainly, is that of the Krausists: Julián Sanz del Río, Ruperto Navarro Zamorano, José Alvaro de Zafra, and Lorenzo Arrazola, initially. Their background was the law, they had read—in French—the works of Ahrens, a German professor of Göttingen who had had to leave the country for political reasons and became established in Brussels and later in Paris: the *Cours de Psychologie* and the *Cours de Droit naturel ou Philosophie du Droit*. The first of these books was the result of a course entrusted to Ahrens in Paris by Guizot, at the suggestion of Cousin, in 1834, and published in 1836–

[1] J. López-Morillas, *El krausismo español*, 85ff.

38; and its aim was to present German philosophy to the French mind, especially the philosophy of Krause,[2] who had recently died (1832).

This is especially significant. Interest in things German went along, in Spain, with a reaction against everything French. López-Morillas, in his book *El krausismo español* ["Spanish Krausism"], entitles two consecutive chapters "Germanophilia" and "Galophobia."[3] Sanz del Río's dislike for French thought, and in particular for Cousin, is well known;[4] later, Giner de los Ríos was to express himself with equal aversion.[5] But, in the first place, this was necessary even to draw away

[2] See my study "El pensador de Illescas," in *Ensayos de teoría* (1954) (*Obras*, IV).

[3] Chapters 5 and 6, pp. 85–121.

[4] In one of the *Cartas inéditas de D. Julián Sanz del Río*, written from Heidelberg on May 30, 1844, Sanz del Río refers to his visit in Paris at the end of July of the previous year, and says, "When I passed through Paris, I scarcely had time to form a clear and solid judgment on the state of philosophy in France; but though I cannot yet determine my thought fully, I shall say only that as a pure science, and an independent science, it is cultivated neither profoundly nor sincerely; there are those who work in philosophy, but subordinating it to an end which is not philosophy, but, for example, politics, social reform—and even to ignoble ends, such as vanity, etc. I visited one of the chief representatives of the science, M. Cousin, and though I would not presume in the slightest degree to judge him as a man, I will say that as a philosopher, he ended by losing even the slight degree of esteem in which I had held him before. I lament more each passing day the influence which French philosophy and science (a science of fraud and pure appearance) have had among us for more than a century: what has it brought us except laziness about working for ourselves, false learning, and above all, immorality and petulant egotism? And this is all the more lamentable when I think today that the qualities of spirit in our country are infinitely superior in profundity and regularity to those of the French, as well as the fact that, on the other hand, they do not degenerate into a tendency to useless abstraction, as in Germany." (*Cartas inéditas de Don Julián Sanz del Río* [1875], 20–21.) See "El Pensador de Illescas."

[5] In his "Consideraciones sobre el desarrollo de la literatura moderna" (1862), published in his *Estudios de literatura y arte* (Madrid, 1876), Giner points out as characteristics of French literature "superficiality and emphasis" (p. 173); "France, more interested, as we have said, in diffusing than in creating, has distinguished herself in the modern period as much by her powerful influence as by her lack of originality" (p. 176). His objections are weighty and fundamental: "No, in this sense there is no national originality in France, nor can there be. Her proper mission, to bind together and sustain the relationships and total commerce between men and peoples, takes her far from that road. Therefore she lacks social tradition, and, in order to erase it, each period rebels against the tradition which has given it being, imagining—as one philosopher says—that it has been born out of the stones; thus her institutions are rooted in an abstract empiricism, not in the harmony of reason along with the progress of political education; and so, institutions, art, science, society, everything in France is unstable, everything changes, everything is renewed every moment: and in the rapid succession of this agitated change, scarcely a vague memory remains today of what was proclaimed yesterday against all opposition" (p. 180). France, he adds a few pages later, "has

from France—nobody could think of "installation" in German culture
—and Ahrens in fact offered the promise of a "synthesis" of the Germanic and the French, a "transcendence" of French thought without completely departing from it, and ultimately without renouncing the French mentality. And, on the other hand, the Germanism of these men was so narrow that it entailed an impoverishment; I mean that it meant living in a restricted and relatively abstract area, the only one that they could really possess and control. This is one aspect which has not, I believe, been sufficiently emphasized with regard to the Krausists, to whom so many stupid objections, and almost never the most weighty ones, have been made. Be it understood, however, that I do not mean that the view of Germany held by the Krausists was partial and incomplete—in a certain sense it had to be in the beginning, if it was to be effective—but that because of their Germanism *a priori* they tended to *limit themselves* to it instead of integrating it with other dimensions of European culture in which they could have moved with more ease and in which, moreover, Spain was already installed.

Such an attitude could not prosper. And, in fact, we must point out that Krausism as a *doctrine* lasted a very short time. Let us recall some dates. Sanz del Río's journey to Heidelberg took place in 1843; in 1845, back in Spain, the minister Pidal offered him a University chair, which Sanz del Río refused because he did not think that he was sufficiently prepared; he did not hold a chair in Madrid, that of history of philosophy, until 1854; only then did the penetration of Krausism begin, in very narrow intellectual circles. Francisco de Paula Canalejas was to say later that "beginning in 1857, not before, the taste and enthusiasm, not for the Krausist philosophy, but for German philosophy, began to grow rapidly";[6] the end of 1860 was the time when the Krausist school began to exist and to achieve some currency; this is the date of the essay—not very well known—by Francisco de Paula Canalejas, "La escuela Krausista en España" ["The Krausist School in Spain"], a

---

always had a blank book where the first comer could write his ravings, and a mass of persons in all social spheres ready to raise those ravings to doctrine and, which is much worse, to incarnate them in institutions" (p. 213). The influence of women in France has been an additional disturbing factor (pp. 222–25). All this leads Giner to feel that France's long influence on our letters has been prejudicial (pp. 225–45). Elsewhere we shall see to what extent Ortega's idea of French society and history differs from Giner's.

[6] "El Panenteísmo" (in *Revista Europea*, IV, 67 [June 6, 1875], 531). Quoted in López-Morillas, 88.

commentary on two books by Sanz del Río published the same year. These were his *Analítica* ["Analytics"] and his *Ideal de la Humanidad para la vida* ["Humanity's Ideal for Life"];[7] this essay is a presentation of the school, a description of its characteristics and meaning, a résumé of the "principles and definitions" of harmonical rationalism, which Sanz del Río formulated, and which Canalejas believed were being published for the first time. After 1865 things began to get difficult for the Krausists: the campaign of the "living texts," the inclusion of *Humanity's Ideal* in the Index, the dismissal of the Krausist professors in 1867 by the minister Orovio. When, in the following year, the triumphant Revolution returned them to their chairs and they were in a sense "in power," politics outweighed doctrine; in 1869, Sanz del Río died; in 1875, after the Restoration, Orovio again dismissed the Krausists—this time with Giner de los Ríos at their head—and the Institución Libre de Enseñanza ["Free Institute of Education"] was established outside the official University.[8]

But this was not all. At about the same date the Krausist doctrine was abandoned by most of its followers and disciples. From 1875 to 1879 the *Revista Contemporánea* of José del Perojo (born in Cuba in 1852, a disciple of Kuno Fischer in Germany, died in 1908) began to broaden and modify the Krausist picture of German thought; it was the ferment of a tendency which was destined to lead to a much more complex and also more superficial view of German culture. Especially neo-Kantianism in a very broad sense, whose ascendancy was linked to that of Positivism. And it was through this process that French thought began to acquire influence again. The *Revista Europea* and the *Revista de España* contributed to the same transformation of the overall view. It can be said that after 1875, Krausism as a doctrine no longer had currency, although there persisted—more strongly than ever, in fact—the influence of an *intellectual attitude*, especially with regard to education, with peculiar political and religious shadings, through the agency of the Free Institute, which was not exclusively Krausist but attracted the collaboration of persons who were in sympathy with some of the school's qualities without feeling themselves to be linked with it. A document which is extraordinarily representative of the moment is

[7] In *Estudios críticos de filosofía, política y literatura* (1872), 135–64.

[8] See the works of Jobit and López-Morillas which I have mentioned; both take up this question in detail.

Azcárate's *Minuta de un testamento* ["Draft of a Last Will and Testament"], published in 1876.[9]

The diffusion of German culture in the broader forms postulated—but not realized—by men like Perojo, never became consolidated; knowledge of the German language continued to be rare; most of those who tried to enter that world beat a retreat when confronted by the difficulties of the language, or, in the best of cases, the doctrines. And they fell back on the habitual preference for things French, though this was less exclusive, less overwhelming than before, with a consciousness of partiality, and always looking sideways in the direction of other cultures. Think of Menéndez Pelayo's utter ignorance of anything German in his youth, in the period when he wrote the *Heterodox Thinkers*, of his disdain for "the German mists," which he would not have permitted himself—the verb is the correct one—if German culture had had some *currency* in Spain during the early years of the Restoration. In 1891, during his debate with Campoamor on metaphysics and poetry, Valera, who shows considerable admiration for Spanish Krausism—remember what I said about it before—spoke of it as something entirely outmoded. And lastly, we should not forget that whereas the Spanish Krausists felt the enormous prestige of Kantian and post-Kantian German thought, things had changed considerably by about 1875. The Positivist reaction to German idealism had restored a certain amount of prestige to French thought, and neo-Kantianism itself returned to Kant by means of a mental stance which attempted to supersede Positivism but in fact started from its assumptions.[10]

The penetration of German culture into Spain, then, was not fully realized. In 1911, Ortega referred to the Krausists' attempt by speaking of it as something belonging to a past time—therefore without any direct connection with his undertaking—and, moreover, placed it within a broader process, belonging to a situation which was also different. His words are worth recalling:

"But the most important thing . . . is Spain's cultural approach to Germany . . . . Something similar was attempted once before. In the 1870's the Krausists, the only intellectual force Spain has enjoyed during the past century, tried to submit their countrymen's intellects

[9] It was published under the title *Minuta de un testamento, por W* . . . .
[10] See my *Historia de la filosofía* (*Obras*, I): "El problema del kantismo." [English translation, *History of Philosophy*, Dover, New York, 1967.]

and hearts to German discipline. But the attempt bore no fruit because our Catholicism, which has taken on itself the representation and responsibility of Spanish history with respect to universal history, correctly saw in Krausism a declaration of the failure of Hispanic culture—and, consequently, of Catholicism as a power capable of building a people. Both fanaticisms, that of religion and that of tradition, together launched onto the battlefield that host of erudite mercenaries who had set up their encampments before the lumber rooms of the national past. Then famous volumes were published, in which it was said that Spain had possessed and still possessed all the sciences, to a degree comparable to other nations; the tale was told, and oft repeated, of supposed inventions of ours that had been taken advantage of and practically stolen by other countries. In short, the continuity of our cultural production was confirmed so that there would be no need to go out of the country in search of orientation and discipline."[11]

It is true that the Krausists were, *in the end*, heterodox; but we might ask ourselves whether it would not be still more accurate to say that in the end their adversaries succeeded in making them so; it is clear that they forced the Krausists into heterodoxy, in a double sense: by their indefensible conduct—lack of veracity, of justice, use of temporal powers, etc.—and especially by an attitude which eventually abused the name of Catholicism by invoking it to reject everything that was not to their taste, condemning equally things which were absolutely irreconcilable with Catholicism and things which were perfectly compatible with it. Imagine what the intellectual history of Spain would have been if there had been a widespread attitude similar to Valera's when he refers to Msgr. van Weddingen.[12]

As for the other aspect, the invocation of tradition, and the subsequent defense of what came to be called "Spanish science," it is too frequently forgotten that fourteen years before, Gumersindo Laverde and Menéndez Pelayo began their famous debate with Azcárate, Revilla, and—on the other side, the Thomist side—with Pidal y Mon and Padre Fonseca as well.[13] Francisco de Paula Canalejas had defended the study of

[11] "Una respuesta a una pregunta." I, 212.

[12] See above, part I, chapter 1, note 24.

[13] "Del estudio de la historia de la filosofía española" (1862), in *Estudios críticos*, etc., 196–97. See also Luis Vidart, *La filosofía española* (1866). Francisco de Paula Canalejas (1834–83), a native of Lucena (province of Córdoba), a disciple of Sanz del Río, received the doctorate in philosophy in 1858, taught in Valladolid and after

Spanish philosophy, had affirmed its existence, and had evaluated it with exemplary moderation and accuracy, as far from ill-natured negation as from irresponsible inflation:

"Let these summary indications suffice," Canalejas concludes by saying, "to demonstrate that it is feasible to construct the history of Spanish philosophy, and that although we may not find in its pages names like those of Descartes and Leibniz, others may appear which can be compared with some who are much esteemed by modern criticism; and that, although we cannot single out Spain as the cradle of one of those transformations which bear the names of Bacon, Descartes, and Spinoza, yet they offer to the thinking man original traits, tendencies worthy of being taken into account in the history of human thought, and very valuable indications about the life and destinies of this vigorous nationality.

"The undertaking was announced a few days ago: we need only a champion to come to grips with it and give it a happy outcome; and the occasion is very propitious, for just now the people least given to philosophical studies feel that the philosophical spirit is already germinating among us; and in such a supreme moment, which will have a powerful influence on the destiny of our country, it would be a wise counsel and a most useful warning, the counsel and warning which can be deduced from the history of Iberian thought in past ages."[14]

The final paragraph is extremely interesting: Canalejas exudes enthusiasm and confidence; he sees a "philosophical spirit" around him, and thinks that this is the time to revive the modest philosophical tradition of Spain. It is obvious that he is not thinking of selling out the past, of repudiating it, of uprooting himself from it, but of piously recovering and evaluating it, without "taking it for granted" either.

For all these reasons, which in detail are very complex,[15] Krausist doctrine quickly dissolved, and there is a long hiatus in the intellectual approach to Germany. In 1934, when he looked back on his student years in that country and on the function he had exercised with regard to German culture, Ortega said: "When I was twenty years old, Spain

1862 in Madrid, held the chair in general literature (1863) and history of philosophy (1872). Very little has been written about this interesting figure in Spanish thought of the nineteenth century; see Jobit, *Les Éducateurs de l'Espagne contemporaine*, II, 9–12.

[14 Source not given in original.]

[15] I refer the reader once more to the books by Jobit and López-Morillas.

was enormously influenced by French ideas and forms. Add to this a slight influence of certain English things. From Germany there was scarcely anything. The famous Spanish Krausism has been mentioned. But the Spanish Krausists were, as the expression goes, excellent persons and poor musicians. They have influenced Spanish life considerably, and in a noble sense, but of Germany they knew only Krause. They did not even have clear ideas about Kant or Krause's Romantic contemporaries. The reader will understand that to find oneself in a desert with the far from representative Krause, all by himself, without precedents, without consequences, without concomitants, is an excruciatingly comic scene."[16]

The last quarter of the nineteenth century witnessed the dissolution of this attempt at intellectual germanization. Things French took over again, though they had to share their influence with *slight* penetrations by other cultures. Knowledge of the German language did not take root. The *basis* of the formation of Spanish intellectuals was French—remember Unamuno's scornful references to "the green pottery of Alcan"; [*] the basic assumptions were French, and so were the great bulk of the reading, and the great admirations, and the really imitable, that is, the effective, models. Only Ganivet and Unamuno, as we have seen, broadened the intellectual horizon to the ends of Europe, and seasoned this with a new wave of aversion for France. Unamuno, always inclined to extremes, seems to prefer anything else, and places French authors behind English ones (especially poets and Anglican theologians), Scandinavians (Kierkegaard and Ibsen), Italians (Carducci), Portuguese (Antero do Quental, Guerra Junqueiro, Oliveira Martins), Americans (William James, Walt Whitman, Oliver Wendell Holmes). But with all this, something essential was lacking in these authors which could make effective the incorporation of Spain into Europe and the assimilation by Spain of European culture; something which Ortega was to miss from the age of twenty.

33. ORTEGA'S FRENCH FORMATION

Before we go into detail about Ortega's relations with Germany, a

---

[16] "Prólogo para alemanes" (1934) (Madrid, 1958), 25.

[* Translator's note: a reference to the green covers of a certain French publishing house.]

relationship so intense, so well known and, as yet, so inaccurately measured, we must point out something previous and of great importance, the background against which his "Germanism" stands outlined, and which explains and justifies it: his previous French formation and the preservation, to the end of his life, of a very close link with everything French.

In his first adolescent article he spins off a number of names. Who are they? Victor Hugo and Ponsard, Taine, Sarcey, Barbey d'Aurevilly, Sainte-Beuve, Poe, Nietzsche, Carlyle: six Frenchmen, one German, one Englishman, and one American. In his youthful articles, references to French culture pile up thick and fast: Flaubert, Stendhal, Chateaubriand, Remy de Gourmont, Maeterlinck, Mérimée, the Comtesse de Noailles—"I know only four things about her, and that is no little: she is a woman, she is young, she is beautiful, and she is Greek"[17]— Barrès, Gobineau, Renan, Dom Leclerq, Cézanne, Ribot, Bergson, Descartes, Charcot, Debussy, Balzac, Gautier, Père Duchesne, Montaigne, Rabelais, Pascal, Voltaire, Thierry, Michelet, Comte, Zola, Maupassant, Courbet, Corot, Manet, Poussin, Verlaine, Mirabeau .... Ortega's library contained thousands of French books: he had read the philosophers, the poets, the novelists, the politicians, the historians, the authors of memoirs, the travelers.

Undoubtedly, Chateaubriand, Barrès, and Renan exercised the strongest influences on the young Ortega. "I have maintained," he wrote in 1911, "a great love for those French literary figures in whose works I have learned to write, for lack of national teachers. I believe that in the novel, as in painting, they have established a new artistic technique which without them would have waited another century to be discovered: realism in the manner of Flaubert, and Manet's impressionism represent the most accurate, most vigorous, and most admirable aesthetic posture invented by man up to the present day. In a lesser degree, from Chateaubriand to Barrès and from Ingres to Cézanne, many other laudable attempts can be found to give striking and imperishable form to human things—namely, passions and ideas."[18] The name of Chateaubriand, especially as a master of expression—I shall have something to say later about his influence on Ortega's style—appears many times in his pages. He wrote on Barrès at more length twice: on *Colette*

[17] "El rostro maravillado" (1904). I, 34.
[18] "Alemán, latín y griego" (1911). I, 208.

Baudoche and again when Barrès died.[19] He was also to dedicate an entire article to Anatole France.[20] We constantly find the philosophers, especially Descartes and Comte, throughout his work. As for Renan, we must say a word about him here.

"The works of Renan have been with me since my childhood," wrote Ortega in 1909. "On many occasions they have served me as a spiritual water-brook, and more than once have calmed certain metaphysical sorrows which attack young hearts made sensitive by solitude."[21] In this long article, "Renan," in one entitled "La teología de Renan" ["The Theology of Renan"] published a year later, in innumerable references in his early writings, which become more widely spaced as Ortega advances in years, we see the name and figure of a man who, as Ortega sadly said, was at that time almost always put in the same bracket with Taine: "Nothing is more saddening than to hear those two names constantly linked: Taine and Renan. To put on the crowning touch of sadness, I do not know what choice of euphony has placed such a disparate pair in that order."[22] Ortega retained his love for Renan's works, but realized their limitations: of the *Histoire du peuple d'Israël* and the *Origines du Christianisme* he wrote: "Both of Renan's historical works are ruins. But they have fallen nobly, as classical buildings fall in spite of being classic; and today they are living ruins, where we can and do go on a spiritual pilgrimage, sure of unchanging wisdom." And of their author he says that "Renan was a literary man, and perhaps literature did a little damage to the integrity of his scientific conscience. But so very little! For all that, Renan—though he is a second-rate figure in the great perspective of the history of culture—knew how to graft his creative gifts onto the deep, sacred, virgin, gloomy, difficult woods which are the nursery of humanity. Renan, though he never succeeded in inventing an idea—invention was not characteristic of him—did have a thorough apprenticeship in the study of those who produced great works. He was not an original philosopher, but he did drink deeply of the disciplinary problems of scholarship."[23]

Ortega does not accept the claim Renan made when he said: "I want

---

[19] "Al margen del libro *Colette Baudoche*, de Maurice Barrès" (1910). I, 464–68. "Maurice Barrès" (1923). IV, 437–41.

[20] "Leyendo *Le Petit Pierre*, de Anatole France" (1919). II, 223–28.

[21] "Renan." I, 438.

[22] I, 88.

[23] I, 89.

written on my tomb, *Veritatem dilexi*, I have loved the truth." What Renan wants is *to live in zigzags*; he does not go from one truth to another but from a truth to a lie, from a lie to another truth, "and for him neither the point of arrival nor the point of departure is the important thing, but instead this indecisive movement itself, from one extreme to the other."[24] It is the world of the *verisimilar*. And Ortega adds: "Now we can correct Renan's epitaph with the respect and piety owed to the dead; and instead of *Veritatem dilexi*, as he wanted, we can write *Verisimilitudinem dilexit*."[25] And after extracting from this statement its positive sense as well as its limitations, Ortega concludes: "The reader should not forget that I am describing Renan's spirit based on the recollection of reading him some time ago:[26] I cannot be documentally sure of the correctness of what I attribute to him, and still less should it be thought that I share his convictions."[27]

"I owe a great deal, then, to France," Ortega was to write in 1934, "and feel that French influence was very beneficial for Spain at its proper time. This is being said by one who is experienced in 'resistance,' in 'independence.' But what's to be done about it! This is what I think."[28] And then he goes on: "I was saying that at the age of twenty I was submerged in the liquid element of French culture, diving into it so deeply that I had the impression that my foot was touching bottom, and that, *at least for the time being*, Spain could draw no further nourishment from France. This made me turn to Germany, about which there were only the vaguest notions in my country."[29]

The first part of this statement—Ortega's permeation by French culture—is sufficiently documented; the second—his impression of inadequacy—can also be documented; I mean that this impression goes back a long way, proceeds in fact from his youthful years, and was very forcefully expressed; as for the third part of the statement—his orientation toward Germany—we shall have to determine its meaning.

Two articles of 1911, "Alemán, latín y griego" ["German, Latin, and Greek"] and "Problemas culturales" ["Cultural Problems"], state the question sharply. In France a league had been formed for the

[24] "Renan." I, 446.
[25] *Ibid.*, 448.
[26] In 1909; that is, when Ortega was twenty-six.
[27] "Renan." I, 463.
[28] *Prólogo para alemanes* (1934), 25.
[29] *Ibid.*, 29.

defense of French language and culture; a danger of "germanization" was felt; the French language, it was said, was threatened with the loss of its qualities. Ortega took advantage of this circumstance to state his most serious objections to the French culture of the early twentieth century. "Culture," he says, "is something more than that, more than the form of human passions and ideas; it is the creation of new passions and new ideas."[30] This has not been present in nineteenth-century France; there has been a proliferation of formal inventions, accompanied by a diminution of sensitivity for *things themselves*; a predominance of adjectives over substantives; French culture is decadent, which does not mean it is to be scorned. For Spaniards it is a serious matter: "We are like a dying man somebody has offered to teach to dance . . . . *Pardon*, we want to live, to live elemental life, to breathe air, walk, see, hear, eat, love, and hate. We need the exact opposite of what France can offer us: a culture of passions and ideas, not of forms. We need an introduction to essential life."[31]

And, in a marvelous study on the French language, Ortega protests the fact that people say there are human things, the most precious ones, which cannot be expressed. "Whatever is human is what is articulated, expressive; the inexpressible is the infrahuman." "Truly human things are clear, precise, expressible, communicable; in other words, only by means of expression can thinking, feeling, loving reach that ripeness and maturity which we call culture. A very powerful spirit will create a multiform and stimulating language; a poor spirit, a sickly, crawling language, devoid of morality or energy."[32] French "was a marvelous instrument, a tawny old violin, from whose narrow-waisted and baroque body humanity had extracted many exemplary tones."[33] And he names a few: the Montaigne tone, the Rabelais tone, the Descartes tone, the Voltaire tone, the Mirabeau tone, the Chateaubriand tone. At the end of the essay: "Language tries out the magnificent new period, but it realizes that it cannot arch up by itself: it is supported on memory, on legend. The language ceases to be original: it lives largely on memory; Romanticism is archaism."[34] And this happens because the French soul

---

[30] "Alemán, latín y griego." I, 208.

[31] *Ibid.*, 209.

[32] "Problemas culturales" (1911). I, 540–41.

[33] *Ibid.*, 541.

[34] *Ibid.*, 542.

has gone down the slope of archaism and conservatism; and the French language "has been intelligent enough to give a name to its decline, and has called it decadentism."[35] Ortega again calls for *an introduction to essential life*; it is what he does not find in France, which offers the *nuance* instead of the essential, *brioches* instead of bread. Spain, naturally, *but France too*, needs something else. This is what I wanted to emphasize: it is not that Ortega is proposing that Spain turn from one influence to another, but that both France and Spain should go to the sources which can revive their cultures in the necessary way. They will have to turn toward Germany, absorb Germanism; but in the same line in which Ortega says this he adds that "Germanism will have to be superseded," and repeats, "it will have to be superseded; that is not its position today." "Germanic culture," he concludes, "is the sole introduction to essential life." But before he signs the article he still has five more words to add: "But this is not enough."[36]

34. ORTEGA'S GERMAN EXPERIENCE

Ortega had received his degree in philosophy and letters in 1902—the same year in which he began to write for the public; in 1904 he received the doctorate with a thesis on a historical subject: "Los terrores del año mil. Crítica de una leyenda." ["The Terrors of the Year 1000. Critique of a Legend"].[37] (The faculty of philosophy and letters was not yet divided into sections.) Up to that time he had not had particularly close contact with German thought. The only presence he felt closely was undoubtedly Nietzsche, who had achieved wide circulation in Spain ever since the Generation of 1898.[38] Quotations from Nietzsche, references to ideas of his, are frequent in all of Ortega's work, beginning with his first article in 1902. Maeztu, who was very much a Nietzschean in his early years, was undoubtedly the person who oriented him toward Nietzsche. In June, 1908, Ortega wrote to him: "Years ago—do you

[35] *Ibid.*, 543.

[36] "Alemán, latín y griego." I, 209–10.

[37] José Ortega y Gasset, *Los terrores del año mil. Crítica de una leyenda*. Thesis written to fulfill the requirements for the degree of doctor in the faculty of philosophy and letters, in Madrid, 1904. Printed by Establecimiento tipográfico de El Liberal, Marqués de Cubas 7, 1909, 58 pages. It is composed of two parts: "Notas sobre los legendarios terrores del año mil" (pp. 2–52) and "La leyenda" (pp. 53–58).

[38] See Guillermo Díaz-Plaja, *Modernismo frente a Noventa y ocho* (1951), 175ff.

remember?—we used to enjoy setting our imaginations aflame over a page of Nietzsche, and as that chatterer of genius has the gift of all the Sophists to flatter the reader and make him conceited, the suspicion may have occurred to us after reading him that maybe there was something in the two of us of those great men who make history, isolated and adamantine, beyond good and evil. A remembrance of that time, so pleasant and so devoted, often sweeps over me. But in the end we emerged from the torrid zone of Nietzsche, whom, of course, we badly misinterpreted then: today we are two ordinary men for whom the ethical world exists."[39] And in another article written the following month he repeats the same thing on a different plane, less personally, with greater strictness and an effort at interpretation: and after this beginning, he sketches out a first critical view of Nietzsche; that is, a judgment of his influence from outside. A few paragraphs are worth keeping in mind:

"Those of us who are not too old at this juncture have let ourselves be led since childhood to a superfluous and tenacious traffic with the things of the spirit; we find in the recollection of our eighteenth year a warm atmosphere, like an African sun, which burned the walls of our inner dwelling. That was our 'Nietzschean period': it was the time when, cheerfully laden with the fragrant wineskins of our youth, we crossed the torrid zone of Nietzsche. Later we arrived at regions with a softer and more fruitful climate, where we cooled our overheated spirits with the waters from some perennial classic fountain, and all that is left of that district of ideas we crossed, all burning sand and fiery wind, is the memory of an unbearable and unwarrantable heat.

"And yet, we should not be ungrateful. Nietzsche was necessary for us . . . . Nietzsche made us proud. There was a moment in Spain—shameful to say!—when the only plank on which we could save ourselves from cultural shipwreck, from the torrent of Philistinism that day after day washed over our nation, was Pride. Thanks to him a few youngsters could inoculate themselves against the all-embracing epidemic which saturated the national air . . . . Those young Spaniards had to believe that Spain had been born with them, that they had come upon this earth by spontaneous generation, with no help from their ancestors, and, consequently, without the diseased inheritance of what had gone before. Pride moved them to seek a standard that matched their own

39 "¿Hombres o ideas?" (1908). I, 436.

energies, to excavate out of the unyielding earth an estuary through which they could flow freely, without contagion, repudiating the traditional standards and worn-out channels.

"But things have gone somewhat better since, and the spiritual atmosphere of Spain has improved a little .... It is, therefore, a good time to correct our former formation and to rearrange the youthful strata of our souls. Let us agree that history began quite a number of centuries before our arrival ...."[40]

Nietzsche's *torrid* influence, good for self-affirmation, for overcoming Philistinism, was influence on an eighteen-year-old; by the age of twenty-five Ortega had recovered from the old ardor and the old self-sufficient pride. Let us keep the figures, that is, the ages, in mind.

In 1905, Ortega decided to go to Germany, specifically to the University of Leipzig. He has described it deliciously more than once: "A few years ago I went out one day fleeing from the rampant Philistinism of my country, and like a medieval scholar I arrived on another day in Leipzig, famous for its bookstores and its university. According to the custom there, I had an advertisement put in the papers asking for exchange of conversation with a student.

"Among the various offers I received was one from Max Funke, *studiosus rerum naturalium et linguarum orientalium*. His seemed the most picturesque of the offers, and I accepted it. One afternoon Max Funke himself arrived; he was a young man of my age, a Saxon, as brachycephalic as it is possible to be, with wide nostrils and rosy cheeks.

"How can I forget you, Max Funke! How can I forget the walks we took, on frigid winter afternoons, through the Rosenthal, the Valley of Roses, that enormous park, where there were long meadows of greenish black grass, paths of dark-colored earth, tall sleeping trees with their trunks greenish from humidity, flocks of cawing crows, and not one single rose!"[41]

It was the same Rosenthal where, at the age of fifteen, Leibniz had walked, meditating on whether to preserve substantial forms: "Et je me souviens que je me promenai seul dans un bocage auprès de Leipsic, appelé le Rosenthal, à l'âge de quinze ans, pour délibérer si je garderais les formes substantielles."[42]

---

[40] "El sobrehombre" (1908). I, 91–92.
[41] "Una primera vista sobre Baroja" (1910). *El Espectador*, I. II, 116.
[42] Letter to Nicolas Rémond, January 10, 1714.

Many years later Ortega recalled his stay in Leipzig: "I had studied in Leipzig for one semester. There I had my first desperate hand-to-hand combat with the *Critique of Pure Reason*, which offers such enormous difficulties to a Latin brain; there . . . that is, seated on a bench in the zoo, in front of the Canadian elk, which was roaring, at that spring season, threatening the sky with its moist muzzle. A few cages farther along, the elephant, with great patience—'genius is patience'—was letting a keeper file a callus off his forehead. I had already read that the elephant was the Indian symbol for the god of philosophy. The elephant is a philosopher and presses his forehead against the bars of his cage, which is the most a creature can do. That is why he gets a callus. And I was getting one too, making dashes against the bars of the *Critique of Pure Reason* that spring, while deep inside the zoo the ducks chased each other around the pond with wild quacks, busy with their indecent necessities."[43]

In 1909, in an article entitled "Una fiesta de paz" ["A Feast of Peace"], which I have already quoted, Ortega commemorated the fifth centenary of this University of Leipzig, which "has been one of the wombs where the present reality of Germany was engendered." He evoked the "Augusteum" of Leipzig and pointed out the ideal and peaceful mission of the university: "For five centuries the teachers and pupils of Leipzig have lived in the community of that ideal: physical nature, the classical and oriental past, theology, jurisprudence, mathematics, art completely filled their spirits. None of these can be eaten, paid for, kissed: they are like the districts of the divine mystic Jerusalem that the prophets saw reflected in the twilight clouds above the earthly Jerusalem."[44]

In March, 1906, Ortega visited Nuremberg, and his first article on a German subject dates from that time. It was "Las fuentecitas de Nuremberga" ["The Fountains of Nuremberg"], published in *El Imparcial* on June 11. A few pages filled with contentment, with appreciation of past and present, with enthusiasm for an idealism which carries with it no hostility toward the real, but on the contrary, "so fervent a love of reality that we take this reality into ourselves; and, absorbed into our innermost parts, it gives us a sort of quintessential humor which, as it flows from artery to artery and vein to vein, moves us to see every-

---

43 *Prólogo para alemanes*, 32–33.
44 "Una fiesta de paz." I, 126.

thing as divinely constructed and makes us detect a transcendent aroma in things."[45]

"The following semester," continues Ortega in 1934, "I went to Berlin. I lived on a very small Spanish government grant which I had obtained by competition.[46] At that time the peseta was moribund, and when my grant passed the frontier, it shrank so much that I could eat, from time to time, only in the 'Aschinger' automats. On the other hand, I had the libraries, where my voracity was satisfied."[47]

Since Ortega never wrote anything lightly, we should keep in mind the reference to libraries and the lack of reference to the university. The absence of scientific books in Spain was at that time desperate. If we read Ortega's articles in 1908, "Pidiendo una biblioteca" ["Ordering a Library"], and "Asamblea para el Progreso de las Ciencias" ["Assembly for the Progress of the Sciences"],[48] we will see how deeply he deplored this situation. Ortega went to Germany, largely, to read nine or ten hours a day, to absorb thousands of books which could not be found in Spain. When we speak of his experiences in the German university, we do not think so much of courses as of libraries and seminars. This is especially true of Berlin. "When I studied in Berlin in 1906," he wrote in 1933, "there was no great figure of philosophy in any of the chairs in that university. *As chance had it*, Dilthey had stopped giving lectures in the university building some years before, and admitted for his teaching, which he did in his own house, only a few especially well-prepared students. This *chance* was responsible for my not meeting him personally."[49] This surprises many people today, though in itself it is rather amusing, for it would have been surprising indeed if a Spanish lad of twenty-three who was spending a few months in Berlin had got into the elderly Dilthey's inner circle in search of a philosophy that no one suspected at the time, not even those who lived

[45] "Las fuentecitas de Nuremberga" (1906). This essay was not included in the first edition of *Obras completas*. See 2nd ed., I. Also in *Notas*, 7–15.

[46] A stipend of 4,500 pesetas, granted on June 6, 1906, "to pursue studies abroad" from October 1, 1906, to September 30, 1907. Ortega wrote a memoir entitled "Descartes y el método transcendental," which was read in the session of October 26, 1908, in the Zaragoza Congress of the Spanish Association for the Advancement of the Sciences. (Published in Vol. VI, Ciencias Filosóficas [Madrid, 1910], 5–13. Ortega is described there as holder of a chair in the Upper Normal School.)

[47] *Prólogo para alemanes*, 33.

[48] I, 81 ff. and 99ff.

[49] "Guillermo Dilthey y la idea de la vida" (1933). VI, 171.

PART ONE: *The Gerfalcon*

in the same city with him. When we think of the number of people who attended Ortega's courses in Madrid, during the quarter-century of his regular teaching career at the University, and of how long it takes people to realize what is being written or taught, it is rather curious to see the criterion with which some authors with scientific pretensions look on this point of Ortega's relations with Dilthey. But we shall have to return to this later, and in more detail.

Georg Simmel was also teaching in Berlin. He was probably Ortega's only teacher of philosophy in Berlin: "The man with the subtlest mind in Europe around 1910, Georg Simmel, used to say—I have heard him many times, for he was my teacher early in the century . . . ."[50] In 1918, Ortega calls him "that most celebrated professor";[51] he adds that he spoke "with the keenness that is peculiar to him, more subtle than profound, more clever than expressive of genius." And in 1910, when he enumerated the men who ought to be invited to give lectures in Spain, he named as "great thinkers" Bergson, Croce, and Simmel.[52] Subtle and clever rather than profound or a man of genius: could Simmel, whom Ortega always admired so much, be the "introducer of essential culture"? Let us not forget that we are speaking of 1906: Simmel had not yet written his *Sociologie*—whose translation into Spanish was arranged by Ortega—nor the *Hauptprobleme der Philosophie*, nor the *Philosophische Kultur*, nor his books on Goethe, Rembrandt, and Kant, nor, of course, *Lebensanschauung*. His work was still very slim: a thesis on the essence of matter in Kant, a study on social differentiation, the *Einleitung in die Moralwissenschaft*, *Die Probleme der Geschichtsphilosophie*, *Philosophie des Geldes*, and, published in that same year of 1906, the book *Schopenhauer und Nietzsche* which Ortega praised in a commentary. Could this satisfy Ortega's needs in Germany?

The third stage of his German experience was the decisive one: Marburg. From the end of 1906 to the end of 1907 or early 1908, Ortega spent a whole year in Marburg an der Lahn. He returned once more, already holder of the chair of metaphysics in the University of Madrid and recently married, in 1911. His first son was born there, and Ortega gave him the name of Miguel Germán.[53] This was his true

---

[50] "En la Institución Cultural Española de Buenos Aires" (1939). VI, 235.
[51] I, 92.
[52] I, 40.

university experience; here he had teachers: Hermann Cohen and, secondarily, Paul Natorp, the two figures of neo-Kantianism. His stay in Marburg was to leave a very deep impression on Ortega, not only intellectually, not only in the sense of philosophical formation, but personally. That was where Ortega lived German life with ultimate intensity, in the tranquil retreat of the little university city. It was where he reflected upon his previous impressions and interpreted them, where he made certain decisive judgments. Ortega was of the opinion that only one's second stay in a country is truly illuminating and instructive, that only on a second visit can one see the other side of things, realize their limitations, and with those limitations their true shape. What did Marburg represent for Ortega?

35. MARBURG AS "LEVEL"

Although other mentions of Germany from Ortega's pen are relatively abstract, when Marburg comes to his mind, we always observe an intimate closeness, a concretion of vivid details, a special way of focusing his ideas on perceptive impressions, a tendency to describe, which is the sign of a profound feeling of identification. Ortega stayed, studied, even resided, in other places in Germany; in Marburg he *lived*. He could not say of Marburg, in the words of Antonio Machado "but there is no thread that memory knots to the heart."

"Permit me," he wrote in 1915, "to place a private memory before you at this point. Because of personal circumstances, I can never look at the landscape around El Escorial without glimpsing vaguely, like the pattern in a cloth, the landscape of another town, far away and as little like El Escorial as it is possible to imagine. It is a little Gothic city set beside a gentle dark river, ringed with round hills completely covered by dense forests of birch and pine, light-colored beeches, and splendid box trees.

"This is the city where I passed the midpoint of my youth: I owe to it at least half my hopes and almost all my discipline. This town is Marburg, on the banks of the Lahn.

"But I was remembering. I remembered that some four years ago I

[53] *Prólogo para alemanes,* 33–34. Ortega says, "Around 1908, I spent a whole year in Marburg . . . ." But he is referring, at most, to the length of that first stay there; he may have written "until 1908."

spent a summer in that Gothic town beside the Lahn .... I shall never forget those nights when the faraway black sky above the woods filled with bright and restless stars, quivering like babies' flesh."[54]

Always the circumstantial evocation. If in Leipzig it is the cold Rosenthal without its roses, in Berlin the "Aschinger" automats where one could eat for a few pfennigs, in Marburg it is the charm of the old city, with its summer landscape among the forests—undoubtedly these are present in the forest Ortega described "vitally" in the *Meditations on Quixote*, inaugurating a new way of knowing reality[55]—the winter vision of the snow-covered fields, of conversation and friendship: "In his humble attic room in Marburg, at the very top of that steep city, the admirable Nicolai Hartmann plays his cello. I am listening to him. We are twenty-two or twenty-three years old. The always moving voice of the cello, almost like a male human voice, makes its turns and evolutions in the air like a swallow. Through the tiny window I can see the town, which clings to the flank of the hill, descending to the valley, where the Lahn flows by, always singing its wordless song."[56] And later on: "Yes, reader, it is true. I have studied in Marburg and in Leipzig and in Berlin. I have studied deeply, frantically, without reservations and without husbanding my efforts— for three years I was a pure Celtiberian flame that burned, that threw off sparks of enthusiasm inside the German university. I have argued about Kant and Parmenides with Nicolai Hartmann, with Paul Scheffer, with Heinz Heimsoeth; often till midnight, on walks along the snowy road that ended in a level crossing as the express train from Berlin passed, monstrous, its red lamps bloodying for a moment the spotless snow."[57]

Marburg had been for some years the place where German philosophy had attained the greatest intensity. This was true not only because of the quality of the professors in that university, but because of the fact that a philosophical *school* had been established there, one of the two neo-Kantian schools—the other was the School of Baden, which was much less compact.[58] It is not a question of a *general* overvaluation

---

[54] "Meditación del Escorial" (1915). *El Espectador*, VI. II, 552–53.

[55] See my Commentary on *Meditaciones del Quijote* (Madrid, 1957), 285ff.

[56] *Prólogo para alemanes*, 19–20.

[57] *Ibid.*, 23–24.

[58] The School of Baden, or *Süddeutsche Schule*, also dominated by the influence of Kant, was oriented much more toward problems of history and culture. The "philosophy

of the school, but merely a *circumstantial* one; philosophy, as we saw in chapter 2 of the Introduction, had become lost in Europe after the Positivist invasion; about the year 1870, and also later, there had been an effort to recover it, to reestablish the level of philosophical thought, properly speaking. This could only be done effectively through the accumulation of effort, through the progressive superposing of "layers," or strata, which a philosophical school implies. It is to be noted that the most intense and valuable intellectual efforts made in the nineteenth century remained relatively sterile and inoperative so long as they were not gathered up and given strength in a school. Compare the fate of Nietzsche with that of Brentano, the total absence of *immediate* consequences of Kierkegaard or Gratry, the tenuousness of Maine de Biran's or Dilthey's influence.

The principal figure in the School of Marburg was Hermann Cohen (1842–1918), who taught at that university from 1876, the year in which he succeeded Lange, until 1912, when he went to Berlin. Ortega knew him in the last years of his professorship at Marburg, when he had already published his books on Kant (*Kants Theorie der Erfahrung, Kants Begründung der Ethik, Kants Begründung der Aesthetik,* the *Kommentar zu Immanuel Kants Kritik der reinen Vernunft*), was finishing his *System der Philosophie,* of which the first two parts, *Logik der reinen Erkenntnis* and *Ethik des reinen Willens* had already appeared, and was working on his *Aesthetik des reinen Gefühls,* where some slight influence of conversations with his pupil Ortega can be observed.[59]

Cohen was a Jew, one of the most relevant figures in the Jewish intellectual community before World War I, a man with an energetic personality, who dominated the school—that is why he was able to establish it—thanks to a *temperament* which is reflected in Ortega's memories of him. The first reference to Cohen in Ortega's work is full

of values" (*Wertphilosophie*) was much cultivated there; this should not be confused with the "theory of values" (*Werttheorie*), of phenomenological inspiration, whose chief representatives were to be Scheler and Nicolai Hartmann. The great figures of the School of Baden were Wilhelm Windelband (1848–1915), the great historian of philosophy, and Heinrich Rickert (1863–1936), whose most important studies refer to the theory of the natural and historical sciences, or "sciences of culture."

[59] See "Meditación del Escorial," II, 552–53. See also the frequent references to Cervantes in Hermann Cohen's *Aesthetik des reinen Gefühls* (1912), II, especially pp. 112–23.

of admiration and friendly feeling: "At that time Hermann Cohen, one of the greatest philosophers alive today, was writing his *Aesthetics*. Like all great creators, Cohen is of modest temperament, and enjoyed discussing with me subjects relating to beauty and art. The problem of what 'novel' meant as a genre was especially what gave rise to a combat of ideas between us. I spoke to him of Cervantes. And then Cohen interrupted his work to reread the *Quixote*. I shall never forget those nights when the faraway black sky above the woods filled with bright and restless stars, quivering like babies' flesh. I would go to my teacher's home, and find him bent over our book, translated into German by the Romantic writer Tieck. And almost always, when he raised his noble face, the venerable philosopher greeted me with these words: 'But, my dear fellow! This Sancho always uses the same word that Fichte makes the basis of his philosophy.' Quite so: Sancho does indeed often use this word, and when he uses it it fills his mouth: 'hazaña' ['deed'], which Tieck translated *Tathandlung*: an act of will, of decision."[60]

"Hermann Cohen," recalled Ortega at the same time, "told me that he always took advantage of his stays in Paris to go to the synagogue and watch the gestures of the Spanish Jews."[61] And the following year, another small, delicious personal reminiscence: "I recall that the great Hermann Cohen could not abide my not being able to abide Goethe's *Elective Affinities*."[62] But in addition to this, Ortega was conscious of closed-mindedness in Marburg, of impermeability, even in Cohen himself: "In 1907—I am sure of it, with no more likely error than a very slight one serving rather to confirm the veracity of the information —there was not one single philosopher in Germany, among the predominant figures of the time, who had read Bergson. And I never succeeded in getting the great Hermann Cohen to read him, in spite of the fact that Bergson was of his own race."[63] And, still within German thought and the same language, *à propos* of Brentano, who lived in Zürich during his last years: "In Toledo I had occasion to introduce to Einstein this exemplary figure of a thinker, whom he had never come to know, and for the same reasons as mine, in spite of the fact that they lived in the same city. I still recall that in 1911, when I asked Cohen about his contemporary, I

[60] II, 552–53.
[61] "Estética en el tranvía" (1916). *El Espectador*, I. II, 32.
[62] "Para la cultura del amor" (1917). *El Espectador*, II. II, 138.
[63] *Prólogo para alemanes*, 48.

could get nothing out of him but this sentence: 'It cannot be denied that he is a keen intelligence.' All my devotion and gratitude for Marburg are inexorably counterbalanced by the efforts I made to open it up, and make it sail out of its isolation toward the open sea."[64] It should be recalled that, in fact, in the volume published in 1907, *Systematische Philosophie* in *Die Kultur der Gegenwart*, Bergson's name shines by its absence, and the same happens to Brentano's. And yet some pretend incredulity when Ortega says that he had no personal contact with Dilthey during his youthful semester in Berlin . . . .

Besides Cohen, Paul Natorp was in Marburg; he was a generation younger (1854–1924), very specially oriented toward social pedagogy, famous for his studies on Kant and Plato and on the School of Marburg itself. He was much less energetic than Cohen; he combined great erudition with a decided "school" spirit which imposed neo-Kantian patterns on all systems. Ortega referred to this "humorously" once, in spite of the seriousness of the matter: "This Natorp, who was a very good man, simple and affectionate, with the soul of a turtledove and a mane of hair like a Robinson Crusoe, committed the cruelty of keeping Plato shut up in a dungeon for twelve or fourteen years, feeding him on bread and water, putting him to the most awful tortures in order to oblige him to declare that he, Plato, had said exactly the same thing as Natorp."[65] Figures of lesser importance who also belonged to the School of Marburg were Stammler, Vorländer—in 1921, Ortega wrote the prologue for the Spanish translation of his *History of Philosophy*—and, especially, Ernst Cassirer (1875–1945), who in many senses went beyond neo-Kantianism and whose last years were spent teaching in the United States (Yale, Columbia), where he wrote in English.

What did Marburg represent early in the twentieth century? Ortega spoke at length about this in a text which is decisive for his biography and especially for the part Germany played in it. This was the prologue for Germans I have already mentioned, which he wrote in 1934—I heard him read long exerpts from it from the chair of metaphysics in Madrid—intended for a new German edition of *El tema de nuestro tiempo* ["The Theme of Our Time"], and which was never published because, Ortega said, "the events in Munich in 1934 repelled me so much that I sent a telegram forbidding its publication."[66] I shall have

[64] "La metafísica y Leibniz" (1926). III, 433.
[65] *Prólogo para alemanes*, 48.　　　　　　　　[66] *Ibid.*, 13

to return to this piece of writing in other contexts; now I wish only to recall some of the traits of the "physiognomy," if the word serves, of Marburg and of Hermann Cohen:

"Marburg was the stronghold of neo-Kantianism. One lived inside neo-Kantian philosophy as within a besieged citadel, in a perpetual state of 'Who goes there!' Everything around it was felt to be a mortal enemy: the Positivists and the psychologists, Fichte, Schelling, Hegel. They were considered so hostile that they were not even read. In Marburg nobody read anything but Kant, and, previously translated into Kantianism, Plato, Descartes, and Leibniz. Certainly these four names are famous, but it is not possible to reduce all the juices of universal history to the least possible number of drops. The governor of the citadel, Cohen, was a very powerful mind. German and world philosophy owe him a great debt. For it was he who obliged philosophy to raise its level with a great shove, no doubt a rather violent one. This is decisive, for, more than anything else in life, philosophy is level. Cohen obliged thinkers to get into intimate contact with difficult philosophy, and, above all, renewed the desire for system, which is the specifics of philosophical inspiration."[67] "What Cohen did from his chair during those years could not be properly called teaching neo-Kantianism. What he did was, rather, to illuminate it, and incidentally to fulminate against all its enemies, real or imagined. Cohen was an impassioned man, and philosophy had become concentrated in him like electrical energy in a condenser; and the dull chore of an hour in the classroom had become nothing but flashes of lightning and sparks. He was a formidable writer, as he was a formidable speaker. By the time I heard him, his eloquence had been reduced to pure emotionalism. But, be it understood, of the most exquisite kind. It was pure rhetoric, but not *bad* rhetoric, the kind that is lymphatic, flabby, and lacking in intimate truth. Quite the contrary. His sentences were abnormally short for German sentences, pure nerve and operative muscle, the sudden punch of a boxer. I used to feel every one of them like a blow on the nape of the neck.

"The curious thing about these sentences is that they usually did not state the idea which they intended to express. No: they took it for granted that the hearer knew the idea, and the sentence, rather, expressed its emotive connotations, and the desire to run through as with

[67] *Ibid.*, 34–35.

a sword anyone who doubted its truth. He never told us clearly what he meant by 'reine Erkenntnis' or 'Urteil des Ursprungs,' but he did communicate to us all his enthusiasm for these ideas, the emotional respect for their worth, and his boundless disdain toward anyone who would not admit them. His prose, either spoken or written, was of a belligerent kind and, as belligerent things almost always are, was profoundly elegant, though a trifle baroque. I learned from him how to extract the dramatic emotion which in fact lies within every great intellectual problem; better still, which every problem of ideas is. The university professor's highest and most productive mission is to give off this potential dramatic quality and make the students in each class be present at a tragedy."[68]

If we read these passages with some degree of attention, we find that they illumine, more than would appear at first sight, the meaning that Marburg had for Ortega. The fundamental reason that he did not learn *a philosophy* there was . . . that philosophy was not taught. It was taken as a matter of course; one lived on its level and on the basis of enthusiasm; respect for philosophy exemplified in one particular form was contagious. All these things are quite different from the insertion into students' heads of a precise and well-defined doctrine from which reality can be seen. Ortega had to learn philosophy elsewhere than in Marburg, chiefly in libraries; what he learned, in fact, in Marburg was *what philosophy is*: namely, that by which Cohen lived, that which could give fuel to his powerful personality. Therefore, precisely because of this, he had to go beyond Marburg (I mean beyond the philosophy which dominated there) because Ortega *could not live by it*; it could not exercise for him the function it exercised for his teacher. But since— let this not be forgotten—Cohen inspired such limitless respect toward that philosophy, Ortega's reaction could not consist in turning his back on it and ignoring it, but in actually going beyond it, which first of all presupposes mastering it. Ortega had to rethink Kantianism for himself, precisely *so as to be able not to be a Kantian* and not to remain in a mere, negative, and sterile state of *not being able to be a Kantian*, which is quite a different thing. He had to master the whole of German philosophy—German philosophy, to start with—and this obliged him to transcend its particular forms in order to see himself oriented toward

[68] *Ibid.*, 45–46.

things themselves, toward reality; naturally, *from the level of philosophy*, that philosophy to which he had arrived impelled by Cohen's formidable emotive gifts.

As for the dramatic quality, there can be no doubt that this was the lesson which Ortega best assimilated from his teacher. Although it is legitimate to ask whether it was not, rather, a matter of "congeniality"; for intellectual dramatics was a trait of Ortega's from his earliest years, before he knew Cohen and even before he went to Germany. Read his early writings and you will see in them "the dramatic emotion which in fact lies within every great intellectual problem; better still, which every problem of ideas is." There is no doubt that Ortega found in Marburg the corroboration of his deepest feeling, and the assurance that philosophy did not exclude it but demanded it; there was "the great Hermann Cohen" to prove it. Philosophy could be other things; still more, it had to be something other than what was taught or taken for granted there in Marburg; but it had to be *that too*, and if not, it was a deficient philosophy. The combination of intellectual rigor with the dramatic sense, the dramatic sense as *a higher form of intellectual rigor*: for Ortega, this was the great teaching of Marburg, the level with which from that time forward he was to measure all philosophical aspirations— beginning, of course, with his own.

* * *

Now that we have arrived at this point we may well ask ourselves, as a conclusion to this chapter, about what has so often been called Ortega's "Germanism." I have tried to make clear just what Germany meant intellectually to the young Ortega; what "weight" did things German carry with him? Did they not have a disproportionate influence on his soul; did they not lead him at times to distortions in his evaluation and interpretation of German reality, and the total reality of Europe?

Those chapters in the *Meditations on Quixote* in which Ortega expounded his viewpoints on "the Germanic" and "the Latin," especially, have usually had a very bad press. For many people they have been a serious, perhaps unpardonable, objection against their author. For the more benevolent, they have been a youthful sin, perhaps excusable because he loved Germany so much, explainable as the bedazzlement of the young student who, fleeing from the rampant Philistinism of his country, arrives, in the manner of a medieval scholar, in a country where the university really exists. "When I was a boy," Ortega in fact writes, "I read Menéndez Pelayo's books, transfixed with faith in them. In these books there is frequent mention of 'Germanic mists,' which the author contrasts with 'Latin clarity.' On the one hand, I felt profoundly flattered; on the other, a great compassion was born in me for those poor men of the North, condemned to bear a mist within themselves . . . ." "Later," he continues, "I was able to find out for myself that it was simply an inaccuracy, like so many others with which our unfortunate race poisons itself. There are no such "Germanic mists,' and much less any such 'Latin clarity.' They are only a couple of words which, if they mean anything concrete, mean a biased misconception."[69]

This whole passage has almost invariably been interpreted as a proof of Ortega's overweening Germanism, as an arbitrary exaltation of everything German in contrast to the Latin countries and their culture. Some have gone so far as to speak of his "racist" interpretation of culture and history. A hasty and superficial reading of those chapters can, in fact, produce such an impression. But why must reading be hasty and superficial? If this passage is read with some attention, taking in the full meaning of the words, and especially if it is placed in relation to what Ortega had written in the years immediately preceding it—not to what he might have "corrected" later—we can discover the proper measure of his "Germanism."

Ortega rejects the contrast "mists-clarity" and substitutes this other contrast for it: "depth-surface." German culture is a culture of deep realities; Latin culture, of surfaces. But "surface," in Ortega, is not a disdainful or pejorative term, but an essential dimension of reality, as essential as depth, and inseparable from it.[70] Thus he can add: "Strictly speaking, therefore, two dimensions of integral European culture"; that is, far from inviting us to accept Germanic culture and reject Latin culture, he proposes to *integrate* them into a *European* culture.

On the other hand, Ortega believes what we call "Latin culture" is an illusion; instead, it is Greek, which is what interests us; Rome, however, is nothing but a "Mediterranean" people, essentially no different from Carthage, an "Occidental Japan." Ortega did make enormous gains in his esteem for Rome after 1914; from *Invertebrate Spain* (1921) to his articles in *La Nación* entitled "Del Imperio Romano"

[69] *Meditaciones del Quijote*, I, 341.
[70] See below, part 3, chapter 5.

["On the Roman Empire"] (1940), and, still more, in his course, *Una interpretación de la Historia Universal* ["An Interpretation of Universal History"], in the Institute of Humanities (1948–49). There are, then, both a *Mediterranean* culture and a *Germanic* culture. Southern Europe and North Africa functioned, in antiquity, as a homogeneous whole: "The unity of the sea was the basis for the identity of the two coasts." The division of the two shores of the Mediterranean "is an error of historical perspective." "The ideas of Europe and Africa as two enormous centers of conceptual attraction have reabsorbed the respective coasts in historians' thought. It was not noticed that at the time when Mediterranean culture was a reality, neither Africa nor Europe existed."[71] Ideas similar to these can be found, to be sure, in a note in Spengler's *Decline of the West* (1918), though they are somewhat exaggerated: "Here the historian is gravely influenced by preconceptions derived from geography, which assumes a *Continent* of Europe, and feels himself compelled to draw an ideal frontier corresponding to the physical frontier between 'Europe' and 'Asia.' The word 'Europe' ought to be struck out of history. There is historically no 'European' type.... 'Europe' is an empty sound. Everything great that the Classical world created, it created in pure denial of the existence of any continental barrier between Rome and Cyprus, Byzantium and Alexandria."[72]

But Ortega adds: "Europe began when the Germans entered fully into the unified organism of the historical world. At that time Africa became non-Europe, the τὸ ἕτερον of Europe. Once Italy, France, and Spain were germanized, Mediterranean culture ceased to be a pure reality and was reduced to a greater or smaller degree of Germanism." That is, Europe is the Mediterranean (the northern coast) plus germanization. When the Germanic is contrasted to the European, Germany is not being contrasted to France or Spain, but to Europe (*including* Italy, France, and Spain, which insofar as they are European are "germanized"), to the *pure* Mediterranean. This is debatable and not entirely accurate, but it is *something other* than what is usually understood. Similarly, when Ortega gives the blanket description of "Germans" to Galileo, Descartes, Leibniz, Kant, Luther, Rousseau, Donatello, and Michelangelo, this produces a certain amount of irritation in the careless reader; an irritation which is considerably tempered—though perhaps

[71] I, 343.

[72] O. Spengler, *The Decline of the West* [English translation (Knopf, 1946)], Vol. I, p. 16.

it does not disappear altogether, for the statement is too abrupt and in any case should have been shaded and supported—if he has read carefully the passages which precede it and, especially, if he recalls that Ortega had written in 1911: "Those Germans fell upon the Mediterranean empires, and, by making their blood run through Greco-Latin veins, survive in us, the Spaniards, French, and Italians";[73] and also: "What is Germanism but the absorption of Latinism by the Germans throughout the Middle Ages?"[74]

With regard to "racism," Ortega wrote in 1908 in a commentary on Gobineau: "Any attempt to reconstruct history on the hypothesis of inequality of races seems bad to me—but at least this hypothesis has grandeur and depth . . . . The Count of Gobineau's book . . . makes history into a sordid physiological tragedy, but not into a farce . . . . I do not believe this theory is correct; I have mentioned it only to indicate that the explanation of our decline needs reasons as fundamental, at least, as those proposed by Gobineau."[75]

Lastly, the recognition of Germany and her culture—the highest in the world, indisputably, at the beginning of the twentieth century—his admiration for her, his decision to incorporate whatever was substantial in Germany's content (and not the rest), was very far from mere *idolatry* in Ortega, from any noncritical acceptance: on the contrary. Thus, in 1908—that is, *during* his German period, before he *returned* from Germany—after remarking that many people there looked on Impressionism as an enemy of the fatherland, he says, "This phenomenon displays the national vice of intolerance: in this sense, *it deserves, like all nationalism, exquisite contempt.*" And he adds: "The German Empire, like those lake dwellings built over unhealthy and shifting ooze, is constructed on something which is culturally false. The German effort of education is today—not to speak of yesterday!—a tissue of falsifications. From the kindergartens to the seminars in the university, a gigantic industry has been created to falsify men and make them into servants of the empire. There is an imperialist science, a nationalist music, a pandering literature, an idealizing and enervating type of painting . . . . But in contrast to this present-day Germany is the other Germany, the Germany of yesterday and tomorrow: the eternal Germany.

[73] I, 343.
[74] I, 209.
[75] I, 82–83.

And this Germany does not die; if it should die, the only possibilities remaining in Europe for a future worthy of being lived would perish too. The tradition of Leibniz, Herder, Kant, and Virchow continues to influence this land which has been imperialized and treated with brutality, and it will always find a source of inspiration in men of enthusiasm who will be pointed out to you, if you go there, as dangerous men, enemies of the Constitution."[76]

Again, in 1911: "[In Germany] you find the two opposite poles of the European man, the two extreme forms of the Continental emotional range: the materialist, or Southern *pathos*, and the transcendental, or Northern *pathos*. Now salvation lies in liberation from all *pathos*, the transcendence of all unstable and excentric forms. Some time ago I spoke of the *pathos* of the South, and I severely criticized the emphasis of the Spanish attitude. I was misunderstood if my readers took it to mean that I favored the contrary emphasis, the Gothic *pathos*."[77]

And finally, this time in 1910, at the end of his stay in Germany, these words which reflect his deep-rooted, voluptuous, vital acceptance of the Southern character: "These nations (Greece, Rome, Italy, France, Spain) did not admit as true a single word which was not at the same time beautiful and which, furthermore, did not incite to activity." (A formula which could not be bettered, certainly, to describe Ortega's entire work.) "Now," he added, "other peoples, so full of virtues that they are bent like slaves under the weight of them, are trying to impose on us an ideal which is less clear and, naturally, less harmonious. Culture is one, no matter where it is found; the Greek and the Scythian, the Frenchman and the Prussian, are certainly engaged in a common task. But there is a form of culture peculiar to the South of Europe, a Mediterranean mode of loving God, of telling tales, of walking through the streets, of looking at women, and of saying that two and two are four."[78] There can be no doubt that Ortega, though he did not renounce the German element, did everything in his life according to this mode.

[76] I, 96–97. Italics mine.
[77] I, 188.
[78] I, 465.

IV.

ORTEGA'S ACTIVITIES

36. TEMPTATIONS: REGENERATION, EXHORTATION, LITERATURE, ERUDITION, SCIENCE

If we take things in a general way, we can say that the chief temptations which assail an intellectual, and within which many different temptations are included, are these: to shut himself up in an "ivory tower," or to plunge entirely into "the city of men." Both—like almost all temptations—are seductive; both appear to have no little justification. We must remember that it is a question of *two attitudes*, of two ways of installing oneself in life, and particularly in the intellectual world—much more than a question of the *activities* one actually carries out.

Let us consider Unamuno, for example: few men have spent more time shut up in a room—and in a provincial city, to boot—reading books and more books, annotating them minutely, making comments on them. But Unamuno's aim was as far as possible from any "ivory tower," from any aseptic and "professional" exercise of the intelligence; and, as he was a professor of Greek and philology, he took the greatest care not to write a single line on either subject, nothing "technical"—but always to be "in the fight," to do battle in the civil sense, to try to "make everyone live restlessly and yearningly," to produce writings in which his great erudition is covered up by lyricism or arbitrariness, to be above all an *excitator Hispaniae*, though at the price of not having disciples in the strict sense or leaving a body of doctrine behind. Unamuno chose to live in the "city of men," to fight his battle in that city, to talk constantly, to let his voice be heard in every argument whether he was right or wrong, whether he had reflected sufficiently or not, whenever time and the occasion demanded, always with passion and indomitable courage. In "El sepulcro de Don Quijote" ["The Tomb of Don Quixote"], which he placed as a prologue to the second edition of his *Life of Don*

Quixote and Sancho, we can see the "manifesto" of this attitude—impassioned, gesticulating, always tending to the extreme, perhaps insecure.

In contrast to this attitude is the one which affirms the "ivory tower" as a demand of intellectual work in the strict sense. The man who shuts himself away in his tower does not want "to know anything about anything," only to be an intellectual and work at his "science" or perhaps poetry or literature. But it often happens that in the last analysis, when he has all his time free for it, when in its name he has renounced all else —a passion for his country or a political party, for liberty or justice, the capacity for indignation, perhaps even friendship or love—he is afflicted with a strange, inexplicable sterility, and cannot perform that science to which he claims to be exclusively dedicated.

These two temptations, circumstantially diversified, lay before Ortega when he was a lad scarcely out of the University. A whole gamut of activities was possible for him: some were Spanish, immediate and pressing, within his grasp; others were attractive and promising; others, a trifle more remote, European, were glimpsed by the adolescent, and these shone with the light of a more distant and shadowy, but loftier, prestige.

The letter to Unamuno dated January, 1904, written when he was twenty years of age, and which I mentioned earlier, shows the degree to which he was weighing these disquieting possibilities. In it the young Ortega justifies his studious turn of mind, his impassioned devouring of books, in the light of a national activity. He may be an "outdoor man," but to be one effectively he must work nine or ten hours a day in the library. The "ivory tower" is excluded from the outset: if there is one, it is a fortified turret, whence he can begin the battle with adequate resources. Ortega makes his youthful program depend on the Spanish situation; it is this situation, though not this situation *alone*, which will cause him to decide "what has to be done"—a phrase which was to weigh heavily on Ortega's entire trajectory.

But let it not be thought that the straight path was marked out from the age of twenty, and that Ortega was to progress along it without detours. In the years between 1902 and 1914—the latter date a decisive one in so many senses—Ortega was very busy: as a writer of articles, promoter of new reviews, as critic, lecturer, professor. All these activities seemed necessary to him, demanded by the situation in which he lived.

An article written in 1906 clearly shows some of the reasons for it: "Great and small, old and young, wise and innocent, all of us bear within us a more or less fragmentary view of the universe. Culture is no other than the mutual exchange of these ways of seeing the things of yesterday, today, and the future." Let us keep in mind some of the elements in this paragraph: Ortega begins by affirming the existence in *every* man of a vision of the universe, which in principle seems to be individual; but he asserts that it cannot be reduced to this, for culture consists in the *interchange* of such views, in their interaction, therefore in something which goes beyond each individual; it is a matter of *living together*, the end result of a combination of actions; lastly, these *ways of looking at things*—an expression which was to become important in Ortega's philosophy, introduced in a more formal way in the *Meditations on Quixote*[1]—affect the past, the present, and the future, and consequently involve a total interpretation of reality. But circumstantial details follow this generic and theoretical observation: "A sinful rigidity, which has flowered out of vanity, is likely to shut each one of us up inside himself and turn every man into an island. This is an old Spanish sin: I do not know whether to see in it a sequel of the Moorish education of our race, for just as the Moslems keep their women jealously locked up, we hide our own ideas from each other. Perhaps our overweening pride demands that we be Caesar or nothing; perhaps we would wish our ideas to be the definitive, the exemplary, the unique ones; and a shade of lack of confidence makes us prefer to hide them rather than to expose them to failure or indifference. We must learn to flee from any such vice . . . . Although it may seem a painful irony, we are greatly in need of learning to be the last among our fellow citizens, to ponder without rancor or resentment the place that is assigned to us in the republic, where the first are as necessary and useful as the last. Thus, in literature and in all of our life today we can observe an itch for idiosyncrasy and showiness, only conceivable when young and old heads are preoccupied exclusively with being the first on every scale, and consider all other positions despicable. Let us learn to be second, to be third, to be last. Perhaps the profoundest lesson taught by contact with

[1] I, 318. See my Commentary in the edition of *Meditaciones del Quijote* (1957), 241–42, where this expression is related to the *zufällige Ansichten* or *modi res considerandi* of Herbart.

real things, which leaves within us that period when we embrace life as we progress from the age of twenty to thirty, is that life is worth living even though we are not great men."[2]

And a year later Ortega wrote what he called "exhortations addressed to some Celtiberian lads who today are beginning to acquire spiritual methods," with the intention of "offering them a mental rhythm and a dignity with which to confront some few incontinent dogmas which dominate the present-day Spanish consciousness."[3] Once more, the pre-occupation for action upon Spaniards, for public action on the immediate circumstance.

The most immediate possibility, and also the most pressing one, was to raise the banner of *regeneration*; it is well known that Ortega felt its attraction and its call, and I have referred to this above. About his attitude with regard to Costa, his admiration for him, and the fact that he differed from him in *essential* points, I have already said enough. Since Ortega began at a higher level, he could no longer install himself comfortably in positions whose deficiencies were obvious to him; but *he was not unsympathetic to them*, and he could not abandon them, because they were justified and had not been realized. In a certain measure, and from a different position, there is a strain of the "regenerationist" in Ortega which never died out completely—we shall see it throughout his life—and which, of course, became united with other strains in a figure which became more complex and had broader horizons.

It is obvious that the person who exercised the profoundest attraction on the young Ortega was Unamuno. For several years, precisely those of his entry into intellectual and public life, he was oriented toward the kind of action which Unamuno had undertaken: exhortation, revival of the inert Spanish atmosphere, a thorough shake-up of stagnation through an appeal to the deepest springs of action of the race. And all this arose out of a literary temper, out of that contagious tremor of the just and harmonious word, which Ortega handled at the age of twenty with intensity, elegance, and accuracy. But we have already seen how quickly he came to feel dissatisfied with the shape Unamuno's leadership was taking; his reservations accompany his earliest enthusiasm; at a time when this enthusiasm was still almost intact, in 1907, he wrote, using the past tense: "I used to be a traditionalist," and states that "after

2 "Moralejas. I. Crítica bárbara" (1906). I, 45–46.
3 "Teoría del clasicismo" (1907). I, 72.

returning from some peregrinations in the land of the Scythians," he has become convinced that there was enough traditionalism in Spain, that it was very well established, and that the time had come "for us to cease to be traditionalists." Did he write this simply in order not to follow the new current? To take issue, and uphold the opposite argument? No: it was to add something more, to enrich the national consciousness, for "the more ideal themes that are present in a country's consciousness, the greater is its culture."[4]

His stay in Germany, his peregrinations in the land of the Scythians, strengthened Ortega's theoretical vocation. His identification of Europe with science, so characteristic of his attitude between 1908 and 1910, led him, in the sphere of his activities, to point out energetically the need for a scientific discipline for Spaniards. There were no books, no libraries, no science, though there was a handful of scientific men—Cajal, Hinojosa; this, to the twenty-five-year-old Ortega, seemed shameful, and the correction of the situation the most important task to be undertaken. "There is no science in Spain," he wrote, "but there are a good number of credulous youths who are ready to devote their lives to scientific work, with the same emphatic, severe, and fervent attitude with which the priests of classical times sacrificed a white heifer to green-eyed Minerva. We must make it possible for them to live and work. They do not ask for much: they do not conceive of the nation's duty to them as did that coal-seller's wife in Paris, on the eve of the Revolution, who said to a marquise: 'Now, madame, I will ride in a carriage and you will carry the coal.' They want neither an automobile nor a mistress: probably they would not know what to do with these things if they were given them . . . . They wish only to live modestly, but adequately and independently: they wish only to be supplied with the tools for their work: teachers, libraries, travel funds, laboratories, archive services, support for their publications. In exchange they are ready to renounce election as deputies to Parliament, wealthy marriages, and even the presidency of the Council of Ministers. These Spartan and hard-working young men, carelessly dressed, unattractive to women, and probably lacking in good literary style, are the only ones capable of salvaging the last remnants of strict intellectual dignity and ethics that remain in our society."[5]

[4] *Ibid.*
[5] "Asamblea para el Progreso de las Ciencias" (1908). I, 108–109.

At the same date, Ortega senses a possible conflict between two of these forms of activity: literature and science. It is not difficult to see that when he speaks in general terms, he is also thinking of himself, asking himself the essential question: *Quod vitae sectabor iter?*—What road shall I follow in life? And he searches for transpersonal, circumstantial reasons for a decision which ought not to be capricious or purely individual. "In our country today," he writes, "the indisputable right to create good literature does not exist: we are too much obliged to convince and to be concrete. If a man does not feel capable of anything more than literature, let him write it as best he can, and if he succeeds we will crown him with flowers and make celebrations in his honor . . . . Insofar as there is no power of choice, the moral dilemma does not arise. If we can create good literature, but also feel ourselves capable of science, our decision will have to incline indefectibly toward the latter, with no pact made with the former." And he condemns those who, not being Valle-Inclán or Rubén Darío, imitate them "instead of shuffling the archives and reconstructing the history of Spain, or making commentaries on Aeschylus or Saint Augustine. *A man should either cultivate literature, or cultivate precision, or shut up.*"[6]

We can see clearly here the possibilities in the form of temptations which can be, and perhaps should be, resisted. At this particular moment Ortega seems to take a resolute stand in favor of science—perhaps not even excluding scholarship—if, of course, a man has the capacity for it. Is this the last word? Is it not perhaps a temptation like the others? And how to decide between them, how to overcome them?

37. THE HEIGHT OF THE TIMES AS A TALISMAN

In *The Revolt of the Masses*, Ortega's most famous book and undoubtedly *one* of the high points in his work, though not the highest, there is a chapter which bears this title: "The Height of the Times." And in that chapter he analyzes the meaning of this expression, a very common one in Spanish, and one which he in particular often employs: "It is said, for example, that this or that thing does not correspond to the height of the times. That is: not the abstract time of chronology, which

6 "Algunas notas" (1908). I, 112–13. Italics mine.

is all on one level, but vital time, what each generation calls 'our time'; it always has a certain altitude, is higher today than yesterday, or stays at the same level, or falls beneath it. The figure of falling contained in the word 'decadence' proceeds from this intuition. Likewise each person feels, with greater or lesser clarity, the relationship in which his own life stands to the height of the time in which that life is lived. There are men who feel, in the present-day modes of existence, like a ship-wrecked sailor unable to keep afloat. The rapidity of the tempo at which things progress today, the momentum and energy with which every-thing is done, cause anguish to the man of an old-fashioned turn of mind, and this anguish is the measure of the discrepancy between the height of his pulse rate and the height of the period. On the other hand, the man who lives fully and happily within present-day modes is conscious of the relationship between the height of our time and the height of the different ages which preceded it."[7]

The analysis which starts in these terms, and which Ortega was to give its theoretical dimension in 1930, has a long prehistory in his earlier work. This idea of *the height of the times* had been with Ortega since his early youth, and, if I am not mistaken, it had exercised the function in his life of a talisman to preserve him from many temptations. Did it cause him to fall into others? This is a question which we shall also have to pose later in this book.

Beginning with the second article collected in his *Obras*, when he was only twenty years old, there is an unequivocal sense of this temporal level. Writing of Valle-Inclán, Ortega sketches out a theory which we might call "filiation" or "historical affinity" among men. Many, in their style, do not belong to the period in which they live. "There are men who are throwbacks to former periods. We can pin down the moment when some of them should have been born, and say that they are *Louis XV men*, or *men of the Empire*, or *men of the* 'ancien régime.' Taine shows Napoleon as a man of the time of Plutarch. Don Juan Valera is an eighteenth-century man; he has the cold malignance of the Encyclopedists, as well as their noble way of expressing themselves. These are spirits who seem to have been forged in other ages, souls who date back to a time that is dead and make it live again in our eyes better than a history book. These miraculous men have the charm of

[7] IV, 156.

things that are past, and the attraction of a rather precious falsification. Don Ramón del Valle-Inclán is a 'Renaissance' man."[8] In the end, that is the reproach which the twenty-year-old Ortega makes to this admirable writer, saying of him that if he would expand his canvases, if he would lose his tendency to an archaic type of *préciosité*—he is referring, of course, to the *Sonatas*—he would attain full perfection: "Today he is a most individual and interesting writer; then he would be a great writer, a master writer." And he concludes, "How I should rejoice if some day I opened a new book by Sr. Valle-Inclán and did not stumble on 'blonde princesses spinning on spindles of crystal,' or glorious thieves, or unnecessary incests! And when I had finished reading that probable book I would exclaim, giving it a couple of affectionate pats, 'Lo and behold, Don Ramón del Valle-Inclán has stopped telling tall stories and has told us *human* things, *really human ones* in his noble style, the style of a well-born writer.' "[9]

Qualities are not enough: Valle-Inclán has them in the highest measure; but they must be exercised adequately, without evading the situation; he must be, in a word, "at the height of the times"; every archaism, however delicious, is a falsification, a form of unauthenticity. In the passage I quoted before, from Ortega's article "Teoría del clasicismo" ["Theory of Classicism"], when he refers to his traditionalism as something he has left behind, the strongest reason, though not the one he emphasizes most, for his abandonment of that attitude is that "I have become convinced that there already exists in Spain a very strong current which affirms race and the sentimental tradition";[10] now we can see the full meaning of this phrase: since Spain has already arrived there, she must go on; the partial justification of "traditionalism" has imposed itself, has triumphed; the height of the times demands that it must not be insisted upon, not be returned to, but that it must be integrated with what is lacking. This readjustment of conduct to the exigencies of the circumstance acquires, in this context, a precise historical meaning.

With this standard before his eyes, Ortega managed to avoid temptations. Let us understand this properly: to the extent that they are justified, he accepts them—as we have just seen; but *he does not stay*

---

[8] "La sonata de estío, de Don Ramón del Valle-Inclán" (1904). I, 19.
[9] *Ibid.*, 27.
[10] I, 72.

in them; above all, he does not subscribe to any of them in isolation from the others. They are not alien to him, but he does not belong to any of them. His constant purpose is to go beyond each, in a *variable synthesis* determined by the concrete circumstance. This demand, valid for the individual, is still more valid for each society. Spain, the Spain which Ortega encountered, was defined precisely by the fact that it was not at the height of the times; to what point this was the Spanish situation beginning with the early years of the nineteenth century, I have shown in section 4 of the Introduction to this book; and we have also seen that the mission of the Generation of 1898 was, precisely, to cancel this difference in level. In Ortega's actions the Spanish aspect of this standard is decisive: throughout his entire life he was to subordinate every other present circumstance to the Spanish one; I mean that, when there was a difference in level among several demands of "the height of the times"—his personal one, that of Spain, the general European one, or even the Western one—Ortega was always to choose the Spanish one and sacrifice the others to it. I believe that this point of view casts extraordinary light on his biography and the meaning of his whole work. And perhaps, occasionally, he was assailed by doubt whether he had done the right thing, whether this was what he was meant to do. On some decisive points we shall have to ask ourselves the same question, and try to find an adequate answer.

38. COEXISTENCE AND POLITICS

The "up-to-dateness" of all of Ortega's work, his insertion into the Spanish circumstance and the abnormality of that circumstance, inevitably impelled him toward politics. And throughout his whole life there also existed in him a political vocation which we must try to analyze.

He had had, since childhood, what we might call a political education. This expression scarcely has intelligible meaning for Spaniards less than forty years of age, and even for their elders it does not have a full and complete meaning; and the same occurs to the citizens of many European and American countries, where politics ceased to exist some time ago and has been supplanted by a number of other things. In Europe, and even in Spain, at the end of the nineteenth century and up to 1914, politics existed and conformed to certain norms, to certain rules of the game, and, in consequence, to a system of valuations. When we read the ferocious political criticisms of Spanish writers—those of the Generation of 1898, those of Ortega's generation—we cannot suppress a start of surprise: "What are they complaining about?" we mutter. "Why do they exaggerate so?" If we reflect again, we will recall the *level of aspiration* on which they moved, the infinite number of things we have renounced since then, the change that has taken place in the borderline between the permissible and the intolerable. Politics— a politics which seemed abominable to the best men of the time, and they were probably right—*existed*; it had channels in which to flow; it was a "career" subject to its own discipline, which required certain qualities and was susceptible of successes and failures; all of this required a type of education, a certain training in problems, in techniques, in procedures, even in controversies. *El Imparcial*, like all newspapers, was a political as well as a literary daily. Oratory was a political as well as an artistic force. A writer was often a politician, and the two careers intermingled at times; literary merit became political aspiration, and, conversely, there were some who aspired to success in this area in order to be able to publish. Politics was something which could be learned, partly with ideas, partly empirically, through familiarity and "contagion." And coexistence, one of its most important levels, was political coexistence, equipped with a language and a system of attitudes of general significance, channeled into a parliamentary system which, although precarious to a considerable degree, at least assured a *public* character to national life, structured into parties which were ideologically deficient and in many cases corrupt, but which made possible the effectiveness of the existence of the nation as such, and made it impossible for the nation to be passed over and swindled.

None of this has anything to do with the negative opinion held by the best men in Spain with regard to the politics which ruled Spain between 1890 and 1914. Their objections might be, and in fact were, extremely serious and on principle; but they presupposed the acceptance and—if the hypothesis had even been suggested—the enthusiastic defense of the existence of a political life.

As for the modes of participation in that life, this is a delicate question. When Ortega was still very young, and perhaps at the time when he felt the call of politics with a certain urgency, early in 1910, he recognized the possibility that an intellectual might approach politics, at a time when the leaders of the Spanish political parties thought it advisable to ask for the aid of such men. "For an intellectual, the operation of joining a party is not an easy task; a body and even a conscience can fit in anywhere; but a philosophy? Be it good or bad, slack or rigid, any public figure who lives honorably from his thought has a philosophy. How to adjust it to the parliamentary speeches of a party head? To what point is a philosophy compatible with Sr. Maura, with Sr. Moret or Sr. Lerroux?"[11]

During that year Ortega spoke in Bilbao on "La pedagogía social como programa político" ["Social Pedagogy as a Political Program"]. After emphasizing that the Spaniard, unlike other Europeans whose governments function normally, has to address himself first of all to national problems, that the problem of Spain is the primary one, he added, "This problem is, as I say, that of transforming the social reality which lies around us. The instrument which can produce this transformation we call politics. The Spaniard *needs*, therefore, to be a politician first of all."[12] It seems that Ortega is about to launch himself into political action, in spite of his reservations; but he immediately feels the need of making a distinction: "Politics can mean two things; the art of governing or the art of achieving a government and preserving it. Stated another way: there is an art of legislating and an art of imposing certain legislation . . . . It must be repeated over and over that it is an immoral act to become a conqueror of power without having previously created an ideal of government. It is true that politics is action, but action is also movement; it means moving from one place to another; it means taking a step, and a step requires a direction which leads straight to the infinite . . . . We must transform Spain: make of her a different thing from what she is today. What sort of thing? What should that ideal Spain be, toward which we turn our hearts, as the faces of the blind habitually turn in the direction from which a little light comes?"[13]

This means that there is something previous to politics *sensu stricto*, or, if you like, that there is a primary politics which asks itself about social reality, and which is the only one that can give meaning to the politics whose task is to control and rule that reality. Thus Ortega was

[11] "La teología de Renan." I, 133.
[12] I, 498.
[13] *Ibid.*

to make *social pedagogy* the political program of the hour. Education, *eductio, educatio*, is the action of leading one thing out of another, of changing a less good thing into something better: "*Pedagogy* anticipates what man should be, and then seeks the instruments which will permit man to achieve what he ought to be."[14] Ortega was strongly influenced at this particular time by his teachers in Marburg, Hermann Cohen and Paul Natorp; the latter's *Social Pedagogy* is the theoretical background of this lecture. Yet more: the attraction toward Socialism which Ortega displays in these early years also comes from Marburg, and corresponds to the political orientation of his teachers.[15] But at the same time that he affirms the moral supremacy of the Socialist state, he is already aware that it is not a question of whether the true Socialism is that of Marx, "nor much less whether the worker parties are the only highly ethical ones." What Ortega understands by Socialism in 1910 is primarily community as co-operation,[16] as opposed to individualistic selfishness or partisanship. It must be added that Ortega felt a profound respect for Pablo Iglesias, elected a Socialist deputy at that time, whom he considered to be a talented and completely serious man, "two qualities for which, under pain of falling into a horrible cosmic pessimism, we must predict sure success wherever they show themselves."[17] That is, he emphasizes the personal qualities of the founder of Spanish Socialism more than his political doctrine, with regard to which he felt obliged to state reservations as soon as, four years later, he attempted to formulate

[14] *Ibid.*, 500.

[15] "Today it is a scientific truth, acquired *in aeternum*, that the only morally admissible social state is the Socialist state." (I, 509.) This sentence of Ortega's has been quoted frequently, but without clarification of what is understood by Socialism in this context, and which is expressed in very explicit words a few lines above this sentence as well as below it.

[16] "The community of labor need not be purely external: it must be a communion of spirits, it must have a meaning for all who collaborate in it. Community will be co-operation. If society is co-operation, the members of society have to be, before anything else, workers. *In society, the man who does not work cannot participate. This is the affirmation by means of which democracy is clearly defined in Socialism.* To socialize a man is to make him a worker in the magnificent human task, in culture, where culture takes in everything, from digging the ground to composing verses." And he adds, "The worker, if he is not to be a slave, needs to have a lively consciousness of the meaning of his labor. It seems to me inhuman to keep a man in the corner of a shop for thirty years without offering him *a vision of the things which give a noble meaning to his task*." (I, 508–509.) Italics mine.

[17] "Planeta sitibundo" (1910). I, 148.

his personal position. This was to be the "League for Spanish Political Education" founded by Ortega in 1914 and presented in his lecture on "Old and New Politics."

39. THE LEAGUE FOR SPANISH POLITICAL EDUCATION

Nineteen fourteen was the year in which Ortega made his debut in public life. We know that he had carried on twelve years of literary activity, of frequent collaboration on newspapers and magazines, with occasional personal appearances behind a lectern. But all of this, in spite of the assurance which characterized Ortega from his beginnings, and which automatically aroused lively support or no less lively irritation, had an unmistakable flavor of *initiation*, of juvenile pressure upon a world which was still "alien" in the sense that a coast one is approaching by ship is still alien. Youthful activities as such, no matter how well thought out and "mature" they are, no matter what their momentum arises from, are always a form of "coming into port." The foundation of the League for Spanish Political Education has a different meaning; it was one of the undertakings attempted by Ortega which had the fewest visible, but most revealing, results, and it is an undertaking which has customarily been overlooked if not entirely forgotten.

When it was presented to the public, in the "Prospectus" which accompanied the text of the lecture on "Old and New Politics," the League had ninety-nine members.[18] Many of them have been significant names

---

[18] In the original edition of *Vieja y nueva política* (Renacimiento, Madrid, 1914), after the text of the lecture given in the *Teatro de la Comedia* on March 23 of that year and the "Prospectus" of the League, this appendix is added:

"The League for Spanish Political Education is at present composed of the following gentlemen:

Azaña, Manuel.	Baeza, Ricardo.
Alvarez Pastor, Joaquín.	Bernis, Francisco.
A. Santullano, Luis.	Begoña, Ricardo.
Azcárate, Pablo.	Basterra, Ramón de.
Abril, Manuel.	Bernaldo de Quirós, Constancio.
Alvarez, Valentín.	Castro, Américo.
Alarcón, Daniel.	Chacón, José.
Alcayde y Vilar, Francisco.	Covián, Juan.
A. de Lorenzana, Ramiro.	Calvo, Alvaro.
Andrés Monedero, Ricardo de.	Cabañas, Francisco.
Ballesteros, Salvador.	Cases Casañ, Antonio.

in twentieth-century Spanish life; with a few exceptions, they belonged to the same generation as Ortega, and this characteristic, as we shall see,

Campo Cerdán, Angel del.
Cordón Barrera, José.
Carreño España, José.
Carazo Landa, Felipe.
Díez-Canedo, Enrique.
España y Heredia, Eduardo.
Esteban Muñoz, Juan.
Elorrieta, Octavio.
Fernández Zabala, José.
Fernández Ardavín, Luis.
Flórez, Rafael.
Gancedo, Gabriel.
García Morente, Manuel.
Gutiérrez, Luis.
Gutiérrez, Ricardo.
González Magro, Pedro.
García Bellido, Joaquín.
González Tomás, Julio.
Guixé, Juan.
García del Diestro, José.
García Martí, Victoriano.
García y García, Diego.
García Bilbao, Luis.
Gómez, Enrique.
González Blanco, Andrés.
Galarza y Gago, Angel.
Hernández Sampelayo, Jesús.
Hoyos, Luis de.
Herrero Bahillo, Fermín.
Hernández Sampelayo, Jesus.
Laza, Enrique.
Luzuriaga, Lorenzo.
Lafora y García, Juan.
Llorca, Angel.
Molina Ravello, Enrique.
Márquez, Manuel.
Membrillera, Ciriaco.
Membrillera, Inocente.

Mira, Francisco.
Madariaga, Salvador.
Menéndez Valdés, Julio.
Maeztu, Ramiro de.
Machado, Antonio.
Mesa, Enrique de.
Moreno Villa, José.
Neira Fernández, Ricardo.
Navarro Flórez, Martín.
Navarro Tomás, Tomás.
Nuñez Moreno, Francisco.
Onís, Federico de.
Onieva, Antonio.
Ortega y Gasset, José.
Orueta y Duarte, Ricardo de.
Pérez de Ayala, Ramón.
Palomares de Duero, Marqués de.
Palacios, Leopoldo.
Pittaluga, Gustavo.
Puig Campillo, Antonio.
Rivas Scheril [*sic*, read Cherif], Cipriano.
Rojo Arias, Ignacio.
Rego, Angel do.
Ruiz Gutiérrez, Francisco.
Ríos Urruti, Fernando de los.
Roldán Casilari, Andrés.
Serrano Salvador, Fernando.
Sevillano, Virgilio.
Subirana, Luis.
Sánchez Rivero, Angel.
Salinas, Pedro.
Said Armesto, Víctor.
Seco de Lucena, Daniel.
Sanz, Rodrigo.
Tomás Cuesta, Angel.
Tenreiro, Ramón.
Viñuales, Agustín.
Vegue y Goldoni, Angel.

"*The League for Spanish Political Education meets periodically on days and at hours specified in the announcements which will be issued; it sends a bulletin to its members, entitled* Política, *which attempts to strengthen the spiritual ties between them and to establish bases for the study of national problems.*

"*A minimum contribution of three pesetas monthly is requested from the members.*"

"*All communications and contributions should be addressed to Don Manuel G. Morente, calle de Torrijos 3, Madrid.*"

was essential: it was, in fact, the manifesto of a generation, the generation which followed that of 1898 (although Antonio Machado, Ramiro de Maeztu, Enrique de Mesa, and Luis de Hoyos were members of the League). They were predominantly "intellectuals." "The names and professions of a large proportion of our members may call down upon us the unfavorable description of 'intellectuals,' " says the Prospectus,[19] "unless we emphasize from the outset our conviction that politics is not a labor that can be satisfied with the intellect alone, or even through individual action." Some of the members of the League were Manuel García Morente, Américo Castro, Federico de Onís, José Moreno Villa, Ramón de Basterra, Enrique Díez-Canedo, Ramón Pérez de Ayala, Tomás Navarro Tomás, Salvador Madariaga, Victoriano García Martí, Manuel Abril, Lorenzo Luzuriaga, Agustín Viñuales, Valentín Andrés Alvarez, Ricardo Baeza, and—he must not be ignored—Pedro Salinas. But there were also men with an obvious political vocation, such as Manuel Azaña, Angel Galarza, Fernando de los Ríos, and José Carreño España.

The "Prospectus" emphasized both the "required" nature of the task which these men had assumed, and the collective personality of their generation: "an inalienable task, which old errors and present-day tepidity have suddenly caused to fall on the shoulders of one generation."[20] This appears even more clearly in Ortega's lecture. The League is composed of "men who, like myself and a large proportion of those who are listening to me, are 'in the middle of the journey' of life." It is a question of "ideas, feelings, energies, resolutions which are *common*, inevitably, *to all of us who have lived under the pressure of the same system* of historical bitterness; it is a question of *a whole ideology and sensibility, which surely lie in the collective soul of a generation* characterized by not having shown personal haste; one which lacks brilliance, perhaps, but knows how to live with austerity and sadness; one which, not having had teachers, by no fault of its own, has had to remake for itself the very bases of its spirit; a generation which *was born to reflective attention in the terrible year of 1898*, and since then has not seen around itself, much less one day of glory or plenitude, even an hour of sufficiency. And in addition to all this, a *generation, perhaps the first generation, which has never made capital out of patriotic clichés* and which ...

[19] I, 301.
[20] I, 300.

when it hears the word Spain does not recall Calderón and Lepanto, does not think of the victories of the Cross, does not call to mind a vision of a blue sky, and a radiance under it, but which merely feels; and what it feels is grief."[21]

Ortega's appeal to his generation is extremely insistent and deliberate; he uses the word, moreover, entirely without vagueness, in a rigorous way, to the point that what is being sketched out here is a doctrine of generations.[22] The chief demand is for *authenticity*, the only means of preventing historical sterility. "Like each individual, each generation, if it wishes to be useful to humanity, must begin by being faithful to itself."[23] The individual's future is linked to that of the generation, and the generation's future to that of the nation, the society in which it lives. The authenticity of personal life makes each one feel responsible for his country, and at a precise historical level, which is, in fact, that of his generation. "It is a puerile illusion," he adds, "to believe that the everlasting life of peoples is guaranteed somewhere; many races have disappeared as independent entities from history, which is an arena full of ferocities. In history, to live is not to let oneself live; in history, to live is to set oneself to live very seriously, very consciously, as if it were one's trade. Therefore it is necessary for our generation to concern itself in full consciousness, premeditatedly, organically, with the national future. It is necessary, in a word, to make *a forceful call to our generation*, and if those men who make the call do not have positive credentials for calling on it, *then someone will have to call on it willy-nilly*; I, for example."[24]

In what does the absolute novelty of this activity of Ortega's, different from all those he had previously attempted, consist? It is a *political* action. It will be said that it is not entirely new, that he had written at length on the subject of politics, and that he had even spoken of it in the Atheneum in Madrid, in *El Sitio* in Bilbao. But it is one thing to write or speak *of politics*, about it, and it is another thing to *make politics*; and I am not thinking primarily of the theoretical aspect of the first element, as opposed to the practicality of the second, for this activity

---

21 I, 268. Italics mine. The last sentence had been written by Ortega, and he had referred to it previously in the article "La herencia viva de Costa" (*El Imparcial*, 20–II–1911).

22 See I, 271. See also my essay "Vieja y nueva política: El origen de la sociología de Ortega" (1957), in *La escuela de Madrid* [1959], 265ff. (*Obras*, V.)

23 I, 270.

24 I, 270–71. Italics mine.

is also theoretical and doctrinal; since it is a question of political *education*, an exhortation to politics, and as such not so very different from the 1910 lecture in Bilbao, and certainly with a far higher theoretical content. No, what I mean is the following: up till this time, Ortega had acted *personally*, in the role of a private individual; now, when he undertook a fully political action, he was exercising a *transpersonal* function. To begin with, he was speaking in the name of a group of ninety-nine persons who, in their turn, considered themselves to be representative of a generation; and he took good care to announce, anticipating the misunderstandings which persist to this day, that "by new generations I must not be understood to mean only those few individuals who enjoy social privileges by birth or personal effort, but equally the mass of persons of their age."[25] But, further, *politics, by its very essence, excludes the purely personal*: "When he approaches politics, it is a question of honor for the man of ideas to surrender his claim to be an original thinker. A principle, new as an idea, cannot move people. New politics means a new declaration and a new desire for thoughts which, more or less clearly, are to be found already residing in the consciousness of our citizens."[26] Which brings him, we may say in passing, to the earliest formulation of his theory of social beliefs.[27] When he initiated a political activity, Ortega had to leave his personal thoughts aside, in order to leave room for the collective reality which is the true and inmost opinion of one part of society, and he recalled the statement by Fichte to the effect that the secret of politics is *to declare what already exists*.

This is the point of connection between politics and the intellectual function; for to declare what exists, one must know what it is, one must discover it. Only by turning back to national reality can one see what its "true and innermost opinions" are, what Ortega was later to call the basic beliefs of a society. "Politics exists only," says Ortega, "where the great social masses intervene in it; all politics exists for those masses, with them and for their sake."[28] But he begins by addressing the minorities which are more cultured, capable of reflection, and responsible, in order to "transmit their enthusiasm, their thoughts, their concern, their courage, to these great, poor, suffering masses."

Old and New Politics contains the germinal nucleus of Ortega's

[25] I, 271.
[26] I, 269.
[27] See my essay mentioned in note 22.
[28] I, 268.

sociology, an interpretation of Spain and a political program which are closely linked, naturally, to the two previous elements. What is it that we might call, taking both noun and adjective in their strictest sense, the *problematical reality* of Spain? For Ortega, it is the coexistence of two realities which are alien to each other: *official Spain* and *vital Spain*. What do these two expressions mean? Are they equivalent, perhaps, to "the government" and "the nation," as has sometimes been understood? Not at all; further, the significance of this distinction of Ortega's lies in going beyond that habitual contrast and contradicting it. "It is not a question of a government's having drawn away from public opinion in some transitory matter of legislation or exercise of authority, no; it is that the *whole parties* from which those governments came and still come, it is that the *entire Parliament*, it is that *all* those corporations on which the world of the politicians has influence, or is directly influenced —yet more, *even the newspapers themselves*, which are like the machines which produce the atmosphere breathed by that world—*all of them, from right to left and from top to bottom, are located outside and apart from the central currents of the present-day Spanish soul.* I do not say that those currents of national vitality are very vigorous (we shall soon see that they are not), but, whether robust or feeble, they are the only sources of energy and possible rebirth. What I do affirm is that *all those organisms of our society—from Parliament to the newspaper and from the rural school to the University—all that which, uniting them under one name, we shall call official Spain* is the immense skeleton of an evaporated, vanished organism, which stands only because of the material equilibrium of its bulk, as they say that elephants continue to stand after their deaths."[29] "And then, what we are witnessing in our nation today occurs; two Spains that live side by side yet which are entirely foreign to each other: *an official Spain* which stubbornly prolongs the attitudes of a dead age, and another Spain, aspiring, germinal, *a vital Spain*, perhaps not very strong, but vital, sincere, honorable; a Spain which, hampered by the other, cannot enter fully into history. This, gentlemen, is the great fact about present-day Spain, and all the rest are mere details which must be interpreted under the light shed by that fact . . . . Official Spain has no understanding of our new Spain, which, I repeat, will be modest, will be small, will be poor, but which is something other than that Spain; we have no understanding of each

[29] I, 272. Italics mine.

other."[30] "Official Spain consists, therefore, in parties of a ghostly sort who defend the ghosts of a few ideas and who, supported by the shades of a few newspapers, operate spectral ministries."[31] Thus Ortega does not attack *abuses*, which always seemed unimportant to him; in this he differs from Costa, who blamed the ruling classes, the politicians; these have usually governed badly, thinks Ortega, because the Spain they govern is equally sick, for it is a question of *uses* themselves. "*An entire Spain—with its governors and its governed—with its abuses and its uses, is at the end of its dying.*"[32]

Thus, the *new politics* which the League is defending does not seek power above all, but the *growth and nurture of Spain's vitality*,[33] and thus it must be above all a historical attitude. And in contrast to the watchword of the Restoration, which was to maintain order at any cost, Ortega warns that "national vitality takes precedence over public order,"[34] that "our problem is much greater, much deeper; it is not to live with order, but to live first of all."[35]

Given these assumptions, we can understand in what the thirty-year-old Ortega's political action consisted. As "potentialities for modernity" in Spanish public life, he recognizes only the Socialist party and the trade-union movement, which, he adds "we would join if they did not limit themselves, as Socialism in particular does, to dogmatic creeds, with all the drawbacks to liberty possessed by doctrinal religion."[36] In the "Prospectus" he goes into even more detail about his attitude, favorable but at the same time critical, of partial agreement and essential reservations and differences of opinion with regard to Socialism: "The Socialist creed is not adequate either. Even leaving aside its utopian attitudes and the rigidity of its dogmas, which the revisionist trend of the workers' party in other countries condemns, we would not hesitate to accept all its practical statements. In this area we believe that our association will march shoulder to shoulder with Socialism without serious differences of opinion. But we cannot be a party to their negoti-

[30] I, 273.

[31] I, 274.

[32] I, 275. See the reply to the interpretation of "Sancho Quijano" (Salvador de Madariaga) in "Fe de erratas" and "Nueva fe de erratas" (1923). III, 134–40.

[33] I, 276.

[34] I, 276.

[35] I, 279.

[36] I, 277.

ations. *For us, the national problem exists. Still more: we cannot easily separate the question of the workers from the national question.*"[37]

Ortega affirms his primary faith in something that is neither the government nor the state, but *the free spontaneity of society*, and warns against "the fatal tendency in every state to take unto itself the whole life of a society."[38] Two motives, therefore, make him draw away both from socialization and statism: the national question and faith in liberty and spontaneity. And therefore his basic political attitude is *liberalism*, with certain details which distinguish it from the existing liberal party.[39] *"We are certain that a large number of Spaniards agree with us in finding that Spain's fate is linked with the advance of liberalism.* On this point we are not to be surprised in the slightest vacillation. But at the same time we believe that by declaring ourselves as liberals we have not shortened our task by one jot. We can understand by liberalism nothing other than that radical emotion, always alive in history, which tends to exclude from the state any influence which is not merely human, and constantly hopes, in all spheres, for new social forms, and a good greater than past and inherited good. But this perennial emotion needs, in every day of its historical progress, a clear and intense body of ideas from which it can take fire . . . . Therefore it is indispensable today for liberalism to dispose of those ideologies which have influenced it for a hundred years . . . the individualist form of liberalism."[40]

As for forms of government, he does not feel *in principle* bound either to the monarchy or the republic. The only thing he considers immutable and indispensable, along with liberalism, is "the generic, the eternal ideals of democracy";[41] he cannot even allow it to be said that the republic is better in theory: "There is no other theory but the theory of practice, and a theory which is not that is no theory but simply foolishness."[42] "It is a question," he adds, "of structuring Spanish life, of acting

[37] I, 303.

[38] I, 277.

[39] In the original edition of the lecture *La pedagogía social como programa político*, printed as a pamphlet in 1912, there is "A word to the reader" added at the end, reading, "Now, I wish to add one clarification. When I have spoken of conservatives in the preceding pages, I refer to the persons who are given that label in Spain today. When I speak of democrats, of liberals, I am not referring to the persons who are given that label in Spain today."

[40] I, 303.

[41] I, 289.

[42] I, 290.

vigorously upon those last remnants of national vitality. For this purpose, we are beginning to work on the Spain that we find. We are monarchists, not so much because we make a great point of being so, but because she—Spain—is monarchical . . . . On this point, it is not seemly for the twentieth century to take any other posture than an experimental one . . . . The monarchy must justify its legitimacy every day, not only negatively, taking care not to break the law, but also positively, by serving as an impetus to national life . . . . If a formula is required . . . I should say that we are going to take part in politics like monarchists without loyalist tendencies. The monarchy is an institution, and we cannot be asked to make it the inalienable basis, the moral axis, of our political conscience. There are two things higher than the monarchy: justice and Spain. It is necessary to nationalize the monarchy."[43]

Liberalism and nationalization: these are the slogans proposed by Ortega.[44] "Nationalization of the army, nationalization of the monarchy, nationalization of the clergy (I have no time to go into this), nationalization of the worker; I would even say nationalization of those ladies who place their signatures, from time to time, at the bottom of petitions of whose importance and transcendence they are unaware . . . ." But Ortega must warn that "nationalization" has nothing to do with "nationalism," of which he had already said, in 1908, that it "deserves exquisite contempt."[45] "Nationalism," concludes Ortega, "presupposes the desire to have one nation lord it over others, which supposes at least that that nation is alive. But we are not alive! Our aim is very different: we . . . would be just as ashamed of wanting a ruling Spain as of not wanting a healthy Spain, a vertebrated Spain that stands on her feet."[46]

These principles are translated into a political program which is a program of conduct: Spain must be taken possession of, known, explored, actively loved. "We are going to flood the farthest corners of Spain with our curiosity and our enthusiasm; we are going to see Spain, and sow her with love and indignation. We are going to explore the fields in an apostolic horde, live in the villages, listen to despairing complaints in the places whence they arise; we are first going to be friends of those

[43] I, 291–92.
[44] I, 299.
[45] I, 96.
[46] I, 300.

whose leaders we will later be. We are going to create strong social ties with them . . . . We shall strive for an imperious spiritual surge among the best men of each capital . . . . We shall let those fraternal spirits, lost in their provincial inertia, know that they have helpers and defenders in us . . . . We are not in a hurry: haste is the only quality the ambitious usually possess."[47]

These ideas, formulated in his first fully political action, were to stay with Ortega all his life. If, keeping them in mind, we go over his entire public trajectory *up to the time of his death*—his participations, his teachings, his words, his silences—we will see that all of it agrees with this initial program, with absolute coherence. The variations in that trajectory are the very condition of that coherence, of fidelity to that point of view: as circumstances change, there is a gradual change in *what needs to be done*, the action demanded by that *same* imperative of authenticity, formulated as early as the age of thirty. We shall continue to see it throughout this book. We shall see how the same consciousness of the Spanish problem, the same demand for "nationalization" of forms and institutions, the subordination of them all to the service of Spain, the same unrenounceable liberalism, stay with him through so much grief, so much error, so much hope. Ortega's political activity arises out of a radically serious persuasion and emotion, which he formulated in 1914 in words that still stand today: "Every Spaniard bears within himself, like a dead man, one who could have been born and was not born, and no doubt there will come a day— it does not matter when—on which those dead men will choose an hour to arise, and savagely come to settle accounts with you for the murder you have committed."[48]

40. POLEMIC AND CREATION

When we read Ortega now, we sometimes have the impression that he is—and especially was in his youth—a polemical writer. This impression is based on the presence, throughout all his work, of frequent references to intellectual positions foreign to his own with which he disagrees, and still more on impersonal reproaches aimed at science or the intellectual life in its totality, which he accuses of not having clarified or presented basic and visceral problems that should have been their starting point. All this, moreover, is done out of his own personality as a *writer*, and therefore with extraordinary vivacity and emphasis, in striking ways which stick tenaciously in the memory. All this contrasts with the usual practice, in which—especially in Spain, but not only in Spain—intellectual life has lost a large part of its vitality, spontaneity, and flexibility, in which the literary form of discussion has been forgotten; and, when an apparent "literary polemic" arises, it is likely to carry in its wake a grim weight of profound and real hostility which is almost always political.[49] Therefore it will be well to go beyond this first impression of the reader's, and to see to what extent Ortega was polemical.

It must be said that, quantitatively, he was not very much so. If we consider the sum total of his works, we will find that very few pages are concerned with writings of a polemical intent. And these few are primarily dedicated to *clarifying* the meaning of his thought, sometimes merely to stating in detail what he had said before by quoting his own text. Thus, for example, the articles "Algunas Notas" ["Some Notes"], and "Sobre una apología de la inexactitud" ["On a Defense of Inexactness"],[50] in which he turns back to the true meaning of his ideas in a discussion with Maeztu, or in "Unamuno y Europa, una fábula" ["Unamuno and Europe, a Fable"],[51] where he harshly rejects Unamuno's invective against the "simpletons" of europeanization; or, in a clearer way, the two articles "Fe de erratas" ["List of Errors"] and "Nueva fe de erratas" ["New List of Errors"],[52] whose sole object is to show by quoting his own words how "Sancho Quijano," when he referred to "Old and New Politics," had not understood this lecture, and had attributed to Ortega something approximately opposite to his real thought.

Much more frequent and significant in Ortega's work are what we might call "oblique polemical ingredients." We find their root in an undertaking to which Ortega dedicated a large part of his energies and which is what we might call, using the title of one of his essays, *the reform of intelligence*. This reform arises out of a situation in which theoretical thought as such had departed from Spain, and only the action of a few men, especially those of the Generation of 1898, was

---

[49] See my article "La convivencia intelectual como forma de trato," in *El intelectual y su mundo* (*Obras*, IV, 522ff.).

[50] I, 111 ff.

[51] III, 128 ff.   [52] III, 134 ff.

reappropriating it and reacclimating it in Spain. It was necessary, therefore, to lay about oneself on both sides with the rudder, to attack erudition when it presented itself as science (instead of being accepted as a simple, indispensable ingredient for creating science), to combat anachronism, provincialism, inertia. And when the men of 1898, especially Unamuno, either through arbitrariness or loss of enthusiasm, began to be unfaithful to what Ortega believed their enlightening mission to be, when he saw old Spanish vices reappearing under their hands, he considered it his inescapable duty to disagree. He was soon to do something similar with regard to the forms of European intelligence. Ortega's reservations about German thought, despite his confessed admiration for it, were strongly felt, and dated from his student years in Berlin and Marburg. He was soon to have the conviction that the European mind was afflicted with substantial defects, that the Western intellectual minorities had a coefficient of irresponsibility which he felt to be dangerous—immediately, for the future of that very intellectual life; secondarily for the world in which we live. Both fears have been justified in the course of the last decades, perhaps more than Ortega foresaw, at least more than he ever expressed.

What I am interested in emphasizing here is that Ortega's work is never polemical *in its content*. When it is, it takes the form of *rectification*, of *complement*, or of *desideratum*—that is, by recognizing the absence of something which ought to have been done and has not been done. He does this many times—there can be no doubt of it—and very vigorously, almost always motivated by the conviction that a doctrine has been presented in which the essential factor has been omitted. It is true that Ortega's work is sprinkled with such expressions as "this has come nowhere near an explanation," "it seems incredible that this has not been cleared up," "it is shameful that philosophy or history have not posed this question." These practices have frequently aroused irritation against their author. Sometimes, the exigencies of style—to which Ortega was so sensitive—have led him to use expressions which are both extreme and uncompromising, in places where it would have been, in fact, advisable to introduce some restriction or exception. But if we go to the root of the question, we must recognize that he was *almost always* right in his objections, that on the points he criticized—and on other essential points as well—not enough has been said. And it must be added that in the majority of cases, the cure went along with the objection, or at least an indication of where a cure was to be sought. I mean that Ortega was not in the habit of leaving things in mere reproaches, and that on the same page in which he offered a reproach, even an extreme one, to the science of our time, we will find at least a rudimentary reply, a methodical indication, or a clue which, if utilized, would have been able to accomplish this *desideratum*. A sentence from *Meditations on Quixote*,[53] applied to Spain, could be transferred to his entire intellectual attitude: "Isolated negation is an impiety. The pious and honorable man contracts the obligation, when he denies, of building a new affirmation. Or of trying to, be it understood."

In an article of his early maturity, without mentioning himself, Ortega gave an explanation of the reason why his work, so impassioned and so combative, could not be polemical in substance. Ortega, in fact, never formulated a doctrine "in contra"; he liked to repeat that he could not content himself with "antibeing"—the height of modesty— but that he aspired to "being." Not a single one of Ortega's ideas is presented as a "refutation" of someone else's; not one of his writings has as its object the invalidation of a doctrine or system belonging to anyone else. When something seems erroneous or insufficient to him, he remarks on it in passing, justifying the mention as briefly as possible, and then advances toward what he believes to be true and fruitful. Thus he can write: "For the real lover of psychological secrets there is nothing more interesting than to surprise a symptom of weakness, a defensive concern, in the mania for attack. The strong man never thinks of attacking: his primary attitude is simply one of affirmation. The serene affirmation of a doctrine, of a wish, of a desire, is the true offensive of the warrior temperament. Attack is a secondary thing for him, and is always the reply to a fellow human who felt offended by the hearty tranquillity of his affirmation. In intellectual life, this is shown with superlative clarity. The writer who tends too much toward polemics is the one who has nothing to say for himself. For me this has become an infallible sign. It would seem to me to be an incredible heroism if a man replete with new ideas about things, instead of setting them forth, were to occupy himself with combating the ideas of others. The authentic intellectual offensive is the expression of new positive doctrines."[54]

[53] I, 328.
[54] "El deber de la nueva generación argentina" (1924). III, 259.

41. THE PROFESSOR OF PHILOSOPHY
in partibus infidelium AND THE
CONVERSION OF THE INFIDEL

All of Ortega's activities became joined to the one which was to constitute the main bulk of his professional life from the moment he had a profession. In June, 1908, he was appointed holder of the chair of psychology, logic and ethics in the College of Education in Madrid.[55] María de Maeztu has written of his first class, "It is nine o'clock in the morning; the lecture room, with a window overlooking the gardens of the Retiro Park, is occupied by forty students, men and women . . . . Ortega comes into the class with a leather folder in his hand. He takes a small book out of it: it is one of the dialogues of Plato, the "Theaetetus"; before beginning to read it, he explains to the students, as a brief introduction, what his course in philosophy is going to be like. Philosophy, he says, is the general science of love: within the intellectual sphere it represents the greatest force toward an all-embracing connection. In philosophy a shade of difference becomes apparent between understanding and mere knowledge. Philosophy is the opposite of information, of erudition. Erudition is the unity of facts, not in themselves but inside the brain of a person—it is not the investigation of the hidden unity of phenomena. The ultimate ambition of philosophy would be to arrive at a single proposition which would express all of the truth—philosophy is an aspiration, a yearning. It is a sudden discharge of intellectual insight.

"The master's words, clear, precise, and elegant, produce a strange emotion. The students try to take notes in their notebooks; but soon they listen with absorption, their pens hovering over the paper, to the marvel of that philosophical exposition clothed in such richness of images and metaphors. It seems that we are witnessing, not the teaching of a magisterial class, but *the progress of a dramatic theory whose protagonist is the philosopher's very life.* Ortega had studied the philosophy of Kant in Germany with Professor Cohen, and he was to be the man who introduced neo-Kantianism into the lecture rooms of our University. However, Ortega departed from the very beginning from the

[55] By Royal Order of June 24, 1908, at the request of the Central Committee of Primary Education, the Royal Academy of Moral and Political Sciences, the Council of Public Instruction, and the Faculty of Philosophy and Letters of the Central University.

method followed by those great teachers whose lessons we were to hear later in the University of Marburg. Under the guise of a cold, serene, incorruptible objectivity, 'beyond good and evil,' a warm emotion, a contained passion, sprang up from the subsoil as from a hidden spring. He honestly tried to flee, to avoid, all emotionalism; but Ortega was a man of the South, and the fire that burned in his spirit was there, and betrayed his best intentions. Philosophical doctrine, dry as dust, acquired a new vigor, a living, immediate strength. His was not a dehumanized philosophy. In him, pure reason was soon to lose its purity, and become converted into vital reason."[56]

Two years later, Ortega presented himself for the competitive examinations to the chair of metaphysics in the Faculty of Philosophy in the University of Madrid, and on November 25, 1910, he was appointed to it; his predecessor had been Nicolás Salmerón, the Krausist thinker and politician, oriented toward Positivism during his last years of tenure. This appointment was received with enthusiasm in the intellectual circles where Ortega already enjoyed great prestige. Ortega, to be sure, offered to continue his position as professor in the College of Education at no salary, so as not to inconvenience his students, and this offer was accepted by Royal Order. Ortega's salary as professor of the University of Madrid was 4,500 pesetas per year. He had married on April 7 of that year. The year 1910 is the date of his "installation" in two especially important sectors of his life.

Since we have already pointed out many negative aspects of Spanish life during this time, and shall soon have to add others, it would be well to pause for a moment on what these two professorial appointments of Ortega's meant. In my opinion the first is more significant. It is not particularly surprising that Ortega's incomparable superiority should assure his success in a competitive examination for a chair, at a time when there was still public life—a Parliament, a free press, etc.—in Spain; more worthy of attention is the fact that fairly broad circles of opinion were aware of that superiority and reacted to something as unexciting as a chair of metaphysics—but the fact that four institutions, the Central Committee of Primary Education, the Royal Academy of Ethical and Political Sciences, the Council on Public Instruction, and the Faculty of Philosophy and Letters, should have been in agreement

[56] María de Maeztu, *Antología—Siglo XX*, (Buenos Aires, 1943), 85–87. Italics mine. The text gives the date of 1909.

in unanimously proposing the young Ortega, who in June of 1908 had published only a few articles, in which he had shown himself to be independent, critical, an innovator, and a man of abounding personality, is something which is worth emphasizing even fifty years later.

We must point out that before he was appointed a university professor, and after he had been one in the College of Education, Ortega had written in *El Imparcial*—that is, with maximum publicity—a very harsh criticism of the Spanish university, as well as an affirmation of deep and lively faith in the institution of the university. In it Ortega recalls the five hundredth anniversary of the University of Leipzig. He rejects the general opinion that in Spain wars and political unrest had produced a cultural collapse; as if the other countries, he says, had been sleeping on a bed of roses in the meantime. We Spaniards, he says, waste and squander our activity: the terrible economic need, the terrible demands of ambition and of passion, "the most ferocious of which are eroticism and pleasure-seeking," vie for our attention. "In countries where the ethical tradition had not been lost, there were those who abstained amid the excitement; there were quiet and peaceful men in the midst of war; and in the midst of seductions, there were humble folk and chaste folk." And after saying that "there is just as much peace in a state as there is university; and only where there is something of a university is there some element of peace," he concludes, "Many readers will believe, and rightly, that this makes no sense: what comes to their minds under the name of university, is a most mournful reality: a dingy and featureless building, a few solemn men, who, repeating dead words, foist their ineptitude and inner gloom onto the younger generations; some schoolboys who play billiards, loudly demand the score, and, twice a year, are classified into 'passed' or 'failed.' The reader is quite right: if that is the university, instead of finding anything resembling peace there, we should have to consider it as something resembling utter Philistinism." And he concludes the article, after evoking the University of Leipzig: "And meanwhile, in our ghostly University the shade of a professor fiercely calls the roll of the shades of a few students."[57]

When, at the age of twenty-seven, Ortega became part of that University, he was determined that it should cease to be a ghost. But,

[57] "Una fiesta de paz" (1909). I, 124–27.

for this purpose, he took great care to keep its phantasmagoric quality well in mind. In 1914, on the first page of the *Meditations on Quixote*, he calls himself "a professor of philosophy *in partibus infidelium.*"[58] In spite of the efforts of Unamuno, and previously those of the Krausists and of José del Perojo, of the editors of philosophical libraries—Lázaro Galdeano with *La España Moderna* ["Modern Spain"], Daniel Jorro, later Antonio Zozaya—Spain was far from any philosophical activity "at the height of the times." Let us recall Morente's words as he described the situation at the time Ortega began his university teaching: "At that time, philosophy did not exist in Spain. Mediocre devotees of Scholasticism, vague dregs of Positivism, mystical fogs of Krausism, had detoured Spanish thought away from the living trajectory of universal thought, burying it in eccentric, out-of-date, behind-the-times corners. Spain was, it could be said, outside the philosophical movement. She did not even participate in it as a mere spectator."[59]

Under these circumstances, Ortega had to check his tendency to make "technical" philosophy; if he had done so, he would have fallen into a void, would have been "unassimilable." He made rigorous philosophy, although it was also attractive, exciting, and dramatic, in his chair at the University, frequented by a group of well-known men a great deal older than he, along with a few young ones. The chair of metaphysics belonged at that time to the doctoral program of a faculty which had very few students, most of whom went no further than the licentiate. For many years Ortega had very few students. Only in the last years of his teaching career in the University, when I was one of his pupils, were his courses attended by a considerable number of students, never exceeding fifty at most, and there were fewer still in his seminars or commentaries on texts. For some twenty years Ortega's participation in the University was extremely minor, and never exclusively academic. This was essential, however, and Ortega was always conscious of it, to the point that when he interrupted all his activities, even that of writing, on occasion, he continued his university teaching without a break—so long as this was possible with full efficiency and dignity, and not a day longer. But he knew that it was not sufficient, for the university is not an isolated reality, but is always rooted in the country, from which it

[58] I, 311.

[59] Manuel G. Morente, *El Sol*, March 8, 1936. (Collected in *Ensayos* [1945], 204–205.)

receives its sap and vitality; it is a "retreat" in which the country's powers are stored and concentrated, to return to the country as a catalyst. Thus, it was neither sufficient nor possible to create an *isolated* philosophical group, one which we might call "intrauniversity." This was the reason why Ortega could not content himself with lamenting his status as a professor of philosophy *in partibus infidelium* or with commenting on it ironically. He had to do something more profound and more difficult: to try to convert the infidel.

And it must be said that he succeeded. By the time he had been a university professor for ten years, Spain had a hitherto unknown sensitivity for philosophy. Day after day, from the pages of the daily newspaper, from reviews, in books replete with charm and clarity, through the emergence of the first groups of his pupils, Ortega had continued to bring philosophy everywhere. He had made the reality of philosophy intelligible to large groups of Spaniards, almost without pronouncing its name. In his last years as professor at the University, Spain was very probably the country with the greatest receptivity toward philosophy, the one most sensitized to it, and, in consequence, least "provincial" in that dimension and in some others. This has not been lost. Many of the chief philosophical works of this century were translated into Spanish before any other language; points of view have been reached which represent a more advanced level than that of other countries whose tradition is incomparably superior; an eager public makes it possible to publish any book of quality, no matter how difficult it may be, when in other countries no editor—at least no commercial editor—could undertake to do so; this same public attends with a degree of interest unimaginable in other places (and in Spain forty years ago) courses in philosophy which require considerable effort. It would be impossible today, without extreme injustice, to repeat the sentence with which Ortega began his *Meditations on Quixote*. And we must still add the fact that this "conversion" has not been confined to the borders of Spain, but has spread to the "infidel" of the other countries which speak our language.

Only the combination of activity in the University with the career of a writer made this possible. If Ortega had been only one of these things, the result would have been very different. But I have said "combination"; it is not a mere problem of addition. And this gives rise to a question of primary importance: what was the character and function of Ortega's writings?

42. ORTEGA'S WRITINGS AS ICEBERGS

There could be no graver error for the comprehension of Ortega than the *identification* of his writings with his thought; it is one that has been committed so many times that this alone suffices to explain, in large measure, the lack of clarity which exists about Ortega. I mean that, throughout fifty-three years, the length of Ortega's life as a writer, he *expounded* his thought very few times, and almost never —not to say never—his philosophy. Does this mean that Ortega possessed a doctrine apart, to which his writings do not correspond? Not at all: they are absolutely faithful to the mind—and what is still more important, to the biography—of their author, to the point that they represent an extreme of *veracity* in the history of philosophy. I once said[60] that Ortega's writings should always be taken as *icebergs*. Let us take this figure of speech seriously, in its turn.

These writings show only 10 per cent of their reality; the rest, which is the larger part, remains hidden under the surface. Ortega never poured into his works the whole of his thought. It is not that he never "managed" to do so, in the sense that he did not succeed in doing so, that he did not carry out that exposition to the end, that he tried to again and again, dissatisfied with what he had accomplished, like Fichte in his *Wissenschaftslehre*; it is, more simply, that this was not his aim. Throughout his life he wrote *circumstantial*, occasional, studies, in which he went straight to the point, to say something, to communicate to the reader—a very particular reader, whose figure gradually changed over the course of time—certain truths, certain warnings, certain very concrete exhortations. To do so he had to put into play *the totality of his philosophical thought*, which is also in action in his lesser writings, but which is not expressed and formulated, which does not appear in them except in the strict measure indispensable for their comprehension.

Ortega's philosophy is present in his works in a singular way; it is there even when not there, it is "underneath," underlying everything

[60] In *El hombre y la gente: la teoría de la vida social en Ortega* (1957). (In *La escuela de Madrid* [1959], 275.) (*Obras*, V.)

that he says, literally sustaining and nourishing it. It could be said that that philosophy constitutes the subsoil of those writings, but I prefer not to say this and to return to the figure of the iceberg. An iceberg is, in fact, a single block, a single and compact piece; what can be seen is in no sense separable from the submerged part, and there is no break between them; not only is it underneath, but it is also joined to the rest. Furthermore, the submerged bulk of the iceberg can be seen thanks to the transparency of the water; it *gives evidence* of its latent presence, it *is* latent. Lastly, it can be explored, discovered, recognized, by merely diving under the surface a little. This philosophy is not "denied" or buried in a dark subsoil, but appears as soon as one has achieved a certain depth and sufficient illumination. And then it shows its outline, its configuration, its entire reality, which becomes transparent. This is what we are going to do in this book.

Very early, Ortega was in possession of the roots of what was to be his philosophical system. Each fundamental idea, which has its date of pronouncement, almost always turns out to be already "old": one has the impression, at first stylistic—that is, recognizable by its features— that Ortega has not just "arrived at it" but that he has "at last" enunciated it. This impression is usually confirmed, and one fine day we discover indications of that idea some years previously. Why, if he possessed it, did he not formulate it before? How was it that he did not hasten to communicate his thought, being, as he was, very much an author and anything but taciturn? Ortega always had a *horror of haste*; few traits in his character have been more profound and more constant. The mere suspicion that something could be "hasty" made him refrain from doing it. If we do not keep this in mind, we cannot understand Ortega's life, and especially his public action. "Life is haste," he taught again and again; but precisely in haste he saw the failure of all theory and all conduct ruled by an intellectual doctrine. On the other hand, his whole philosophy consisted in avoiding the "Greek calends," the postponement *sine die* of replies to the problems that had been posed. His life ran its course between these two fears, that of haste and that of the Greek calends, and we must understand his work in the light of both. "We are not in a hurry: haste is the only quality the ambitious usually possess,"[61] we have seen that he said in 1914; and fifteen years later, in his course, "¿Qué es filosofía?" ["What Is Philosophy?"], which was

[61] I, 287.

kept in manuscript and not published until after his death, an insistent example of his denial of haste, he repeated: "I am in no hurry to be proved right. The right is not a train that leaves at a certain hour. Only the sick man and the ambitious man are in a hurry."[62]

The deliberate circumstantiality of Ortega's work obliged him to keep in mind the level of his own thought, the situation of the person to whom his words were aimed, that person's capacity for receptivity, the repercussions that could be foreseen. This made him postpone constantly the expounding of many doctrines. I believe that he sometimes was mistaken about the attitude and capacities of his readers, and delayed unnecessarily the presentation of theories which ought to have been adequately formulated by him at relatively early dates.

We must keep in mind, however, that Ortega always wrote motivated by authentic inspiration, never out of inertia and because it was his trade. In the writing of every book there are some dry areas which require effort to traverse, some steppes or unappetizing deserts, temptations to leave the writing unfinished; if to this we add the constant stimulus of new subjects on Ortega's mind—the part of him that was like a bull, as I once said, incapable of resisting the call of the red rag represented by an exciting problem—the fragmentary nature of almost all his works can be explained.

But in each of them, even the less important ones, the integral mass of his thought was in operation, and this was, from a very early date, a systematic philosophy, the compact bulk of that iceberg whose tip alone emerged above the waves.

[62] "¿Qué es filosofía?" (course given in 1929) (1958), 220.

Part Two

THE WRITER

I.

ORTEGA'S STYLE

43. LITERATURE AND PRECISION

Ortega began to write for the public in 1902, at the age of nineteen. After 1904 he did so continuously. That is, he began very soon after the writers of the Generation of 1898, was almost of the same "social age"[1] as a number of them, and very quickly made connections with them on a basis of equality—except for Unamuno, nineteen years older than he, whose leadership Ortega recognized. Probably this explains Ortega's tendency to relegate Unamuno and Ganivet to a generation he calls the generation of 1857[2] (one to which Barrès, Shaw, etc., would also belong),[3] and in consequence to set them apart from the other writers of 1898—Valle-Inclán, Azorín, Baroja, Maeztu, the Machado brothers—who appeared to him to be on a different level.

He was, therefore, inside this immediately preceding literary tradi-

---

[1] See my article "Constelaciones y generaciones" (1953), in *Ensayos de convivencia* (*Obras*, III, 198 ff).

[2] Ganivet was born in 1865 and died in 1898; he was, therefore, a year younger than Unamuno; but the year 1862 has been repeated as that of his birth in many books, and it is the date Ortega gives, which perhaps explains his grouping the two Spanish authors with Barrès and Shaw. I would not accept 1857 as the central birth date of that generation, as indicated by Ortega, but believe that it is 1856 (see my article "La generación de 1856" in *El oficio del pensamiento*). Unamuno and Ganivet would *not* belong to it, but to the following generation, that of 1871, *together with the other members of the "Generation of 1898."* Is the generational link which Ortega establishes between Shaw and Barrès on the one hand, and Unamuno and Ganivet on the other, a simple error, then? Is it based only on an error of date with regard to Ganivet, and of Ortega's having adopted 1857 instead of 1856? I do not think so. In my opinion, Shaw and Barrès belong to one generation and Unamuno and Ganivet to another, but certain functions carried out *in Europe* by the generation of 1856 are accomplished *in Spain* by the following generation. (See above, Introduction, I, 8, "The crisis of 1898.")

[3] Prologue to *Cartas finlandesas* and *Hombres del Norte*, by Angel Ganivet. VI, 370 ff.

tion; he collaborated with them and with the men of his own generation in the reviews of the period—*Vida Nueva, Alma Española, Faro*—and in *El Imparcial*. Valera was by this time very old; he died, still writing, in 1905, attentive to what was going on around him, sensitive to the art of Pío Baroja, so different from his own; but with a certain inclination toward some writer-diplomats with little inspiration or spirit. Ortega speaks of "the cold and correct books of some new writers in the Ministry of State which inspire and protect the soul of Don Juan Valera, that smiling, blind God Pan who still survives in the sterile garden of Spanish letters, like the broken white statue of a heathen deity."[4] This was undoubtedly one reason why Ortega did not feel very much attracted to Valera; another more important reason was that, since Valera was a writer who was still alive and producing, Ortega paid more attention to his recent work, which did in fact show the defects for which Ortega reproached it. Except for the novels—relatively late works— Valera's early writings had been gradually becoming, if not lost, badly outdated; today we see the sum total of his work in perspective, but while he was alive, attention was paid to his more recent work; therefore the Valera who might have been able to arouse interest in Ortega was, in particular, the Valera prior to 1870, a Valera who had not yet given in to the leveling and disillusioned pressures of the Restoration. Ortega's regard for him was lukewarm and distant, and I have the impression that he was not aware of certain resemblances and coincidences which existed between them, and which were certainly very inconspicuous in Valera's last years, when he was writing a benevolent, somewhat frivolous, and very disenchanted kind of criticism.

Galdós' influence was, by its very nature, less probable. First, because he was almost exclusively a narrator, at most a dramatist, and Ortega never wrote either fiction or poetry; in the second place, because Ortega entered literary life just at the time when there was a shift away from Galdós, for a reason that was justified, though partial and insufficient: the critics missed in him what I have called "quality of style," this quality being what the Generation of 1898 restored; Valera—and almost solely Valera—had retained it.

Among the "reigning" writers, members of previous generations— of the generation of 1826, Valera; that of 1841, Galdós; of 1856, Menéndez Pelayo, Clarín, Ortega's own father, Ortega Munilla—only

---

[4] "La *Sonata de estío*, de Don Ramón del Valle-Inclán" (1904). I, 26.

Costa and Menéndez Pelayo had authentic prestige for the young Ortega. I have already demonstrated the stylistic influence of Costa, traces of which seem evident to me in Ortega's prose. Later on I shall have to discuss in more detail in what these traces consisted. As for Menéndez Pelayo, whom Ortega read as a boy, "transfixed with faith," it is licit to speculate that frequent reading of him in Ortega's years of stylistic formation served to counterbalance somewhat the tendency to the short sentence imposed by the Generation of 1898. Menéndez Pelayo was a spirited writer, both facile and copious, with a considerable volume of work; but he was not very rigorous, tended to be old-fashioned in his language, and, worst of all, frequently lapsed into clichés. The task of returning its pristine quality to the language, which the writers of 1898 undertook with such exceptional intensity and success, the high level which they set for themselves, left Menéndez Pelayo "out-of-date" when he was scarcely more than thirty years of age, and he never succeeded in becoming "up-to-date" again. I do not know whether sufficient notice has been taken of this, which could explain many things, among them the intellectual and literary trajectory of Menéndez Pelayo himself. His "classicism," his hastiness, his character (almost continuously polemical and rhetorical), with a rhetoric (*sit venia verbo*) of a very conservative tenor—all this placed him outside the mainstream, locating him in a tradition which was mediocre in the literary sense and rather thankless. This caused the undoubted literary talent he possessed to become in the end infertile—as, for that matter, happened with all his other talents, except that of historian, in the strict sense, of our letters.

Ortega, therefore, was formed along with the authors of the Generation of 1898 as well as the older or more precocious members of his own generation—Juan Ramón Jiménez, Pérez de Ayala. That is, once again —just as in the sphere of thought—almost without teachers and, though not without elders, without *seniors*. He joined in the renovation of writing carried out by the Generation of 1898 in a "cumulative" attitude toward it and a "polemical" one toward what had gone before it, contributing his personal touches and a level which was no longer exactly the same as before.

But with some essential differences. The first was that the writers of the Generation of 1898, except for Unamuno and Ganivet, had a formation that was primarily *literary* and *Spanish*. Their formation in the

university was either nonexistent or unimportant, and had few consequences. Valle-Inclán, Azorín, Baroja, and the Machados were purely
literary writers: Maeztu, more of an ideologue, was above all a journalist and lacked refined and rigorous intellectual techniques. Their readings were almost exclusively in Spanish and French—English in the
case of Maeztu. Even in the case of Ganivet and Unamuno, the situation
is not *entirely* different, for various causes contributed toward weakening
their very different formation. Both were products of the university,
knew classical languages and a number of modern ones, had a vast range
of reading in all of them, were familiar—especially Unamuno, incomparably more so—with European thought, including philosophical
thought. But their professed traditionalism, and their desire to avoid
any "scientific" air and even all doctrine—Unamuno's irrationalism in
particular—caused this formation to remain in a certain degree hidden
or placed in parentheses, denied and therefore unexpressed; and in
consequence it did not act—or acted only in a slight degree—on their
literature.

Ortega, in contrast, felt from the beginning like a man of doctrine.
The first thing he wrote, after five or six articles, was a doctoral thesis.
Since his youth he had had an ample background of reading in foreign
languages: French, of course, but followed immediately by German
(Nietzsche, Goethe, Hebbel, Heine, Schopenhauer)—I am referring
here to reading of literary significance; and secondarily English and
Italian, and, of course, Greek (Plato, Herodotus, Thucydides, Polybius)—and Latin (Cicero, Seneca). His reading in French was very
broad and covered a large span of time; the names of Chateaubriand,
Renan, and Barrès have often been emphasized, and properly—more
because he mentioned them than because any special trace of them is
discernible—but they were by no means the only ones. We should have
to think of Montaigne and Descartes, of Pascal—in spite of Ortega's
reservations, which he expressed *because* he had read him—Voltaire,
Rousseau, all the Romantics, and the marvelous doctrinaire writers
(Constant, de Tocqueville, Royer-Collard, Guizot), and Baudelaire,
Verlaine, Mallarmé. And there was something else, which no one has
noticed so far as I know: Ortega had behind him an enormous number
of readings which were neither literary nor theoretical, without which
we cannot understand very important aspects of his personality: history

books—especially *chroniques* and memoirs—and books on travel, in all languages.

A second difference is that the members of the Generation of 1898—except for Maeztu—had almost always lived in Spain and did not undergo the profound experience of other countries. I am not counting Ganivet, who died "before," in the year of 1898 itself, and who did have the experience of living abroad; but he did not bring it back to Spain and assimilate it, because he did not return. Nor am I counting Antonio Machado, in spite of his stays in Paris, because he did not really profit from this experience. It will suffice to recall the sentence with which he began his article "Gentes de mi tierra" ["Folk of My Land"], so revealing of a common attitude among Spaniards: "During the time I have lived in Paris, more than two years, on my own, I have had dealings with few Frenchmen; but, on the other hand, I have been able to observe a number of traits of my own country."[5] Azorín's and Baroja's travels through Europe, hasty and coming late in their lives, cannot be compared with Ortega's studies in Germany, which conditioned his briefer stays in other countries.

But, in particular, the greatest difference between Ortega and his seniors was that, being by vocation and irremediably a *writer*—and we shall soon see what this meant—he could not be a *littérateur*. And since a writer is a man who makes literature, he was forced to invent a new image for that profession to overcome the contradiction. I have already mentioned what he wrote in 1908: "A man should either cultivate literature, or cultivate precision, or shut up,"[6] in a context where he was insisting that if there is a choice between them, a moral dilemma is posed, and that if we are capable of both literature and science, we will have to incline toward the latter, *with no pact whatever made with the former*. And, in 1924, he wrote from another point of view, "A man whose production consists of a delicious literary flow, a poet, a novel-maker, a stylist, can content himself with being read. But I am none of those things."[7] Which did not mean that he was not *also* a man of letters in some sense, at least in an instrumental way and as a means of seduction and persuasion toward philosophy: "I found it necessary

---

[5] *Obras completas de Manuel y Antonio Machado* (3rd ed., Madrid, 1957), 1197.
[6] I, 113.
[7] "El deber de la nueva generación argentina." III, 255.

to seduce my readers toward philosophical problems by lyric means"[8]—
and later, in a more intrinsic linking: "I do not give myself airs about
anything. But *man of letters, man of ideas, theorizer, and an amateur
of science* are not things which I aspire to be, but which—what the
devil!—I am, I am to my very roots . . . . *The figure of speech and
melody in the sentence are tendencies in my being which cannot be
gainsaid;* I have brought them to my University chair, to science, to
café conversation, just as, vice versa, I have brought philosophy to the
newspaper. What am I to do about it? What Sr. Prieto thinks of as a
bright-colored necktie I have put on, turns out to be *my spinal column*
itself, showing through."[9] And this duality, so clearly "overcome" in
principle and in his early youth, eventually became "my delight, the
irony of my life."

We shall see how far this went. We shall see what the *literary condition* of Ortega's philosophy is. And further, guided by his hand, not
only by his theory about it, but beyond theory, by the reality itself of
the philosophy he created, we shall come to discover that *only with
literature can one attain a certain higher precision,* that to cultivate

---

[8] "Ni vitalismo ni racionalismo" (1924). III, 270. The complete passage is particularly significant, and is worth recalling to mind; it reads as follows: "There is no
solution but to approach philosophy ever more closely—philosophy in the strictest sense
of the word. Until now it was convenient for the Spanish writers who were cultivators
of this science to try to hide the dialectical musculature of their philosophic thoughts by
weaving a flesh-colored film over them. It was necessary to seduce readers toward
philosophical problems by lyrical means. The stratagem has not been without result.
There exists today in the Spanish-speaking world a broad circle of people who are
already close to philosophy. It is, then, a good time to take the second step and begin
to speak of philosophy philosophically. But, of course, we must enter the new terrain
cautiously, inch by inch. Long experience of a University chair, the lectern, and the
press has given me quite an unfavorable opinion about the philosophical capacity of the
people of our countries at the present time. Philosophy can only live by breathing an
air that is called mental rigor, precision, abstraction. It belongs to the high-altitude
fauna, and needs a sharp mountain breeze, a bit rarefied and very penetrating breeze."
And he even adds, "I would prefer to have as readers the hunters of the chamois, who
know how to make just the right leap on the granite crag, not an inch to one side or
the other. But I have not found such readers. And still less among professional intellectuals. What predominates is the coarse mentality that squashes the tiny insect of the
articulated idea between its thick peasant's fingers. It does not pain people to squash
ants, nor to mix up concepts." We shall have to return to this passage from several
different points of view. Let it be noted here.

[9] "Una cuestión personal" (1931), in *Rectificación de la República* (Madrid, 1931).
(In *Obras* [1932], p. 1352.)

precision, the only solution is to cultivate literature. What literature? That is the question.

44. STYLE AS INSTALLATION

The importance of literary style arises from the fact that it is a manifestation—the most visible and patent manifestation—of a life style. It has a value which is "physiognomical," like the expression on a face. The point of departure of a literary style is, first of all, the language—just as that of a human face is the biological inheritance. Language is already "style" in itself, for it is a mode of "installation" in reality, out of which a person speaks (and, secondarily, writes); but it is not, of course, individual style. Language is always "this language of the moment"; it bears within itself the historical experiences of the race; it has created the "gestures" which correspond to these experiences, to their adaptation to different circumstances—think, for example, of the variation of the language, not to mention the literature, of any European country as it progressed from the Middle Ages to the sixteenth century, or after any of the great crises of its history, or, if you will, the difference between British and American English, or the Spanish of Spain and that (or perhaps *those*) of Spanish America; the historicity of style is, therefore, previous to literature, and consequently to the "history" of literature. Analogously, personal expression is superimposed—not only on the inheritance, but on the *age* of the face—and is, we might say, the "instrument" which will permit the speaker to strum a strictly individual melody. Any adequate study of a literary style must begin by isolating the elements which proceed from the language as such—from its precise historical vicissitude and the reigning literary level—before it can arrive at the personal modulation of the author under study. To what does this respond?

The generic forms of "installation"—race, social class, historical period—are distilled into a personal mode of expression which *realizes* them by integrating them with elements of the individual circumstance. To begin with, these are psychophysical, for the expressive factors are decisive; in the second place, they are biographical, and naturally include the aim which gives form to all biography. This personal installation is translated into a "temper," which not only is qualified, but has the possibility of quantification; that is, it admits of *degrees*, and the variation of these in the course of time. The Spanish language recognizes this, when it says of someone that he is "muy templado" ["in good temper"] as well as when it says that now he is "destemplado" ["out of temper"]. This vital temper is, if I am not mistaken, the root of style, and style is its expression; but we must add that style is from the outset *programmatic* (I mean, desired and sought), and man "takes sides" with it, "chooses" within it—and this corroborates, or eventually modifies, his temper. In other words, style becomes in its turn a constitutive and determining factor of his temper. In the true writer—later we shall inquire with some precision into what this means—style builds itself a habitation in which to lodge, within which it lives; and consequently style, the result of that basic and original "installation," functions secondarily as a decisive factor of installation.

This is why style has an importance that goes beyond aesthetics and psychology. In a philosopher, style usually seems secondary and almost irrelevant. But I believe exactly the opposite: style—or its "absence" on occasion, which is a peculiar form of style—is the basic assumption of all philosophy, since in that "installation" and that "temper" the primary life pattern and the primary interpretation of reality are given, which philosophy attempts to formulate in the sphere of meanings. Style is a substratum, and therefore an intrinsic part, of all philosophical doctrine, and at the same time a guideline which might permit one to measure the degree of authenticity of its realization.

Elsewhere[10] I have pointed out the important differences which exist between the concepts "circumstance" and "situation." The situation does not include all the elements of the circumstance, but only those which determine a concrete *level*; but, on the other hand, the situation is created by an element which is not circumstantial, but belongs to the "I": the aim, which is what articulates the situation and gives it its character as such. Very well: style is the most adequate expression of the situation thus understood. And its variation—style is a *mode of making*, concretely a mode of writing, a dynamic and not a static reality —corresponds to the *unstable* quality (by definition unstable) of the situation, which consists in being "one among several" (a unique situation is a contradiction in terms) and in being unable to persist. The determination of the peculiarity of a style and its history would be the

[10] *Introducción a la Filosofía,* I, 9 (*Obras,* II). *La estructura social,* I, 6.

proper method of pursuing the series of situations in which a life takes place and, in this particular case, the trajectory of a philosophical work, which is intrinsically literary.

Undoubtedly, this is easier said than done. There are no techniques to carry out this type of research. The studies commonly called "stylistic," no matter how great their interest may be, use results as their point of departure, and do not pose the antecedent problems, which are fundamental ones, the only ones which permit us really to explain those same results. Furthermore, an "intraliterary" presentation of the problem is not sufficient, not even in the case of literary writings—not to mention whether we can come to grips with it in a philosophical work. What would be worthy of being called a "physiognomy" of philosophy has yet to be written,[11] and it could be established only by a complex and very elaborate method, and after a long series of unsatisfactory fumblings and attempts. It is not to be expected, therefore, that in this context we can do anything more than postulate such a physiognomy, and briefly note the point to which, I believe, it might be oriented.

45. THEMES AND STYLE

The writer normally feels a greater or lesser number of stimuli; they are the *themes* on which he might possibly write. Generally, he actually writes about only a few of them; if he is a responsible writer, he has sufficient justification for this; but this is not enough; what happens most frequently is that an author feels more than sufficiently justified to write about some themes; more than this, he may think that he is "obliged" to do so, and yet he may never do so. This means that the *justification* we are discussing here is a *vital* and rather complex one; it is necessary for the incentive of a given theme to destroy the balance of other forces and resistances, and unleash the author's action. Without counting external motives—public ones, for example—we would have to keep in mind the writer's "inertia" with regard to certain themes, his "avidity" in relation to others, the fleetingness or persistence of his interest—all of which does not have too close a relationship with the

[11] My *Biografía de la Filosofía* (*Obras*, II) is in some measure an attempt to do this, though at a distance and consequently in very broad strokes. See also my article "Ferrater y su diccionario" (*La Nación*, Buenos Aires, February 8, 1959).

PART TWO: *The Writer*

objective difficulty of the work in each case. Therefore, when we confront an author, we would do well to enumerate first of all—having some reasons for doing so, of course—what he did *not* write. For example, Ortega never wrote—so far as is known, that is, publicly at least —any poetry, in spite of the fact that he had not only sensitivity for it, but also a personal lyricism which penetrates his work and gives a "poematic" character to many fragments of his prose. Nor did he ever write a novel, although he had theorized at such length about it, and, what is more, in a passage inquiring about the possibility of wisdom and its relationship to silence—"that great Brahmin"—he concluded by asking himself, "But, why not begin little by little, slowly, this new culture, this very latest 'scienza?' The first thing to do would be to meditate on what form of expression would be most adequate. Dialogue? Memoirs? Or, perchance, the novel? May not the novel exist, perhaps, as a language which had to mature in the school of art in order to be one day the primary expressive form of the great Brahmin?"[12]

With regard to poetry, Ortega probably felt it to be *personally* unjustified; that is, he felt it insufficiently; the poet's component of irresponsibility—"divine irresponsibility"—undoubtedly seemed to be too far distant from his own *dharma*; I do not mean the generic *dharma* of the "philosopher," but his own intransferrable *dharma*, which consisted in the affirmation of the intellectual's responsibility, in the concrete sense of justifying everything by deriving it from life. I think that Ortega must have felt that to *set himself* to writing verse would have been unauthentic.

As for the novel and memoirs, the question is more delicate. It is clear that Ortega did not feel that these genres were alien to him, and even that he planned on writing them. Once, when speaking of the accumulation of knowledge of one's fellow man which a person amasses in life, he said, "But no matter what portion of this knowledge has been vouchsafed to us, *it is a pity to carry it unspoken to the grave*; it is a pity not to leave it for others, and 'said' forever. After all, it is the knowledge of what was closest to us; it is our wisdom applied to concrete life, *vital science par excellence*. Year after year we have been amassing this booty, into which we skimmed the riches of our passing life. We wrote books on one subject or another, on the stars or on the Aztecs. And yet we silenced this gift of knowledge which life had made to us as we lived it. I find

[12] "El silencio, gran brahmán" (1925?). *El Espectador*, VII. II, 627.

that it is ungenerous not to return that life to life. Thus, I feel that *every man capable of meditation ought to add to his professional books another book that would communicate his vital knowledge.*"[13] And in 1928 he wrote again, "Some day, when I write my memoirs, I shall try to do so in what I feel to be the proper way. Memoirs, or their substitute, the novel, in which we recount our life, have as their object, after all, to save that life, to prevent its absolute volatilization. We want, in gratitude, to return to life what life has given us, or what we have wrenched out of life: to return it after having meditated about it and distilled it. And so the motto for my future memoirs and novels will be this: "¡Neblí, neblí, suelta tu presa!" [*"Falcon, falcon, release thy prey!"*][14]

In some measure Ortega wrote certain fragments or anticipations of what he planned to do. Since his early youth he had sporadically introduced into his writings "fictitious personages" who corresponded more or less to himself. The first of these is *Rubín de Cendoya, Spanish mystic,* who came to life in 1906[15] and survived until 1911.[16] Rubín de Cendoya, "an obscure man, a fervent man," a mystic and a Celtiberian, who wanders over the Guadarrama mountains and goes to Segovia, to whom Ortega writes about classicism, supposedly from Germany, while Rubín, his *alter ego,* stays behind among the mountains of Celtiberia; who was born in Cordova[17]—let us not forget Ortega's Andalusian roots —who wanders about the countryside of Castile, and to whom the cowherd Rodrigálvarez makes his confidences on the highlands of Sigüenza, Berlanga de Duero, and Medinaceli, on whose "desolate and threatening height" the anonymous singer of *Mio Cid* gave his song to the air, like a falcon screaming from a crag: "Let us not do things wrong! For Spain, Don Rubín, is a rosebush."[18] Rubín de Cendoya, a Spanish mystic, "a man so gentle and spiritual that he could, like Francis of Assisi, live for a whole week on the song of a locust,"[19] and who talks of *The Saint* and modernism beside the fountain of Neptune near the Prado Museum, while enjoying "the most intense of his enthusiasms: spatial aesthetics," and confesses that "men are not productive except when

---

[13] *Ibid.*, 625. Italics mine.
[14] "Intimidades. La Pampa . . . promesas." *Ibid.*, 630.
[15] "La pedagogía del paisaje." I, 53ff.
[16] "Tierras de Castilla." *El Espectador*, I. II, 41ff.
[17] I, 68.
[18] II, 46.
[19] "Sobre *El Santo*" (1908). I, 429ff.

they are religious" and that "Every man who thinks, 'life is a serious thing,' is a religious man at heart."

There was also (fleetingly) *Doctor Vulpius*, a German and a professor of philosophy, a subtle and metaphysical man, with whom Ortega spoke of art: "We used to go for a walk every afternoon in the Leipzig zoo, that damp and solitary place, covered with greenish black grass and planted with tall, dark trees. From time to time the eagles uttered a great legionary and imperial cry; the 'Wapiti,' or Canadian elk, lowed, homesick for its broad cold prairies, and not uncommonly, a pair of ducks chased each other over the water with lascivious gabbling, to the scandal of the honest folk among the bigger and more decorous animals."[20] Doctor Vulpius too? I believe that the answer—and the key to this personage who passes through Ortega's works and disappears, like those characters in novels from whom we hope for so much and who then evaporate—lies in these words written four years later: "My soul comes from known parents: I am not only Mediterranean. I am not inclined to confine myself within the Iberian corner of myself ... Why does the Spaniard insist on living anachronistically within himself? Why does he forget his German heritage? ... Do not force me to be only a Spaniard, if by Spaniard you mean only a man of the light-drenched coast. Do not force civil wars into my bosom; do not stir up the Iberian in me, with his harsh, hairy passions, against the blond, meditative, and sentimental German who breathes in the twilight zone of my soul. I aspire to make peace between my inner men, and I urge them toward a collaboration."[21]

And another of his "inner men"—an unrenounceable facet of himself —was *Olmedo*: "For my taste, an admirable man. He is intelligent and he is not intellectual." "That is why it is a delight for me to meet Olmedo, to see him arrive smiling, preceded by the double-edged foil of his glance—a cutting and almost cynical glance, which seems to lift the skirts of everything to see what they are like underneath. Olmedo is a banker and a man of the *grand monde*. When he flashes across my existence, which is after all squalid, as befits an intellectual, he seems to me like a glittering meteorite which comes laden with golden stardust."[22]

But in particular, in a more intense and perfect mode, Ortega's last

---

[20] "Adán en el Paraíso" (1910). I, 473.
[21] *Meditaciones del Quijote*. I, 356–57. See my commentary in the edition cited.
[22] "Paisaje con una corza al fondo" (1927). VI, 142–44.

"personage" is *Gaspar de Mestanza*, "one of the few interesting Spaniards who have been born in the last hundred years," whose memoirs
Ortega began to write about 1936.[23] These "do not have a narrative, but
rather an analytical, intent." In Spain, Mestanza "suffered excessively,
and his nation and his race appeared to him from afar purified in the
essentiality of memory and the monumentality of distance." "With a
superb disdain for clichés, he goes straight for the viscera, and discovers
tremendous secrets of this Spanish soul, so old and yet so imperfectly
known. For if Mestanza avoided contact with his countrymen, he nevertheless felt an enormous curiosity about them. He was, along with
Francisco Alcántara, the first to penetrate the Peninsular soil in depth,
to discover the deep and lost towns." Another unmistakable facet of
Ortega's, who was initiated by no other than Alcántara into these penetrations of the Spanish earth, which he came to know inch by inch, even
to details such as the tree and the bird on the wing and the gray or violet
rock, and the "cereal gold" around the towns, appalling towns perhaps,
where so many Spaniards, "our brothers," lived.

If Ortega did not write memoirs or novels it was doubtless due to the
limitations of life, the painful renunciations it imposes on us. He probably never found time and leisure for the dedication which such works
demand in their full manifestation; he could not allow his experiences
to accumulate until the new inspiration welled up in him—each genre
requires its own kind of inspiration. It is not rash to suppose, moreover,
that this would have brought up the question of literary forms, in which
he would have been forced to be an innovator. Ortega's work has remained incomplete even with respect to the genres that he did cultivate,
even with respect to the books which he wrote and did not finish; his
work appears much more fragmentary if we think of it as ideally completed by his *desiderata*, by those forms and those themes which were
postulated internally, perhaps expressly desired, and which he never
began. These form a sort of border or frame within which the written
work acquires its true meaning. Beside the many volumes written by
Ortega we must place the memoirs and novels he should have written,
that he *must* have written in order to have fully realized his programmatic "I."

And lastly, we must add that he did not write philosophical *treatises*
either, and scarcely wrote books *of* philosophy. But we shall have to

[23] "Memorias de Mestanza" (1936). V, 471-85.

speak of this in another context, as part of the analysis of that philosophy itself.

Ortega had, and from a very early age, a consciousness of this whole area of problems. In an essay of extraordinary *theoretical* importance, perhaps never read from this point of view, his "Ideas on Pío Baroja," Ortega wrote as early as 1915:

"A writer's style, that is, the physiognomy of his work, consists in a series of selective acts which he executes.

"The world opens its limitless circle all around the artist. All past, present, and future things are there. The material and the spiritual, the sad and the joyous, the North and the South are there. All the words in the dictionary are there, ranged in rows like artillery, each with its meaning ready to be fired. And we see how the writer, among all those innumerable things, chooses one and makes it a general object, the central theme of his work. In this first choice, style begins to be formed: it is the decisive choice .... There is a previous and latent affinity between the most intimate being of an artist and a certain portion of the universe ....

"The style of language—that is, the selection of the lexical and grammatical fauna—represents only the most external part, and the one, therefore, least characteristic of the literary style taken as a whole .... The speech of our period in history imposes its general structure on us, and the transformations which the greatest innovator of speech may have succeeded in making are nothing if they are compared with his originality on the other levels of creation."[24]

And thus he could add, years later, that "all style starts from an assumption; *style is assumption*."[25] Ortega's themes are going to appear as the result of a *choice*, of a series of *selective acts* which arise out of his vital plan. From something which, in the last instance, is not chosen, and which is proclaimed in the small individual shadings that the author imposes on communal and ordinary language. Let us try to see how.

46. ORTEGA'S LITERARY TEMPER

A reader of Ortega, one who knows the physiognomy of his prose as one knows a person's face, previous to all analysis, can identify any fragment

[24] II, 68–69.　　　　　　　　　[25] *Goethe desde dentro* (1932). IV, 390.

of it without difficulty; that is, he recognizes his *style* in it without hesitation, intuitively. And now it would be a matter of finding out in what this style consists, why the reader recognizes and identifies this scrap of prose. Perhaps a good way to do so would be to isolate certain chosen examples and examine them. But then a difficulty occurs: to consider them as chosen, to select them out of the totality of his writings—does this not presuppose having the answer already, being already in possession of a criterion with regard to that style which is being sought? The ideal thing would be to find examples which were of high quality in themselves and from the outset, examples which would isolate themselves spontaneously and without an arbitrary act of judgment on our part. I believe that it is not impossible to find such examples; it would suffice to examine his early writings, those in which his style is not yet formed and fixed, which vacillate between various tendencies; those which are, in a word, immature. It is *their* indecision which allows us to escape from our own. In those first texts, written at the age of twenty, which are still not fully "Ortega" because the writer Ortega does not yet exist, this style *announces itself* in sentences which stand out and approach us in a manner unmistakably *his*. Those turns of phrase, those expressions, those ways of saying things in which we immediately identify what are later to be the privileged examples in which the peculiarity of a style can be isolated; we can place them in a test tube and analyze them. It is as if, in a heap of children's pictures, we should suddenly find the one which resembles the adult whom we know well, and should search in it for his germinal traits.

The first known article written by Ortega, "Glosas" ["Glosses"], published in the review *Vida Nueva* on December 1, 1902, when its author was nineteen years old and had just taken his degree in philosophy and letters, is clearly immature, somewhat disorganized, and excessively juvenile; its style is unsure and aims in a number of directions; but it is of extreme interest, not so much for its intrinsic value as for the fact that there appear in it—merely appear, but that in itself is sufficient —a whole series of *themes* which are to be permanent ones in his later work; and further, because—and this is what interests us at the moment —a skilled ear can perceive here and there intimations of what the writer who made his presence felt in the article was going to be like. It begins as follows:

"*On personal criticism.* I was speaking yesterday with a friend of mine, one of those admirable men who dedicate themselves seriously to hunting down the truth, who aspire to *breathe metaphysical certainties*: a poor chap.

"He said, 'Have you read the criticism So-and-So made about such-and-such a work?'

"I have read it, my dear chap; it is delicious."[26]

Further on he says, "I am not talking, however, about dead religions, about the gods who *made their exit with their creeds under their arms*.[27] And later, "The crowd as a mob, as a *foule*, is impersonal because of the sum of its abdications; it is involuntary, *stupid as a primitive animal*."[28] Or, "What value is there today, after the *great massacre of mysteries*, what value is there in an action whose author does not show himself?"[29] "*Sorrowful and miserable mobs whose eyes seek the bronze serpent*."[30] "*Men with mysterious frowns and burning eyes*."[31]

A year later, in February, 1904, Ortega published his article "*La Sonata de estío, de Don Ramón del Valle-Inclán*" ["Summer Sonata, by Don Ramón del Valle-Inclán"]; here it is not a question of occasional sentences, but of a stylistic continuity; the melody of the sentence is basically that of the mature works, the figures of speech frequently have an Orteguian stamp, the use of adjectives already shows traces of the techniques which were to be dominant in his later writings. Here are merely a few examples: the men of the Renaissance "knew how to give a flavor of *gallant malice* to their terrifying narratives";[32] Valle-Inclán "is thin, *thin to the point of inverisimilitude*, and has a long beard with *mysterious purple reflections in it*, above which looms a pair of magnificent tortoise-shell spectacles."[33] "Rapidly, like a gaucho galloping across the horizon, a Mexican bandit whisks through the story, *his conscience swollen with murders . . . .*"[34]

After this time, Ortega continues to take possession of himself, to illuminate new areas of the language, personal cadences, as a habitual attitude. "When we entered the Low Countries, *we let fall the melancholy of our mysticism*, which is the deepest dregs of the Spanish soul, *on the broad white flesh of the Flemings*."[35] The mystics "have been the lookouts of humanity who, *hoisted aloft in dreams or in ecstasy*,

[26] I, 13.
[27] I, 14.
[28] I, 15.
[29] I, 16.
[30] I, 17.

[31] I, 17.
[32] I, 19.
[33] I, 19.
[34] I, 20.
[35] "El poeta del misterio" (1904). I, 31.

have raised the cry of alarm when they descried the rosy mists that announce a landfall. The scholars, with all their impedimenta and their *tired-camel gait*, get to the promised lands centuries later than the seers."[36] Maeterlinck's dialogues are "open like skylights on the unknown."[37] "The countryside shivers with pleasure under the breeze's hand."[38] On the Comtesse de Noailles: "I know only four things about her, and that is no little: she is a woman, she is young, she is beautiful, and she is Greek."[39] "I know that many men feel a chill of desolation when they enter their homes, for there they hear more clearly than in other places *the dragging, rusty, vulgar noise life makes as it turns on its hinges.*"[40]

The articles I have quoted are "literary." In that same year, 1904, Ortega wrote a scientific and purely academic study: his doctoral thesis. This text, which almost no one has read or, in consequence, utilized, is of special interest for us: here there is no question of "making literature," which could explain certain stylistic peculiarities; far from being a newspaper article, it is a university study not intended for public notice (it was printed in 1909, probably in a very limited edition, never circulated, and up to the moment has not been reprinted). If, as we believe, there is a certain type of expression which has an effective value as "physiognomy," and responds to a personal installation in language and reality, a life factor and an interpretation of reality, it should also be found here. Let us see whether this is so. The thesis begins as follows—as in the previous examples, I shall italicize the passages which seem to me to be especially significant:

"In the history of the Middle Ages there is one page which *stirs the imagination* like few others, an unsettling page, which relates one of the moments in which humanity has found itself most oppressed, most in anguish. *Upon an accumulation of real misfortunes,* some historians have *woven the marvelous tapestry of a legend.* This legend is the one which sees the men of the tenth century abandoning their life-sustaining labors and *fleeing in dark droves to the calm and miraculous secret of the cloisters.*"[41] "The legend of the millennium is completely incorrect;

---

[36] I, 32.

[37] I, 32.

[38] "El rostro maravillado" (1904). I, 33.

[39] I, 34.

[40] I, 37.

[41] *Los terrores del año mil* (1904). Madrid (1909), 3.

descriptions of it do not embody real events. But *these events absolutely could have taken place.*"[42] This tone does not change in any essential way: "souls which love turbulent things";[43] "There are men who go to bed free and when they wake up find that they are slaves";[44] "the man who is nothing and can possess nothing, whose life is worth only a farthing, will always be an *anguished and suffering figure.*"[45] In feudalism, "the soil is distributed *as a prize for the soul*";[46] "the serfs of the glebe were fastened to the ground like a tree or a stone."[47] "Tirelessly they wage war and conquest; *a raid is a pleasure; policies are made with the broadsword.* A representative figure, a great lord named Tibaldo el Zizañero, crosses the history of the tenth century, a tireless champion, *drunk on skirmishes.*"[48] "Only one difference is admitted between men: muscle. There are muscular men and anemic men; no more. *Cunning died in Rome and has not been born again.*"[49] "But both these groups were free men; beside them an oppressed, neglected people vegetated, carrying them on its shoulders; *the serfs, the perennial beast of burden of history.*"[50] The whole thesis abounds in expressions and turns of phrase of the same sort. That this style responds to Ortega's deepest feelings, that in it he realizes himself and discovers his vital "temper," his mode of living reality, can be documentally proved by a few lines from *The Terrors of the Year 1000* which we will see sounding forth, almost identically, at the end of their author's literary trajectory.

It is a passage which is revealing as few others are. Ortega speaks of the tenth century, of the episcopal and convent schools, where religious subjects were studied exclusively or almost exclusively, the sciences were scarcely cultivated, and classical antiquity was exiled as a matter of doctrine. "And it stirs the mind to imagine," he adds, "those libraries with their solid carved chairs and their beautiful desks, with *the shining pates of the Scholiasts and the purplish tonsures of the students bent over them*; the light, descending with indefinable clarity from the tall windows, enfolded the peaceful thoughts of the Fathers of the Church, so unflaggingly pondered, while neglected and as if lost, there between Rufinus and Saint Jerome, beside the 'Confessions' of Saint Augustine and Boethius' 'Consolations,' the old books of classic bronze guarded

[42] *Ibid.*, 3.
[43] *Ibid.*, 4.
[44] *Ibid.*, 5.
[45] *Ibid.*, 6.
[46] *Ibid.*

[47] *Ibid.*
[48] *Ibid.*, 7.
[49] *Ibid.*
[50] *Ibid.*, 10–11.

the secret of the sins and joys of pagan life."[51] And in Ortega's definitive and most mature book, his posthumous work *La idea de principio en Leibniz y la evolución de la teoría deductiva* ["The Idea of Principle in Leibniz and the Evolution of the Deductive Theory"], written almost entirely during 1947, we find these lines: "Now let us counterimagine a monastery of the thirteenth century, in the chilly center of Europe or the mists of Hibernia; and in the walks of its cloister, where ogival arches take a bite at the sky and permit us to see the well in the middle of the mystical garden in the patio, *the old teacher-friars overseeing the disputations of the young novices with their purplish tonsured pates, as if they were Platonic ephebes.*"[52] At the other end of Ortega's literary career, at forty-three years' distance, the same image reappears, with the same characteristics, the identical central life-factors around which the scene is organized. Note that in both cases it is a question of a deliberate image: "It stirs the mind to imagine . . . ." "Now let us counterimagine a monastery . . . ." Ortega has just been evoking a Greek discussion; in both passages there is a stage setting, with slight variations —the library in his thesis, the cloister in his later book, and in both there is an appeal to visuality and to illumination: "the light, descending with indefinable clarity from the tall windows . . . "; "ogival arches take a bite at the sky and permit us to see the well . . . "; lastly, and above all else, the stylistic nerve center of both scenes is literally the same: old and young men making disputations, *tonsures purplish* with the cold: "the shining pates of the Scholiasts and the purplish tonsures of the students"; "the old teacher-friars overseeing the disputations of the young novices with their purplish tonsured pates, as if they were Platonic ephebes . . . "; not even the element of "pate" has been lost, which together with "tonsure" and "purplish" form the stylistic nucleus; in the later text the three are grouped in an ultimate condensation, in a single phrase.

In these expressions, all of them from his nineteenth to twenty-first years, in literary newspaper articles or in a doctoral thesis, Ortega's literary temper shows through. We find already, from the outset, the writer he was to be. In these literary attitudes a personality, a way of looking at reality, of speaking it, that is, of living it and interpreting it, is discovered and at the same time realized. What Ortega was one day

---

[51] *Ibid.*, 23.
[52] *La idea del principio en Leibniz y la evolución de la teoría deductiva*, § 20, p. 243.

to call, adding that it was even more important than philosophy, "our cosmic sensation."[53]

47. INNUMERABLE REFLECTIONS

In what does the peculiarity of that literary style consist? Can we isolate a general meaning which constitutes, if we can put it that way, the active principle of this way of writing? *To utter*, in the broadest meaning of this term, is to make things patent, to show them, therefore to *interpret them*. All utterance is interpretation, presentation of reality in a certain foreshortening. There is no such thing as "neutral" utterance: what seems to be neutral is something else: a gray interpretation, usually in the form of clichés and made up of commonplaces, clumsy and alien to the author, but just as much of an interpretation as any other. The writer who does not have a personal style intervenes in reality like anybody else, with the sole difference that *it is not he who intervenes*, but his readers through him, and they take as obvious the modifications exercised on the real by other men, petrified in the language and the reigning modes of expression. Conversely, the true writer interprets things deliberately; he makes himself responsible, we might say, for the foreshortening in which he presents them, for the emotional tone in which they are experienced, for their linkages or their lack of connection. This has nothing—or little, if you prefer—to do with the margin of innovation which the period permits to the individual writer; it is evident that at certain times the author is subject to very strict norms, to a general discipline of utterance which limits personal interpretation; this was the case in the eighteenth century, for example. But if we look closely, we see that this is not precisely correct: rather, the limitation affects the instrumental *means* which the author must make use of in order to carry out this individual modification; and precisely because of this, the modification requires greater skill. Think of the two different innovations carried out by Voltaire and Rousseau, enormous in their content and significance, but accomplished with a paucity of means, without fanfare, almost under their breath, within a very strict literary discipline; in lesser degree, something similar occurs with Cadalso and Moratín— especially, of course, in their letters and accounts of travels, where the

[53] *El tema de nuestro tiempo* (1923). III, 200.

discipline was freer; and Goethe himself, with his fantastic power of creation, permits himself fewer liberties with regard to means than any writer from 1830 to 1920, for in these last cases the *nonsubjection to a guideline is the guideline itself*, the discipline that is in fact reigning, which imperiously demands the breaking of all discipline, so that any possible personal innovation *begins beyond this*.

Compare Huxley's sentence with Hemingway's; or Miró's with Baroja's; or Victor Hugo's with Stendhal's. Are not their authors' aims fully present in them? Do we not have the general interpretative patterns of the three languages, the three linguistic "tempers" of English, Spanish, and French, broken down into irreducible forms, which correspond to an equal number of ways of living reality, and, therefore, of projecting oneself personally? What does Ortega intend, we can now ask ourselves; what does Ortega intend when he writes as he does?

To begin with, something he has in common with every authentic writer: to make pristine the expressions of the common language—it is the condition of all expression—and to *appropriate it to himself* by means of small indentations and even mannerisms which give it a personal accent. It is the function which, for the present, the voice has in speech—something psychophysiological—to which correspond the melody of the sentence and the selection of vocabulary and the use of the margin of freedom given by grammar in the written word. When Ortega writes—to return to the examples we have already quoted—"my dear chap," employing the phrase "Señor de mi *ánima*" instead of the more customary "alma"—when he finds Valle-Inclán thin "to the point of inverisimilitude," he confers novelty on a trivial expression or emphasizes personally, giving it an emphasis worthy of it, something as unextraordinary as the thinness of the author of the *Sonatas*. The same could have been said of the contrast between the "accumulation of real misfortunes" and the "marvelous tapestry of a legend" woven by the historians.

But there is more. Ortega, beginning with his first printed lines, begins what I would call the *dramatization of concepts*. If "dead religions," are mentioned, this is abstract and static, and arouses only what Husserl calls "significant mention"; but if "the gods who made their exit with their creeds under their arms" is added, the novelty and plasticity of the expression, the personalization of the subject, the tonality of decline, renunciation, and withdrawal which appears in it, bring the process itself to life with special effectiveness. Similar effects are obtained by formulas such as those used when presenting the mystics as lookouts who cry the alarm, "hoisted aloft in dreams or in ecstasy"; the figure ceases to be a cliché when it is strengthened by the word "hoisted": its literal meaning, its adjustment to the function of the lookout, clashes with the metaphorical crow's nest of dream or ecstasy, and presents these in an unexpected context, as something to which one might "climb" so as to see from there; and the contrast with the scholars' "tired-camel gait" accentuates the ascensional function of mysticism, its lightness and dynamism, its possibilities for discovery. The word "mystic" is pulled out of the inert world of mere meanings and goes to live in a situation which is even "stage-set"—in a strict dramatic form; that is, in the Antipodes of the dictionary. It is equally meaningful to say of the mob that it is "stupid as a primitive animal" or to call the serfs "the perennial beasts of burden of history": functionalization, dramatization in plastic form of a "meaning," of a concept.

A further step is the "osmosis," if I may permit myself the expression, between psychic or spiritual contents and material or somatic references, whose interaction reciprocally penetrates meanings. This occurs with the expression "his conscience swollen with murders," or still more when he notes that "we let fall the melancholy of our mysticism" on the "broad white flesh of the Flemings"; the reader glimpses a Danaë painted by Rubens receiving on her rosy skin the immaterial shadow of that otherworldly melancholy, and both realities are reinforced, intensified, and at the same time dialectically opposed, unreconcilable, in perpetual struggle.

Lastly, there are the metaphors. This is a theme so important in a general sense, and so especially important in Ortega, that I shall have to treat it independently later on; but I cannot dispense with saying a word here about its function as a *mere* ingredient of style, as it appears in Ortega's first, germinal writings. There is a character who crosses the narrative of *Summer Sonata* "like a gaucho galloping across the horizon"—let it be stated in passing that the gaucho appeared twelve years before Ortega's first visit to Argentina; a great lord is "drunk on skirmishes"; the men of the tenth century flee in "dark droves" to the calm and miraculous secret of the cloisters; he speaks of "the dragging, rusty, vulgar noise life makes as it turns on its hinges." Unexpected and violent juxtapositions of words make concepts emerge from their usual haunts, "crossbreed" them with other very different concepts, and thus *connections* come into being which the reader did not count on, new *foreshortenings* in which things and words change attitudes and replace their outworn and lifeless face for a new one. When he says "dark droves," the image of the flock of sheep is associated without more ado with that of the friars, and in two words the homogeneity, the gregariousness, the earth-colored habit, the mass flight to a cloister which is both spiritual refuge and sheepfold—all these come alive. And the figure about life takes in monotony, repetition, dailiness, vulgarity, irritations, and difficulties, all grasped intuitively in a single mental movement.

The analysis could go on indefinitely. But it is not essential. The more urgent task, it seems to me, is to ask ourselves what the meaning of these procedures is, or, if you like, the extent to which these attitudes are not deliberate but proceed from spontaneity. For me there is no doubt: what Ortega is aiming at is to fix and multiply the *reflections* of reality. In other words, to cause each element of the real to be effectively present, acting, in person, radiating its possibilities, establishing connections with all the connections of each element and of all the other elements. This is not simple conjecture: it is the abbreviated formulation of the operations we have just reviewed; as if this were not enough, we have Ortega's own testimony. As early as 1900 he had written, "The true criticism consists in raising the work or author being studied to another power, changing them into the example of a special form of humanity and obtaining from them, by this procedure, *a maximum of cultural reflections*."[54] And especially, at the beginning of the *Meditations on Quixote* when he draws up the program of "salvations," he explains his proposal clearly: "To place the materials of all kinds, which life, in its perennial ebb and flow, will toss at our feet like the useless debris of a shipwreck, *in such an arrangement that the sun will throw off innumerable reflections from them*."[55]

This is the reason for Ortega's style. The presentation of the thousand facets of reality, of its multiple foreshortenings, possibilities, potentialities, making them shine in the sun. If the style is coruscating, it is because this characteristic of it is the condition for the reflection of reality. The uncovering function which belongs to truth as *alétheia*—and which Ortega was to formulate in an early version in 1914, at a time when

[54] "Renan." I, 449. Italics mine.
[55] I, 311. Italics mine.

European philosophy knew hardly anything about this concept and had no intention of reviving it and using it—was already in play through the agency of his literary style. Each label used by Ortega, each figure of speech, each transposition, reveals an aspect of reality either named or alluded to; it makes reality new, presents it reborn before our eyes, *ready to have thought act upon it in a creative way*, not to have thought fall back on it in an inertial way.

But we must take seriously the figure of speech in which Ortega defines his style, the justification for his innumerable images: it is a question of *the sun's* making reflections upon things; its shining and its heat are essential; the dead indication of things with a school pointer will not do. The unveiling of reality, its patentization, cannot be attained except from a certain adequate temper, and in the end it turns out that this has to be a *literary* temper. The unexpected result is that the "sober," "cold," "objective" attitude, which seems proper to science, is less scientific. The truth is uncovered, made manifest, only by making things glow and perhaps even burn. In an essay in which he reflected upon his own life, Ortega said something which seems to me to be one of the profoundest and most important truths that he has shown us: "the set of teeth with which one devours a culture is called enthusiasm."[56] This is why I said something before that might have seemed to lack justification and truth: that only by means of literature can a certain kind of higher precision be attained, and that to cultivate true precision there is no solution but to cultivate literature.

[56] "Prólogo para alemanes" (1934), 30.

II.

THE METAPHOR

48. THEORY OF THE METAPHOR

Metaphors accompany Ortega's prose from the very first page. This is a fact which is sufficiently well known and of such importance that it is considered to be the defining characteristic of his literary style. But intellectual attention to the theme of the metaphor, which very soon settles into a theory, is almost as early in his work. Ortega is spontaneously metaphorical, by the irresistible impulse of his literary inspiration, out of the very depths of what I have called his "temper"; he is also metaphorical deliberately and as a matter of principle, with full consciousness of being so and of the significance which this has. The two things are inseparable, for the metaphors an author uses are not just any metaphors, and Ortega's are conditioned by that theory—that is, by the function which they assume in his work. They cannot be studied, therefore, unless we have clear ideas about what they mean for him, and this in its turn is not possible except out of a comprehension of his philosophy. There is a double relationship, operating both ways, between his philosophy and the metaphor: Ortega makes a philosophical theory of the metaphor, and, on the other hand, in his writing the metaphor is the express instrument of philosophical investigation and, what is more, a philosophical expression of reality. It will be essential, therefore, to move on different planes, to go forward and then backward, and in some measure to anticipate doctrines whose full meaning will be visible only later on.

I have already cited a number of Ortega's metaphors in writings not later than 1904; that is, of his nineteenth to twenty-first year. Now we shall have to investigate the fact that during those same years he began to reflect on the metaphoric process of style. The first occasion was offered, and this is understandable, by Valle-Inclán. "He hatches his images steadfastly, to make them entirely new," says Ortega of this writer.[1] And he attributes his technique to the influence of foreign writers. The Spanish tendency had been to almost allegorical comparison, faithful to the Roman tradition. In Spanish prose the figure of speech is rare; when there is one, it is likely to be "an integral comparison of the whole primary idea, wedded to the total second idea."[2] The reason for this, Ortega believes, is that our literature and even our language have been *chiefly* oratorical, rhetorical. What Valle-Inclán does is very different: "He employs unilateral figures of speech almost exclusively; that is, figures which arise, not from the whole idea, but from one of its sides or edges."[3] It is a matter of *uniting very separate ideas by a slender thread*, as when Valle-Inclán says of a miller that he is "cheerful and picaresque as a book of old saws," etc.

A few years later, Ortega was to construct a theory of the metaphor. Apparently an *aesthetic* theory; in reality—as we shall soon discover unexpectedly—a general *philosophical* theory, one of the first points on which he was to demonstrate his original philosophical thought; and as always—except, perhaps, for the last period in his life—set forth in a manner veiled by a certain timidity which seems unlikely, yet which is one of the keys to understanding Ortega's work.[4] The text in which Ortega confronts the metaphor thematically is the "Ensayo de estética a manera de prólogo" ["An Essay on Aesthetics in the Form of a Prologue"], which he used as a preface in 1914 to *El Pasajero* ["The Passenger"], by José Moreno Villa. A few years ago I called attention to this decisive text, whose implications had passed unnoticed, so far as I know, until then. "Ortega is proposing," I said in that commentary,[5] "a theory of metaphor. The connection between poetry and metaphor is very close; only slightly less close, Ortega thinks, is the connection between metaphor and philosophy. . . . The theme of the metaphor is, then, a tremendous philosophical theme, not only a literary one; but,

---

[1] "La *Sonata de estío* de Don Ramón del Valle-Inclán." I, 24.

[2] *Ibid.*, 25.

[3] *Ibid.*

[4] See, for example: "The reader should realize that he is dealing here with a man whose timidity is as great as his audacity, and who advances through life in an uncomfortable rhythm of forward impulses and abrupt halts." *Prólogo para alemanes* (1934), 82.

[5] "Conciencia y realidad ejecutiva" (1956). In *La Escuela de Madrid*, 255ff. (*Obras*, V.)

conversely, without philosophy we cannot really ascertain what metaphor is; thus, when Ortega urgently asks himself this question, he has to precede his theory of metaphorical expression with a short antestructure of strict philosophy." This structure is nothing less than the doctrine of *executive reality*, with which he demonstrates the impossibility of phenomenological reduction, the unreality of *consciousness*, and arrives at the reality of "my *life*."[6]

It is from this position that Ortega interprets the phenomenon of art. "Let us think," he says, "of what a language or system of expressive signs would be like if its function were not to consist in narrating things to us, but in presenting themselves to us as executing themselves. Art is such a language; this is what art does. The aesthetic object is an innerness insofar as it is an aesthetic object—it is everything insofar as it is *I*. I am not saying—take care!—that the work of art uncovers the secret of life and of the being; I do say that the work of art pleases us with that peculiar delight which we call aesthetic because it *seems* to us that it makes the innerness of things, their executive reality, patent to us—compared with which the other messages given us by science *seem* to be mere diagrams, remote allusions, shadows, and symbols."[7]

Ortega analyzes the quality of duality—of separation between the thing known and the subject who knows—in every cognitive act, be it vision or image or concept. There seems to be an exception only in the case of transparent objects; within the glass there seems to be a compenetration: "In transparent things, the thing and I are one."[8] In art, analogously, we are given "an object which combines the dual quality of being transparent and the fact that what shows through in it is not something else, but itself."[9] "Very well then," he continues, "this object which is transparent to itself, the aesthetic object, finds its elemental form in the metaphor. I would say that the aesthetic object and the metaphorical object are the same thing, or rather, that the metaphor is the elemental aesthetic object, the beautiful cell."[10]

---

[6] I have shown that in this essay Ortega first went beyond phenomenology, though he does not name it. A year before, he had expounded phenomenology without making a criticism of it. ("Sobre el concepto de sensación", [1913].) As we have not reached this theme as yet, it will suffice to leave its ultimate implications noted here.

[7] "Ensayo de estética a manera de prólogo" (1914). VI, 256.

[8] *Ibid.*, 256.

[9] *Ibid.*, 257.

[10] *Ibid.*

Ortega begins with a concrete example: a line of poetry by the Catalan poet López Picó, which says that the cypress

és com l'espectre d'una flama morta.
["is like the specter of a dead flame."]

Strictly speaking, he tells us, there are three metaphors: "the one which makes the cypress a flame, the one that makes the flame a specter, and the one that makes the flame a dead flame";[11] to simplify, Ortega limits himself to the first. The metaphorical object here is not the cypress nor the flame nor the specter, for they are real images. "The new object which comes out to meet us is a 'cypress-specter of a flame.' Well, that cypress is not a cypress, or that specter a specter, or that flame a flame."[12] The only thing left of the cypress and the flame is the real note of identity between the lineal diagrams of both; there is a real resemblance, and thus it has been believed that the metaphor is an *assimilation* of very different things. But this is a mistake: if we insist upon what both things possess of real resemblance, the charm of the metaphor melts away and what is left is an unimportant geometrical observation. The real resemblance is necessary, but not sufficient. It is a question of forming a new object which Ortega calls the "beautiful cypress" in contrast to the real cypress. In order to accomplish this, two operations are performed: the annihilation of the real cypress and its endowment with the characteristic of beauty. First, the poet seeks an unimportant real resemblance, and by dwelling upon it affirms the absolute identity; as this is absurd, the process accentuates the real lack of resemblance. The metaphor lives by the clear knowledge of nonidentity. Ortega recalls, quoting Max Müller, the method of metaphorizing in the Vedas, even without the "as" of the comparison, with only the naked negation of identity. Instead of saying "firm as a rock," the Vedic poet says *sa parvato na acyutas* (*ille firmus, non rupes*); the hymn *Non suavem cibum* is sweet, but it is not something to eat; the river comes roaring along, but it is not a bull. It is, Ortega concludes, the method of *tollendo ponens*, which annihilates things insofar as they are real images. The second operation consists in this: "Once we know that the identity is not in the actual images, the metaphor stubbornly insists on giving it to us. And it shoves us into another world where this is apparently possible."[13]

The image has two faces: image of *a thing*, and *my* image; in this

[11] *Ibid.*, 259, note 2.　　[12] *Ibid.*, 257.　　[13] *Ibid.*, 259-60.

sense, while it is being *executed*, the image is a moment of my I; this is what Ortega calls sentiment. We see the image of a cypress through the image of a flame, *we see it as a flame*, and, conversely, the images are mutually exclusive, but in the poem they penetrate each other; we have, says Ortega, "a case of transparency which is established in the sentimental place of both. The cypress-sentiment and the flame-sentiment are identical." "The metaphor, then," he adds, "consists in the transposition of a thing from its real place to its sentimental place." And the final conclusion: "Each metaphor is the discovery of a law of the universe."[14]

This last sentence jerks the theory of the metaphor out of its pure aesthetic context and gives it greater implications; if we join it to the philosophical "antestructure" with which Ortega has preceded it, this can make us think that when we speak of metaphors, we are dealing with something more than art and aesthetics.

This is of course true, and we have a *previous* and especially important confirmation of this suspicion. Five years before, in an essay written in 1909, long before Husserl propounded the theory of phenomenology and of consciousness as reality in his *Ideen* (1913), Ortega had referred to the metaphor in these lines:

"Out of the arsenal of human sensations, sorrows, and hopes, Newton and Leibniz extracted infinitesimal calculus; Cervantes, the quintessence of his aesthetic melancholy; Buddha, a religion. These are three different worlds. The material is the same in all of them; only the way of working it varies. In the same way, *the world of the verisimilar is the same world as that of real things, subjected to a peculiar interpretation: the metaphorical interpretation.*

"*That boundless universe is built with metaphors.* What riches! From the small and latent comparison, which was the origin of almost all words, to the enormous cosmic myth which, like the divine cow Hathor of the Egyptians, feeds a whole civilization, *we find scarcely anything but metaphors in the history of man.* Take out of our lives everything which is metaphorical and we will be nine-tenths diminished. *That flower of the imagination, so fragile and minute, forms the immutable layer of subsoil on which this our daily reality rests,* just as the Caroline Islands rest on coral reefs."[15]

[14] *Ibid.*, 261
[15] "Renan" (1909). I, 449. Italics mine.

PART TWO: *The Writer*

The metaphor is, therefore, *an interpretation of reality*; and we live in a universe built chiefly of metaphors; furthermore, these metaphors are the foundation of everyday reality, the *immutable layer of subsoil* over which we live. This is the origin in Ortega's thought of his theory of interpretations as forms of vital reality, and, at the same time, of the notion of *beliefs*. Nor is this passage a passing coincidence: in his lecture on *Old and New Politics* Ortega speaks, with the same expression he had used here, of "that *subsoil reality* which comes to constitute, in each period, in each instant, the *true and inmost opinion* of part of society." He goes on to speak of "*our true, inmost, decisive opinions*," of "*the dark and inmost depths of our personality.*"[16] And now we have just seen that that subsoil, that depth on which our life is based and which is reality for us, consists of *metaphors*.

The consequence is disturbing and paradoxical: the metaphor is something that man makes; it is a translation or transposition that man carries out, and therefore the result of a human operation; and, notwithstanding, that fragile flower of the imagination is the subsoil of our life, the base on which our life rests, to the point that Ortega even says that our universe is "built with metaphors." How is this possible? An adequate reply cannot be given here. It will be necessary to wait many years to find the key to this difficulty in Ortega's work. That key consists, no less, *in the idea of being and reality* which makes up the ultimate nucleus of Ortega's metaphysics. But we should keep in mind from this point onward these statements made by Ortega in 1909, for they show to what extent the doctrines of his maturity proceed from certain original intuitions which he reached very early and which are the ones that define the trajectory of his thought. It would not be excessive to interpret this trajectory as the effort to possess conceptually, and therefore to justify, an early vision of reality.

But if this is true, the metaphor, in addition to its aesthetic and literary value—in addition to, but not apart from it—has a strictly intellectual function. What is this function?

49. METAPHOR AND KNOWLEDGE

In volume V of *El Espectador* an essay written in 1924 was published entitled "Las dos grandes metáforas" ["The Two Great Metaphors"];

[16] I, 269. Italics mine.

but we shall have to warn at the outset that the ideas are not those of 1924 nor are there two metaphors: in 1916, invited by the Spanish Institution for Culture, Ortega gave a course of lectures in Buenos Aires; one of the lessons in this course was entitled "The Three Great Metaphors."[17] A summary of it can be seen in the *Annals* of that institution.[18] The essay in *El Espectador* has the following subtitle: "On the Occasion of the Second Centenary of Kant's Birth"; undoubtedly, Ortega took a few pages from his course of eight years before, perhaps making some changes in them, and published them. Why, however, does one metaphor disappear, and instead of three, there are only two? Why is it precisely the new one which is missing, the one Ortega proposes as the expression of his personal philosophy? This is still another case which demonstrates the iceberg quality in Ortega's writings: he shrank from expounding his philosophy, out of consideration—whether he was right or not is another question—for the circumstances, and delayed as much as possible the formal presentation of his most personal and original ideas, which are very often hard to find in his writings. We must add, however, that finding them is almost always possible, and that a bit of attention and some knowledge of the matter are usually sufficient to locate them.

Ortega says in this essay, "When a writer censures the use of metaphors in philosophy, he simply reveals his ignorance of what philosophy is and what metaphor is. No philosopher would dream of expressing such censure. The metaphor is an indispensable mental tool; it is a form of scientific thought . . . . Poetry is metaphor; science uses nothing more than metaphor. Also, it could be said, nothing less."[19] Ortega notes that Aristotle does not reproach Plato for the use of metaphors, but does reproach him for using some concepts—such as "participation" —that aspire to strictness but turn out to be only metaphors. The objection to the metaphor in itself is always based on a misunderstanding: "The spirit which is inept or uneducated in meditation will be incapable, when he reads a philosophical book, of taking as only a metaphor the thought which is only metaphorical. He will take *in modo recto* what is said *in modo obliquo*, and will attribute to the author a defect which, in reality, he is contributing himself. Philosophical thought, more than any

[17] See *Prólogo para alemanes*, 76.
[18] *Anales de la Institución Cultural Española* (Buenos Aires, 1947), I, 175–76.
[19] "Las dos grandes metáforas." II, 379.

other, has to change constantly, subtly, from the direct sense to the oblique sense, instead of stiffening into one or the other."[20]

Now let us look a little more closely into what Ortega understands by metaphor, and what will allow him to take it as a procedure with cognitive value. Let us not forget that we are dealing here with ideas expressed in 1916. At that date, the most advanced theory of the metaphor was that of Hermann Paul in his *Prinzipien der Sprachgeschichte*. What did Paul understand by metaphor? Is the passage in which he explains it worth quoting?

"The metaphor is one of the most important means for the *creation of denominations* for complexes of representations, for those for which *adequate designations do not yet exist*. But their application is not limited to the cases in which such an external necessity is given. Even when an already existing denomination is available, *an internal impulse leads us to prefer a metaphorical expression*. The metaphor is precisely something which flows necessarily out of human nature and imposes itself, not only in poetic language, but also especially in colloquial, popular language, which always tends toward *graphic expression* and *picturesque characterization*. This also makes many metaphors commonplace, although not as easily as in the cases in which the lack of any other designation is a factor.

"It is evident that for the creation of metaphor, in the measure in which it is natural and popular, there is generally recourse to those circles of representations which are most strongly present in the soul. What is most distant from comprehension and interest becomes more intuitive and familiar by means of something which is nearer. In the choice of the metaphorical expression, therefore, the individual diversity of interest is shown, and in the sum total of metaphors which have come to be usual in a language, one can recognize which interests have been especially powerful among the people."[21]

---

[20] *Ibid.*, 380.

[21] Hermann Paul, *Prinzipien der Sprachgeschichte*, (5th ed., Halle a. S., 1920), § 68, pp. 94–95. Italics mine. The German text reads as follows: "Die Metapher ist eines der wichtigsten Mittel für Vorstellungskomplexe, für die noch keine adäquaten Bezeichnungen existieren. Ihre Anwendung beschränkt sich aber nicht auf die Fälle, in denen eine solche äissere Nötigung vorleigt. Auch da, wo eine schon bestehende Benennung zur Verfügung steht, treibt oft ein innerer Drang zur Bevorzugung eines metaphorischen Ausdrucks. Die Metapher ist eben etwas, was mit Not wendigkeit aus der menschlichen Natur fliesst und sich geltend macht nicht bloss in der Dichtesprache, sondern vor allem auch in der volkstümlichen Umgangssprache, die immer zur

Ortega goes considerably beyond this from the outset. "In science the metaphor has two uses of different rank. When the research worker discovers a new phenomenon—that is, when he forms a new concept—he needs to give it a name. Since a new word would not mean anything to other people, he has to fall back on the repertory of ordinary language, where every word is already attached to a meaning. So as to make himself understood, he chooses the word whose usual meaning has some resemblance to the new meaning. Thus, *the term acquires the new meaning through and by means of the old one, without abandoning it.* This is its metaphorical aspect."[22] This is the way, he explains, that we speak of "association" of ideas, or of "idea" (that is, aspect), to designate what our intellect does not see, but rather perceives. Ortega notes, however, that "metaphor" means transposition, but that many transpositions are not metaphors: namely, those in which "a word changes from having one meaning to having another, but abandoning the first";[23] thus, "*moneda,*" money, (from the temple to Juno Moneta, near which there was a mint in Rome), "candidate" (from *candidatus,* dressed in white), "*grève,*" strike, (from *grève,* a sandy bank, and the Place de Grève in Paris where the unemployed used to gather). That is, the survival of the original meaning within the new and metaphorical one is essential to the metaphor. This happens when, for example, we speak of "the depths of the soul": here the word "depths" is not used in its spatial meaning, but indirectly, to signify spiritual phenomena, when strictly speaking there is no depth. We use the word improperly, and knowing that we do so, with consciousness of the double meaning; it is an effort for us to think of this reality of the soul—not only to name it—and this is the second use, the one which

---

Anschaulichkeit und drastischer Charakterisierung neigt. Auch hiervon wird vieles usuell, wenn auch nicht so leicht wie in den Fällen, wo der Mangel an einer andern Bezeichnung mitwirkt.

"Es est selbstverständlich, dass zur Erzeugung der Metapher, soweit sie natürlich und volkstümlich ist, in der Regel diejenigen Vostellungskreise herangezogen werden, die in der Seele am mächtigsten sind. Das dem Verständnis und Interesse ferner liegende wird dabei durch etwas Näherliegendes anschaulicher und vertrauter gemacht. In der Wahl des metaphorischen Ausdruckes prägt sich daher die individuelle Verschiedenheit des Interesses aus, und an der Gesamtheit der in einer Sprache usuell gewordenen Metaphern erkennt man, welch Interessen in dem Volke besonders mächtig gewesen sind."

[22] "Las dos grandes metáforas." II, 380. Italics mine.

[23] *Ibid.,* 381.

is most profound and essential, of the metaphor in knowledge: "We inevitably need it in order to think about certain difficult objects ourselves. Aside from being a means of expression, the metaphor is an essential means of intellection."[24] "The metaphor is a truth, it is a knowledge of realities. This implies that in one of its dimensions poetry is research, and that it uncovers facts as positive as the habitual ones of scientific exploration."[25]

But poetry and science use the metaphor in very different ways, to a certain degree in opposite ways. Two *concrete* objects are brought together, which can be perceived separately; following one of Lope de Vega's figures of speech, Ortega takes the example of the jets in a fountain which are equated with crystal lances. Both have common abstract qualities: color, form, thrust; if this *partial* identity is stated, the result is a scientific truth, as when Newton affirms the identity of the behavior of the stars and certain numbers. But the Pythagorean who said that stars are numbers or the poet who identifies jets and crystal lances goes beyond this: the poetic metaphor *totally* identifies two concrete things, and that "exaggeration" is what gives it its poetic value. "The metaphor begins to radiate beauty where its true portion ends. But, vice versa, there is no poetic metaphor without a discovery of effective identities."[26] The metaphor, he adds, "permits us to give a separate existence to the least accessible abstract objects. Hence their use is all the more indispensable the further away we move from the things we handle in the ordinary traffic of life."[27]

[24] *Ibid.*, 382.

[25] *Ibid.*, 383.

[26] *Ibid.*, 385.

[27] *Ibid.*, 386. It is extremely interesting to read what had been said many years before by Archibald Henry Sayce (1845–1933), an English theologian and philologist, a professor of Assyriology at Oxford, in his *Introduction to the Science of Language* (London, 1880; 4th ed. 1900), II, 181: "Three-fourths of our language may be said to consist of worn-out metaphors. In no other way can terms be found for the spiritual and the abstract. *Spirit* is itself 'the breath'; the *abstract*, that which is 'drawn apart.' Our knowledge grows by comparing the unknown with the known, and the record of that increase of knowledge grows in the same way. Things are named from their qualities, but those qualities have first been observed elsewhere. The *table*, like the *stable*, originally meant something that 'stands,' but the idea of standing had been noted long before the first table was invented." (Quoted by Philip Wheelwright, *The Burning Fountain. A Study in the Language of Symbolism* [Indiana University Press, Bloomington, 1954], 119 and 379. On the subject of the metaphor, things of great interest will be found in chapters 5 and 6 of this book.)

The human mind has been formed according to the order of biological urges. To dissociate the psychic factor from the body has meant a painful effort of abstraction. We have arrived at the "I" by means of "my flesh" and "my body," "my heart" and "my breast." "The possessive pronoun precedes the personal pronoun. *The idea of 'mine' is previous to that of 'I'.*"[28] (I italicize this thesis, which many believe to be a recent discovery.) Therefore, almost all psychical terminology has to be metaphorical. The harder it is to conceive an object, the more intimately it is tied to others, the more necessary is the metaphor. If there were some reality that were indissolubly mingled with any other, it would be the exemplary and extreme case. Nothing would throw more light on the cognitive function of the metaphor; and, conversely, the only way of discovering that reality and taking possession of it would be to make use of the metaphorical procedure. Precisely here, Ortega's theory of the metaphor culminates; and at the same time a central discovery arises in his philosophy.

50. THE THREE GREAT METAPHORS

"There is one object," says Ortega, "that is included in all the rest, that is in them as their part and ingredient, just as the red thread is braided into all the cables of the Royal British Navy. This universal object, ubiquitous, omnipresent, which no matter where another object is found inevitably presents itself, is what we call consciousness.

"We cannot speak of anything at all which is not found in relationship to us, and this minimum relationship with us is the conscious relationship. The two most different objects one could possibly imagine have, notwithstanding, the common note of being an object for our minds, of being objects for a subject.

"Given this situation, it is understandable that there is nothing more difficult to conceive, perceive, describe, and define than that universal, ubiquitous, omnipresent phenomenon: consciousness. It will, then, be included as an inevitable accessory in every other phenomenon, monotonously, indefectibly, never going away. If, thanks to the fact that humidity sometimes occurs along with cold, but at other times along with heat, we have succeeded in distinguishing cold from humidity, how

[28] II, 387.

are we going to succeed in determining that area of appearance, consciousness? If there is any case in which metaphor is inescapable, there is no doubt that it is here.

"This universal phenomenon of the relationship between subject and object, which is realization, can be conceived only by comparing it with some particular form of the relationships between objects. The result will be a metaphor. And we always run the risk that, when we interpret the universal phenomenon by means of some other, more accessible, one, we may forget that it is a question of a scientific metaphor and may identify, as in poetry, the one thing with the other. The error in this matter is especially dangerous. For on the idea which we form of consciousness depends our whole concept of the world, on which, in their turn, depend our ethics, our politics, our art. I say that *the whole edifice of the universe and of life rests, in the end, on the tiny ethereal body of a metaphor.*"[29]

This page, which I have chosen to quote literally, is the explanation of that statement of 1909 according to which *the universe is built with metaphors*, that we scarcely find anything but metaphors in the history of man, and that this flower of the imagination, so fragile and minute, forms *the immutable layer of subsoil on which this our daily reality rests*. A basic metaphor, the one which makes us understand our relationship with all reality, and, therefore, the nature of reality for us, is the keystone of our universe.

In this fashion Ortega reconstructs the whole history of the philosophic past, beginning with Greece, by following two great metaphors, whose poetical content is minimal: one dominates the ancient period and its medieval prolongation; the second, the modern period, since the Renaissance. "For ancient man, when the subject realizes an object, he enters with the object into a relationship analogous to that which exists between two material things when they collide, with one leaving its print upon the other. *The metaphor of the seal which leaves its delicate imprint on the wax* becomes fixed very early in the Hellenic mind, and is destined to guide for many centuries all the ideas of men."[30] "As early as the *Theaetetus* of Plato," adds Ortega, "there is mention of the *ekmageîon*, the wax tablet, where the scribe leaves literal prints engraved by his stylus.[31] And this image, repeated by Aristotle—*On the*

29 *Ibid.*, 388–91. Italics mine.
30 *Ibid.*, 390. Italics mine.

Soul, book 3, chapter 4[32]—will have repercussions throughout the Middle Ages; and in Paris and in Oxford, in Salamanca and in Padua, for centuries, the teachers will inject it into a legion of youthful heads."[33] "According to this interpretation," continues Ortega, "subject and object would find themselves in the same situation as any two corporal things whatever. *Both exist and survive independently of each other, and outside of the relationship into which they sometimes enter.* The object which we see exists before being seen, and continues to survive when we no longer see it; the mind continues to be mind, though it neither sees nor thinks anything. When mind and object come together, the object leaves its mark imprinted on the mind. *Consciousness is impression.*"[34] This is the original metaphor out of which the *ancient* interpretation of reality is to be organized, which is perpetuated throughout the Middle Ages—and to this day often aspires to come to life again. "This doctrine understands the consciousness or relationship between subject and object as a real event, as real as the collision between two bodies might be. Thus it has been called *realism.* Both elements are equally real, the thing on the one hand, the mind on the other, and the influence of the thing on the mind is real."[35] At first sight, Ortega observes, this attitude is impartial; but to accept the possibility that a material thing can leave an imprint on another which is immaterial is to treat the latter as if it were the former; it is to take seriously *the comparison with the wax and the seal*; the subject is damaged, its condition is not respected. It is *materialism* which persists in the bosom of all the philosophies of "realistic" and Aristotelian inspiration, no matter how "spiritualistic" they may call themselves. "From such a seed springs *the ancients' concept of the world. For it, 'to be' means to find oneself a thing among other things* .... The subject is only one of many things immersed in the great 'sea of being,' as Dante expressed it. Its consciousness is a little mirror, where nothing is reflected but its surroundings. The 'I' does not have a large role to play in the ancient idea of the

[31] The chief passage is in the *Theaetetus*, 191 c:Θὲς δή μοι λόγου ἔνεκα ἐν ταῖς ψυχαῖς ἡμῶν ἐνὸν κήρινον ἐκμαγεῖον, etc.   Δυνάμει δ'οὕτως ὥσπερ ἐν γραμματείῳ ᾧ μηθὲν ὑπάρχει ἐντελεχείᾳ γεγραμμένον.

[32] *De Anima*, III, 4, 429 b 31 ff.:

[33] "Las dos grandes metáforas." II, 390.

[34] *Ibid.*, 390. Italics mine.

[35] *Ibid.*, 390.

world . . . . *The I, imploring hand of the blind man*—Aristotle says that the soul is like a hand—must go on feeling out the paths of the universe to make them the channel of its humble progress."[36]

This is the first metaphor; the figure of the wax tablet. But it is an inadequate interpretation, and the Renaissance "takes a full turn" when it realizes this. "When the seal molds the wax, we have equally before us the seal and the imprint it has left. We can, therefore, compare the one with the other. But when we see the Guadarrama range, we can see only its impression in us, not the thing itself."[37] To speak of objects outside our consciousness is an assumption; there is no doubt that things are, in some sense, "in us"; but their existence outside us is problematical. "Descartes makes up his mind to the great innovation. The only certain existence of things is that which they have when they are thought. Things die, therefore, as realities, to be reborn only as *cogitationes*. But 'thoughts' are no more than states of the subject, of the I itself, of *moi-même, qui ne suis qu'une chose qui pense*. From this point of view, the relationship of consciousness has to receive an interpretation opposite to antiquity's. *The seal and the wax tablet are supplanted by a new metaphor: the container and its contents.* Things do not come to the consciousness from without, but are *contents* of it, *ideas*. The new doctrine is called idealism."[38]

Consciousness, says Ortega, is something generic: there are many forms of realizing things: seeing, hearing, etc., or even indulging in fantasy, or thinking. Ancient philosophy paid attention to *perception*; modern philosophy fixes on the *imagination. Consciousness is creation.* Goethe, Leibniz, Kant, Schopenhauer, Nietzsche, all exalt fancy, imagination, *Einbildungskraft*, representation, fantasy, dreams. Leibniz calls man *un petit Dieu*. "Fichte will not be content with less than saying: the I is everything."[39]

The essay of 1924 ends here; but not the lesson of 1916. In the latter *Ortega makes the criticism of the second metaphor and proposes the third*; that is, he goes beyond *realism* and *idealism*. "This point of view is as an age-old illness of which we must be cured"; "we must abandon subjectivism." "Positivism is not really Positivism because it does not simply hold to the facts as they become patent. We must aspire to a super-Positivism." Hence a third interpretation of the consciousness

---

[36] *Ibid.*, 390–91.
[37] *Ibid.*, 391.

[38] *Ibid.* The last italics are mine.
[39] *Ibid.* 392.

is derived, *the basic thesis which today is the vehicle for the reigning philosophy of life,* expressed "for the first time" in Ortega's words. What is the new metaphor? Literally this:

"Consciousness, far from being a relationship of container to content, and subject and object the same thing, is a relationship of exclusion. Subject and object are incompatible; they are the two most different things there could be. *The object and I stand confronting one another, but one is outside the other, the two are inseparable from each other.* The metaphor which corresponds to this third interpretation—as opposed to the wax tablet, which was the first, and the glass with its contents, which was the second—could be one of those pairs of deities frequent in the Mediterranean mythologies, like Castor and Pollux, who are called *Dii consentes* and also *Dii complices,* the matched gods who had to be born and die together. Just so does the universe appear as duplicated. We emerge from the eternal monotony of the I, where everything appeared to be included, and objects appear before us in infinite variety."[40]

But this means the elimination of consciousness. Subject and object are at once irreducible and inseparable; whereas realism *makes the I simply one more thing,* and idealism *includes everything in the I,* Ortega's point of view affirms the *coexistence* of subject and object as *dii consentes,* matched gods who must live and die together, and *no more.* Realism erroneously supposed that I can compare the seal with its imprint on the wax tablet, as two equivalent "things"; whereas the reality is that the seal would be present to me only in its imprint; idealism supposes that, besides the I and the object, consciousness is there as the surrounding agent of their "contents." What is really there is *I with the thing,* what Ortega had called in his "Essay on Aesthetics" *executive reality,* to which corresponds in the *Meditations on Quixote,* in that same year of 1914, the formula *I am I and my circumstance,* metaphorically expressed four years before in the title itself of "Adán en el Paraíso" ["Adam in Paradise"]. The third metaphor is the way to think about a difficult and hard-to-grasp reality: that reality which Ortega will make great efforts to conceptualize throughout his entire lifetime.

Note that what we have somewhat hastily called the third metaphor

---

[40] *Anales de la Institución Cultural Española,* I, 175–76. Italics mine. The last passage has been placed between quotation marks as a direct quotation, not a resumé or paraphrase, of Ortega's lecture.

is not a single metaphor. *The metaphor which knows itself to be one possesses a plurality of facets.* The one taken unjustifiably as an identification exaggerates itself and goes beyond the truth; the cognitive metaphor knows that the coincidence between its terms is only *partial*, which, seen from the other side, means that it has to *integrate itself* with what we might call the *complementary metaphors*, until we reach what I should propose to call formally a *metaphorical system* or repertory of images which need each other and clarify each other mutually. Each of them makes us think in a certain direction, and leads to the discovery of one aspect of reality; but the connection of this aspect with others requires a new metaphor in its turn. Thus, the metaphors already described are completed in Ortega, at about the same date, by a third and essential one: the metaphor of light. The presumed "duplication" of the universe is only the point of departure. "No, no," writes Ortega in the *Meditations on Quixote*, "*man has a mission of clarity upon the earth*. This mission has not been revealed to him by a God, nor is it imposed from without by anyone or anything. He bears it within himself, *it is the very root of his constitution*." And later on: "The concept is clarity inside life, light shed on things. No more. No less."[41]

This correction of metaphors is philosophically decisive. For in them lies, germinally, the general interpretation of reality in which philosophy consists. It would be illusory to believe that a formula, even a strictly conceptual one, can contain a philosophy. "The proposition which sums up a philosophy," I have written elsewhere,[42] "is not separable from the totality of the philosophy, but rather its mission is to 'liberate' the intellective energy accumulated in the whole doctrine. It is not that Ortega's philosophy is included in the thesis 'I am I and my circumstance,' but that this sentence is understood only when it serves as a center of condensation for all that philosophy, and its enunciation suddenly actualizes and orders this doctrine, and thus makes possible its real intellection." Well, that function of *condensation* and subsequent *liberation* can be realized only by means of a system of lived allusions and references, which include an aura of feeling, so that the *single* concept would be insufficient. The formula of a philosophy has to be *also* metaphorical, by intrinsic necessity, and all the great philosophical

---

[41] *Meditaciones del Quijote.* I, 357–58. Italics mine. See my Commentary on *Meditaciones del Quijote*, 356ff.

[42] Commentary on *Meditaciones del Quijote*, 356ff.

condensations have been so. And, finally, the "ironic" character of all metaphor makes it, when it is recognized as such, avoid falling into the absolutist error of being taken for *reality itself*. The function of what we might call *original metaphor* of a philosophical doctrine consists in this.[43]

[43] In his lecture "Hegel y el problema metafísico" (1931), published in 1933 and included in the book *Naturaleza, Historia, Dios* (1944), Xavier Zubiri has referred to this problem as follows:

"In a marvelous essay, my teacher Ortega said that philosophy had lived on two metaphors: the first is precisely this Greek metaphor: man is a piece of the universe, a thing that is there. And upon this quality of *being there* that other quality of his, the quality of knowing, is based and supported. Knowing means that things make their imprint on human consciousness; knowing is impression. Well, then: Descartes cuts the connection which links knowing to what man is, and changes knowing into the very being of man; *mens sive animus*, he said. The 'animus' or 'spiritus' has become 'mens,' knowing.

"At this moment the second metaphor makes its appearance, in which man is not a piece of the universe, but something in whose knowing is contained all that the universe is.

"Is this philosophical situation defensible? . . .

"Thus, perhaps the time has come when a third metaphor, also an ancient one, can impose its happy tyranny—we do not know for how long. It is not a question of treating human existence either as a piece of the universe or even as something virtually enveloping the universe, but rather that human existence has no other intellectual mission than that of illuminating the being of the universe; man would not consist in being a piece of the universe, or in something enveloping it, but simply in being the authentic, the true, light of things. Therefore, what things *are*, they are only by the light of that human existence. According to this third metaphor, what 'is constituted' in the light is not things, but their being; not what is, but what may be; but, reciprocally, that light illuminates, underlies, their being, the being of things, not of the I; it does not make them pieces of me. It only makes them 'be'; *en photí*, in the light, said Aristotle and Plato, is where things actually acquire their true being." (*Naturaleza, Historia, Dios*, 298–300.)

The idea of "liberation" by means of a discharge of lived allusions, to which I refer in the text, has very old antecedents in Ortega: "There is nothing so worthless that it cannot be ennobled by injecting into it the essence and aroma of a portion of the universe. When we have loved or suffered, there are small things all around us which are everlastingly linked to the memory of our pleasure or our grief. And so men, as they grow old, weep perhaps for an old, out-of-date waltz played by a blind man on the street, or, seeing the trembling of the first leaf that Spring puts on the tree, feel their temples perfumed with the sweet-smelling memory of their youth. Every word of poetry is a storehouse of innumerable emotions, which, when we read or hear it, discharges upon us, as if we had opened the door of a haymow. Sexual pleasure consists in the sudden emptying of some glands, of the fluid which has collected very slowly. In the same way, when a brushstroke, a melody, or a verse suddenly lets fall its whole charge of emotions upon our fancy, we feel aesthetic pleasure." ("Renan" [1909]. I, 424.) And again, several years later: "Sexual pleasure seems to consist in a sudden discharge of nervous energy. Aesthetic enjoyment is a sudden discharge of

Up to this point we have been observing the general theory of metaphor, as it appears in Ortega's early work, and his cognitive interpretation of it, culminating in the condensation which he makes of the history of philosophy (Greek-medieval, modern, and the philosophy which is beginning now) in relation to three great metaphors. But there is also in Ortega an application of the notion of metaphor to the understanding of certain literary procedures, and especially of poetry. And, on the other hand, there is his personal use of the metaphor in his philosophy and his literature.

In 1919, Heinz Werner's book, *Die Ursprünge der Metapher*, was published. This book, which according to Bühler "produced a sensation among the specialists,"[44] did not escape Ortega's attention. In *La deshumanización del arte* ["The Dehumanization of Art"] he refers to it at considerable length. One of the roots of the metaphor, according to Heinz Werner, lies in the spirit of "tabu." "There has been a period in which fear was the greatest human inspiration, an age dominated by cosmic terror. During this age the need was felt to avoid certain realities which, on the other hand, were inescapable .... And since for primitive man the word is a little like the thing of the same name, the necessity arose not to name the tremendous object upon which the 'tabu' had fallen. Hence it was called by another name, mentioning it in a hidden and surreptitious way .... This was metaphorical evasion. Obtained in this tabulike form, the metaphorical instrument can then be employed for the most diverse ends."[45]

The decisive word here, for Ortega, is not *tabu*, but *evasion*. In this context he is interested in poetry, which he defines as "an evasion of the everyday names for things," and of which he was also to say that *today* (1925) it is "the advanced algebra of metaphors."[46] Werner's theory of tabu explains very satisfactorily this evasive facet of metaphorical expression. But Ortega does not adopt this theory—strictly speaking he had already gone beyond it, as we have seen; and in this same passage

---

allusive emotions. Analogously, philosophy resembles a sudden discharge of intellectual insight." (*Meditaciones del Quijote*, I, 317–18.)

[44] Karl Bühler, *Teoría del lenguaje* (Spanish translation by J. Marías [1950], 395). See the entire chapter Bühler writes on "The Linguistic Metaphor," 386–401.

[45] *La deshumanización del arte* (1925). III, 373.

[46] *Ibid.*, 372.

he says things which are independent of it and have greater implications: "The metaphor is probably the most fertile power that man possesses. Its efficacy goes so far as to touch the edges of thaumaturgy, and it seems like an implement which God forgot and left inside one of His creatures when He created it, as the absent-minded surgeon leaves an instrument inside his patient's abdomen after an operation. All the other powers leave us confined inside the real, inside what already is. The most we can do is to add or subtract some things from others. Only the metaphor makes evasion possible, creates imaginary reefs among the real things, the flowering of islands lighter than air."[47]

This is what really matters to Ortega, what is in the line of his general theory. And it is a bit surprising that, carried away by his interest at the time he wrote this passage—which was to explain poetry and in general *the dehumanization of art* in the third decade of the twentieth century—he abandons what he has just said and adds, as a transition toward the statement of Werner's theory: "It is really strange, the existence in man of this mental activity which consists in supplanting one thing by another, not so much in order to arrive at the latter, as to try to flee the former. The metaphor whisks one object out of sight by masking it with another, and it would make no sense unless we saw underneath it an instinct which leads man to avoid realities."[48] I have quoted in reverse order so as to show more clearly what I am trying to demonstrate. The chapter in Ortega's book is called "El 'tabú' y la metáfora" [" 'Tabu' and the Metaphor"]; in it he will expound Werner's doctrine, which he accepts in principle at least, and which he uses to explain the metaphor as "the most radical instrument of dehumanization,"[49] which is precisely what interests him on this occasion. And for this purpose he does violence to what he had just said, which is personally his and of much greater implications, and in a sense vitiates it. How can the chief thing be to *flee* from realities, and not to *arrive* at others? How can the decisive thing be the instinct to *avoid realities*, if the metaphor is something quasi-divine, an "implement of creation," the most fertile power that man possesses? The valuable factor in evasion is its quality of *liberation* of one form of reality in order to create *imaginary reefs* among real things. These reefs, these new "realities" that man

[47] *Ibid.*, 372–73.
[48] *Ibid.*, 373.
[49] *Ibid.*, 374.

can create, are what interest him. Shortly before this, Ortega had said that the mission of the poet is "to invent what does not exist." "The poet augments the world, adding to the real, which is already there by itself, an unreal continent. 'Author' comes from *auctor*, the one who augments. Romans gave this name to the general who conquered a new territory for his country."[50]

The thing could not be clearer. Whether or not it is true that *one* of the roots of the metaphor is found in the spirit of tabu,[51] what gives metaphor its formidable importance is not the moment of *evasion*, which at most can be a condition for its exercise, so that the imagination can "come unstuck" from habitual and everyday reality, but the moment of invention, discovery, uncovering, illumination, reflection of light, creation, and augmentation of existing things.

This aspect is the one which has most importance in the actual metaphors which appear constantly in Ortega's writings. A minute analysis of them would be enormously interesting, but it would force us into a focus which is not that of this book. We must, however, examine some of them, and try to discover their physiognomy, their genesis, and their double function—aesthetic and cognitive. For this purpose we would do well to complete the theory of the metaphor which Ortega worked out along with some other ideas, derived in part from the consideration of his own metaphors.

I refer, in the first place, to the theory of the concept which I sketched out in my *Reason and Life*.[52] Here I am interested only in the following aspect of it: the reality of what I call "things" is not something which is simply given, in an abstract or absolute way, but includes *perspective*. "The reality 'cat,' " I wrote in that book, "is strictly speaking different for me, for a flea lurking in the cat's fur, and for a parasite inhabiting its intestines; and a possible cat which would be one and the same for all is a convention; it is, in all strictness, a *theory* or interpretation, founded on the multiple reality *cat*. Without departing from human life—not to force things too far—we have already seen how thunder and lightning are different things for the men of different historical

[50] *Ibid.*, 371.

[51] See the discussion of Werner's theory in Bühler, 395–400.

[52] *Introducción a la Filosofía* (1947). *Obras*, II, chapter 2, pp. 34, 35; IV, 37; V, 45; VI, 53; VII, 61.

groups; and, for myself, a river is something which quenches my thirst, something which bars my way when I find it in my path, something which defends me when it comes between me and an enemy; three different vital realities, which *provide a base* for an *interpretation* of mine, whose result is the *concept* of river, which will possibly be 'single' but which is a new element that I use to handle the other three realities."[53] If we look at the thing from the other side, the identity of concepts and the expressions which signify them, although not an error, must be taken as something partial, a reflection of the persistence, in each of the situations, of common elements, which are very far from exhausting their significant reality. Expressed with greater strictness, it is necessary to distinguish between the *logical scheme* of the concept—invariable, abstract, not applicable to the situation—and its effective *significant function*, or what I have called the *concipient concept*, the one which has the function of conceiving concretely, circumstantially, a certain reality.

The greater number of words, even *technical terms*, are outworn metaphors, in which their metaphorical character has been erased and forgotten, which are no longer lived as metaphors. Well, metaphorical expression re-injects into terms their original character, and thus gives concepts, beyond their abstract scheme, their concipient function. The metaphor is a power of repristination of concepts, which saves them from the skeletal structure into which they inevitably fall, and gives them back their original function: that of conceiving reality—in a certain foreshortening, in a real and irreplaceable perspective.

After an analysis of one of the culminating forms of Ortega's expression, I summarized, in the book I have mentioned, the role played by metaphors in that expression: "Nor can they be 'plastic' or morphological; still less can they become stereotyped, as is traditional in literature, until they turn into those overfamiliar metaphors which eventually become reduced to epithets; for the function of metaphors is not a simple indirect allusion to objects, but an *interpretation* of them, a placing of objects in a certain foreshortening, to make meanings—in themselves universal and invariable—assume a precise circumstantial value. No longer, then, are there 'fixed' and rigid things; there are only dynamic ingredients of a reality constituted by essential mobility: each 'thing' is,

[53] *Ibid.*, III, 34.

literally, *many things*; it has no being 'in itself,' but gradually acquires one in the different vital *functions* which it assumes; and this is the thematic use of the metaphor."[54]

Now we can try to understand what the metaphors which adorn Ortega's writings are like, and what they mean. In one of the earliest of them, Ortega says that the dead leave us a heritage of "the bulging quiver of their virtues."[55] These six words give us a whole interpretation of the virtues and their function: something dynamic, projective, which requires a target, with a quality of repertory and possibility, offered as something to be made use of, etc. If Ortega had *said* all this, the result would be different, and furthermore it would alter the structure of what he wrote; he *cannot* say it, for that is not his intention, it is not to the point, and anyway if he said it he would become identified with it and would have to justify it, and this would bring in its train impermissible changes in the text; he simply *suggests* it; this is the way the metaphor shows the virtues; it places them, merely by mentioning them, in that precise foreshortening, orients the reader's life experiences, launches their associations, puts him in the way of expanding with his own personal content that laconic *nominal*, not apophantic, mention. In another passage he says that Julio Cejador, who was professor of Latin in the Instituto of Palencia, "is off there teaching preterites and supines to little Celtiberian angels."[56] The connotations of the word "Celtiberian" (in large part those which Ortega has injected into it stylistically), joined with the connotations of the term "little angels" say more than a page of prose could about Cejador's situation: uncouthness, limitations, lack of intellectual interest, rude manners, innocence, involuntary tenderness.

Sometimes the metaphors are more complex, or rest on deeper assumptions. When Ortega speaks in the *Meditations on Quixote* of the "Spaniards' inmost dwelling place," he is expressing by this a whole interpretation of a national society and its function with respect to individual lives; and when he adds that "it was conquered some time ago by hatred, which is still there, drawn up like artillery, making war on the world," he takes advantage of the possibilities of the previous metaphor in order, by the use of a new one, to define in an intuitive form one essential vicissitude of Spanish society, as a result of which "our souls pass through life making bitter faces, suspicious and slinking as

[54] *Ibid.*, V, 48.   [55] I, 59.   [56] I, 67.

cunning, hungry dogs,"[57] which is simply a condensed *aperçu* of collective psychology.

Analogously, when he writes, after having constructed the theory of the forest which I have analyzed in detail elsewhere,[58] "The forest opens up its depths around me. A book is in my hand: *Don Quixote*, an ideal forest,"[59] this metaphor is the only way in which the light which the previous doctrine has captured can be thrown upon the *Quixote*, in a suddenly intelligible form.

At times the function of the metaphor is the maximum condensation of a whole doctrine. This is the case of his chapter headings, or even the titles of essays or whole books: "The Myth, Ferment of History"; "Adam in Paradise"; *Invertebrate Spain*; *The Atlantides*; "The High Tide of Philosophy"; "The Strangulation of *Don Juan*"; "Under the Ruined Arch"; "Toward a Topography of Spanish Arrogance." Only in metaphorical form is it possible to suggest in a few words the content of a theory; it is obvious that one runs the risk that the metaphor may be understood not metaphorically but literally, and that a meaning may be conferred upon it improperly, by simultaneously—and this is what the metaphor consists of, as we have seen—suggesting and discounting. How much of the bad reputation of *Invertebrate Spain* has arisen simply out of a lack of metaphorical sense? And the same thing happens with titles which are not *strictly* metaphorical, either because a partial or erroneous sense of some of their terms slips into the understanding of them—*The Revolt of the Masses*—or because what is simply descriptive is taken to be preceptive—*The Dehumanization of Art*. But these risks —which always go along with being a writer, and which consist in the fact that people who read do not know how to read—do not dim the brilliance, and therefore the extreme effectiveness, of metaphorical titles.

Sometimes the metaphor has very complex functions, as when it gives a new cast to expressions which were *originally metaphorical*, but which have lost their aliveness as such. Then, when a new, "fresh" metaphor is superimposed upon them, the new metaphor emphasizes the metaphorical nature of the other expressions and makes the combination come alive again, and prevents formulas already minted and outworn

[57] I, 312.

[58] Commentary on the *Meditaciones del Quijote*, 285–311.

[59] I, 337 (p. 83 of my edition without the commentary).

from being accepted in a passive way. An example will explain this more clearly: "War fluidifies the human element, which always tends to crystallize in the souls of the Philistines, *like saltpeter in damp corners.*"[60] "To fluidify" and "to crystallize" are, undoubtedly, metaphorical expressions, but they are so elementary and commonplace that they are constantly repeated without attention to what they say; when Ortega adds the last comparison I have italicized, he interrupts the merely expressive, not figurative, line of thought, and causes the reader to recover the intuition on which those modes of expression are based. A similar effect is obtained by what we might call the reinforced or intensified metaphor, in which a slender metaphor, one almost totally lacking in effectiveness, is "taken seriously" and continued. The figure of "retirement" or "retreat" to explain states of mind has functioned for a long time almost as a cliché, and has lapsed into a function of mere abstract mention; but Ortega writes: "When there is no joy, the soul retires to a corner of our bodies and makes its lair there. From time to time it gives a pitiful howl or shows its teeth to the things that go by."[61] That Ortega does this as a matter of method and with full awareness, as well as treating it as a literary inspiration, is proved by the passages entitled "Geometría en la meseta"[62] and "Geometría sentimental."[63]

At the very least, Ortega's metaphors insure intensity and effectiveness: "Romanesque cathedrals were constructed in Spain to the rhythm of swords falling on the bodies of the Moors."[64] Or: "The Tartar Empire lasted as long as the life of the blacksmith who had riveted it together with the iron of his sword."[65] But sometimes it is much more: what he presents in a brilliant and intuitive form, under the guise of emotion, could be "justified" conceptually and in detail, could be taken literally in its meaning, by transferring it to other language; on occasions, Ortega does this himself: "Rodrigálvarez, meanwhile, talks along with the slow rhythm of the mules' gait. *He moves among proverbs like a crossbowman among the battlements.* For this man Rodrigálvarez lives, like all the men born in these harsh lands, perpetually on the defensive. Each proverb serves them like a trench, and in the short space left open between two of them, they hurl their deadly shaft. The imprecision of speech and thought, so characteristic of peasants, makes particularly easy for them the ambushes where they hide their intentions

[60] II, 29.
[61] II, 31.
[62] II, 245.
[63] II, 462–64.
[64] II, 43.
[65] III, 56.

and powerful instincts. They are 'guerrillas' in speech as well as in battle."[66] We could say the same when Ortega proposes, "An ideal which at the same time would be a spur!"[67] or says of Lucifer that he is "God's snob."[68] Or when he defines the tramp with a series of conceptual terms and secondary metaphors which declare one central and nuclear metaphor: "The tramp is a man who does not stay in one place; a fugitive from all customs, he arrives, takes a look around, and leaves. *He is a Don Juan of the small towns, of trades and of landscapes.* He crosses all places without staying in any of them. He has the dynamic soul of an arrow that forgot about its target after it was in the air."[69]

I am purposely using examples from the first half of Ortega's literary career, during which his literary style was established. Although it has sometimes been said, it is not certain that this style is less metaphorical in his late works: *rather, the contrary.* A certain greater degree of sobriety in his style, which is indisputable, has frequently been wrongly interpreted in this sense, since the fact is that it consists in something quite different. For it must be said that *metaphor is sobriety,* that it is born precisely out of a defined wish for conciseness. Successful metaphors save innumerable explanations, avoid circumlocutions, permit the writer to go straight to where he wants to go. Ortega tries to go *by the shortest road*; this expression recurs in his writings: when he speaks of the *Poem of the Cid,* he says, "The anonymous singer who—like a falcon screaming from a crag—gave this song to the air on the desolate and threatening height of Medinaceli, knew how to take us along the shortest road to the inmost depths of an eternal reality . . . ."[70] The purpose of the "salvations" is: "given a fact—a man, a book, a picture, a landscape, an error, a pain—to take it by the shortest road to the plenitude of its meaning."[71] This is what he does when he calls the Roman Forum "that ten-centuries-long *tertulia,*"[72] or writes, "Movement is life spending itself, it is death disguised, slyly entering life"[73]; or, "Let us be poets of existence, who know how to find the perfect rhyme for their lives in an inspired death."[74]

The metaphor, like Ortega's style in general, undergoes some variation throughout his work. An evolutionary examination would not, however, be proper, for it would be unexplained and unjustified. Certain

[66] II, 45–46. Italics mine.   [69] II, 123. Italics mine.   [72] II, 324.
[67] II, 87.   [70] II, 42.   [73] II, 170.
[68] II, 713.   [71] I, 311.   [74] II, 425.

changes are understood only in the light of philosophical positions at which Ortega arrived later in his life. Only after expounding them could we return to his style and his metaphors. Moreover, I was interested here only in showing their generic quality and their function, and in illustrating this with a few examples. Later I shall collect many concrete metaphors; I mean, in order to analyze their intellectual significance or their literary function. I wish only to state that Ortega's metaphors have played an important role from the beginning, as an *indispensable* point of convergence of literature with philosophy. Many people have taken *only as metaphors* what were really *metaphorical pronouncements*;[75] others, however, have taken literally and straight-

[75] A particularly significant example is offered by the different interpretations of the passage in which Ortega introduces, in the *Meditaciones del Quijote*, the idea of *circumstance*. I shall quote the whole passage, followed by two of the most recent commentaries on it, José Gaos' and mine. This is what Ortega says:

"Circumstance! *Circum-stantia!* The mute things which are close around us! Near us, very near us they raise their silent faces with an expression of humility and yearning, as if begging us to accept their offer, and at the same time as if ashamed of the apparent simplicity of their gift. And we walk blindly among them, our gaze fixed on faraway enterprises, planning the conquest of distant diagrams of cities. Few readings have moved me as much as those stories where the hero advances, swift and straight as an arrow, toward a glorious goal, oblivious of the anonymous maiden who is secretly in love with him, and walks beside him with a humble and suppliant face, carrying in her white body a heart on fire for him, a red-and-yellow coal where incense is burned in his honor. We would like to signal to the hero, so that he would cast one glance toward that burning flower of passion which is growing at his feet. All of us are heroes in varying degrees, and all of us inspire humble loves around ourselves.

> *I have been a fighter*
> *And this means that I have been a man,*

shouts Goethe. We are heroes, we are always fighting for some distant goal, and as we go we trample on sweet-smelling violets." (I, 318; pp. 35–36 in my edition.)

Gaos' commentary is as follows:

"This is not an ordinary passage. It is the passage that explains one of the two cardinal concepts of the conception of philosophy which Ortega explains in the prologue and which the *Meditaciones* begin to realize, and which always continued to be an important concept in Ortega's philosophy. And the explanation lies solely in the concept of 'the mute things that are close around us,' which contains a personification. The rest is a tirade made up of figures of speech, one following on the heels of another, which, with their narcissistic eroticism, their affected pathos and their superabundant rhetoric, half-extraordinary and half-vulgar, have always struck me as verging on the shoddy." ("Los dos Ortegas," 1956, in *Sobre Ortega y Gasset* [1957], 91.)

My commentary on the same passage reads as follows:

"We must emphasize the stylistic trademarks with which Ortega introduces this concept: first, the use of the exclamation mark: second, the use—uncommon in Spanish—

forwardly what was a *metaphorical utterance*; proper comprehension of Ortega falls between these two, and asks only that we do not forget what he has said, that we do not renounce any of the means he has used in order to make himself understood.

of the word in the singular. This is a stylistic recourse which attracts the attention to a word and shades its meaning; thus, Ortega often says 'la tiniebla' ['the shadow'], 'el Alpe' ['the Alp']. In the present case, it is a question of avoiding the triviality with which this word is often used, and which is reflected in its definition in the Dictionary of the Academy, and of giving this word the fullness of its meaning; thus he takes it in its literal Latin sense, and with the value of a neuter plural: *circum-stantia*. 'The mute things which are close around us!' The circumstance is everything that surrounds us, that which is *circum me*, around me, about me. It is a purely functional concept, and one which prejudges nothing, but which takes reality in all its immediacy and purity; in this sense, much more fundamental than *Umwelt*. Ortega's description immediately adds a few notes of lively interest: *mute* things lift their *silent* faces; that is, circumstance, therefore, has no voice or meaning—we shall soon see the implications of this. But neither is it a question of an inert and passive 'being there,' but rather that things are an *offering* and a *gift*. We are oriented toward something; the figures of speech come thick and fast: with his eyes fixed on faraway, *planned* enterprises, the hero advances like an *arrow* toward a *goal*. Offer and project are the initial traits with which Ortega sketches out the dialogue between circumstantial reality and the subject whose circumstance it is." Commentary on the *Meditaciones del Quijote* (1957), 248–49.

III.
LITERARY GENRES

52. THE PROBLEM OF LITERARY GENRES

When an author sits down to write, he has already accomplished an essential part of his task before he has put a single word on paper; he is going to write a certain type of work: a novel, a drama, a comedy, a treatise, an essay, a sonnet, a newspaper article, memoirs . . . . These are what are generally called "literary genres." Well, early in this century, in 1902 to be precise, Benedetto Croce published a book which was to have many consequences: *Estetica come scienza dell'espressione e linguistica generale* ["Aesthetics as the Science of Expression and General Linguistics"]. In it he denied the true reality of literary genres. After this any treatment of them had to start by taking this invalidation into account, though it has been more frequently invoked than known in detail and discussed concretely.[1]

---

[1] See the chapter "Critica della teorica dei generi artistici e letterarî." Croce says that "il trionfo più cospicuo dell'errore intellettualistico è nella dottrina dei generi artistici e letterarî che ancora corre nei trattati e perturba i critici e gli storici dell'arte." The whole chapter, which is important to this theme, should be read; the nucleus of its argument is as follows: "—Qual'è la forma *estetica* della vita domestica, della cavalleria, dell'idillio, della crudeltà, e cosí via?—Tale, denudato e ridotto alla più semplice formola, è il problema assurdo, che la dottrina dei generi artistici e letterarî si propone; in ciò consiste qualsiasi ricerca di leggi o regole di generi. Vita domestica, cavalleria, idillio, crudeltà e simili, sono, non già impressioni, ma concetti; non contenuti, ma forme logico-estetiche. La forma non si può esprimere, perché è già essa stessa espressione. O che cosa sono le parole: 'crudeltà,' 'idillio,' 'cavalleria,' 'vita domestica' e via enumerando, se non le espressioni di quei concetti?" And finally Croce concludes, summing up his doctrine: "La condanna filosofica dei generi artistici e letterarî è la dimostrazione e la formolazione rigorosa di ciò che l'attività artistica ha sempre operato el il buon gosto sempre riconosciuto . . . . Chi poi discorre di tragedie, commedie, drammi, romanzi, poemi, poemetti, liriche e cosí via, tanto per farse intendere accennando alla buona e approssimativamente ad alcuni gruppi di opera su quali vole, per una ragione o per un altra, richiamare l'attenzione, certo non dice nulla di scientificamente erroneo, perché egli adopera *vocaboli e frasi,* non stabilisce *definizioni*

Ortega was concerned with the subject from a very early age. He had two reasons for this interest: his own activity as a writer and his critical thinking, concentrated especially on the novel. As early as 1910 he wrote, "Leaving for another occasion the discussion with Benedetto Croce as to whether literary genres exist or not, I firmly believe that they do. The artistic task, like the task of living, is individual; but just as biology needs the concept of the species in order to approach the organic individual, descriptive aesthetics needs the concept of the literary genre in order to approach the book which can be called beautiful. And just as, in one way or another, the motive for the appearance of a zoological species must be sought in the physical milieu, so we must inquire in the psychological milieu for the origin of a literary genre. There is a reason for finding elephants in the tall grass, and a reason for picaresque novels in the Spanish language."[2]

But it is in the *Meditations on Quixote* that he formulates his theory of genres. Ortega set out to write a "short treatise on the novel," which appears to be *Don Quixote*'s most external feature; but to ask oneself what the novel is presupposes "a discourse on the essence of literary genres." And he adds: "The subject is held to be mere rhetoric. There are some who deny even the existence of literary genres."[3] The allusion to Croce is clear. When Ortega affirms this existence, he is going to have to make clear in what sense, other than that of ancient poetics, he understands literary genres.

Ortega does not accept literary genres as "certain rules of creation to which the poet had to adjust himself, empty diagrams, formal structures within which the Muse, like a docile bee, deposited its honey."[4] He does not admit the separability of what he calls "content" and "form," as if there were preexistent forms into which a content could be "poured." The figure of the bee and the hive is sufficiently eloquent. The interpretation of genres proposed by Ortega is very different from the traditional one, but his affirmation of them—as opposed to Croce—is conclusive. Content and form are not one and the same thing; Ortega recalls and

---

e leggi. L'errore si ha solamente quando al vocabolo si dia peso di distinzione scientifica: quando, insomma, si vada ingenuamente a cadere nei tranelli che quella fraseologia suol tendere." *Estetica come scienza dell'espressione e linguistica generale*, (4th ed., 1912), 42–46.

[2] "Una primera vista sobre Baroja" (1910), *El Espectador*, I. II, 119.

[3] *Meditaciones del Quijote*, I, 365.

[4] *Ibid.*

accepts Flaubert's statement: form arises out of content as heat rises from fire; and he improves upon it by saying that form is the organ, and content the function which creates it; and, dwelling on this metaphor, he arrives at a first definition: "literary genres are poetic functions, directions in which the process of aesthetic generation gravitates."[5] That is, "content or theme" and "form or the apparatus which expresses that theme" are *different and inseparable*: to separate them is as erroneous as to annul the difference between them. This difference is the same as that which exists between a direction and a road: "To set off in a certain direction is not the same as to have walked to the goal we have set for ourselves."[6] "Thus," he goes on to say, "a tragedy is the expansion of a certain fundamental poetic theme, and only that theme: it is the expansion of the tragic." The near-tautology of this expression is essential: tragedy is the expansion of the tragic. Both things are, in fact, *the same*, but in different ways: a manifest, articulated, developed form (tragedy) of what was only a tendency or pure intention (tragic theme). The expression which Ortega used before is the decisive one: "directions in which the process of aesthetic *generation* gravitates"; the literary genre consists precisely in the generation of the work arising out of its theme, in its *genesis*. An age-old use of the term "genre" as merely formal (genres and types) has made us forget the genetic moment included in its root. The literary genre is the path along which, out of the "content" of a certain precise theme, the corresponding work of art is *engendered*.

Now Ortega can introduce his authentic definition: "I understand, therefore, by literary genres, something opposite to ancient poetics: certain fundamental themes, irreducible among themselves, true aesthetic categories."[7] It is not a question of aesthetic categories in a purely formal sense, as a repertory of rules or laws—compare Croce's idea— but in the fundamental sense of the very substance of aesthetic reality. The epic poem is not a *poetic form*, but a *substantive poetic content*. His explanation of the lyric is still clearer: it is not "a conventional idiom into which something already said in a dramatic or novelistic idiom can be translated, but, simultaneously, a certain thing to be said and the sole manner of saying it fully." That is, that immediately after disappearance of literary genres had been decreed, Ortega shows them to

[5] *Ibid.*, 366.   [6] *Ibid.*   [7] *Ibid.*

be necessary, inevitable, fundamental, simply by asking himself serious-ly *what they are.*

And there is more. "Man is always the essential theme of art." And then genres, thus understood, become "broad vistas observed from the cardinal points of human existence." This allows us to understand all the implications of literary genres in Ortega's thought. It is a question of the different *dimensions* of man, his fundamental possibilities, which are tendencies or directions and acquire a certain actualization, a mani-festation or visibility, in the different genres. These, far from being mere conventions, are explicit manifestations of cardinal aspects of hu-man existence, and constitute after their fashion what we might call an "anthropology." The word is not to be found in this text of Ortega's, but the idea is there: Ortega adds that "each period brings with it a radical interpretation of man," and amends his own expression by saying that "it does not bring this interpretation with it, but rather each period *is* just that," and this is the reason why each period prefers a certain genre. Each period is an interpretation of man, and one of the funda-mental modes in which man *executes* and realizes himself is the most authentic genre, the one which the period creates or re-creates. The *historical* condition of literary genres, which are not an abstract and timeless world of "forms" and "rules," causes the "anthropology" which they constitute to be concrete also, the manifestation and the temporal development of the "cardinal points," the fundamental ten-dencies which constitute man.

This is—giving it its full implications, carrying it as far as it will go—the theoretical presentation of the problem of literary genres in Ortega. In 1914, in his first book, it appears thus formulated. This means that these ideas influence all of his literary production. Now we shall have to ask ourselves what Ortega does with the literary genres which he him-self cultivates, how he realizes them, to what innovations he subjects them.

53. THE FORM OF ORTEGA'S WRITINGS

The reader will recall what we have observed of the deliberate circum-stantiality—that is, accepted and sought for its own sake—of all of Ortega's work; and he will also have in mind what the situation of the intellectual world in Spain was at the time Ortega began his public activity. Spain was at that time the *only* "market" for his writings, and was always the *chief* one: something we must keep in mind constantly. Since in Spain there was no living philosophical tradition, and the public's receptivity toward "technical" philosophy was almost nonexistent, the literary genres habitually cultivated in Spain did not seem to him to be adequate. It must be added that they did not seem appropriate in other countries either: from a very early stage in his career Ortega was conscious of the deficiencies of the "literary" uses of German thought, which was the model, and also, for different reasons, those of French and English thought. For many years Ortega reserved his "technical" philosophy for the University, where it was possible to effectively create a minority which in its turn would make possible other modes of dealing with philosophy. And so he wrote *newspaper articles*, for years exclusively, and throughout the greater part of his life in considerable measure.

This is Ortega's most important literary genre, since even many of his books were originally series of articles published in newspapers in Spain or South America, and must be interpreted from this point of view. The reasons Ortega published mostly articles were many; in addition to those I have just mentioned, the fact that ever since the nineteenth century the daily newspapers in Spain have had an illustrious tradition, and therefore *general acceptance*. The best Spanish writers have frequently collaborated on newspapers, and have formed their public within them. Newspaper articles, furthermore, have been an indispensable source of income for many writers: professors' salaries in Spain have always been inadequate to live on, not to mention in adequate style *intellectually*. A fact not sufficiently stressed—certainly, it is overlooked by those living in other countries—is that Spanish libraries were early in this century, and continue to be today, totally inadequate—because of their poverty and lack of facilities—for research and for any form of effective intellectual life; the Spanish scholar must possess a considerable personal library, of several thousand volumes—Ortega's eventually numbered more than twenty thousand—many of them foreign books, the majority of them old, very costly, and difficult to acquire. The proportion of his income that a Spanish intellectual spends on books is extraordinary. In a period when there was no likelihood of having supplementary income which did not represent work already completed, when sales of scholarly books were minimal, the only normal source of income for a writer consisted of writing for newspapers, which paid reasonably well and, moreover, promptly. For the greater part of his life Ortega, until international reputation and translations made the total sales of his books very large, lived "from day to day"—or behind-hand—and always depended on his contributions to the press. To this must be added the prestige of the periodical publications to which Ortega contributed most frequently: *El Imparcial*, *El Sol*, and *La Nación* of Buenos Aires, which were an unexcelled medium for diffusing his ideas, and one which assured "impact" on the readers whom Ortega hoped to influence, transform, and educate toward philosophy, those whom he wished to "convert" to it. "Toward this domain of light cast on themselves and their surroundings, I wished to mobilize my country-men," wrote Ortega in 1932, when he reviewed his work as a whole. "It is the only thing in which I have faith; only it will bring out the Spaniard's quality and cure him of that sleepwalking in which he has been indulging for centuries. But this propaganda of enthusiasm for mental light—*lumen naturale*—had to be made in Spain in a way neces-sitated by her circumstances. In our country, neither the University chair nor the book had social efficacy. Our people do not accept the faraway and the solemn. What reigns there is the purely everyday and common. The man who wishes to create something—and all creation is aristocracy —must succeed in being an aristocrat in the public square. This is why, submitting to the circumstance, I have caused my work to appear in the intellectual public square represented by the newspaper. I need not say that I have been constantly criticized for this. But there must be some merit in my resolve, when foreign presses have made full-fledged books out of these newspaper articles."[8]

These requirements condition the nature of Ortega's articles. Each of them had to be, of course, *intelligible* in itself; that is, to be a mean-ingful autonomous unit, not a fragment or chapter of a larger whole which would be necessary for comprehension. On the other hand, since a unitary doctrine of a philosophical, and therefore systematic, nature underlay them, this doctrine had to be in some sense "aimed," so that it would continue to act in the comprehension of each of the articles. Further, though autonomous, the articles were *connected*. The reader

---

[8] "Prólogo a una edición de sus obras" (1932). VI, 354–55. See also *Prólogo para alemanes*, 76ff.

confronted each one, and had to understand it in itself; I mean, without exceeding its bounds, without having to keep other writings in mind; but the comprehension of them transcended the contents of the article, and became a minimal possession of the general doctrine which sustained it. Thus, when these articles were *added up*—in the first place in the reader's mind, in many cases in the pages of a book composed of a collection of them—the result was the constitution of the doctrine as such, with its internal unity, and then each of its elements or ingredients automatically came to occupy a place in the higher organism thus formed. This is, neither more nor less, the constitutive requirement of a genre which we may call the *philosophical article*: if there is no question of a "sufficient" unity, it is not an article; if the general philosophical doctrine which permits its systematic articulation with the rest is not present, then it is not *philosophical*, no matter how many ideas it may contain.

Ortega had to reconcile brevity with his conviction that "any proper opinion takes a long time to express"[9]: from thence arise the exigencies of his style and the structure of his articles. Remember what I said about the metaphor as sobriety. On the other hand, it is a frequent occurrence that an article or essay of Ortega's begins with a phrase in which he sums up a whole doctrine. For example, "Muerte y resurrección" ["Death and Resurrection"], in which he is to speak of El Greco and other things, begins as follows: "All our acts, and thinking is an act, are like questions or answers which are always referred to that portion of the world which exists for us at each instant. *Our life is a dialogue, where the individual is only one speaker; the other is the landscape, the surroundings.*"[10] The theory of human life as the dialogue of the "I" with the circumstance, and incidentally the doctrine of the circumstantiality of every vital act, are summed up in a single sentence. What is the function of this extreme "condensation" in the article? For the unprepared and "innocent" reader, who does not suspect that a philosophical theory is being slipped over the threshold of his consciousness, like an episode of a novel in installments, this sentence signifies an observation of no great implications, but one which is perfectly intelligible, which he understands in a trivial but not inaccurate way, and which from then on is destined to operate in his mind, perhaps to take root in it, like a seed. For the reader who is better prepared, or simply more familiar

9 "Verdad y perspectiva" (1916), *El Espectador*, I. II, 17.
10 "Muerte y resurrección" (1917), *El Espectador*, II. II, 145.

with Ortega's work, this observation refers the article to an area of ideas already known to him, and adds a new viewpoint to the consideration of a portion of reality upon which he had already tried out his views, in other foreshortenings. Thus, the reader of *La Nación* who began to read "No ser hombre de partido" ["On Not Being a Party Man"] finds that a whole—and very strict—metaphysical theory of human life as a project, vocation, and destiny is being pumped into him in a few lines: "The reader's 'I' is, in the first place, a project of life. But there is no question of a project *he* has thought of, freely chosen. He does not find this project already formed when he finds himself in life. The ancients used, confusedly, a term whose true significance coincides with the one I have called the vital project: they spoke of Fate and believed that it consisted in the things which happen to a person . . . . Our radical being, the project of existence in which we consist, classifies and gives different meanings to everything which is around us. And thus it turns out that the real Fate is our own self. What happens to us, fundamentally, is being who we are."[11] Is it conceivable that a German scholar, a *Forscher* or *Gelehrte*, would seek this philosophical doctrine (which, indeed, anticipated European thought by several years) in an article out of a daily newspaper which announces that it is going to speak merely of the inadvisability of being a party man? And as this is *constant*, and happens hundreds of times throughout Ortega's writings, this alone explains a large part of his public activity.

But there is another side to the question: this structure of utterance often prevented Ortega from developing his ideas, and at other times obliged him to state them and then pass on, putting off dealing with them until another occasion. Since *each* delay was justified, this had the effect of strengthening his habit of putting things off, and the relative normality of his acceptance of the habit. And this has been fatal for certain decisive aspects of his thought. In an article written in 1917, "Para la cultura del amor" ["For the Culture of Love"] (keep the title in mind!) there is a note which says, "The idea of the *person* is one of the victims of the nineteenth century. It has been wiped out of the common culture. How many *persons* have a clear idea today of what it means to be a *person*? And yet, on this idea depends a whole piece of the future. It is not possible to go into the question deeply just now."[12]

[11] "No ser hombre de partido" (1930). IV, 77.
[12] II, 141.

Not now; but when? I shall say at once, in anticipation, that Ortega's philosophy represents, in my opinion, the most earnest effort to understand man as a *person*, a name "taken in vain" by almost all philosophies, and very particularly by those which characterize themselves as "spiritualist," those which insist on the "thingification" of the personal; but it is obvious that Ortega never found an occasion to attack head-on the question which he "postponed" in this note at the age of thirty-four. We could give numerous examples: let us quote only one more here, a close and decisive one: "At bottom, man is credulous; or, which amounts to the same thing, the deepest stratum of our lives, the one which sustains and carries all the others, is made up of beliefs." And he attaches a footnote: "Let us leave untouched the question of whether underneath this deepest stratum there is not still something more, a metaphysical depth which not even our beliefs can reach."[13]

The article, as Ortega understands it, must have a "principle," which cannot be only logical, but must be a vitalizing principle. In other words, it must be a *dramatic unity*. On the other hand, its brevity obliges it to be visual or *intuitive* rather than *dialectical*. It must be based on evidences rather than on "linkages" of ideas, so prone to inert thought and terminological mechanization. These "literary" demands have influenced, I believe in an extremely favorable way, Ortega's philosophy itself, have preserved it from innumerable risks and temptations, on which forms of contemporary thought of very high quality have foundered. The necessity of a "plot" for each article has caused Ortega always to write a very alert kind of philosophy, one which does not lose sight of reality, which does not get entangled in its own ideas, spinning a cocoon that turns out to be their tomb: the silkworm should not be the totemic beast of the philosopher.

This dramatic character of Ortega's articles makes comprehension of them possible even though they may be difficult—when a book, or a lecture, is especially difficult this must be compensated for, if one wishes them to be understood, by a heightening of dramatic technique—and it also permits, at times demands, that they be long. Ortega introduced, in Spain and in Latin America, the intellectual newspaper serial, packed with doctrine, passionately interesting to read, finished in form, written in delicious prose, whose dramatic "argumentative" connections—together with the dramatic quality of their doctrine—constituted their

[13] *Ideas y creencias* (1936). V, 388.

dialectical nerve center in the authentic sense of the word, and permitted the long connected series which in the end became books. The newspaper serial acquired, in the sphere of thought, the impassioned and even urgent characteristics of the "folletín," which is the Spanish translation of the word *feuilleton* when used in connection with novels.

In 1914, when Ortega planned a series of publications for the first time, he called them *essays*: "Under the title of *Meditations*, this first volume announces essays on various themes . . . ."[14] These are the meditations which he calls "salvations" in the same preface. Of the essay, even though warning that his receive their impulse from philosophical desires, he says that "it is science minus the explicit proof."[15] This definition responds to a larger genre in Ortega's work. It has frequently been understood in a minimal or negative form, emphasizing the absence of proof; but there is no such absence, for Ortega immediately adds, "For the writer there is a question of intellectual honor in not writing anything susceptible of proof unless he possesses that proof. But it is licit for him to blot out of his work any clearly demonstrable *appearance*, leaving the proofs merely *indicated elliptically*, in such a way that the person who needs them *can find them*; but in such a way, on the other hand, that they do not interfere with the expansion of the *intimate warmth with which the thoughts were thought*. Even books whose intent is exclusively scientific are beginning to be written in a less didactic and pedantic style; footnotes are suppressed insofar as possible, and the rigid mechanical apparatus of proof is dissolved into a more organic, emotional, and personal style."[16]

The decisive factor in the essay is its *theme*. A newspaper article is decidedly a foreshortening, a single facet of the reality dealt with. The fertility of the point of view, of the "focus," is essential to it; its unity is the unity of a flash of enlightenment—this is why the worst thing that can happen to a newspaper article is to be boring; no piece of writing *ought* to be boring, but the article *cannot* be so without turning into a caricature of itself—which does not exclude its more strictly fragmentary quality. The essay is something else: it is defined by the delimitation of a theme, by its own internal structure, which is precisely the structure which is

[14] *Meditaciones del Quijote.* I, 311.

[15] *Ibid.*, 318.

[16] *Ibid.* Italics mine. I have shown in my commentary on this book how these comprobations can be found, if one looks for them.

going to organize it as a piece of writing, the structure which is going to constitute its internal movement, what I have called its "plot." When, in his "Meditación del marco" ["Meditation on the Picture Frame"], Ortega says that he needs to write just one page to complete a volume of *El Espectador*, and is searching for a theme, he is fully conscious of this. "The reader does not suspect the difficulties a man goes through in order to write a single page. All the things in the world are so marvelous! There is so much to say about the least among them! And it is so painful to chop the limbs off a subject arbitrarily, and offer the reader a torso sprouting with stumps!"[17] This delimitation of themes was Ortega's greatest talent as a writer. This is why his themes have been able to pass into the collective consciousness, into the "public domain," like minted coins; we sometimes think that the titles are brilliant, but it is much more than that: it is the themes themselves, the articulations of reality; when he has once touched on them, then we see them as he does, we think of them in the shape which he gave them, or, still better, which he discovered in them. The anatomy of the real shines through and becomes visible under his pen. This has been his greatest and most far-reaching influence. Apart from his strict philosophical doctrines, assimilated by very few persons, Ortega has introduced into the minds of his contemporaries themes, and ways of thinking about them, which have become, since his time, *the very form of reality*. Invertebrate Spain, the mass-man and his revolt against himself, the dehumanization of art, the ideas of castles, of the triple reality—vitality-soul-spirit; the pairing of ideas and beliefs, the idea of generations, of the interesting man, the idea of circumstance, the contraposition between man and people, and so many more, are themes which belong by now, not to a repertory of "subjects," but to the effective contents of our world, which thus appears to have been shaped by his hand. This is the cause of the inexplicable irritation which Ortega has always produced in a certain type of mind.

Then there are the *books*. What are Ortega's books like? To be entirely correct, we should have to say that he never wrote one. Those which ought to be considered as books because of their length, do not quite manage to be books because of their structure; I mean that they are incomplete: the *Meditations on Quixote* includes only the prologue, the preliminary meditation, and the first one, and the

[17] II, 301.

other two are lacking; *The Theme of Our Time* is merely the development of the first lesson in a course of lectures, filled out with a number of appendices; *Invertebrate Spain* and *The Revolt of the Masses* are unfinished; the last chapter of the latter book is entitled: "Now We Come to the Real Question"; *En torno a Galileo* ["Concerning Galileo," translated under the English title *Man and Crisis*] or *El hombre y la gente* ["Man and People"], which arose out of courses of lectures, are only part of what they should have been; *The Idea of Principle in Leibniz*, besides having been interrupted, was in need of articulation and structuring, and Ortega was well aware of it.

The fact that, in spite of all this, these books are the most absorbing that the philosophy of our time has produced, does not detract from the fact that Ortega never succeeded in writing a *book* in the sense that he felt he should have. Many reasons—biographical, collective, philosophical, merely casual—prevented him from doing so. To write a book demands a temperament rather more ascetic than Ortega's, a capacity for not asking too much of inspiration, for being able to write when one is not in the full spate of enthusiasm, perhaps crossing stony wastes in the process. Ortega's almost voluptuous enjoyment of his themes, which he felt very intensely and which made him, not only an intellectual, but a writer in the full sense of the word, too frequently distracted him toward incidental questions, and especially toward new subjects, to the detriment of the internal economy of his books. Before he had finished them, he would feel attracted and drawn toward other themes. And, above all perhaps, his innovations in style and in the re-creation of the minor literary genres, the article and the essay, absorbed his attention and his capacity for many years, and he never achieved—because his literary trajectory had long breaks in it and ended prematurely—the maturation of a new genre in philosophical books, such as was postulated by his earlier discoveries; such as was sketched out, though not realized, in his literary work as a whole.

54. THE INVOLUTION OF THE BOOK TOWARD DIALOGUE

Ortega himself declared his aim as a writer at one solemn moment in his life, precisely at the time when he took up the question of the translation of his work into foreign languages: "The involution of the book toward dialogue: this has been my aim."[18] What does this mean?

Ortega picks up Goethe's idea that the written word is a substitute for the spoken word. "Ideas," "thoughts," are abstractions; true reality is the idea or thought of a particular man, especially if authentic realities are being referred to; then those thoughts or ideas are inseparable from the man who thinks them, and cannot be understood if we do not know *who* has said them. Analogously, says Ortega, an idea is a bit stupid if we do not take into account *who* is the one being spoken to. *Lógos* is *dialógos*, *lógos* from the point of view of the other, of one's fellow: *argumentum hominis ad hominem.* "This has been, since my early youth," says Ortega, "the simple and obvious standard which has governed my writing. All utterance says something—this commonplace is recognized by everyone—but, in addition, every utterance says that something to somebody—the professors, the German *Gelehrte*, know this as well as I do, but, cruel and disdainful, they are apt to forget it."[19] "I am present," he continues, "in each one of my paragraphs, with the timbre of my voice, my gestures, and . . . if one puts his finger on any of my pages, he will feel the beating of my heart." But this is not the decisive point; it is not a question of a "gift," Ortega says, and still less that he, like Chateaubriand, obliges the reader to encounter him; on the contrary: "Everything arises from the fact that I *place* the reader in my writings, insofar as is possible, that I take him into account, that I make him feel just how he is present to me, how he interprets me in his concrete and anguished and disoriented humanity." *This is the involution of the book toward dialogue*; this is what Ortega was trying to do in all his literary genres, what probably kept him from finishing any book; that is, kept him from doing it authentically and energetically throughout the entire architecture of a book, faithful at once to this attempt and to all its objective demands.

Ortega tells of something his friend Nicolai Hartmann, his young fellow student in Marburg, once said to him, interrupting for a moment the "moving, almost human" sound of his cello: "You, my dear Ortega, have intellectual altruism."[20] Ortega almost never wrote merely to be writing something. This conviction must have been a good guide for his readers, and has probably avoided innumerable false scents on the part of those who write about him. In a text of the Marburg period,

18 *Prólogo para alemanes*, 19.   19 *Ibid.*   20 *Ibid.*, 20.

toward the end of it—that is, around 1911—this expression, *intellectual altruism*, appears with a breadth of meaning which has not, so far as I know, received any attention. Ortega speaks of "a defect I am likely to find in Sr. Cejador; a defect which, were I not so hostile to those presumed psychologies of peoples, I would dare to recognize as a characteristic of our race, at least of the most traditionally Spanish thinkers, both of today and yesterday . . . . They lack intellectual altruism. A man possesses intellectual altruism when he lovingly causes his intelligence to progress toward the heart of things in such a way that in passing he dissolves himself in them, when he attempts to transubstantiate himself in his fellow man, even though momentarily, in order to assimilate that man's opinion in all its original complexity . . . . All things, and among them those animate things we call our fellows, are a series of invitations for us to emigrate out of ourselves and live outside ourselves, even though temporarily. . . . Lacking this virtue, the exercise of comprehension is difficult, for in the end intellectual altruism is nothing more than the habit of finding out about things."[21]

This explains a paradoxical fact: that Ortega's books which are most fully "books," those which are closest to being effectively and completely books, are . . . courses. Thus, *Man and Crisis* and "What Is Philosophy?"—especially the latter—were courses given in 1933 and 1929; and also "An Interpretation of Universal History" and *Man and People* were his two courses in the Institute of Humanities, from 1948 to 1950. Why is this so?

Ortega's courses were composed of lectures or lessons, which in their turn were *dramatic unities*. In each of them, whether they were written previously and then read, or spoken extemporaneously, or a mixture of the two, Ortega carefully *anticipated* his listeners. The speaker's communication with his public was such that he rarely caused a more *personal* impression than when he was speaking to an audience—the forty or fifty students in a university lecture room or the thirteen hundred listeners in the Institute of Humanities. The presence of the reader is always relatively abstract; that of the listener is much more real and concrete, even when it is only anticipated, for his image is, of course, much more precise. In large measure Ortega foresaw the reality of the lecture, and "rehearsed" it—in imagination, of course—like an actor; I mean that he imagined the reaction of each listener and

---

[21] "Observaciones" (1911). I, 165.

the effect of his words, voice, and gestures upon that listener. In the texts he wrote to be read in public, the system of punctuation Ortega used—and which can be observed in his published courses—was not strictly "orthographic," but rather declamatory, and resembled a dramatic script. For example, the use of the dash—a long dash—indicating pauses and transitions, the dramatic rather than logical—unless it is *also* logical—structure of the text.

This refers, of course, to each one of the lectures; but the nature of the entire course, which is also "plotlike" and dramatic, gave adequate tension to the sequence of lectures and assured the continuity in which Ortega as a writer was sometimes lacking. For in his lectures he sought not only a logical development, but also a *biographical* unity with his hearers, whom he had to carry along with him and by whom he had to be led in his turn. The course showed the nature of the book as an *undertaking*, and a "coexistential" undertaking, if the adjective serves. For we are likely to forget that, although thought is engendered in solitude, the book (as a communicative function) originates in the sphere of coexistence; and the mutual isolation of writer and reader weakens the awareness of that condition which intrinsically belongs to the act of writing, and which in the lecture or the lecture room springs up anew and conquers the audience.[22]

By 1932, Ortega was well aware that it was necessary to write *books*. Largely, because the interlocutor in that dialogue of which writing

---

[22] The value of Ortega's oratory did not escape Unamuno. When speaking of one of Ortega's articles on the problems of theatrical performance, he says, "And this has the same value as a lecture which is well read and pronounced by its author, compared to the same thing which one reads silently at home. And Ortega y Gasset himself knows the difference very well, for he is an extremely fine lecturer, a marvelous reader or reciter of his essays. Does he believe that even for a man who is capable of perceiving the superior qualities of one of Ortega's essays, that it is the same thing for him to read it by himself, in his house and silently, or to hear him, the author, read it? Of course not." ("Teatro y cine" [1921], in *De esto y aquello*, IV, 387.)

I have described elsewhere the impression his oratory produced on me the first time I heard one of his classes, in 1932: "When I came into the lecture hall I saw his face for the first time: grave and yet friendly, furrowed with deep wrinkles, with something of the peasant and the Roman emperor combined. His eyes were light in color, penetrating but not hard; they pierced, not like steel, but like light. From time to time his face lighted up in a gay, warm smile, with a flash of Spanish wit. He began to speak. Maybe it was his voice which first told who Ortega was; all of him was in it. Grave, sometimes hoarse; low dramatic notes at the end of his sentences; full of expressive shadings. The words seemed to roll out between his teeth, to come out of his lips, aimed precisely at each one of us. Words, in his mouth, were more truly words than in the

consists had changed: now it consisted not only of Spaniards, or of readers of the Spanish language in general, but of foreigners, especially Germans, Englishmen, North Americans; in principle, and after that date, of readers in every country. "Without my intending it, and even against my will," wrote Ortega, "groups of readers have been formed outside my country to whom I must pay attention. In order to influence them, I need weapons of larger caliber and scope than newspaper articles, although these are an essential instrument in every country today. The most likely thing, therefore, is that my future work will consist primarily in the forging of books . . . a type of book that goes beyond newspaper articles, which has learned from them, and not the pre-newspaper book, which belongs to a certain European past, the so-called Contemporary Age so anachronistic today, but which did not exist in our Middle Ages or in the baroque period, the most glorious in Europe."[23] Well, it was precisely at this date that Ortega's *normal* activity as a writer was interrupted; that is, he stopped publishing regularly and frequently. It will be said that external causes influenced this: political upheavals, greater participation in public life, civil war and emigration, the consequent difficulties and hindrances of publishing in Spain. All this is obvious and very true, but I believe that it is not a sufficient explanation. I believe that Ortega felt the necessity of writing books, but not just any books—rather, books which would be "at the height of the times"—and that he never had sufficient leisure to conceive them and bring them into being adequately for one very decisive reason, among others: the "involution of the book toward dialogue" presented an unexpected and very serious difficulty: the figure of the other interlocutor, who had suddenly become problematical. To whom was he to speak? Who was, between 1932 and 1955, that person to whom Ortega had to address himself, the one who had to collaborate with him in his written utterance; in short, who was the *Western reader?*

mouth of anyone else. Not in vain was Ortega one of the last two rhetoricians of our time—the other was Churchill. Ortega's hands, on the table, also said their share with sober, elegant Mediterranean gestures: gravity and grace combined in one motion." ("Ortega: historia de una amistad" (1955), in *La Escuela de Madrid* [1959], 218.) (*Obras*, V.)

See also Azorín's article "Ortega o el orador," in *Cuadernos de Adán*, II (Madrid, 1945.)

[23] "Prólogo a una edición de sus obras" (1932). VI, 355–56.

IV.

RHETORIC

❧

Rhetoric has had "a bad press" in the twentieth century. Occasionally a word turns into a lightning rod which draws down on itself all attempts at *disqualification*. This happened to the word "metaphysics" in the nineteenth century: it was enough to say that something was metaphysical for it to be automatically disqualified, discarded, rendered unworthy of attention (the last was the most important thing). It must be recalled that between 1920 and 1935, approximately, the proscribed word among Spanish writers was . . . "literature," which at the time was contrasted to "poetry" and aroused nothing but scorn. At about the same date—perhaps a few years earlier—this role had been filled by the word "rhetoric," with a somewhat wider scope: I mean that all unauthentic poetry was called "literature," and "rhetoric" was used to disqualify any piece of writing, either in verse or prose, which did not satisfy the demands of the moment.

There is a passage in which Ortega uses "rhetoric" approximately in this sense. It is a text of 1915, his "Ideas on Pío Baroja"; the great positive virtue of this writer, Ortega says, is the absence of rhetoric. And he adds: "The man who manages to write without rhetoric is a great writer: *tertium non datur*. For rhetoric cannot mean pomposity or reconditeness: there can be pompous and recondite styles without rhetoric. I would say: any style or bit of style which is inexpressive is rhetoric. . . . And rhetoric is that sin of not being faithful to oneself, of hypocrisy in art. The purist, for example, is a born rhetorician."[1]

But in other places Ortega considered rhetoric from other points of view; and not only did he later effect a "reconciliation" with rhetoric, but in an article written five years previously, and which is a dialogue

---

[1] *El Espectador*, I. II, 97–98.

with "Rubín de Cendoya," we find very different views. Here Ortega is speaking, as in the case of Baroja, of *sincerity*; he says of it that "it is, after all, the least costly of virtues; to say what one feels is frequently nothing but proof of a lack of imagination." "One must, of course," he adds, "tell the truth; but truth is not felt, it is invented.[2] To express the truth which we have succeeded in inventing at the cost of enormous effort is certainly a high and forceful virtue peculiar to our species! Divine Veracity, active virtue, you move us not so much to tell the truth as to search for it before we speak it!"[3] And a little later: "Parliaments are censured, most of all, because they dilute the nation's energies in rhetoric." "Don't go on, don't go on. But what do those people believe? Do they believe that humanity is imbecilic? That it has lived for twenty-five centuries concerning itself with rhetoric, so that now rhetoric turns out to be a cheap trick? ... Rhetoric and good manners are the last two conventions, the last two cultural yokes human beings would like to throw off, so that in two strides they can go back to the womb of the jungle and start hopping around before the rising sun, the way the baboons do in the long grass."[4]

Is there a contradiction in these two positions of Ortega's? Let us try to understand his thought *circumstantially*; to do this we should also have in mind other texts of the same period, which show the point of view from which he said what he said. In the essay on Renan, written in 1909, we can find a number of clues. At that time Ortega was concerned with *chabacanería*, or Philistinism, as a national problem: "Philistinism is the Spanish reality at the moment. And we can state that it consists exclusively in our having drawn away from everything that means transcending the momentary, from everything that exceeds the bounds of the individual or of an instinctive collectivity.... An extreme symptom of Philistinism can be found in the *zeal* for sincerity we all

---

[2] An idea which later was to sound forth in Antonio Machado's lines:

> "Se miente más de la cuenta
> por falta de fantasía:
> también la verdad se inventa."
> ["We lie more than we should
> for lack of imagination:
> truth is invented too."]
> (Proverbios y cantares, XLVI.)

[3] "Planeta sitibundo" (1910). I, 147–48.

[4] *Ibid.*, 149.

feel nowadays; it is a fad which has been imposed on us, and to whose success that supreme hermit, Don Miguel de Unamuno, has contributed not a little, for among the echoing stones of Salamanca he is initiating a torrid youth into fanaticism. Sincerity, it seems, consists in everyone's duty to say what he thinks, in fleeing from all conventionalism, whether it is called logic, aesthetics, or good breeding. It is obvious that sincerity is the demand of those who feel weak and cannot breathe, in a severe atmosphere, between firm and adamantine limits, of people who would like a more permissive and softer world."[5] That is, Ortega at this time was combating *what was called sincerity in the Spain of 1910*, and what seems to him to be a desire for Philistinism and lack of rigor, abandonment to the spontaneous, a renunciation of "being in good trim." Is it that the virtue of being sincere did not interest Ortega at the time? Of course it interested him, but since at that time something else went by the name of sincerity, he intended to recover *veracity*, love for truth itself, a higher quality than speaking it; Galileo was to be his example: "Galileo was forced to recant before a tribunal inspired, not by the Church, as is usually said, but by intrigues of private groups, especially stirred up against him; and yet, he loved the truth with so ardent and fruitful a love that the wise souls who are being born even today are no more than offshoots of his virile contemplations. But he had discovered a natural law; what did it matter whether he proclaimed it? *Eppur si muove*: the law is there, whether man will or no. All those who came after him will find it."[6]

Is he advocating the opposite when he praises Baroja for his sincerity and lack of rhetoric? I think not; if we read him carefully, we note that two *similar* expressions are no more than similar, and perhaps go in opposite directions. Sincerity, as the word is used, and which Ortega rejects, is "everyone's duty to say what he thinks"; what he praises in Baroja and which seems to him "the sublime attitude" is something else: "to feel what we feel and not what we are ordered to feel."[7] Not *to say*, but *to feel*; one can say what one feels, and, notwithstanding, be that which one feels to be false, unauthentic, a "pose," cliché, or slogan; in short, what we are ordered to feel. What he praises in Baroja is *authenticity*, fidelity to what he calls the *unsubornable base*. When he attacks

[5] "Renan" (1909). I, 456–57.
[6] *Ibid.*, 445.
[7] II, 99.

rhetoric, he refers to the opposite tendency, not "sincerity" in that sense, but authenticity, fidelity to one's own truth.

A more complex and consequently a more accurate treatment of the problem is found about the year 1924, in his two essays "Sobre la sinceridad triunfante" ["On Sincerity Triumphant"] and "Fraseología y sinceridad" ["Phraseology and Sincerity"]. In both, Ortega tries to pin down the nature of the period in comparison with others, and particularly in comparison with "modern times"—1500–1900—defined as the "Age of the phrase, or phraseology"; on the other hand, he contrasts the desire for sincerity in "classicism," which is composed of commonplaces, of impersonal and conventional modes. In our time, he says, "the predominance of a new ethical climate began, harsh and alien, which quickly caused the death of all the 'phrases.'" "The phrase, in this bad sense of the word, is every intellectual formula which exceeds the bounds of the reality described in it."[8] The phrase rounds off reality, as a fortune is rounded off, often fraudulently. European life during these centuries has been ruled by *phrases*. These have been very useful, and have permitted the organization of Europe and many other things. Nor is it the fact that they are errors, that they are false: rather, they are *falsifications*; medieval thought, says Ortega, erred more than modern thought, but it falsified less. The phrase replaces reality with unequivocal unrealities, and is the great simplifier. "Phraseology is nothing but utopianism as an intellectual method."[9] Rationalism and phraseology are *inert intellect* which is expressed and then not adjusted to the real. This is why classicism is not possible without a dose of insincerity, and we must imagine, conversely, *a period of radical sincerity*. These are two modes of being which Ortega presents without praise or vituperation, conscious of the problems posed by both. Sincerity will bring with it "a prelude of cynicism triumphant," and "it is probable that, under its protection, there will be transitory invasions of fabulously archaic souls, of human types who have been socially buried for a long time, kept in the cellars of the collective body."[10]

During some periods the "good action" is good because it repeats a *model*; that is, it is valued because *it is not individual*; at other periods, sincerity is valued, the effort *not to conform to the model*. "Can a classicism based on sincerity be imagined?" Ortega asks himself. "Is it not

[8] "Fraseología y sinceridad." *El Espectador*, V. II, 473.
[9] *Ibid.*, 475.
[10] *Ibid.*, 481.

a contradiction in terms?"[11] Ortega is well aware of the seriousness of the problem, but also realizes its inevitable and undeferrable nature. It is not possible to go backward, to revive faith in "phrases." Although the "barbarian" is still more archaic, the maker of phrases is desperately so. "The area of sincerity, once conquered, must be preserved, and upon it must be built a new home for men, a new culture with a finer curve, with more dimensions, one which is better adjusted to the shape of the real. For this purpose, the disciplined solidarity of those who are capable of creating it is important. For the task is a dangerous one: it is a war on two hostile fronts: the 'phrase' and barbarism."[12]

This amounts to saying that it is necessary to create a new rhetoric, an *authentic rhetoric*, one which will not consist in fraudulently rounding off reality, but in giving it power, becoming involved with it, making it give off the reflections of which it is capable. Ten years later, Ortega saw clearly that this was practicable. In 1934, speaking of his teacher Cohen, he says: "He was a formidable writer, as he was a formidable speaker. By the time I heard him, his eloquence had become reduced to pure emotionalism. But, be it understood, of the most exquisite kind. It was pure rhetoric, but not *bad* rhetoric, the kind that is lymphatic, flabby, and lacking in intimate truth. Quite the contrary."[13] Here we see how it is not rhetoric itself, but bad rhetoric, which consists in un-authenticity, which lacks "intimate truth." This is a degenerate rhetoric, one that no longer performs its function. What is this function? I prefer not to load my own idea of rhetoric onto Ortega's, though I believe that it corresponds fairly exactly to certain tenets of his. We need only recall what he himself says in one of his essays, "Temas de viaje" ["On Travel"], precisely in 1922, where he does not use the word rhetoric, but where he profoundly defines its role in human life:

"We forget that ideas have two faces and two different values or efficacies. On one of its faces the idea aspires to be the *mirror of reality*; when this aspiration is confirmed, we say that it is *true*. Truth consists in the objective value or efficacy of the idea. But on its other face, *the idea takes over the subject*, the man who is thinking it; when it coincides with his intimate temper, with his character and desires, although it may not be true, although it may lack objective value, it possesses a subjective

---

[11] "Sobre la sinceridad triunfante" (1924). IV, 516.
[12] II, 482.
[13] *Prólogo para alemanes*, 45.

efficacy, giving intellectual satisfaction to the spirit. *I would counterpoise to the truth, or objective value of the idea, its vitality or subjective value.*

"For the majority of persons this extremely delicate and almost superfluous function of ideas which consists in their truth is, strictly speaking, unknown. *Ideas exercise, within their vital economy, a function which is solely organic, no less marvelous than the other. They are vital organs which the organism—the individual, people, or period—knows how to mold in order to confront existence . . . .*"[14]

This is why the thinker, the philosopher, the intellectual, if he writes, has to be a *writer*. If he is not, his ideas, though they may have objective value, will lack subjective value; they may perhaps be true, but they will lack vitality; and then they will not be justified in their attempt at *communication*, for the writing will not fulfill its proper function. Thought, the personal investigation of truth, is one thing; the task of writing it is another. Certain forms of doctrine have failed, either absolutely or after a certain period in history, owing to lack of expressive quality, because they have not fulfilled that function of vital economy which permits them to "confront existence." Whatever their "truth" may be in the technical sense of the word, they lack vitality, and insofar as they are written they are unjustified. And in the last instance we should have to ask if it is certain that they in fact possess the truth, whether they are capable of uncovering and unveiling the real (*alétheia*), whether they contain that *authenticity* which permits *the truth of life*. It might happen that, because of literary deficiencies, a system of ideas which was technically correct might be vitally and really false.

56. EROSIONS

"Good writing consists in constantly making small erosions in grammar, in established usage, in the reigning standards of the language. It is an act of permanent rebellion against the social environment, a subversion. To write well implies a certain fundamental recklessness."[15] These words of Ortega's explain his literary procedures very well. What I have just shown proves the necessity for them. This system of erosions constitutes the peculiarity of a style; they are also the methods which

[14] II, 362–63. Italics mine.
[15] "Miseria y esplendor de la traducción" (1937). V, 430.

assure that vital efficacy of the written word. The tendency of language —and, even more strongly, of the written word—is automatization, mechanization, and consequently inertia. A language is what *is* said, what *is* spoken; it is something necessarily transpersonal, and which runs the constant risk of becoming impersonal. When this occurs, expressions become inert and inoperative. It becomes less and less likely that they will contain what Husserl calls *significant realization*, and they become reduced to mere *mention*. We might say that, just as water always flows downhill, so language always tends toward the cliché. In speech, the individual expressive elements—voice, glance, gestures, appearance—in part counterbalance this tendency and renew the personal value of what is spoken; in writing, the collective powers very definitely predominate, and only the *style* as such can restore their original quality of *spokenness* —spoken *by someone*, naturally.

In the first place, and beginning with the most elementary aspect, there is the choice of words. For the moment we are not to think of the *invention* of words, of the "neologism." This is an exceptional procedure, for it does violence to the very nature of language—the fact of its not being invented, but of *being there*—and the tendency toward neologism is an indication of an author's literary and linguistic insecurity. I have written elsewhere,[16] "As for neologisms, even the most sparing use of them seems excessive. Not only because of linguistic scruples, which are highly respectable, but still more because of a strictly intellectual scruple—that is, a very concrete theoretical fear: the neologism falsely leads to the deceptive illusion that it is the equivalent of a concept; when a phenomenon which one is trying to investigate is given an artificial name, and one which does not belong to the language, the mind tends to accept it calmly, and to suppose that that phenomenon, once baptized, is already known and possessed. The reality, however, is usually quite different: the artificial and 'technical' name, invented for the express purpose of designating a problematical thing, permits its 'manipulation,' permits operating with it mechanically and perhaps automatically, making it function as a known and thoroughly understood quantity in new contexts and situations, appealing to it as a solution and explicative principle, when perhaps it cries aloud for explanation and clarification. The neologism, when it becomes too much of a temptation, not only does violence to the very condition of language, but transforms theory

---

[16] "Solencia e insolencia" (1955), in *El oficio del pensamiento* (1958), 139.

into a sort of 'verbal magic.' " This means, on the other hand, that the neologism goes in the opposite direction from the metaphor; and in fact, the writer who has a propensity for the neologism usually falls into the habit of using it because he is incapable of using the metaphor.

What I call the *choice* of words is the effective selection of those existing in the language. Language is, of course, a usage, and properly speaking those words which are no longer used, but are "in disuse," do not belong to it; these words are, at most, the past of the language. An archaism, for example, the opposite of a neologism, has in common with the neologism the fact that it avoids *living* language. But there are many grades of usage. The writer may correct the *incipient* lack of usage by placing in circulation, by "gingering up," a word which is still alive. He may prefer the less hackneyed word to the one which has become a cliché and is covered with a crust of triviality; sometimes, in order to do this, he can choose a legitimate but less frequent form. A few examples from Ortega will clarify what I mean. The image of a "source" is one of the most overworked in our time, a cliché; it first became mannered in poetry and in certain forms of "artistic" prose, and on the other hand it has come into technical use by scholars, for example as when the "sources" of an author or a doctrine are spoken of; it has lost, therefore, a large part of its radiating force. Well, in this sense Ortega frequently uses the word "hontanar," which is alive in the language though little used; it has extraordinary phonetic beauty, able to make any context vibrate. The same occurs with the adjectives "peraltado" ["elevated"] and "señero" ["isolated"], which have later become trivialized, and, what is worse, have been used indiscriminately.

Occasionally, Ortega performs a mild linguistic change. For example, he prefers the form "rigoroso" to the usual "riguroso." Why? Out of a simple desire for correctness? Perhaps; but in any case the reader, attracted by the less outworn variant, notices the word, and especially the presence of its original element: *rigor*. The word "riguroso" is often used in the form of a made phrase "luto riguroso" ["strict mourning"], "riguroso incógnito" ["strict incognito"]—without any express reference to rigor; as this is what interests Ortega, his linguistic choice is intellectually effective. The same could be said of his use of the singular in words which are usually employed in the plural: "la tiniebla," "el Alpe," "la circunstancia" [for "tinieblas," shadows, "Alpes," Alps, and "circunstancias," circumstances]. Sometimes he makes certain changes in words or syntax, as when he says "adherir a," giving it a shade of meaning very different from the normal, reflexive use ("adherirse a").

Finally, Ortega is notoriously inclined toward the use of certain linguistic forms which are in themselves erosions of grammar or the general rules of language: *idiomatic expressions*. A good proof of the interest he took in this subject is the colloquium on such expressions which he organized and directed at the Institute of Humanities in 1948–49. Their frequent occurrence in his writings is well known. By this tendency he did no more than to follow the Spaniard's natural propensity, in which the cultured language is constantly made more vivid by colloquial expressions; and, conversely, the refined forms are neither foreign to popular speech nor—in large measure—incomprehensible for any speakers. Contrary to what happens in other languages—such as French up to about thirty years ago—where the two types of speech are mutually exclusive, and at most produce a sudden and exaggerated invasion of colloquialism and even vulgarism in the literary language, Spanish maintains a constant osmosis between them. Ortega, in spite of the theoretical nature of his writings and his awareness that idiomatic expressions represent considerable difficulties for translation, was never willing to sacrifice the fullness of intensity and effective expression which they assure. Think of the prologue to *Las Aventuras del Capitán Alonso de Contreras* ["The Adventures of Captain Alonso de Contreras"], written as late as 1943, and which perhaps represents Ortega's peak as a writer.

57. WRITING AND THE WRITER

Ortega's social image was, quite as much as that of a "philosopher" or "professor," that of a writer. It was certainly the earliest image, and was always, perhaps, the most relevant. For Ortega was a *writer*, not simply *an intellectual who writes*. These are two very different things. We must keep in mind the Spanish situation early in this century, which was very far from being that of today. At that time there were many *writers* in Spain—not *great* writers, of whom there are always few, or even *good* writers, who are never numerous; today the "men who write" are legion, and they frequently write well, but writers are very few. And, as a consequence of this, they cause a certain unease in a society accustomed to their absence. A vague feeling of discomfort tinged with irritation is felt in the presence of the writer, in the measure that he is one—and, especially, if he is also an intellectual *sensu stricto*; that is, a man who lives by thinking. It would be interesting to set down in detail in what this phenomenon consists, and what its causes are; but this would carry us too far afield.

"The man who writes" is engaging in an activity which does not—not even partially—constitute his personality; I mean that he is what he is apart from his writing; first he *is*—whatever he is—and then he writes. The result is that strictly speaking he does not write *out of himself*, but, at the very most, out of what he has done, what he knows, etc. The writer, on the other hand, even though he may not be *solely* a writer, does not have a personality which is separable from this condition; it could be said that he only *is*—fully—when he is writing. He engages in this operation out of his personal center: the writer is implicated in what he writes (I mean in his writing), and not only in "what he has written" (opinions, a thesis, etc.). This presence of his on the page gives that page a personal and intimate character which confers attractiveness and intensity upon him, but which at the same time is felt by some societies to be somewhat "immodest" and disturbing. Let me make it clear that I am not thinking—on the contrary—of the author who talks about himself, who makes confidences or shows off his innermost feelings; the most reserved and timid of them—Azorín, for example—insofar as he is a *writer*, has this characteristic. No matter how circumspect his pages may be, he is there 100 per cent, *forming himself in those pages*, and this makes him different from the man who has his previous and different personality, and one fine day—even though it be every day—sits down with pen and paper to write certain things. To be a writer, then, presupposes a certain mode of *installation* in the world— and not only in the world of letters—which often becomes problematical, not only in reference to the social atmosphere, but, what is more serious, with regard to what affects this same mode of installation. The position of the writer in Spain today is difficult, much more so because of a faulty system of pressures—excessive and stupid pressure where it should not be applied, lack of pressure where it is needed—than because of the lack of clear ideas about what that mode of installation is, which leads to archaism, imitation, or caricature as soon as a very rigorous demand for authenticity is lost.

As we all know, about the year 1900 there were in Spain a few eminent writers who were, moreover, extremely eminent: those of 1898.
There have been few times when the *condition* of the writer, not merely
his qualities, has been so fully realized. But in addition to those half-
dozen writers of genius, there were some dozens who were not, who
were often no more than mediocre, and yet who, when we chance to read
them nowadays, produce in us an unmistakable impression of belonging,
in the lower ranks, to the same species: though less gifted, less rich in
dedication, their task was the same: they were "birds of a feather," even
though their plumage is discolored and abused. The economic insecurity
of writers—both good and bad—was extensive; but a certain insecurity
is very probably the condition of this species of "bird," at least of their
constitution and origin—we might even say of their "breeding." And
so, of course, is independence; this does not mean that on occasion
the writer does not "sell himself"; but, first of all, he sells himself *after
being in existence*, after he has (independently) become a writer; and
second, he sells *himself*—that is, he performs a further independent act,
even though it is a shameful one, and the merchandise he delivers is
precisely that independence which he had possessed up to that moment;
in other words, this species of bird is not bred in captivity, and at most
he can make the decision of going into the cage on his own two feet.
"The primary prescription for the writer's trade," wrote Ortega in 1927,
"is not to give service to any party, and to flee the disgraceful support
of all of them. It is a prescription and not the opposite, an attitude which
one may either hold or evade. (What is disgraceful, of course, is not the
party, but its support of the writer. The writer must live without support, in midair, in a deluded attempt to resemble the Holy Spirit and
the archangel, both of which are feathered species that live in the air.)"[17]

It would be interesting to follow the vicissitudes of the writer in
contemporary Spanish society. Suffice it to say that ever since the Generation of 1898 the species is becoming less frequent, and the individuals
who become writers in the fullest sense more exceptional, although
there are more and more men who write well—and in some cases very
well. But meantime there are fewer and fewer first-rank writers who are
only writers. Unamuno was not simply a writer either, nor was Ortega;
but both, in the measure that they were writers, were writers wholly and
uncompromisingly; I mean, without diluting that condition with the

[17] "El poder social" (1927). III, 488.

condition of being professors, for example. Insofar as they were writers, they were *at the mercy of the elements*, and they moved in the world of letters naked and unprotected; for example, they were judged *by what they did*—by what they actually wrote—and not by their supposed possibilities, by what they *might be able to do*. This is, in fact, one of the essential differences between the writer and the "man who writes"[18]: the former is always an *actual* reality; the second, who is "already" and previously to writing anything, what he is, may live off *potentialities*, and at times may not *realize* them. Already, in Ortega's generation, this plenitude of the writer's condition had begun to be less frequent, and since his time the tendency has become accentuated. This results in the loss of the *professional* nature of the writer, even in an economic sense: the writer lives—at least substantially—from his pen, and on the free market, which means that he must maintain a certain volume and quality of production.

It is evident that the *writer's* condition, in a strict and professional form, can only be assumed, normally, as a fundamental *vocation*. In some societies it is possible that other, peripheral stimuli may attract a man toward it, and make possible the existence of the "false" writer who seems to be one because he is "gifted." In Spain this has never been likely. The reasons for not being a writer are so strong that only a lively vocation and a certain lack of common sense can overcome them. This vocation arises out of the deepest roots of the person, out of strata which are less exalted, but perhaps more basic, than those which determine the *intellectual* vocation. The writer is always helplessly a writer, moved by an impulse in which his psychophysical condition and his life program

[18] I am not forgetting that when Unamuno used these two expressions he gave them a meaning almost exactly opposite to the one I give them; for example, in the article "El oficio de escribir" (1924), in *De esto y aquello*, IV, 617ff., and in other articles on a similar theme at the same period. But the oppositeness is more apparent than real: when Unamuno says "the man who writes and not the writer," what he is emphasizing is the *man*, the existence of a personality behind the "office" which converts it into a true *officium*, a duty, an obligation. "Not in the sense of an occupation—*métier* in French—not in the sense of potboiling. The task of writing is an office, it is duty, it is the obligation toward the human community, in which we live and move and have our being. Even though it is right for the priest to live off the altar." And when he says, "not a writer, but a man who writes, that is, with style," it is easy to see what he means by this. As when he adds, referring to Bernal Díaz del Castillo, "that man who, after having been a soldier by trade, molded himself to the trade of writer when his hand could no longer wield the sword; that man was a man who wrote and not a writer. And what strength of style!"

PART TWO: *The Writer*

converge. If the expression "incarnate spirit" has a fully comprehensible meaning, the writer embodies it. And therefore literary style, true rhetoric, is the intrinsic convergence of the letter with the spirit; it is *the letter which is spirit*.

Ortega was very deeply aware of these roots of writing. "I have nothing to do with Freud," he wrote in 1934, "whose work, it seems to me for many reasons, ought to be known in Spain, but for which I have always felt a rather evanescent interest. Therefore, very far indeed from Freud is my suspicion that in general literary style as such (and therefore, insofar as it is something by itself, different from thought, insofar as it is an expressive function) has in man some relation to his virility. Expressed in an exaggerated and somewhat grotesque form: the function of writing—I insist—not that of thinking, is a secondary sexual characteristic, and is in large part controlled by the evolution of sexuality in the individual. Every writer *pur sang* knows that the operation of writing, the actual *writing*, invests his body with sensations which are close to being voluptuous. Who knows whether, in some degree and measure, the writer *writes* as the peacock spreads his tail, and the stag bellows in autumn!"[19]

I would say that writing, rather than being a *sexual* dimension, is *sexed*, in the sense that this condition—differentiated from "the sexual," which is a private and restricted activity within the total economy of our life—is the radical mode of *installation* of each individual, consisting in the separation of human life into two sexes, each one of which implicates or complicates the other, in the form of a polar distinction.[20] And if we recall what I said before about style as installation, we can better understand that relationship, pointed out by Ortega, between the operation of writing and the deepest roots of the person.

[19] *Prólogo para alemanes*, 44–45.
[20] See J. Marías, *La estructura social*, VII, 52.

V.

THE ORIGINAL MOTIFS

58. THE AGE OF TWENTY-SIX AND
INDIVIDUAL SPONTANEITY

Among Ortega's deeply rooted ideas about the ages of human life is the idea that the age of twenty-six is, approximately, the moment when the intellectual has the first intuition of what is going to be his theme or capital idea. Even in the "Prólogo para alemanes" ["Prologue for Germans"], written in his full maturity, he stresses this, precisely in order to explain the genesis of his personal thought. It is surprising how much he insists upon it, a number of times even in such a short piece of writing. "The group of young men who were learning the uses of philosophical warfare in the citadel of neo-Kantianism, between 1907 and 1911, were no longer neo-Kantians by the time they reached the age of twenty-six —a date which is apt to be decisive in the vital career of a thinker."[1] And a little later he adds, "Nicolai Hartmann must be a couple of years older than I, and Heinz Heimsoeth about my age. Therefore, in 1911 we were all about twenty-six, a decisive date in the intellectual evolution of a person, as I have said before without hinting at the reasons. It is the moment when a man—for the moment I am referring to the philosopher —begins to be not merely receptive with regard to the great problems, but begins to exercise his spontaneity. Look in the biography of thinkers and you will find with surprising frequency that the date of their twenty-sixth year is the one in which the intellectual *motifs* which were later to constitute their original work made their germinal appearance. The fact that at that age the concrete ideas which we are later to sustain and develop come to us is not the essential, or even the most important thing. Concrete ideas are not, strictly speaking, anything but concretions of certain generic positions which become, as it were, multiparous wombs

[1] *Prólogo para alemanes*, 43.

of those and other ideas. Therefore it is not a question of certain ideas *occurring* to us at that age, but rather that we suddenly discover in ourselves, already installed and without our knowing where it has come from, a certain decision or will that the truth should possess a certain meaning and consist in certain things. That decision, which we do not feel responsible for having taken, but find within us, making up a sort of mental ground upon which we must live, is the vital level which establishes every generation in the evolutionary process of human history. Therefore it is not something which *occurs* to us, but precisely something which we are."[2] And still further on, Ortega returns to the theme: "But this common awakening—about the year 1911—was also the sign of separation. The age of twenty-six—the figure must be taken with a certain amount of looseness—is the moment of most essential departure for the individual. Up to that time he lives in the group and of the group. Adolescence is cohesive. During it, man neither can be alone nor knows how to be. He is governed by what I have called 'the instinct of coetaneity,' and lives submerged within the herd of the young, in his 'age class.' But at that point in the course of his life, the individual sets out toward his exclusive destiny, which is, at its root, solitary. Each one is going to fulfill after his own fashion the historical mission of his generation. For each generation is, after all, no more than this: a certain mission, certain precise things *which must be done*."[3]

I have quoted these passages at length because they prove, in the first place, the importance which Ortega attached to these ideas, and further because they contain details of some interest. On the one hand, Ortega insists on the date 1911; on the other, the—approximate—age of twenty-six. Well, he reached the age of twenty-six in 1909; the insistence on both of these figures, which are not strictly in accordance, shows that both had value for him: no doubt he was referring to 1911 as the decisive date for the Marburg *group*, and on the other hand had unmistakable memories of his personal situation localized around the year 1909. Let us pass over for the moment what pertains to his German friends and fellow students—we shall have to return to this later—and try to fix his personal situation.

The year 1908 is the first in which Ortega had a sustained literary activity; apart from unsigned published pieces which have never been

[2] *Ibid.*, 46–47.
[3] *Ibid.*, 58–59.

collected, in this year alone he published more than in all the previous years since 1902. Among the writings of that year are two interesting ones, the long article entitled "Assembly for the Progress of the Sciences," published in *El Imparcial*, and his first "technical" philosophical work, his memoir "Descartes y el método transcendental" ["Descartes and the Transcendental Method"], presented in the Zaragoza Congress of the Spanish Association for the Progress of the Sciences, on October 26, 1908.[4] Earlier in this book, I have spoken at length of the first article; the second is an obviously youthful piece of work, but it is substantial and well documented, with frequent quotations in Greek, Latin, German, and French. Well, this study is *Kantian*; if pressed, I will even say that it was Ortega's only Kantian piece of writing. I mean by this that it is derivative, that it responds to the ideas reigning in Marburg, within the ambit of which the twenty-five-year-old Ortega's thought moves.

After the following year, things changed. In 1909 his most important piece of work is the article "Renan." In 1910—a fruitful year—"Adam in Paradise." Both represent a new level. Both signify what we might call a *declaration of independence*. In the former as well as the latter article, Ortega draws away from the teachers of his youth: from French, the faraway teacher of his adolescent reading, and from his face-to-face teachers in Marburg; the fact that he does so respectfully with regard to Renan and that he does not *try* to draw away from Cohen, does not obviate the fact that after this date he *progresses toward himself* and diverges from them. The paragraph with which he concludes "Renan" is significant: "The reader should not forget that I am describing Renan's spirit based on the *recollection of reading him some time ago*: I cannot be documentally sure of the correctness of what I attribute to him, *and still less should it be thought that I share his convictions*. Pantheism, diluted as was natural for a nineteenth-century thinker, seems to me, however, to constitute the general tone of his spirit, or at least of Renan's way of approaching things."[5] Renan is a nineteenth-century thinker, read some years before and whose convictions are not shared. But also, if we look carefully, we observe that in this essay the distance with regard to Marburg is still more apparent; concretely, the

---

[4] Published in *Actas de la Asociación Española para el Progreso de las Ciencias*, (Madrid, 1910), VI, 5–13.

[5] I, 463. Italics mine.

reaction against *subjectivism*, which in this article and in "Adam in Paradise" is carried to such an extreme that the notes added in 1915 are placed there to temper it. "In general," says Ortega, going to the point after a short preamble, "I cannot conceive that men can be more interesting than ideas, persons more than things. An algebraic theorem or a great old boulder in the Guadarrama Mountains is apt to have more significative value than all the employees of a ministry."[6] And a little later, he makes this statement, no less: "The subjective, in short, is an error." With a note added in 1915: "This is a thought that seems very doubtful to me today."[7] "I dare say," he continues, "that the fundamental, insuperable, and decisive school for us must be the Imitation of Things." But he is forced to add in the next line: "And what are we to do with the subjective, with the *I*, with this mystical yapping voice, so restless, so demanding, that gnaws at our vitals and howls within us at every hour of the day, like a starveling, and does not leave us in peace or quietness of mind? To be sure, it also has its rights, even though they may be transitory and not very precise."[8] And after speaking of the "secret leprosy of subjectivity," and admonishing himself in a note of 1915, "I repeat that this is blasphemy," he concludes, "We also need the Imitation of Subjects."[9] Opposed to subjectivism, yet conscious of its error, of the injustice of "objectivism"; unable to be an idealist, but feeling remorse for moving in the direction of being a realist, Ortega vacillates between the Imitation of Things and the Imitation of Subjects, knowing how to do no more than to add them together. It is clear that, insofar as the fundamental question is concerned, he has come to his twenty-six years "at the mercy of the elements."

"Adam in Paradise" represents something different. It is still written, of course, from the assumptions of Marburg, and in large part using Marburg's terminology; but only a nearsighted view would see no more in it. What is important is to find those "multiparous wombs" of ideas, that "decision or will that the truth should possess a certain meaning and consist in certain things," that "mental ground" or "vital level" which was to condition all his later life and thought. That basic reality continues to be "disclosed" sporadically, generally from different angles; its expression is usually faulty, because it is usually interpreted from the thinker's assumptions at the time—from the repertory of received ideas

[6] I, 438.
[7] I, 440.
[8] I, 441–42.
[9] I, 442–43.

—and at the same time assimilating that expression into the motifs which have led to this discovery. In Ortega's case, the received assumptions are those of Marburg; the occasions of discovery, chiefly three: phenomenology—and the knowledge that it is not sufficient or ultimately acceptable —which is to lead to the idea of "executive reality" as opposed to Husserl's "consciousness"; the biological idea of *Umwelt*, coming especially from Uexküll, which serves to "precipitate" the Orteguian idea of circumstance; and meditation on art, a subject to which Ortega paid much attention during those years. Ortega's profound intuition does not "proceed" from any of these presumed "sources," but was "awakened" by these *stimuli* in a convergent manner.

59. "ADAM IN PARADISE": INTUITION OF HUMAN LIFE AND THE ORIGINAL METAPHOR

This essay, "Adam in Paradise," deals with a theme in art. Ortega's immediate intention is to clarify what happens in Zuloaga's paintings; to do this he must sketch out a theory of art, and this task carries him far beyond the confines of his theme. We shall leave the examination of these artistic ideas for a later section; what interests me at the moment is to see the fundamental intuition which flourishes here and there, in the process of "vivifying"—the highest mode of foundation—all of Ortega's doctrine.

A thing is not something solitary; each thing is related to the rest, it is what it is in function of others; the essence of each thing is resolved in pure relationships. Ever since the Renaissance, the category of substance has gradually been dissolving into the category of relationship, and thus there has been transition from the *res* to the *idea*, from realism to idealism. "Each thing is a crossroads: its life, its being is the sum of relationships, of mutual influences in which all the others are found. A stone at the edge of a path needs the rest of the universe in order to exist."[10] No great perspicacity is required to discover that this doctrine corresponds to neo-Kantian teachings, when Ortega says in a note of 1915: "This Leibnizian and Kantian concept of the being of things irritates me a little now." But it would be of more interest to think for a moment about what this means. And what occurs to me is the follow-

[10] I, 478.

ing: (1) When Ortega merely says that this concept "irritates me a little," this indicates that he has already moved some distance away from it, but that it does not seem to him simply to be an error or a "blasphemy" —rather something of which he can make use, although it is insufficient and inexact; (2) the fact that Ortega, departing from his usual practice, has placed notes to his own text of "Renan" and "Adam in Paradise" showing corrections and disagreement—this seems to indicate that these writings were important to him *theoretically* and that he wished to cleanse them of their youthful errors; and (3) if Ortega took the trouble to place these notes to some passages with which he does not agree a few years later, and which he even formally repudiates, and does not do this with other very significant ideas, one may draw the conclusion that he continued to adhere to them and that these ideas, the ones which he retained without criticism, are the important thing for him. What are these ideas?

"The proof that things are nothing but values is obvious," says Ortega at one point in this essay. "Take any thing whatsoever, apply to it different systems of valuation, and you will have an equal number of different things instead of a single one." The terminology he uses is inadequate: it is not a question of "values" or "valuation"; if these words are taken literally, we will not understand what Ortega is *seeing* and as yet does not know how to name. He himself shows that he is not thinking of values, immediately following this: he is about to exemplify what he has just stated, and it is not a question of valuation, but of something else: "Compare what the earth means for a peasant and for an astronomer: for the former it is enough to *tread* the planet's reddish skin and *scratch* it with his plow; his earth is a *path*, some *furrows* and a *field of grain*. The astronomer must *determine exactly the place* which the globe occupies at every instant within the *enormous supposition of sidereal space; the point of view of exactitude* obliges him to convert it into a *mathematical abstraction*, into a case of universal gravitation. The example could be extended indefinitely."[11] These are not valuations; they are *interpretations*, and not only *mental*, but *vital* ones: it is the peasant's mode of life which differs from that of the astronomer. Their points of view must be taken in all strictness; I mean that when this expression is used, one is apt to pay attention only to the "view," forgetting the "point"—that is, the *real situation*—in this case the vital situation of the

[11] I, 471. Italics mine.

peasant or the astronomer; they are not mere visual images, but effective real perspectives. This is why he adds, "Therefore this supposed immutable and unique reality with which we can compare the contents of artistic works does not exist: *there are as many realities as there are points of view. The point of view creates the panorama.* There is an *everyday reality* forged out of a system of lax, approximative, vague relationships, sufficient for the uses of day-to-day living. There is a *scientific reality* forged out of a system of exact relationships, imposed by the need for exactitude. Seeing and touching things are, after all, nothing but ways of thinking them." Ortega calls "supposition" what Husserl was to call *Einstellung.* But the decisive point is that one reality corresponds to each; that is, that reality is constituted according to the different vital perspectives, and consists, to that extent, in interpretations. It is what Ortega means by the expressions "insufficient," "value," and "valuation."

He gives new proof of this when he returns to his starting point: art. "Every art is born out of the differentiation of the fundamental need for expression which exists in man, which is man."[12] "Man bears within himself an heroic, a tragic problem"[13]: whatever he does, all his activities, are only functions of that problem, steps he takes in order to solve it. And it is of such a caliber that there is no way of giving it pitched battle: by following the maxim *divide et impera*, man divides it into segments and gradually solves it by parts and by stages." "We must ... indicate *in what the human problem consists*, the problem out of which, as out of a basic core, all man's acts derive."

The second of the chapters into which this essay is divided begins with these words: "With the vague idea of seeking a formula which defines the ideal of painting, I wrote the first article, entitled "Adam in Paradise." *I do not quite know why I called it that*; by the end of the article I had got lost in that dark forest of art, where only the blind, like Homer, have seen clearly. In my confusion I grasped at the memory of an old friendship: Doctor Vulpius, a German, a professor of philosophy .... I asked my friend to write *something which could justify the title of my first article.*"[14] And, in fact, Adam and Paradise appear very late in the article; indeed, the point of departure is the title, as we shall

---

[12] I, 474.

[13] I, 475. Italics mine.

[14] I, 472–73. Italics mine.

very soon see: an *original metaphor*; what Ortega calls "something which could justify the title" is, neither more nor less, the explanation of that metaphor, which in its turn clarifies the theory of the interpretations or perspectives of reality.

"One day among days, as the Arabic tales say, there in the garden of Eden . . . God said, 'Let us make man in our image.' This event was of supreme importance: man was born, and suddenly immense sounds and noises rang through the length and breadth of the universe, lights shone in all its corners, the world was filled with odors and tastes, of joy and suffering. In a word, *when Man was born, when he began to live, universal life began too . . . .*

"*When Adam appeared in Paradise, like a new tree, this thing we call life began to exist.* Adam was the first being who, by living, felt himself live. *For Adam, life exists as a problem.*

"What is Adam, then, with the greenness of Paradise *all around him, surrounded* by animals; *off there in the distance*, the rivers with their darting fish, and still *farther off* the mountains with their stony bellies, and *then* the oceans and other lands, and the earth and the other worlds?

"*Adam in Paradise is life pure and simple*; he is the feeble prop of the infinite problem of life.

"Universal gravitation, universal grief, inorganic matter, organic series, the whole history of man, his yearnings, his exultations, Nineveh and Athens, Plato and Kant, Cleopatra and Don Juan, the corporal and the spiritual, the momentary and the eternal and that which endures . . . all pressing down upon the red fruit, suddenly ripe, of Adam's heart. Do we understand all of what the systole and diastole of that little organ means, all those inexhaustible things, all that which we express in a word whose boundaries are infinite, *LIFE*, made concrete, condensed in each one of its pulsations? *Adam's heart, the center of the universe*; that is, *the universe, whole, in Adam's heart*, like a liquor bubbling in a glass.

"*This is man: the problem of life.*"[15]

This is the conceptual expression of the image of "Adam in Paradise"; the idea of *circumstance*. Adam appears among innumerable preexistent living beings, and yet *life*—in a new sense—begins with him. For him life exists as a *problem*, as awareness, as feeling himself living, what he will later call concern. Adam has greenness *all around him*, he is *surrounded* by animals; and then there is a series of *terms* of his circum-

---

[15] I, 476–77. Italics mine.

stantial perspective— "off there," "still farther off," and "then," etc.—
until the perspective includes the other worlds, all of Nature, history,
art, the eternal. *Adam in Paradise* says in 1910, in a figure of speech,
what in 1914 is expressed in concepts: *I am I and my circumstance.*

But after saying that man is the problem of life, Ortega must ask
himself what life is; he must seek an adequate idea of it. *In 1910 he does
not as yet possess this.* When he says "all things live," he does not mean
this in any mystical sense. On the other hand, he does not accept the
point of view of science, which "seems to reduce the significance of the
word *life* to one particular discipline: that of biology."[16] And this biological life cannot be clearly defined. In this context, Ortega tries to
clarify the notion of life, but in a way which is inadequate and which
he himself disqualifies in his 1915 note. He must return to the immediate theme, art; and only at the end of the essay do some further details
on life appear, and these again arise out of the figure of Adam in Paradise. And Ortega writes: "Life is an exchange of substances; therefore
it is to colive, to coexist, to entangle oneself in a fine-meshed net of
relationships, to support one thing upon another, to mutually nourish
each other, to get along together, to fulfill one another."[17] And later:
"In man, *life is duplicated*: his movements, his members, are at once
spatial life and signs of affective life."[18] "Adam in Paradise. *Who is
Adam? He is everybody and nobody in particular*: life. Where is Paradise? It does not matter: *it is the ubiquitous stage setting for the immense
tragedy of living.*"[19] Life as *tragedy*, and Paradise as the *setting*. This
is to be the theme of Ortega's philosophy, as he stated it metaphorically
at the watershed of his twenty-six years.

But what is that original metaphor, *Adam in Paradise?* The third
metaphor stated by Ortega in his lectures in Buenos Aires in 1916—
neither more nor less. Let us recall what was said in section 50: "The
object and I stand confronting one another, but one is outside the other,
the two are inseparable from each other. The metaphor which corresponds . . . could be one of those pairs of divinities . . . who are called
Dii consentes and also *Dii complices*, the matched gods who had to be
born and die together. Just so does *the universe appear as duplicated.*

[16] I, 477.
[17] I, 488.
[18] I, 499, Italics mine.
[19] I, 499. Italics mine.

We emerge from the eternal monotony of the I, where everything appeared to be included, and objects appear before us in infinite variety."[20] That essential duality, that duplication of ingredients which need each other reciprocally, that coexistence, that infinite variety of objects around the subject and irreducible to it—all this is contained in the metaphor of 1910. After that date Ortega's work will consist in extracting all the philosophy that belongs to that new level where it appears installed at the time when he begins his personal thought. When he reflects on the title of his essay, he says, "I do not quite know why I called it that." Perhaps the young philosopher did not know it yet; no doubt the writer did.

[20] *Anales de la Institución Cultural Española* (Buenos Aires, 1947), I, 175–76.

Part Three

TERRA FIRMA

I.

THEORY AND ITS REQUISITES

In 1914, Ortega arrives at what we might call terra firma. And this is true in many senses. In a number of different dimensions, it is only at this time that his image begins to solidify. Everything that has gone before becomes intelligible only from this level where his significance appears. Therefore it seems to me to be a grave error of method, rendering any effort sterile, to study *separately* Ortega's most youthful writings. We have observed the occasional character of all of them, the "iceberg" quality which defines them; this is true to an extreme degree in his early writings, in which Ortega's thought is not *expressed*, although it is *prefigured* in them. Yet more: to speak of Ortega's "thought" before 1914 is extremely equivocal: we cannot call what an author is thinking at a certain moment his "thought." If Ortega had died in 1913, we would never have been able to speak of his *thought*, no matter how rich his youthful ideas may have been—and we have already seen how rich these were, and how by 1910 he had achieved the basic intuition of what his philosophy was to be. For the same reason, to give the name of a "period" to the stage prior to 1914 seems to me to be ambiguous and confusing; still more so if it is given theoretical value— that is, if we describe as a "thesis" or "doctrine" the progress toward an intellectual position in which Ortega was later to install himself. Ortega was not like Schelling, a thinker in whom one system was supplanted by another; he had only one system throughout his life, with a coherence which does not exclude variation—rather, the contrary; it demands variation and the internal biography of that system.[1]

[1] This is why, in spite of the fact that it represents a great effort in reading and making use of Ortega's youthful writings, and is done with detailed care though not always with accuracy, Fernando Salmerón's long book *Las mocedades de Ortega y*

On the other hand, it is significant that Ortega published in book form only a few of his writings of the period 1904–12, in the volume entitled *Personas, obras, cosas* ["Persons, Works, Things"], in 1916, *after* his first real book, and with a clear judgment of them as "antecedents." He goes back to those works as something belonging to the past; it is, he says, a farewell to his early youth, and if it seems justifiable to him to emphasize this and place special emphasis on it, this is for a transpersonal reason: "My early youth was not mine; it belonged to my race. My youth has been consumed entire, like Moses' burning bush, on the edge of the road traced through history by Spain. Today I can say this with pride and with truth. Those ten youthful years of mine are mystical pages swollen only with Spanish anguish and Spanish hopes."[2] That is, the *theme* of Ortega's youthful work is not a theme of theory: it is Spain, the Spanish circumstance. It is obvious that Ortega's method of confronting this circumstance consists in thinking and in bringing the theory to it; but the organizational center of that youthful work is not a philosophical doctrine, but his own theme, and the doctrine will arise precisely out of that theme, will be constituted in it. It is just that circumstantial quality of his thought which is going to fall back upon that thought and bring it to the new idea: *to think as to circumstantialize.* But if, instead of starting off from that *reality* which makes Ortega think, one pays attention directly to the resulting "ideas," their quality of being justified and profound will not be understood either. Ortega's initial thought is, rather than a "doctrine," the form of action in which he engages when confronted with, and in view of, his circumstance; and the truly original feature of that thought, the thing which places it from the outset on a different line from the reigning thought in Europe—and naturally in Spain—is, neither more nor less, its *origin*: what is lost if it is considered as an "ideology"; first, because it is not fully an ideology; second, because at most it would be simply one more ideology.

On the other hand, the *intellectual* torso of that youthful work, what we might call the *germ* of the future philosophical doctrine, is the pre-

---

Gasset (Mexico, 1959) does not cast much light. As for José Ferrater Mora's book *Ortega y Gasset. Etapas de una filosofía* (Barcelona, 1958) (English edition, *Ortega y Gasset. An Outline of His Philosophy* [New Haven and London, 1957]), in spite of being as shrewd as all Ferrater's books are, it suffers from having introduced an "objectivist" phase which is not justified, and which beclouds our understanding of Ortega's trajectory.

[2] I, 419.

cipitate of that circumstantial confrontation, its conceptual possession: what is expressed metaphorically in "Adam in Paradise" and analogously in the metaphor of the *Dii consentes*, who are born and die together, reciprocally conditioned; and as a consequence of this the doctrine of the interpretations of reality, made up of the different modes of "supposition," installation, or perspective. To speak of "objectivism" to designate Ortega's presumptive youthful doctrine seems unjustified to me, for the few "objectivist" expressions found in those writings are only the manifestation, the opposite swing of the pendulum, of his rejection of subjectivism, and they are formally disqualified by their author almost immediately afterward. Not only in the notes we have already quoted, but in the Prologue to *Persons, Works, Things*, where he says, "In all essential points, I can be in agreement today with the thoughts borne by this volume. I find only one serious exception, which corresponds to two or three observations I have slipped in, at the bottom of the same number of pages: I refer to the value of the individual and subjective. Today more than ever, I have the conviction that subjectivism was the disease of the nineteenth century, and Spain's disease to a superlative degree. But polemical ardor has frequently caused me to commit a tactical error, which is also a substantial error. To wage war on subjectivism I denied the subject, the personal, the individual, all its rights. Today it would seem closer to the truth and even to tactics to recognize these things in all their fullness, and to assign to the subjective a place and a task in the universal hive."[3] *In all essential features* Ortega is in agreement with his early thoughts; are we then to define this period by the sole point with which he very quickly came not to feel in agreement, the point which, even at the time he formulated it, he no longer felt in agreement with? Then let us not forget that on the same date and in the same piece of writing in which he proposed the Imitation of Things, he added that we also need the Imitation of Subjects.[4]

In 1914, Ortega made an unequivocal move to "strike out on his own"; rather, he made several. Let us remember that in March of that year he gave the lecture entitled "Old and New Politics," his first fully *public* act and one in which he represented himself as the spokesman for his generation; at the same time, he published his first *book, Meditations on Quixote*; in the third place, in that book he announced a whole

[3] I, 419–20.
[4] "Renan" (1909). I, 441 and 443.

series of further volumes, a collection of *Meditations*; lastly, in that same sentence he presented himself—something he had never done before—as a professor of philosophy; he is undoubtedly being ironic when he adds that he is one *in partibus infidelium*, but we should not overlook the fact that he chooses this time to establish the fact after having been a professor for six years in the College of Education and for four years in the University. What do these four actions mean, and why does he perform them at that date?

Ortega had just turned thirty years of age: it is the age, according to his own doctrine, when a man begins his historical activity *sensu stricto*, the period of "gestation" and struggle with the previous generation, the one which is "in power." Up to a short time previously, Ortega had placed his hopes on Unamuno; he had said that he served the same cause; he had become irritated with him and reproached him sharply, because he believed that Unamuno was not fulfilling his proper mission. Now he is about to initiate, on his own account and *in the name of his generation*, an independent course of action. He will continue to count on Unamuno—perhaps more than before, and in a more friendly fashion; but at a greater distance and from his own personal position; it is also at this time that he plans and begins to write studies of the other men of 1898: Baroja, Azorín; this implies a certain distance in respect to them—to the extent that they are "themes"—and at the same time the need to confront their work so that he may speak a *mot juste* about it from his own perspective. It should be added that in 1915 he was to be editor of a review, *España*, representative of his generation; and that, after leaving it a year later, he would begin in 1916 the publication of a personal "review": *El Espectador*. Later I shall have a word to say about the reasons for this latter move.

But there are other reasons, of a strictly theoretical kind, which we must take into account. In 1913 two books were published, enormously different and enormously distant from each other, but—and to note this is what is characteristic of historical consideration—very close to each other within Ortega's vital perspective: Husserl's *Ideen* and Unamuno's *Del sentimiento trágico de la vida* ["The Tragic Sense of Life"]. Their effects were destined to be, paradoxical as this seems, convergent. The *Ideen* represent the *theory* of phenomenology—the *Logische Untersuchungen* were only its practice, its reality; and furthermore, in the *Ideen*, beyond the phenomenological *method*, the phenomenological *philosophy* noted in its title appears—*Ideen zu einer reinen Phänomenologie und phänomenologischen Philosophie*—which is in fact an *idealism*, the idealism of pure consciousness, or *reines Bewusstsein*.[5] In that year, Ortega took possession of phenomenology and realized its inestimable value and its limitations; he realized what Husserl's innovation in method signified, its indispensable nature, but he also realized what it would mean to adhere to his philosophy. At the same instant—this seems almost impossible, but it is obvious and we shall see this in its proper place—he placed himself *beyond* phenomenology, preserving, naturally, everything in it that represented a permanent acquisition.

As for *The Tragic Sense of Life*, it is clear that it meant to him the most intense and vibrant formulation of irrationalism, the most uncompromising, energetic, and sharp opposition between reason and life. An exciting and deeply felt book, full of "palpable hits" and truths, of persuasive force, capable of launching Spanish thought onto a path which Ortega had thought was closed to it. It was the most vigorously flung gauntlet, the most unavoidable challenge to the proofs in which Ortega was beginning to install himself. I believe that the impact of *The Tragic Sense of Life* was one of the strongest stimuli that "precipitated" Ortega's personal philosophy. Urged on by Unamuno's work, with no hope of bringing Unamuno into the path he, Ortega, felt would be fruitful, without faith in the possibility of a discussion with him, his only outlet was a reply which would be *independent* and yet at a distance, the confrontation of Unamuno's thesis with another that was juster and truer, able to come to terms with its irrationality. Ortega *never* spoke, so far as I know, about *The Tragic Sense of Life*; and, since it was the book that it was, this means only that he thought about it too much, so much that he was not able to express it, but only to *do* it: be it understood, to make the adequate response to a doctrine he judged to be erroneous; and that response could only be a *different* doctrine, one of equal or greater caliber, whose function was not to "refute" the previous one, but rather to "*absorb*" it. Strictly speaking, Ortega's dialogue with Unamuno, when matters became sufficiently serious, consisted in ceasing to discuss, and yielding the floor to reality itself, in making his voice heard in a new theory which would respond to Unamuno's without answering it.

[5] See J. Marías, *Historia de la Filosofía* (*Obras*, I, 395–409) and *Introducción a la Filosofía* (*Obras*, II, chapter 4, p. 40).

By about 1914, Ortega was isolated. Isolated from his teachers in Marburg, from Husserl's phenomenology, in which he could not install himself because he saw it as full of errors, from his onetime master and rival Unamuno, with whom he felt a need to have things out but on whom he could not count. This situation made him feel "adult"; thus he had to "strike out on his own" and *begin to exist out of his own self*, unsupported by a tradition or his own age group.

The level on which he found himself, defined by the terms of what for him was going to be the problem, was that of the *idealism of consciousness* and the *irrationalism* which, in the name of life, denies reason without being able to dispense with it. The two positions presuppose, beyond their *content* in the strict sense, two very necessary and—needless to say—divergent ideas about what *theory* is. Before taking up a discussion of these concrete doctrines, Ortega had to establish certain demands or requisites of theory as such, which were to condition what this theory could discover and its manner of justifying this; or, expressed in other terms, of verifying it, making it true. He had to start off, then, with something previous to *a* philosophy, from a *level* of intent as to what philosophy is. This is the starting point of Ortega's originality, of something previous to the theses of his philosophical thought, and which sustains these theses and makes them possible. To trace the line of that level is equivalent to tracing the contours of the terra firma on which he set foot for the first time in 1914, with the *Meditations on Quixote.*

61. CLARITY, VERACITY, AND SYSTEM

In Ortega the demand for clarity is not only a standard for the expression of his thought and his dealings with others—"clarity is the philosopher's courtesy"—but the very condition of philosophy. It is, as we shall see, one of the essential themes of the *Meditations on Quixote,* where it is equated with that of profundity, and its result is the various species of clarity;[6] where it appears as the mission of man on earth, that it is the root of his constitution, so that light is an imperative.[7] The decision for clarity which accompanies Ortega from his beginnings emerges from his deepest philosophical convictions and from the very

[6] I, 332.
[7] I, 356ff.

root of his personality, which is expressed in those lines by Goethe which Ortega has more than once made his own:

> *I declare myself of the family of those*
> *who from obscurity to clarity aspire.*

Together with this imperative, there is another which deserves special attention: that of *veracity*. Ortega has reflected on this theme, especially when he clarified his relationship to the German philosophical tradition. Ortega speaks of a German generation, previous to that of his neo-Kantian masters and much more interesting, which encountered extreme philosophical despair following Positivism, with only two masters— deficient ones, for various reasons—Lotze and Trendelenburg. This group of philosophers[8] was composed of Sigwart, Teichmüller, Wundt, Brentano, and Dilthey. Except for Dilthey—"who did not fully realize that he had it"[9]—these men did not have a philosophy. They were strongly influenced by Anglo-French thought, which imposed on them "a mental ground, a fundamental disposition: empiricism." "The manner in which Brentano and Dilthey, especially the latter, were empiricists," adds Ortega, "continues even today to be the future of philosophy."[10]

These men who were so different coincide, according to Ortega, in the following repertory of intellectual themes:

"1. They are all rabidly anti-Kantian, in contrast with the generation which was to follow them.
"2. They tend to affirm that the whole comes before its parts.
"3. That activity comes before the thing.
"4. That the whole, and dynamism or activity, are, nevertheless, something given, factitious, and not posited. Therefore they are anti-Kantian. For them, then, the categorical is 'empirical'; it is a fact.
"5. That it is necessary to transcend intellectualism.
"6. They recognize the psychic factor as the preferred reality on which the world must be constructed.

[8] Ortega presents them as a generation, but without doing so formally. He notes that the accurate pin-pointing of the chronological date of a generation is a very difficult problem, and speaks of giving his indications "a purely approximate and conventional value." I incline to suspect that the philosophers mentioned belong to two generations, those of 1826 and 1841.

[9] *Prólogo para alemanes*, 40.

[10] *Ibid.*, 41.

"7. Therefore, they would base all philosophy on psychology.

"8. But on a psychology considered from the outset as a fundamental science, and, consequently, on the basis of its possible utilization in philosophy."[11]

The divergences and differences between them are enormous, but the differences exist precisely *on those themes.* Ortega notes that, in spite of the impossibility of making Wundt and Dilthey agree on the priority of the whole over the parts, "Dilthey's basic idea and the 'law of Schöpferische Synthese' and the aperception or 'voluntarism' of Wundt, are two forms of *feeling* a completely new idea in the history of thought. The new feature here, let it be said, was above all that the totality, the synthesis, the *Zusammenhang* was a simple fact, whereas in Kant it is precisely the symptom of that which is not fact but action of the subject, a subjective addition to what is given and factitious."[12]

The young scholars of Marburg in the years 1907 to 1911 were no longer neo-Kantians by the time they reached their twenty-sixth birthday, as we have seen. Ortega refers specifically to Nicolai Hartmann, Heinz Heimsoeth, and himself. Why were they not? When Ortega thinks about his youth, he makes it plain that at that time they *felt* or had a presentiment of something which they could as yet neither think nor formulate. This was the question of *veracity.* The neo-Kantian philosophies, and those related to them, the only ones then *reigning,* "produced a strange effect on us, which we dared not confess to each other: they seemed . . . . *forced.*"[13] Those philosophies—profound, serious, acute, full of truths—did not seem *veracious.* Many things which were not true for those who affirmed them were forced to take on the guise of truth. There was a good deal of "orthopedia," says Ortega, in that style of thinking. This leads him to introduce, beside the *truth-error* dilemma, another question: the veracity of the philosopher. "Veracity is nothing but the thirst for truth, the yearning to arrive at what is certain."[14] It is not enough to say that the man who lacks veracity is simply a liar. It may happen that he feels other desires than those which lead to the truth. In philosophy veracity has been taken for granted, and its quantity, the coefficient of veracity possessed by the different philosophers, has not been questioned. For example, German idealism, marvelous from a philosophical standpoint, represents a minimum of veracity; the post-Kantians were determined to conquer

11 *Ibid.,* 41–42.　　　　13 *Ibid.,* 48.
12 *Ibid.,* 42.　　　　　　14 *Ibid.,* 55.

the kingdom of a system, come what might. "Genius and Shameless-ness in Transcendental Idealism" is the title of a study which Ortega considered to be urgently needed. The neo-Kantians also had "insufficient scrupulosity and an excessive zeal to be right."[15]

The reaction of what Ortega calls the "youthful group of 1911" was, in this respect, one which he formulates in these terms: "A commitment to veracity, to subjecting the idea strictly to what is presented as real, without additions or rounding-off."[16] We must keep these words in mind for, if they are "transposed," if they are taken in another context and from a slightly different perspective, they express with considerable exactitude a basic principle in Ortega's philosophy, which leads him to the very center of his innovation. Later we shall see this clearly. As an example of veracity, Ortega gives us Hartmann, who, when things begin not to be clear, turns to the reader and tells him, "I know no more on this point." And on other occasions he has recalled Lotze's phrase in his *Metaphysics*: "God knows a great deal more about this." The names of Dilthey, Husserl, and Ortega himself, within contemporary philosophy, exemplify better than any other explanation what veracity in a philosopher means.

The second element in the reaction of the young men of Marburg to the reigning philosophy was the "wish for a system, which is so difficult to bring into harmony with the resolution I mentioned before."[17] Ortega notes that the Romantics craved system "like a sweet-meat, for its resemblance to a ripe, round, sweet, and juicy fruit," while for them it had the aspect of "the harsh specific obligation of the philosopher." And he adds these biographically decisive words: "System, thus felt, could not be a youthful production. Hence there was a tacit agreement, which each of us must have made inside himself, to leave the ripe fruit for the hour of ripeness, which (as Aristotle remarks with a terrifying excess of precision) is the age of fifty-one." Ortega wrote this in 1934, just at that age. Might not all this be an a posteriori explanation, first to vindicate the value of system in philosophy, and second to justify the delay in his personal formulation of it? But the fact is that when he was twenty-five years old, in 1908, three years before that date of 1911 to which he always referred, he had written:

[15] *Ibid.*, 56.
[16] *Ibid.*
[17] "Algunas notas" (1908). I, 114–15. Italics mine.

"I believe that among the four or five immovably certain things that men possess, is that Hegelian statement that truth can only exist in the shape of a system . . . . Hegel's statement not only does not exclude the idea of development; rather, . . . Hegel has constructed the system of evolution more profoundly than anyone else. To demand a system, as I do, has nothing to do with the Scholasticism of the Sorbonne. Truth, for Hegel, is never exhausted; the Idea evolves tomorrow, just as today and yesterday; it is, as Kant and Fichte would say, a task and a problem which are infinite. But it is necessary at every instant that the truth of the world be a system; or, what is the same thing, that the world be a *cosmos* or universe. System is unification of problems, and in the individual it is unity of consciousness, of opinions. This was what I meant. It is not licit to leave opinions floating in the spirit like drifting buoys, without any rational links between them . . . . It is not decent to keep water-tight compartments in the soul, without any communication among them; the hundred problems which make up the view of the world must live in conscious unity. *It is possible, naturally, not to have a system ready; but it is obligatory to try to form one. System is the thinker's honor.*"[18] That is, the youthful Ortega places system in the future, but he places it there as an inexorable duty, and therefore as his life task. At the proper place we shall see how Ortega's demand for system is still more profound than this, and how it will be some time yet before he discovers the *ultimate* reason why philosophy must be systematic.

Lastly, Ortega points out one more conviction shared by his youthful group, the conviction that it was necessary "to launch the ship and abandon, not only the province of Romantic idealism, but the whole idealist continent."[19] This is, he adds, the most radical thing that the European can do today, for by doing so he abandons not only a space but a time: the Modern Age. Ortega recalls that in 1916 he wrote an essay entitled *Nada moderno y muy siglo XX* ["Nothing Modern, and Very Twentieth Century"]; since one cannot go backward, his motto was that of Cromwell's soldiers: *Vestigia nulla retrorsum.* "The young men of that year bought a ticket to the unknown—'Ins Unbekannte, niemals Betretene'—the path never trodden."[20]

18 *Prólogo para alemanes*, 56.
19 *Ibid.*, 57.
20 *Ibid.*

"But," the fifty-one-year-old Ortega continues to reflect, looking back on his youth, "did we have *concrete positive* reasons to *know* that idealism was no longer the truth? We had, to be sure, many *negative* reasons, many objections to idealism. But this is not enough. Living truth is not bound by the rules of the Scholastic disputation. And it has not been fully proved that an idea is erroneous so long as one does not possess the other clear and positive idea that we are going to put in its place. Naturally we did not have such an idea. But this is the odd thing; we did have perfectly clearly, unequivocally . . . the hollow of the new idea, its contour, just as in a mosaic the missing piece makes its presence felt by its absence."[21] We know that this was literally true: we have seen how dissatisfaction with idealism and subjectivism appears in Ortega; how it appears for a moment that he is going to *backslide* into realism or "objectivism," but—*Vestigia nulla retrorsum*—there is no escape, there is no retrogression, one cannot "go back" either in life or in history; no "neoism" exists when one has authentic veracity. There is, metaphorically prefigured, the missing piece: *Adam in Paradise*, the I surrounded by everything else, the different interpretations of the real which correspond to an equal number of other "suppositions" or visual perspectives, life as coexistence and dialogue with the distinct and inseparable; what soon will be those *Dii consentes, I and my circumstance.*

62. PHILOSOPHY AS THE GENERAL SCIENCE OF LOVE

The first definition of philosophy which we find in Ortega's writings is this: *the general science of love.* There is nothing vague about the meaning of this: it is the condensation of the doctrine set forth in the prologue to the *Meditations on Quixote* and developed throughout that book.[22] The two words most often repeated in these pages, and which are reciprocally explained, are *connection* and *love.* At the beginning of this book, Ortega announces a series of "salvations"; this literary genre responds to the intellectual proposition of making each thing the center of the universe, of binding some things to others, of concentrating one's gaze on each of them in such a way that the sun gives off "innum-

[21] *Ibid.*, 58.

[22] In this section I use many ideas and some passages from my commentary on the edition of *Meditaciones del Quijote* (Madrid, 1957).

erable reflections." On the first page, Ortega revives "the beautiful name Spinoza used," *amor intellectualis*: he is going to write some essays on intellectual love.[23]

The proximity of love and philosophy has a tradition which stems from the origins of philosophy, even from its name; at some moments that linkage acquires particular importance: thus in Plato, whose philosophy has an *erotic* character and where the *éros* is assimilated to the philosopher; in the Aristotelian *philía*; in the Augustinian idea of *agápe* or *caritas* as the path of truth (*non intratur in veritatem nisi per caritatem*), explained by the quality of *sapientia* or wisdom which belongs to God (*si sapientia Deus est, verus philosophus est amator Dei*); in Saint Anselm, whose motto *fides quaerens intellectum* is inseparable from love, since in him faith which is alive and *operosa* consists in *dilectio*; in Spinoza, who makes philosophy culminate in *amor intellectualis Dei*. But in Ortega this linkage has characteristics of its own. In the first place, the idea of *connection*, an "all-embracing connection," which is not simply a love of the subject for things, or a vague love of things among themselves. For Ortega, love is "love for the perfection of the thing loved."[24] In Spinoza something different was being dealt with: *amor* is *joy* accompanied by the idea of its exterior cause, and joy is the progress *of man* to a greater *perfection*; that is, it is a question of the perfection *of the lover*, who when he becomes more perfect becomes joyful and loves the cause of this joy. For Ortega, it is a question of the perfection *of the thing loved*. This is not the decisive point, however; rather that this perfection is not *intrinsic to the thing*, that each thing must emerge from itself, must enter into *connection* with the rest in order to attain its perfection (which ties in with the ideas in "Adam in Paradise"). "Blessed be things! Love them, love them! Each thing is a fairy whose inner treasures are clothed in poverty and commonness, and a virgin who must fall in love in order to bear fruit.... The important thing is that the theme be placed in immediate *relationship* with the elemental currents of the spirit, with the classic motifs of human concern. Once *interwoven* with them, it is transfigured, transubstantiated, *saved*."[25] Love binds us to things. The characteristic which comes over a thing when it is loved is that it seems *indispensable* to us; this means that we cannot admit of a life in which we could exist

[23] *Meditaciones del Quijote*. I, 311.
[24] *Ibid.*, 312. Italics mine.   [25] *Ibid.*, 313.

and the loved object could not; in other words, that we consider it as a part of ourselves. "In love there is, consequently, a broadening of individuality which absorbs other things into it, which fuses them with us. This bond and interpenetration cause us to enter deeply into the properties of the beloved object. We see it whole, it is revealed to us in all its worth. Then we see that the beloved object is, in its turn, part of something else, which needs it, which is linked to it. Indispensable for the loved object, it also becomes indispensable for us. Thus love gradually binds one thing to another and all things to ourselves, in a firm essential structure."[26]

The final formula is the decisive one: *one thing to another and all things to ourselves*. When we arrive at this point, we can understand what I wrote in section 31 of this book: *to think as to circumstantialize*. Ortega's philosophy is intrinsically circumstantial; it consists, as a doctrine, in being circumstantial. To philosophize is precisely to *circumstantialize*, to make what is "out there" circumstance or world, a loving connection in the perspective of the living subject, with its near and its far, its more and its less, its large and its small: its *hierarchy*. And therefore Ortega can conclude: "In this sense I consider that philosophy is the general science of love; within the intellectual sphere it represents the greatest impulse toward an all-embracing connection."[27] The key word here is *all-embracing*: this is the peculiar quality which the *philosophical* connection has, as distinct from all others. On it is based the *systematic* character which we saw postulated before. And so Ortega says a little later: "The ultimate ambition of philosophy would be to arrive at a single proposition in which all of the truth would be expressed."[28] In what sense this may be possible, and what the function of this single proposition would be, will only become clear later on. Now we must ask ourselves what form of *knowing* is demanded by philosophy, whether philosophy is an all-embracing connection and the general science of love.

63. ERUDITION, COMPREHENSION, AND THEORY

Since very early in his career Ortega had shown a lack of confidence in erudition, or a dissatisfaction with it; that is, a conviction of its insufficiency and—if it is considered as an adequate form of knowing—its

[26] *Ibid.*, 316.   [27] *Ibid.*, 317.   [28] "Nueva revista." I, 142.

error. From the European level to which he aspired he wrote in 1910: "To say Europe . . . is to take with equal respect a most erudite book by the great Menéndez Pelayo and to write in the margin of the last page: *Non multa sed multum.*"[29] And at about the same date he greeted the publication of Menéndez Pidal's *La epopeya castellana* ["The Castilian Epic"] as a triumph over insufficient erudition: "A new culture is being formed in the subsoil of the Peninsula. A few hardworking men are quietly carving out a new soul for Spain, a lofty continental spirituality. Ramón Menéndez Pidal has chosen the most dangerous material with which to make Europeanism. This substance is so difficult to grasp that it is precisely to those who dealt with it before his time that we owe this way of looking at the world, which I would call a barbarous traditionalism, a sort of Celtiberianism, which for thirty years has hindered our integration into the European consciousness. A host of erudite mercenaries had set up their encampments before the lumber rooms of the national past . . . . Menéndez Pidal has broken with these habits, and thanks to him, Spanish philology has passed under the influence of a different sign of the Zodiac."[30]

But the place where he contrasts erudition and other ways of knowing, and indicates its limits, is in the *Meditations on Quixote.* "Philosophy," he says, "is the opposite of the concrete piece of information, of erudition." Not that he disdains erudition: it was the kind of science adequate to the times in which philology had not found reliable methods to discover in the mass of historical events the unity of their meaning. The greatest possible number of pieces of information was gathered in the mind of one individual; these thus achieved a sort of "ragbag" unity, and their spontaneous associations shed a certain amount of light. "This unity of facts, not in themselves but inside the brain of one person, is erudition." To return to it would mean a regression for philology, "as though chemistry were to go back to alchemy, or medicine to magic."[31] Persons who are *merely* erudite are becoming rare, he says, and soon we will witness the disappearance of the last mandarins. Erudition occupies, therefore, the outer circle of science; it is limited to the accumulation of facts, whereas philosophy represents the opposite tendency: pure synthesis. Naturally, this does not mean that erudition is not *necessary*, that those facts ought not to be collected; what it means is that science begins after the collecting is finished and one has begun

[29] I, 146. [30] I, 317. [31] I, 317.

to do something else. What is inadmissible in erudition is not erudition itself, for it is useful and even admirable, but the fact that it tries to be what it is not—science—and perhaps to dispense with science. Ortega explains his point of view several years later in the clearest way possible, also with regard to Menéndez Pidal: "The greatest worth of Menéndez Pidal's work is not the indefatigable exploration or the accumulation of information. If his work contained no more than this, it would not deserve the divine name of science, with the purity such a name demands. Science is not erudition, but theory. A scholar's efforts begin to be science when he mobilizes the facts and the knowledge in the direction of a theory. For this he needs a great combinatory talent composed of equal measures of rigor and boldness. This is, in my opinion, the admirable gift of our Menéndez Pidal, at once daring and cautious under his flourishing beard, which is beginning to turn to pure silver .... Gentlemen, once more, science is not mere knowledge! Science consists in replacing the knowledge which seems so sure by a theory; that is, by something that is always problematical. Or, expressed in another way: science is that which always leaves room for discussion."[32]

That "all-embracing connection" which is philosophy leads Ortega to contrast "mere knowledge" and "understanding." We know many things which we do not understand; all wisdom based only on facts is uncomprehending, and can be justified only when brought into the service of a theory. Today, those paired terms, *knowing* and *understanding*, make us think of Dilthey (*Erkennen und Verstehen*); but in him and his school something quite different is being dealt with. In Dilthey and in the *immediate* Diltheyan tradition, *Verständnis* is a form or species of knowledge, in which, first, not only the pure intellectual processes intervene, but the other psychic energies co-operate; and, second, starting off from external data—from a child's stammering phrase to the *Critique of Pure Reason*, from a piece of marble to a gesture—one reaches the knowledge of something previous, of a psychic life, stemming from one's own, which permits one to relive and reproduce the lives of others, or perhaps even the lives of those who have gone before us.[33]

---

[32] "Orígenes del español" (1927), in *Espíritu de la letra*. III, 512–13.

[33] I reproduce here fairly long selections from one of the notes in my commentary on the *Meditaciones del Quijote*, 234 ff., which I think it important to state here:
The distinction between understanding and "mere knowing" is particularly relevant

today; but in 1914 its intellectual tradition was extremely tenuous. It derives, as we know, from Dilthey (*Erkennen und Verstehen*), but much time and effort were necessary before the concept of *Verstehen* or *Verständnis* achieved any kind of currency, because of the slowness with which Dilthey's work spread, became known and, above all, properly understood and used. In the *Ideen über eine beschreibende und zergliedernde Psychologie* (1894), the distinction is already sketched: *Dies bestimmt schon die Natur des Verstehens unserer selbst und anderer. Wir erklären durch reine intellektuelle Prozesse, aber wir verstehen durch das Zusammenwirken aller Gemütskräfte in der Auffassung* (*Gesammelte Schriften*, V, 172). In a later work, *Die Entstehung der Hermeneutik*, some interesting details are given: "Wir nennen den Vorgang, in welchem wir aus Zeichen, die von aussen sinnlich gegeben sind, ein Inneres erkennen: *Verstehen* . . . . Dies Verstehen reicht von dem Auffassen kindlichen Lallens bis zu dem Hamlet oder der Vernunftkritik. Aus Steinen, Marmor, musikalisch geformten Tönen, aus Gebärden, Worten und Schrift, aus Handlungen, wirtschaftlichen Ordnungen und Verfassungen spricht derselbe menschliche Geist zu uns und bedarf der Auslegung . . . Das Verstehen zeigt verschiedene Grade. Diese sind zunächst vom Interesse bedingt. Ist das Interesse eingeschränkt, so ist auch das Verständnis." (G.S., V, 318–19.) The additions to the manuscript of this study, *not published until 1924*, constitute the strictest formulation, perhaps, of Dilthey's idea of *understanding*: "Verstehen fällt unter den Allgemeinbegriff des Erkennens, wobei Erkennen im weitesten Sinne als Vorgang gefasst wird, in welchem ein allgemeingültiges Wissen angestrebt wird.—(Satz 1.) *Verstehen nennen wir den Vorgang, in welchem aus sinnlich gegebenen Ausserungen seelischen Lebens dieses zur Erkenntnis kommt.*—(Satz 3.) *Das kunstmässige Verstehen von schriftlich fixierten Lebensäusserungen nennen wir Auslegung, Interpretation.*—(Satz 5.) *Verstehen, in dem nun anzugebenden weiten Umfang genommen, ist das grundlegende Verfahren für alle weiteren Operationen der Geisteswissenschaften.*" (G.S., V, 332–33.)

All this, most of it unknown, had had very few repercussions. The expression is not even included in Husserl's *Ideen* (1913). The meaning given to the terms *Verstehen* and *Verständnis* in Benno Erdmann's *Logik* (2nd ed., 1922, p. 300) has a connection with the mental operations carried out beneath the threshold of consciousness (*unterhalb der Schwelle des Bewusstseins*) and has nothing to do with Dilthey's ideas. However, in 1912, Benno Erdmann published an article on "Erkennen und Verstehen" (*Sitzungsberichte der Berliner Akademie*, p. 1240 ff.). The book by A. Stein, *Der Begriff des Geistes bei Dilthey* (1913), written from the point of view of Rickert, is entitled *Der Begriff des Verstehens bei Dilthey* only in the second, revised, edition (1926). As late as 1924 this term was still a novelty: in Heinrich Maier's notes to the fifth edition of Christoph Sigwart's *Logik* (1924), when he speaks of the philosophy of history and its methodology, he emphasizes the fact that "in the last few years" psychological and logical thought has been brought to bear, in a penetrating way, on the peculiarity of knowledge of spiritual realities, "which have also recently been called 'understanding' (das man neuerdings auch 'Verstehen' nennt),'' and quotes, along with Erdmann's essay, the *Lebensformen* of E. Spranger (1914) and the article by Spranger in the homage to Volkelt (1918): "Zur Theorie des Verstehens und zur geisteswissenschaftlichen Psychologie." Maier sees the underlying assumption of knowledge in the sciences of mind, in a "transference" ("Sichhineinversetzen") to other lives, an inner reproduction of them under the guise of living them in representation. "The key to 'Verstehen,' " adds Maier, "therefore lies in the internal experience itself of the person who understands."

It is interesting to see, then, that from the outset the theme undergoes substantial modifications in the *Meditations on Quixote*. (1) Ortega does not contrast "knowledge" of the natural with "comprehension" of the spiritual, but already moves within the orbit of the spiritual and human; and what he contrasts is erudition or information and philosophy, the "knowledge of facts," which is uncomprehending, and "theory," in which comprehension is produced. (2) What interests Ortega is *connection*. And he contrasts the "external unity" of phenomena inside the scholar's head with their unity "in themselves"; that is, in the synthesis of the theory: it is the postulate of system, whose concrete character—one which is very different, as we have seen, from the traditional idealist system—will appear later. (3) Ortega emphasizes the instantaneous and total, sudden nature of philosophical intellection, which is an abrupt clarification of the enormous perspective of the world: "This maximum illumination is what I called comprehension";[34] that is, what Ortega calls *theory* is system and at the same time total vision, contemplation, *theoría* in the Greek sense of the word, not a simple concatenation of logically combined theses, although these are also necessary: theory exists, in fact, when one succeeds in thinking, suddenly and all at once, a "treasure of significance," which has been prepared by a long labor of exploration and meditation. Observe with what *requisites* philosophical knowledge is postulated in Ortega's first book.

But this is still not enough. That *theoretical* connection, which Ortega contrasts with the connection possessed by facts inside the scholar's head (as in a ragbag) is simply the unity of facts "in themselves." Is this the only alternative? More: do facts "in themselves" have a connection? Let us not forget what we observed a few pages back: the point of departure is *love*, which binds "one thing to another and *all things to ourselves*"; that is, circumstantially. In theory, as Ortega understands it and expresses it beginning with the *Meditations on Quixote*, mere logical foundation, simple "concatenation," does not suffice. For the effective connections of the real are not a chain, but the

(Ch. Sigwart, *Logik*, II, 851.) In another note he adds that "all the peculiarity of historical knowledge in the sciences of mind, of the spiritual 'Verstehen,' if it is to be scientifically reliable, presupposes a deep familiarity with the nature of the human psyche and a vast psychological experience" (pp. 862–63).

[34] I, 317.

systematic and reciprocal vivification of the ingredients of a circumstantial and concrete drama. Only from the "plot" do we discover the function of the elements—characters, stage settings, emotions, static relationships—of any dramatic structure. When we deal, then, with the circumstantial connection effected by love, *theory is one more connection.* This quality forms part of every authentic theory, and Ortega discovers it at the beginning of his first book: if you prefer, we can say that after that first book, *theory is intrinsically dramatic.*

64. THE FIRST PHILOSOPHICAL JUSTIFICATION OF THE *Meditations on Quixote*

We must emphasize the fact that Ortega's philosophy is presented for the first time in a book on *Don Quixote.* A certain anomaly with regard to established norms seems to dominate his philosophical production. I am not going to say that, from the point of view of its general comprehension and utilization, this has not had its disadvantages (although today it is not easy to see clearly what the results would have been if it had adapted to more academic standards). But, in any case and from the strictly doctrinal and theoretical point of view, it must be said that this feature, the fact that it was initiated and presented in a book which makes reflections on *Don Quixote*, has not been a drawback for that philosophy, but one of its intrinsic demands, whose meaning may yet become clear.

The reason Ortega approaches *Don Quixote* to meditate about it is not, of course, a personal whim, or a pleasure, or a more or less respectable curiosity, or a mere desire for "knowledge"—historical or literary knowledge, for example. We may summarize under a few headings the steps which led Ortega to launch his personal philosophy in this way.

1. It is a question of *knowing what to hold to*, of achieving the necessary orientation to be able to live, the fundamental origin of philosophy.

2. In order to do this, one must emerge from himself, must have recourse from the "I" alone to what, after this date, Ortega formally entitles *the circumstance.* This circumstance is primarily Spain: "the individual cannot orient himself in the universe except through his race, for he is submerged in it like a drop of water in the passing cloud."[35]

---

[35] I, 361.

By "race" he understands, as we have already seen, a historical way of interpreting reality, an original version of the human factor. This is why Ortega states that "the heartbeats of patriotic concern" will be found even in the furthest corners of his essays: "If the most intimate and personal of our meditations are explored, we will be surprised making attempts at a new Spain with the humblest gleams of our soul."[36]

3. Spain becomes intelligible in certain essential experiences, and perhaps the greatest of these is *Don Quixote*. "When a few Spaniards are gathered together—sensitive to the ideal destitution of their past, the sordidness of their present, and the bitter hostility of their future—Don Quixote descends among them, and the melting heat of his mad countenance brings those dispersed hearts together, strings them as if on a spiritual thread, nationalizes them, establishes a common ethnic sorrow behind their personal tribulations. 'Where two or three are gathered together in my name,' said Jesus, 'there am I in the midst of them.' "[37] For the foreigners who have studied *Don Quixote*, he was "a 'divine curiosity': he was not, as he is for us, the problem of their destiny."[38] We must concentrate on *Don Quixote* "the greatest of questions: My God, what is Spain?"[39] We must save—in the teeth of tradition, beyond tradition as it is presented to us, which has "consisted expressly in the progressive annihilation of the possibility of Spain"[40]—we must save what is Spanish, "a lofty promise which has been fulfilled only in extremely rare cases," "the primary substance of the race, the Hispanic core, that simple Spanish terror in the face of chaos," to find, "like an iridescent gem, the Spain that might have been."[41] And since Cervantes is supremely Spanish, if we were to know in what his style consists, we would possess it all. "If some day someone should come along and reveal to us the shape of Cervantes' style, it would suffice for us to prolong its lines along the other collective problems, and thus awake to a new life. Then, if there is courage and genius among us, we would be enabled to make the new Spanish attempt in all purity."[42]

4. But in order to understand Cervantes and *Don Quixote radically* —that is, in their root—we have to see the book in its connection, binding it lovingly to all that makes it real and intelligible.

[36] I, 328.
[37] I, 326.
[38] I, 360.
[39] I, 360.
[40] I, 362–63.
[41] I, 363.
[42] I, 363.

5. This radical form of comprehension cannot be given by any form of penultimate knowledge; what is necessary is that all-embracing connection of which we have spoken. In short, only *philosophy* can do it.

6. But, on the other hand, we have seen that to philosophize is to circumstantialize, to make of each thing a circumstance or world, presided over by its effective hierarchy. And since *Don Quixote* represents a maximum point in the hierarchy of Spanish circumstances, this philosophical consideration brings us back to it. For national, "ethnic" reasons —in the sense of the historical race, be it understood—*Don Quixote* was the inescapable theme of a meditation aroused by the question, "What is Spain?" For reasons which this time are philosophical, Ortega must also confront Cervantes' book with a Spanish form of thought defined by its circumstantiality. Observe that little is left to chance or whim in this book which seems to be literary, but in reality is subject to an adamantine intellectual standard, whose multiple facets are built on an exact and clairvoyant geometry.

This is the philosophical justification of the *Meditations on Quixote*, the justification for the fact that Ortega initiated his philosophy with them. But, although this seems sufficient, it is only half of that justification. A little later on, another justification, still more profound and philosophical, will become clear to us.

II.

THE IDEA OF CIRCUMSTANCE

The circumstantial character of Ortega's thought, of which he had such a clear consciousness from very early in his career, led him to the formation of the concept of *circumstance*, which became one of the pillars of his philosophy. Its use developed with growing precision within his work, and it has been incorporated into the repertory of terms of all the philosophy which proceeds from Ortega either directly or indirectly, to the point that it has become one of the concepts used in the Spanish-speaking world to understand reality, even from a not strictly philosophical point of view, and in that context, in cultivated circles generally. As far as I know, it had never been used before in philosophy, nor has it been used subsequently except in reference to Ortega or the philosophers who have followed in his footsteps.

As we shall see, the *concept* of circumstance, taken in its strict sense, is in fact exclusive to this school—in the broadest sense of the word. But this does not mean that it lacks all philosophical antecedents. Other terms have pointed toward realities which are *partially* coincident with that reality which Ortega calls circumstance. Explicitly, the French word *milieu*, the English *environment*, and the German *Umwelt*. All three were first used in biology, and thence extended, analogously, to other spheres. It is worth stating that the term "circumstance" does not have a primarily biological meaning, but a human one, and above all a historical or political meaning.

The term *milieu*, in this sense—derived from the meaning it has in physics when, for example, an "aqueous medium" is being described— seems to have been introduced into biology by Geoffroy Saint-Hilaire, and, through the works of Blainville, it appears in Auguste Comte, in the lessons of his *Cours de philosophie positive* dedicated to biology.

Comte accepts with enthusiasm the "philosophical definition of life" proposed by Blainville: "le double mouvement intestin, à la fois général et continu, de composition et décomposition," and feels that it lacks only "une indication plus directe et plus explicite de ces deux conditions fondamentales co-relatives, nécessairement inséparables de l'être vivant, un *organisme* déterminé et un *milieu* convenable."[1] A little later on, in a note, he states that by *milieu* he understands "non seulement le fluide où l'organisme est plongé, mais, en général, l'ensemble total des circonstances extérieures, d'un genre quelconque, nécessaires à l'existence de chaque organisme déterminé."[2] The use of the notion of *milieu* culminates in Taine, who makes it a key for his sociological and historical explanations; and it dominates, indirectly, the nineteenth-century novel from Balzac to, especially, Zola, who was directly influenced by Taine and Claude Bernard.

The English word *environment* has passed from the biological to the human in another form, this time by a primarily psychological route, as in William James. We need only recall his *Great Men and Their Environment* (1880); in his *Psychology* (1902), an even more penetrating abridgment of his *Principles of Psychology*, he introduces as a decisive factor in the study of mental events the *physical environment*. The great defect, says James, of the old rational psychology was that it took the soul to be an absolute spiritual entity with certain faculties of its own; today we see that our internal faculties adapt themselves in advance to the characteristics of the world in which we live; mind and world have evolved together.[3] Hence the role of the concept of *adjust-*

---

[1] *Cours de philosophie positive*, III (1838), lesson 40, pp. 295–96.

[2] *Ibid.*, 301.

[3] William James, *Psychology*, chapter 1: "*Mental facts cannot be properly studied apart from the physical environment of which they take cognizance.* The great fault of the older rational psychology was to set up the soul as an absolute spiritual being with certain faculties of its own by which the several activities of remembering, imagining, reasoning, willing, etc., were explained, almost without reference to the peculiarities of the world with which these activities deal. But the richer insight of modern days perceives that our inner faculties are *adapted* in advance to the features of the world in which we dwell, adapted, I mean, so as to secure our safety and prosperity in its midst . . . . Mind and world in short have been evolved together, and in consequence are something of a mutual fit." "On the whole, few recent formulas have done more service in psychology than the Spencerian one that the essence of mental life and bodily life are one, namely, 'the adjustment of inner to outer relations.' "

ment, which comes from Spencer, but which has a long period of development in English-language psychology and sociology.

Finally and especially, *Umwelt*, literally the world around one, or the surrounding world. This concept appears in Husserl (*Ideen*, §§27, 28, and 29), and its meaning is the world, not as an alien physical reality, but the world insofar as it surrounds me; and it is not only a world of things but of values and possessions, a practical world. And when I suspend the natural attitude (*natürliche Einstellung*), or rather, superimpose other particular attitudes, such as arithmetic for example, I obtain "ideal surrounding worlds" (*ideale Umwelten*).[4]

But the term *Umwelt* had been used before in Germany, not by a philosopher but by a biologist who was concerned with philosophy and had been a stimulant for it: Jakob von Uexküll. Uexküll's influence on Ortega has been considerable, and has been expressly stated by the latter on several occasions: "I ought to declare," he has said, "that ever since 1913 these biological meditations have exercised a great influence on me. This influence has not been merely scientific, but heartfelt. I know no suggestions more effective for imposing order, serenity, and optimism on the disarray of the contemporary soul than those of this thinker."[5] And elsewhere[6] he had referred to Uexküll in relation to the idea of the "vital milieu" in biology, including human biology.

In 1909, Uexküll published his book *Umwelt und Innenwelt der Tiere*. In it he introduces a new viewpoint in biological studies; he proposes the substitution of the *anthropocentric* concern for another in which the *animal's* point of view is taken. With this, he says, all that has seemed obvious to us disappears: Nature as a whole, the earth, the heavens, the stars, all the objects which surround us; only those factors remain which exercise influence on the animal, determined by its struc-

---

[4] Husserl's description of the "surrounding world" from the point of view of the natural attitude is extremely shrewd and sharp; the decisive factor, as we shall see, is that his assumptions permit what he calls "disconnection" (*Ausschaltung*); that is, the transition from the natural attitude to the phenomenologically reduced attitude. This possibility, admitted by Husserl, influences the nature of *Umwelt* and makes its being *Welt*, that is, its *worldliness*, and with still greater reason its circumstantiality, problematical.

[5] "Prólogo a *Ideas para una concepción biológica del mundo*, de J. v. Uexküll" (1922). VI, 310.

[6] "Biología y pedagogía. El *Quijote* en la escuela" (1920). *El Espectador*, III. II, 289–91.

tural plan (*Bauplan*); thus, around each animal there arises "a new world, completely different from ours, its *Umwelt*."[7] This perspective is applied by Uexküll to the study of different animal species, the factors of which, as well as the structure of their respective *Umwelten*, he tries to define. Thus, for example, he says: "The world surrounding the *paramecium* is limited to two things: a liquid containing a stimulus and one not containing a stimulus, where the stimulus may be either chemical or mechanical."[8] A general formulation appears later: "The sum of all the stimuli which an animal receives thanks to the structure of its receptors constitutes its *Umwelt*."[9] The *Umwelt* contains prejudicial elements as well as favorable ones (*Schädlichkeiten neben Nützlichkeiten*).[10]

Uexküll's aim had been to introduce into biology a more rigorous and fruitful concept than those of *milieu* or *environment*, in the form in which these appear in Darwinism, and in fact his notion of *Umwelt* was a considerable step forward. But he soon found out that this term was again being used in the old sense of *milieu*: that is, that Uexküll's fine conceptual distinctions were being wiped out, and that under the new expression only the old, crude concept of the "medium" was being retained. To correct this, in his *Ideas for a Biological Conception of the World*, he introduced two paired concepts, *Merkwelt* and *Wirkungswelt*:

"The world which surrounds the sense organs of the Jacobean oyster would, in this case, contain only a single object. This world is entirely the work of the organization of the Jacobean oyster; if its organism were changed, this world would also have to change. Now, since the organi-

[7] J. v. Uexküll, *Umwelt und Innenwelt der Tiere* (Berlin, 1909), 6: "Unsere anthropozentrische Betrachtungsweise muss immer mehr zurücktreten und der Standpunkt des Tieres der allein ausschlaggebende weren.—Damit verschwindet alles, was für uns als selbstverständlich gilt: die ganze Natur, die Erde, der Himmel, die Sterne, ja alle gegenstände, die uns umgeben, und es bleiben nur noch jene Einwirkungen als Weltfaktoren übrig, die dem Bauplan entsprechend auf das Tier einen Einfluss ausüben. Ihre Zahl, ihre Zusammengehörigkeit wird vom Bauplan bestimmt. Ist dieser Zusammenhang des Bauplanes mit den äusseren Faktoren sorgsam erforscht, so ründet sich um jenes Tier eine neue Welt, gänzlich verschieden von der unsrigen, seine *Umwelt*."

[8] "Die Umwelt von Paramaecium beschränkt sich auf zwei Dinge: Flüssigkeit mit Reiz und Flüssigkeit ohne Reiz, wobei der Reiz chemisch oder mechanisch sein kann." *Ibid.*, 47.

[9] "Die Summe aller Reizen, die ein Tier dank der Bauart seiner Rezeptoren empfängt, bildet seine *Umwelt*." *Ibid.*, 55.

[10] *Ibid.*, 119.

zation of all animals is different, it follows that this world varies from animal to animal.

"In order to designate this world, which is the product of the organism, I have attempted to introduce the word *Umwelt*. The word has become naturalized rather quickly, but not the idea. This term is employed nowadays to designate that which immediately surrounds a living being, in the same sense as the word *milieu* was formerly used. Thus it has lost its peculiar meaning.

"It is a totally useless endeavor to try to fight the use of language, nor does the expression 'surrounding world' correspond with sufficient exactitude to the concept attributed to it. Therefore I wish to replace it with the term 'perceptible world,' *Merkwelt*, and to mean by this that there is a special world for each animal, which is composed of distinctive notes gathered by that animal from the external world.

"The perceptible world, *Merkwelt*, which depends only on the sense organs and central nervous system of the animal, is completed by the 'world of effects,' *Wirkungswelt*, which includes those objects to which the animal's eating and moving arrangements are accommodated.

"If we try to include the world of effects and the perceptible world under the name of surrounding world, it can easily be done; but one should realize immediately that no unity results from the two of them together, but that the animal's organism is absolutely necessary, for it is what creates the dependence between these two worlds."[11]

I believe that the strictly biological meaning of this theory of Uexküll's about the "surrounding world" is completed and acquires all of its implications if we keep in mind some of his ideas which I have quoted elsewhere,[12] and which are extremely close to some of those which have acquired the greatest prominence within the philosophy of the last few decades; hence, the following passages, referring to the ideas of *function* and *service* as a condition of vital realities: "Everything which we designate with a certain word—such as, for example, a chair or automobile— is not unequivocally determined by the note of color, hardness, smell, or taste, or by its shape in space, but by its *function*. The chair is an object in which to sit; the automobile, an object in which to be transported from one place to another."[13] "Everywhere we find a human function, to

[11] *Ideas para una concepción biológica del mundo* (Madrid, 1922), 52–53.
[12] Commentary on *Meditaciones del Quijote*, 245–46.
[13] *Ideas para una concepción biológica del mundo*, 55.

which the object gives support with its opposite function. The chair serves to sit in, the staircase to ascend; to move from one place to another, the automobile, etc. We can speak of a chair-being, a stair-being, and an automobile-being without fear of misapprehension, for the service performed by human products is, strictly speaking, what we refer to under the word which designates objects. It is not the shape of the chair, of the automobile, of the house, that is designated by the word, but the service it performs. The significance of the object for our existence lies in its service."[14]

What can we gather from these clarifications of Uexküll's about the concept of *Umwelt*? First of all, we must note that it is a concept which is correlative with another: *Innenwelt*, internal world; this consists of the totality of the effects produced in the nervous system by the factors of the *Umwelt*. In addition to both of these, *Umwelt* and *Innenwelt*, is the *Bauplan*, the structural plan, which controls it all, and whose investigation is for Uexküll the correct and certain basis of biology.[15] The concept of the organism in Uexküll is based upon this, and is different from that of Jennings, for whom "an organism is a complex mass of material, in which certain processes take place; to the aggregate or system of these processes we give the name of life": and the result is that for him "the animal is an event."[16] For Uexküll there are, then, two "worlds," linked by the organism, which in its turn is defined by a structural plan; and the first world (*Umwelt*) appears as split in its turn into the "perceptive" world (*Merkwelt*) and the world of "effects" (*Wirkungswelt*), both resulting from selective operations of the organism, which, therefore, is in no way identified with the *Umwelt*. And *the organism, insofar as it consists in a structural plan, is what is decisive*. Which means in its turn that Uexküll's idea, no matter what its degree of penetration and refinement, is *intrabiological* and has no meaning except within the sphere of study of an organism as such. Any

---

[14] *Ibid.*, 59.

[15] "Ebenso objektiv wie die Faktoren der Umwelt sind, müssen die von ihnen hervorgerufenen Wirkungen im Nervensystem aufgefasst werden. Diese Wirkungen sind ebenfalls durch den Bauplan gesichtet und geregelt. Sie bilden zusammen die *Innenwelt* der Tiere." "Über der Innenwelt und der Umwelt steht der Bauplan, alles beherrschend. Die Erforschung des Bauplanes kann meiner Überzeugung nach allein die gesunde und gesicherte Grundlage der Biologie abgeben." *Umwelt und Innenwelt der Tiere*, 6–7.

[16] *Ibid.*, 30.

attempt to pose the problem in another dimension would oblige us to go beyond his concept of *Umwelt*.

If we now turn our attention to Husserl, we find, on a very different plane, a singularly close analogy. He insists that, in the concept of *Umwelt*, it is not a question of a mere "world of things" (*Sachenwelt*), but, *with the same immediacy*, a world of values, a world of possessions, a practical world (*Wertewelt, Güterwelt, praktische Welt*); close at hand also are things as "objects of use" (*Gebrauchsobjekte*): "table," "books," "glass," "vase," "piano," with their friendly or hostile or serviceable characteristics, etc.[17] On the other hand, each *Umwelt* is "constituted" within an *Einstellung*, an "installation" or "attitude," and both elements are correlative. The arithmetical world, for example, exists for me only when and while I am in the arithmetical *Einstellung*, and what we call the "natural" world also corresponds to what Husserl calls the "natural attitude" or *natürliche Einstellung*, which is precisely the attitude which is modified and altered by the transition to another, and especially can be placed "in parentheses" by means of phenomenological reduction.[18] That is, the selective function of the organism understood as a *Bauplan* or structural plan corresponds to the different *Einstellungen*, and the *Umwelt* is in each case conditioned by those selections or suppositions. The chief difference resides in the singleness of the organism in contrast to the plurality of possible *Einstellungen*, but what really corresponds in Husserl to the idea of organism as *Bauplan* in Uexküll's biology is the great supposition of *consciousness*, within which all the possible *Einstellungen* are constituted. Every *Umwelt* is, therefore, conditioned and in some measure "given" by that general "supposition," be it the organism or the consciousness. To the "intrabiological" quality of the notion of *Umwelt* in Uexküll corresponds the "intraconsciousnessal"—*sit venia verbo*—or merely intentional (if that is a better word), quality in Husserl.[19] We shall see to what extent this is decisive when we compare it with the Orteguian idea of circumstance.

[17] *Ideen zu einer reinen Phänomenologie und phänomenologischen Philosophie*, I. § 27.

[18] *Ibid.*, 28–29.

[19] There are very interesting ideas in book 2 of the *Ideen*, published for the first time in 1952 (Husserliana, Band IV, Martinus Nijhoff, Haag), Zweiter Abschnitt, Erstes Kapitel (p. 97 ff.) and Beilagen VII and X (pp. 318 ff., 321 ff.).

66. THE NOTION OF CIRCUMSTANCE IN ORTEGA

The theory of circumstance appears in Ortega in the *Meditations on Quixote*. The concrete form in which this notion is introduced, and therefore the foreshortening in which it is presented in this decisive context, must be kept in mind. Only thus can we attempt to understand what Ortega is thinking when he uses the term "circumstance"; other previous contexts will confirm for us the trajectory of this idea in his thought—that is, where it came from.

Ortega mentions the *themes* with which the *Meditations* he is about to present are to be concerned: besides the "glorious matters," "the most unimportant things," small manifestations in which the soul of a race is revealed. We must be careful not to confuse the large and the small; that is, we must affirm the *hierarchy* "without which the cosmos returns to chaos"; but, once this is assumed, we must also turn our attention to what is to be found *near* our person. And he at once introduces the concept of circumstance—*circum-stantia*—with the stylistic qualities which I have pointed out before.[20] Ortega thinks that one of the most profound changes in the twentieth century, compared to the preceding one, will be the mutation of "our sensitivity with regard to circumstances." This consideration leads him to sketch out a theory of *perspective* and of *culture*, which we shall examine later. And then he adds: "We must search for our circumstance, precisely in what it possesses of limitation, of peculiarity, the one right place *in the immense perspective of the world*. We should not remain in perpetual ecstasy in the presence of hieratic values, but gain for our individual life the proper place among them. In short: *the reabsorption of the circumstance is the concrete destiny of man*." And he continues: "My natural outlet *toward the Universe* opens out over the Guadarrama passes or the countryside around Ontígola. This sector of circumstantial reality *forms the other half of my person*; only by means of it can I become integrated and be fully myself."[21]

It is only now that a marginal reference to biology appears, evidently an allusion to Uexküll: "The most recent biological science studies the living organism as a unit composed of the body and its particular medium: so that the vital process does not consist only in an adaptation

---

[20] *Meditaciones del Quijote*, I, 318–19. (See note 74, chapter 2, part 2 of this book.)
[21] *Meditaciones del Quijote*. I, 322. Italics mine.

of the body to its medium, but also in the adaptation of the medium to its body. The hand tries to form itself to the material object in order to grasp it firmly: but, at the same time, each material object conceals a previous affinity with a particular hand."[22] This is all: there are no more biological references in the theory of circumstance; it is simply an illustration, a confirmation of his point of view by means of a focus *analogous* to that of the biologists; and this consideration is marginal to the point that the only example he adduces is human. Still clearer is the way in which the most important formula of all is introduced: "I am I and my circumstance, and if I do not save it, I do not save myself. *Benefac loco illi quo natus es*, we read in the Bible. And in the Platonic school the task of all culture is given to us as follows: to 'save the appearances,' the phenomena. That is, to seek the meaning of that which surrounds us. Having prepared our eyes by gazing at the map of the world, we must return them to the Guadarramas. Perhaps we find nothing profound. But let us be certain that the defect, and the sterility, come from our own gaze. There is also a *lógos* of the Manzanares River . . . ."[23] The Bible, Plato, meaning, the *lógos*—where is biology? The local references are geographical proper names—that is, a *historical landscape*; it is not the biological function of river water, but the *lógos* of the Manzanares. Nor is it only what is close by, but the fact that it is a question of locating oneself *circumstantially* in the *immense perspective of the world*, and one must go from the map of the world to the Guadarramas.

Lastly, the meaning of what Ortega calls circumstance is clarified by keeping in mind another text in the same book: the circumstance cannot be understood only in a geographical, or a physical, or an organic, way. Ortega writes: "The external world! But, are not the worlds which are not of the senses—the deep lands—also external to the subject? Undoubtedly: they are external, and are so to an eminent degree."[24] The circumstance includes the external world and the *internal* one, all that which is *external* to the subject—not to his body alone; consequently, all that which is not *I*, all that which I find around myself, *circum me*. What is not of the senses, the world we call "internal," is external to the second "I" in the expression "I am I and my circumstance"; therefore it forms part of this circumstance, and it can only be said that it forms part of myself in the sense of the first "I," the one which designates my whole personal reality. The circumstance—he had said earlier—*forms*

[22] *Ibid.*, 322. [23] *Ibid.* [24] *Ibid.*, 349.

the other half of my person; this person is that designated by the first *I*, of which the *subject "I"*—the second one—is only a dynamic ingredient, and totally opposed. This notion of circumstance cannot be reduced to the notion of *Umwelt*, either in Husserl's intentional sense or in Uexküll's biological sense.

On the other hand we must note that the meaning of *circumstance* is not sufficiently determined so long as we are not clear about the basic meaning of the *I*; only in this way can we understand the ultimate character of *human life*; Ortega does not give us details in this context, and it has been possible to believe that they are not there; we shall see that this is not the case, and that such details are present in this book as well as in other writings which belong to the same "level." As for the rest, the thesis "I am I and my circumstance and *if I do not save it, I do not save myself*" contains the *philosophical* reason why Ortega treats Spain thematically, and in addition the justification for patriotism in general.

The significance of the Orteguian idea of circumstance becomes still more clear if we glance at its *prehistory*. Strictly speaking, its history begins, metaphorically, in the passages in "Adam in Paradise" which we analyzed before. But the trajectory which leads Ortega to the plenitude of this idea illumines its meaning. It is not a question of biological motifs. In an article written in 1908, in fact, he rejects the use of the biological to understand the human, and does so precisely with regard to the idea of "medium": "The spontaneous! . . . that is, unless I misunderstand it, the ultimate innerness of character, *the immediate reaction of the I to the influences of the medium* in order to establish vital equilibrium . . . . *No organic realities . . . . To use biological similes when referring to moral entities is something completely discredited . . . .*"[25] When the natural reality appears, it presents itself in a strictly human form—that is, under the guise of a *landscape* and not a medium; speaking of a possible "pedagogy of landscape," Ortega wrote in 1906: "Landscapes have created half my soul for me, and if I had not lost long years living in the gloominess of the cities, I would be a better man now, and a more profound one. Tell me the landscape in which you live, and I will tell you who you are."[26]

The intuition of circumstance appears even more clearly in a passage

---

[25] "Pidiendo una biblioteca". I, 84. Italics mine.
[26] "Moralejas. III. La pedagogía del paisaje." I, 35.

written in 1909, where the idea of landscape is associated, in its most profound form as stage setting, with the theme of perspective and interpretations, which constituted the doctrinal nucleus of "Adam in Paradise" and which is mingled with the expression of the idea of circumstance itself in the *Meditations on Quixote*—I have omitted it only for reasons of simplification, with the intention of combining the two dimensions later on. Speaking of centaurs—a theme which lasts throughout Ortega's life and which always produced an extraordinary intellectual and literary excitement in him—he writes, "What sort of world did Father Chiron conceive of, as he galloped over the emerald meadows? A world of human visions belonged to his human torso; an equine universe to his horse's loins. The nerves of man and steed were joined at their very centers, and the robust veins poured into a single heart the theology of the European and the neigh of the stallion. Poor heart, always vacillating between a filly and a Bacchante! What was truth for one half of him was not true for the other half; if he went into a city and came to the public square, his lips must have formed the words, 'This is the agora,' while his hooves beat out the message, 'This is a racecourse.' "[27]

And finally, in a text of 1911 in which he speaks about the orator, always the man who takes care to inform himself about the circumstances, he gives for the first time a direct idea of circumstances; I mean, using that very word: "What are *circumstances*? Are they merely these hundred persons, these fifty minutes, this unimportant question? *Every circumstance is contained within another, broader one*; why believe that ten meters of space is all that surrounds me? And the meters that surround those ten meters? A serious oversight, a miserable stupidity, to deal only with a few circumstances, when *in truth everything is around us*! I am not in sympathy with the madman and the mystic: the man who arouses all my enthusiasm is *the man who takes the circumstances into account, so long as he does not forget any of them.*[28] *Everything surrounds us*; everything which is not myself presents itself to me as circumstance; and what man has to do in the face of this is to *deal with it*. In this brief paragraph we find the clearest antecedent for the doctrine which, announced as early as "Adam in Paradise," is strictly formulated in the *Meditations on Quixote*.

[27] "Renan." I, 446.
[28] "Vejamen del orador." I, 557.

The idea of circumstance in Ortega does not come from biology, and consequently not from Uexküll; previous to his possible influence, and also to that of Husserl, it cannot be reduced to the thought of either; the vital and intellectual context in which it appears shows that it arises from other areas. Uexküll's influence, to which Ortega refers in no uncertain terms, is not the "source" of the idea of circumstance, but a lateral stimulus which confirms the original intuition and completes its later conceptual development.

67. THE RADICAL MEANING OF CIRCUMSTANCE AND THE PROBLEM OF THE WORLD

If we compare the two terms "circumstance" and "Umwelt," we will find a very important difference: the first is merely *functional and not interpretive*; the second includes what we might call its *worldly* interpretation. *Um-welt is "the world around"* or the *"surrounding world"*; circumstance (*circum-stantia*) in the singular, with the value of a neuter plural, is "What is around"—no matter what that may be. That *what is around us is the world*, is something that goes beyond the strict evidence: this evidence reduces itself to something more limited: *that the world is around us*. I mean that the identification of "what is around us" with "the world" is not allowable, for it leaves out possible realities which, even though they are "intraworldly," are not "world," as well as those others which may be "extraworldly."

In the case of Uexküll we saw how an *Innenwelt* was contrasted to the *Umwelt*, an internal world to the surrounding world; that is, it could not even be said that the *Umwelt* was the "world of the animal," for the animal has another, internal, world. What is the link between the two, or, if you prefer, in what does the "worldlike" quality of both reside? It is the organism which makes both be "worlds," and, precisely, the "worlds of that animal." In Ortega, on the other hand, *the human organism is an ingredient of the circumstance*, and only in a derived sense and *cum grano salis* could it be said of that organism that it is a "world." The "internal worlds" in the sense that this expression has when it is used with regard to man, the worlds "not of the senses," are also "circumstance"; they are external to the subject, which, naturally, is not the organism.

As for Husserl, a single consideration suffices: the *Ich-Umwelt* (I-world around) contrast is merely intentional and not real; the proof of this lies in the fact that Husserl admits the possibility of "*Einklamme-rung*" or "*Ausschaltung*," of the "putting in quotation marks" or "disconnection" in which the *epokhé* or phenomenological reduction consists, and which affects equally the I and its *Umwelt*, so that both are disconnected or *ausgeschaltet*, and succumb equally to the *epokhé*. And the result of this reduction is *pure or transcendental consciousness* (*reines oder transzendentales Bewusstsein*), as a "phenomenological residue" (*phänomenologisches Residuum*) which includes along with the "pure I"—phenomenologically reduced—its life experiences and their designed objects.[29]

Circumstance is none of these things, for its character is strictly *real* and not merely intentional; it consists of the totality of that which I find around me and with which I have to cope, no matter what it may be, whether it is "world" or not, and which is in principle and absolutely *irreducible* to myself, but without which I do not exist. And this radical interdependence makes a sufficient determination of the circumstance impossible, so long as the problem of the reality of the I is not posed;[30] in Ortega the I cannot be exhausted in being a mere "subject of intentional life experiences." Therefore a basic clarification of the question will be possible only from a more radical point of view than that of these two terms, "I" and "circumstance"; and this is precisely the explanation of the true meaning of the *Meditations on Quixote*'s central thesis—which presupposes, let it be said in passing, the invalidation of the assumption of phenomenology—*I am I and my circumstance.*

[29] *Ideen*, §§ 31–33.

[30] After this was written, my friend Pedro Laín Entralgo showed me this curious text by Münsterberg: "Das Wirkliche ist jederzeit Gegenglied und Zentralglied zugleich. Ich und Umgebung bilden eine unauflösliche Koordination in dem thatsächlich Vorgefundenen. Die Frage ensteht, was das Ich sei." (*Grundzüge der Psychologie* [Leipzig, 1900] I, 22.) Ortega's thesis consists in going beyond this "co-ordination" and answering the question of "what the I is" by making it go back to another question of a different type, a more radical one—What am *I*?—and answering, "*I* am I and my circumstance."

On the meaning of the opposition between *Individuum* and *Umgebung* in the theory of pure experience (*Empiriokritizismus*)of R. Avenarius (1843–96), see Überweg, IV, 390 (1951).

III.

THE IDEA OF PERSPECTIVE

68. THE PHILOSOPHICAL TRADITION

The concept of *circumstance* in Ortega is linked with that of *perspective*. This union is essential; I mean that to take them in an isolated manner has caused these concepts to be quite sterile in the philosophies—and these are very few—in which they have appeared. The idea of circumstance demands, in some measure, the presence of perspective, even though there is an attempt to avoid it. The selective character of Uexküll's *Bauplan* establishes, to be sure, a certain "point of view" in the constitution of the *Umwelt*. In Husserl the *Einstellungen* represent an analogous function, but these are, so to say, "consecutive" to the *Ich-Umwelt* duality, and are superadded to that original design. But, above all, *the notion of perspective has not been taken circumstantially*, but rather the opposite; it has usually functioned as a means of evasion of circumstantiality. When Ortega, however, says, "We must seek for our *circumstance* . . . the one right place in the immense *perspective* of the world," he introduces a new concept, different from the modest previous philosophical tradition. What is this previous tradition?

The classic antecedent is Leibniz. In the piece of writing in which Ortega introduces the idea of perspective *as a theme*[1]—the idea had been utilized very profoundly many times by that date—he quotes the passage from *Monadology* in which Leibniz's notion appears most clearly: "Et comme une même ville regardée de différents côtés paraît tout autre et comme multipliée perspectivement, il arrive de même que, par la multitude infinie des substances simples, il y a comme autant de différents univers, qui ne sont pourtant que les perspectives d'un seul selon les différents points de vue de chaque monade."[2] Some previous

---

[1] "Verdad y perspectiva" (1916). *El Espectador*, I. II, 18.
[2] *Monadologie*, 57.

texts throw more light on the meaning of this doctrine in Leibniz. It is an important idea for him that bodies and their appendages are "well-founded phenomena" or "the foundation of appearances." "Tous les corps et tout ce qu'on leur attribue . . . sont seulement *des phénomènes bien fondés, ou le fondement* des apparences, qui sont différentes en différents observateurs, mais qui ont du rapport et viennent d'un même fondement, comme les apparences différentes d'une même ville vue de plusieurs côtés."[3] The image also appears in Leibniz's notes on the article *Rorarius* in Bayle's Dictionary: "Enfin lorsqu'on dit, que chaque monade Âme, Esprit a reçu une loi particulière, il faut ajouter, qu'elle n'est qu'une variation de la loi générale qui règle l'univers; et que c'est comme une même ville paraît différente selon les différents points de vue dont on la regarde."[4]

The idea of perspective also appears in a different context: in that passage of the *Théodicée* in which Leibniz tries to explain "apparent disorder" in what has reference to man. God has given him, along with intelligence, an image of divinity. God allows men to operate within their "little compartment," and enters it only in a concealed way, "car il fournit être, force, vie, raison, sans se faire voir." Hence free will "plays its part," controlled by God, Who behaves in respect to those "little gods He has been pleased to produce" as we behave toward children. "L'homme y est donc comme un petit dieu dans son propre monde, ou Microcosme"; he does marvels, or makes great mistakes, and man, when he errs, "s'en trouve mal"; but God changes all the defects of the little worlds into a greater adornment of His great world. "C'est comme dans ces inventions de perspective, où certains beaux dessins ne paraissent que confusion, jusqu'à ce qu'on les rapporte à leur vrai point de vue, ou qu'on les regarde par le moyen d'un certain verre ou miroir."[5]

In a note added by Ortega to his quotation from the first passage from Leibniz, he adds two more references and a warning that the sense in which he speaks of perspective is very different: "Since in these volumes we shall have to speak very frequently of *perspectivism*, I think that it is important to state that this doctrine has nothing in common with the

---

[3] Gerhardt, III, 622. Quoted by E. Cassirer in *Leibniz' System in seinen wissenschaftlichen Grundlagen* (1902), 369.

[4] Gerhardt, IV, 553.

[5] *Théodicée*, 147.

one Nietzsche has propounded, under the same name, in his posthumous work *The Will to Power*, or with the one which Vaihinger has sustained, following Nietzsche, in his recent book *The Philosophy of the As If*. Moreover: whatever references there are to monadological idealism in the paragraph I have quoted from Leibniz should be discounted."[6] What are these contemporary doctrines? Are they the only ones? On what points does Ortega's doctrine depart from them? Let us try to find out.

Perspectivism—under that name—had appeared, or reappeared if you like, in the next-to-last decade of the nineteenth century, around 1880. In Nietzsche's work, first in *Die fröhliche Wissenschraft* (1881–82, second edition 1886); then, more thematically, in the posthumous writings published under the title *Der Wille zur Macht*.[7] Nietzsche's central idea is very different from that advanced by Leibnizian perspectivism: consciousness, for him, does not properly belong to man's individual existence, but rather to what is communal and gregarious nature in him ("Mein Gedanke ist, wie man sieht: dass das Bewusstsein nich eigentlich zur Individuell-Existenz des Menschen gehört, vielmehr zu dem, was an ihm—Gemeinschafts- und Herden-Natur ist");[8] our actions are, at bottom, personal, unique, limitlessly individual, in a manner which is incomparable; but "as soon as we transfer them to consciousness, *they no longer seem so . . . .* This is the authentic phenomenalism and perspectivism, as I understand it: the nature of *animal consciousness* carries with it the fact that the world of which we can be conscious is only a world of surfaces and signs, a generalized, vulgarized world." ("Unser Handlungen sind im Grunde allesamt auf

---

[6] II, 18.

[7] In the octavo edition of Complete Works (*Gesamtausgabe in Grossoktav*), Leipzig, 1894ff., C. G. Naumann and then Alfred Kröner, in volumes XV and XVI (1911). In that edition the title of these texts was *Der Wille zur Macht, Versuch einer Umwerthung aller Werthe*. Karl Schlechta has recently demonstrated that the order in which these fragments have been arranged, their presentation, and even the title of the presumed "collection" are very doubtful, owing to manipulations which may alter their meaning. See his book *Der Fall Nietzsche* (Munich, 1958). In his excellent edition: Friedrich Nietzsche, *Werke in drei Bänden* (Munich 1954–56), Schlechta has published all these writings under the title *Aus dem Nachlass der Achtzigerjahre* (vol. III, pp. 415–925), in the order indicated by the chronology of the manuscripts. In my notes here, I refer to this edition.

[8] *Die fröhliche Wissenschaft* ("La gaya scienza"), 5. Buch, 354. (Schlechta's ed., II, 221.)

eine unvergleichliche Weise persönlich, einzig, unbegrenzt-individuell, es ist kein Zweifel; aber sobald wir sie ins Bewusstsein übersetzen, *scheinen sie es nicht mehr* ... Dies ist der eigentliche Phänomenalismus und Perspektivismus, wie *ich* ihn verstehe: die Natur des *tierischen Bewusstseins* bringt es mit sich, dass die Welt, deren wir bewusst werden können, nur eine Oberflächen- und Zeichenwelt ist, eine verallgemein-erte, eine vergemeinerte Welt.")[9]

In the posthumous writings, the theme of perspective appears in a rather different form, in relation to *truth* and knowledge. This *per-spective world (perspectivische Welt)*, says Nietzsche, this world for the eye, the taste, and the ear, is very deceptive when it is compared with a much finer sensorial apparatus. But its characteristics of compre-hensibility, inclusiveness to the sight, practicability, and beauty begin to cease when we refine our senses; the order of finality is an illusion. The more superficial and coarse one considers the world to be, *the more valuable it appears*, the more precise, beautiful, and full of significance; the more deeply we consider it, the more our esteem for it disappears, *the lack of significance draws nearer. We*—exclaims Nietzsche—have created the world which has value; and therefore, *veneration for truth is the result of an illusion.* Everything is false! Everything is per-mitted! And he concludes, "Only with a certain dullness of vision, with a desire for simplicity, can we constitute 'the beautiful,' the 'worthwhile': in themselves they are *I know not what*."[10]

Knowledge is understood from the point of view of vital usefulness—almost always understood biologically—and this is the reason why his

---

[9] *Ibid.*

[10] "Diese perspektivische Welt, diese Welt für das Auge, Getast und Ohr ist sehr falsch, verglichen schon für einen sehr viel feineren Sinnenapparat. Aber ihre Verständ-lichkeit, Übersichtlichkeit, ihre Praktikabilität, ihre Schönheit beginnt *aufzuhören,* wenn wir unser Sinne *verfeinen:* ebenso hört die Schönheit auf beim Durchdenken von Vorgängen der Geschichte; die Ordnung des *Zwecks* ist schon eine Illusion. Genug, je oberflächlicher und gröber zusammenfassend, um so *wertvoller,* bestimmter, schöner, bedeutungsvoller *erscheint* die Welt. Je tiefer man hineinsieht, um so mehr verschwindet unsere Wertschätzung—*die Bedeutungslosigkeit naht sich! Wir* haben die Welt, welche Wert hat, geschaffen! Dies erkennend, erkennen wir auch, dass die Verehrung der Wahrheit schon die *Folge* einer *Illusion* ist—und dass man, mehr als sie, die bildende, vereinfachende, gestaltende, erdichtende Kraft zu schätzen hat.

"Alles ist falsch! Alles ist erlaubt!

"Erst bei einer gewissen Stumpfheit des Blickes, einem Willen zur Einfachheit stellt sich das Schöne, das 'Wertvolle' ein: an sich ist es *ich weiss nicht was.*" (*Aus dem Nachlass der Achtzigerjahre,* Schlecta's ed., III, 424.)

perspectivism tends toward the *annulment of the difference between truth and error*, wanting to go *jenseits von Wahr und Falsch*. For Nietzsche truth is the *type of error* without which a certain species of living beings could not live. Value for life decides, in the last instance. And something still more serious: "There are many eyes. The Sphinx also has eyes: and consequently there are many types of 'truths,' and consequently there is no truth."[11] The opposition between the true and the apparent world ("die wahre und die scheinbare Welt") is reduced by Nietzsche to value relationships (*Wertverhältnisse*). "We have projected," he adds, "*our* conditions for preservation as *predicates of being in general*." Out of our need to be stable in our belief in order to prosper, we have caused the "real" world not to be a world of change and becoming (*keine wandelbare und werdende*), but a world "that is," "ens" (*seiende*).

Nietzsche's ideas on perspectivism appear later in Hans Vaihinger's famous book, quoted by Ortega, *Die Philosophie des Als Ob*, which takes up the question precisely in the context of the ideas of fiction, illusion, and deception, and adduces other passages from Nietzsche.[12] We shall see how, in fact, all this has very little to do with the idea of perspective as Ortega understands it. But first, we shall have to consider the "perspectivism" of another nineteenth-century philosopher in whom the theme acquires much larger implications: Teichmüller.

Gustav Teichmüller (1832–88), a thinker whose interest is much greater than his present fame would seem to indicate, a disciple of Trendelenburg and Lotze, a professor at Basel and then at Dorpat, in Estonia—which resulted in his influence on Russian philosophy at the end of the last century—belongs to the intermediate group between his teachers and the neo-Kantians, to which Ortega has referred with great interest. Teichmüller, a man of vast knowledge, full of felicitous and penetrating intuitions, published his most important book in 1882: *Die wirkliche und die scheinbare Welt. Neue Grundlegung der Metaphysik*. Modifying the division of philosophical systems which Trendelenburg had proposed, he considers three directions: so-called *materialism*, "de-

---

11 "*Wahrheit ist die Art von Irrtum*, ohne welche eine bestimmte Art von lebendigen Wesen nicht leben könnte. Der Wert für das *Leben* entscheidet zuletzt.

"Est gibt vielerlei Augen. Auch die Sphinx hat Augen—: und folglich gibt es vielerlei 'Wahrheiten,' und folglich gibt es keine Wahrheit." *Ibid.*, 844.

12 *Die Philosophie des Als Ob* (1911) (4th ed., 1920), 780 ff.

mocritism" and empiricism; so-called *idealism*; and, finally, so-called *monism*, which he sometimes calls Spinozism.[13] "All these systems are *projective* representations of the content of our knowledge and, as knowledge is necessarily related to the point of view—literally, the 'ocular point,' *Augenpunkt*—of the subject, merely *perspective* images." And this leads him to deny that existence and the substantial being (*das Existiren und das substanziale Sein*) can be found in any of those systems, and to contrast these ideal perspective images of the world to the *subject*, which is found in the "ocular point," and only by means of a fiction is it "overturned" and projected upon the surface of images. For Teichmüller this subject is "the substance sought in vain in its ideal objective content." "The shadings of the different systems, and also all their so-called oppositions of principle, disappear, therefore, in the face of this new point of view, after which all of them can only have value as perspective images."[14] What Kant calls the "dogmatism" of certain philosophical positions which he censured, he would have done well to call "perspectivism," for those doctrines produce only *bloss perspectivische Weltbilder*, merely perspective images of the world.[15]

Teichmüller makes constant use of the idea of perspective or point of view. He speaks of "intuition or perspective image" (*Anschauung oder perspectivisches Bild*); he shows that the idea of diversity or distinction is not of the senses, but is a point of view (*die Idee der Verschiedenheit*

[13] G. Teichmüller, *Die wirkliche und die scheinbare Welt*, xv–xvi.

[14] "Deshalb sind alle diese Systeme *projectivische* Darstellungen unseres Erkenntnissinhaltes und, da die Erkenntniss notwendig auf den Augenpunkt des Subjects bezogen ist, bloss *perspectivische Bilder*. Da nun in der ganzen erkennenden Thätigkeit, sowohl in den sinnlichen Anschauungen, als in den sogenannten Ideen und Principien, nur unser Erkenntnissgehalt gegeben ist, der nur ein ideelles Sein als Erkenntnissinhalt hat, so leugne ich, dass von und in irgend einem dieser Systeme das Existiren und das substanziale Sein gefunden werden könne, und setze diesen ideellen, perspectivischen Bildern der Welt das Subject entgegen, welches sich im Augenpunkte befindet und nur durch eine Fiction 'umgeklappt' und mit auf die Bildfläche geworfen wurde. Dies Subject ist die vergeblich in seinem objectiven ideellen Inhalt gesuchte Substanz. Die Nüancen der verschiedenen Systeme und ebenso alle ihr sogenannten principiellen Gegensätze verschwinden daher für diesen neuen Standpunkt, von welchem aus sie alle nur für perspectivische Bilder gelten können." *Ibid.*, xvi–xvii.

[15] "Die Lehren, welche Kant als 'Dogmatismus' und als die Erkenntnisskräfte überschreitend tadelt, überschreiten zwar nicht die Erkenntnisskräfte, projiciren aber die metaphysischen Begriffe nach Aussen und erzeugen bloss perspectivische Weltbilder, und wenn Kant statt '*dogmatisch*,' was er freilich von seinem Standpunkte aus nicht konnte, 'perspectivisch' gesagt hätte, so würden wir bei ihm schon auf festem Boden stehen." *Ibid.*, xviii.

aber ist nichts Sinnliches, sondern ein Gesichtspunkt).[16] But we must not lose sight of the function which this represents within his thought. The "so-called external world," he says, is properly the content of our consciousness itself (*der Inhalt unseres Bewusstseins selbst*), and therefore it does not matter whether one says that the I projects this world outward or extracts the I from that world.[17] The world, as it appears to our eyes, is always and everywhere ordered *perspectively*, and neither the microscope nor the telescope can show us the order of relationships that we take to be true. Reality is determined only by thought, and this same concept of reality (*Wirklichkeit*), in opposition to appearance (*Schein*), does not pertain to the senses, but only to thought.[18] That is, perspective always appears in Teichmüller as *mere* perspective, as perspective *only*,[19] as *appearance opposed to reality*.

The conclusion could not be clearer. For Teichmüller, idealism, materialism, and Spinozism are on the same line or series; all of their *Weltanschauungen* are *perspectives*, since they only introduce us into the image of the world as it appears in this or that manner (*so oder so*) from our point of view. All that image of the world is only *ideal being*, as the content of our cognitive activity for the point of view "turns over" and projects upon the surface of the object, and thus we find ourselves in an *apparent* world, as though we were contemplating the world simply in a mirror, and beyond the objects we see there, including our own reflected image, as though we were to forget ourselves completely as a real person, who looks out from the mirror and lives there.[20] The

---

[16] *Ibid.*, 19–20.

[17] "Denn da die sogenannte Aussenwelt eigentlich der Inhalt unseres Bewusstseins selbst ist, so ist es ganz einerlei, zu sagen, das Ich projicire diese Welt nach Aussen hin, oder es ziehe sich das Ich von dieser Welt zurück." *Ibid.*, 131.

[18] "Die Welt, wie sie für das Auge erscheint, ist immer und überall perspectivisch geordnet und weder Mikroscop noch Teleskop kann uns die Ordnung der Verhaltnisse zeigen, welche wir für de wirkliche halten. Die Wirklichkeit wird also nur durch das Denken festgestellt, wie ja schon dieser Begriff der Wirklichkeit im Gegensatz zum Schein nicht der Sinnlichkeit, sondern dem Denken angehört." *Ibid.*, 183.

[19] *Ibid.*, 333.

[20] "Wir stellen deshalb den Idealismus mit dem Materialismus und Spinozismus in eine Reihe und erklären alle diese Weltanschauungen für *perspectivisch*, weil sie uns in das Weltbild, wie es uns von unserem Standpunkte so oder so erscheint, aufgehen lassen. Dies ganze Weltbild hat aber, wie wir nach den obigen Untersuchungen wissen, nur *ideelles Sein*, als Inhalt unserer erkennenden Thätigkeit, in welcher das Subject verschwunden ist, da der Gesichtspunkt, wie man in der Perspective sagt, 'umgeklappt' und mit auf die Fläche des Objects geworfen wird. Mithin befinden wir uns dabei in

real world, on the contrary, the one Teichmüller is inquiring into "in order to put an end to the enchantment," (*um dem Zauber ein Ende zu machen*) is something different. As soon as we ask ourselves this sober question, "all the spectral perspectivist world immediately disappears, and we return to ourselves and awake as from an anguished dream." And that real world is "our I, our substantial being" (*Unser ich, unser substanziales Sein*), for "there is no other source for the concept of a substance except the I," and only by analogy with the I do we rightfully accept other entities. Then, and only then, illusion disappears, and thus we again find ourselves in the *real* world. "Thought which is deceived by the perspectivist conception now separates the real world from the apparent one, and achieves a firm basis of its deception and is able to give an account of its knowledge."[21]

This was the state of the question, if we analyze the texts and do not rely on hearsay, when Ortega introduced the notion of *perspective* into his system. And now we shall have to ask ourselves what meaning this idea has in Ortega's thought.

69. ORTEGA'S NOTION OF PERSPECTIVE

We have already seen that the idea of "point of view" appears in Ortega in 1910, in "Adam in Paradise." There, it is linked to the notions of

einer *scheinbaren* Welt, wie wenn wir die Welt bloss im Spiegel betrachteten und über den dort geschauten Objecten, unser eigenes Spiegelbild eingeschlossen, uns als wirkliche Person, die da schaut und lebt, ganz vergässen." *Ibid.*, 346.

[21] "Wir fragen daher jetzt, um dem Zauber ein Ende zu machen, woher denn eigentlich *die Dingheit selbst* stammt, die wir den ideellen (materialen oder idealen) Objecten zuschreiben, ohne sie doch bei genauerer Analyse darin finden zu können. Kaum aber stellen wir diese nüchterne Frage, so verschwindet sofort die ganze perspectivische Gespensterwelt und wir kommen wie aus einem ängstlichem Traum wieder zu uns und wachen. Wir sehen dann, dass es unser Ich, unser substanziales Sein ist, das uns bestbekannte, sichere und unveräusserliche, dessen Bild wir im Spiegel der Objecte erblickten. Denn es gibt, wie oben nachgewiesen, gar keine andere Quelle für den Begriff einer Substanz als das Ich. Nach der Analogie mit dem Ich nehmen wir mit Recht andere Wesen ausser uns an . . . . Idem wir diesen Zusammenhang erkennen, verschwindet die Illusion, und damit zugleich befinden wir uns wieder in der *wirklichen* Welt und werden uns unseres Wollens, Thuns und Denkens bewusst. Das durch perspectivisch Auffassung getäuschte Denken scheidet nun die wirkliche von der scheinbaren Welt und kommt zu einer festen Gewissheit und zu einer sicheren Ruhe, weil es den Grund seiner Täuschung erkennt und von seiner Erkenntnis Rechenschaft zu geben weiss." *Ibid.*, 346–47.

PART THREE: *Terra Firma*

"supposition" or "system of valuation" in the sense of what he was later to call "interpretations." I mean that the notion of "point of view" does not have an immediate meaning, *of the senses*, limited to perception. Rather, the opposite: "Seeing and touching things are nothing, in the end, but ways of thinking them";[22] that is, perception is referred to "thinking" in a broad sense, which includes all manner of interpretations. But this is not the most important thing; rather it is the relationship between point of view and reality. According to the different systems of valuation—says Ortega, using an inexact expression—one has "an equal number of different things instead of a single one," and the decisive result is formulated without attenuations: "And so this supposed immutable and single reality with which we can compare the contents of artistic works does not exist: there are as many realities as there are points of view. The point of view creates the panorama."[23] This last expression, apparently so bold, is, if we examine it carefully, a tautology: the vision is included in the *pan-orama*; there is no panorama without it, and therefore none without a point of view. One could only object to the verb "to create," which could make us think of an idealist attitude; but there is no such attitude: Ortega *starts off with things*: "Take any thing whatsoever, apply to it different systems of valuation. . . ." That is, the point of view creates the panorama *as such*, its condition of being such a panorama, which without a point of view could have no reality.

But all this is, once more, prehistory. The notion of perspective appears formally, using this precise term, in the *Meditations on Quixote*. The first text is as follows: "When will we become open to the conviction that the definitive being of the world is neither matter nor soul, that it is not any particular thing, but a perspective? God is the perspective and the hierarchy: Satan's sin was an error of perspective. Well then, the perspective becomes perfected through the multiplication of its terms and the exactness with which we react in the presence of each of its hierarchical ranks."[24]

With this paragraph alone, Ortega turns his back on the idea of perspective introduced into contemporary philosophy by Nietzsche, Vaihinger, and Teichmüller, and poses the question in a different,

[22] "Adán en el Paraíso." I, 471.
[23] *Ibid.*
[24] *Meditaciones del Quijote*, I, 321–22.

almost an opposite, form. For the first thing he says about perspective is that the definitive *being* of the world consists in it; that is, the first attribution of perspective is not to *knowledge* or any of its aspects, but to *the real*. Nor does he say that matter and soul are not real; rather, that the *definitive* being of the world does not consist in them, because this is not "any particular thing." This places us very far from any subjectivism, from any reduction of the real and the subject who observes it: from any "phenomenalism," from any projection of the subject and its point of view. In fact, the opposite is being deal with: a reality with a rigorous structure of its own, to which one must hold in order to attain the truth. Perspective is made perfect by the multiplication of its terms and the exactness with which we react to each of its hierarchical ranks; that is, there is a structure of the real, which only presents itself perspectively, which needs to be integrated from multiple terms or points of view, and which demands *exactness* in our reaction. And when he adds that "God is the perspective and the hierarchy; Satan's sin was an error of perspective," he takes the attitude contrary to Nietzsche's when he attempted to place himself *jenseits von Wahr und Falsch*. Every time that a particular point of view is built into an absolute one, instead of placing it in its proper place within the total perspective, an error is committed which consists in usurping God's point of view—if the expression can be permitted—which is precisely the infinitude of all possible points of view, the hierarchical integration of all perspectives. This is why I often say that all claims to "absolutism of the intellect," to the affirmation of a particular system to the exclusion of all the rest, are forms of "Satanism," no matter how innocuous and even pious the intention may be.

Whereas in Nietzsche or Teichmüller perspective is contrasted to reality and means appearance, convention, illusion which vanishes when the perspectivist vision is suppressed, *in Ortega perspective is the condition of the real and the possibility of access to its truth*. Falsity consists in evading the perspective, in being unfaithful to it, or in making a *particular* point of view absolute; that is, *forgetting the perspective quality of every vision*. Or, expressed in other words, the need for each perspective to be integrated with others, for perspective means *one among various possible perspectives*, and a single perspective is a contradiction.

The problem is posed with even greater clarity in the initial essay in

El Espectador, "Verdad y perspectiva" ["Truth and Perspective"], in 1916. This is a particularly interesting piece of writing; in it, Ortega tries to justify the title he has chosen for that publication, and therefore the relationships between theory and reality, between life and the contemplation of life. Therefore he must introduce *directly* the notion of truth, which is the central theme of the essay: veracity, the obligation of truth, the right of truth, which must be reaffirmed, and with it the mission of contemplative men, the *philotheámones* or friends of gazing, the speculatives, the theorizers, the philosophers. Not that the theoretical attitude is the highest one. "The only thing which I affirm," says Ortega, "is that from time to time theory must open her clear eyes upon spontaneous life, and that then, when theory is formed, it should be formed with all purity, with all tragedy." *El Espectador* "speculates, looks—but what he wishes to see is life as it flows before him."[25]

The theme of perspective arises in this context. That is, out of the claim to the maximum demands of truth; perspective is precisely the concept which is going to permit Ortega to make sure that truth is not going to escape him, contrary to the philosophical positions which used perspectivism to evade the truth. "Theory was justly criticized as drab, for it concerned itself only with vague, remote, and schematic problems. The history of the science of knowledge shows us that *logic, oscillating between skepticism and dogmatism, has usually started off from this erroneous belief: that the point of view of the individual is false.* The two contrasting positions stemmed from this: thus it could be held that *there is no other point of view than the individual one, therefore truth does not exist—skepticism*; thus it could be held *that truth exists, therefore one must take a supraindividual viewpoint—rationalism.*"[26] Ortega denies both opinions, or theses, because he does not accept their *assumption*; but we shall very soon see that his not accepting their assumption does not consist in "denying" it either, but in understanding it in a different way; that is, that in his turn he is going to go underneath this assumption in order to discover his own assumptions, and to show that they are neither valid nor adequate. *El Espectador* will try to separate himself from both solutions equally, for he disagrees with the opinion which gives rise to them. The individual point of view seems to me to be the only point of view from which one can look at the

[25] II, 17–18.
[26] II, 18. Italics mine.

world in its truth. Anything else is a trick."[27] And, after bringing in the quotation from Leibniz mentioned above, he adds, *"Reality, precisely because it is reality* and because it is outside our individual minds, can only reach these minds by multiplying itself into a thousand faces or clusters." Note what this means; when Ortega is about to defend the individual point of view, he stops talking about "myself" and evokes the irreducible nature of reality. *Perspective is not justified by my always being in a certain point of view or situation, but by the condition itself of reality.* The problem is transferred, then, from subjectivity to reality, to its own structure. This is true to the point that, when one is not dealing with true reality, even though the conditions of the subject remain the same, the perspective is not imposed; think, for example, of abstract knowledge *in its aspect of being abstract*; thus, in mathematical knowledge taken in an *intramathematical* way—that is, without causing it to be rooted in life. The subject of that knowledge is not different in any way from the subject of any other; it is the object upon which one is operating which *is not real*. This would justify Husserl's position in his *Logical Investigations*, especially the criticism of psychologism and the demand for "pure logic": his attitude would depend on the *previous elimination of reality* through *epokhé, Einklammerung,* or *Ausschalltung,* "abstention," "placing in parentheses," or "disconnection." Whether or not this is possible is another question, which we will take up at the proper time. What interests me here is to show that Ortega's perspectivism does not come from subjectivity but from the measure in which subjectivity is conditioned by the structure of the real, which naturally contains the subject, not because of its quality of being a subject but because of its quality of being real and effective, and therefore it ceases to impose itself as soon as "subject" and "object" cease to function as *real*.

The two views of the Guadarrama range, from El Escorial and from Segovia, are different, and by this token they are real. If the mountains were a fiction, the two views might coincide, "but reality can only be looked at from the point of view which each person occupies, fatefully, in the universe. The reality and the point of view are correlative, and just as reality cannot be invented, the point of view cannot be feigned either."[28] It is a question of *eliminating fiction*; again, the opposite from

[27] II, 18.
[28] II, 19.

Nietzsche and Vaihinger. Reality cannot be feigned, nor can the point of view. Those who proclaim themselves more or less "fictionalists" or subjectivists are disposed toward making reality phantasmagorical; but those who profess "objectivism" or "realism" are no less disposed to *feign the point of view*, and by so doing, if we look closely, they *disqualify the reality* they are talking about; one could speak of an *evacuatio realitatis* which all the realists perform, and which consists, literally, in taking its name in vain, in juggling the point of view from which one has access to it, the point of view from which it is constituted as that reality and, therefore, which permits it to be named.

"The truth," Ortega continues, "the real, the universe, life—whatever you want to call it—is broken up into innumerable facets, into countless surfaces, each one of which presents a face to an individual. If this individual has known how to be faithful to his point of view, if he has resisted the eternal temptation to exchange his retina for another which is imaginary, what he sees will be a real aspect of the world.

"And vice versa: each man has a mission for truth. Where my pupil is, there is no other: what my pupil sees of reality is not seen by any other. We are irreplaceable, we are necessary. 'Only among all men does the human come to be lived,' says Goethe. Within humanity each race, within each race each individual, is an organ of perception different from all the rest, and is like a tentacle which gropes its way into bits of the universe inaccessible to others.

"*Reality, therefore, is offered in individual perspectives.* What may be in last place for one, is found for another in the first rank. The landscape arranges its sizes and its distances in relation to our retina, and our heart distributes the accents. *Visual perspective and intellectual perspective are involved in the perspective of valuation* . . . .

"*El Espectador* will watch the panorama of life from out of his heart, as from a promontory. He would like to make the attempt to reproduce, without deformations, his private perspective. Whatever clear ideas are in it will emerge as such; but whatever dreams are there will also emerge as dreams. *Because one part, one form of the real is the imaginary, and in every complete perspective there is a plane where the things we desire live their life.*"[29]

Vision, intelligence, valuation, imagination, desire, are ingredients of perspective. But neither is perspective *static* nor *passive*; it is not

[29] II, 19. Italics mine.

limited to "reflecting" speculatively a reality which is simply there, but acts upon it; and further, reality is in part *not there*. Stated more strictly: *my reality* is also reality; it is a part, or, better still, *a constitutive ingredient of reality*.

This shows that Ortega's notion of perspective "has nothing in common," in fact, with the doctrines of Nietzsche, Vaihinger, or Teichmüller; even in the last-named, whose ideas are much more interesting, the idea of "the perspective" is disqualified by the affirmation of the "substantial I" as the only effective reality. As for Leibniz, his doctrine is not an antecedent of Ortega's either, unless we take this word in an heuristic sense, as an incitement, suggestion, and stimulus; I mean that Leibniz' doctrine is different, and irreducible. The reason is clear: the monadological idealism of Leibniz annuls the very nerve center of the Orteguian notion of perspective; the reason why there is a perspective multiplication of the universe is "la multitude infinie des substances simples," of *windowless* monads which represent the universe by virtue of an internal *vis repraesentativa*. In Leibniz, then, perspective does not arise from the condition of reality, but from the irreducible plurality of the monads, and those that are minds and consciousnesses do not have real communication either among themselves or with the totality of the universe. Thus there is in Leibniz, in the last instance, an appeal to a *privileged* and exempt point of view, "une même ville *paraît* différente selon les différents points de vue dont on la regarde," and for this reason, finally, "dans ces inventions de perspective" the pictures seem only confusion until they are brought "à leur *vrai* point de vue."

In Ortega, the idea of perspective has a different root. Without going beyond the level of the *Meditations on Quixote* and "Truth and Perspective"—that is, between the years 1914 and 1916, when for the first time Ortega takes philosophic possession of his original intuition—we find that the word "reality" lacks meaning for us outside of the perspective in which it is constituted and organized, in which *it is real*. We can say that for Ortega *reality only exists as such perspectively*, and that on this fact is based the possibility of its truth.

IV.

HUMAN LIFE

❧

70. THE IDEA OF HUMAN LIFE AND THE "PHILOSOPHY OF LIFE"

The two concepts we have analyzed, circumstance and perspective, are inseparable in Ortega's mind, and their fecundity resides in this. We have seen how the notion of circumstance arises in his thought linked with that of perspective, and that the latter idea appears, in its turn and even more energetically, linked with the former. And it would be an error to think that they separate later, and that *perspectivism* in its mature form is "liberated" from the circumstantial condition; rather the contrary, for that theory is introduced at the moment when Ortega decides to make circumstance the nucleus and moving force of his philosophy, in a book which he calls, no less, *The Theme of Our Time*, and which begins with the theory of historical generations.

Very well, then: circumstance and perspective are two relatively abstract concepts, in the sense that they are not sufficient, nor is their mutual reference sufficient. Both are *aspects* or ingredients, perhaps dimensions, of a higher *reality* from which they must be understood and which confers upon them the fullness of their meaning; they are, in their turn, instruments used by Ortega to achieve the intellectual apprehension of that reality *with* which, in principle, he does not find himself, precisely because he finds himself *in* it. This reality is *human life*—the expression used, for the moment and for the sake of clarity, in a slightly inaccurate manner.

This might lead us to think that Ortega's thought is a form of what has been called a "philosophy of life," or *Lebensphilosophie*. In the Introduction to this book (chapter 2) and elsewhere[1] I have referred in detail to this philosophical tendency. It must be stated that Ortega

---

[1] In particular, *Biografía de la Filosofía*, VI (*Obras*, II).

❅ 380 ❧

has never associated himself with it, nor has he invoked its pertinence; rather, he has referred to it on occasion as something entirely alien. And, in fact, the connection of Ortega's philosophy with *Lebensphilosophie* is minimal; beginning with the fact that what Ortega understands by "life" has scarcely anything to do with the "life," or *Leben*, of *Lebensphilosophie*. Only later on will we have more proof of this, and it would be an error to add the content of later speculation here, when we are speaking of the origin of this idea; what we need to do, on the other hand, is to confine ourselves very closely to the state of the question on each of the "levels" at which it appears, on condition that these are real levels and not arbitrary temporal sections. However, I would like to state from the outset, so as not to lose sight of the place where we are going, that the distance between "life" in Ortega and in *Lebensphilosophie* is so great, that it is not a question merely of their possessing different ideas or interpretations of a reality, but that they designate different realities; that is, it is not that they think *different things* about the same life, but that they call different realities by this name; and, if pressed, I would even say that *Lebensphilosophie* does not call by this name a *reality* in the strict sense, but certain "interpretations" from which it starts out, and which are interpretations, of course, of something which pulses under them, and toward which they indirectly aim; that something is, in fact, *life*, but life will only manifest itself when one comes to it with an adequate method, which these thinkers never possessed; therefore, when it is said that they were the authors of the "discovery" of life, we must make it clear that, like Columbus's caravels on his first voyage, they discovered only islands, indicators of a continent, but that they did not succeed in setting foot on terra firma. And it is worth stating in advance that the most recent European philosophy, since it has originated in the tradition of that "philosophy of life," and has never achieved adequate method, is still in the state of having failed to transcend those interpretations, in order to discover human life in what it possesses of reality, in what Ortega was to call *radical reality*.

A proof of what I have just said—the difference between the idea of life in Ortega and in *Lebensphilosophie*—and one which is totally pertinent, because it refers precisely to the beginnings, is the decisive fact that Ortega *does not at first give the name of "life" to the reality he has discovered*. If he had started off from "philosophy of life," he would have used this term from the beginning, and would have defined it in his own way and in a personal context; that is, he would have received the "theme," and would have explored it, investigated it, and clarified it by himself. But this was far from being the case; it was a long time before he used the word "life" in the philosophical sense it was later to have in his thought, and he does so only after having utilized other expressions, when he realizes that the reality of which he is speaking and to which he has been referring for a number of years is neither more nor less than *life*, not in the sense in which the philosophers have used this word, but in the more immediate and radical sense that it has in language.

Naturally, Ortega had employed the word "life," just as everyone does, since he began to speak or write, and innumerable cases in which he uses it can be found in his writings; and, since the basic meaning which it has in language is the designation of what Ortega one day will come to call "life," it is not impossible to find in his youthful writings sentences which seem to be "antecedents" of his philosophical discovery, but which it would be a misconstruction to take as such. These antecedents are found in his work, to be sure, though not necessarily—or even normally—joined to the expression "life," but rather under other names. Ortega *arrives* at that reality; he designates it with expressions proceeding from the different perspectives from which he discovers it; and only later, in the early maturity of his doctrine, does he find that what he has found is better named than in any other way by the elemental and age-old words which man has used ingenuously, and which he has habitually debased by converting them into "clichés": *life, to live*.

71. "I AM I AND MY CIRCUMSTANCE"

In chapter 2 of this part of this book, I observed that the meaning of circumstance does not become clear until the problem of the reality of the I whose circumstance it is, is adequately posed—in other words, so long as it is not wholly understood that this circumstance is always *my* circumstance. This is what gives emphasis to the phrase which Ortega was to come to consider, much later, the most condensed expression of his philosophic thought, and which we must examine at some length.

In it, the concept "I" functions twice, or three times if you like, for we must add the "my" which is perhaps the first element we must take into account. Let us not forget that for Ortega "Man begins to know himself through the things that belong to him. The possessive pronoun precedes the personal pronoun. The idea of 'what is mine' is previous to that 'I.' "[2] When Ortega speaks of "my natural outlet toward the universe"—"This sector of surrounding reality *forms the other half of my person*; only through it can I be integrated and be fully myself"[3]—he shows clearly that the *person* is not *only I*, but includes the surrounding reality; and, therefore, I am only fully *I myself* in a circumstantial form—that is, integrated with and in *my* circumstance. This clarifies the meaning of the famous formula which Ortega introduces some lines farther on. The word "I" has two functions; only the first is strictly *real*, is the totality of my person, and includes the "other half" of it— namely, the circumstance. The second I is "insufficient": it is only an element or ingredient, inseparable from the circumstance, precisely the moment of the "I-ness" of man which *does not exhaust his reality*. This second I, which could be identified with the "I" of idealism—not even this is rigorously exact—is the *subject* of living, *center* of a circumstance; this, in fact, is constituted by being around—*circum*—an I: its mode of being is to "circle" or "circum-state"; it is, then, the I which gives the circumstance its character as such; therefore it is unitary, and, in short, vital; but, on the contrary, the circumstance is only constituted around an I which is not simply defined by being its "center," which is not just any I, but an *I myself*, capable of entering into itself, and who is *some-one*. This is what the expression "my circumstance" means: the possessive does not indicate a mere localization, but an effective possession; because I am I myself, because I have a selfhood and am master of myself, I can have something which is *mine*. We might say that I am "defined" by my circumstance, but that my circumstance does not define me; in other words, it circumscribes me, I *am* only with my circumstance; it conditions me, but it does not exhaust my reality, does not *determine* it. My true reality is not given when my circumstance and an abstract I, a mere dot, the pure subject of the circumstance, are given. Neither the moment of "I-ness" nor the moment of "subjectivity" exhausts my personal reality. I, in the real sense of the term, am not a mere subject or support of circumstance; I am not only "the thing

---

[2] II, 387.

[3] *Meditaciones del Quijote*, I, 322. Italics mine.

which" lives in it, but the *person who* makes his life with it, giving that *who* its strict personal meaning. That is, man, besides being an "I" and the "subject" of his vital acts, support of his world, is also a *person*, and that condition of his is precisely *circumstantial*.

If Ortega had simply said "I and my circumstance," he would not have achieved the philosophic innovation which he accomplished in the *Meditations on Quixote*. That formulation would be acceptable, in the last instance, to a realistic attitude, or rather an idealistic one, provided that the fact that the subject is referred to an object is not lost sight of. When Fichte speaks of the contrast "I and not-I" (*Ich und nicht-Ich*), or when the *mature* Husserl, carrying Brentano's idea of intentionality to its ultimate consequences, corrects the Cartesian *cogito* with the formula *ego cogito cogitatum*, they have still not superseded the sphere of mere "reference"—in the case of Husserl, explicitly an intentional reference—to reach an affirmation of *reality*. The decisive point is the first *I* of Ortega's formula, the one which does not simply "mean," but which designates or *denominates*, which points out *me*, my reality, and of whom it is said that "*I am* I and my circumstance." This first *I*, which cannot be abstract, is a *position* of reality, and thus an article cannot be placed in front of it: as soon as we said "the I," we would have suspended its real and effective function, and would have supplanted it by something entirely different. But it is not even a positing "I" in Fichte's sense (*setzend*), which, as it posits itself, "posits" the not-I; rather, this "I," polarized to the circumstance, far from positing it, is *posited with it* (if you like, *com-posited* with it), both as ingredients of that primary reality which is *I*—the first I in the formula—as a person made up of both.

Does the formula of the *Meditations on Quixote* really mean this? Is it licit to confer these metaphysical implications on an expression which many have understood in a trivial way, in a "geographical" or "biological" sense? Is it not rather that Ortega, many years later, may have noticed the coincidence of his youthful expressions with some theses of later German philosophy and reworked them, investing them with a meaning they did not have originally? Were these not at most a lucky chance, an intuition if you will, detached from any strictly philosophical content, arising out of a reflection upon Spanish life and upon a work of literature?

In order to answer these questions we must abandon for the moment this book, *Meditations on Quixote*, and explore the state of the author's mind at about that time. It is a question of applying, once more, the methodological principle which advises us to consider Ortega's writings as icebergs: we must go under water, and try to come to know the bulk which surfaced in those paragraphs of the *Meditations*, and reverberated with that surprising thesis: "I am I and my circumstance."

72. THE EXECUTIVE BEING AND PHENOMENOLOGY

When Ortega recalled the disagreement of the youthful group in Marburg with the neo-Kantianism its members had received from their masters, and the need they saw to "row toward the imaginary coast," he remarks that success was improbable. "However," he adds, "fate had made us the gift of a prodigious instrument: phenomenology. That group of young men had never been neo-Kantian, strictly speaking. Nor had we entirely given ourselves over to phenomenology. Our desire for system prevented us from doing so. Phenomenology, because of its own consistency, is incapable of achieving a systematic form or shape. Its inestimable value lies in the 'fine structure' of fleshy tissues which it can offer to the architecture of its system. Thus, phenomenology was not a philosophy for us: it was . . . a piece of good luck."[4] Ortega adds that he began to study phenomenology seriously in 1912;[5] in 1913 the *Jahrbuch für Philosophie und phänomenologische Forschung* appears, and in it the *Ideen*; in that first volume—it seems unbelievable—the first part of Scheler's *Ethics* was also published, and it was to continue in the second volume, in 1916. Well, in that same year, 1913, Ortega published two articles on phenomenology: one, the inaugural speech in the philosophical section of the Congress of the Spanish Association for the Progress of the Sciences, on "Sensación, construcción e intuición" ["Sensation, Construction, and Intuition"][6]; the other, a series of articles "Sobre el concepto de sensación" ["On the Concept of Sensation"], which appeared in the *Revista de Libros* between the months of June and September.[7]

The first of these two studies, "Sensation, Construction, and Intui-

---

[4] *Prólogo para alemanes*, 58.

[5] *Ibid.*, 66.

[6] Asociación Española para el Progreso de las Ciencias. Congreso de Madrid. Volume I, 1913, pp. 77–88.

[7] I, 245–61.

tion," attempts to pose the initial problem itself of philosophy, the problem which constitutes the approach to it. It is a question of determining the scientific ambit which is specifically called philosophical. Every science propounds "another whose particular theme is 'theory' itself; if all the sciences are 'transitive,' this one must be 'reflexive' science, the only one which has this character. Hence its unique position with regard to all the others."[8] This theory could also be called science without assumptions. But Ortega warns that this does not mean that in this science suppositions are entirely excluded: it can take them, if it proves them later, and need not even prove them, on condition that it does not consider them as proved truths in another science; this happens when, as in Descartes, one supposes a truth not as a truth but as a mere supposition. "*Philosophy*," writes Ortega, "*is born, therefore, into a desperate situation. It has to earn its living, one might say, from the cradle. Hence its radicalism.* It is not permitted to philosophy to support itself on any capital fund or inheritance of certainties, of acquired truths. What we are accustomed to call common sense is a decanting of *traditional evidence* which serves as a firm foothold to the vacillations of our spirit in the practical matters of life. In this sense, as Kant has mentioned, philosophy is the opposite of common sense, of *evidence by tradition*. Its purpose consists precisely in *perforating that common sense*, in superseding it, and in restoring the philosophic meaning at any cost."[9]

Ortega wishes to show "the three radical positions which philosophy takes today with regard to its deepest problem." It is a question of finding an *exemplary cognitive function* which by its own nature gives its contents, immediately, the value of truths. And, correlatively, he was to call "being, truth, reality, objectivity" the genuine content of that function, what we grasp through that function.

Since these functions are the functions of a subject, they can be arranged in a scale, from the minimum to the maximum activity. The minimum is *pure reception*, where there is no intermediary between subject and object; that is, the object is not *represented* by anything, but is *present*. If this receptive function were to exist, the problem would be solved, for "where the object itself is found, there is no room for

8 "Sensación, construcción e intuición"; *loc. cit.*, 78.

9 *Ibid.*, 79. Italics mine. See the relationship between these ideas and very late writings of Ortega's, such as the Prologue to Bréhier's *History of Philosophy* and his posthumous book, *La idea de principio en Leibniz y la evolución de la teoría deductiva.*

error"; this would be the analytical, definitory, symptom of the sought-after truth. This is, says Ortega, the position of the *radical empiricism* of Mach and Ziehen. The original meaning of knowing is not systematization, reasoning, or judgment, for these demand an activity, a spontaneity in the subject which draws away from what is received and "substructs" an ideal object in place of the primary one. Nor is representation sufficiently original. Mach confines himself to sensation. The first attitude which it is possible to take with regard to science without assumptions, to the science of theory, is: "being is what is felt; knowing is the correlative function, feeling."[10] Ortega warns that this solution is open to suspicion because it is the manifestation of a period; the essence of knowing is sought on the boundary where man as agent disappears, becoming a mere passivity. "Is it not symptomatic of a whole cycle of European civilization, this lack of confidence with regard to man, and this attempt to correct and rectify the specifically human by means of the infrahuman?"[11] Ortega accepts the principle that "strictly speaking, we could only call knowledge that subjective function in which the being itself is given to us," and in this he feels that empiricism is correct; but he warns that Mach's empiricism is unfaithful to its own tendency, for it considers as the definitive reality what it calls "elements," the contents of pure sensation, without seeing that "pure feeling" and its correlate are limit concepts, problems, not *single realities* which can serve as a point of departure. "To isolate a pure sound we need physical and physiological methods and all the reflective apparatus of introspection. So that pure sound and pure sensation, far from being *given* to us, are constructions of systematic science." "In short, *radical empiricism is contradictory in itself*; it postulates as being the pure being of the senses, founded on the belief that the function, in the cases when we reach it, is merely dative. But it happens that this dativeness and its content are, in their turn, a result of the whole scientific conceptuation, and therefore of active and constructive thinking."[12]

The consequence of this is very serious: if it is impossible for being to reach us without subjective deformation, if the object cannot be *given*, one must either renounce knowledge or transform the correlative terms "being" and "knowing"; that is, it would be absurd to seek being as

[10] *Ibid.*, 79–80.
[11] *Ibid.*, 80.
[12] *Ibid.*, 81. Italics mine.

something different from knowledge, something which reaches it from outside. Whereas for common sense there is a subordination between being and knowing, and the conditions of knowledge follow those of being, and knowledge adjusts itself to being, we can now see that "being lacks meaning outside of its mutuality with knowing," that "the correlation is strict; both terms live dependent on one another, without any sort of primacy"; "because there is being, there is knowledge . . . because there is knowing, there is being." Mach skirted, against his will, a metaphysical position. "Metaphysics," warns Ortega, "in the bad sense of the word."

The only solution left is this radical one: "Nothing aspiring to the title of 'being' is *given* to knowledge, if by 'given' we mean entering into the knowledge of something which at first is extraneous to it, and which, nevertheless, will later, as it enters, constitute an element of knowledge." "It cannot admit as 'determined,' as 'being' something, what does not receive its determination from the purely spontaneous activity of knowledge." "Here is," concludes Ortega, "the position of critical idealism which, arising out of Kant, is sustained today by Cohen and Natorp. The first of these has even said, breaking with the last shreds of empiricism still existing in Kant, that *the stuff of knowledge is not the raw material of the sensations. Hence the passive function of feeling is completely excluded from the system of cognitive acts.*"[13]

This seems hard to admit: that knowledge lives off itself without receiving anything from outside. Idealism finds a solution when it eliminates the factitious and, in fact, biological, point of view:

"*Knowledge is not a process, but an ideal object.* The psychological act of being aware of a real proposition is a very different thing from the 'meaning' of that proposition."[14] Being is *ab origine* immanent to knowing. "Thus, after we have burned the boats of all recourse to transcendence, knowledge appears as a *construction*, and being as what has been constructed."[15] Thus this idealism picks up the Platonic tradition and the tradition which, awakened by Plato, reappears in the Renaissance with Descartes and Galileo: knowing consists in "saving appearances." Saving: that is, fixing them in a system of connections. If in Plato the decisive factor was the idea, in Kant it is "the transcendental

13 *Ibid.*, 82–83. Italics mine.
14 *Ibid.*, 83. Italics mine.
15 *Ibid.*, 84.

unity of aperception"; the essential factor is *unity*; in Leibniz, analogously, "consent" is mentioned.

But Ortega does not remain installed in this idealist solution of his neo-Kantian teachers. He notes—and let us not forget that we are in 1913—"two extremely serious points." The first, suggested by Nicolai Hartmann—here the closeness of the youthful Marburg group, recalled by Ortega in his maturity, becomes visible—is the *need for the cognitive function to start off from a problem,* a need which is "unpalatable to idealism." "A problem is not simply a void; it is a something; it contains some determination no matter how simple and imprecise it may be." There is no such thing as a first problem; there is no such thing as a "problem in itself"; in each stage of the progressive series, the former solution is a problem. "It might make some sense to say," adds Ortega, "that *history is the history of what has been a living problem for men, and which is no longer one for us.*"[16]

The other difficulty is still more serious: "Is the quality of construction, such as we have described it, enough to define knowledge? . . . the two terms whose 'consent' makes up knowing, must previously find themselves in some way present to the subject so that the subject can confirm their coincidence. And in its turn this coincidence or consent is not a construction either, but we simply notice it, we are aware of it. So that the cognitive function may well be, in its totality, a construction of the object; but each one of its steps or moments requires *a simple intuition of the terms placed in relation.*"[17] Ortega analyzes the case of the impossible object, for example the round square, which is "something for me" when I have been able to formulate the judgment of it as impossible. Before reaching that judgment, something was hanging over me. "That something could not be a given truth; it might not even be truth, as the round square was not a truth. But with this, the only result would be that *there is an even deeper and more primary plane than that of constructive truth or nontruth, than being and nonbeing.*"[18] (We shall soon see the *remote* consequences of this in Ortega's thought, far beyond the assumptions of the *Gegenstandstheorie* of Meinong, whom he quotes in this context, in addition to Lask; when Ortega brought this idea to its full development, he was to introduce one of the essential

[16] *Ibid.,* 86. Italics mine.
[17] *Ibid.,* 86–87. Italics mine.
[18] *Ibid.,* 87. Italics mine.

themes of his metaphysics, perhaps the most profoundly innovative one.)[19] Any judgment, for example, is superimposed on the terms *themselves*, which place themselves *in person* before our intuition. *"Intuition is, consequently, a function still more previous to that in which we construct being or nonbeing.* The *passivity* of which empiricism spoke reappears, in consequence. But in what a different sense! For empiricism, passivity was synonymous with sensation and had no more original content than that of the senses. *Intuition takes in all the intellectual degrees."* "The correlate of intuition," he adds in a note, "is *essence* not subject to space, time, or predication of reality."[20] This is the principle established by Husserl. "Its very novelty," says Ortega, "makes for the fact that we still do not see clearly its limits and its constitution." "Let us leave for the immediate future," he concludes, "the proof of whether the theory of theory will be achieved or not, exempt from assumptions; this theory Edmund Husserl is now in the process of preparing, in partial studies which for their precision and fundamentality have no peers today. Perhaps with the principle of intuition a new period in philosophy will be opened."[21]

In this first article, Ortega examines the three positions—the empiricist, neo-Kantian, and phenomenological—and places his hopes on the last of the three. Intuition represents the justification of the partially correct demands of the empiricism of sensation and the idealism of construction. I was interested in emphasizing, however, that Ortega takes up the problem in a very broad dimension, and that, in spite of his admiration for Husserl, he does not go over to Husserl's side without further ado. He must ask himself about its "constitution" and its "limits," which are not clearly seen as yet. His study "On the Concept of Sensation" answers the first question to some degree; the second was to remain unexpectedly and implicitly answered in one of Ortega's most disconcerting pieces of writing, a year later.

"We are witnessing," says Ortega, "a renaissance of what Schopenhauer called man's 'metaphysical need.'" And he notes that in 1912 he gave some public lectures on this subject at the Madrid Atheneum. But now he is interested in speaking of the thesis of a disciple of Husserl's,

[19] See my essay "Realidad y ser en la filosofía española" (1955), in *La Escuela de Madrid.* (*Obras*, V.)

[20] "Sensación, construcción e intuición", *loc. cit.* 87–88. Italics mine.

[21] *Ibid.*, 88.

Heinrich Hoffmann (*Untersuchungen über den Empfindungsbegriff*, 1913). "The influence—greater every day—of 'phenomenology' on psychology tends to separate in the latter, in the most profound and healthy sense, description from explanation." Ortega writes "phenomenology" in quotes; the novelty of the expression is still total; indeed, in the first of these articles, he speaks of "a strange term, 'sensible intimacy'—'das sinnliche Erlebnis' ";[22] a short time later, in the fourth article, he introduces the term "vivencia" ["life experience"] to translate *Erlebnis*, which has become naturalized in our language, and which has not achieved an equivalent in other languages. "I am taking advantage of this occasion," he says in a note, "to ask for help in a question of terminology from those who take an interest in Spanish philosophy, if, as I believe, *Spanish philosophy simply means philosophy explained in words fully meaningful for Spaniards* . . . . This word, 'Erlebnis' was introduced *by Dilthey, I believe*. After having turned it over in my mind for years, hoping to find some word already existing in our language sufficiently capable of transcribing it, I have had to desist and try to find another. The problem is the following: in sentences like 'to live life' and 'to live things,' the verb 'to live' acquires a curious meaning. Without abandoning its value as a deponent, it takes a transitive form signifying that type of immediate relationship into which the subject enters or can enter with certain objectives in mind. But, what to call each actualization of this relationship? I do not find any other word than 'vivencia.' Everything which arrives with such immediacy to my 'I' that it enters to form part of it, is a 'vivencia.' Just as the physical body is a unit of atoms, so the I, or conscious body, is a unit of 'vivencias.' I realize that this word sounds unpleasant, like all new words. However, it already exists in compounds such as *convivencia* [living together], *pervivencia* [survival], etc., and follows similar forms. Thus, from *existir* [to exist], *existencia* [existence] from *sentir* [to feel], *sentencia* . . . . I beg of the philologists, therefore, to take an interest in this petition. So long as another, better term cannot be found, I shall continue to use 'vivencia' as an equivalent to 'Erlebnis.' "[23]

In the third of these articles, Ortega introduces the decisive question: "What is phenomenology?" I doubt very much whether, in any country outside of Germany, this question had been answered at such an early

[22] "Sobre el concepto de sensación" (1913). I, 248.
[23] *Ibid.*, 257. Italics mine.

date and with such precision and familiarity. I am not interested in its details, but only in two or three points of special interest. Ortega starts off with Husserl's notions of *essence* and *essential intuition*, which he explains as follows:

"There is a 'natural way' of carrying out the acts of consciousness, whatever these may be. This natural manner is characterized by the *executive* value which those acts have. Thus the 'natural posture' in the act of perception consists in accepting as existing in truth before our eyes a thing belonging to an ambit of things which we consider effectively real and which we call 'world.' The natural posture in the judgment 'A is B' consists in the fact that we firmly believe that an A exists which is B. When we love, our consciousness lives unreservedly in love. This efficacy of our acts, when our consciousness lives them in its natural and spontaneous attitude, we call the *executive* power of those acts.

"Now let us suppose that, just at the point when our consciousness has carried out an act of perception, as it were, *in good faith*, naturally, it were to turn back upon itself, and instead of *living* in the contemplation of the sensible object, were to occupy itself in contemplating its perception itself. This perception, with all its *executive* consequences, with all its affirmation that there is something real in front of it, will remain, we might say, in suspense; its efficacy will not be definitive; it will only be efficacy as a *phenomenon*. Note that this reflection of the consciousness upon its acts (1) does not disturb them: perception is what it was before, only—as Husserl says very graphically—it is now placed in parentheses: (2) it does not attempt to explain them, but merely sees them, just as perception does not explain the object, but witnesses it in perfect passivity.

"Well, all the acts of consciousness and all the objects of those acts can be placed in parentheses. The whole 'natural' world, or science insofar as it is a system of judgments carried out in a 'natural manner,' is reduced to *phenomenon*. And here phenomenon does not mean what it does in Kant, for example—something which suggests another substantial something behind it. Phenomenon here is simply the virtual quality which everything acquires when from its natural *executive* value one passes to the contemplation of it in a speculative and descriptive posture, without giving it a definite character.

"That pure description is phenomenology."[24]

[24] *Ibid.*, 253–54.

In this quotation I have italicized the word *executive*, which Ortega uses four times, to signify what is opposed to the merely "speculative," to what is "placed in parentheses," to the phenomenologically reduced, in short. Then Ortega explains the character of "consciousness of" as that within which all objects are constituted, and among them, "as one object among others," the object "human consciousness."[25] "Reality," he adds, "is 'consciousness of' reality: consciousness could hardly be a reality in its turn."[26] Against this backdrop it is easy to understand that disconcerting text of Ortega's to which I referred above, and which until recently[27] had never been interpreted, so far as I know, from this point of view. The supersession of phenomenology and the idea of consciousness appear in it very clearly. Let us examine it.

This article, dating from 1914, is the "Ensayo de estética a manera de prólogo" which Ortega used as an introduction to José Moreno Villa's book of poetry, *El Pasajero*. Few cases are more revealing of the qualities of Ortega's writings. Is it possible that a prologue to a book of verses should take up the thorny questions in which we are entangled? And who would think of going there to look for a critique of phenomenology, which at that time was the last word in European philosophy, something up-to-the-moment, or rather to the future, since its theory had just been formulated at the time? And we shall still have to add that Ortega does not *name* phenomenology in this prologue. What he is dealing with is the *metaphor*; I have already explained in detail the part of his work which refers to this theme; the connection of metaphor with poetry is, naturally, very close; only slightly less close is the connection which links metaphor with philosophy. Without philosophy we cannot understand what metaphor is; and Ortega, in order to try to do so, has to precede his theory of metaphorical utterance with a short antestructure of formal philosophy. It is no coincidence that its content is precisely what it is: Ortega—we now see—was concerned with the problems raised by this enormous fact of phenomenology. He has dealt with it in writing in the two examples I have examined; in principle, it was a question of *expounding* Husserl's philosophy, of presenting to Spanish readers this recent and brilliant creation of German

[25] *Ibid.*, 254–55.

[26] *Ibid.*, 257

[27] See my essay "Conciencia y realidad ejecutiva: la primera superación orteguiana de la fenomenología" (1956), in *La Escuela de Madrid*.

thought; it was neither opportune nor urgent to hasten to write criticism or reservations—Ortega never had this itch, so characteristic of those who are incapable of creating, those who feel impatient to rush in with their "objection," their little correction, so that there can be no doubt that they too have their personality which is not ready to accept anything created by their fellow man. But in the depths of Ortega's thought decisive difficulties were taking root, which affected the very assumptions of phenomenology. Those difficulties and the response to them are the *backdrop* of Ortega's thought when he writes about the metaphor, in connection with Moreno Villa's poems. They are the iceberg's mass of ice, whose peak *occasionally* emerges in this prologue. He has no need to speak of phenomenology; neither is he in a hurry to make a radical criticism, one which would bring into question the basic assumptions of contemporary philosophy in a way which would be premature with regard to Husserl's work, still in full spate of formation, and which, in addition, *would not be understood*, for a fundamental reason: because it would make no sense with regard to the problem itself. Therefore Ortega limits himself to building his theory of metaphor on a philosophical foundation which *means*—though he does not state this—the criticism of the possibility of *phenomenological reduction* and the idea of *consciousness*. We shall not take up the question of whether this manner of presenting his philosophical discoveries was an adequate one or not, whether it would have been better to present this criticism directly and explicitly, along with the personal position which he upheld. The time to pose this problem will come later, at another stage in this book; just now I am only interested in pointing out that that was the way it was, and to discuss in detail the contents of this criticism and the intellectual motives for it.

What I have called the "philosophical antestructure" in the strict sense, placed by Ortega before the theory of metaphor, includes chapters 2–4 of the "Essay on Aesthetics," and the titles of these chapters are: "The 'I' as Executive Factor," " 'I' and My I," and "The Aesthetic Object." I prefer to quote the most important passages directly, for it is of great interest to have Ortega's words before us in all their literalness:

"We can use, utilize, only things. And vice versa: things are the points where our utilitarian activity is inserted. Very well; first of all, we can place ourselves in a utilitarian attitude with regard to all things but one: I.

"Kant reduces ethics to his well-known formula: behave in such a way that you do not use men only as a means, in such a way that they are like the ends of your own acts . . . . Kant's imperative . . . seeks to have other men be *persons* for us, not utilities, *things*. And this dignity of being a person comes over something when we act upon the immortal commandment of Scripture: love thy neighbor as thyself. To make something an *I myself* is the only way it can cease to be a thing."[28]

Ortega contrasts *thing* and *person*. *Thing* is what is utilizable; as for person, there is only, for the moment, one clear example: *I*, I myself. Not—be it noted—"the I"; when I confront another man, I can choose between treating him like a *thing* or like an *I*. How is this possible? Naturally, only because *the other is not strictly speaking I*, but is so only in a fictitious way. "But, it seems," continues Ortega, "it is given to us to choose, in the presence of another man, another subject, between treating him as a thing, utilizing him, or treating him as an 'I.' Here there is a margin for free will, a margin which would not be possible if the other human individuals were really 'I'. The 'thou,' the 'he,' are, then, fictitiously 'I.' In Kantian terms, we would say that my *good will* makes other 'I's out of 'thou' and 'he.' "[29]

Ortega has said that the only thing which we *cannot* convert into a thing, even though we want to, is *I*, and points out that this must be taken literally. On the one hand, he shows the change of meaning introduced into a verb by its use in the first person, compared with the meaning it has in the second or third. "I walk" and "he walks" use the same verb, "walk," which means the same thing in both expressions to some degree, and thus the identical verb is used in both; but whereas his walking is a reality that I perceive in an exterior sense and with my eyes, my walking is primarily a reality which is invisible and has nothing to do with space: the effort, the impulse, the muscular sensations, etc. "One might say that in the form 'I walk' I am referring to walking seen from inside of what walking is, and in 'he walks,' walking seen in its external result . . . . There is, then, an 'I-walking' which is completely different from 'others walking.' "[30] This is important, but not decisive, nor does it lack antecedents both in recent and more remote philosophical tradition. From Fichte and Maine de Biran to Bergson, this evidence

[28] "Ensayo de estética a manera de prólogo" (1914), VI, 250.
[29] *Ibid.*, 250.
[30] *Ibid.*, 251.

had been becoming imposed upon philosophy; on the other hand, Husserl, in his *Ideen*, when he is about to explain the peculiarity of the phenomenological method, refers explicitly to *Ichrede*, to speech in the first person. It is also clear that in some verbs—to desire, to hate, to feel pain—the primary significance is the one they have in the first person. This is not the most important thing: what is important is that Ortega then adds:

"This now clarifies, in my opinion, *the distance between 'I' and every other thing, whether it be an inanimate body or a 'thou,' a 'he.'* How would we express in a general way that difference between the image or concept of pain and pain as feeling, as hurting? Perhaps by observing that they *are mutually exclusive*: the image of a pain does not hurt; still more, it places the pain at a distance, replaces it by its ideal shadow. And vice versa: pain hurting is the opposite of its image; at the moment when it becomes an image of itself, it ceases to hurt."[31]

When he reaches this point, Ortega's expressions are not entirely precise, and they are not the ones he would have employed in later years; but the idea is surprisingly clear: "*I* means, then, not this man as different from another, nor much less man as different from things, but everything—men, things, situations—insofar as they are taking place, being, executing themselves." "Now we see why we cannot place ourselves in a utilitarian posture in the presence of the 'I': simply, because *we cannot place ourselves in its presence*, because the state of perfect compenetration with something is indissoluble, because it is everything insofar as it is innerness."[32]

Ortega is fully aware that he is not expressing his intuition adequately, and corrects himself. For example, he writes, "Everything, looked at from inside itself, is *I*." And he immediately adds, "This sentence can only serve as a bridge to the strict comprehension of what we are seeking. Strictly speaking, it is not exact."[33] What is he seeking? So that we will not get lost, I am going to follow only the essential line, leaving unessential or deficient developments to one side.

"When I feel a pain, when I love or hate, I do not see my pain nor do I see myself loving or hating. In order for me to see *my* pain, it is necessary for me to interrupt my situation as a hurting being and change

[31] *Ibid.*, 252. Italics mine.
[32] *Ibid.* Italics mine.
[33] *Ibid.*

into a seeing 'I.' This I which sees the other, hurting I, is not the true I, the executive one, the present one. The hurting I, to speak precisely, was, and now is, only an image, a thing or object which I have before me.

"Thus we reach the last step of the analysis: 'I' is not man in opposition to things, 'I' is not this subject in opposition to the subject 'thou' or 'he'; 'I,' in fact, is not that 'me myself' *me ipsum*, that I think I know when I practice the Delphic precept: 'Know thyself.' "[34]

The original sin of the modern age, says Ortega, was *subjectivism*, "the mental illness of the age which begins with the Renaissance and consists in the supposition that what is nearest to me is I—that is, what is nearest to me in the sense of knowledge, is my reality or I insofar as it is reality." In Fichte this reaches the maximum degree, "and under his influence a period elapsed during which, at a certain hour in the morning, inside German lecture halls, the world was pulled out of the I the way one pulls a handkerchief out of one's pocket." And "perhaps at those moments, like the vague outline of a coast, the new manner of thinking appeared, free from that preoccupation.

"So," Ortega concludes, "we arrive at the following unyielding dilemma: nothing can be made the object of our comprehension, nothing can exist for us, if it is not changed into an image, into a concept, into an idea—that is, if it does not cease to be what it is, to be transformed into a shadow or scheme of itself. *We have an intimate relationship with only one thing: this thing is our individual, our life*, but this intimacy of ours, when it changes into an image, ceases to be intimacy . . . . *The true intimacy, which is something insofar as it is executing itself*, is as far from the image of the external thing as it is from the internal thing." "Intimacy cannot be our object or the object of science, either in practical thinking or in machinelike representing. And, nevertheless, it is the true being of each thing, the only sufficient factor, and the one whose contemplation would fully satisfy us."[35]

There is yet more. If we contrast *executive* intimacy to narration, we find that "Narration makes everything a ghost of itself, puts it at a distance, transfers it beyond the horizon of the present. What is narrated is a 'was.' And the *was* is the schematic form left in the present by what is not there, the being of what no longer is—the cast skin left behind by

[34] *Ibid.*, 252–53.
[35] *Ibid.*, 254. The first italics are mine.

the snake."[36] And finally, when he has already launched into the analysis of the metaphor, Ortega continues to accumulate evidence pointing in the same direction: "While my vital act of seeing the cypress is being *executed*, the cypress is the object which exists for me; what I may be in that instant constitutes for me an unknown secret."[37] "This subjectivity exists only in the degree that it occupies itself with things .... put more clearly: style proceeds from the individuality of the 'I,' but it is verified in things."[38]

In the interests of brevity, permit me to repeat here the conclusion of my essay "Consciousness and Executive Reality," in preference to drawing it out with an unnecessary paraphrase:

These long quotations have been necessary in order to make clear the significance of what Ortega was trying very hard to communicate in 1914. Remember that phenomenology suspends the "natural attitude," in which there are real acts of mine related to real things in an also real world; it places everything "in parentheses" and, instead of *living* perception, for example, it contemplates perception itself. Phenomenological reduction is described by Ortega as the elimination or suspension of the *executive*, in order to hold to the phenomenon in the sense of the *virtual* character which everything acquires when one passes from its executive and natural value to contemplating it in a speculative and descriptive posture. In other words, when all of it—subject, act, and object—is reduced to pure *consciousness*.

A year after the publication of the *Ideen*, Ortega comes to the point of saying that when I contemplate my "vivencias," my "life experiences," the *I* who is subject of them stops being properly speaking *I*, and becomes an image, thing, or object. On the other hand, the true *I*, the executive, the present *I*, is the one which sees and contemplates the previous one, the one which *was* the subject of the "vivencia" described and contemplated. Or, inverting the terms, the I who considers, contemplates, and describes; that is, the I which is executing the phenomenological reduction, far from having succumbed to it, and become an "athetic" I and one in parentheses, is *true, executive*, and *present*, unreduced and irreducible. *I* means *executiveness*, presence, full reality. It is not a question of "the I," or of the man, but of *the true intimacy which*

[36] *Ibid.*, 255–56.
[37] *Ibid.*, 260.
[38] *Ibid.*, 263.

is something insofar as it is executing itself; and that is *our life*—not as an image, but precisely in its very execution, which in its turn is possible only *while it is occupying itself with things.*

This means that as soon as Ortega thought phenomenology through, he went beyond it in its content of idealist philosophy, of affirmation of the consciousness as absolute reality, or, as Husserl says, "nonrelative" consciousness. The elimination of the executive factor is illusory, for reality *itself*—that is, not its image or concept—is executivity; when the phenomenologist believes that he is dealing with a phenomenologically reduced I, with an I-consciousness, it is his executive I, fully real, which operates with a past image of his I, which was also executive before. Expressed in different and more exact words, under the illusion of consciousness appears reality, the only reality with which we have an intimate relationship, *our life while it is being executed*; that is, living.

Because—and this is decisive—when he eliminates the possibility of phenomenological reduction, when he sees that there is no escape from the executive, Ortega does not fall back on what Husserl calls "the natural attitude" (*natürliche Einstellung*) in the sense of realism. The Orteguian position consists precisely in *superseding things*, and therefore superseding all realism. What Ortega reproaches in the presumed suspension of the executivity which is I, is, neither more nor less, what it implies of "*thingification*," even though an ideal thing is being dealt with. "The hurting I, to speak precisely, was, and now is, only an image, a thing or an object which I have before me." A thing or an object which *I* have before me, and I am not *nor can I be* a thing. Remember that this was the essential point: that *I* am the only thing which "not only do we not wish to, but we cannot convert into a thing." That irreducible reality, which can never be "thingified," or objectified, for then it ceases to be what it is and becomes a mere image of itself, in its narrated or described past, is not consciousness, but quite its opposite: I executing myself, not mere subjectivity, but inasmuch as I concern myself with things; in sum, *my life.*

And so, in 1914, when the theory of phenomenology was only a year old, Ortega had gone beyond the notions of reduction and consciousness, to affirm the personal and executive reality of *human life.*

* * *

This was Ortega's thought at the time he wrote his formula "I am I and my circumstance." These were the problems which were pressing in upon him and which he was discussing with himself. The image of the *Dii consentes*, of the Dioscuros, the metaphor of Adam in Paradise expressed conceptually in the formula *I am I and my circumstance*, are replies to the question about primary reality, which phenomenology had posed with such extreme refinement within the great assumption of idealism. The bulk of the submerged iceberg, support of the famous thesis of the *Meditations on Quixote*, is no other than the original presentation, beyond idealism, but without thereby falling back into realism, of the central problem of metaphysics.

Haste or ignorance has often tried to see in this thesis an isolated "lucky hit," lacking philosophical meaning. When it is regarded in its effective *context*, that of the book in which it appears and that of its author's thought at that particular time, it appears as the culmination of long intellectual efforts of the most rigorous and "technical" type, of a discussion at very close quarters with philosophical tradition and the most recent positions which European thought had reached during those very months. And now we can see the justification of the idea of the *essay* which Ortega formulates precisely in the *Meditations*: "science, minus the *explicit* proof"; for, as we have also seen, "for the writer there is a question of intellectual honor in not writing anything susceptible of proof unless he possesses that proof. But it is licit for him to erase from his work any clearly demonstrable appearance, leaving the proofs merely indicated elliptically, in such a way that the person who needs them can find them, but in such a way, on the other hand, that they do not interfere with the expansion of the intimate warmth with which the thoughts were thought."[39]

Was Ortega right? We have just seen that he did possess the proof; that the person who needed it could find it, is obvious. Perhaps he was mistaken on one point: he probably thought that those who did not content themselves with the warm and heartfelt form of the "essay" really *needed* the proof, and thus were capable of seeking it. The experience of forty-five years leads us to believe that these persons were very few; that there were a great many more of those who preferred to "feel the absence of" a proof which they neither needed nor were capable of seeking, perhaps not even of comprehending when someone finds it and makes it plain.

[39] *Meditaciones del Quijote*, I, 318.

73. THE REALITY OF THE I AND
THE REALITY WHICH I AM

I was saying before that the decisive feature of the formula "I am I and my circumstance" is not the simple copulative duality "I and my circumstance," but the first *I* which designates or denominates *me*, which is not a mere signification, or *Bedeutung*, and of whom it is said that *it is* "I and my circumstance," so that this last expression seems to enunciate or analyze what *I* am; or, looking at things from the other side, "I" and "circumstance" are *really* linked in that reality of the first I—that is, in that reality which I am. Thus, once we understand the strictly philosophical background of that thesis, we must pause for a moment on the question of the *different reality* of the first "I" and the second "I."

If I am "I" and my circumstance, this means that, from the point of view of the first "I," the reality of the second is *insufficient*, needy; of what? precisely of the circumstance. This is what the second member of Ortega's thesis means: "and if I do not save it, I do not save myself." The reality of the second "I" appears, then, subject to its coexistence with the other term, both related to each other, so that both are insufficient. Let us not forget that the term "circumstance" is unintelligible apart from the "I" of whom it is, around (*circum*) which it is. The circumstance consists in *being around* the I, and this I is circumstantial; that is, it is intrinsically related to that circumstance, constituted by that reference.

But we must ask ourselves: where does one find a foothold? It is illusory to take "I" and "circumstance" *separately*, and to try to "make them agree." As often as philosophy has tried to do so—under other names—it has had to fall back on a "trick." How? In one of these three ways: (1) By taking the "I" as *just one more thing* to which some special property is attributed—for example, reason—*which does not affect its quality of reality*. This is what realism does in all its forms, for it "thingifies" the I, it resolves it into a thing, as when Boethius defines the person *rationalis naturae individua substantia*, "an individual substance (or thing) of a rational nature"; that is, that *a person is a thing like other things*—like others insofar as it is a thing, be it understood, insofar as it is reality—although of a particular nature; namely, a rational one. (2) By reducing the circumstance or world to the I, as all idealisms do, causing it to be the mere correlate of a subject, or, if you like, *a position of the I*, a derivation of the I insofar as it is reality.[40] (3) By eliminating the question itself, through the *de-realization* of all of it, as phenomenology tries to do, and trying to hold to mere *intentionality*. But this is no solution either, for, in the first place, Husserl "absolutizes" consciousness when he makes it "relative to nothing," and with this, obviously, it remains inside idealism, and therefore within the previous position, since the "objects" are exhausted in being intentional objects; and, in the second place, this "suspension" of executiveness, that "disconnection" or "placing in parentheses" in which the *epokhé* or phenomenological reduction consists, is illusory *from the point of view of reality*, since what is *executed* in an act is not in its turn reduced, and by an *executive I* which is not the same, which, *in a new act*, can be the object of reduction.

Very well, then, if there is no possible "composition" of the I and the circumstance, this means that both are *already* "com-posed"; that is, that they are "moments," "ingredients," or whatever you want to call them;—in short, subordinate and secondary realities with regard to another primary reality from which they are discovered and found, and in which the deficient and needy reality is rooted. This reality is, in the terms used by Ortega in 1914, the *I* as an executive position of reality, as a subjectivity which "only exists while it is occupied with things"; that is, *as not only subjectivity*, but primary position which includes, and therefore can distinguish, "I" and "things." In short, opposed to *the reality of the I*—its "I-ness," its "subjectivity," its "polarity" as opposed to things, for the moment—*the reality which is I*, defined by very different attributes: position, executivity, priority with respect to *its* ingredients, intrinsic duality.

All this appears in Ortega's original discovery. Naturally, the dis-

---

[40] Descartes vacillates between the two positions when he says, on the one hand, "Je connus de là que j'étais une substance dont toute l'essence ou la nature n'est que de penser, et qui, pour être, n'a besoin d'aucun lieu, ni ne dépend d'aucune chose matérielle" (*Discours de la méthode*, IV partie), and, on the other, "Possunt autem substantia corporea, et mens, sive substantia cogitans, creata, sub hoc communi conceptu intelligi: quod sint res, quae solo Dei concursu egent ad existendum. Verumtamen non potest substantia primum animadverti ex hoc solo, quod sit res existens; quia hoc solum per se nos non afficit: sed facile ipsam agnoscimus ex quolibet ejus attributo," etc. (*Principia philosophiae*, I, 52.)

covery of a reality is not the same as its exploration and the construction of an adequate theory about it. This was to be the intellectual task of his life, and *not only of his*, but perhaps that of a whole stage of philosophical thought. But already on this *level* of his philosophy, about 1914, defined by the *Meditations on Quixote* and the writings which, seen in this perspective, appear as complementary to it, we find the body of that theory, unequivocally formulated. For the moment, formulated in a decisive concept, introduced into a theory which was not well understood for so many years and which is, if I am not mistaken, the key to the *concrete* and real sense, not merely the formal sense, of the theory which has occupied us up till now, and the one which most fully anticipates what was to be the nucleus itself of Ortega's philosophy, its most fruitful and innovative principle.

74. THE REABSORPTION OF THE CIRCUMSTANCE

In the *Meditations on Quixote*, the theme of circumstance is, as we have seen, inseparable from that of perspective; and both appear linked, on the one hand, to what Ortega calls "individual life," "the immediate," and on the other to "meaning," "spirit," or even *lógos*.[41] "Culture," he writes, "offers us objects already *purified*, which once *were spontaneous and immediate life*, and today, thanks to reflective efforts, *seem to be* free of space and time, of corruption and caprice. They form, as it were, a zone of *ideal and abstract life*, floating above our *personal, always hazardous and problematical, existences*. Individual life, the spontaneous, the circumstance, are different names for the same thing: those portions of life from which the *spirit* they enclose, their *lógos*, has not been extracted."[42] Hazard and problem are the characteristics of personal, individual, circumstantial life; the opposite attributes—exemption from space and time, from caprice and corruption—correspond to those portions of it which are subject to the *lógos*, worked out by culture. Notice, however, that Ortega says that such portions *seem* to be like this; that is, that they cannot be taken, in ultimate seriousness, apart from that individual and problematical life. "Thus, social life, like the other forms of culture," he adds, "is given to us *under the guise of individual life*, of the immediate. What we receive today, already adorned with

[41] *Meditaciones del Quijote*, I, 320–23.   [42] I, 320. Italics mine.

sublime aureoles, had in its season to be narrowed and shrunk in order to pass through the heart of a man."[43] This text, which reproduces the central intuition of the passage in "Adam in Paradise"[44] on which I commented before, already contains the formulation of one of the permanent theses of Orteguian philosophy: faced with the traditional consideration *sub specie aeternitatis*, Ortega shows that the primary consideration—the one on which, in the last instance, that traditional consideration must be founded—is, on the contrary, *under the guise of individual life*. The consequence is this: "All that is general, all that is learned, all that has been achieved in culture, is only the *tactical turn* which we must make in order to adapt ourselves to the immediate."[45] This expression is not a chance hit or an improvisation, but corresponds to what he had said in another context a few months before: "The general is no more than an instrument, an organ, to see the concrete clearly; *its goal is in the concrete, but it is necessary* . . . . For culture is nothing but that premeditated, cunning *turn taken by thought—* which is a generalizing in nature—*in order to throw the chain securely over the neck of the concrete*."[46] That is, what matters is the concrete, the immediate, the circumstantial; but in order to "take charge" or "know what to hold to" with respect to it, it is not enough to *have it there*; but one must *return* to it, in an essential, premeditated tactical turn, which is the ultimate substance of what is called, in a radical sense, *culture*, of which in its turn Ortega will say that it is two things: *clarity* and *security*. Now we can understand this thesis, which has been so stubbornly overlooked.

Ortega insists that we must seek for our circumstance, precisely in what it possesses of limitedness and peculiarity, in what is concrete, individual, and immediate in it, "the one right place in the immense perspective of the world"; and he also insists that, instead of going into ecstasies over hieratical values, we must conquer for our *individual life* its proper place—that is, its circumstantial place—among these values. And he concludes: "In sum: *the reabsorption of the circumstance is the concrete destiny of man*."[47]

[43] I, 321. Italics mine.

[44] I, 476–77.

[45] I, 321. Italics mine.

[46] *Vieja y nueva política*, I, 285. Italics mine.

[47] I, 322. Italics mine.

Note that it is not a question of the destiny of man "in general," in the sense in which Fichte speaks, for example, of *die Bestimmung des Menschen*, a destiny which could be made specific in a number of others, such as that of the learned or scholarly man—*die Bestimmung des Gelehrten*—but of the *concrete* destiny of man, the destiny of each one; and of this destiny Ortega says that it consists in the *reabsorption* of its circumstance. What does this mean? Note that, although this is a decisive concept, it appears only three times so far as I recall, in all of Ortega's work: here, in another passage of the same book on which I shall comment soon, and in a third place[48] in which these two are referred to retrospectively. This means that that *expression* was later supplanted by others, and presents us with the problem of pursuing its development under other names, no doubt more adequate to the evolution of the doctrine itself.

Man, the hero, he had said previously, "advances swift and straight, like a dart, toward a glorious goal"; we march "projected" toward the far distance; circumstance asks of us that we accept its "offer."[49] The reabsorption of the circumstance consists in its *humanization*, in its incorporation into this project of man's; that is, man makes himself *with the things that are offered to him*; he makes *life* with them, his life; he appropriates them by projecting into them meaning and significance—in short, *lógos*. The *destiny* of man, of each man, when he is faithful to his situation—that is, his *concrete* and circumstantial destiny —is to impose his personal project on the real, to give meaning to what does not have meaning by itself, to extract the *lógos* from what is inert, brutal, and "illogical," to convert that which is simply "out there around me" (circumstance) into true *world*, into *personal human life*. The reabsorption of the circumstance consists in this: man, who for the moment is simply there, among things and with them, making his life with them as something outside himself, executes an appropriation of them by personalizing them, "worldifying" them, if the expression is allowable, in terms of his project, which is the mode of realizing that "tactical turn" in which "one throws the chain over the neck of the concrete" and thus incorporates and "reabsorbs" it. Thus, the relationship of the I to the circumstance is not a mere intentional reference, or even a simple "coexistence," but a mutual belonging, only from the

---

[48] *Prólogo para alemanes*, 61, 77.
[49] *Meditaciones del Quijote*, I, 319.

point of view of which does each of the two terms have meaning—and subordinated reality. And this cobelonging is not inert or static, but is *project and offer*, and in consequence *reabsorption*; that is, a *task*, a reality which, so far from being a thing, is *executive* reality that takes place along with things and in virtue of which these things acquire meaning.

Is this interpretation faithful to the meaning of Ortega's texts? Does it not, perhaps, at least project upon the idea of the reabsorption of the circumstance details which proceed from other, much later, levels of his thought? If people had read carefully the *Meditations on Quixote*, in its entirety, without separating the first part from the second, without considering this second part as merely "literary," and therefore taking seriously what it says, they would have arrived many years ago at the point of understanding these concepts, and would have seen that such an interpretation is fully justified, without the need of going outside this book. For the passage I have commented on is inseparable from another at the end, in which the idea of "reabsorption" reappears and is explained. Ortega is speaking of the hero and tragedy; and from this point onward let it be noted—I shall justify it a little later—that both characteristics necessarily belong to human life, so that what he says about them can be applied to *all life*. The hero is defined by his aspiration to be somebody, by a project, part, or role which he has chosen.[50] And Ortega says, "Since the quality of the heroic is based on *the will to be what one not yet is*, the tragic hero has *half his body outside reality*. If we give his legs a pull and return him completely to reality, he becomes a comic character. With difficulty, by dint of effort, the noble heroic *fiction* is added onto *real* inertia: all of that fiction lives by *aspiration*. Its testimony is the *future*. The *vis comica* is limited to accentuating that aspect of the hero which faces toward pure materiality. Through fiction, *reality advances*, it is imposed on our sight and *reabsorbs the tragic role*. The hero made this role *his very being*; he became fused with it. *Reabsorption by reality consists in solidifying, materializing the aspiring intention upon the body of the hero*."[51]

Now we see what is meant by "reabsorption." We are dealing now with the other side: first we saw the reabsorption *of the circumstance*, by means of its humanization and personalization by the project; now

[50] I, 392–94.
[51] I, 395–96. Italics, except for *vis comica*, mine.

we find the reabsorption of the man—of the project—*by the circumstance*. The two aspects are inseparable; and this characteristic of inseparability is the one expressed in the prefix "re–." Ortega does not say simply "absorption" of the circumstance, because man absorbs it while he is at the same time absorbed by it; the result of that dramatic dialogue between the two is precisely the absorption of that which also absorbs—therefore reabsorption. Reality does not allow itself to be controlled easily; strictly speaking it never allows itself to be controlled completely; it is *irreducible*—thus man is a utopian being, as Ortega is to say later; that reality advances by confronting the project or role with which the I, which is its very being, is fused, and in a certain measure, more or less, solidifies, materializes that aspiring intention, made out of the future. Expressed in other words, whereas man tries to "humanize," to "personalize," circumstance and make a *world* out of it—which means a *human* world—reality "thingifies" man, solidifies him, and thus despoils him of his human character properly speaking, that of invention and aspiration. This is the authentic human condition, the undertaking always begun and always frustrated, unrealizable and unrenounceable, which consists in *living*, in trying to be a man. Now we shall see how Ortega, even before he introduces the notion of *life* thematically, must go through a process of defining its attributes and characteristics, and thus gradually constructing his thesis.

75. HEROISM AND TRAGEDY

The theme of heroism is a persistent one in the *Meditations on Quixote*. When Ortega speaks of "the hero" who advances swift and straight toward a goal, there is no narcissism or mere literature in this, but the insinuation of an intellectual theme of the first rank. "All of us, in different measure, are heroes,"[52] he adds; and elsewhere: "Nothing hampers heroism—which is the spirit's activity—like thinking of it as being tied to certain specific contents of life."[53] If this is true, if we are all heroes and heroism is not limited to particular contents of life, this means that Ortega gives the name of heroism to one dimension or characteristic of all human life. When he spells out his doctrine, then, he is initiating—under another name—the theory of that life.

[52] I, 319.   [53] I, 323.

Ortega speaks of the fact that "that which is not—the project for an adventure—governs and composes harsh reality." The man—and in the last instance, all men—who wants adventure does not content himself with reality; he makes it and reshapes it in the light of that project which is not he, but is what he aspires to be. Ortega contrasts this project with custom, tradition, and the biological instincts; that is, nature, society, and history, what is "real," what is "thing" in man. "Being a hero consists in being one's own self. If we resist the fact that heredity, that what lies around us, imposes certain actions on us, it must be that we are seeking to concentrate on ourselves, and only on ourselves, the origin of our acts. When the hero wants, it is not his ancestors in him or the uses of the present which want, but he himself. *And this wanting of his to be himself is heroism.*"[54] The many possible projects depend upon one which is original and radical; the project of oneself. It is himself whom the hero projects, and this project draws in others. Contrasted with the external pressures of *what is other*, is the *selfness* of the hero who wishes to be *himself* and cause his acts to emerge out of himself. That is, the hero is the authentic man. Under the guise of heroism, Ortega introduces the idea of *authenticity*, which he has just defined in strict terms; he contrasts yielding to inertia and collective pressures, the different forms of "socialization," with the idea of authenticity. And this explains the sense of the previous statement that all of us, in some measure, are heroes: all of us are in some degree authentic; life contains a certain degree of authenticity and a certain degree of unauthenticity. Remember the role played later, in Husserl's philosophy, by the concepts of *Eigentlichkeit* and *eigentliche und uneigentliche Existenz.*

This is why Ortega can also speak of "the practical, active originality of the hero" as the most profound originality. We may well ask why Ortega calls the authentic man a "hero"; there is no lack of reasons, and Ortega points them out here. "His life is a perpetual resistance to the habitual and customary. Each movement that he makes has first had to *conquer custom and invent a new kind of attitude.*" "Such a life is a perennial pain, *a constant tearing himself away from that part of himself* which is given over to habit, the prisoner of matter."[55] Resistance and invention, then, constitute authenticity: they are the two faces

[54] I, 390. Italics mine.
[55] I, 390.

of authentic life, which in order to claim its originality, to make its acts emerge from its *selfness*, needs previously to free itself from the pressures and temptations of the social surroundings, from custom, from habit, from what others do—that is, from the ordinary man (remember what Heidegger was to call *Man*). But the decisive point is that it is not only a question of a resistance with regard to what is external and outside oneself, but that one must tear oneself away from part of oneself; that is, the person is made partially extrinsic, alienated, made unauthentic. It is not enough to reclaim the I from what is not itself; rather, the fact is that what is not itself conditions the I and in a certain sense "integrates" it. Once more, it is the double aspect of reabsorption, its essential "to and fro" which is a constitutive part of human life. Resistance to pressures, the tearing away of the unauthentic part of one's own life, "reabsorbed" by the circumstance—especially the social circumstance—original invention and project of oneself; this is, for Ortega in 1914, life as heroism or authenticity.

This dimension is prolonged and made explicit in another: what he calls *tragedy*. "*The hero is the man who wants to be himself. The root of the heroic is found, therefore, in a real act of will* .... The tragic subject is not tragic ... inasmuch as he is a man of flesh and bone, but only inasmuch as he *wants*. *Will*—that paradoxical object which begins in reality and ends in the ideal, for *one only wants what one is not*—*is the tragic theme.*"[56] Ortega emphasizes the *real* nature of the act of will; what the hero wants is *to be himself*; therefore *he is tragic insofar as he wants to be himself*—therefore not as a "thing," as a natural entity, of flesh and bone, but as an *aspiration* or *project* of himself. And when Ortega speaks of "will," we must not think of a psychic "faculty," for this is fully real and not at all paradoxical, but in this *projective aspiration* that "wants what it is not"—so far, of course—which moves within the unreality of the imagined and programmatic.

This idea of tragedy necessarily causes Ortega to turn away from Greek tragedy, whose religious dimension, which is not very well understood, makes it difficult to understand. For Ortega, "the intervention of fate is not necessary."[57] If this were so, determinism could be a substitute for destiny; but it is not—on the contrary, it annuls tragedy. The ordinary spectator of a tragedy cannot escape from the impression that

[56] I, 392. Italics mine.
[57] I, 393.

all the bad things happen to the hero because he holds obstinately to a certain plan. "Fatality, therefore, does not exist, or rather, what fatally happens, happens fatally because the hero has allowed it to happen. The misfortunes of the *Constant Prince* were fated after the point when he decided to be constant, but he is not fated to be constant."[58] And he adds these essential words: "In the tragic, then, far from originating in fatality, *it is essential for the hero to desire his tragic fate*. Therefore tragedy looked at from the vegetative life always has a fictitious quality. All the grief arises from the fact that the hero refuses to give up *an ideal part, an imaginary role which he has chosen*. The actor in the drama, it could be said paradoxically, plays a role which is, in its turn, *the representation of a role*, even though he plays it *in earnest*."[59]

That authentic I consists, therefore, in being a project, an aspiration, a vital program, a character in a novel, a part or role. And there is more; it is essential that the hero *desire* his tragic *fate*; that is, it is not a question of simple *choice*, still less of a *gratuitous* choice, as has been said in France thirty years later; man feels himself to be "summoned," called to be *someone*, and this is vocation, fate; but this is not *imposed* upon man, but *proposed*; man does not choose his fate, and that is why it is fate; but he must choose *to be faithful to it or not*; that is, in Ortega's very words, *to want it or not*; and the consequence that he extracts is that *the man who wants his fate is authentic*; he is the man who adheres to himself, the hero.

A few lines farther on, Ortega achieves greater precisions, which anticipate—with the exception of certain errors—the European philosophy of the last two decades. The nature of the heroic "lies in *the will to be what one is not as yet*"; thus the tragic character "has half his body outside of reality"; which means that half is *inside* it. "With great difficulty, by dint of effort, the noble heroic fiction is superimposed on the inertia of the real: all of it lives from aspiration. Its witness is the future."[60] The hero "anticipates the future and appeals to it. His atti-

---

[58] I, 393.

[59] I, 393–94. Italics mine. Sartre's works after 1943 present again and again ideas which seem to be *in part* mere developments or repetitions of these ideas in the *Meditations on Quixote*, even though they eventually lead in a very different direction. See *L'Être et le néant*, especially pp. 69–127, and also *L'Existentialisme est un humanisme*.

[60] I, 395. As for Sartre, he writes, "Je ne suis pas celui que je serai. D'abord je ne le suis pas parce que du temps m'en sépare. Ensuite parce que ce que je suis n'est pas le

tudes have a utopian significance."[61] To human life in the most characteristic and authentic qualities it possesses—which Ortega calls heroism here—belong *futurition* and *utopianism*, two characteristics which are going to play such a large role in his later thought.

This means that as early as his first book Ortega had discovered the unique and irreducible peculiarity of *human life*, different from every other reality, and of course from all merely biological life. We have seen how the formula "I am I and my circumstance," besides arising out of a solid treatment of the deepest and most technical problems of the philosophy of that time, is expanded and articulated in a series of views which show the fundamental characteristics of human life as such, its conditions or requisites. The only thing lacking—and this proves that Ortega's starting point was not what was then called "the philosophy of life," and which, as we have seen, had almost nothing to do with his philosophy—is this name, for Ortega had not yet arrived at that ultimate simplicity for which he has been so often reproached and in which his greatest profundity lies. The mode of being of human life is visible to Ortega in certain of its extreme forms, those which he shares to some degree, and which display his most authentic consistency. *The structure of life is revealed to him under the guise of heroism or tragedy*. Reality and unreality, a mode of being what one not yet is, living with half one's body outside reality, attempting to carry out a project, wanting to be

fondement de ce que je serai. Enfin parce qu'aucun existant actuel ne peut déterminer rigoureusement ce que je vais être. Comme pourtant je suis déjà ce que je serai (sinon je ne serais pas intéressé à être tel ou tel), *je suis celui que je serai sur le mode de ne l'être pas*." (*L'Être et le néant* [1943], 69.) He also speaks of "un premier projet de moi-même qui est comme mon choix de moi-même dans le monde" and of the "projet unique et premier qui constitue mon être" (*ibid.*, 77). Or, he states that "il s'agit de constituer la réalité humaine comme un être qui est ce qu'il n'est pas et qui n'est pas ce qu'il est" (*ibid.*, 97). But though these statements do not add anything to what Ortega said in 1914, Sartre departs essentially from Ortega—and also departs, if I am not mistaken, from the reality of things—when he adds, in the same contexts, "rien ne peut m'assurer contre moi-même, coupé du monde et de mon essence par ce néant que je *suis*" (*ibid.*, 77); or, "cet être se constitue comme réalité humaine en tant qu'il n'est rien que le projet originel de son propre néant" (*ibid.*, 121). Or, even more explicitly: "L'homme, tel que le conçoit l'existentialiste, s'il n'est pas définissable, c'est qu'il n'est d'abord rien" (*L'Existentialisme est un humanisme*, 22); or, finally: "l'homme n'est rien d'autre que son projet, il n'existe que dans la mesure où il se réalise, il n'est donc rien que l'ensemble de ses actes, rien d'autre que sa vie" (*ibid.*, p. 55). See my essay "El pensamiento y la inseguridad," in *Ensayos de convivencia* (*Obras*, III).

[61] I, 396.

oneself, to be authentically what one must be, because one has freely chosen to do so, "practical" originality, "part" or role in which the subject consists, reabsorption of the circumstance, material and inert reality and fictitious reality of the projective will, fate freely desired. All this appears in the *Meditations on Quixote* as a theory of the hero or the tragic character, not—not yet—as a *theory of human life.*

V.

THEORY OF REALITY

76. THE FOREST AS A VITAL REALITY

In Ortega's writings between 1914 and 1916, a theory of reality is unequivocally formulated which can be carried out only by means of a noticeably innovative method, one which came to be called a short time later, thematically, *vital reason*. The same thing happens with this expression that happens with the other decisive expression, as we have seen, in his philosophy: *human life*. Neither of the two expressions has been "invented," deliberately introduced as a "term." On the contrary: we could say that they have been "shrunk from," that Ortega has reached their *objects*, the realities which correspond to them, without seeking "technical" names for them, and that each expression, relatively late, has been the result of an effort to find a fully adequate name. We might say that Ortega has *reached the point* of seeing that the term "life," in its primary and least intellectualistic and theoretical meaning, is the one which best indicates the reality first discovered under other, less direct, names, and that analogously he has been *forced* to call the form of reason which he had in fact reached, "vital reason," in order to avoid its confusion with the reigning theories about reason, and because this expression had been formed undeliberately in his writings on the subject. The theory of reality, as Ortega understands it, is inseparable from that method which makes access to it possible; but, as Ortega first brings the method into play and then reflects upon it, we will do well to follow this order and try, insofar as it is possible, to present each dimension separately. For what is important here is to show the two theories, that of reality and that of reason, *in statu nascenti*, as they originate in Ortega's early philosophy.

The preliminary Meditation in the *Meditations on Quixote* begins with something which is as surprising in a book of "literary criticism," as this one seems to be, as in a philosophical investigation, which is what it primarily is: the description of a forest, "La Herrería" ["The Smithy"] in El Escorial, to be exact, a spot closely associated with Ortega's life, for he frequented this place as a youth. This is essential, for he is dealing, in fact, with a forest which has been *lived*, and his analysis and the theory of its reality arise out of this characteristic, as we shall see. The mere "notion" of a forest, such as can be found in a dictionary—"place containing trees and bushes," says the dictionary of the Royal Spanish Academy—or an "image" of one, which could serve for a phenomenological description and the attempt to reach its essence, or *Wesen*,[1] would not be sufficient. There are certain basic experiences which make possible that kind of intellectual approximation; but when we say "experiences," we must be careful not to insist on their quality of realization or execution, for, as we shall soon see, it is essential for them not to have been executed. It is a question of *vital* experiences which include, beyond the sphere of what is called, in a narrow sense, "pragmatic," all the forms of "dealing" with reality, including, of course, those which are purely mental, imaginative, conceptual, and negative—for example, all the modes of abstention and privation.

The expression of these experiences in a broad sense, and consequently their interpretation and conceptuation, obliquely formulates a method—in the literal and etymological sense of path or road—whose first reality is, naturally, *to be traveled on*. Normally the method is established by its *exercise*: "We make the road as we walk"; and only the retrospective view discovers it, in the form of footprints. Thus, theories about philosophical methods tend to be late, with respect to their invention and application; the most considerable and closest example is phenomenology, fully realized in the *Logical Investigations* and formulated as a

---

[1] Husserl says, in a passage which is very important with regard to method, "Das Eidos, das *reine Wesen*, kann sich intuitiv in Erfahrungsgegebenheiten, in solchen der Wahrnehmung, Erinnerung usw., exemplifizieren, ebensogut aber *auch in blossen* Phantasiegegebenheiten, Demgemäss können wir, ein Wesen selbst und originär zu erfassen, von entsprechenden erfahrenden Anschauungen ausgehen, *ebensowohl aber auch von nicht-erfahrenden nicht-daseinerfassenden, vielmehr 'bloss einbilden' Anschauungen.*" *Ideen*, § 4, p. 12. (In Gaos's translation: "The *eidos*, the *pure essence*, can be intuitively exemplified in empirical data, in data of perception, memory, etc., but equally well *in mere data of fancy*. We can, therefore, in order to apprehend an essence in itself and *originally*, start off from the corresponding empirical situations, *but equally well from intuitions that are not experimentative*—which do not seize upon something which is in existence—but rather 'merely imaginative.'" (*Ideas*, 23.)

theory only in the *Ideas*, thirteen years later. In this case, the "attitude" or "installation" from which one arrives at the forest means that the forest at which one has arrived is not a "thing"—or a combination of things—or a mere "object," but what we might call a "lived forest"; that is, a *concrete* reality rooted in my life, which is concrete too. All the rest consists of abstractions or constructions, abstract or "thingified" interpretations of what a forest radically and authentically is. When Ortega says that in every language its name preserves an aura of mystery which, strictly speaking, is untranslatable, since the German *Wald* is not the same as the Spanish *bosque*, etc., he is showing what *vital* reality is being referred to, in what measure something so much "mine" as *its* aura of mystery belongs to it.

This is much more than the theory of *Zuhandensein* as opposed to *Vorhandensein* which Heidegger introduced in *Sein und Zeit*, or the "existential" descriptions found in Sartre and his followers;[2] it is a question of new forms of access to the real—and correlatively, of new aspects or modes of reality; but the radicality of Ortega's point of view, as we shall see immediately, is much greater. What Ortega shows, what constitutes the nerve center of his "description," is that *I necessarily enter into the description of the forest*, and that that description is not possible unless it includes a reference to me. In other words, it would not be possible—except fraudulently and by "cheating"—to describe a forest *by itself*. And the reason for this is that *without me there is no forest*. Does this mean that the forest is a "subjective" reality? By no means: it is something perfectly real and objective, a reality with which I find myself and with which I have to come to terms, as much "outside of me" as I am "in" the forest. Am I "part" of the forest, then? Not at

---

[2] To take an example, let us recall the passage in Sartre where he interprets fear (it is not this interpretation which interests me, but the description on which it is based): "Ce soldat qui fuit, il avait toute à l'heure encore autrui: l'ennemi au bout de son fusil. La distance de l'ennemi à lui était mesurée par la trajectoire de sa balle et je pouvais, moi aussi, saisir et transcender cette distance comme distance s'organisant autour du centre 'soldat.' Mais voilà qu'il jette son fusil dans le fossé et qu'il se sauve. Aussitôt la présence de l'ennemi l'environne et le presse; L'ennemi, qui était tenu à distance par la trajectoire des balles, bondit sur lui, à l'instant même où la trajectoire s'effonde; en même temps, cet arrière-pays qu'il défendait et contre lequel il s'accotait comme un mur, tourne soudain, s'ouvre en éventail et devient l'avant, l'horizon accueillant vers quoi il se réfugie." *L'Être et le néant* (1943), 356. See also certain analogous descriptions in his novels—the root in *La Nausée*, some passages in *L'Âge de raison*—or in the works of Simone de Beauvoir—*L'Invitée*, *Le Sang des autres*.

all. If this were the case, it would mean accepting the forest and I myself as "things"; on the other hand, there is no way of seeing in what measure or in what sense I could be considered as an "element" or "ingredient" of the forest, in possible addition to others. What does not exist or have meaning is the forest "in itself"; neither "in itself"—as realism would suppose—nor "in myself"—as an idealist attitude would tend to think. In fact, Ortega's philosophical innovation, which here *is executed* before being strictly formulated, consists in going beyond those two forms of "thingifying" thought—whether one is dealing with some things, or with others, with extended things or thinking things, of the thing called "forest" or the "thing" called "consciousness" —on which the philosophy which some believe to be the last word is now, anachronistically, falling back, when it is not the last word but rather the next-to-last. The forest is something fully real, different from me, with which and in which I find myself, with which I have to come to terms, which is irreducible to me; but this presumed forest "in itself" does not exist, for it is a hypothesis which in the last instance is contradictory. The forest needs me in order *to be*; to be itself, to be that forest, of course. My possibilities *as such*—Ortega was later to say— as they *confront* a portion of the real, of what there is, constitute *the being of the forest*. The forest is the result of a private dialogue between the I and a certain portion of circumstance, and without those ingredients, its reality—which is of another order—does not become established. Let us see how this can be.

The lines—apparently a purely literary paragraph of description of El Escorial—with which this Meditation begins already contain some points of interest. Ortega refers to this landscape in various seasons of the year, in a "temporal description" which suggests a reality, as I said before, "lived" over a long period of time and not only perceived as it is at present. The images employed suggest what might be called "distant perspectives," which contribute unexpected associations and thus expand the compass of comprehension, broaden the elements which might intervene in the total life experience; "Here, Spring passes through swift, instantaneous, and exaggerated—like an erotic image through the steely soul of a monk."[3] But, in particular, Ortega is already proceeding to a "vitalization" of the landscape, which appears from the outset as incorporated into human life. Thus, he tells us that there are

[3] I, 329.

places of wonderful silence, which is never absolute silence. And the reason is that when this absolute silence falls, the external absence of sound is replaced by organic sounds—the pounding of the heart, the throb of blood in the temples, the stir of air in the lungs. Expressed in other words, when the *external* circumstance falls silent, then the one which normally lies hidden appears: the *internal* and organic circumstance, which is also circumstance, though usually it is not "paid attention to" and is therefore forgotten. Thus, traditional thought has obstinately been able to commit the error of taking *together* the I and a portion of the circumstance—namely, the organic one—and contrasting it with the rest of the circumstance, taking both as things.

"He can't see the forest for the trees." This German adage—*Er sieht den Wald vor lauter Bäumen nicht*—which seems to be a joke, is the starting point. "Forest and city," says Ortega, "are two essentially deep things, and depth is condemned, fatally, to become surface if it wishes to show itself."[4] "Around me now I have as many as two dozen grave oaks and graceful ash trees. Is this a forest? Certainly not; what I see is some trees of a forest. The true forest is composed of the trees that I do not see. *The forest is an invisible nature*—that is why, in every language, its name retains an aura of mystery." "I *can* get up now and take one of these indistinct paths where I see the blackbirds crossing. The trees I saw before *will be* supplanted by others like them. The forest *will gradually* come to pieces, falling apart in a series of *successively* visible segments. But *I will never find it* wherever I am. *The forest flees from one's eyes*." "The forest is always *a little beyond* where we are. It has just gone away from where we are, and only its still-fresh *footprint* remains. The ancients, who projected the silhouettes of their emotions into corporeal and living forms, peopled the forests with fugitive nymphs. Nothing could be more exact and expressive. As you walk along, let a quick glance fall on a clearing in the thicket, and you will find a quivering in the air as if it were hastening to fill the hollow left by a slender naked body as it fled." "From any one of the places in it, the wood is, strictly speaking, a *possibility*. It is a path down which we *might* go; it is a spring from which a faint sound reaches us, in the arms of silence, and which we *might* discover a few steps farther on; it is snatches of song sung in the distance, by birds perched on branches which we *might* reach. *The forest is a sum of possible acts of ours which,*

[4] I, 330.

as we performed them, would lose their genuine value. The part of the forest which is before us is only a pretext for the rest of it to be hidden and distant."[5]

This "description" of the wood is as little as possible like what we usually understand as description: namely, description of what "is there." Ortega constantly refers to what is "not"—present—but to the past (the "footprint") and the future (possibilities); and to what is not "there" but "off there," farther off, hidden and latent. That is, for him the *vital* reality "forest," the forest *as a forest*—not seen in other interpretations: as "land" or "a group of trees" or "a certain amount of lumber," etc.—consists in *possibility*. And yet, *it is a reality*. And with this Ortega introduces an "ontological" theme—let us accept this word for the moment—of supreme importance, a word destined to have long repercussions in his later work and all the thought inspired by him: that of *realities* which consist in being *possibilities*. The last sentence I have italicized is decisive: "The wood *is* a sum of *possible acts* of ours which, as we performed them, would lose their genuine value." That is, that reality would cease to be what it is and would become another, a different type of reality from that which consists in possibility. The forest is only an example; if we take this idea in its widest scope, we will see that it is a characteristic of purely human realities: the city, history as such, one's fellow man, in a special way the *other* sex with regard to each of the sexes.[6] Very well, then: possibility is always *my* possibility—it is not a question of "potentialities"; therefore the reality of the forest—its own reality—involves *me*, without being in the least subjectivized by this. The forest is not an invention of mine, it is not something I can do anything about, I find myself with it absolutely; but I find it only by finding myself in and with it, and only with me is it that forest. The forest and I are two *irreducible* realities—it is useless to try to "take the forest out" of me or to "include me" in the forest—but they are *indigent*, needy; we need each other reciprocally to be who we are. The theory of the forest is only an exemplification of the thesis "I am I and my circumstance," which has been in operation ever since its formulation in all of Ortega's metaphysics.

[5] I, 330–31. Italics mine.

[6] See, for example, Zubiri's admirable study "Grecia y la pervivencia del pasado filosófico" (in *Naturaleza, Historia, Dios* [1944], especially 393ff.), and also some passages in my book *La estructura social*, chapter 7.

77. THE STRUCTURE OF REALITY

Ortega makes use of the forest to disclose one characteristic of certain realities—indeed, of all realities: the depth-surface duality, or, in another form, latency-patency. It is a question of a *structural* principle of reality—and, correlatively, of knowledge: manifestation or *patency* has to take place in the form of superficialization of what lies deep and, inasmuch as it is deep, latent. Hence the fact that for Ortega certain negative characteristics are not negative, but acquire positive meaning. The "invisibility" of the forest or the city are not negations, but the very condition of depth, needy of patentization. "Invisibility," writes Ortega, "being hidden, is not a merely negative characteristic, but a positive quality which, when it is shed upon a thing, transforms it, makes a new thing of it."[7] From the point of view of formal ontology this would make no sense. Compare it with the Aristotelian notion of privation, or *stéresis*,[8] or with the Scholastic conception according to which darkness is a mere *ens rationis*.[9] Ortega affirms the necessity of holding to reality *just as it is*, of recognizing that *each thing has its own condition*, that there are *different kinds of clarity*, and not only the clarity of surfaces. It is a question of carrying to its ultimate consequences one methodical demand of phenomenology, which Ortega makes his own: "Absolute positivism versus partial positivism," he says, in the manner of Husserl, in the first *Espectador*, when he defends the right of the imaginary along with the perceptible, of the centaur along with the

---

[7] I, 331–32.

[8] Aristotle, *Metaphysics*, V, 22.

[9] See, conversely, the *vital* interpretation of darkness which I have expounded elsewhere: "Some things *hide* others. The vital determination of the occult or hidden has a primary visual significance. There is, finally, the radical form of invisibility which is lack of light; that is, expressed in vital terms, darkness, shadow, which is not, as some Scholastics think, *ens rationis*—it might be, just possibly, from the point of view of physics—but a positive vital reality, with which I find myself and with which I have to deal as with any other reality. In my life, I find darkness as an irreducible reality, one which is even the object of visual 'perception.' And darkness is, neither more nor less, the image of *nothingness*, probably its psychic and historical origin. Nothingness as positive reality, as the negation of reality, is being sustained in it and depends on it: it is the kind of reality—positive, therefore—which total negation possesses, of itself. Analogously, darkness is the form of visible—or visual—presence of invisibility itself, as such. When we open our eyes upon darkness, *we see that it cannot be seen*." "La interpretación visual del mundo" (1956), in *El oficio del pensamiento*, 56.

real rose, of the manner in which each form of reality presents itself.[10] Each thing has its own condition and not the one which we might like to demand of it or impose upon it; not to know this is the "cordial sin" which is derived from lack of love; nothing is more opposed to the philosophical attitude, if philosophy is the general science of love. This is an attitude which Ortega maintains tenaciously throughout the whole course of his work: respect for reality, the decision not to supplant it by utopianism, Greek kalends, wishful thinking, and other temptations of thought, especially the thought of the last two centuries. Fidelity to the real—satisfaction in it, letting things reveal their own structure—is the chief demand of philosophy. Remember what we observed before about "veracity" as an attitude of the philosopher: it is nothing but the ethical aspect of that intellectual requisite; and I say aspect, because both things are really only one.

Ortega tells us that, even having recognized the fugitive, absent, and hidden nature of the forest, its quality as a combination of hidden possibilities, this is not sufficient to possess the whole idea of the forest. Why? Here one of the most serious problems of knowledge slips in, and simultaneously the theme which eventually will be the distinction between *radical* realities and *radicated* realities. "*If the deep and latent is to exist for us, it must present itself to us,* and this presenting of itself must be in such a form that it does not lose its quality of depth and latency."[11] I hear different sounds in the wood, the water running and the birds singing; the water that flows at my feet and the oriole that sings over my head have full intensity and brilliance; but I hear other sounds which are lacking in these qualities. "Without the need of deliberating, I scarcely hear them, I enclose them in an act of ideal *interpretation* and cast them far away from me: *I hear them as distant.* If I limit myself to receiving them passively in my hearing, these two pairs of sounds are equally present and close by. But the different sonorous quality of both pairs invites me to place them at a distance, attributing a different spatial quality to them. *It is I,* then, *by an act of mine, who keep them in virtual distension*; if this act were lacking, distance would disappear and everything would occupy, undifferentiatedly, a single plane. Hence, *distance is a virtual quality of certain things that are present,* a quality that they acquire only by virtue of

10 "Conciencia, objeto y las tres distancias de éste." *El Espectador,* I. II, 50–64.
11 I, 334. Italics mine.

an act of the subject's. *The sound is not far away;* I make it far away."[12] This shows my intervention or co-operation in the constitution of perceptive reality. Passively, all sounds are equally "present," but my interpretation maintains them in *distension* and lives them close by or far away; that is, it simultaneously recognizes and projects a *structure,* which *it would not have without me,* but which is the *structure of reality.*

What distance shows with regard to space is revealed analogously for time in the life experience of *faded color,* which Ortega analyzes marvelously. "What color do we see when we see a faded color? The blue which is before our eyes we see *as* having been a more intense blue, and this seeing the present color along with the past one, through what it was before, is an active vision which is not like the reflection in a mirror; it is an *idea.* The fading or dulling of a color is a new and virtual quality which comes over it, giving it a sort of temporal depth. Without the need of reasoning, in a single and momentaneous vision, we discover the color and its history, its hour of splendor and its present ruin."[13] If perception were purely sensorial, none of this would happen; it is what happens with the mirror, which reflects only the *present.* (Nor should we lose sight of the fact that among the qualities which Parmenides discovers in the being is included that of "presence"—*parón*—corresponding to the vision of the *noûs;* at the base of this discussion of Ortega's is implied the transcending of Eleatism.) In a passive and receptive or inert manner, when I look at a blue, I can see only *that* blue; but the fact is that when I *see* a faded color—and in fact I do see faded colors—I see in the present dull color, *another* more intense and brilliant color that *was,* a past color which in some fashion survives in the present. Where? is what we must ask ourselves. Not, naturally, in the color itself as a mere perceptive reality; nor is it a matter of reasoning or inference; it is not that we *see* the present color and *think* that it must have been more intense before; we see it, equally and simultaneously, as blue and as faded; we see it as *faded blue,* and here the adjective does not designate a mere chromatic quality, for that color is not in the spectrum, but a *vital* quality; the old color survives in *human* vision, which is always intellective, interpretative—in a word, historical. When *man* perceives, he has necessarily to interpret, and thus he can instantaneously *be present* in the fading of the color.

[12] I, 334–35. Italics mine.   [13] I, 336–37.

Ortega has a clear awareness of this. Hence his doctrine is rounded out by the recognition that there are different *planes of reality*, and by the *interpretive and intellective* nature of vision, and, in general, of perceiving. "If there were nothing but passive seeing, the world would be reduced to a *chaos of luminous dots*. But over and above passive seeing there is an active seeing, *which interprets by seeing and sees by interpreting*; a seeing which is looking."[14] Plato, he adds, called these seeings which are looked at *ideas*. The third dimension of the orange is only an idea, and "God is the ultimate dimension of the meadow" when a very religious man says that he sees God in the blooming meadow or in the vaulted surface of night; it is the *ultimate plane of reality*, necessary to all integral perspective, as Ortega was to maintain throughout his work. But the philosophically decisive consequence that must be extracted from this is that if there were no more than passive seeing, the world would be reduced to a chaos of luminous dots; and since that is not a world, if there were nothing more than that sort of seeing, *there would be no world*. The only real and human seeing, active seeing or looking, *is* interpretation, and *that is why there is a world*. There is no interpretation without vision, or vision without interpretation. *Perception is interpretive and interpretation is perceptive*. Thus what we call "things" are *interpretations*—interpretations, of course, of *reality*.

This theory of reality is unequivocally formulated, in extremely precise terms, which for their part implicate—or, using expressions later introduced by Ortega, "complicate"—man's cognitive activity. There is, says Ortega, a *patent world*, which is the world of *pure impressions*; but there is also a *world behind it*, made up of *structures of impressions*, "which, though it is latent in relation to the first world, is not for that reason less real," and which requires something more of us than opening our eyes.[15] The culmination of this theory is the concept of *foreshortening*. Depth—Ortega now takes this notion in its most general sense—whether visual or auditory, whether of space or of time, is always presented in a surface. And then this surface has two values: one, material; the other, virtual. According to the virtual value, the surface, without ceasing to be one, "spreads out in a deep sense"; that is what Ortega calls *foreshortening*. "Foreshortening," he concludes, "*is the organ of visual depth*; in it we find a limit case, where *simple vision is fused with a purely intellectual act*."[16]

[14] I, 336. Italics mine.   [15] I, 335.   [16] I, 337. Italics mine.

This concept of *foreshortening* is a singularly fruitful one, and very recent doctrines of human perception and intellection could be reduced to it. It contains the two aspects or dimensions of perception, or, if you like, of intellection. Foreshortening is, at one and the same time, *seeing* and *what is seen*. Expressed more precisely: *reality is seen in foreshortening*—that is, *perspectively*—and this means: (a) concretely (since the point of view is always *this and no other*); (b) intellectively (from a certain interpretation). But, on the other hand: *reality is foreshortening*; I mean, reality is constituted and I have to come to terms with it insofar as it manifests itself and exists for me perspectively. This notion of foreshortening, which Ortega takes in its broadest sense— although his point of departure consists of *examples* which are by preference visual and also aural—contains possibilities that are far from having been exploited. We would, of course, have to work out an adequate theory, and especially a theory of the "analogous" or "homologous" forms of foreshortening. But it should not be believed that Ortega takes only these first steps, which are not to be despised. This idea of reality brings him to the concept of *structure*, so often used in this context, which must be considered separately.

78. STRUCTURE AND INTERPRETATIONS: REALITY AS A GENERIC FUNCTION

The theory of reality which I am trying to formulate strictly, is tied up with the doctrine of perspective. Let us recall that for Ortega, "the definitive being of the world is neither matter nor soul, that it is not any particular thing, but a perspective." The notion of foreshortening derives from the visual—like perspective—but Ortega takes both ideas in a general sense and with all their possibilities. The two are connected, in turn, with the notions of patency and latency on the one hand, depth and surface on the other, and they converge in the idea of *structure*, which had already appeared when he spoke of the latent, or background, worlds made up of "structures of impressions," but which he later introduces more formally and rigorously, as a key concept of this theory of the real.

"A *structure*," says Ortega, "is a *thing of the second degree*; I mean, a combination of things or simple *material elements*, *plus an order* in which those elements are disposed. It is obvious that the *reality* of that order has a value and a significance which are different from *the reality possessed by its elements* . . . . Things united in a relationship form a structure."[17] The essential feature of this definition is that for Ortega there are no "things" or "elements," which happen to dispose themselves in certain structures, but that what Ortega understands by *structure* is a *reality* which *includes* the elements, in a certain order, disposition, or relationship. That is, structure is not the *disposition* of the elements, but a *reality*, a thing of the second degree, made up of those elements in their order. We could say, in a formula: structure=elements+order. The immediate consequence is that the "thing" by itself, the *naked* element, has very little *reality*. Ortega himself extracts this consequence immediately: "How unimportant a thing would be if it were only what it is in isolation! How poor, how barren, how blurred! One might say that there is in each thing a certain secret potentiality to be much more, which is freed and expanded when one thing or other things enter into a relationship with it. One might say that each thing is fertilized by the rest; that they desire each other, like male and female; one might say that they love each other and aspire to a marital relationship, *to join together in societies, in organisms, in structures, in worlds.*" *Effective* realities are not, then, elements or isolated things, but the arrangement of these in different ways; we might say that the elements are elements *of* the structures; and the enumeration of these structures made by Ortega is sufficiently expressive of the breadth of his conception: societies, organisms, edifices, worlds—that is, "the natural," biological or not, as much as the human, and also that which results from voluntary human action.

But the decisive factor, and the one which emphasizes the meaning of all this doctrine, is what Ortega then adds: *"What we call 'Nature' is no other than the maximum structure into which all material elements have entered."*[18] This is the key to the whole interpretation: *Nature* is the "maximum" organization, that is, the sum, the organization of the highest order, and at the same time the one into which *all* material elements enter, not only a portion of them. We are dealing, then, with a *structural hierarchy*: among the *material* structures, nature is the greatest one, and all the rest are subordinated to it; they are *partial* and

17 I, 350. Italics mine.
18 I, 350. Italics mine.

of an *inferior order* insofar as their complexity goes. I mean that this supreme structure is made up of other structures which "function" within it as elements, even though they in their turn are made up of other simple elements. These intermediate structures are organisms, societies, etc. Strictly speaking, the only *real* permanent material structure would be nature, for the other structures function as elements *of* it; which means that their quality of being *natural structures* would arise from this.

Is this sufficient? Not at all. If Ortega were to take this higher structure which is nature as a mere *factum*, without trying to explain it, to justify it, he would not have gone beyond the point of view of "things," though he would have gone beyond things in their isolation. I mean that he would not have transcended any other idea of reality. Once more, the *I* intervenes in this constitution, without *subjectivizing* it thereby. The concepts of "reflection" and "meaning" are added to those previously introduced to explain the genesis or constitution of those kinds of reality. "When we open our eyes—you must have observed—there is a first instant in which objects rush distortedly into our field of vision. It seems that they expand, stretch, break up as though they were a gaseous body tormented by a gust of wind. But bit by bit order enters in. First the things which are in the center of our vision settle down and become fixed, then those on the edges of our vision. This settling down and fixing of their outlines comes from *our attention*, which has *ordered* them; that is, *has spread a net of relationships* between them." One might think of an attitude depending chiefly on Kantianism: it would be our subjectivity which would establish relationships among elements which are chaotic in themselves, in order to construct a world with them. But this is not so; we are not dealing here with a subjective order, but with the very *structure* of the real, *which includes me*, certainly. "A thing cannot be fixed and confined except with others." That is, I do not "set" arbitrary or at least subjective relationships on my own, but *I discover them in things.* "If we continue to pay attention to an object, it will become more and more fixed, for we shall be *finding in it more reflections and connections of surrounding things. The ideal would be to make each thing the center of the universe.*" What does this last sentence mean? Attention does not *impose* relationships, but *discovers* them as it tries out different points of view. The reflections and connections are really there; they are reflections and connections *of surrounding things.* To make each thing the center of the universe means to take it as a point of view in order to discover the totality of its real connections; precisely this conferring upon it of a central position leads us to abandon it in order to test this perspective with each one of the others. The essential thing about the sentence I have quoted is that Ortega speaks of "each thing," and therefore of all things successively. It is not a question of petrifying the central position of *a* thing, or of any of them, for that would be equivalent to hieratizing the perspective; but of the opposite, of making each—unstably—assume the perspective.

"And," he concludes, "this is the *depth* of something: what it contains of a *reflection of the rest,* of *allusion* to the rest. The reflection is the form most accessible to the senses of the *virtual existence of one thing in another.*" Depth and *reflection* appear here as the virtual existence of one thing in another; that is, the form of structure *that the senses can apprehend;* like the notion of perspective, they express metaphorically the intrinsic condition of the real. Reality is seen foreshortened, perspectively. Later, Ortega will reach the point of saying that perspective, far from being the deformation of reality, is its *organization;* except for the formula, the idea is already here: reality is fundamentally *structure,* irreducible to the *mere* elements, which as such do not have full reality, since their order or disposition has to be added to them; and these are not anything "added" to them from outside, created by the subject, but consist in the virtual existence of some *in* others, whose sense symbol is the *reflection.* (Elsewhere Ortega writes, not long after this: "Do not aspire to create things, for this would be an objection against your work. A created thing can only be a fiction. Things are not created; they are invented in the good old sense of the word; they are found.")[19]

And behind the reflection, the *meaning.* "The 'meaning' of a thing is the supreme form of its *coexistence with the rest;* it is its dimension of depth. No, it is not enough for me to have the *materiality* of a thing; I need, further, to know its 'meaning'; that is, the mystic shadow which *the rest of the universe casts upon it.*"[20]

This idea is made explicit much later on, at the end of the *Meditations on Quixote,* whose two parts are so strictly connected that separating them hinders their comprehension. Here the "sense" of things is for-

[19] II, 27.   [20] I, 351. Italics mine.

mally contrasted to their "materiality," as two aspects of them. "Things have two aspects. One is the 'sense' of things, their meaning, what they are when they are *interpreted*. The other is the 'materiality' of things, their positive substance, what constitutes them before and apart from all *interpretation*."[21] Here the theory of reality and its interpretations are prefigured—and even with the use of the decisive term. And note that "materiality" and "sense" are inseparable; that is, reality is not contrasted with its interpretations, for these *belong to it*, they partake *of* reality, are simply one of its *aspects*. There is, then, a *naked* reality previous to all its interpretations, and an *interpreted* reality, or, which is the same thing, a reality with meaning. It is what Ortega had previously called its "salvation," the "reflections" which the sun calls forth from "matter of all kinds";[22] it is, in another context, the theme of *reabsorption of the circumstance.*

In later writings, Ortega was to employ other formulas for the same ideas; he was to say that what is given to us is the circumstance as pure facilities and pure difficulties for living, upon which we project our projects and thus interpret them and make "things" of them; he was also to say that man "makes his world," that he is "a born fabricator of universes." All this had been found when he analyzed *Don Quixote*, especially with regard to the windmills, in his first book. The problem which Ortega poses himself in all its sharpness is that of the *necessity* of interpretation of the real. The flour mills of Criptana gesticulate at the west, upon the line of the horizon. "These mills," he says, "have a meaning: as 'sense' these mills are giants." It will be said that Don Quixote was insane, but this does not solve the problem for us; the fact that we disqualify *that* interpretation does not affect its interpretive character or the generality of this condition; for Ortega continues to ask about giants in general: where did humanity get them from? Even though the mills are not giants, where do giants come from, since they do not exist and never have existed *in reality*? In any case, it is a question of an interpretation of something which humanity has achieved. Consequently, every time we refer to a reality, we do so out of a "sense," therefore out of an interpretation. And then, what is that which Ortega has called "materiality"? Can it be the absence of all interpretation? No; it is an interpretation, no more and no less than the rest. What interpretation? This: "the thing when it is not interpreted," resulting from an

[21] I, 385. Italics mine   [22] I, 311.

effort, a very painful one certainly, to look at the real from a certain foreshortening.

Only this finally clarifies Ortega's theory of reality. The apparently literary passages in the first Meditation, "Short Treatise on the Novel," contain some of the most rigorous explanations of this theory, in which the first mature version of Ortega's metaphysics is sketched out. "*All things*, out of their inert materiality, make signals, as it were, which we *interpret*. These interpretations become *condensed* until they form an objectivity which amounts to a duplication of the primary, the so-called *real*, objectivity. A perennial conflict arises from this: the 'idea' or 'sense' of each thing and its 'materiality' try to fit, one inside the other. But this presupposes the victory of one of them. If the 'idea' triumphs, 'materiality' is supplanted and we live in a state of *hallucination*. If materiality gains the upper hand, and, penetrating into the vapor of the idea, *reabsorbs* it, then we live in a state of *disillusionment*."[23] I have italicized the most illuminating aspects. Ortega presents this doctrine in the most general way possible; as I have already pointed out several times, the particular determinations he has been considering are no more than cases or examples in which the condition of the real becomes visible; all things make signals, and we respond with interpretations. Thus a "duplication" appears, whose meaning now becomes clear: there are in fact two "realities": one is the "so-called" real; the other, the combined total of interpretations. The quality of reality is not exclusive to the first of these; not only does Ortega point this out, but also the fact that the second constitutes an *objectivity*, something different from me, which I find in my path as an object. There is still one key word, which seems to me to be the most significant: interpretations are *condensed* until they form an objectivity. That is, since material elements are not, properly speaking, reality, but rather this quality belongs only to their structure, in the same manner an isolated interpretation would remain under the threshold of "objectivity," would lack the necessary consistency. That condensation is what might be called its "worldification," the establishment of a stratum of "consistent" reality, with which we have to come to terms—the definitory quality of the real. Thus, this conflict which Ortega describes as perennial; that is, as a condition of human life: the struggle between the "idea" or "sense" and materiality, or between the interpretation pro-

[23] I, 386. Italics mine.

jected by me upon the real, and the inertia of the real. The situation can be one of dynamic equilibrium or of complete triumph of one of the two terms; if this last occurs, and the idea triumphs, materiality is passed over and supplanted; in other words, a certain interpretation is imposed, even though this be by exercising violence on materiality; this is the situation of Don Quixote, who projects the interpretation "giants" onto the reality which moves its colossal blades on the Manchegan plain; in a less extreme form, with ups and downs, with alternatives, it is the *predominant* situation in some societies or epochs; then we live *in a state of hallucination*, in perpetual instability, always on the brink of finding that trampled-down materiality will return to claim its rights. If the opposite occurs, if it is materiality which imposes itself, interpretations are defeated by the inertia which weighs upon them, the idea or project is *reabsorbed*, and then we live *in a state of disillusionment*. The word illusion possesses here, as compared to the merely negative meaning which it has in some languages, the dual and ambiguous meaning, positive and negative at the same time, which it has in Spanish; it is at once, and unexpectedly, mirage, fiction, deception, and also project, incitation, hope. It is not in vain that Spanish calls the loss of illusion "desengaño." The figure of the hero who has half his body outside reality (and, therefore, the other half inside it), the dramatic tension between the project which advances and tries to reabsorb the circumstance as opposed to the inert materiality of that circumstance which "reabsorbs the tragic role," anticipated what, in a more technical form, this theory has to say about the real.

I noted before that materiality is also an interpretation, that which consists in taking the thing *insofar as it is not interpreted*. Ortega studies this possibility with regard to *realism*. "There are *distances, lights, and slants* out of which the sensitive material of things reduces the sphere of our interpretations to a *minimum*. A concretizing force impedes the movement of our images. The inert and rough thing spits out of itself whatever 'senses' we wish to give it: it is there, confronting us, affirming its *mute, terrible materiality* in the face of all the phantoms. This is what we call *realism*: to *take* things to a certain distance, *place* them under a light, to *slant them* in such a way as to accentuate that aspect of them which slopes toward pure materiality."[24] It is a question of degree, on the one hand: of accentuating, of reducing our interpretation to a

---

[24] I, 386. Italics mine.

minimum; but, on the other hand, there is nothing more *active*: I have italicized the words with which Ortega indicates the *operations* which I must execute in order to "not interpret" the real and all the perspectivist images which it accumulates. The "inert and rough thing" spits out whatever senses we wish to give it . . . except one: that which we have given to it when we interpreted it as mute, terrible materiality. Therefore Ortega has to add that reality can only enter into art by making an active and combative element (that is, a dramatic element), out of its very inertia and desolation. The indifference of realism with regard to things, its attitude—which seems paradoxical—that one is as good as another, has its justification precisely in this, which leads Ortega to a last important discovery: that it is not, properly speaking, things which interest him. And then, what?

Ortega speaks of the characters in the realistic novel, and points out that they lack attraction; then the question arises of how it is possible that the representation of them can move us; and Ortega answers, "It is not *the* realities which move us, but their representation; that is, the representation of *the* reality in them. This distinction is, in my mind, decisive: the poetic quality of reality is not reality as this or that thing, but reality as a generic function."[25] This passage is of supreme importance. Ortega distinguishes between *the* reality and *the* realities; this distinction has a precise meaning: it is the difference which exists between *things* and reality as *generic function*; that is, what those things *possess of reality*, what makes them "those realities." And this is inseparable from the I which must deal with them and interpret them. All objects, adds Ortega, have an imaginary aura around them; namely their interpretations, under which an attempt is made to show their pure materiality. Man aspires, wants, imagines; all of this, *if it is taken as sufficient*, bows before that "ultimate instance," which in its turn is not sufficient either. The meaning of poetic realism is the insufficiency of culture, of whatever is noble, bright, aspiring. Wrapping around it "lies the barbarous, brutal, mute, meaningless reality of things . . . . It is real, it is there: in a terrible way, it is sufficient unto itself. Its strength and its only meaning are rooted in its presence. . . . reality is a simple and terrifying 'being there.' Presence, lying there, inertia. Materiality."[26]

[25] I, 387.
[26] I, 387. In my commentary on the *Meditaciones del Quijote*, I have compared

All this, however, is only one side of the real, because it is the result of a certain human perspective. In the human drama *the* reality is represented. This clarifies the text we discussed before, according to which the definitive being of the world is neither matter nor spirit, nor any particular thing, but a *perspective*; even this expression is insufficient; we have already seen that that notion had to be integrated with the notion of circumstance, and how circumstance in its turn was not clarified except by means of a theory about the reality of the I and of that in which both *are rooted* and achieve their *polar* effectiveness as *Dii consentes*. What Ortega has often called "the transcending of substantialism"—and which, let it be said in passing, means only what it says, and therefore *not* elimination of *substance* without further ado—has, for the moment, a perfectly clear and controllable meaning: to have recourse from *things* as a presumed ultimate reality to that in which they are rooted and from which they derive. Definitive being is not "any particular thing"; one must appeal from "this or that thing" to reality as a *generic function*, from things to *their* reality. He first said that that reality, *the* reality, which is represented in literary characters, is a perspective; we have also seen that it is presented under the guise of heroism or tragedy. All these expressions, which Ortega gradually abandons as unsatisfactory, point unequivocally to what is to be the central theme of Ortega's mature philosophy, what he later was to call simply *human life*.

Therefore its key is the *character*, who is the person who confers its

with these texts of Ortega's the central passage in Sartre's *La Nausée*, the basic text of "Existentialism" (1938):

" . . . je ne peux pas, je suffoque: l'existence me pénètre de partout, par les yeux, par le nez, par la bouche . . . .

" . . . l'existence s'était soudain dévoilée . . . c'était la pâte même des choses . . . ; la diversité des choses, leur individualité n'était qu'une apparence, un vernis. Ce vernis avait fondu, il restait des masses monstrueuses et molles, en désordre—nues, d'une effrayante et obscène nudité . . . .

"Ce moment fut extraordinaire:j'étais là, immobile et glacé, plongé dans une extase horrible . . . . L'essentiel c'est la contingence. Je veux dire que, par définition, l'existence n'est pas la necessité. Exister, c'est *être là*, simplement; les existents apparaissent, se laissent *rencontrer*, mai on ne peut jamais les *déduire* . . . .

"Il faut que ça vous envahisse brusquement, que ça s'arrête sur vous, que ça pèse lourd sur votre coeur comme une grosse bête immobile—ou alors il n'y a plus rien du tout.

"Tout était plein, tout en acte, il n'y avait pas de temps faible . . . . Monde tout nu qui se montrait tout d'un coup . . . . Ça n'avait pas de sens, le monde était partout, présent, devant, derrière." (*La Nausée*: Mercredi. Six heures du soir.)

characteristic of "world" on what would not have it without him. When Ortega considers reality and fiction, real world and imaginary world, in the incident of the retable of Maese Pedro, and says that "Don Quixote is the edge where both worlds meet, forming a bevel,"[27] he is following out the consequences of the central thesis of the *Meditations*: "world" is circumstance, and this means *my* circumstance, and *I* am "I" and my circumstance. In words which may be clearer, both worlds, the real world and the world of adventure, "communicate" in the life of Don Quixote because both are *his* circumstance; therefore—although precariously, for Don Quixote is insane—they constitute *a world*. To live is, in fact, to be in *a* world, precisely because this world is primarily defined by its characteristic of circumstance, by its function of *being around*. We could say that the characteristic of unity in the world *insofar as it is a world* is *analytical*, to the point that the "other world," in the measure that it is an ingredient of my life, is integrated into my circumstance, which therefore includes a plurality of planes and strata of reality. It is, then, human life which establishes the connection of all of the ingredients of the real as *such and such a world*; and this means that all the different senses in which something is "real" are rooted in it, and that all realities, as such, are constituted in it. This is the justification of Ortega's later thesis, according to which my life is *radical reality*.

[27] I, 382.

VI.
TRUTH AND REASON

❧

Up to this point we have been observing the rigorous and systematic linking together of the first version of Ortega's philosophy, which appears to have been unequivocally possessed and formulated about 1914–16, especially, though not exclusively, in the *Meditations on Quixote*. The different stages we have considered—theory, circumstance, perspective, human life (under the guise of "heroism" or "tragedy" as forms in which its form of reality is revealed), and finally reality itself— have been examined successively, and each in its turn has illumined the ones that have gone before. Now we must close the cycle and study the route which has made it possible to reach the point where we are now; or, expressed in other words, the method of investigation we have employed, the one which gives the preceding chapters their full theoretical justification. Only by means of this method, which is no different from the same ideality discovered by Ortega, has that discovery been enabled to have a metaphysical, not a merely descriptive, scope, or, at most, one which could serve as an introduction to a later metaphysic.

We saw that *reality is seen foreshortened, or perspectively*, but that at the same time—the example of the forest served to demonstrate this —*reality is foreshortening*, or, if you prefer, *exists perspectively*. The concepts utilized by Ortega—connection, intellectual love, latency, and patency (or depth and surface), coimplication of vision and interpretation (or perception and intellection), finally foreshortening and structure—lead back, for the moment, to the concepts of *light* and *illumination*, in the context of which is going to arise the first *philosophical* use —so far as I know—of the notion of truth as *alétheia*. But we must add that from this point onward Ortega's theory of truth, on this level of his thought, does not reduce itself to the idea of *alétheia*, but anticipates another, deeper, and more complex idea which was to occupy a relevant place in later phases of his philosophy. This notion of truth is not simply enunciated, but serves to set in motion a coherent doctrine, from which culture and some of its particular forms, such as art, are interpreted, *derived from the reality of human life*. And the articulation of this doctrine leads in its turn to a general theory of thinking, in which themes such as those of meditation, concept, myth, and science are clarified, and which culminates in a first sketch of what was to be the deepest nucleus of Ortega's philosophy: *vital reason*.

We shall have to see—although this theory is only outlined, and, in fact, at this level Ortega does no more than to *arrive* at it—how it had already been functioning for a long time, and how in its turn its explicit "discovery," prepared over a long period of time, reacts upon all that has gone before and constitutes the effective apprehension of reality and human life.

All these doctrines were formulated by Ortega with very little insistence; thus many of them passed over people's heads without being seen. When Ortega at times pointed them out, most people limited themselves to seeing the *points* toward which his gaze had been directed, and usually concluded that there was no more in them than that: isolated points, mere coincidences. The reality is exactly the opposite: the difficult thing would be to isolate an unconnected coincidence in Ortega's philosophical writings during this stage: they are composed of a dense, almost inextricable network of connections, a fact I tried to emphasize a few years ago in my commentary on the *Meditations on Quixote*; the nature of this commentary—some *notes* to the passages in that book—gave him an immediate and constant justification, when one compares it with the text commented upon; but on the other hand it imposed a *formal lack of connection*, the fragmentation of a thought obliged to follow the meanderings of the book in discontinuous form. Now it is necessary, by picking up, as before, many elements in that commentary, to present this doctrine in its *historical context*, on the one hand, and in its *internal connection* on the other.

80. HISTORY AND PREHISTORY OF THE INTERPRETATION OF TRUTH AS "*alétheia*"

Ortega presents the theme of truth in the *Meditations on Quixote* within the context of the ideas of *illumination* and *discovery*. "He who wishes to show us a truth," he writes in the chapter entitled "Trasmundos" ["Worlds Beyond"], "should not tell it to us: let him simply allude to it with a brief gesture, a gesture which starts an ideal *trajectory* in the air, along which we glide until we *arrive* at the feet of the *new* truth."[1] It is a question, then, of "arriving" at the truth by following a certain path; but what interests us is the last italicized adjective: a *new* truth. Why new? It will turn out that *truths in the strict sense are always new.* "Truths, once known, acquire a utilitarian crust; they no longer interest us as truths, but as useful formulae. That pure and sudden illumination which characterizes the truth is present only in the instant of its discovery. Hence its Greek name, *alétheia*—it originally meant the same thing as the word *apocalypse* did later—that is, discovery, revelation, more properly unveiling, the removal of a veil or cover. He who wishes to show us a truth, should place us in a situation where we will discover it for ourselves."[2]

This is the 1914 text. Note that Ortega does not pause on the Greek idea of ἀλήθεια, does not take care to document it—but simply uses it to confirm his interpretation of truth as novelty, illumination, and discovery. But the introduction of this Hellenic notion is not less formal and deliberate because of this, or less insistent: Ortega piles up expressions which, taken together, translate the Greek term, and in addition he clarifies the significance of this ancient word, its "original" meaning —he says implicitly that it is not the normal meaning of the word in classical Greek—with the more controllable and clearer meaning which the word *apocalypse* had *later*. This text reveals, then, familiarity with that interpretation of *alétheia*, and at the same time an indirect interest in it: the etymological corroboration of his own theory, which is to be developed later.

Well, in 1927, Heidegger published *Sein und Zeit*. In this book he introduced thematically the idea of *alétheia*, in an insistently etymological context; and since that date he has used it and commented on it

---

[1] *Meditaciones del Quijote*, I, 335. Italics mine.
[2] I, 335–36.

in many of his writings. It has passed over from Heidegger to other authors, and the concept has had unexpected good fortune. Over the course of the last thirty years it has become a concept in current usage and almost a commonplace. But, in spite of this, the idea is affected by a considerable degree of obscurity. In the first place, it is unproved, and in general not even known, where this etymological interpretation comes from; it is given as obvious or as a "known fact," when it is not made to appear as the personal interpretation of the author who is using it. In the second place, it is automatically assumed that in Greek philosophy the word *alétheia* had that etymological meaning, as the basis of the meaning of "truth" in the trivial sense or in the sense of "concord"; but it is not documented with texts in which such a meaning is made clear, or even those in which it would be easy to trace such a meaning. I shall try to summarize briefly the history of that interpretation, including its little-known "prehistory," and to show in some Greek texts a glimpse of that meaning which seems to resist being documented.

Heidegger's doctrine of truth also arises out of the idea of *light*, and goes from that to the idea of *discovery*. The intermediate steps are the components of the word "phenomenology": *phainómenon* and *lógos*. "Phenomenon" is derived from the verb *phaínesthai*, and means what is shown, what is patent; but *phaínesthai* is in its turn a middle form of *phaíno*, "an den Tag bringen, in die Helle stellen"—to bring to light, to illumine—and the root of this verb is φα,—like φῶς *phôs*, light, clarity.[3] The "true being" (*Wahrsein*) of the *lógos* as *aletheúen* means, on the other hand, taking out of its hiddenness (*Verborgenheit*) the entity which is being talked about and allowing it to be seen, *discovering it* (*entdecken*) as not occult, not hidden, or un-covered (*Unverborgenes*) or *alethés*. Falsehood is also interpreted as *pseúdesthai*, to deceive in the sense of *covering over* (*verdecken*), placing something in front of something else and making it pass for what it is not.[4] That is, the same terms

---

[3] "Der griechische Ausdruck φαινόμενον auf den Terminus 'Phänomen' zurückgeht, leitet sich von dem Verbum φαίνεσθαι her, das bedeutet: sich zeigen; φαινόμενον besagt daher: das, was sich zeigt, das Offenbare: φαίνεσθαι selbst ist eine *mediale* Bildung von φαίνω, an den Tag bringen, in die Helle stellen: φαίνω gehört zum Stamm φα- wie φῶς, das Licht, die Helle, d. h. das, worin etwas offenbar, an ihm selbst sichtbar werden kann." Heidegger, *Sein und Zeit*, § 7 A, p. 28.

[4] "Das 'Wahrsein' des λόγος als ἀληθεύειν besagt: das Seiende, wovon die Rede ist, im λέγειν als ἀποφαίνεσθαι aus seiner Verborgenheit herausnehmen und es als Unverbor-

which Ortega had put into play in his interpretation of *alétheia*, though *not all* of them, for some which add essential dimensions are lacking.

Later, in *Sein und Zeit* itself, Heidegger tries to clarify "the original phenomenon of truth,"[5] by following the same concepts of *Entdeckt-heit, Unverborgenheit*, and enunciation in the *lógos* (*apóphansis*). This *is the true* and original meaning of *ἀ-λήθεια*. "The translation by the word 'truth,'" he adds, "and especially the theoretical definitions of this expression, mask the meaning which the Greeks posited as 'obvious' (*selbstverständlich*) underlying the terminological use of *ἀλήθεια*, as a prephilosophical comprehension."[6] There is no further justification of this meaning, which does not turn out to be so "obvious."

This is not the place to follow the evolution of the idea of truth as *alétheia* in Heidegger, and still less in other authors who have taken it from Ortega, from Heidegger, or from both. Let a few references suffice. In Heidegger's very important work *Das Wesen der Wahrheit* (1943), he follows the thread of the concept of "the open" (*das Offene*,) which again characterizes *alétheia* as *Unverborgenheit*, and, with still greater precision, *Entborgenheit* and *Entbergung*, in which to the negative prefix *un–* the more expressive prefix *ent–* ("*dis–*") is added. (Recall that Ortega said, "discovery, revelation, more properly unveiling, the removal of a veil or cover.") On the other hand, this Heideggerian writing insists on the connection between truth and freedom (*Freiheit*).

In his study entitled *Platons Lehre von der Wahrheit* (which dates in oral form, Heidegger says, from the 1930–31 academic year, appeared in *Geistige Überlieferung*, and was printed separately in 1947), he returns insistently to the idea of *alétheia*. And in *Einführung in die Metaphysik* (1953) he points out once again that *alétheia* is *Unverborgenheit*, and that when we translate this Greek word as "truth," we misunderstand it; and he remarks that "now the Greek word *alétheia*

---

genes (ἀληθές), sehen lassen, *entdecken*. Im gleichen besagt das 'Falschsein' ψεύδεσθαι soviel wie Täuschen im Sinne von *verdecken*: etwas vor etwas stellen (in der Weise des Sehenlassens) und es damit ausgeben *als* etwas, was es *nicht* ist." *Ibid.*, B, p. 33.

[5] *Ibid.*, § 44, pp. 219ff.

[6] "Die Übersetzung durch das Wort 'Wahrheit' und erst recht die theoretischen Begriffsbestimmungen dieses Ausdrucks verdecken den Sinn dessen, was die Griechen als vorphilosophisches Verständnis dem terminologischen Gebrauch von ἀλήθεια 'selbstverständlich' zugrunde legten." *Ibid.*, 219.

is slowly beginning to be translated literally."[7] (Thirty-nine years after the publication of the *Meditations on Quixote*.)

Lastly, he takes up the subject many times in his essays "Logos," "Moira," and "Alétheia" (published in his book *Vorträge und Aufsätze*, 1954), and here he introduces a new theme—new in Heidegger, for we shall see at once that it is extremely old: the connection of *alétheia* with *léthe*, oblivion.[8] There is also a reference to the "visibility" (*Sichtbarkeit*), proffered by *alétheia*, placed in connection with natural light, *lumen naturale*, which here is the "illumination of reason" (*Erleuchtung der Vernunft*).[9] The last of the essays I have mentioned comments on fragment 16 of Heraclitus (Diels): τὸ μὴ δῦνόν ποτε πῶς ἄν τις λάθοι; "Wie kann einer sich bergen vor dem, was nimmer untergeht?" ("How would it be possible for one to hide from what never sets?"), and interprets the *patency* of *alétheia* as the opposite of the "hiddenness" of oblivion (*léthe*).

The most recent authors, with very few exceptions, have not referred to Ortega, in spite of the fact that the interpretation of *alétheia*, philosophically formulated, appears in his work in 1914 and has scarcely progressed since then. The references, if there are any, are to Heidegger or to some other, later utilization of his work; not even in books dedicated to studies of Greek philosophy is it easy to find anything older and more original.[10] This is surprising, for the *etymological* interpretation of *alétheia* is much older.

---

[7] "Indem Seiendes als ein solches *ist*, stellt es sich in die und steht es in der *Unverborgenheit*, ἀλήθεια, Wir übersetzen, und d. h. zugleich, wir missdeuten dieses Wort gedankenlos mit 'Wahrheit.' Zwar beginnt man jetzt allmählich das griechische Wort ἀλήθεια wörtlich zu übersetzen." *Einführung in die Metaphysik*, 77–78.

[8] "Das Entbergen aber ist die Ἀλήθεια. Diese und der Λόγος sind das Selbe. Das λέγειν lässt ἀληθέα. Unverborgenes als solche vorliegen (B 112). Alles Entbergen enthebt Anwesendes der Verborgenheit. Das Entbergen braucht die Verborgenheit. Die Ἀ-λήθεια ruht in der Λήθη, schöpft aus dieser, legt vor, was durch diese hinterlegt bleibt. Der Λόγος ist *in sich zumal* ein Entbergen und Verbergen. Er ist die Ἀλήθεια. Die Unverborgenheit braucht die Verborgenheit, die Λήθη als ihre Rücklage, aus der das Entbergen gleichsam schöpft." "Logos," in *Vorträge und Aufsätze*, 220–21.

[9] "Moira," *ibid.*, 252.

[10] See, for example, Werner Marx's book *The Meaning of Aristotle's "Ontology"* (1954), which says of this question, "There is, however, an older meaning of *alétheia* alive in Aristotle's works. In pre-Socratic tradition, *a-letheia* seems to have implied a state of manifestedness in which *Lethe* has been overcome, a state of un-concealedness:

In the first place, in my commentary on the *Meditations on Quixote* I took it back to Nicolai Hartmann in 1909. In his youthful book *Platos Logik des Seins*, he collected, à propos of Plato, the etymological implications of *alétheia*, as Platonic "survivals" of the old meaning which, moreover, he did not document in pre-Socratic philosophy. For Hartmann, in *alétheia* the original, literal meaning survives as simple negation of *lanthánein* or "being hidden"; *a-lethés* is the "not hidden" (*unverborgen*). But, further, he places this idea in express relationship to the "mythical image of Lethe," of oblivion, and of the "field of oblivion" (*tô tês Léthes pedíon*) of which Plato speaks in *The Republic*; in Plato *alétheia* is lost, and must be recovered in a "reminiscence" (*Wiedererinnerung*) in which the *alétheia* of the being is reconquered.[11] Hartmann, then, shows this etymological significance of *alétheia* in all strictness, using the same expression as Heidegger's *unverborgen*, and, further, adds the insistent reference to the meaning of "oblivion" and

and *aletheuein* correspondingly meant: to un-conceal, to partake of the state of *Lethe*. The un-concealing effort on the part of man presupposes in a sense the state of uncon-cealedness within which this activity can act: it presupposes that there is something that can be gathered as *alétheia*" (p. 16). Note Marx's hesitation: "seems to have implied," and the absence of documentation. On the other hand, the only bibliographical items adduced by Werner Marx to support this meaning of "truth" are *Sein und Zeit* and K. Riezler's *Parmenides* (1934).

[11] "Bei Plato hat ἀλήθεια noch vielfach den ursprünglichen, wörtlichen Sinne, der einfache Negation des λανθάνειν ist: ἀ-ληθής—'unverborgen.' Est ist einer von jenen bedeutsamen Begriffen, die bleichsam handgreifliche Beispiele der in der Begriffsbildung sich betätigende Methode des Nichtseins sind, indem ihr Gebrauch sie als durchaus positiv zeigt, während ihre Etymologie noch den negativen Ursprung erkennen lässt. Im weiteren Verlaufe der Sprachentwickelung verschwindet das Bewusstsein dieses Ursprungs fast ganz. Bei Plato und den Aelteren lässt die Anwendung es noch zuweilen als lebendig erkennen. An Stellen, wo fundamentale Erörterungen im Gange sind, hat es Wert, auf solchen negativen Ursprung Gewicht zu legen, zumal es in solchen Fällen sowieso der Sache nach ein seiendes Nichtsein herauskommt—wie sich an der ὑπόθεσις sogleich zeigen wird—. Für diese Auffasung der ἀλήθεια spricht auch folgendes. Λήθη bedeutet (nach Phäd 75 D) ἐπιστήμης ἀποβολή, das "Verlorengehen" eines Wissens. Folglich muss die ἐπιστήμη in ihrer Nichtverlorenheit sein: das ist der genaue Sinn von ἀλήθεια—was der durchgehend enge Zusammenhang von ἐπιστήμη und ἀλήθεια bei Plato bestätigt. Man vergleiche hiermit auch das mythische Bild der Λήθη. Die Seelen der Gestorbenen müssen, ehe sie zu neuem Leben wieder auf die Welt kommen, durch das 'Feld der Vergessenheit' hindurchgehen (τὸ τῆς Λήθης πεδίον Rep. 621 A). Dort verlieren sie also die ἀλήθεια die sie von Anbeginn geschaut haben. So kommen sie des Wissens beraubt zur Welt, um auf dem mühevolle Weg der 'Wiedererinnerung' das von der Λήθη Verschlungene wiederzugewinnen: Die ἀλήθεια des Seienden." *Platos Logik des Seins* (1909), 239.

its opposite (wholeness of memory or its recovery), which later will also be found in Zubiri[12] and in Heidegger, even with the mention of the *Léthe*, the "field of oblivion." However, in all of them, and of course in Hartmann, some moments are lacking which we will examine later in Ortega; and in Hartmann the presence of the essential theme of *light* is missing. Hartmann's interest, and consequently his interpretation, goes in another direction: that of the *negative* character of the notion of *a-létheia*, which his etymological analysis makes clear, underneath the positive sense of the word in normal, even in philosophical, usage; Hartmann tries to show that this meaning is preserved in certain exceptional passages in Plato and—as he says without documenting the statement—in other, older thinkers.[13] But the most significant point is that there is no reference to *alétheia* in the section entitled "Das Phänomen der Wahrheit" in his *Grundzüge einer Metaphysik der Erkenntnis* (1925). That is, Hartmann is interested in the theme only in a *historical* context, and makes no use of that notion in his own philosophy, in which, therefore, any *philosophical* (and not merely etymological) interpretation is lacking. The first text in which a philosophical use is made of

[12] "Out of love for precision, it would not be amiss to say that the *primary* meaning of *alétheia* is not 'uncovering,' 'patency.' Although the word contains the *root* la-dh-, 'to be hidden,' with a -dh- suffix of condition (Latin, *lateo* de *la-t*, Benveniste; Old Iranian, *rahú-* the demon who eclipses the sun and the moon: perhaps Greek *alastós*, he who does not forget his sentiments, his resentments, violent, etc.), the word *alétheia* has its origin in the adjective *alethés*, of which it is the abstract. *Alethés* derives in its turn from *lêthos, láthos*, which means 'oblivion' (only passage, Theocritus 23, 24). Originally, then, *alétheia* meant something without oblivion; something in which nothing has fallen into oblivion; 'complete.' (Kretschmer, Debrunner.) The only patency to which *alétheia* alludes is therefore simply that of memory. Hence, because of its element of completeness, *alétheia* later came to mean simple patency, the uncovering of something, truth." *Naturaleza, Historia, Dios* (1944), 29n.

[13] In a later work, Hartmann in fact returned to the idea of *alétheia*, this time with special reference to a passage in the *Phaedo*, 99e; he says, "Die Bedeutung von ἀλήθεια ist hier, wie öfters bei Platon, nicht 'Wahrheit' in unserem Sinne, sondern 'Unverborgenheit' oder 'Offenbarsein.' Denn wahr oder unwahr können im strengen Sinne nur Vorstellungen, Meinungen oder Urteile sein, nicht aber die Dinge, die deren Gegenstände sind. Das Wahrsein basteht im Zutreffen auf den Gegenstand; dass dieser aber seinerseits noch einmal auf sich selbst oder auf etwas drittes zutreffe, ergibt keinen Sinn. Man muss also ἀλήθεια in der ersten Bedeutung des Wortes versehen, welche die Negation des Verborgenseins (λήθη) ist. Der Sache nach stehen dann Unverborgenheit und Wahrheit streng komplementär zueinander, indem 'wahr' eben diejenige Erkenntnis ist, in der die Verborgenheit des Gegenstandes aufgehoben und er selbst 'offenbar' geworden ist." *Das Problm des Apriorismus in der platonischen Philosophie* (1935), 17, note 2.

the notion of *alétheia* continues to be, as far as my information goes, that of Ortega in 1914.

On the other hand, we must look for the discovery of the etymological meaning at least three decades earlier. The oldest discussion of the theme which I have been able to discover is found in Teichmüller, where it at last appears as justified and documented from the linguistic point of view. In his *Neue Studien zur Geschichte der Begriffe* (1879), Teichmüller refers to the connection which Rassow thought he had seen between λήθη and ἀληθής; and notes that Walter, in his book *Die Lehre von der praktischen Vernunft in der griechischen Philosophie* (1874), had immediately rejected "that play on words so truly repugnant for the philosophical consciousness."[14] "For me," comments Teichmüller, "it is certainly doubtful also whether one ought to attempt an etymology here; but if it were true, this would not be 'dégoutant,' but would have to be noted with interest and satisfaction. The gods too, says Plato, like jokes and games. Hate and horror are not good guides for interpretation."[15] This context appears to suggest that at that time this was a total novelty. And a long note of Teichmüller's confirms it, in which he adds that "Since investigating the truth is more important than an ingenious game, I will permit myself here to communicate the etymology of my linguistic colleague and friend Leo Meyer, who has kindly given me permission to publish the following." And then he gives that etymological note, extremely detailed and with express references to *lêthos*, or, in the Doric form, *lâthos* (oblivion), and some highly interesting suggestions. Teichmüller considers that, with Leo Meyer's linguistic explanations, the matter is cleared up, and that therefore it is necessary to admit that the concept of truth among the Greeks was originally *negative*, as an elimination of the lie, deceit, concealment, etc.[16] That is, the result which Nicolai Hartmann was to formulate thirty

---

[14] "Während Rassow die λήθη in etymologischer Verbindung mit ἀληθής stehend glaubte, straft Walter (S. 448) sofort diesen 'für das philosophische Bewusstsein wahrhaft degoutanten Wortwitz.'" Teichmüller, *Neue Studien zur Geschichte der Begriffe* (1879), III, 233.

[15] "Es ist mir zwar auch zweifelhaft, ob hier eine Etymologie beabsichtigt sei: aber wenn es doch so wäre, so würde sie nicht 'degoutant' sein, sondern mit Interesse und Vergnügen notiert werden. Auch die Götter, sagt Plato, lieben ja Scherz und Spiel. Hass und Abscheu sind aber keine guten Wegweiser der Interpretation." *Ibid.*, 233–34.

[16] Since, if I am not mistaken, this is the first time that an etymological explanation of *alétheia* has been given, and since the word has proved so fruitful, I think it is of

years later. This seems to me to be the origin of this famous interpretation of truth which, paradoxically, remains quite concealed and not at all obvious. And not only in contemporary philology, but also in pre-Socratic philosophy. This is the other aspect of the question.

It is not easy, in fact, to find texts in which *alétheia* or *alethés* appears clearly as the "not hidden," "uncovered," "manifest" or "patent." Hence the statement, so often reiterated in these last decades, that this is why the Hellenic meaning of truth always turns out not to be very clear. But some passages can be found in which this meaning *can* be seen; and I italicize the *can*, for in fact it has been seen very few times, and even today it is usually passed over. The connection between *alethés* and

---

interest to transcribe Teichmüller's entire note in reference to this question, a question so much debated later and so evanescent:

"Da die Wahrheit zu erforschen aber noch interessanter ist, als ein geistreiches Spiel, so erlaube ich mir, die Etymologie meines linguistischen Collegen und Freundes Leo Meyer hier mitzutheilen, der mir das Folgende freundlich zur Veröffentlichung überliess.

"'Ἀληθής ist ohne Zweifel zusammengesetzt aus ἀ (αν) privat. + *λῆθος n. (wie ἀσθενής, 'schwach, kraftlos' aus ἀ + σθένος 'Kraft,' ἀκηδής 'unbesorgt, vernachlässigt,' sorglos aus ἀ + κῆδος 'Sorge,' ἀταρβής 'unerschrocken, furchtlos' aus ἀ + τάρβος 'Schrecken, Furcht,' ohne Zweifel auch ἀ-τρεκής aus ἀ + *τρέκος ['Verdrehung? oder ähnlich], ἀκριβής 'genau' aus ἀ + κρῖβος [etwa 'Ungenauigkeit'] und viele andre ähnlich).

" *λῆθος 'Vergessenheit, Vergessen' ist ganz unbelegt: die dorische Form λᾶθος für die auf Theocrit 23, 24 verwiesen wird, findet sich an dieser Stelle gar nicht, sondern statt ihrer τὸ λᾶθον, das *Ahrens* 'oblivionem afferens' erklärt. Man darf aber mit Bestimheit für λῆθος die Bedeutung vermuthen '[absichtliches] Vergessen, [absichtliches] Auslassen, Verheimlichung' wie in λάθρα, λάθρῃ 'in Verheimlichung, heimlich', das mit λῆθος, λήθω, λανθάνω zur selben Wurzel λαθ gehört. So im Homer schon il. 2, wo überall *absichtliches* Verheim lichen, kein zufälliges Vergessen. So bei 515: ὁ δὲ ῥοί παρελέξατο λάθρῃ, od. 15, 430: ἀνὴρ ὃς ἐμίσγετο λάθρῃ ss., wo überall *absichtliches* Verheimlichen, kein zufälliges Vergessen. Homer auch ἀληθὴς γύνη (il. 12, 433) 'ehrliches Weib, eigentlich 'Weib ohne Verheimlichung,' d.i. das nichts verheimlicht, und häufiger (il. 6, 832; od. 14,125ff.) ἀληθέα μυθήσασθαι und Aehnliches, 'Worte ohne Verheimlichung sprechen,' d.i. solche bei denen nichts verheimlicht wird."

"Mir schein diese Erklärung *Leo Meyer's* die Sache zu erledigen. Man muss demnach annehmen, dass der Begriff der Wahrheit bei den Griechen ursprünglich *negativ* war. Indem der Grieche von der Befürchtung ausging, dass ihm Lüge, Verstellung, Verheimlichung, Betrug entgegen komme, verlangte er die Beseitigung dieser Heimlichkeiten d. i. Wahrheit." *Ibid.*, 233–34.

This is the note; I think that the word *alétheia* has never been cleared up etymologically in so complete, so explicit, and so penetrating a fashion as in this page, written in 1879, representing the co-operation of a forgotten philologist and an obscure and almost completely forgotten philosopher. It has seemed only right that I should call them to mind, and thus bring them again into the presence of truth.

phainómenon (what appears or shows itself) can be discovered in Leucippus and Democritus, according to references by Aristotle. However, in the context in which they appear within Aristotle's work, that connection tends to vanish—and thus has escaped many commentators—because Aristotle interprets the sentences of the Atomists from the point of view of his own concern: that of distinguishing the "true" from the "sensible appearance." Thus, in *De generatione et corruptione*: Δημόχριτος δὲ καὶ Λεύχιππος . . . . ἐπεὶ δ'ᾧοντο ταληθές ἐν τῷ φαίνεσθαι. And in *De Anima* he says of Democritus: ἐκεῖνος μὲν γὰρ ἁπλῶς χυχὴν ταὐτὸν καὶ νοῦν· τὸ γὰρ ἀληθὲς εἶναι τὸ φαινόμενον.[18] Most commentators feel uneasy when faced with these passages: on the one hand they see them as "sensualism" or negation of "objective truth"; on the other, they do not fail to see that in doing this, both they and Aristotle are doing a certain amount of violence to the pre-Socratics, imposing upon them a distinction which they themselves had not made. That is, that in spite of this uneasiness, it does not occur to them to take *alétheia* in the sense of uncovering, unveiling; that is, *phainómenon* in the literal sense of what appears or manifests itself, what is patent, and what has had a veil or cover removed from it.[19]

[17] Aristotle, *De generatione et corruptione*, I, 2, 315 b ff. In Didot's edition it is translated as follows: "Democritus autem et Leucippus . . . ceterum quoniam quae apparent, ea vera esse putabant."

[18] Aristotle, *De Anima*, I, 2, 404 to 27 ff. In Didot: "is enim animam et intellectum simpliciter idem esse putabat: etenim id quod sensibus appareret, verum esse censebat."

[19] Hicks translates the passage in question as follows: "The latter, indeed, absolutely identified soul and mind, holding that the *presentation in the senses* is the truth." But in his commentary he states, "This proposition, which recurs as the doctrine of 'some' thinkers 427 b 3, is understood by A. to mean the denial of objective truth, and to it he opposes his own position, etc." See all the discussion of this passage, *Aristotle de Anima*, edited by R. D. Hicks, Cambridge (1907), 218–19. Hicks's translation is very probably correct and justified as a translation *of Aristotle*; that is, of what Aristotle thought and understood; but as a translation *of Democritus* it is problematical; that is, as a translation of mentions and references from Democritus included by Aristotle in his text. Tricot, on the other hand, translates: "le vrai est ce qui *apparaît*," and establishes in a note that Democritus "contrairement à ce que prétend Aristote, il mantient la distinction du vrai et du faux, de la connaissance sensible et de la connaissance rationelle" (*De l'Âme*, Paris [1934], 17). A particularly explicit form of Democritus' interpretation according to aísthesis is found in a passage of Philopon's, in his commentary on the *De anima* (see H. Diels, *Die Fragmente der Vorsokratiker*, 6. Aufl., Demokritos A 113, volume II, pp. 110–11.)

With regard to the problem—a very delicate one—of the interpretation of the pre-Socratic texts when they function within a context of a later philosopher (for example Aristotle, who inevitably projects his own problems onto them), it is well

I have felt it useful to present in some detail, which has been so sadly lacking, the history of this notion of truth as *alétheia*, which Ortega introduced into his philosophy at a date as early as 1914. He was, as far as I know, the first to do so. But now the important thing is to ask ourselves what the function of that notion of truth is, within Ortega's philosophy.

81. TRUTH AND REALITY

The many terms which Ortega uses to translate *alétheia* are, as we have seen, significant. In the first place, he adduces another Greek term as an explanation of *alétheia*, as a later equivalent of its "original" meaning: *apokálypsis*. It is the only place I know of where the two roots are related to each other. And the fact is of interest. The word *a-létheia* has a *negative* quality: it is the *not* hidden (if one thinks of *lanthánein*) or the *not* forgotten (if we use *léthos* or *léthe*); and in both cases there is a question of something *passive*, being hidden or forgotten. On the other hand, *apokálypsis* is something different: it is *un*-covering, the result of an action which consists in *un*-covering (*apó*) what has been covered or hidden (*kalyptein*). Ortega insists upon this: uncovering, revelation, *properly speaking, unveiling* (he adds), the removal of a *veil* or cover. This is the meaning of *apokálypsis*.

And, while it is so difficult to find that original use of *alétheia* in Greek philosophy, in the introduction of Parmenides' poem we find that same expression *kalyptein*: "The Daughters of the Sun (*Heliádes koûrai*), after leaving the dwelling place of the night and drawing back with their hands the veils from their heads (*kráton ápo khersì kalyptras*), hastened to lead me to the light (*eis pháos*)."[20] Perhaps the

---

to keep in mind what Ross says in his commentary on Aristotle's *Metaphysics*: "Bonitz argues that Aristotle attaches too much importance to isolated phrases of early thinkers. Certainly neither Empedocles nor Democritus nor Parmenides nor Anaxagoras can fairly be charged with consistent sensationalism . . . . They did not deliberately identify thought with sensation, but in their time the two things had not been clearly distinguished, so that it was impossible for them to be definitely either rationalists or sensationalists." *Aristotle's Metaphysics*, ed. by W. D. Ross (Oxford, 1924), I, 275.

[20] Diels, I, 229 (Parmenides B i, verses 9–10):

'Ηλιάδες κοῦραι, προλιποῦσαι δώματα Νυκτός,
εἰς φάος, ὠσάμεναι κράτων ἄπο χερσὶ καλύπτρας.

most interesting passage of all is a verse of Critias,[21] in the fragment of his satirical drama *Sisyphos* which has been preserved, where he explains in a rationalist way the origin of belief in the gods. There, in a single verse, four essential words are found together: *pseudôs, kalyptein, alétheia,* and *lógos*:

$$\chi\epsilon\upsilon\delta\epsilon\hat{\iota}\ \kappa\alpha\lambda\acute{\upsilon}\chi\alpha\varsigma\ \tau\grave{\eta}\nu\ \dot{\alpha}\lambda\acute{\eta}\theta\epsilon\iota\alpha\nu\ \lambda\acute{o}\gamma\omega\iota:$$[22]

hiding the truth with false words.[23] The covering and uncovering correspond to falsity and truth, and it is the word, the *lógos*, which brings them into being.

Therefore, in Ortega the theme of truth leads back to that of reality; let us not forget that it was by following a theory of reality, determined by the concepts of depth and surface, latency, patency, and, in a word, foreshortening, that Ortega reached the point of posing the problem of truth. "For us," he says elsewhere in the *Meditations on Quixote*, "real is what is accessible to the senses, what the eyes and ears keep feeding into us; we have been educated by a spiteful age which had laminated the universe and made of it a *surface*, a pure *appearance*. When we seek reality, we seek appearances. *But the Greek understood by reality quite the opposite: real is the essential, the profound and latent*; not appearance, but *the living springs of all appearance*."[24] Ortega contrasts the attitude dominant in his time, and against which he reacts, to that of the Greeks; the identification of the real with that which is accessible to the senses, which is the point of view of Positivism in all its forms, including its late survivals at the beginning of this century; it "laminates" the universe, reduces it to surface and appearance—that is, strips it of true reality. The ultimate expression of the Orteguian sentence we have quoted is the deepest interpretation of *alétheia*; Ortega does not limit himself to the presumed philological evidence—we have already seen how tenuous it is, and how generally

---

[21] Critias, born about 460 and died 403 B.C., belonged to an aristocratic family in Athens and was related to Plato's mother; he was a close friend of Socrates and the Sophists, was very active politically, and was one of the Thirty Tyrants; he died fighting Thrasybulus. He wrote elegiac poems and tragedies.

[22] Diels, II, 388 (Kritias B 25, verse 26).

[23] Diels translates this verse: "mit lügnerischem Wort die Wahrheit verhüllend." Kathleen Freeman (*Ancilla to the Pre-Socratic Philosophers* [Oxford, 1948], 158): "covering up the truth with a false theory."

[24] *Meditaciones del Quijote.* I, 373. Italics mine.

unknown this very tenuousness is—but understands its metaphysical significance: the truth is true *reality (alethès ón)*, that which is patent; that is, it makes patent or manifests *what truly is*; expressed in other and basically more exact words, that which *gives life to appearance*, that from which appearance arises, the *living springs of appearance*. This expression, *living spring*, would translate admirably what the Greeks understood by *physis*, that from which springs or arises what is shown and uncovered in its appearance, and which for this reason can be interpreted as principle (*arkhé*). Recall the use of the word "hontanar" ("source") in Ortega's work.

But this is not enough. We must ask ourselves how this unveiling of reality is possible, how it is possible to go beyond the surface to reach the latent and make it patent, how it is possible to possess that profound reality and bring it to the surface, to place it in the light and thus to make it true.

82. THEORY OF THE CONCEPT

Ortega recognizes that there are "two breeds of men: meditators and sensual men"; for the latter the world is "a surface casting off reflections"; the others "live in the dimension of depth." "Just as for the sensual man," he continues, "the organ is the retina, the palate, the tips of the fingers, etc., the meditator possesses the organ of the concept. The concept is the normal organ of depth."[25] This is the beginning of the theory of the concept which Ortega outlines in the *Meditations on Quixote*. The concept is an *organ*, which is equivalent to those of the *senses*; these belong to the surface; the concept, to depth. Let us return to that linkage between the sensorial and the intellectual which is the nucleus of Ortega's doctrine. We saw before that foreshortening is "the organ of *visual* depth," the limit case in which "simple *vision* is mingled with a purely *intellectual* act";[26] therefore the *concept*, the normal organ of depth, is the intellective correlate of *foreshortening*.

If we take this seriously, it would mean that the *isolated* concept of an *isolated* thing would not make sense. And this is the way we must take it, in fact. The usual interpretation of the concept makes of it "a repetition or reproduction of the thing itself, reduced to spectral matter . . . . Compared with the thing itself, the concept is no more

[25] I, 349–50.   [26] I, 337.

than a specter, or even less than a specter." No one in his right mind, comments Ortega, can possibly think of exchanging his fortune in things for a fortune in specters. "The concept cannot be thought of like a new, subtle thing destined to take the place of material things."[27]

What is the mission of the concept, then? What is its relationship to things? The decisive point is that the concept does not refer to each isolated thing, but to *things in their connection*. The impression of a thing, says Ortega, gives us its matter, its flesh; "the concept contains everything which that thing is *in relation to other things*, all that greater treasure with which an object is enriched when it becomes part of a structure."[28] What exists between things is the content of the concept, and what there is between them is, for the moment, their *limits*. But Ortega next asks himself where the limits of the object are. Not within itself: if there were no more than a single object, it would be limitless. One object ends where another begins. Is the limit, then, in the other object? No, because this other object is in the same situation of having to be limited by the first. Ortega arrives at a first definition of the concept, derived directly from that elementary proof that it is related to structure—that is, to things in connection: "limits are new virtual things which are, as it were, interpolated and interjected between material things, schematic natures whose function consists in defining the boundaries of beings, bringing them together so that they can live side by side and at the same time placing them at a distance so that they will not merge and become annihilated. This is what the concept is: no more, but no less either. Thanks to it, things enjoy mutual respect and can come into union without invading each other."[29]

Not only, then, does the concept not coincide with the *mere* sensorial impression, but it does not even have to do with *the same thing* as the impression. The concept, in fact, and for the moment, exceeds *each* thing; if there were no more than one thing, it would not make the slightest sense to speak of a "concept" of it. Limits are not *in* things; neither in this thing or in that thing; the concept has to go beyond *this* thing, and consequently beyond *every* thing as such, precisely in order to be able to return to them in their reciprocal relationship, in a new and effective manner; once more, the "tactical turn" which is the *leitmotiv* of all of Ortega's theory of knowledge. The expressions used by Ortega to define the concept are significant: they are virtual things which are

[27] I, 353. [28] I, 352. Italics mine. [29] I, 352.

"interpolated and interjected" (the affinity with the idea of "interpretation" is evident); they are "schematic natures" (*skhêma* is figure, configuration) which define the "boundaries of beings." This idea of
delimitation was to have decisive developments in the writings of the
following decade, when Ortega formulated his idea of the *being* as
different from *reality* or what *there is*.[30]

The mission of the concept is not to supplant the thing, or to displace
the intuition, the real impression. It retains only the *scheme*, the *limits*
which outline the real substance. And those limits mean no more than
"the relationship in which an object finds itself with respect to others";
"the concept expresses the ideal place, the ideal space corresponding to
each thing within the *system of realities*." Things as impressions are
fleeting, fugitive, they slip away from us and we do not possess them;
the concept does not give, or have any need to give, what the impression
gives: the flesh of things; but the impression will never give what it is
the concept's proper function to give: the form, the physical and moral
meaning of things. In other words, Ortega makes a double mental movement: (a) to place the concept at a distance from the thing, to show that
it is in no way its "equivalent"; (b) to make it inseparable from the
thing insofar as the concept is inexorably related to the thing for which
it exists, and, at the same time, the thing needs the concept. Concept
and thing are *irreducible* and *irreplaceable*. The "meaning" which the
concept gives is the *connection* in which the *lógos* consists, and which
is the chief theme of philosophy as the general science of love, as an
effort toward an "all-embracing connection" as Ortega defines it in the
first pages of the *Meditations on Quixote*; that notion, presented somewhat abruptly there, is made explicit and is developed in this theory of
the concept.

All this becomes still clearer if we keep in mind the further explanations in which this theory culminates. If, says Ortega, we restore to
the word *perception* its etymological value (its allusion to "catching,"
"grasping"), "the concept will be the real instrument or organ of the
perception and apprehension of things . . . ." "It therefore exhausts its
mission and its essence by being, not a new thing, but an organ or apparatus *for* the possession of things." And finally: "Each concept is
literally an organ with which we grasp things."[31] Only in *context*, that

---

[30] See "Realidad y ser en la filosofía española," in *La Escuela de Madrid*. (*Obras*, V.)
[31] I, 354.

is, by virtue of the *limits*, or rather, within *the system of realities*—according to the expressions which Ortega has just used—is true apprehension or captation—perception—of things made possible. We can perceive, then, only because the concept is added to the impression: strictly speaking, to perceive is to *conceive*. But, be it noted, this *instrumental* interpretation of the concept, as an *organ* for the apprehension of things, deprives it of substantivity and makes impossible any form of rationalism.

"Only *by means of the concept* is a vision complete," Ortega concludes; sensation gives us only the shapeless and pliable matter of each object; it gives us the *impression* of things, *not the things themselves*."[32] This is decisive, and anticipates very recent developments in present-day philosophy: it is not that Ortega places the vision *next to* the concept (remember the Kantian comparison between *Anschauung* and *Begriff*), but the effective and complete vision, the true vision, capable of giving us *things* and not their mere *impression*, is vision *by means of* the concept, the one which "sees" with the concept; that is, the vision is, strictly speaking, sensation *and* concept simultaneously. It could be said, in a certain sense, that this theory is the reverse of that of "intellectual intuition," which idealism used and abused so much: here *vision*—perceptive, physical, sensorial vision—if it is really vision, is *conceptual*. And, so far from exercising itself upon mere isolated things—in that case it would go no further than its impressions—it can operate only in *context*, or, in Ortega's own words, *within the system of realities*.

This is, in its essential nucleus, Ortega's doctrine of the concept in 1914; but it is only the first step in a more complex and closely coherent theory, in which each step is systematically linked with the rest, and which leads to the idea of vital reason.

83. CULTURE AS SECURITY

What is the *vital function* of the concept? It is a question of the *apprehension* of things; now we must ask ourselves in what this consists, and what its purpose is. Only if we succeed in deriving its contents from human life will concepts become intelligible, only then do they have "meaning." Ortega believes that all necessity, if it is given full develop-

[32] I, 354. Italics mine

ment, becomes an ambit of culture. This culture, he adds, offers us objects already *purified*, which at one time were spontaneous and immediate life, and which now *seem* free of space and time, of corruption and caprice. "They form, as it were a zone of ideal and abstract life, floating on our always hazardous and problematical personal existences."[33] On the other hand, he adds: "The specifically cultural act is the creative one, the one in which we extract the *lógos* of something which was still meaningless (*il-logical*). Acquired culture has value only as an instrument and weapon for new conquests," and "all that is general, all that is learned, all of what is attained in culture is only the tactical turn which we must make in order to convert ourselves to the immediate."[34]

It is a question, then, of escaping from true reality, which is hazardous, problematical, and insecure, in order to conquer a new zone of unreality in which to install ourselves, safe from the limitations and insecurities of our individual lives. But as we are committed to this reality, it is only a question of a trick, an instrument to return to things, to make possible that *tactical turn* which will permit us to dominate and possess them. And this is achieved through the *lógos*—that is, the "meaning" which establishes connections, which gradually links "one thing to another and everything to ourselves, in a firm essential structure."[35] These statements by Ortega in the prelude to the *Meditations on Quixote* now acquire a much clearer and stricter meaning, and link up with the theory of the concept. Let us see how.

"Only when something has been *thought* does it fall into our *power*. And only when elementary things are *subdued* can we progress toward more complex ones.

"Every step toward the *control* and increase of moral territories presupposes the *peaceful*, definitive *possession* of others on which we can *support* ourselves .... If nothing is *secure* beneath our feet, all our higher conquests will fail.

"This is why an *impressionistic* culture is condemned not to be a progressive culture .... Each impressionist of genius re-creates the world out of nothingness, there where another predecessor of genius left it."[36]

33 I, 320.   35 I, 313.
34 I, 321.   36 I, 354. Italics mine.

In these quotations we can clearly see the connection between thought (concept) and possession, control; in a word, security, as opposed to the instability and discontinuity of impression. Ortega, thinking circumstantially, links these ideas with his interpretation of Spanish culture. Every Spanish genius has arisen anew out of chaos; he is an Adam, a first man—like Goya. Thus Spanish culture is a frontier culture, without a yesterday, without progression, *without security*. "It is a fact," he adds, "that the best products of our culture contain an ambiguity, *a peculiar insecurity*."[37]

But culture, properly speaking, is the opposite, and this appears in its exemplary and original case within Europe, in Hellenic culture. "On the other hand," says Ortega after characterizing what is specifically Spanish, "the *preoccupation* which, like a new restlessness, begins to arise in the breasts of the Greeks, and then spreads to the peoples of the European continent, is the preoccupation for *security, firmness*— τὸ ἀσφαλές. Culture, for the dark-eyed men who meditate, argue, sing, preach, dream, in Ionia, in Attica, in Sicily, in Magna Graecia, *is the firm as opposed to the uncertain, is the fixed as opposed to the fleeting, is the clear as opposed to the obscure*. Culture is not all of life, but only the moment *of security, of firmness, of clarity*. And the Greeks invent *the concept as an instrument*, not to substitute for vital spontaneity, but to *assure it*."[38]

This text could not be more explicit. Culture is security, *tò asphalés*. In the European philosophy of the last thirty years, this idea has acquired unaccustomed importance. But its origins in Greece are clear: Ortega quotes Plato;[39] as for Aristotle, I have based all my interpretation of his *Politics* on the central concept of security, or *aspháleia*, which separates it from the other *politeíai* as "ideal constitutions" which are relatively utopian, and on the other hand I have shown the decisive function of politics for the total interpretation of Plato's and Aristotle's philosophy.[40]

---

[37] I, 355. Italics mine. Chapter 1 of Américo Castro's *La realidad histórica de España* (1954) is called "España, o la historia de una inseguridad."

[38] I, 355–56. Italics mine.

[39] *Phaedo*, 100 d-e; 101 d.

[40] See my introductions to the *Politics* (1951) and the *Nicomachean Ethics* (1960), editions of the Instituto de Estudios Políticos, Madrid. See also *Biografía de la Filosofía.* (*Obras*, II.)

"Culture," Ortega was still to add, " . . . is that mode of life in which, by an act of self-reflection, life acquires polish and order. Thus the works of culture can never retain the problematical character connected with everything which is simply living. In order to control the intractable torrent of life, the sage meditates, the poet trembles, and the political hero builds the fortress of his will."[41] But this culture, though *necessary*, is not *sufficient*. Ortega, who has been called "culturalist," has reacted with the greatest decision—and, what is more important, from deep-rooted motives—against all "substantivation" of culture, against all idealist idolization of it. Culture exists *in order to* apprehend reality, in order to enable us to live in reality, and is affected by unreality, which is inherent in it as its proper and instrumental condition. "Culture tries to establish itself as *a separate and self-sufficient world*, to which we can transfer our deepest feelings. This is an illusion, *and only when looked at as an illusion*, only when placed on the earth as a mirage, *is culture put in its proper place*."[42]

The instrumental nature of the concept is extended to all culture; it is a question of the "tactical turn" which permits us to take possession of the concrete, to control it, to possess it; this is how security is achieved. Well then, the radical form of this human security is the *clarity* in which the meaning, or *lógos*, of things *appears* or manifests itself, is made *patent*; and thus these are left arranged in *context*, forming part of a *structure*—that is, within the *system of realities*—in short, *interpreted*, seen *foreshortened* or *perspectively*. All the concepts which Ortega has been introducing become closely linked together here, in a systematic unity. It is the dual meaning of the expression, which Ortega always used so often, "knowing what to hold to," which includes, together with the moment of security (to hold to) that of clarity (to know): *it is a security which consists in clarity*. In other terms, this theme will appear in Ortega's maturity under the guise of the idea of the *being* as a plan for this "*holding to*" with respect to things, as that interpretation which permits us to know what to hold to in relation to the real; that is, with respect to what *there is* and with which we have *to have it out*, by accounting for it. Now we shall have to see in what this clarity consists, and what its role is in our life.

[41] I, 357.
[42] I, 385. Italics mine.

84. LIGHT AS AN IMPERATIVE AND MISSION OF CLARITY: THE ROOT OF MAN'S CONSTITUTION.

Chapter 12 of the preliminary Meditation, "Light as an Imperative," contains one of the most important moments of the *Meditations on Quixote* and one of the centers of articulation of Ortega's thought. It deals, in the first place, with the fact that there are several sorts of clarity: "There is certainly a peculiar way in which surfaces are clear, and another in which deep things are clear. There is a clarity of impression and a clarity of meditation."[43] Ortega wrote this in 1914; we have seen how his thought was bent on Husserl's phenomenology; it is not too bold to suggest that he was thinking of the famous article *Philosophie als strenge Wissenschaft*, published in *Logos* in 1911, where Husserl, in the first *theoretical* writing about the phenomenology which he had brought into being, had contrasted "clarity" with "depth": depth—*Tiefsinn*—he said, is a matter of wisdom (*Weisheit*); conceptual clarity (*begriffliche Deutlichkeit und Klarheit*) belongs to strict theory (*strenge Theorie*).[44] It is true that in this passage Husserl refers *directly* to the depth of doctrine (*Tiefsinn*), rather than to that of things (*Tiefe*); but, in spite of this observation, his aspiration to "clarity" is evident, in the sense of absolute patency, which responds, further, to the radical nature of phenomenology, which tends to reduce the real to its characteristic of "object," or *Gegenstand*. If we compare with this attitude the description and analysis of the forest made by Ortega in the *Meditations*,[45] we see that there is an important difference: that analysis might seem to be phenomenological, but it already goes beyond phenomenology, and precisely because it is more faithful than phenomenology itself to its postulate of "absolute Positivism," of *Selbstgebung*; that is, of allowing things to present themselves *as they are*—for example, essentially latent; that is, without excluding the fact that, no

[43] I, 356.

[44] "Tiefsinn ist ein Anzeichen des Chaos, das echte Wissenschaft in einen Kosmos verwandeln will, in eine einfache, völlig klare, aufgelöste Ordnung. Echte Wissenschaft kennt, soweit ihre wirkliche Lehre reicht, keinen Tiefsinn. Jedes Stück fertiger Wissenschaft ist ein Ganzes von den Denkschritten, deren jeder unmittelbar einsichtig, also gar nicht tiefsinnig ist. Tiefsinn ist Sache der Weisheit, begriffliche Deutlichkeit und Klarheit Sache der strengen Theorie. Die Ahnungen des Tiefsinns in eindeutige rationale Gestaltungen umzuprägen, das ist der wesentliche Prozess der Neukonstitution strenger Wissenschaften." (*Logos*, Band I, Heft 3. [1911], 339.)

[45] See above, section 76.

matter how much this may do violence to the theory, *they may not be clear*. Ortega begins the chapter by stating that he is not too intellectualistic, and that he has showed this by his theory of the concept. In fact, intellectualism and rationalism consist in demanding of things that they adjust themselves to the intellect's mode of being. Theory, on the contrary, is fully theory only when it accepts the troublesome contingency that things are neither so easy nor so docile; reason, unlike rationalism, does not demand of reality that it be rational, but that reason itself be rational, and that its role is to account for *reality*, no matter what reality is like, perhaps even if it is irrational.

Clarity, that tranquil spiritual possession in which our consciousness controls images and overcomes the fear that the object we have grasped may elude us, is given to us by the concept. "All cultural endeavor is an *interpretation*—elucidation, explanation, or exegesis—*of life. Life is the eternal text*, the burning bush beside the road from which the voice of God speaks to us. *Culture*—art or science or politics—is the *commentary*."[46] Culture is, then, *interpretation of life*; this theme, which had such long resonances later, is introduced here in the most rigorous way. The terms which Ortega uses are insistent and significant, and are more or less those which the most recent philosophy in Germany is to use again and again: reality and interpretation, text and commentary, more clearly still, exegesis (Dilthey had already spoken of *Hermeneutik*, and Heidegger was to do so much later, as well as speaking of *Auslegung*); clarification of life (the second part of Jaspers's *Philosophie* [1932], is in fact called *Existenzerhellung*). The vital is problematical, restless, insecure, and culture is the instrument for its control; any elaboration of life, not only the intellectual but the artistic and the political, is *interpretation*. Science, art, and action appear linked by a vital radical function: they are the three modes of interpretation, and, consequently, of security and certitude; different ways of *knowing what to hold to*, of introducing order into spontaneous life, or, if you prefer, of seeking its *lógos*, its meaning. We could say with equal truth that they are three different modes of *reabsorption of the circumstance*, which is, we must not forget, the concrete destiny of man.

For this, and nothing else, is what it is all about. The paragraphs which Ortega wrote immediately following those I have just quoted constitute the radical nucleus of this doctrine, which in its turn illumi-

[46] I, 357. Italics mine.

nates the one set forth in the previous chapters. *"Man has a mission of clarity upon the earth. This mission has not been revealed to him by a God nor is it imposed on him from without by anybody or anything. He carries it within himself; it is the very root of his constitution . . . .* Clarity is not life, but it is the fullness of life . . . . Clarity within life, *light shed upon things, is what the concept is.* No more. No less. *Each new concept is a new organ which opens within us upon a portion of the world* which was silent and invisible before. *The man who gives you an idea increases life and dilates the reality around you.* The Platonic notion that we do not look with our eyes, but through or by means of them, is literally correct: *we observe with concepts. Idea* in Plato meant point of view."[47]

What does this passage mean? Only by keeping it in mind can we look backward and understand anew, in a tighter circle—what I have called the "Jericho method"—some previous doctrines. The interpretation of truth as *alétheia* now becomes fully intelligible. Recall that *before* he arrived at the notion of truth, Ortega had pointed out the quality of sudden *illumination* which truth possesses in its uncovering. Very well, then, the profoundest justification of the view that truth is uncovering, or patency, is that man's *mission,* the one which belongs to him *intrinsically,* with no external imposition or possible evasion, the mission which it *constitutively* and *radically* is ("the very *root* of his *constitution*"), is *clarity.* To be a man is to illuminate, clarify, cast light on things, and thus to uncover them, reveal them or unveil them, to make them patent and place them on view, to make them *true.* Ortega said before that truths, once known, acquire a utilitarian *crust,* and no longer interest us *as truths,* but only as useful formulae. This is literally the case: they cease to be true as such, in the sense of *alétheia,* since they are left "covered" with a *crust*—a particularly graphic and forceful expression— and lose their quality of patency and clarity.

We should keep in mind the form in which ideas very similar to these appear in Heidegger's *Sein und Zeit.* He refers to the "ontically" figurative way of speaking about the *lumen naturale* in man; and according to him, it means only "the ontological-existential structure" of the *Dasein* or existing. Only to a being thus existentially enlightened, he adds, does the present (*Vorhandenes*) become accessible in the light, or concealed in the darkness. And finally he concludes that existing, or

[47] I, 357–58. Italics mine.

Dasein, is its opening, or breach (*Erschlossenheit*).[48] And as if this were not enough, elsewhere Heidegger refers to this passage and states that only with that *Erschlossenheit,* or opening, of the *Dasein* is the most fundamental phenomenon of truth attained, and even adds that, "Insofar as the *Dasein* essentially *is* its own opening, and as an opening it opens and uncovers, it is essentially 'true.' *Dasein* is 'in the truth.' " And he is very careful to make clear that this thesis has ontological meaning, that "the opening of its most proper being belongs to its existential constitution."[49] All the derivation Heidegger makes of truth, which he previously took from the Greek notion of *alétheia,* and the result that "truth only 'is there' insofar and while there is existing,"[50] and that all truth, insofar as its mode of existential being is concerned, is relative to the being of existing,[51] is founded on these theses I have quoted, which seem to coincide, almost literally, with those which Ortega had formulated in the *Meditations on Quixote.*

But it would be an error to believe that these two doctrines, so close to each other in one aspect, coincide completely. They are near each other, but go in divergent directions. Ortega says that "man has a *mission of clarity,*" that "*this mission* is the very root of his constitution." And this implies: (1) that the very root of man's constitution *is* mission (an idea which was to dominate Ortega's later works, and especially those he wrote about 1930); (2) that clarity is not something which goes along with man, automatically *given,* as a mere "faculty" or "gift," but

48 "Die ontisch bildliche Rede vom lumen naturale im Menschen meint nichts anderes als die existenzialontologische Struktur dieses Seienden, dass es *ist* in der Weise, sein Da zu sein. Es ist 'erleuchtet' besagt: un ihm selbst *als* In-der-Welt-sein gelichtet, nicht durch ein anderes Seiendes, sondern so, dass es selbst die Lichtung *ist.* Nur einem existenzial so gelichteten Seienden wird Vorhandenes im Licht zugänglich, im Dunkel verborgen. Das Dasein bringt sein Da von Hause aus mit, seiner entbehrend ist es nicht nur faktisch nicht, sondern überhaupt nicht das Seiende dieses Wesens. *Das Dasein ist seine Erschlossenheit.*" *Sein und Zeit,* § 28, p. 133.

49 "Sofern das Dasein wesenhaft seine Erschlossenheit *ist,* als erschlossenes erschliesst und entdeckt, ist es wesenhaft 'wahr.' *Dasein ist* 'in der Wahrheit.' Diese Aussage hat ontologischen Sinn. Sie meint nicht, dass das Dasein ontisch immer oder auch nur je 'in alle Wahrheit' eingeseins. *Wahrheit 'gibt es' nur, sofern und solange Dasein ist.*" *Ibid.,* p. 226. "Seines eigensten Seins gehört." *Ibid.,* § 44, p. 221.

50 "Das Dasein ist als konstituirt durch die Erschlossenheit wesenhaft in der Wahrheit. Die Erschlossenheit est eine wesenhafte Seinsart des Daseins. *Wahrheit 'gibt es' nur, sofern und solange Dasein ist.*" *Ibid.,* p. 226.

51 "*Alle Warheit ist gemäss deren wesenhafter daseinsmässiger Seinsart relativ auf das Sein des Daseins.*" *Ibid.,* p. 227.

that it is a *mission*, something that man *has to do*; in short, a *something-to-be-done* (*quehacer*). As early as this, the demand of Ortega's method to *derive* everything from human life appears; in contrast to the idea of a *Seinsverständnis* or "comprehension of the being" which would belong to man automatically, as contrasted with the Aristotelian conviction that all men tend toward knowledge *by their nature*, Ortega will have to make great efforts to *justify* every dimension or activity of human life.

And furthermore, human life does not reduce itself to clarity. Clarity is *internal* to life, is "light shed upon things"; man illumines reality, and that light is the concept—that is, the *intellective vision* of the real, which perceives or grasps things in their limits, in context or (which is the same thing) within the system of realities. Thus the doctrine of light, or clarity, culminates in the idea of an *opening upon the world*. The concept causes what before was invisible and tacit to be made manifest, or patent. And when Ortega says that an idea "increases life and dilates reality," he expresses himself metaphorically, but with supreme rigor. Let us return to the old thesis of the *reabsorption of the circumstance* as the destiny of man: to be a man is to *have to* reabsorb the circumstance in order to live, to incorporate it into his project, to humanize it; and this can be done only by "shedding light" upon it, opening oneself upon it and thus making it visible and audible, with a voice (when before it was tacit and invisible) with *lógos*, or meaning, thus increasing life by dilating the "reality around us"—that is, the circumstance as such. This is the concrete way in which the dynamic dialogue between the I and the circumstance takes place, the *dii consentes* of the third great metaphor: the imperative of *light shed upon things*.

85. THE ULTIMATE JUSTIFICATION OF THE *Meditations on Quixote*

As we reach this point, we shall have to remember what I said in section 64 about justification for the fact that Ortega's philosophy was first presented in a book *on Don Quixote*; I said there that the six reasons enumerated certainly constituted a philosophical justification for the *Meditations on Quixote*, but that strictly speaking they were only half of it; now we can see what was still missing then.

Under the guise of heroism or tragedy, the structure of human life was revealed to Ortega, showing itself in a series of visions which display its particular attributes. All of this, as we have seen in detail, appears as a theory of the hero or the tragic character, and only at a few moments, and not deliberately—therefore far from all terminological use—does Ortega present it as "life." This is not, however, simple lack of maturity, mere "not having arrived" thematically at the theory of human life. Ortega demonstrates again and again that we are all heroes in some measure, that heroism is not limited to certain specific contents, that will is the tragic theme, that that possibility of tragedy and heroism underlies everything, always—that is, that heroism and tragedy belong essentially and intrinsically to man, that they are, if you will, privileged modes of life, perhaps close to those which Jaspers and other philosophers have later called "limit situations" (*Grenzsituationen*).

Very well, then, the theme of Don Quixote was obligatory in a *circumstantial* type of thought motivated from Spain, a thought which aspires to know what to hold to. But, on the other hand—and this is what is important to us just now—*Don Quixote is the paradigm of that consistency*, the example in which it becomes visible and intelligible. Why? Why a fictional character, a creature of art, in preference to a real man? Precisely because of that: because Cervantes interpreted that human manner of being, that singular consistency, illumined its *lógos*, its meaning, "shed light" upon it, unveiled it and patentized it when he re-created it imaginatively. Ortega has full consciousness of this, although he appears to say it in a different context—what I am doing in this book is, very largely, pointing out the subterranean connections: "The work of art," he says, "has, no less than the other forms of the spirit, this *clarifying* mission, *light-bearing*, if you will. An artistic style which does not contain *the key to the interpretation* of itself, one which consists in a mere reaction of one part of life—the individual heart—to the rest of life, will produce only doubtful values. In the great styles there is something resembling a stellar, or high-altitude, atmosphere, in which life is refracted as conquered and overcome, *shot through and through with clarity*."[52] This idea is not new in Ortega. In 1906 he had spoken of "that superexistential and saving idea of art, that metaphysical intention in its elaboration of beauty."[53] But this is almost nothing;

[52] I, 358–59. Italics mine, except for *light-bearing*.
[53] I, 50.

in "Adam in Paradise," he had expressed himself much more clearly: "Each art is born out of the differentiation of the *radical need for expression which exists in man, which is man* .... Man bears within himself a *heroic, a tragic problem*: whatever he does, *all his activities, are only functions of that problem*, steps he takes in order to solve it .... Science is the solution of the first stage of the problem: ethics is the solution of the second. Art is the attempt to resolve the last corner of the problem."[54] And still more: "The infinitude of relationships is inaccessible; art seeks for and produces a fictitious totality, a *semblance* of infinitude .... The *Quixote*, for example, leaves in us, like divine dregs, *a sudden and spontaneous* revelation which permits us to see effortlessly, in a single glance, a very broad ordering of all things."[55]

Don Quixote, in fact, is the example in which that condition of man's is made patent, "is revealed suddenly and spontaneously." He is real, he belongs entirely to reality, but in this reality he includes—says Ortega —his indomitable will, and this is a will for adventure. He is a *frontier nature*, and in his nature we discover that human condition which consists in existing with half one's body outside reality and half inside. And in Don Quixote, a fictional being, created by art, human life shows itself exempt from the inert elements which normally cover it, illuminated with the clarity shed on it by Cervantes, interpreted and placed in its *truth* or *alétheia*. This is the ultimate *methodical* justification of the *Meditations on Quixote*, understood as what we have seen that they are: a first approximation to a *metaphysical theory of human life*.

86. TRUTH AND AUTHENTICITY: THE PROJECT AND THE UNSUBORNABLE CORE

The keystone linking the theory of human life with the theory of truth is a concept which goes beyond the notion of *alétheia*, and which appears on the same "level" of Ortega's thought. In 1911 he had already presented life as consisting in *choice*, in preference, and had pointed this out in passing as a root of unhappiness: "Someone, when He placed us on the planet, did so with the plan that our hearts should be a preferring

[54] I, 474–75. Italics mine.

[55] I, 481. Italics mine, except for *semblance*. See the passage in Heidegger's *Holzwege* (1950), 25, and also the one on p. 29. They are quoted in my commentary on *Meditaciones del Quijote*, 362.

machine. We spend our lives choosing between *one thing and another*. A painful fate! A prolonged, insistent tragedy! Yes, a tragedy: for to prefer presupposes the recognition of both terms subject to choice as goods, as positive values. And even though we may choose what seems best to us, we always leave a niche in our desire which ought to have been filled by that other good, postponed . . . . Life takes on meaning when one makes of it an aspiration not to renounce anything."[56] Five years later, in 1916, he establishes the idea of the *project* as man's condition and the measure of his reality; that is, the demand for authenticity: "No, no; duty is not unique and generic. Each of us brings our own *inalienable and exclusive* duty . . . . I can want fully only that which arises in me as a desire of all my individual person . . . . We saw before that the individual face is at once the *project of itself* and a more or less complete realization. Thus, in ethics I believe that I see every man who passes before me as confined *within a moral silhouette of himself*: it shows what his individual character would be in perfection . . . . Let us not measure each man, therefore, except *against himself*: what he is as reality with *what he is as a project*. 'Become what you are.' This is the proper imperative . . . ."[57]

These doctrines, which we have been uncovering in writings where they were not to be expected—an article on travels through Castile, an essay on feminine beauty inspired by the passengers in a Madrid streetcar—where the *Gelehrte* have not gone to find them and where Spanish readers have not encountered them, culminate in the doctrine of the *unsubornable core*, an expression used by Ortega to designate the ultimate reality of our life—namely, its authenticity. This idea did not appear in works of a scientific bent either: first, in 1914, in a political lecture, "Old and New Politics"; two years later in the "Ideas on Pío Baroja." Let us look into it.

Ortega speaks of "our true, inmost, decisive opinions," of "those unexpressed and inner opinions," of the demand that each generation, like each individual, be "true to itself."[58] And soon after this, when he speaks of *loyalty*, he speaks of "that insubornable core which never allows itself to be completely disoriented."[59]

[56] "Tierras de Castilla" (1911). (*El Espectador*, I. II, 44.)
[57] "Estética en el tranvía" (1916). (*El Espectador*, I. II, 37.) Italics mine.
[58] *Vieja y nueva política*, I, 269–70.
[59] I, 278.

But this is no more than a prelude to the theme. It appears in the study on Baroja, one of Ortega's youthful writings which has the greatest *philosophical* implications, but which no one, so far as I know, has ever made use of. In a chapter entitled "Vital Balance," Ortega speaks of what happens to one's life as the age of thirty approaches. "An *imperative of truth*" appears in it, and "a sort of repugnance toward the phantasmagorical." "It is the age at which we cease to be what has been taught us, what we have received within the family, in school, in the commonplace of our society . . . . Now, suddenly . . . *we begin to want to be our own selves*, sometimes with full consciousness of our deepest defects. We want to be, above all, *the truth of what we are*, and very especially we resolve to make perfectly clear what we do not like about the world. Then, pitilessly breaking through the *crust of received opinions and thoughts*, we call upon *a certain unsubornable core* which exists in us. *Unsubornable*, not only with regard to money or flattery, but even with regard to *ethics, science, and reason*. Scientific conviction itself . . . takes on a superficial aspect if it is compared with the affirmations and negations which *this substantial core inexorably carries out*."[60]

A whole theory of life—a second version of it, this time with regard to the idea of authenticity—begins to take shape; just as in the *Meditations on Quixote*, it arises out of the concepts—so similar also—of heroism and tragedy. Ortega discusses happiness, and says that "confronted by things, the subject is pure activity. Call it soul, consciousness, spirit, or what you will, *what we are* consists of a bundle of activities, of which one is carried out and the others aspire to be carried out."[61] He rejects, on the other hand, the idea that desires constitute all of our personality,[62] and in passing renews the idea of the executive being which he had set forth two years earlier: "In a certain sense, *to live and to feel oneself living are two incompatible things*."[63] Finally, in a chapter entitled, in fact, "The Unsubornable Core," he returns to the theme more profoundly.

"I was speaking before," writes Ortega, "of a certain unsubornable core which exists in us. *Generally this ultimate and extremely individ-*

---

[60] "Ideas sobre Pío Baroja" (1915). (*El Espectador*, I. II, 72, 73.) Italics mine.

[61] II, 78. Ortega's choice of the word "haz" (a bundle or fagot) is misleading and inexact; what he wishes to emphasize is the active quality of *that which we are*, and the plurality of the activities we carry on.

[62] II, 79.

[63] II, 80.

ual nucleus of personality is buried under the accumulation of judgments and sentimental manners which fell upon us from outside. Only a few men gifted with a peculiar energy succeed in glimpsing in certain instants the attitudes of what Bergson would call the *profound I.*"[64] And he contrasts to this what he calls, using Baroja's favorite word, *farce*. "We give the name of *farces*," says Ortega, "to those realities in which reality is counterfeited. This supposes that we distinguish two planes of reality: one external, apparent, manifestative; another internal, substantial, which manifests itself in the other. That first reality has the inescapable mission of being an adequate expression of the second, if it is not a farce. This internal reality, in its turn, has the mission of being manifested, being exteriorized, in the former, if it is not a farce also. Example: a man who stoutly defends opinions which at bottom he cares nothing about, is a *farceur*; a man who really holds those opinions, but does not defend and make them patent, is also a *farceur*."[65] Note that this is only an application in human terms of the general theory of superficial and profound, patent and latent, realities, and their reciprocal relationships. On the other hand, I do not believe that Sartre, in his most felicitous moments of contrast between authenticity and farce, has taken one step farther than this old article in *El Espectador*.

"According to this," Ortega concludes, "the *truth* of man lies in the exact correspondence between the action and the spirit, in the perfect congruity between the external and the internal."[66] This is the complement of the theory of truth as *alétheia*, as uncovering or patentization. In his course *Man and Crisis*, given in the University of Madrid in 1933, one of his lectures, which was published that same year, bore the title "La verdad como coincidencia del hombre consigo mismo" ["Truth as the Coincidence of Man With Himself"]. This is the interpretation foreshadowed in this old text of 1916, corresponding to the first mature level of his thought. In the later course there was only the maturation of ideas that were already very old, possessed for a long time. And, in addition, there is no opposition to the idea of *alétheia*, but a deepening and complementing of it. Above all, application of the theory, specifically, to *human reality*: it is a question, in fact, of a correspondence, a congruity or coincidence of man with himself, of the external part of

[64] II, 82. Italics mine, except for *profound I*.
[65] II, 82–83.
[66] II, 83.

man with his innermost part. But that relationship is intrinsic and necessary, for man consists of *both things*; Ortega has just said that one reality has the *inescapable* mission of expressing or manifesting the other, and the latter has the mission of being expressed, exteriorized, manifested by the former. This congruity cannot be a *mere* congruity; rather, that constant patentization of its innermost self belongs to human life; that is, the expression and execution of projects, the reabsorption of the circumstance. Authenticity, the coincidence of man with himself is only the adequate way of making patent what is latent in man; in other words, the human form of *alétheia*.

87. THE DAWN OF VITAL REASON

This unveiling or uncovering in which truth consists is an action I perform. And if it means moving from the patent to the latent, in order to make it patent in its turn, this signifies a *movement*, a path which I have to traverse. A static vision, therefore, an act of *mere* intellection, does not suffice, for this is no more than an abstract of the more complex reality in which it occurs and where it could be artificially isolated. Perspective, on the other hand, is not *unique* or static; I was saying before that it is always *one among several*; but this means that those other perspectives are acting in each one, present in some manner in it, and that the effective reality of one supposes its integration with the others, therefore a *going* from one to another, *passing* from one to another. It is what I call "the Jericho method," recalling a figure frequently used by Ortega. As early as the *Meditations on Quixote* he had said, "A work of the scope of *Don Quixote* has to be taken as Jericho was taken. Our thoughts and our emotions must travel in broad swings, slowly tightening around it, with noises like ideal trumpets sounding in the air."[67]

Farther on, Ortega clarifies these metaphorical expressions when he sketches out a theory of the literary and intellectual genre to which his first book belongs, and which is to be the genre of a whole series of future publications: the *meditation*. The whole passage is worth quoting, for it is one of those which shed most light on Ortega's attitude toward method at this date:

[67] I, 327.

"Impressions form a *superficial tapestry*, where *ideal paths leading toward another, deeper reality* appear to debouch. The meditation is the *movement* in which we abandon surfaces, like the coasts of terra firma, and feel that we are being launched into a more tenuous element, where there are no material footholds. We *go forward* holding on to ourselves, keeping ourselves in suspension *thanks to our own efforts* within an ethereal orb peopled with weightless forms. A lively suspicion goes with us that, at the slightest vacillation on our part, all that orb would come tumbling down, and ourselves with it. When we meditate, the spirit must hold itself *in total tension*; it is a painful and integral effort.

"In meditation, *we gradually open a path* among masses of thoughts, *separating* some concepts from others, making our glance *pierce* the imperceptible gap left open between the most closely related ones, and once we have put each in its place, we *stretch imaginary springs* between them to keep them from getting confused again. Thus *we can come and go* as we please through the landscapes of the ideas which present their clear and radiant outlines to us."[68]

I have italicized the most revealing expressions. It is a question here of something active, of a path or march, which presupposes an effort, an essential *coming and going*. Well then, the discovery of *reason* in Greece consisted in the discovery of this possibility. In contrast to the *moîra* which *reveals itself* when it pleases, which makes patent what was latent, although *I* cannot go, for there is no *path*, reason supposes the possibility of *unveiling* the path, of placing it actively on view, of *going* to the latent and *returning* again from there to the patent, to things. "The upward road and the downward road are one and the same," said Heraclitus.[69]

Expressed in other words, intellection does not present itself except in the form of the *connection* and *movement* which are proper to *reason*. When Ortega defined philosophy as "the general science of love," he explained it by saying, "In love there is a broadening of the individuality which *absorbs* other things into it, which fuses them with us. This *link and compenetration* makes us enter very deeply into the properties of the beloved object. We see it whole; it is revealed to us in all its worth. Then we see that the loved object is, in its turn, part of something else, which needs it, and which is *linked* to it . . . . Thus love *gradually links one*

[68] I, 340–41. Italics mine.
[69] See *Introducción a la Filosofía*, VIII, and *Biografía de la Filosofía*, I. (*Obras*, II.)

thing to another and everything to us, in a firm essential structure."[70] This connection is not only that of things among themselves—what we saw before as *structure*—but *envelops me*—"one thing to another and everything to ourselves." Thus it is a question of *circumstantial perspective*; that is, real and not fictitious; and thus things present themselves as *realities*, not as mere *objects*, as happens in phenomenology, for which they are mere intentional correlates of a pure consciousness.

Now we can understand some theses in which this theory culminates. Ortega speaks of the concept, which cannot consist in being a new, subtle thing destined to supplant material things, whose mission does not lie in dislodging intuition, the real impression. And he adds, "*Reason cannot*, need not aspire to take the place of life." "This very *opposition*, so much used today by those who are unwilling to make an effort, *between reason and life*, is already suspicious. As if *reason were not a vital and spontaneous function*, out of the same line of descent as seeing or touching!"[71]

In sections 16 and 17 of this book I have showed the relative justification of that *irrationalism* which is the object of an ill-humored allusion of Ortega's. In section 24 I have tried to give details about his relationship with Unamuno, to whom he refers very directly in the sentence quoted above. *The Tragic Sense of Life* had just been published, written in 1912 and published (undated) the following year, one year before the *Meditations*. In this book Unamuno "impassioned, irritating, and a genius, perspicacious and irresponsible," as I have said of him elsewhere, had given irrationalism its most forceful, intense, impassioned, and effective formulation and perhaps its happiest formulation: "For to live is one thing and to know is another, and as we shall see, perhaps between them there is such an *opposition* that we can say that *all which is vital is antirational, not merely irrational, and all which is rational, antivital*. And this is the basis of the tragic sense of life."[72] "And it is that, strictly speaking, *reason is the enemy of life*. Intelligence is a terrible thing. It tends toward death as memory tends toward stability. The living thing, that which is absolutely unstable, absolutely individual, is strictly speaking unintelligible. Logic attempts to reduce everything to

[70] I, 313. Italics mine.
[71] I, 353. Italics mine.
[72] *Del sentimiento trágico de la vida*, 38.

identities and types, wants each thing to have only one identical content in any place, time, or relation where we encounter it. And there is nothing which remains the same in two successive moments of its being. My idea of God is different each time that I conceive it. *Identity, which is death, is the aspiration of the intellect. The mind seeks what is dead, for the living thing escapes it*; the mind attempts to freeze the fugitive current into blocks of ice, tries to immobilize it. To analyze a body, we must diminish or destroy it. *To understand something we must kill it, make it turn stiff* in our minds .... *How, then, can reason give access to the revelation of life? The combat of life with reason* is a tragic combat, it is the basis of tragedy. And truth? Is it lived or is it understood?"[73] And he still insists, "*All which is vital is irrational, and all which is rational, antivital*, because reason is essentially skeptical."[74] And finally, after having insisted that, in spite of everything, faith, which is life, and reason need each other mutually, he concludes, using the same expression that was to be the formula of Ortega's system, though here it is inverted, "And, however, faith is neither transmissible nor rational, *nor is reason vital*."[75]

Ortega writes within this European philosophical situation and within this precise Spanish circumstance. I suggested some time ago that *The Tragic Sense of Life* was a polemical stimulus for Ortega, that it perhaps obliged him to mature his incipient theory of vital reason in order to contrast it with that attractive, fascinating formulation of irrationalism. I have stated that, given the idea of reason then current, irrationalism was justified and reasonable. It was necessary, therefore, to take things at a deeper level, to arrive at a new idea of reason, to rise above irrationalism, but not to fall back into rationalism, in relation to which irrationalism was right, but to go beyond both and "give an account" of them. And in fact, in that ill-tempered phrase the two words "reason" and "vital" appear together in Ortega for the first time. The literary form of the phrase reveals: (1) impatience; (2) a long and habitual conviction; (3) the reference to *a different point of view*, which alters the posing of the question and which has, in fact, been overlooked, has not been known, purely because it is so elementary and so radical. Ortega

[73] *Ibid.*, 92.

[74] *Ibid.*, 93.

[75] *Ibid.*, 115. (I quote from the first edition, which could have been available to Ortega at the time he wrote *Meditaciones del Quijote*. All italics are mine.)

indicates, as clearly as if with a pointing finger, the fact that, no matter what opinion one may have of reason, no matter what its later relationships with life may be, or its possibilities with regard to life, *reason begins by being a vital function*, something that man does *as he lives*, just as in seeing or touching; that is , that far from being something apart from life, something which comes to it from without, reason, from the outset and for the moment, *is given in life*, is constituted in it, and in that radical and orginal sense it is of course *vital*.

And is it only this? In the first programmatic article in *El Espectador*, in 1916, an article so laden with philosophic substance, Ortega was to say, "To accentuate this difference between contemplation and life . . . was necessary. Because *El Espectador* has a second intention: he speculates, looks—but what he wishes to see is life as it flows before him."[76] And in the same *Espectador* he was to say—had written a year before— "The first commandment of the artist, of the thinker, is to look, look well at the world around him. This imperative of contemplation, or *amor intellectualis*, suffices to distinguish the ethic of the spectator from that established by the *activists*, despite their multiple points of similarity."[77]

But all this, no matter how great its value, is programmatic. There could be no greater error than to pursue the matter no further than this. For Ortega *has set vital reason in motion* in the investigation of human life, and reality in general, that we have examined step by step. Theory is intrinsically *dramatic*, as we saw when we considered its requisites. It must be *circumstantial*, understanding this notion in a *biographical* sense, on the one hand, and on the other a *real* and not merely intentional sense, far, therefore, from any sort of utopian and abstract thinking. That theory is constituted only in a *perspective*, in contrast with the reigning image of it, which Unamuno so cavalierly rejects—accepting, however, the fact that it is like that. In Ortega all vision is perspective, and perspective is justified by being the condition itself of reality, since *reality exists as such only in a perspective manner*. The concrete destiny of man, the condition of life, therefore, is the *reabsorption of the circumstance*, its humanization by means of a project, its *apprehension* by means of a system of *connections*, thanks to the instrument of the *concept*, within the *system of realities*. But this is *reason*, and that reason

[76] "Verdad y perspectiva." (*El Espectador*, I.) II, 18.
[77] "Ideas sobre Pío Baroja." (*El Espectador*, I.) II, 96.

is not something distinct from life, but is life itself in its function of apprehending reality by linking "one thing to another and everything to ourselves." This is what *vital reason* means, at least at the moment when Ortega discovered it and set it in motion.

In 1914 or 1916, on the first mature level of his philosophy, Ortega does not define it, nor does he construct his theory; he only *names* it and shows it *executively*: the theory of the forest, which I have chosen to follow step by step, is the first example in which what was to be the method of Ortega's philosophy and perhaps a good part of the philosophy of the future, *vital reason*, is shown at work.

* * *

About 1930, Ortega talked about the publication of a book which was to be entitled *Aurora de la razón vital* ["Dawn of Vital Reason"]. It was to be the full and public manifestation of a doctrine which had been germinating in his thought for many years. As we have explored the icebergs of his writings, we have found that the dawn of vital reason coincided with Ortega's first possession of a mature philosophy, much more coherent and systematic than it might seem to the untrained or careless glance.

When we reach this level, we find that during the two-year period 1914–16 Ortega had unequivocally formulated a personal philosophy, the anticipation of many doctrines of the following decades, and, above all, of those which were to be, up to the present, confined to himself and his philosophical descendants.

Once in possession of these mental instruments, Ortega's theory had to keep on growing at the same rate as his life, as a function of that life. The development of his thought could not be abstract or merely logical; I mean that his later ideas could not arise out of ideas—either his or others'—but out of reality. The reabsorption of the circumstance presented itself as the concrete destiny of the man Ortega, committed to observing the world around him; he already possessed a path for this, possible new ways of looking at things, an instrument for their possession, in order to link them lovingly and understand them within the system of realities. This was the task which faced Ortega's circumstantial thought in the following decade. Ortega had to *give an account* of the reality around him, and only this reality could expand his reason, create with its inexhaustible riches and its own systematism the plenitude of his philosophical system.

The man Ortega was a vocation, a certain aspiration, an unrenounce-able project of being the man he had to be, in a particular circumstance. At this moment, he possessed himself and could say, like Don Quixote, "I know who I am." But his philosophy was to discover what he was beginning to know even then: that man, properly speaking, not merely *is*, but rather *lives*; and that living is *what we do and what happens to us*; it means having to swim, a shipwrecked man afloat in circumstance, accounting for it, knowing what to hold to; and for each man it means being able to be, authentically and freely, faithful to his destiny.

INDEX